Volvo 140 Series Automotive Repair Manual

by J H Haynes

Member of the Guild of Motoring Writers

Models covered:

UK:

Volvo 142 & 142S 2 door saloons. 1778 cc & 1986 cc

Volvo 144 & 144S 4 door saloons. 1778 cc & 1986 cc

Volvo 144E & 144GL 4 door saloons. 1986 cc Petrol injection

Volvo 145 & 145S Estates. 1986 cc

Volvo 145E Estate. 1986 cc Petrol injection

USA:

Volvo 142S 2 door sedan. 108.5 cu. in. (1778 cc) & 121 cu. in. (1986 cc)

Volvo 142 ('73 on) 142GL & 142E 2 sedans. 121 cu. in. (1986 cc) Petrol injection

Volvo 144S 4 door sedan. 108.5 cu. in. (1778 cc) & 121 cu. in. (1986 cc)

Volvo 144 ('73 on) 144GL & 144E* 4 door sedans. 121 cu. in. (1986 cc) Petrol injection

Volvo 145S Station Wagon. 121 cu. in. (1986 cc)

Volvo 145 ('73 on) & 145E* Station Wagon. 121 cu. in. (1986 cc) Petrol injection

These models designated 'E' and fitted with petrol injection for California only.

ISBN 978 0 85733 595 1

© **Haynes North America, Inc.** 1975, 1976, 1977, 1981, 1982, 1987
With permission from Haynes Group Limited

(129-10U6)

Haynes Group Limited
Haynes North America, Inc

www.haynes.com

Acknowledgements

Before writing this book, the Author conducted, and assisted with, the strip-down of a Volvo 142. The mechanical work involved was carried out by Brian Horsfall - a skilled mechanic; at the same time, Les Brazier took the photographs which illustrate this book. Both were unremitting in their efforts to ensure that the procedures established would be those best suited to the D-I-Y man, and that these procedures, would also be clearly illustrated in the form of photographs. For their help and forbearance the Author is very grateful.

The Author also acknowledges with gratitude the help and encouragement received from Tim Parker and Rod Grainger who edited the text.

A number of illustrations in this book are used by kind permission of Volvo Concessionares Limited; and Castrol Limited have been generous in the provision of lubrication details.

Our thanks to the Champion Sparking Plug Company Limited for the provision of spark plug photographs. The bodywork repair photographs used in this manual were provided by Lloyds Industries Limited who supply 'Turtle Wax', 'Dupli-Color Holts' and a range of other Holts products.

Finally, we all have cause to be grateful to Jenny Jones who turned the Author's faltering dictation into readable typescript.

About this manual

Its arrangement

This book is divided into 13 Chapters. Each Chapter is divided into sections. The sections contain serially numbered paragraphs.

All the illustrations carry a caption. When the illustration is designed as a figure the reference number consists of the Chapter number, followed by a sequence number; the sequence starting afresh for every Chapter. Photographs have a reference number in the caption - this reference number pinpoints the section and paragraph in that Chapter to which the photograph refers. Almost invariably the existence of this photo is indicated in the paragraph by direct reference in the text, or the words "photo" or "see photo" in brackets.

When the left-hand side or right-hand side of a car or component is mentioned, this is to be taken as if the viewer was looking in the forward direction of travel and the component normally fitted in the car.

Getting the best from your manual

Before starting a job, read all the relevant parts of the manual - and indeed any irrelevant parts which you think might be useful. As well as providing information, it will help you to check that you have all the tools, and all the spares that you will need. The ideal time to do this is on the Friday night if you are going to do the job over the weekend - not the Friday night before you start but the previous Friday night. This will allow you a full week to get all of the materials which will be needed. Obviously this manual will be used as the actual work is carried out: in order to make on the spot references. When the manual is being put to this use, it is a good idea to cover the open pages with polythene or a sheet of glass to prevent it from becoming stained with oil or grease.

Whilst every care is taken to ensure that the information in this manual is correct, no liabilty can be accepted by the authors or publishers for loss, damage or injury caused by any errors in, or omissions from, the information given.

The tools for the job

The Volvo needs metric spanners. (Some early models may require AF spanners). You will see from this book that you can do almost anything if you possess a set of open-ended spanners and a set of cranked ring spanners. If, having bought these you still have money to spend, don't buy a box full of gleaming socket heads with a ratchet holder - instead, buy yourself a hub puller, which can also be used for the gearbox and timing gear (you can see the sort of tool needed in our illustrations) and a torque wrench.

Torque wrenches, pullers and other specialised tools are pricey items - therefore, you will not find them easy to borrow. However, one possible source should not be overlooked - many local car clubs lend tools to their members, and it could well be that a subscription to such a club would cost you less than buying a torque wrench.

One most useful 'tool' which we hope you have already bought or are about to buy is the Haynes Owners Workshop Manual for your car.

Contents

Your Volvo

Sweden has a very harsh environment for many months of the year, and for this reason, most things made in Sweden are very ruggedly constructed. This characteristic is reflected in the solidity, reliability and attention to detail which is synonymous with the name Volvo. It is interesting to note that many of the components used in the Volvo are manufactured in Great Britain and exported to Sweden.

Volvo cars are made to last - and so are their designs. The 140 Series was introduced in 1966, but though this may show in small details of the appearance - such as the instrument panel before it was given its 1973 facelift - the engineering design more than holds its own with the majority of later introductions.

Some of the features of the 140 Series have recently appeared on other makes where they have been hailed as significant advances - for example, extra safety features in the body construction and disc brakes all round. Exhaust emission control has been available on Volvos for a number of years, and alternators have been fitted as standard since 1967.

There is something very satisfying about unobtrusive good breeding. We were very aware of this as we worked over the car (which appears in many of our photographs) devising and checking the maintenance methods described in this manual. We are sure that you, the Volvo owner-maintainer, will feel the same way, arriving at the conclusion that you possess a car which, though it may not have an immediate trendy impact, reveals your good taste to people of discernment.

Volvo 145 Estate

Volvo 144 Saloon

Buying spare parts and vehicle identification numbers

Buying spare parts

Spare parts are available from many sources, for example: Volvo garages, other garages and accessory shops, and motor factors. Our advice regarding spare part sources is as follows:

Officially appointed Volvo garages - This is the best source of parts which are peculiar to your car and are otherwise not generally available (eg complete cylinder heads, internal gearbox components, badges, interior trim etc). It is also the only place at which you should buy parts if your car is still under warranty - non-Volvo components may invalidate the warranty. To be sure of obtaining the correct parts it will always be necessary to give the storeman your car's engine and chassis number, and if possible, to take the 'old' part along for positive identification. Remember that many parts are available on a factory exchange scheme - any parts returned should always be clean! It obviously makes good sense to go straight to the specialists on your car for this type of part for they are best equipped to supply you.

Other garages and accessory shops - These are often very good places to buy materials and components needed for the maintenance of your car (eg oil filters, spark plugs, bulbs, fan belts, oils and greases, touch-up paint, filler paste etc). They also sell general accessories, usually have convenient opening hours, charge lower prices and can often be found not far from home.

Motor factors - Good factors will stock all of the more important components which wear out relatively quickly (eg clutch components, pistons, valves, exhaust systems, brake cylinders/pipes/hoses/seals/shoes and pads etc). Motor factors will often provide new or reconditioned components on a part exchange basis - this can save a considerable amount of money.

Vehicle identification numbers

1 Although many individual parts, and in some cases sub-assemblies, fit a number of different models it is dangerous to assume that just because they look the same, they are the same. Differences are not always easy to detect except by serial numbers. Make sure therefore, that the appropriate identity number for the model or sub-assembly is known and quoted when a spare part is ordered.

2 The final drive assembly has a number of its own which is carried on a plate fastened to the left hand side of the casing. This plate gives the drive ratio, part number and serial number of the unit. The gearbox carries a similar plate on its underside giving the type designation, part number and serial number.

3 The engine serial number appears on the left-hand side of the engine at the top of the cylinder block just below the cylinder head, between the distributor and the crankcase breather (see photo). Just in front of this pad is another pad carrying two engraved figures. These are the last two digits of the engine part number. The first four figures of this number appear on the cylinder head casting immediately beside this pad. In fact the cast numbers on the engine shown were, "4969" and the engraved numbers "20", meaning that the engine part number was "496920". The serial number (which may be difficult to read in the reproduction) was "7327".

4 The type designation and chassis number of the vehicle are stamped on the front right-hand door pillar or on a plate attached to the left-hand door pillar, inside the vehicle as shown in our photograph.

5 The vehicle type designation and the code numbers for colour and upholstery, together with the model number, appear on a very obvious plate on the extreme left of the scuttle not very far from the bonnet hinge (photo).

6 A little way in front of this plate is another much less obvious plate bearing the body number. It is fixed to a curved box section.

Bsp 1. This is the engine serial number ("7327"). The rest of the whole engine number will be found in the same position nearer to the front of the engine

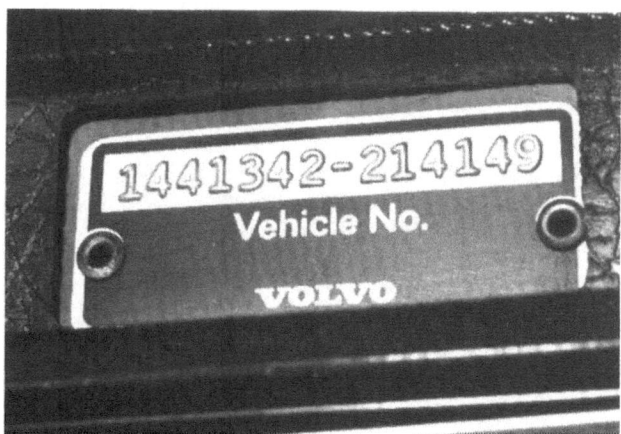

Bsp 2. Type designation and chassis numbers - this plate is attached to a door pillar

Bsp 3. This plate repeats the vehicle type designation number and also gives code numbers for paintwork and upholstery

Routine maintenance

Introduction

1 Routine maintenance is a chore - however enthusiastic an owner or ardent a car lover you may be. A better name for it is preventive maintenance. This does not make it any less of a chore, but it is one of those chores which pays off.

2 It does this in three ways:

a) It reduces wear and lengthens car life by ensuring that all parts that need it are properly lubricated.

b) It ensures that all small adjustments which make so much difference to the performance of the car - and in some cases neglect of these may mean disaster - are always correct.

c) Most important of all, carrying out maintenance you give your car a thorough inspection.

3 The maintenance tasks described below are in the main those recommended by Volvo, but we have added a few more to the list which practical experience has convinced us are well worth doing.

4 The recommended time intervals are applicable in temperate climates where the roads are reasonably dust-free and for yearly distances of 12,000 - 24,000 miles (20,000 - 40,000 kms). They may need to be modified where environmental conditions are extreme or distances driven are very much greater.

2 Weekly, before a long journey, or every 250 miles (400 kms)

1 Check the engine oil level which should be up to the "Max" mark on the dipstick. Top up the oil in the sump with Castrol GTX. On no account allow the oil to fall below the "Min" mark on the dipstick.

2 Check the battery electrolyte level and top up as necessary with distilled water. Make sure that the top of the battery is always kept clean and free of moisture.

3 Check the coolant level in the expansion tank. Top up if necessary with the same mixture as is already in there - do not top up antifreeze solution with water. Persistent need to top up indicates leakage somewhere and should be investigated without delay.

4 Check the tyre pressures - and that includes the spare. The correct tyre pressures depend on the type of tyre you are using and the loading of your vehicle. Your Volvo agent, or indeed, any garage who deals in the make of tyre you are using, will be able to give you this information. Keep your spare tyre at the highest pressure you use; you can always let it down a bit when you fit it, but pumping it up may be more difficult.

5 Refill the windscreen washer container with perfectly clean water. If you want to add antifreeze, use the sort specially made for windscreen washers. Check that the jets are operating correctly.

6 Check the working of your windscreen wipers. If you have a 145 of course, these last two tasks are twice as difficult.

7 Check all of the lights - notably brake lights. When a car brakes suddenly, the car behind it needs all the warning it can get.

8 Talking of brakes, check the level in the brake fluid reservoir. Top it up to "Max" if necessary.

3 Every 6000 miles (10000 kms) or six months

1 You are going to be thoroughly dirty by the time you have finished the tasks described in this section, so we suggest that you lubricate the bodywork while you are still clean. Normally, only the items shown ringed in Figs. R.M.1 and R.M.2 are lubricated at six month intervals, the remainder being dealt with every 12 months. If however it has been a long, hot summer we advise you to do the lot (Figs. R.M.1 - R.M.4)

2 Don't leave out your weekly check (Section 2).

3 Run the engine until it is hot and drain the engine oil. Out of the sump you will get approximately 5.7 Imperial pints (6.9 US pints or 3,25 litres). You will need a bigger container than this implies because you also remove the oil filter and this holds another 0.7 Imperial pints (1.0 US pints or 0.5 litres). Fit a new filter (see Chapter 1).

4 Wipe the top of the carburettor suction chamber and top up the carburettor until the fluid is within 0.25" (6 mm) from the top (see Chapter 3).

5 Check the carburettor adjustment as described in Chapter 3.

6 For fuel injection engines, carry out the adjustments described in Chapter 3, Sections 67 and 68. Check the cooling and heater system for signs of leakage. Be sure that all hose clips are tight and that none of the hoses shows signs of cracking.

7 Carburettor engines: clean the filter in the fuel pump.

8 Check the fan belt for signs of wear. If necessary set the tension as described in Chapter 10.

9 Lubricate all the throttle control linkages and such like with the oil can.

10 Check the adjustment of the handbrake and footbrake. Inspect the discs and pads for wear and signs of scoring (see Chapter 9). If you have made any appreciable adjustment to the handbrake, or in any event if you did not inspect them last time, remove the rear brake drums and examine the drums and linings.

11 Carefully examine all the brake hydraulic pipes and unions for signs of leakage and see that flexible hoses are not able to chafe against any part of the car when the steering is turned through both locks.

12 Lubricate the moving parts of the handbrake system with Castrol GTX from an oil can.

13 Clean and adjust the spark plugs (see Chapter 4).

14 Check the state of charge of the battery with a hydrometer. If it is not fully charged, and there is no immediate explanation of this (as, for example a slack fan belt) have the battery checked by a local garage or preferably a specialist. If it is not very good, you will have to consider replacement. Clean the battery terminals and smear them with petroleum jelly to prevent corrosion (see Chapter 10).

15 Check the alignment of the headlights and adjust if necessary (see Chapter 10).

16 Wipe round the filler plug on the steering box and check the oil level which should be up to the bottom of the plug hole. Top up if necessary with Castrol Hypoy or similar.

17 Check the tyre wear pattern in case this indicates that your front suspension is out of alignment. If it does, the remedy is

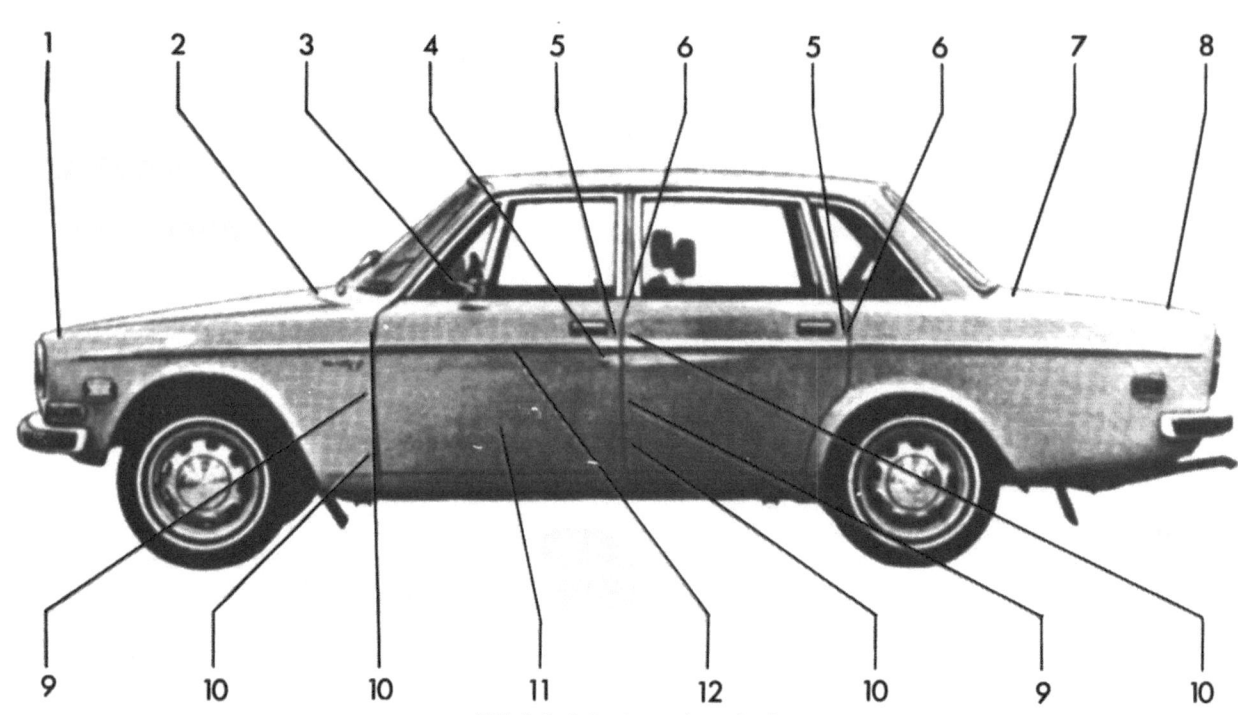

RM. 1 Lubrication points - body

No.	Lubricating point	Lubricant
1	Bonnet catch	Paraffin wax
2	Bonnet hinges	Oil
3	Ventilation window catch and hinges	Oil
4	Keyholes	Lock oil
5	Striker plate	See Fig. RM3
6	Outer sliding surface of door lock	Paraffin wax
7	Trunk lid hinges	Oil
8	Trunk lid lock	Oil

No.	Lubricating point	Lubricant
	Keyholes	Lock oil
9	Door stops	Paraffin wax
10	Door hinges	Grease
11	Front seat runners and catches	Paraffin wax and oil
12	Window winders	Oil and grease
	Locks	Silicon grease
	(Accessible after door upholstery panels have been removed.)	

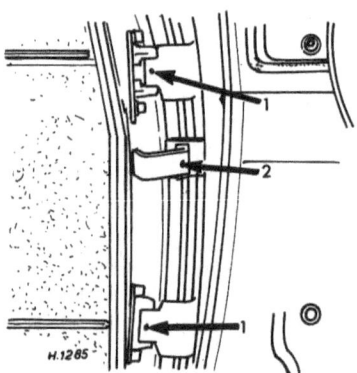

RM. 2 Lubrication points - door

1   Hinges   2   Door stop

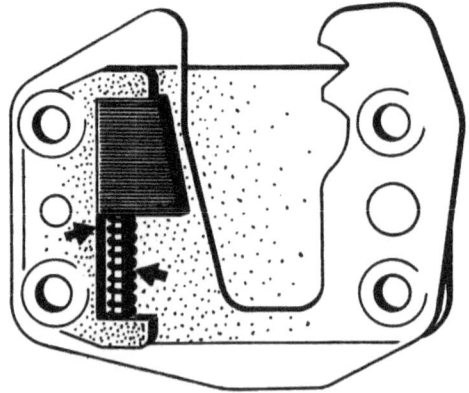

RM. 3 Lubrication points - door latch

Inner sliding surfaces, spring and pin lubricated with molybdenum disulphide grease

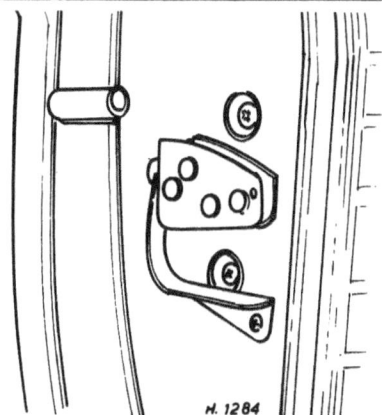

RM. 4 Door lock and guide plates - apply paraffin wax

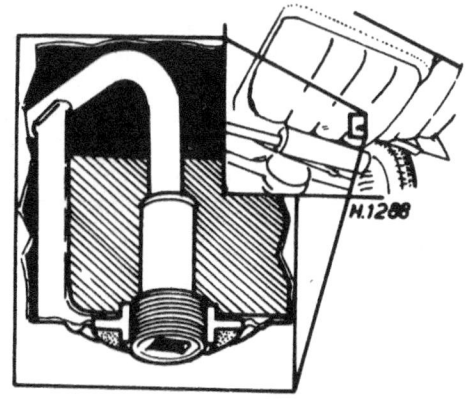

RM. 5 Filter in fuel tank

obvious and should be applied as soon as possible.

18 You cannot put off grovelling underneath the car any longer. Start by wiping round the filler plug of the final drive and checking its oil level. It should come up to the filler hole. If necessary top up with recommended oil.

19 Check that the rubber seal covering the junction between the propeller shaft and the splined shaft on the end of the gearbox or transmission is undamaged. If it has been damaged, it should be replaced and a new seal filled with molybdenum disulphide grease (Castrol MS3). Check the universal joints for excessive play. Generally speaking, if such play is apparent it would already have made its presence felt by causing vibration in the transmission system.

20 For cars with manual gearboxes, whether or not they are fitted with overdrive, wipe round the filler plug and check the oil level which should be up to the filler hole. If necessary top-up with recommended oil. For cars with automatic transmission, stand the car on level ground with the engine idling and 'P' selected. Withdraw the transmission dipstick and wipe it clean with a nylon cloth before replacing it. Withdraw the dipstick again and check the fluid level: if the engine is at normal operating temperature use the 'Warm' graduations, if the engine has only been running a short time, use the 'Cold' graduations. Add automatic transmission fluid as necessary, through the dipstick tube.

21 Check the exhaust system for signs of leaks. If you find small blow holes, you can apply a little Holts Silencer Seal or Gun-Gum as a temporary measure, but they are a sign that corrosion is well advanced and you will soon have to replace the pipe. Check all exhaust mountings for tightness.

22 Check and if necessary adjust the clutch free play (see Chapter 5). At the same time check the condition of the clutch cable and give it a touch of oil.

4 Every 12000 miles (20000 kms) or 12 months

1 Carry out the complete body lubrication routine illustrated in Figs. RM1 - RM4.
2 Carry out all the tasks described in Sections 2 and 3 except that instead of cleaning and adjusting the spark plugs you renew them.
3 Service the crankcase ventilation system (see Chapter 3, Section 30).
4 Clean the filter in the fuel tank (see Fig. RM5).
5 Change the discharge line fuel filter - fuel injection engines (see Fig. 3.68).
6 Check and if necessary adjust the valve clearances (Chapter 1, Section 37).
7 Check the engine compression. This is best carried out by a Volvo agent using specialised apparatus.
8 Adjust the throttle valve switch - fuel injection engines (see Chapter 3, Section 48).

9 Thoroughly examine all electrical connections and fuel lines for signs of deterioration and damage.
10 Service EGR system where this is fitted (see Section 8).
11 Where the engine air cleaner is fitted with a plastic sleeve, remove and clean or change this sleeve. (Note: Do not confuse this sleeve with the plastic sleeve in the filter for the evaporative control system).
12 Check and adjust ignition points and (in the case of fuel injection engines) trigger contacts (see Chapter 4).
13 Examine all ball joints in front suspension and steering (see Chapter 10) replace any that are worn.
14 Fuel injection models: Ensure that orifice in inlet manifold nipple (distributor vacuum pipe connection) is unobstructed.

5 Every 24000 miles (40000 kms) or 18 months

1 Carry out the complete six month service described in Sections 2, 3 and 4 with the exception of the oil level checks - (Sections 3.17 and 3.18) which are replaced by the oil changes described in this Section.
2 Having driven the car until the oil in the transmission and final drive is thoroughly warm, drain and refill both these systems. You will need 1.3 Imperial pints (1.6 US pints or 0.75 litres) of recommended oil for the manual gearbox where overdrive is not fitted, 2.8 Imperial pints (3.4 US pints or 1.6 litres) of the same for the manual gearbox fitted with overdrive, 11.3 Imperial pints (13.5 US pints or 6.4 litres) of recommended oil for the automatic transmission BW35, and 2.3 Imperial pints (2.7 US pints or 1.3 litres) of recommended oil for the rear axle. Note that where a limited slip differential is fitted the rear axle must be filled with oil to specification MIL-L-2105B with additive suited to limited slip differentials.
3 Change all air filter elements.
4 Change foam plastic element in Evaporite venting filter (Chapter 3, Section 34).
5 Change coolant and pressure test cooling system (see Section 7).
6 Examine the hub bearings for wear and replace as necessary (see Chapter 8, Section 8 and Chapter 11, Sections 2, 3 and 4).
7 Remove the starter motor, examine the brushes and replace as necessary. Clean the commutator and starter drive (see Chapter 10).
8 Test the engine compressions, and if necessary remove the cylinder head, decarbonise, grind in the valves and fit new valve springs (see Chapter 11).
9 Replace EGR valve where fitted (see Section 8).

6 Every 36000 miles (60000 kms) or three years

1 Carry out the 12000 mile service described in Section 4.
2 Replace the seals and air filter in the brake servo-cylinder (Chapter 9, Section 12).

3   Completely drain the brake hydraulic fluid from the system. Give the brakes a thorough overhaul as described in Chapter 9, preferably renewing all seals and flexible hoses throughout the braking system.

7   Pressure testing the cooling system

1   It is a simple matter to pressure test the cooling system provided that you have a tyre pressure gauge which is accurate at pressures of 10 lb/in^2 (0.7 kg/cm^2) above atmospheric. All you need to do is to obtain a spare radiator cap which fits the filler hole on the radiator. If this is not possible, you could use a cap which fits the expansion tank, but if you do this you will be unable to include the expansion tank cap in your test.
2   Drain the cooling system and pump it up with a tyre pump to a pressure of just under 10 lb/in^2 (0.7 kg/cm^2) on the B20 engines or 4 lb/in^2 (0.28 kg/cm^2) on B18 engines.
3   The system should be able to hold this pressure for at least 30 seconds without noticeable drop. If it does not, examine for leakage. The cap on the expansion tank may be at fault and you should make sure that it is all right. The simplest way is to

replace it temporarily with another cap or stopper which seals the system 100%.

8   EGR System - maintenance

1   The exhaust gas recirculation system comprises a valve worked by a vacuum which connects the exhaust manifold to the inlet manifold under conditions of high vacuum, thus ensuring that a considerable part of the exhaust gases are sucked back into the engine when the throttle is set fairly low.
2   A diagram illustrating its situation and section is given in Fig.RM6.
3   To test the system, with the engine idling, connect the distributor vacuum line to the vacuum connection of the EGR valve. The engine should now stop or begin to run rough. If this does not happen, check all hoses and pipes for clogging. If no clogging is found, replace the EGR valve and retest.
4   The maintenance procedure is to clean all hoses and pipes in the system every 12,000 miles (20,000 kms) and replace the EGR valve every 24,000 miles (40,000 kms).

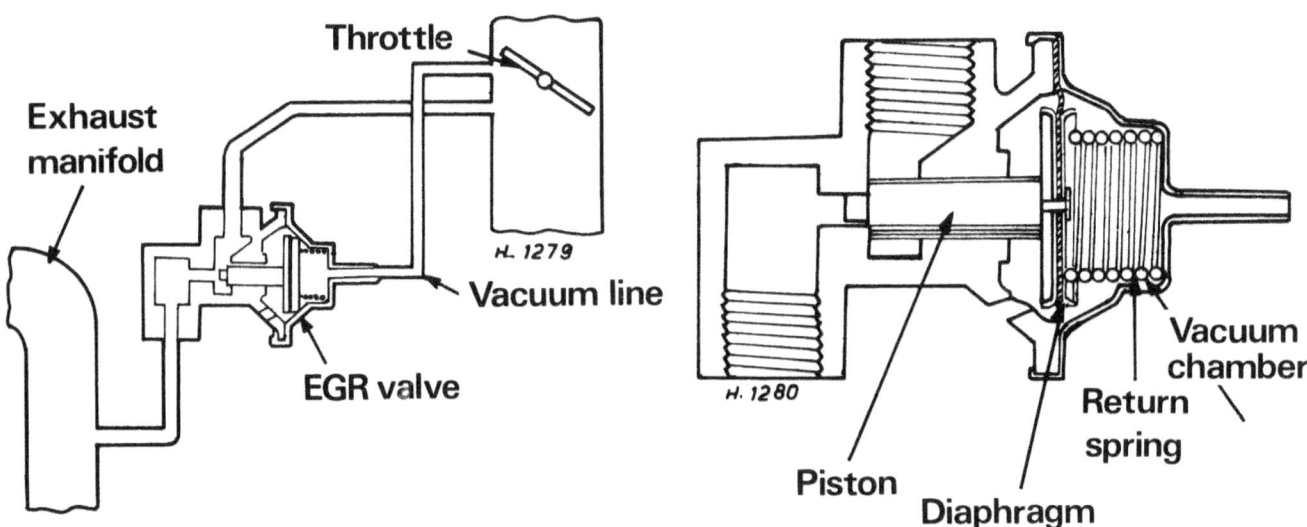

RM. 6 Exhaust gas recirculation system
(left) Diagram of system   (right) Details of E.G.R. Valve

Recommended lubricants and fluids

Component	Castrol Grade
Engine	Castrol GTX
Gearbox	Castrol GTX
Rear axle	Castrol Hypoy B
Wheel-bearings	Castrol LM Grease
Brake fluid reservoir	Castrol Girling Universal Brake and Clutch Fluid
Steering box	Castrol Hypoy Light
Carburettors	Castrol Everyman

Lubrication chart

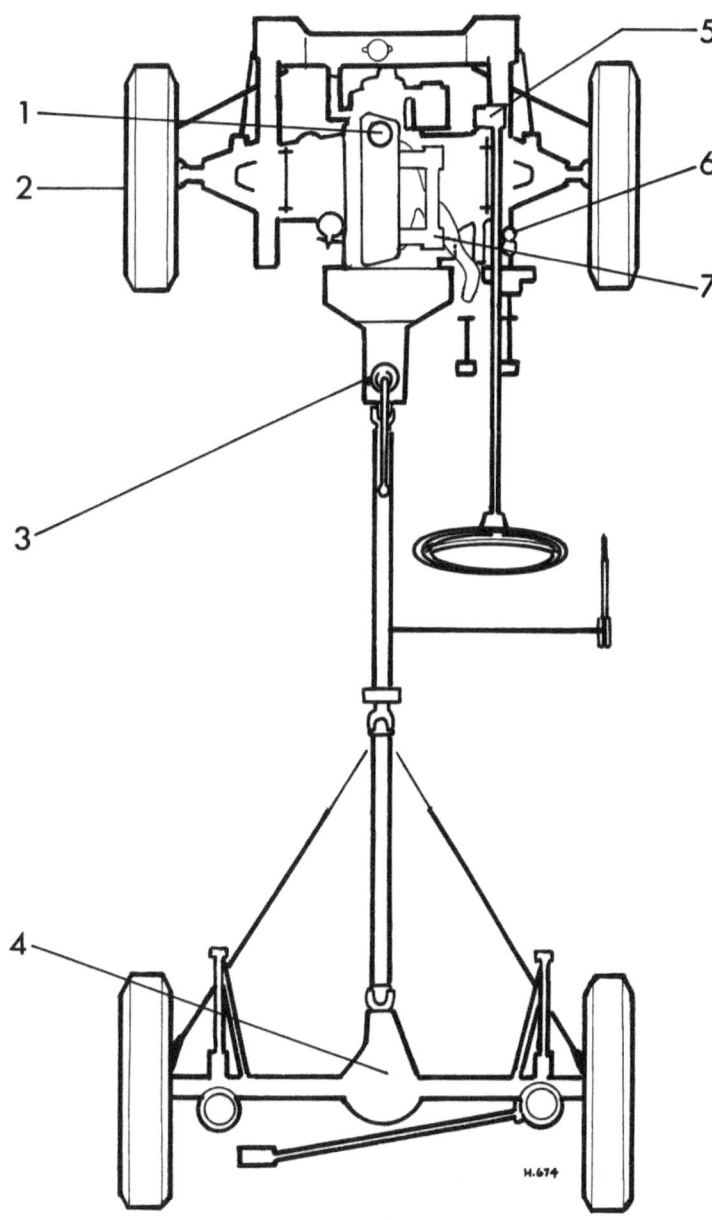

H.674

Key to Lubrication points

1 Engine
2 Wheel bearings
3 Gearbox
4 Rear axle
5 Steering box
6 Brake fluid reservoir
7 Carburettors

Chapter 1 Engine

Contents

Specifications

General specifications (B18 engines)

	B 18A	B 18B
Type	B 18A	B 18B
Performance, HP at rpm:		
SAE	85/5000	115/6000
DIN	75/4700	100/5066
Max. torque, lb ft. (kgm):		
SAE	108(15)/3000	112(15.5)/4000
DIN	105(14.5)/2300	107(14.8)/3500
Compression pressure at 250 - 300 rpm (warm engine turned over with starter motor)	156 - 185 lb./sq. in. (11 - 13 kg/sq. cm)	170 - 200 lb./sq, in. (12 - 14 kg/sq. cm)
Compression ratio	8.7 : 1	10.0 : 1
Number of cylinders	4	4
Bore	3.313 in. (84.14 mm)	3.313 in. (84.14 mm)
Stroke	3.150 in. (80.0 mm)	3.150 in. (80.00 mm)
Capacity	1780 cc	1780 cc
Weight	Approx. 341 lb. (155 kg)	Approx. 341 lb. (155 kg)

General specifications (B20 engines)

	B 20A	B 20B	B 20E	B 20F
Type	B 20A	B 20B	B 20E	B 20F
Performance, HP at rpm:				
SAE	90/4800	118/5800	135/6000	112/6000
DIN	82/4700	100/5500	124/6000	
Max. torque, lb ft. (kgm):				
SAE	119(16.5)/3000	123(17)/3500	18.0(130)/3500	123 (17.0)/3500
DIN	115.7(16)/2300	112(15.5)/3500	17.0(123)/3500	116 (16.0)/3500

Compression pressure at 250 - 300 rpm (warm engine turned over with starter motor)	156 - 185 lb./sq.in. (11 - 13 kg/sq.cm)	170 - 200 lb./sq. in. (12 - 14 kg/sq.cm)	170 - 200 lb./sq. in. (12 - 14 kg/sq.cm)	156 - 185 lb./sq.in. (11 - 13 kg/sq.cm)
Compression ratio	8.7 : 1	9.5 : 1	10.5 : 1	8.7 : 1
Number of cylinders	4	4	4	4
Bore	3.500 in. (88.90 mm)	3.500 in. (88.90 mm)	3.5008 in. (88.92 mm)	
Stroke	3.150 in. (80.00 mm)	3.150 in. (80.00 mm)	3.150 in. (80.00 mm)	
Capacity	1990 cc	1990 cc	1990 cc	
Weight	Approx. 341 lb. (155 kg)	Approx. 341 lb. (155 kg)	Approx. 341 lb. (155 kg)	

Pistons

Material	Light-alloy
Permissible weight difference between pistons of one engine	0.35 oz. (10 gr.)
Piston length:	
B 18, early models	3.29 in. (83.5 mm)
B 18, later models	2.79 in. (71.0 mm)
B 20	2.79 in. (71.0 mm)
Running clearance - B 18	0.0008 - 0.0016 in. (0.02 - 0.04 mm)
- B 20A, B	0.0014 - 0.0020 in. (0.03 - 0.05 mm)
- B 20E, F	0.0016 - 0.0024 (0.04 - 0.06 mm)
Piston ring gap:	
B 18 engines	0.010 - 0.020 in. (0.25 - 0.50 mm)
B 20 engines	0.016 - 0.022 in. (0.40 - 0.55 mm)
Compression rings:	
Number of rings	2
Width	0.078 in. (1.98 mm)
Side clearance in groove:	
B 18 engines	0.0021 - 0.0032 in. (0.054 - 0.081 mm)
B 20 engines	0.0017 - 0.0028 in. (0.045 - 0.072 mm)
Oil scraper ring:	
Number of rings	1
Width	0.186 in. (4.74 mm)
Groove clearance	0.0017 - 0.0028 in. (0.045 - 0.072 mm)
Gudgeon pins:	
Arrangement	Fully floating with circlips at both ends
Fit in con rod	Sliding fit
Fit in piston	Push fit
Gudgeon pin diameter:	
Standard	0.866 in. (22.00 mm)
0.002 in. oversize	0.868 in. (22.05 mm)
0.004 in. oversize	0.870 in. (22.10 mm)
0.008 in. oversize	0.874 in. (22.20 mm)

Cylinder head

Height between cylinder head joint face and face for bolt heads - B 18	3.46 in. (88 mm)
- B 20A	3.41 in. (86.7 mm)
- B 20B	3.39 in. (86.2 mm)
- B 20E	3.34 in. (84.9 mm)
- B 20F	3.42 in. (87.0 mm)

Valves

Inlet valves:	
Seat angle in cylinder head	45°
Valve seat angle	44.5°
Seat width in cylinder head: - B 18	0.055 in. (1.4 mm)
- B 20	0.080 in. (2.0 mm)
Valve head diameter - B 18	1.58 in. (40 mm)
- B 20 (earlier models)	1.654 in. (42 mm)
(later models)	1.732 in. (44 mm)
Stem diameter: - B18	0.3419 - 0.3425 in. (8.685 - 8.700 mm)
- B 20	0.3132 - 0.3138 in. (7.955 - 7.970 mm)
Valve clearance: - B 18	0.016 - 0.018 in. (0.40 - 0.45 mm) (warm)
	0.020 - 0.022 in. (0.50 - 0.55 mm) (cold)
- B 20A, B 20E and B 20F	0.016 - 0.018 in. (0.40 - 0.45 mm) (warm and cold)
- B 20B	0.020 - 0.022 in. (0.50 - 0.55 mm) (warm and cold)
Exhaust valves:	
Seat angle in cylinder head	45°
Valve seat angle	44.5°
Seat width in cylinder head: - B 18	0.055 in. (1.4 mm)
- B 20	0.080 in. (2.0 mm)

Valve head diameter: - B 18 and B 20 ... ... 1.38 in. (35 mm)
Stem diameter: - B 18 ... ... 0.3403 - 0.3409 in. (8.645 - 8.660 mm)
      - B 20 ... ... 0.3120 - 0.3126 in. (7.925 - 7.940 mm)
Valve clearance: - B 18 ... ... 0.016 - 0.018 in. (0.40 - 0.45 mm) (warm)
      0.020 - 0.022 in. (0.50 - 0.55 mm) (cold)
      - B 20A, E, F ... ... 0.016 - 0.018 in. (0.40 - 0.45 mm) (cold and warm)
      - B 20B ... ... 0.020 - 0.022 in. (0.50 - 0.55 mm) (cold and warm)

Valve guides
Length:
  B 18, Inlet and Exhaust ... ... 2.48 in. (63 mm)
  B 20, Inlet ... ... 2.047 in. (52 mm)
  B 20, Exhaust ... ... 2.323 in. (59 mm)
Inner diameter:
  B 18 ... ... 0.3435 - 0.3441 in. (8.725 - 8.740 mm)
  B 20 ... ... 0.3200 - 0.3210 in. (8.000 - 8.022 mm)
Height above cylinder head face:
  B 18 ... ... 0.83 in. (21 mm)
  B 20 A and B ... ... 0.689 in. (17.5 mm)
  B 20 E and F ... ... 0.705 in. (17.9 mm)
Valve stem running clearance:
  B 18, Inlet ... ... 0.0010 - 0.0022 in. (0.025 - 0.055 mm)
  B 18, Exhaust ... ... 0.0026 - 0.0037 in. (0.065 - 0.095 mm)
  B 20, Inlet ... ... 0.0012 - 0.0026 in. (0.030 - 0.067 mm)
  B 20, Exhaust ... ... 0.0024 - 0.0038 in. (0.060 - 0.097 mm)

Valve springs
Free length ... ... 1.81 in. (46 mm)
Fitted length ... ... 1.57 in. (40.0 mm)
  With load of ... ... 60 - 70 lb. (27.2 - 31.8 kg)
Fitted length ... ... 1.18 in. (30 mm)
  With load of ... ... 172 - 191 lb. (78.2 - 86.8 kg)

Lubricating system
Oil capacity:
  With oil filter ... ... 6.5 Imp. pints (8 US pints; 3.75 litres)
  Without filter ... ... 5.75 Imp. pints (7 US pints; 3.25 litres)
Oil pressure at 2000 rpm.
  (Engine warm) ... ... 36 - 85 lb./sq. in. (2.5 - 6.0 kg/sq.cm)
Oil filter:
  Type ... ... Full flow
  Make ... ... Wix or Mann
Oil pump:
  Type ... ... Gear-type pump
  Gear end float ... ... 0.0008 - 0.004 in. (0.02 - 0.10 mm)
  Radial play ... ... 0.0032 - 0.0055 in. (0.08 - 0.14 mm)
  Backlash ... ... 0.006 - 0.014 in. (0.15 - 0.35 mm)
  Number of gear teeth 9
Relief valve spring:
  Free length - B 18 ... ... 1.28 in. (32.5 mm)
  Free length - B 20 ... ... 1.54 in. (39 mm)
  Fitted length - B 18 ... ... 0.89 in. (22.5 mm)
    With load of ... ... 17.6 lb. (8.0 kg)
  Fitted length - B 20 ... ... 0.83 in. (21.0 mm)
    With load of ... ... 13.7 - 17.1 lb.(6.2 - 7.8 kg)

Crankshaft
End float - B 18 ... ... 0.007 - 0.0042 in. (0.017 - 0.108 mm)
     - B 20 ... ... 0.0018 - 0.0054 in. (0.047 - 0.137 mm)
Main bearing running clearance:
  B 18A ... ... 0.010 - 0.030 in. (0.026 - 0.077 mm)
  B 18B ... ... 0.0015 - 0.0035 in. (0.038 - 0.089 mm)
  B 20 ... ... 0.0011 - 0.0033 in. (0.028 - 0.083 mm)
Big end bearing running clearance:
  B 18 ... ... 0.0015 - 0.0032 in. (0.039 - 0.081 mm)
  B 20 ... ... 0.0012 - 0.0028 in. (0.029 - 0.071 mm)
Permissible out-of-round of main bearing journals ... ... 0.0020 in. (0.05 mm)
Permissible out-of-round of big end bearing journsls ... ... 0.0020 in. (0.05 mm)

Main bearings
Main bearing journals:
  Diameter standard - B 18 ... ... 2.4977 - 2.4982 in. (63.441 - 63.454 mm)
      - B 20 ... ... 2.4981 - 2.4986 in. (63.451 - 63.464 mm)

Undersizes	-	B 18	...	...	...	...	...	...	0.010, 0.020, 0.030, 0.040 and 0.050 in.
	-	B 20	...	...	...	...	...	...	0.010, 0.020 in. only
Main bearing shells:								
Thickness - Standard	...	...	...	...	...	...	...	0.0781 - 0.0784 in. (1.985 - 1.991 mm)
Undersizes	...	...	...	...	...	...	...	0.010, 0.020, 0.030, 0.040 and 0.050 mm)

Big end bearings

Big end bearing journals:								
Diameter standard	-	B 18	...	...	...	...	...	2.1295 - 2.1300 in. (54.089 - 54.102 mm)
	-	B 20	...	...	...	...	...	2.1299 - 2.1304 in. (54.099 - 54.112 mm)
Undersizes	-	B 18	...	...	...	...	...	0.010, 0.020, 0.030, 0.040 and 0.050 in.
	-	B 20	...	...	...	...	...	0.010 and 0.020 in. only
Width	...	...	...	...	...	...	...	1.2579 - 1.2618 in. (31.950 - 32.050 mm)
Big end bearing shells:								
Thickness - Standard	...	...	...	...	...	...	...	0.0722 - 0.0725 in. (1.833 - 1.841 mm)
Undersizes	-	B 18	...	...	...	...	...	0.010, 0.020, 0.030, 0.040 and 0.050 in.
	-	B 20	...	...	...	...	...	0.010 and 0.020 in. only

Connecting rods

End float on journal	...	...	...	...	...	0.006 - 0.014 in. (0.15 - 0.35 mm)
Length between centres	....	...	...	...	...	5.710 ± 0.004 in. (145 ± 0.1 mm)
Permissible weight difference between con rods of one engine						0.21 oz. (6 gr.) max.

Camshaft

Number of bearings	...	...	...	...	...	...	3
Running clearance	...	...	...	...	...	...	0.0008 - 0.003 in. (0.020 - 0.075 mm)
End float	...	...	...	...	...	...	0.0008 - 0.0024 in. (0.020 - 0.060 mm)
Camshaft marking:							
B 18A, B 20A	...	...	...	...	...	...	A
B 18B, B 20B	...	...	...	...	...	...	C
B 20E, B20F	...	...	...	...	...	...	D
Bearing journal diameter:							
Front	...	...	...	...	...	...	1.8494 - 1.8504 in. (46.975 - 47.000 mm)
Centre	...	...	...	...	...	...	1.6919 - 1.6929 in. (42.975 - 43.000 mm)
Rear	...	...	...	...	...	...	1.4575 - 1.4567 in. (36.975 - 37.000 mm)
Valve clearance for valve timing setting (cold engine)							
B 18A, B 20A	...	...	...	...	...	...	0.043 in. (1.1 mm)
B 18B, B 20B	...	...	...	...	...	...	0.057 in. (1.45 mm)
B 20E, B 20F	...	...	...	...	...	...	0.055 in. (1.40 mm)
Inlet valve should then be open:							
B 18A, B 20A	...	...	...	...	...	...	10° A.T.D.C.
B 18B, B 20B	...	...	...	...	...	...	0° T.D.C.
B 20E, B 20F	...	...	...	...	...	...	5.5° B.T.D.C.
Radial clearance	...	...	...	...	...	...	0.008 - 0.0030 in. (0.020 - 0.075 mm)
End float	...	...	...	...	...	...	0.008 - 0.0024 in. (0.020 - 0.060 mm)
Timing gear:							
Backlash	...	...	...	...	...	...	0.0016 - 0.0032 in. (0.04 - 0.08 mm)

Flywheel

Permissible axial throw, max.	...	...	...	...	0.002 in. (0.05 mm) at a diameter of 5.9 in. (150 mm)

Torque wrench settings

								lb ft.	kgm
Cylinder head	...	...	...	...	...	...	...	61 - 69	8.5 - 9.5
Main bearings	...	...	...	...	...	...	...	87 - 94	12 - 13
Big end bearings	...	...	...	...	...	...	...	38 - 42	5.2 - 5.8
Flywheel	...	...	...	...	...	...	...	33 - 40	4.5 - 5.5
Spark plugs	...	...	...	...	...	...	...	27 - 33	3.8 - 4.5
Camshaft nut	...	...	...	...	...	...	...	94 - 108	13 - 15
Crankshaft pulley bolt	...	...	...	...	...	...	...	51 - 58	7 - 8
Oil sump bolts	...	...	...	...	...	...	...	6 - 8	0.8 - 1.1
Alternator bolts	...	...	...	...	...	...	...	45 - 75	6 - 10
Oil filter nipple	...	...	...	...	...	...	...	32 - 40	4.5 - 5.5

1 General description

The Volvo 140 series has used basically the same engine throughout. It started life as the B18, which was produced in two versions, the low compression B18A and the high compression B18B. The different compression was obtained by the use of a different cylinder head.

Starting with the 1969 series, the bore of the engine was increased, and it became the B20. This has been produced in four types; the B20A with a compression ratio of 8.7:1, the B20B with a compression ratio of 9.3:1, the B20E with a compression ratio of 10.5:1 and, most recently of all, the B20F which has reversed the trend and has the same compression ratio as the B20A.

As with the type B18, differences in compression are produced by using different designs of cylinder head.

The high compression B18B and B20B use a different camshaft from the low compression engines B18A and B20A. A third type of camshaft is used by the B20E and B20F engines which are designed for fuel injection. The camshafts for low compression, high compression and fuel injection engines are marked A, C and D respectively.

The engine is a four cylinder, water-cooled, overhead valve unit, the valves being pushrod operated by a three bearing camshaft. It employs alloy pistons and a five bearing crankshaft. The big end bearings are replaceable shells.

The three bearing camshaft is made of special grade cast iron and has case hardened cams. It operates the valves through the normal mechanism of tappets, pushrods and rockers. There are no inspection covers for the valve tappets since these are accessible after the cylinder head has been removed.

The connection rods are made of drop forged steel and have precision machined bushes at the little end which act as bearings for the gudgeon pins.

The pistons are made of light alloy and have two compression rings and one oil scraper ring. The upper compression ring is chromed in order to reduce cylinder wear.

The cylinder head is bolted to the block - ie there are no studs in the block. All the combustion chambers are machined throughout and have separate inlet and exhaust ports, one for each valve. The valves themselves have chromed stems and run in replaceable valve guides to which they are sealed with rubber seals.

The cylinder block is made of special cast iron and is cast as a single unit. The cylinder bores are machined directly in the block. The oilways in the block are arranged so that the oil filter, which is of the full flow type, is directly attached to the right hand side of the block.

The engine has a 'force' feed lubrication system. Pressure is provided by a gear pump driven from the camshaft and fitted under the crankshaft in the sump. The pump forces the oil past the relief valve (itself fitted inside the pump), through the oil filter and then through oilways out to the various lubricating points. All the oil supplied to the lubricating points first passes through the oil filter.

This quick glance at the B18, B20 engine series reveals a design which, though technically unadventurous, is lifted out of the rut by its concern for quality and reliability.

When, in later Chapters, we come to consider fuel and ignition systems, we will find that these are by no means old fashioned - just the reverse in fact. This bold combination of new ideas and well-established principles has produced in the Volvo 140 - particularly in its latest manifestations - a car with real individuality and character.

2 A closer look at the engine

Fig. 1.1 shows a "cut-away" view of the engine. Those who are contemplating an engine overhaul for the first time would be well advised to study this figure carefully in conjunction with the observations made in this section.

Fig. 1.1 Cutaway view of the engine (B20)

1 Cold air hose
2 Hot air hose
3 Flap, constant air temperature device
4 Fuel line
5 Temperature sensor
6 Valve guide
7 Valve spring
8 Retainer
9 Valve collet
10 Exhaust valve
11 Connection for crankcase hose
12 Valve stem seal
13 Intake valve
14 Oil filler cap
15 Carburettor (Stromberg)
16 Damping device
17 Air cleaner
18 Hose for crankcase gases
19 Vacuum hose for distributor
20 Choke wire
21 Rocker arm
22 Rocker arm shaft
23 Spring
24 Push rod
25 Bearing bracket
26 Rocker arm casing
27 Cylinder head
28 Rubber terminal
29 Spark plug cap
30 Seal
31 Vacuum hose
32 Vacuum governor
33 Distributor
34 Condenser
35 Valve tappet
36 Clamp bolt
37 Flywheel casing
38 Cylinder block
39 Gear wheel
40 Pilot bearing
41 Flywheel
42 Flange bearing shell
43 Sealing flange
44 Reinforcing bracket
45 Bush
46 Sump gasket
47 Oil pump
48 Main bearing cap
49 Delivery pipe
50 Main bearing shell
51 Crankshaft
52 Sump
53 Piston rings
54 Big end bearing cap
55 Connecting rod
56 Camshaft
57 Piston
58 Big end bearing shell
59 Small end bearing shell
60 Gudgeon pin
61 Washer
62 Spacing ring
63 Camshaft gear
64 Nut
65 Crankshaft gear
66 Hub
67 Washer
68 Bolt
69 Pulley
70 Key
71 Seal
72 Fan
73 Oil nozzle
74 Key
75 Timing gear cover
76 Coolant inlet
77 Gasket
78 Water pump
79 Gasket
80 Pulley
81 Alternator
82 Sealing ring
83 Cylinder head gasket
84 Tensioner
85 Water distributing pipe
86 Thermostat
87 Coolant outlet
88 Throttle spindle guard
89 Air cleaner
90 Carburettor (SU)
91 Manifold
92 Brake servo connection
93 Ventilation hose connection
94 Ventilation hose
95 Clamp

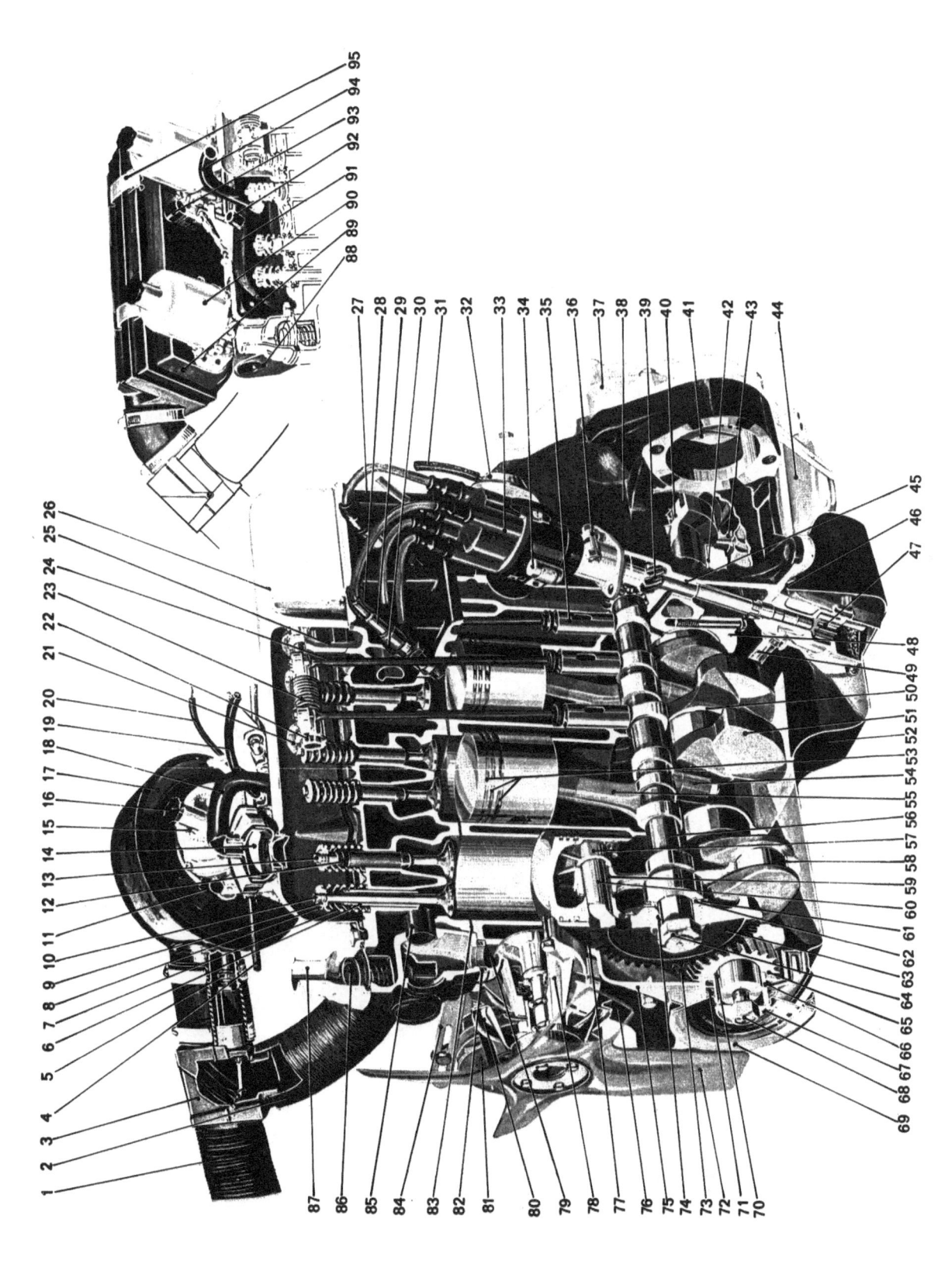

The crankshaft, which does not look like a shaft at all in the figure because most of it is hidden by the main bearings on which it runs or the connecting rods which drive it, has a gearwheel on the front end which drives a larger gear attached to the camshaft. The camshaft operates the valves by pushing on tappets, which in turn operate pushrods which work on rockers whose far ends push the valves downwards to open them. As the valves only have to be opened on alternate revolutions of the crankshaft, the camshaft is geared to run at half the speed of the crankshaft.

It is very important that the valves should open at exactly the right time in the cycle of operation, and that their rate of opening and closing should be carefully controlled. All this is taken care of by the shaping of the cams and the relationship between the camshaft and the crankshaft. In order to ensure that this relationship is correct when the engine is reassembled after dismantling, the camshaft gear and crankshaft gear are marked.

You can see that there is not much you can do about the valve timing, especially as the inlet and exhaust valves are all controlled from the same camshaft. If the camshaft is in good condition, the gears are correctly meshed, and the valve clearances are right you can rest assured that all is well. Valve clearances are important because the cams on the camshaft are designed to move the tappets comparatively slowly at the start and finish of a lifting cycle; if the clearances are too great the excessive hammering, as well as being noisy, can lead to wear and damage of the camshaft face, which is case hardened, ie it is extremely hard right on the surface but the hardness does not go very deep.

The other engine function which must be carefully timed is, of course, the ignition. This is gear driven from the camshaft and so maintained in a fixed relationship to the valve timing, but provision is made for adjusting the timing by having the distributor in a clamp so that it can be turned relative to the crankshaft, and in addition to this there are automatic timing controls within the distributor itself. The distributor is driven by a 1:1 skew gear from the camshaft, and so revolves at the same speed as the camshaft, ie half engine speed. Thus in two revolutions of the crankshaft the rotor arm selects each of the cylinders once. During this time the contact breaker has to produce four sparks; hence the familiar four-cornered cam which operates it. Because of the steep profiles of this cam, wrong setting of the points clearance has a noticeable effect on the ignition timing.

An extension to the spindle of the distributor drive pinion forms a handy means of driving the oil pump which sits in the sump.

The camshaft has a further function which is not shown in Fig.1.1. An extra cam (just behind the pair that drive the valves of number 1 cylinder) drives the petrol pump which is bolted to the outside of the crankcase. This is fully described in Chapter 3.

The flywheel and clutch are dealt with elsewhere. The toothed ring on the outside of the flywheel engages with a pinion on the starter motor. This is bolted to the casing with two bolts and has been removed in Fig. 1.1.

3 Engine removal - when is it necessary?

1 Because engine removal is a bothersome job for the ordinary owner whose lifting tackle may well consist of nothing more than a barely adequate pulley block, he will naturally want to do all he can with the engine still in place. The Volvo owner is fortunate in that he can remove the complete front section of the car (Chapter 12, Section 9) and this gives him very good access to the front of the engine. This means that such jobs as replacing the camshaft or timing gears present no problems with the engine in the vehicle. Removing the sump is a little awkward and has a section to itself later on (Section 44). Once it is removed, you can deal with the big end bearings, and with these removed and the head off you can push the conrods up the cylinders and remove the pistons.

2 This means that you can get at the engine sufficiently well to give it a thorough examination in order to decide whether, for example, it needs a re-bore or the crankshaft needs grinding, to say nothing of carrying out quite a range of repairs, without having to take the engine out of the car. Nevertheless, if you are faced with replacing the crankshaft or main bearings or if you have got to do anything on the flywheel more difficult than straightforward replacement of the clutch assembly, you will have to take the engine out.

4 Removing the engine

1 The engine will go in and out quite easily with the gearbox attached. There is no need to take off the front section of the body. However, we recommend that you take the gearbox off before you remove the engine. If overdrive is fitted this has to be removed even if you leave the gearbox on, and the bulk and weight of the automatic transmission where this is fitted makes its removal a must, (photos).

2 What we did when working on the car shown in the photographs was to take the engine out with the flywheel housing and gearbox detached and put it back again with the gearbox fitted, and we think that this is the best way. Lowering the engine into the vehicle is a much less awkward process than lifting it out and the presence of the gearbox at this stage is less

4.1a The engine coming out of the car ...

4.1b ... and going back

of a hindrance; in addition to this, refitting the gearbox and any necessary clutch alignment is much easier done with the engine on the bench than when you are on your back underneath the car.

5 Engine removal - sequence of operations (carburettor engines)

1 Remove the bonnet as described in Chapter 12, Section 7. Remove the radiator shroud (photo).
2 Drain off the engine oil into a suitable container that is clean, does not leak, sits underneath the sump and holds 7½ imperial pints, 9 US pints or 4¼ litres. This will hold the oil comfortably. You will find the drain plug right at the back of the sump.
3 Drain off the coolant. There is a drain cock on the side of the cylinder block just behind the oil filter but there isn't one on the radiator. Take the filler caps off the expansion tank and the

radiator to ensure complete drainage. Often the radiator does not have a proper filler cap but simply a screw-in plug (photos).
4 Unclip and remove the expansion tank, disconnect the radiator hoses from the engine, remove the radiator fixing bolts (one at either side) and lift it out (photos).
5 Slack off the fan belt by loosening the fixing bolts for the alternator or dynamo and moving it along its strut, remove the fan belt, unscrew the nuts fixing the fan, remove it together with any spacers and the fan pulley. Sometimes you will find more elaborate fan arrangements than we have shown, but removal will present no difficulties (photos).
6 Disconnect the positive lead from the battery. Take the battery right away at this stage though this isn't essential (photo).
7 Detach the high tension lead from the ignition coil and remove the distributor cap with all its leads attached (photos).
8 Disconnect the fuel pipe from the petrol pump and plug both pipe and pump (photo).

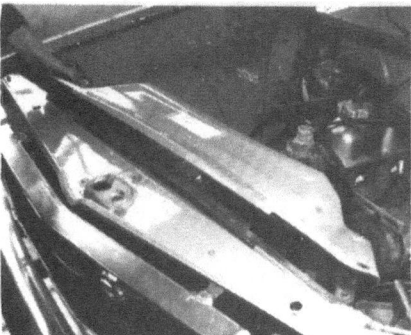
5.1 Removing the fan shroud

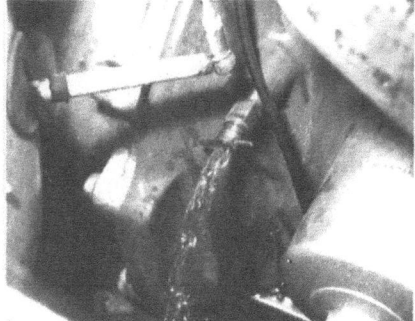
5.3a Draining the coolant

5.3b There is no need for a filler cap on the radiator because you normally top up via the expansion tank

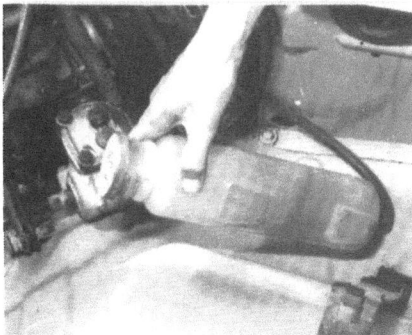
5.4a Removing the expansion tank

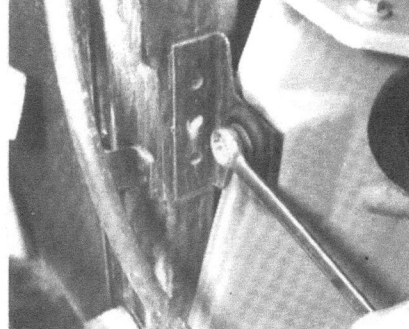
5.4b The radiator is held by one bolt at each side

5.4c Out comes the radiator

5.5a The alternator has been moved along its strut far enough to allow the fan belt to be moved

5.5b The fan is removed ...

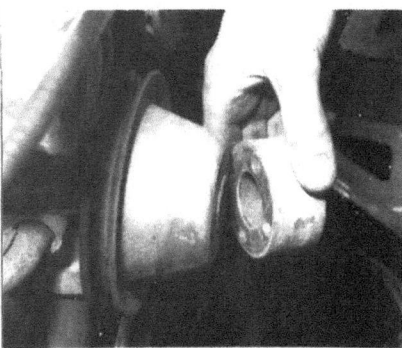
5.5c ... followed by a spacer (or may be a viscous variable speed device) ...

5.5d ... and the fan pulley is removed

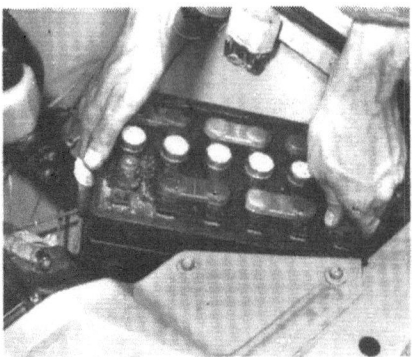

5.6 We like the battery out of the way

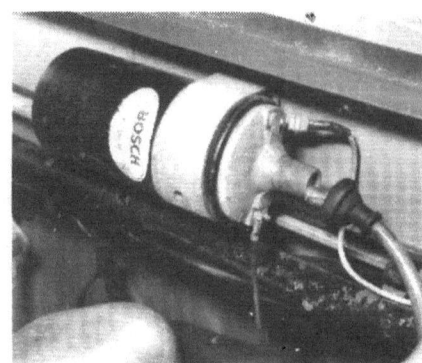

5.7a Detach the high tension lead from the coil

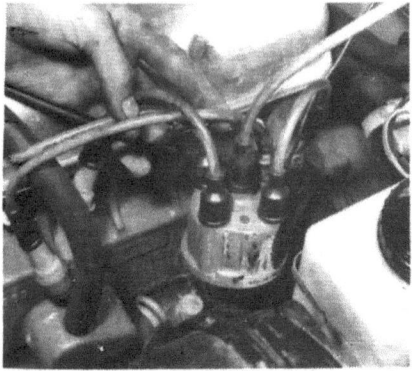

5.7b Remove the distributor cap and leads

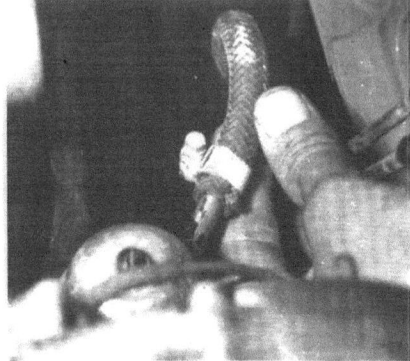

5.8 The fuel pipe coming off the petrol pump

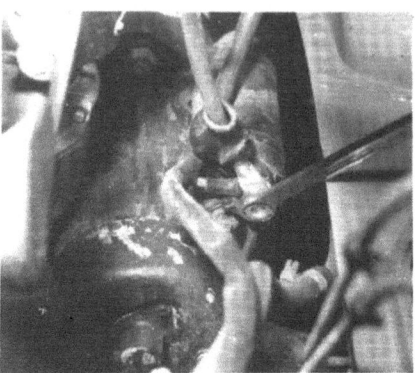

5.9a Starter motor leads

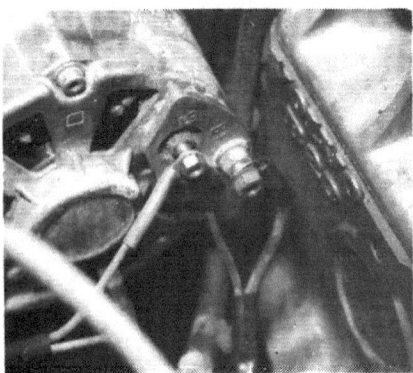

5.9b Alternator leads

5.10a This is the warm air connection for the air intake system. The picture shows first stage of exhaust pipe removal

5.10b The cool air comes in here. The hose just pulls out

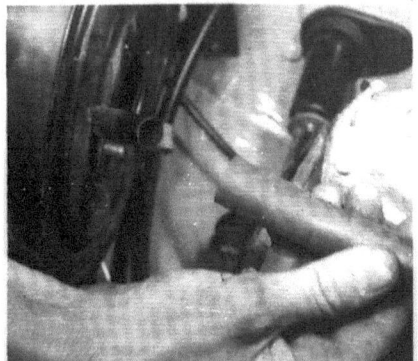

5.10c This hose goes to the crankcase breather

5.10d The crankcase breather

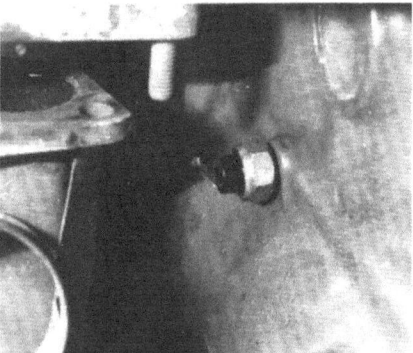

5.12a The oil pressure sensor is near the exhaust pipe flange

9 Remove the leads from the starter motor and the alternator or dynamo (photos).

10 Remove the air cleaner and its associated intake hoses. The warm air hose is attached to the pre-heater plate where the exhaust pipe meets the manifold and the cold air hose pulls out of a hole not far from the radiator bracket on the right-hand side of the car. A further hose leads to the crankshaft breather and can be detached at either end (photos).

11 Remove the pre-heater plate and disconnect the exhaust pipe (photo 5.10a).

12 Disconnect the leads from the oil pressure sensor and the water temperature sensor (photos).

13 Disconnect the choke wire from the carburettor or carburettors, disconnect the throttle control rod from the linkage attached to the manifold, pull out the hose from the vacuum brake servo and disconnect the heater hoses from the pipe ends at the back of the engine (photos).

14 From here proceed to Section 7.

6 Engine removal - fuel injection engines

1 Carry out operations Nos. 1 to 6 of Section 5.

2 Remove the hose for the pressure sensor from the inlet duct, the fuel hose for the cold start valve from the distributor pipe and the fuel hoses from the pipes at the fire wall, (photo).

3 Remove the plug contacts from the cold start valve, the throttle valve switch and the coolant temperature sensor (photo 6.2) Fig. 1.2.

4 Remove the air intake hose (photo 6.2).

5 Remove the leads from the air temperature sensor (Fig.1.3).

6 Remove the earth lead (if one is fitted) from the inlet duct.

7 Remove the bolts holding down the pressure regulator. Alternatively, if it is mounted as shown in Fig.1.4, disconnect the hose joining it to the distributor pipe; Disconnect the complete injector and distribution pipe assembly by turning the locking rings on the injectors anti-clockwise and withdrawing them from the block (Fig.1.5). The complete assembly will still be fastened to the body by its cable harness but can be placed out of the way of the engine, for example on the container for the windscreen washer fluid. Before you do anything else, cover the ends of the injectors so that no dirt can get in and plug the inlet ports in the engine.

8 Disconnect the throttle cable from the throttle control and remove the bracket holding its casing from the inlet duct to

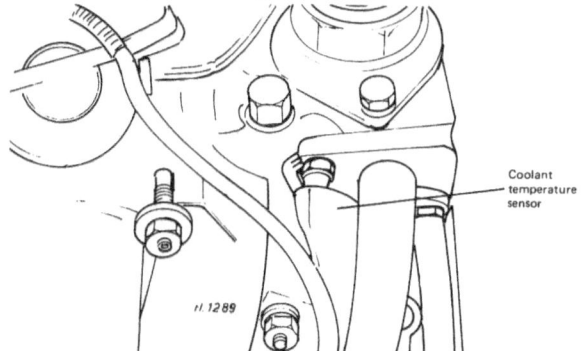

Coolant temperature sensor

Fig. 1.2. Coolant temperature sensor

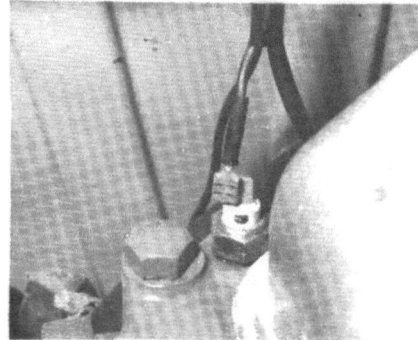

5.12b The water temperature sensor is at the right hand rear corner of the cylinder head

5.13a The choke lead

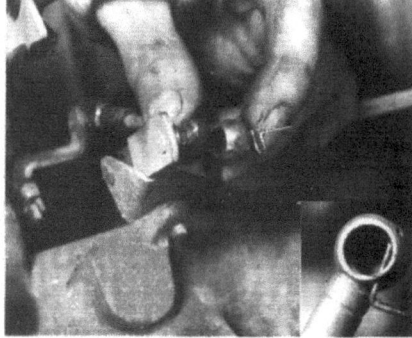

5.13b The throttle linkage and its clip

5.13c The hose to the brake servo simply pulls out

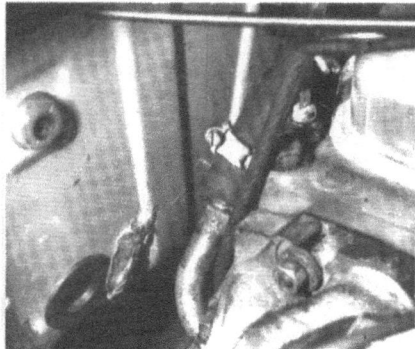

5.13d The connections to the heater were a problem to our photographer - he had to wait for this one until the engine was coming out

6.2 Connections to inlet duct
A - hose to pressure sensor
B - hose to cold start valve
C - cable for plugs to cold start valve and throttle valve switch
D - vacuum pipe to distributor
E - air intake hose

6.7 If you look at the pressure gauge as shown in Fig.1.4 you will be able to spot it in this photo

6.8 Throttle control wire and bracket holding it

7.4 Undoing the nut on an engine front mounting

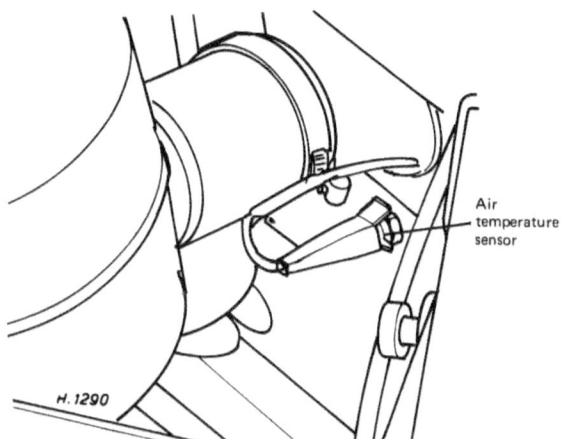

Air temperature sensor

H.1290

Fig. 1.3 Inlet air temperature sensor

Fig. 1.4 Pressure regulator - alternative mounting to that shown in photo 6.7

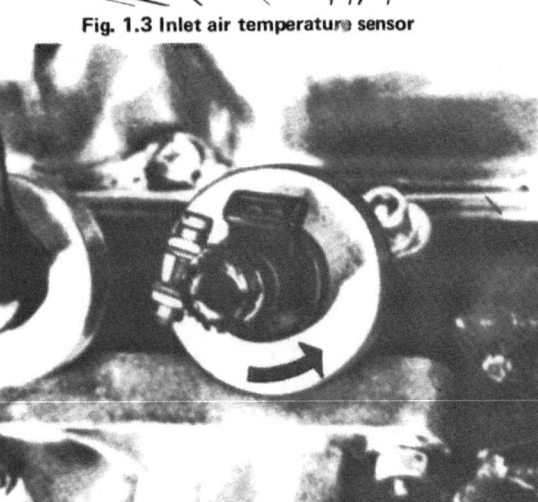

Fig. 1.5 Removing injector

which it is fastened by two screws (photo).

9 Remove the leads from the oil pressure sensor, the water temperature sensor and the alternator (see photos 5.12a, 5,12b and 5.9b).

10 Pull out the hose from the vacuum brake servo and disconnect the heater hoses from the ends of the pipes at the back of the engine (see photos 5.13c and 5.13d).

11 Remove the ignition leads from the spark plugs and the distributor cap from the distributor. Remove the ignition coil high tension lead and take off the distributor cap complete with its leads (see photos 5.7a and 5.7b).

12 Proceed to Section 7.

7 Engine removal (continued) - all types

1 If you have carried out the instructions in Section 5 for a carburettor engine or Section 6 for a fuel injection engine the following instructions will complete the job for either type.

2 Remove the overdrive (if fitted) gearbox or automatic transmission as described in Chapter 6.

3 Alternatively, if you intend to remove engine and gearbox as a unit, carry out the operations described in Chapter 6.

4 Remove the lower nuts from the engine front mountings (photo).

5 Rig up your lifting tackle. As you can see by looking again at photographs 4.1a and 4.1b we use something that the owner really ought to have - a length of plastic covered steel cable terminated with selfgrip hooks. Use a beam and hoist, or a tripod. If you use a tripod, be sure that the legs are tied together so that there is no fear of its collapsing. Unless you are very sure of your lifting tackle, as a result of previous experience, take things very carefully at first; lift the engine up a little way and see how things are stretched and how the engine balances. After one or two false starts you will soon achieve the results shown in the photographs (4.1a and 4.1b). You can do it all on your own, but it is much better to have an assistant.

8 Dismantling the engine - general

1 The essential preliminary to dismantling an engine is cleaning. The ideal way to do this is to brush the engine all over with paraffin or, better, 'Gunk' or a similar commercial solvent. Allow it to stand for a while and then hose it down. Where the dirt is thick and deeply embedded, work the solvent into it with a wire

brush. If the engine is very dirty a second application may be necessary here and there. Finally, wipe down the outside of the engine with a rag. If you are not able to hose down the engine in this way, cleaning is much more laborious, but however laborious it is , it will pay you in the long run. After all, the engine has got to be cleaned at the end of the dismantling process, so it might just as well be as clean as possible at the start.

2   Clean each part as you strip the engine. Try to ensure that everything you take off - down to the smallest washer - goes back exactly where it came off and exactly the same way round. This means that you should lay the various bits and pieces out in a tidy manner. Nuts, bolts and washers may often be replaced finger tight from where they were removed.

3   Most parts can easily be cleaned by washing them in paraffin and wiping down with a cloth, but do not immerse parts with oilways in paraffin. They are best wiped down with a petrol or paraffin dampened cloth, and the oilways cleaned out with nylon pipe cleaners.

4   Reuse of old gaskets is false economy. You will be bound to get oil and water leaks, if nothing worse. Always use genuine Volvo gaskets obtainable from your Volvo agent. Volvo say that you should not use jointing compound with any of their gaskets.

5   Do not throw the old gaskets away as you strip the engine down. You may need them for checking the pattern of new ones or as templates for making gaskets for which you cannot get hold of replacements. Hang up the old gaskets as they are removed.

6   In this Chapter we have described the order in which we stripped down the engine shown in most of the photographs. Where it seems necessary we have explained why we removed or did not remove certain parts at certain times. Generally speaking when stripping an engine it is best to work from the top down at least once you have removed the gearbox. Support it with wood blocks so that it stands firmly on its sump or the base of

the crankcase to start with. When you get to the stage of removing the crankshaft and connecting rods, turn it on its side and carry out all subsequent work with it in this position.

9   Dismantling the engine on the bench

1   Assuming that the engine is out of the car and on the work bench, first of all remove the inlet and exhaust manifolds for a carburettor engine or the inlet ducting and exhaust manifold in the case of a fuel injection engine and pull out the pipe that goes from the water pump along the side of the block to the heater. Once this is done there ceases to be any difference between fuel injection engines and carburettor engines, and the instructions which follow are equally applicable to both (photos).

2   It is a good idea to start with the more cumbersome items as the remainder of the engine then gets progressively easier to handle. If you have not already removed the gearbox, do so now by removing the bolts round the edge of the flywheel housing. Two of these anchor the starter motor which will now be freed (photos).

3   Remove the rocker arm casing which is held down by small screws round its edges. Remove the four screws holding down the rocker arm assembly and lift it off. Take out the pushrods and put them in a safe place. There is no advantage in keeping them in order though this is a good idea for valves. Remove the thermostat. Unscrew the bolts holding down the cylinder head and place it on one side. Lift out the tappets with pliers (photos).

4   It is now easy to remove the water pump. Notice how it is sealed to the cylinder head by two rings. It can of course be removed and fitted with the cylinder head in position (photos).

5   The fuel pump (on a carburettor engine) and the crankcase breather are easy to deal with. The crankcase breather is fastened

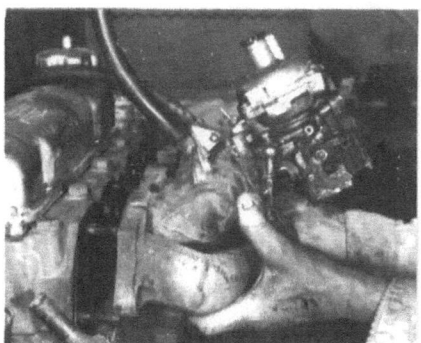

9.1a Removing the manifold

9.1b This pipe pulls out of the water pump (you can see the ring seal inside the pump) ...

9.1c ... and is clamped by a manifold fixing nut

9.1d Don't forget these when you reassemble!

9.2a Two of the bolts securing the fly wheel housing

9.2b The starter motor is released when the fly wheel housing is removed

9.3a Taking off the rocker casing

9.3b Taking off the rocker shaft assembly

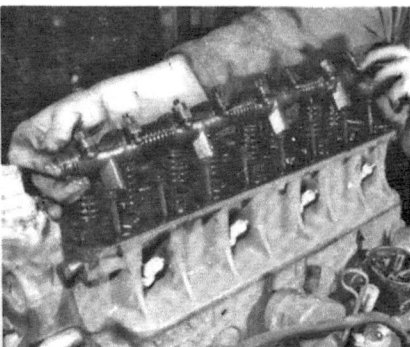
9.3c ... is quite simple

9.3d Out come the push rods

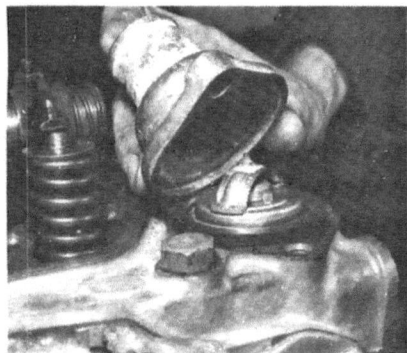
9.3e Removing this cover ...

9.3f ... lets us get at the thermostat

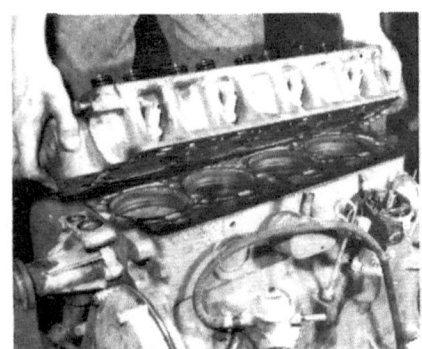
9.3g The cylinder head is removed

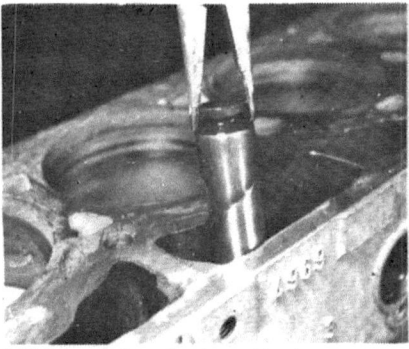
9.3h Then it is a simple matter to remove the tappets

9.4a The water pump has a gasket between it and the cylinder head

9.4b These rubber rings seal the water pump outlets to the cylinder head

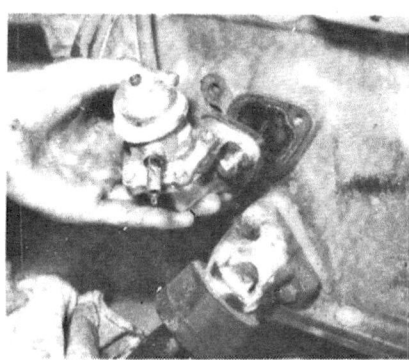
9.5a The fuel pump is removed ...

9.5b ... likewise the crankcase breather

to the case by a single screw (photos). The oil filter simply unscrews. The neat way in which the alternator is fixed makes its removal a simple matter (photo).

6 As the distributor is timed, its removal is better left until you have taken off the timing case. This enables you to note the position of the rotor arm shaft for a given timing setting and so ensure that the timing is the same when you replace the distributor.

7 Before removing the crankshaft pulley, note the index mark on the timing cover and the figures on the edge of the pulley which indicate degrees before or after top dead centre for No 1 (front) and No 4 (back) pistons (see photo). This is not sufficient for checking the setting of the rotor arm in the distributor because you don't know which of these cylinders is firing.

8 Take out the central bolt and draw off the crankshaft pulley (photo).

9 Remove the timing case cover (photo) and take out the

spring clip, retaining washer and felt ring. These have to be removed to permit the correct aligning procedure to be carried out when refitting, and in any event the felt ring should be replaced.

10 With the timing cover removed, we can set the timing for checking the position of the rotor arm. Rotate the crankshaft until the timing dot on the crankshaft gear comes opposite the mark on the camshaft gear as shown in the photograph.

11 Mark the position of the distributor shaft which carries the rotor arm and also mark the position that the distributor assembly occupies relative to its clamp - just in case you want to loosen the clamp later on. Now undo the fastening bolts and lift out the clamp and assembly as a unit. Follow this by lifting out the driving gear which is operated by the camshaft (photos).

12 Remove the nut from the camshaft and pull off its timing gear as shown in the photograph. Be careful not to push the camshaft backwards - certainly you should not hammer it - because the hole in which it runs at the back of the cylinder

9.5c Take out the bolt attaching the alternator strut to the body, slacken but don't remove the bottom nut ...

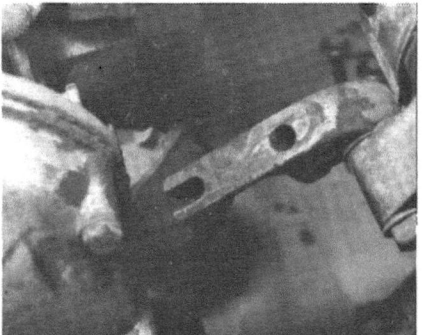
9.5d ... and lift the alternator off

9.7 Timing marks on the crankshaft pulley

9.8 Remove the central bolt and the pulley will come off without difficulty

9.9a The timing cover can now be removed

9.9b ... revealing the timing gears

9.10 The timing marks aligned

9.11a Withdrawing the distributor assembly

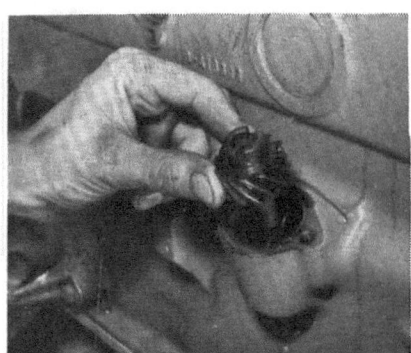
9.11b Distributor drive gear is lifted out

block is supposed to be sealed off for life and it certainly won't be if you hammer the camshaft against it. You can see the seal (or most of it) in the top left hand corner of photograph 9.15a). Now remove the thrust flange and the spacer ring behind it, and you can then withdraw the camshaft (photos). Now pull off the sleeve (called by Volvo a 'hub') - you will probably be able to start it on its way by getting a bit of purchase under the two holes on the timing gear. These holes are threaded, and bolts screwed into them can form the basis of a simple device for pulling the timing gear off. If however you are removing the crankshaft you can easily take it off later which is what we did.

13 Unscrew the bolts holding the clutch housing to the flywheel a little at a time, keeping them all in step to avoid the risk of distorting the clutch housing. Mark the clutch housing and flywheel to identify position for replacement, and remove the clutch assembly from the flywheel (photos).

14 Stop the flywheel from turning by wedging it with a screwdriver as shown in the photograph, undo the six bolts holding it to the crankshaft and lift it away, (photo) marking flywheel and shaft to identify position.

15 Undo the wired bolts holding on the sealing flange and remove it (photos).

16 Remove the reinforcing plate and the sump. Undo the bolts fastening the oil pipe to the crankcase and remove the oil pump. Its delivery pipe simply pushes into a hole in the crankcase and it is sealed by a rubber ring.

17 Before proceeding any further have a look at the bearing caps. You will see that they are marked, either with dots as are shown in several of our photographs for example 9.18a, or with stamped figures, to indicate their positions. When the bearing caps are refitted they must be put back in the same places and the same way round as they were before. The big ends are marked 1, 2, 3 and 4, the front one (in accordance with time-honoured convention) being No 1. The five main bearings are marked 1 - 5, No 1 being at the front. It is easy to see which way round the caps are meant to be because of the shape of the pads which carry the dots. Often these pads are circular, in which case it may be more difficult to remember how the caps have to go. If you are in doubt, put your own marks on. You should also find a mark on one side of the connecting rod and a corresponding mark on the same side of the bearing cap which enables you to be sure that the piston as well as the bearing cap goes back the same way round as it came out. If you cannot find such marks, make them yourself. When you remove the shells, mark them too, so that you can tell where they came from if a later inspection reveals faults.

18 Now for each of the connecting rods in turn, remove the bearing cap and shell, and push the connecting rod up the cylinder, steadying the piston with the other hand as it emerges. Take great care when doing this that things do not get banged about or scratched, and in particular that the skirt of the piston does not knock against the connecting rod (photos). Remove the main bearing caps with their shells, and the crankshaft can be lifted out of the crankcase. Pull off the timing gear, now a very simple matter (photos).

19 Removal of a retaining clip and protecting ring at the back end of the crankshaft reveals the pilot bearing for the clutch (photo). There is no need to remove this in order to inspect it thoroughly, and we suggest that you only remove it if you intend to replace it. It then does not matter if the removal process damages the bearing. If you have not got a puller which will do the job, a suggested method is to fill the cavity behind the bearing with thick grease, push a circular drift which is a pretty good fit into the bearing, and give the drift a good blow with a hammer. The pressure exerted by the grease will then drive the bearing out.

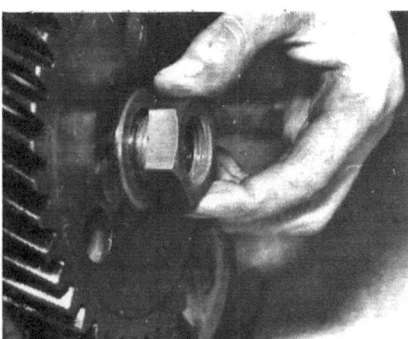

9.12a Undoing the central nut on the camshaft

9.12b Pulling off the timing gear (be careful - it is a fibre gear)

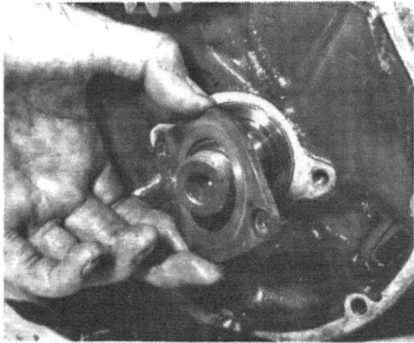

9.12c Remove the flange and the spacing ring behind it

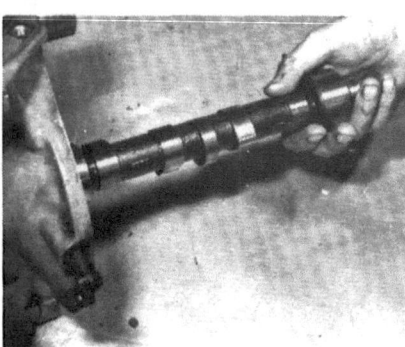

9.12d and you can then remove the camshaft

9.12e The sleeve or "hub" that takes the crankshaft pulley. Note the key that also keys the timing gear. Just under the tip of the thumb you can see the nipple which directs oil on to the gears

9.13a Removing the clutch housing

9.13b The clutch assembly comes away

9.14a How to hold the fly wheel steady while undoing the centre bolts (they were being done up while this was being taken)

9.14b The fly wheel is lifted away

9.15a The wired bolts holding on the sealing flange

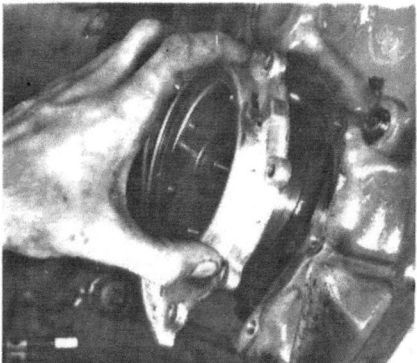

9.15b Removing the sealing flange

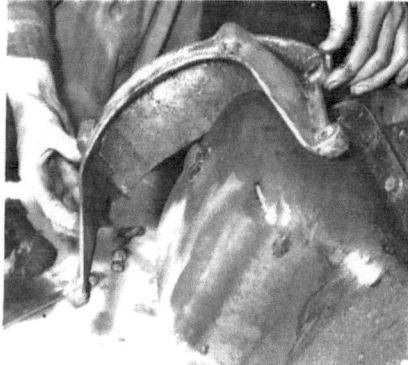

9.16 a Removing the reinforcing plate - when this is off the sump can be removed

9.16b Oil pump removal

9.16c Note the rubber seal on the oil delivery pipe

9.18a Taking off the bigend bearing cap note the dot marks on the main bearing cap indicating numbers 3 and 4 (number 1 is at the front)

9.18b The piston emerging from the cylinder

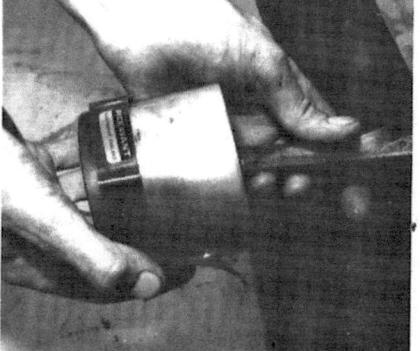

9.18c This photo (taken on re-assembly - hence the ring clamp on the piston) shows how to handle a piston and connecting rod. No fear of damage if you do it this way!

9.18d Removing the main bearing caps. Number 1 is still in place though its bolts have been taken out

9.18e The rear main bearing cap and shell. This is the only one which has flanges

9.18f At last the crankshaft can be lifted out

9.18g With the crankshaft out of the engine it is easy to pull off the timing gear

9.19 The pilot bearing for the gearbox input shaft

10.2a Compressing the valve springs

10.2b When the spring is compressed the collets can be removed ...

10.2c ... the retainer and spring lifted off ...

10.2d ... the rubber seal removed ...

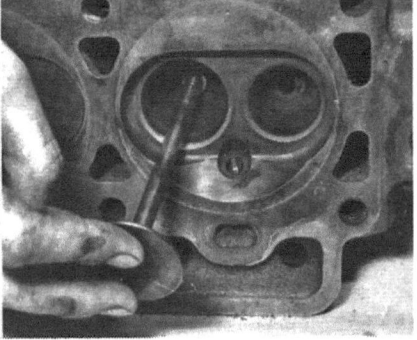

10.2e ... and the valve is withdrawn from the cylinder head

10 Overhauling the cylinder head and valves

1   Clean the oil and grease off the cylinder head and remove the carbon from the combustion chamber and valve heads with a scraper or rotary wire brush.

2   Remove the valves by compressing the valve springs until the collets are free of the recesses in the spring retainers, remove the collets, release the pressure on the spring, lift off the spring and its retainer. Push the valve through the valve guide and remove it. If the valve seems a tight fit in the guide, this may be because the upper part of the stem has dirt or carbon on it. Give it a clean in this case. Remove the rubber seal from the end of the valve guide (photos). Keep the valves in the order in which you removed them. A good idea is to stick them through holes in a piece of thick paper. We like to stand them up when we have done this, and slip the spring and retainer belonging to each valve over the

stem. Then if we find anything amiss with a valve seat we know at once which valve and spring to look at.

3   With the valve removed, clean out any remaining carbon from the ports. This done, examine the valve seats. If they are only slightly pitted you will be able to make them smooth again by grinding the valves against the seats as described in the next Section. Where bad pitting has occurred they will have to be re-cut - a job for the specialist. Grinding the valves is described in Section 13.

4   Check the valve guides with the valve stems to ensure that they are a good fit; the valve stems should move easily in the guides without slop or side play. Worn guides can be extracted and new ones installed. The guides should project above the adjacent surface of the cylinder head by the amounts shown in Fig. 1.6. After fitting new guides, check that they are free from burr and that the valves move easily in them. Note that guides for B20 engines are different from those for B18 engines. Be

sure to have the step end of the B20 guides at the top.

5 Examine the valves, checking them for straightness and noting the condition of their faces. Slight pitting can be removed by grinding in, but if it is serious the valves will have to be refaced by a specialist.

6 Remove the carbon at the tops of the cylinder bores and polish them. Now examine them for scoring, scratching and wear. Start by carefully examining the top of the bores. If they are worn you will detact a very slight ridge at the top of the cylinder at the highest point the piston reaches. Using an internal micrometer, measure the maximum diameter of the cylinder just below this ridge and compare it with the diameter at the bottom where no wear has taken place. If the difference between these diameters exceeds 0.010" (0.025 mm) you need a rebore. If you have no micrometer, remove the rings from a piston and insert it in its cylinder about ¾" (19 mm) below the top of the bore. If you can slide a 0.010" (0.025 mm) feeler gauge between the top of the piston and the cylinder on the right-hand side just below the ridge you need a rebore. If the wear is less, the diameter difference or feeler gauge thickness will be correspondingly reduced. If it is around .004" (.010 mm) you can buy and fit special rings designed to cope with small amounts of cylinder wear and stop the engine burning oil.

7 Reboring, followed by the fitting of over-sized pistons is a job for specialists. Your Volvo Agent will be able to arrange for this to be done for you.

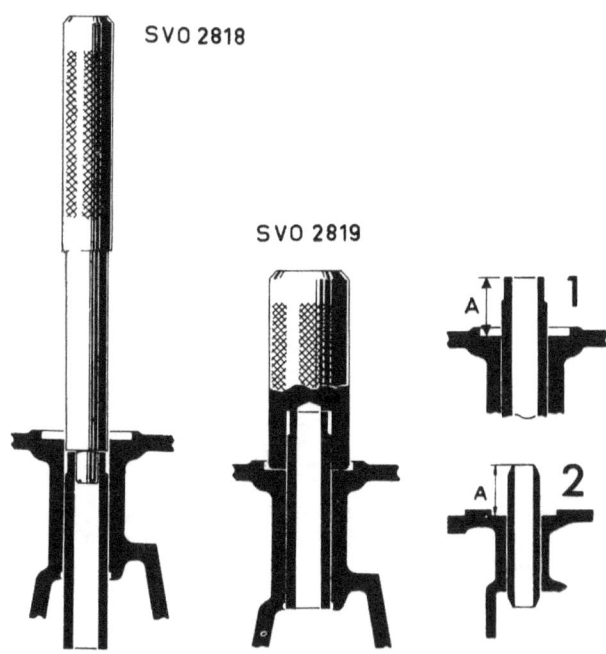

Fig. 1.6 Replacing valve guides

1 —B20
2 —B18
A = 0.827" (20.1 mm) B18
    0.689" (17.5 mm) B20A - B
    0.705" (17.9 mm) B20E - F

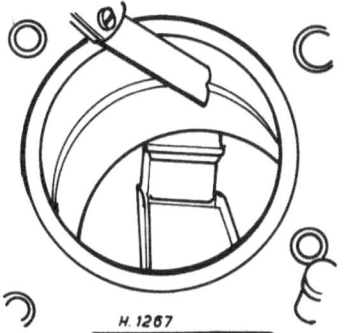

Fig. 1.7 Measuring the piston ring gap

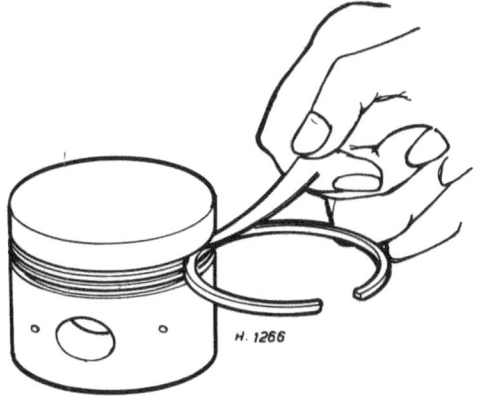

Fig. 1.8 Checking piston ring clearance in groove

11 Pistons and piston rings - examination and renovation

1 If the old pistons are to be refitted, carefully remove the piston rings and then thoroughly clean them. Take particular care to clean out the piston ring grooves. Do not scratch the comparatively soft material of the pistons in any way. Piston rings can be easily removed by raising one end and slipping a thin metal strip (such as an old feeler gauge of around 0.020" (0.05 mm) underneath it. Slide the strip round the piston easing the ring out of the grooves as you go. Fitting pistons is considered in detail in Section 24, paragraph 4.

2 If new rings are to be fitted to the old pistons, then the top ring should be stepped so as to clear the ridge left above the previous top ring. If a normal but oversize new ring is fitted it will hit the ridge and break, because the new ring will not have worn in the same way as the old.

3 Before fitting the rings on the pistons, put them in the cylinder bore at a point below the bottom limit of their travel and check their gap. (Fig.1.7). This should be between 0.016 - 0.022" (0.40 - 0.55 mm). If the ring gap is too small rub down the ends of the ring with a very fine file until it is correct. To keep the rings square in the bore for measurement, line them up with a piston in the bore.

4 Check the fit of the piston rings in the grooves by rolling them round the groove and inserting feeler gauges (Fig.1.8). For correct clearances, see specifications at the beginning of this Chapter. Note that of the two compression rings, the chromium plated one goes at the top. The scraper ring, which is grooved fits in the bottom groove.

5 In engine manufacture the cylinders are all machined simultaneously and because of this have very slight differences in diameter, This is allowed for by selecting pistons to fit each bore, this is why it is so important when refitting old pistons that they should be replaced in the cylinders that they came from.

12 Gudgeon pins

1 The gudgeon pins are retained in the pistons by circlips and can easily be pushed out of the pistons when these are removed. When you separate the connecting rod from the piston, mark the connecting rod so that you can refit it the same way round. There is no need to mark the piston as this has a small slot (which must always face forwards when the piston is in the

engine) on the top.

2 The fit of the gudgeon pin in the connecting rod should be such that it can be pushed out with light thumb pressure but should have no noticeable looseness. It should fit in the piston so that you can push it through by hand, against light resistance. If the gudgeon pin hole in the piston is worn, an over-sized gudgeon pin must be fitted. In this case the holes must be reamed out in line to the correct measurement (see paragraph 4).

3 If the bush in the connecting rod is worn, it can be pressed out and a new bush pressed in. The new bush must be reamed to the correct fit.

4 Reaming is best carried out by someone who has suitable machinery and experience. If you do not come within this category, have it done through your Volvo Agent.

13 Grinding in the valves

1 Grinding in is essential when fitting valves whether these, or their seats, be new or old. As well as removing every trace of scoring, it ensures that the valve face and the seat have exactly the same slope and hence a reasonably wide area of contact. Where new valves are being fitted to correctly re-cut seats, grinding is still essential, because - as you can see from the specifications at the start of the Chapter - a valve face is cut to

an angle which is very slightly less than that of the face in the cylinder head and consequently the contact area is very small (see Fig.1.9). The correct area of contact is obtained by grinding.

2 Valve grinding is a simple matter, needing only fine and coarse carborundum paste, an inexpensive tool and a great deal of patience. Fig.1.10 illustrates the procedure. Place the cylinder head upside down on a bench with a block of wood at each end to give clearance for the valve stems.

3 Smear a trace of coarse carborundum paste on the seat face and apply a suction grinding tool to the valve head. Press lightly on the tool, and rub your hands together about a couple of dozen times; then lift the valve from the seat and give it a quarter or half a turn before repeating the process. When a dull, matt, even surface finish is produced on both the valve seat and the valve, wipe off the coarse paste and carry on with fine paste, lifting and turning the valve as before. When a smooth unbroken ring of light grey matt finish is produced on both valves and valve seat faces, the grinding operation is complete (photos). Aim to get a surface 0.08" (2.00 mm) on B18 engines and 0.055" (1.4 mm) on B20 engines. If the seat is too wide, you can reduce the width by carefully rounding off the corners with an oil stone.

4 When the grinding is complete, clean away every trace of grinding compound with paraffin or petrol. Take great care that none is left in the ports or the valve guides.

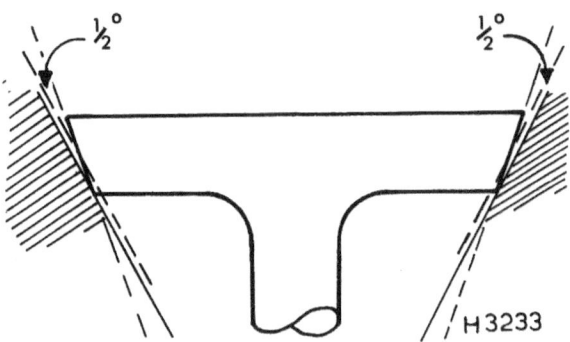

Fig. 1.9 Diagram of valve and seat. When the valve and seat are newly cut, the valve angle is slightly steeper than the seat angle (the difference is exaggerated in the diagram). Contact only occurs at the corners and grinding progressively removes these corners until the correct seat width is obtained.

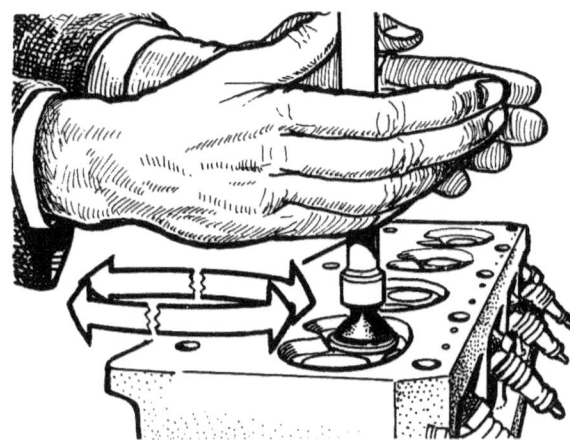

Fig. 1.10 Valve grinding using hand suction tool. Lift off seat occasionally to spread grinding paste evenly over seat and valve face.

13.3a Grind patiently until you get a smooth even seating surface like the one on the right of the tool ...

13.3b ... and the same thing on the valve

14 Rockers and rockershaft - overhaul

1 Remove the circlips from the ends of the shaft and take off the springs and rockers. Remove the plugs from the ends of the shaft and give it a good clean paying special attention to the oil holes through which the rockers are lubricated. Check the shaft for straightness by rolling it on a flat surface, and for wear which will show as ridges where the rocker arms were running. If any wear is present or the shaft is appreciably distorted, replace it. Wear is likely to have occurred only if the rockershaft oil holes have become blocked.

2 Check the rocker arms for wear on the rocker arm bushes. There should be no appreciable play between the rocker arm and the shaft. If there is, the bushes in the rocker arms can be pressed out and replaced, but after replacement they must be reamed to fit the shaft correctly. Unless you are equipped and experienced this is a job best left to your Volvo Agent.

3 Check the tip of the rocker arm where it bears on the valve for cracking or serious wear. If none is present the rocker arm may be refitted. Otherwise replace it - grinding the face is only a short term remedy because the arm is case - hardened.

4 Check the pushrods for straightness. If bent they must be renewed.

15 Tappets

Clean these thoroughly and look them over for any indentation on the end that bears on the camshaft. Check that they are a reasonable fit in the cylinder block. It is very unusual to find anything wrong with the tappets, but you should look them over just the same.

16 Camshaft

1 The camshaft and its bearing bushes in the cylinder block are another part of the Volvo engine which seems virtually everlasting. If there is noticeable play between the camshaft and its bearings, they will have to be replaced, but this is a highly specialised job, involving as it does the reaming of three bushes in line - definitely a task for the specialist.

2 The camshaft itself should show no sign of wear. If very light scoring marks are present they can be removed by gently rubbing down with a very fine emery cloth or an oil stone. The greatest care must be taken to keep the cam profiles smooth.

17 Timing gear - overhaul

1 The Volvo timing system is simplicity itself: only two gears and nothing to adjust. If the fibre gear on the camshaft is worn it will have to be renewed: unfortunately this will mean renewal of the crankshaft gear also as the gears are not available separately.

2 Take out and clean the oil spray nipple which can be seen just under the thumb in photo 9.12e.

18 Crankshaft and bearings - examination and renewal

1 Inspect the bearing shells for signs of general wear, scoring, pitting and scratches. The shells should be a matt grey in colour. If any trace of copper colour is noticed, you can be certain that the bearings are badly worn, because the white metal is plated onto a copper coloured underlay.

2 The purpose of inspecting the shells is to give some indication of where you may find wear on the crankshaft. Even if they appear perfect, they should be replaced. In fact it is a very good idea to change big end bearings every 25 - 30,000 miles and main bearings at 50,000 miles irrespective of bearing wear. This will ensure that your crankshaft lasts for 100,000 miles or more before it needs regrinding.

3 The bearing shells will have figures stamped on them to indicate their size, and naturally you will be sure that the shells you buy are of the same size as the ones you took out.

4 Examine the bearing surfaces on the crankshaft for signs of scoring or scratches and check their ovality with a micrometer. Take measurements at a number of positions on each surface, paying particular attention to the surfaces for which the bearing shells show signs of wear. You will of course know which bearing shells belong to which surface because you marked the shells when dismantling. If you get differences in diameter of more than .002" (0.05 mm) on the main bearing surfaces or .003" (0.07 mm) on the big end surfaces the crankshafts must be reground. It is probably worthwhile regrinding the crankshaft if you find that the bearings are worn and the crankshaft ovality appreciably more than half these figures.

5 Regrinding the crankshaft and subsequent fitting of under sized bearing shells is a job for the specialist. If you receive your reground crankshaft with the bearing shells fitting to the surfaces, be sure that you do not change them round when refitting.

6 Never make any attempt to cure a noisy big end by filing the bearing cap and/or working on the bearing shell.

19 Flywheel and starter ring

1 The ring gear is a shrink fit on the flywheel. Replacing it needs care but is not really very difficult. Remove the old ring by drilling through it at the root of the gear teeth at two diametrically opposite points, being careful not to drill the actual flywheel. Drill as big a hole as you can and then break the ring with a hammer and cold chisel.

2 Heat up the new ring in the oven, setting the thermostat to 220°C (430°F). If possible, put the flywheel in the refrigerator for an hour or so at the same time.

3 Before the ring has time to cool, fit it over the flywheel and clamp it in position so that as it cools down it will be accurately positioned.

4 After refitting a ring, the flywheel (ideally the flywheel assembled to the crankshaft) should be balanced. Any out of balance is rectified by drilling on the flywheel close to, but not on, the joint between the wheel and the ring gear.

5 Do not be tempted to heat the ring gear with a flame. It is case hardened and if the temperature is raised much above 220°C locally the casing will be softened.

20 Oil pump - overhaul

1 Dismantling the oil pump is perfectly straightforward; pull the delivery pipe out of its socket, remove the wire clip and take off the perforated cover. Undo four screws and remove the lower part of the body (exposing the view of the pump seen in Fig. 1.11) and withdraw the relief valve spring, valve ball and gears.

2 Wash the parts in petrol and wipe them dry with a non-fluffy rag.

3 Check the bushes for wear by fitting the driven gear into position and checking its play. This should be undetectable, the gear being perfectly free to revolve.

4 Fit the other gear and measure the tooth flank clearance with a feeler gauge (Fig. 1.12). This should be between 0.006 - 0.014" (0.15 - 0.35 mm). If wear has occurred, replace the bushes and if necessary the driving shaft which comes as a unit with its gear. The new bushes should be reamed after pressing in.

5 The relief valve spring is an important component and should be checked against the specifications at the beginning of the Chapter. If it does not come up to scratch, renew it. Note that the ball valve is progressive in action, and even at quite slow speeds there should be a certain amount of oil flowing past the ball.

6 The sealing rings at the ends of the delivery pipe are not just any old rings - they are made of special rubber and are manufactured to very close tolerances. Use only genuine Volvo

Fig. 1.11 Oil pump components

1 Pump body   4 Valve bore
2 Spring for relief valve 5 Hole for oil pipe
3 Gear

parts if you replace them. They are very unlikely to need replacement unless you have managed to damage them when dismantling the pump. When you are reassembling the pump, coat the rings with soapy water.

21 Oil filter and oil cooler

The oil filter contains a paper element and incorporates its own relief valve which allows the oil to by-pass the element, if through neglect this has become so dirty as to offer excessive resistance to the flow of oil. The whole assembly screws on to the cylinder block and is replaced complete.

The B20E engine is fitted with an oil cooler. This is placed between the oil filter and the cylinder block. A diagram is given in Fig. 1.13.

22 Engine reassembly - general

1 To ensure maximum life with minimum trouble from a re-built engine, not only must every part be correctly assembled but everything must be spotlessly clean, all the oilways must be clear, locking washers and spring washers must always be fitted where needed and all bearings and other working surfaces must be thoroughly lubricated during assembly. Before assembly begins, renew any bolts or studs whose threads are in any way damaged, and wherever possible use new spring washers.
2 All bearing caps should be assembled with new bolts.
3 Be sure that where the instructions call for pressing on bearings, pressing in bushes, pressing on gears and so forth, you have suitable tools for doing the job. In most cases you can make these up with suitable bolts, lengths of tubing, washers, bridging pieces etc. The point is that taking things off is generally speaking easier than putting them on, and in any case if you are removing a bearing which has already been condemned it doesn't matter whether you damage it or not. When you are replacing things however, you do not want the replacement to be damaged in any way. In the case of replacement bearings or replacement gears, there is no reason why you should not have a rehearsal

Fig. 1.12 Oil pump - measuring tooth flank clearance

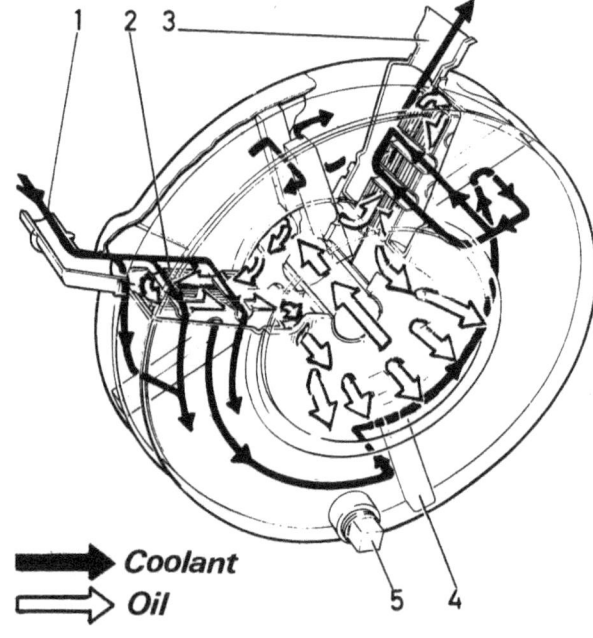

Coolant

Oil

Fig. 1.13 Oil cooler

1 Coolant inlet   4 Rubber seal
2 Discs   5 Coolant drain plug
3 Coolant outlet

with the old ones.

4   Be sure you have got all the gaskets you need. If you have followed our advice and hung up all the old gaskets you have an instant check.

5   Finally, when reassembling this engine you should regard a torque wrench as a necessity, not a luxury. The bolts and nuts for the big ends and main bearing caps do not carry cam washers or split pins; they rely on accurate torque setting to stretch them just enough to ensure a really shakeproof assembly.

23 Crankshaft - replacement

1   Make sure that the crankcase is thoroughly clean and that all the oilways are clear. A look at Fig. 1.14 will show you how the oilway system runs - from the oil pump to the filter, from the filter through the crankcase to holes in the seats for the main bearings, and upwards through the cylinder head (when this is in place) to the valve guides and rocker arm shaft. The nipple which lubricates the timing gear is connected to the main oilway

system, and a further oilway provides lubrication for the shaft of the distributor drive gear. Inject oil into the oilways here and there with your forcefeed oil can or plastic bottle; this will have the two-fold benefit of checking that the oilways are clear and getting a bit of oil into them before you start assembly. Do the same with the crankshaft - it is particularly important to get as much oil as possible into the crankshaft oilways.

2   Remove every trace of protective grease from new bearing shells.

3   Wipe the seats of the main bearing shells in the crankcase clean and place the appropriate bearing shells on them. Notice that the bearing shells have tabs on the back which fit into grooves in the seat, so there is only one way in which they can be fitted (photo). If by any chance you are refitting the old bearings in spite of our recommendations to fit new ones, be sure that you replace them in the same order they were in before. Watch the order too if you are fitting bearings whose positions on a reground crankshaft were specified.

4   Oil the shells generously and place the crankshaft on top of them - be sure that it is the right way round (photos).

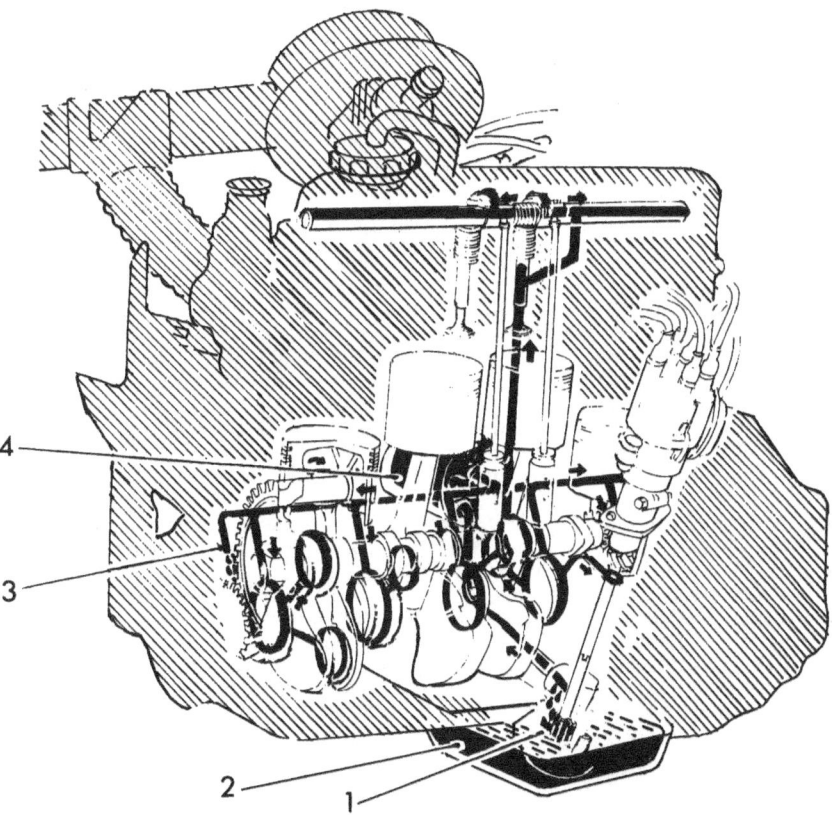

Fig. 1.14 Lubricating system

1   Oil pump   3   Nozzle
2   Sump   4   Oil filter

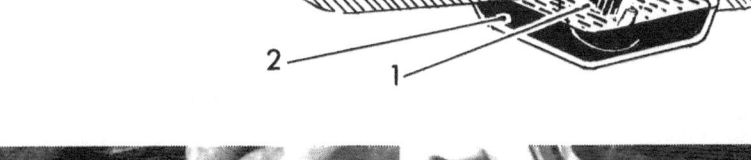

23.3 Note how the cap on this big end bearing shell fits the groove in the seating

23.4a Oil the bearing shells well ...

23.4b ... and then place the crankshaft on them

5 Wipe the bearing cap housings and fit their shells into them, keeping an eye on the order if necessary.

6 Oil the bearing surfaces of the crankshaft generously and fit the bearing caps over them, ensuring that they locate properly. The mating surfaces must be spotlessly clean or the caps will not seat correctly.

7 As each cap is fitted, put a new pair of fixing bolts through the holes and screw them up finger tight. Be sure the caps are fitted in their right order and the right way round as was discussed in paragraph 17 of Section 9.

8 When all the caps are fitted and the nuts finger tight, check that the crankshaft rotates freely without any suggestion of high spots. If it does not, there is something wrong and you should not go any further in the assembly until you have found out what it is. The most likely cause is dirt on one of the bearing shells.

9 Tighten the bolts to a torque of 87 - 94 lb ft (12 - 13 kg m). Recheck the crankshaft for freedom of rotation.

10 Check that the crankshaft end float lies within the specifications at the beginning of this Chapter.

24 Pistons and connecting rods - reassembly

1 We have already considered the overhaul of the pistons, connecting rods and gudgeon pins and it only remains to assemble the connecting rods, gudgeon pins and pistons before fitting them into the cylinder block. As a final check that the connecting rods are the right way round, make sure that when the mark on the connecting rod lines up with the corresponding mark on the bearing cap and the cap itself is right way round, the piston is placed as in Fig.1.15 with the slot in the head facing forwards.

2 Assemble the connecting rods and gudgeon pins to the pistons, inserting the circlips with proper circlip pliers.

3 Check that the piston ring grooves and oilways are thoroughly clean and that the clearance between piston rings and the edges of the grooves is correct (see Section 10 and Fig.1.8).

4 Fit the piston rings to the pistons, remembering that the top compression ring is chromium plated and the oil control ring with its ridges and slots goes at the bottom. Piston rings should always be fitted over the top of the piston and not from the bottom. A simple method is to place three narrow strips of thin metal - old feeler gauges of about 0.020'' (0.051 mm) are ideal - at equal distances round the piston and slide the piston rings over these. Stagger the gaps in the piston rings equally round the piston. Be very careful not to scratch the piston or damage the grooves when fitting piston rings. Mind too that you do not let

the connecting rod bang against the piston as this may damage or distort it. Remember that the pistons are made of alloy and are comparatively soft.

5 Insert the pistons into the cylinders from the top, using a device like the one shown in the photograph to clamp the rings. If you haven't got the correct tool it is a very simple matter to make a substitute. We have used a large jubilee clip with success. Whatever you use, make sure that you do not scratch the piston. Gently tap the piston through the piston ring compressor into the cylinder as shown in the photo. Ensure that each piston is the correct one for the bore and that the front of the piston (with the slot) faces forwards. Lubricate the piston well with clean engine oil.

6 As each piston is fitted, wipe the big end bearing seat on the connecting rod perfectly clean and fit the shell bearing in position with its locating tap engaged with the corresponding groove in the connecting rod. The procedure and precautions are exactly the same as those needed for fitting big end bearings as described in Section 23.

7 Generously lubricate the corresponding surfaces on the crankshaft with engine oil and draw the connecting rod on to it.

8 Fit the bearing shell to the connecting rod cap in the same way as with the connecting rod itself.

9 Generously lubricate the shell bearing and offer up the connecting rod bearing cap to the connecting rod. Joint the cap to the rod with new fixing bolts and nuts.

10 Tighten the retaining bolts evenly - in other words tighten each bolt a little at a time alternately to the specified torque.

25 Camshaft and timing gear - reassembly

1 Oil the camshaft well and insert it into the block, being careful to keep it straight so that the edges of the cams (which are very sharp) do not hit the bearing bushes and damage them. This is an operation that should be taken gently.

2 When the camshaft is in place, fit the spacing ring over the end and follow this by the retaining flange. Bolt the retaining flange to the block and bend the tab washers over the bolt.

3 Fit the camshaft gear to the shaft, not forgetting the woodruff key. Press it on gently, using a tool which depends on a bolt screwing into the centre of the crankshaft, see Fig.1.16. Don't hammer it on - see Section 9 paragraph 12 for the reason. Take care with this gear - it is a fibre one and can easily be damaged. Put the nut on the camshaft (there is no washer) and tighten it to 94 - 108 lb ft (13 - 15 kg m). Do not try to prevent the gear from turning by putting a screwdriver between the

24.5 Tap the piston gently into the cylinder past the ring clamp

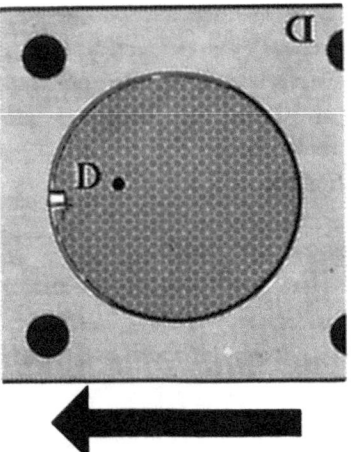

Fig. 1.15 The slot in the piston faces forward. (The letters identify selected pistons in new engines).

teeth. Some sort of device carrying two bolts which you can push into two of the holes in the gear will do the trick with perfect safety.

4 Turn the camshaft and the crankshaft so that when you fit the crankshaft gear with the key in its correct position the timing marks will line up as shown in photo 9.10. Press the gear onto the crankshaft, noting that the key will stick out in front of the gear and engage with the sleeve which you fit next (see photo 9.12e).

26 Distributor - refitting

1 With the timing marks aligned, fit the drive pinion for the distributor in the position required for the distributor rotor to take up the position that was marked for it when the engine was taken apart (see Section 9, paragraph 10). Oil the pinion and its shaft well before fitting them. Fit the distributor flange, using a new gasket. This fitting is the reverse of the dismantling process dealt with in Section 10.

2 Just in case you are not sure as to the position of the rotor we mention here that when the timing marks are coincident cylinder No 4 is at the top end of its compression stroke. Hence the rotor should be selecting the plug on No 4 cylinder and the points should just have opened.

27 Oil pump - refitting

This is a very simple matter - the driving dog on the oil pump must engage with the dog on the shaft of the distributor drive spindle, and the delivery pipe must be pushed home into its socket in the crankcase. Oil the pump well before assembly and ensure that the flange on the pump is bedding against its mating surface in the crankcase before you fasten it down.

Fig. 1.16 Fitting the camshaft gear

28 Rear sealing flange - refitting

1 Wipe the surface of the cylinder block clean, smear the new gasket very lightly with grease so that once placed on the surface it will not move about and carefully position the gasket on the cylinder block (photo).

2 Refit the sealing flange, but do not at this stage have the felt ring fitted into the flange. Fit the bolts with their spring washers but do not tighten them for the moment.

3 Carefully centre the sealing flange, using feeler gauges to ensure that the distance between the sealing flange and the end of the crankshaft is the same all the way round. Be very careful when moving the flange not to damage the gasket.

4 When you have got it right, first of all do up the bolts finger tight and then tighten them up with a spanner as you would a cylinder head - each one a little at a time, in crosswise order. Finally, wire them up (see photo 9.15a).

5 Oil the felt ring well and fit it into the flange, following it with the washer and circlip. Make sure that the circlip is properly embedded in its groove.

6 Later models are fitted with a rubber lip type oil seal. This seal can be fitted to earlier models provided the seal housing is changed also.

29 Sump - refitting

1 Ensure that the sump is really clean and that every trace of old gasket has been removed from the flanges on the sump and the crankcase.

2 Smear the crankcase flange lightly with grease and fit the gasket to it, making sure that you have got it the right way round so that it does not block up the drain hole from the rear sealing flange. You can see the correct position in the photograph.

3 Lightly grease the flange on the sump, refit the sump and the reinforcing plate, not forgetting the spring washers on the bolts. Tighten the bolts to a torque of 6 - 8 lb ft (0.8 - 1.1 kg m) (photo).

30 Fuel pump - refitting

1 Make sure that the mating faces of the fuel pump, cylinder block and spacer are free of all traces of old gasket.

2 Thread the fixing bolts and their spring washers through the flange on the pump and slide the gaskets and spacer onto the bolts, a gasket on either side of the spacer (photo).

3 Fit the assembly to the cylinder block, tightening up the bolts securely.

31 Flywheel and clutch - refitting

1 Clean the mating faces of the crankshaft, flywheel and (in the case of automatic transmission) the spacing and support plates. Refit the flywheel (and support plates if present) to the

28.1 A new gasket for the sealing flange

29.2 A new gasket for the sump. Note position of slot

29.3 The sump and reinforcing plate re-fitted

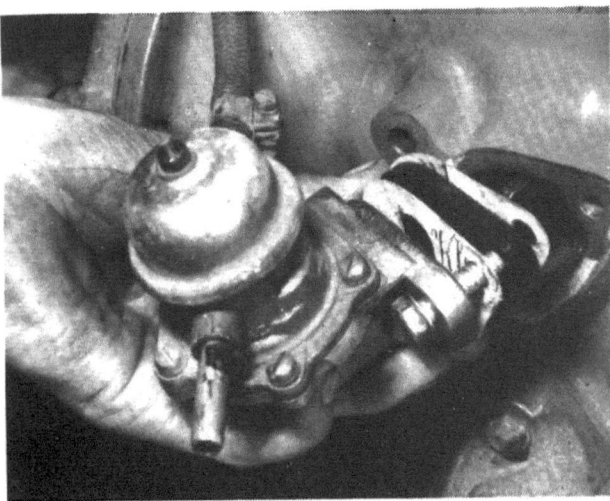

30.2 Gaskets and spacer for fuel pump

crankshaft, taking note of any position marks you made when dismantling. Tighten the bolts to a torque of 36 - 40 lb ft (5.0 - 5.5 kg m) (see photo 9.14a).

2   Refit the clutch disc and pressure plate assembly and lightly secure it in position with its fixing bolts.

3   The clutch disc must now be carefully lined up with the crankshaft pilot bearing, as this bearing supports the input shaft from the gearbox which is splined onto the clutch disc. Ideally, you could use for this a shaft whose diameter at the end was such that it just fitted into the pilot bearing, the rest of the diameter being of a size just to go through the splines in the clutch disc. Of course you have probably got on the bench not very far from you the ideal thing - the input shaft on the gearbox itself. We used the gearbox with the bellhousing removed when we were reassembling the engine of the car in the photographs. When you have done the lining up, tighten the clutch securing bolts by easy stages in a criss-cross order.

32 Refitting valves and springs to the cylinder head

1   Unless there has been some renewal, each valve and spring should be put back in the guide from which it was removed.

2   Fit each valve and valve spring in turn, wiping down and lubricating the valve stem as it is inserted into the guide.

3   As each valve is inserted, slip a new rubber sealing ring over the stem and onto the top of the valve guide.

4   Slip the spring over the stem of the valve and fit the retaining

cap into the top of the spring. Position the compressor so that the bottom part of it bears on the head of the valve. Depending on what sort of compressor you use, you may have to rig up some arrangement of wooden wedges or the like to achieve this. Whatever you do, be careful not to scratch the valve head, the combustion chamber or the mating surface of the cylinder head.

5   Compress the valve spring until the cotters can be slipped into place in the cotter grooves. You may find it helpful to grease the cotters which sometimes had the annoying habit of falling out of the grooves at the critical moment and disappearing under the bench.

33 Water pump - refitting

1   The water pump is simply screwed to the cylinder block, a gasket being required even though there is no water outlet from the pump into the side of the block. The two sealing rings are placed in the grooves at the top of the pump and will be compressed by the cylinder head when it is fitted (see photo 9.4b).

2   Fitting the water pump when the head is removed as we are doing here is somewhat simpler than fitting it with the head in position, because you have to push the pump up against the head, ensuring that the rings are properly located, as you put in the bolts. This may well have to be done of course if the pump has been removed for some reason when the head has not been taken off.

34 Tappets - refitting

1   Lubricate the tappets generously, inside and out, and insert them in the bores beofre fitting the cylinder head (photo)

35 Cylinder head - refitting

1   Check that both the cylinder block and cylinder head mating faces are perfectly clean and completely free from all traces of old gasket.

2   Generously lubricate each cylinder with engine oil.

3   Always use a new cylinder head gasket. The old gasket will be compressed and incapable of giving a good seal.

4   Do not smear grease or gasket cement on either side of the gasket.

5   With both mating surfaces spotlessly clean and dry, place the gasket on the cylinder head right way up (photos) and carefully align with the bolt holes.

6   Lower the cylinder head on to the gasket, being careful to align the holes accurately. Volvo suggest that you put guide pins in the cylinder block to help you, but the trouble saved by using guide pins is less than the trouble taken to prepare and insert them.

34.1 The well-oiled tappet goes home

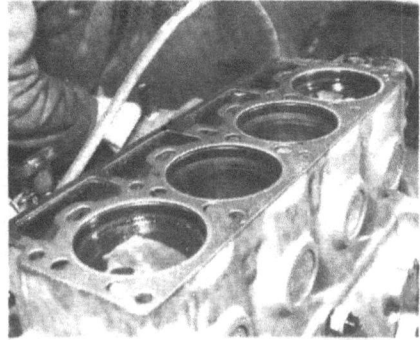

35.5a The cylinder gasket is put on ...

35.5b ... the right way up

7 Tighten the cylinder head bolts in the order shown in Fig.1.17 to a torque of 29 lb ft bringing them up to this in gradual stages. This is not the final tightening value; there will be two further stages of tightening first after the rocker arm assembly has been fitted and finally after running the engine. These will be dealt with in due course.

36 Rocker arms and rocker shaft - assembly and refitting

1 Assembling the rocker arms on the rocker shaft is simply a reversal of the dismantling process and calls for no particular comment. Squirt oil into the rocker shaft and oil all the bits and pieces generously.
2 Fit the pushrods, making sure that they are sitting on top of the tappets. Turn the crankshaft to such a position that the pushrods are all lower than the block ie that the valve would be closed if the rocker assembly were fitted.
3 Fit the rocker arm and shaft assembly to the cylinder head.
4 Volvo do not lay down a torque wrench setting for the rocker shaft fixing bolts. We feel that it is a good idea if they are evenly tightened with a torque wrench and suggest a setting of 25 lb ft (3.4 kg m).

37 Further cylinder head tightening and valve clearance adjustment

1 When the rocker arm assembly has been refitted as just described, tighten the cylinder head nuts in the proper order (Fig.1.17) to a torque of 58 lb ft (8.0 kg m). Adjust the valve clearances between limits 0.002'' (0.05 mm) greater than those laid down in the specifications. The correct setting will be made when the final cylinder head tightening is carried out after the engine has been run. The simplest method of setting the

clearances is to use two feeler gauges, one for the lower limit and one for the upper limit. Adjust the clearances so that the thicker feeler gauge will not go between the rocker arm and the valve and the thinner one will fit in quite easily.
2 It is important that the clearance of a valve is set when the tappet operating it is well away from the peak of its cam. This can be done by carrying out the adjustments in the following order, which also avoids turning the crankshaft more than necessary.

Valve fully open	Check and adjust
Valve No 8	Valve No 1
Valve No 6	Valve No 3
Valve No 4	Valve No 5
Valve No 7	Valve No 2
Valve No 1	Valve No 8
Valve No 3	Valve No 6
Valve No 5	Valve No 4
Valve No 2	Valve No 7

3 Just in case one of our readers doesn't know how to set the valve clearance, we show a photograph of it being done. The lock nut on the rocker arm is slackened off and the screw turned to raise or lower the rocker on the pushrod. If you use two feeler gauges as we have suggested you will soon learn what the fit of the thin one feels like when you have set the clearance so that the thick one won't go in.

38 Timing gear cover and crankshaft pulley - refitting

1 Though we have fitted the timing gears we have not so far dealt with the timing case cover. The photo shows the preliminary to fitting it - a new gasket fitted to a clean surface very lightly smeared with grease. Fit the cover to the cylinder block, making sure that its mating surface is perfectly clean and very lightly greased, and do up the bolts finger tight.
2 Align the cover so that the crankshaft extension is perfectly central in it. You should be able to insert a 0.004'' (0.02 mm) feeler gauge comfortably all round it. Recheck this after fully tightening the fixing bolts.
3 Fit a new felt ring (well oiled). Follow this with the retaining washer and circlip. Check that the circlip is properly embedded in its groove.

39 Oil filter and oil cooler

1 Refitting the oil filter is a simple matter - just screw it on till

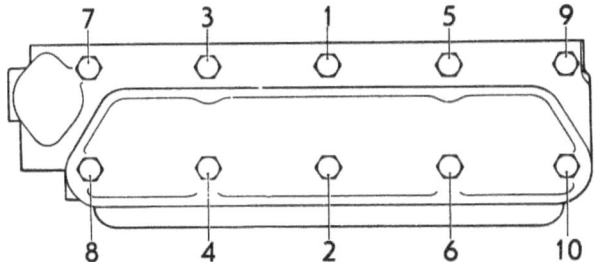

Fig. 1.17 Tightening sequence for cylinder head bolts

7   3   1   5   9

8   4   2   6   10

37.3 Adjusting the valve clearance

38.1 Preparing to fit the timing case cover

it touches the crankcase or the oil cooler if fitted and then give it a further half a turn. Do not overdo the tightening or you may damage the sealing and cause an oil leak.

2 Where an oil cooler is fitted and has been removed, particular care must be taken when it is refitted if oil leaks are to be avoided. The rubber ring which seals it to the crankcase must, of course, be renewed. The groove in the oil cooler into which it fits and the mating surface on the crankcase must both be thoroughly cleaned and degreased, using carbontetrachloride or a similar cleaning fluid. Remove any deposits left by the cleaning fluid with perfectly clean rag. Once this has been done, do not touch the surfaces with your fingers.

3 Coat the groove with a thin even layer of an adhesive such as Pliobond 20 which is resistant to oil up to temperatures of 140°C (280°F). Place the rubber ring in the groove, if possible, by handling it with tweezers only. Coat the mating surface on the crankcase with a very thin even layer of adhesive.

4 Be quite sure of the position you want the cooler to occupy (the drain plug should be at the bottom) thread it over the pipe and push it straight onto the crankcase. Press it there for a moment, then put on the washer and retaining nut. With the nut tightened to a torque of about 7 lb ft (1 kg m) check that the cooler is in good contact with the cylinder block all round. When you are tightening the nut, hold the cooler so that no turning torque is exerted on the sealing ring.

5 Leave the adhesive to set, and then finally tighten the nut to a torque of 23 - 25 lb ft (3 - 3.5 kg m).

6 The oil filter screws onto the thread protruding from the cooler fixing nut.

40 Other fitments

1 The remaining fitments call for no special instructions. Provided mating surfaces are absolutely clean, with no more than a thin smear of grease used to keep the thinner gaskets in position, you cannot go wrong. The fitting procedures are simply the reverse of dismantling.

2 When you fit the thermostat, remember to fit the clips that carry the clutch cable and the fuel pipe.

3 Fitting the alternator and water pump pulley brings us to the problem of tensioning the fan belt. Settle for 0.5" (13 mm) of lateral movement at the mid-point position between the alternator pulley and the crankshaft pulley. Don't have the belt too tight - if you do the alternator and water pump bearings wear rapidly. On the other hand, if the belt slips because it is too loose, it will get hot and very soon pack up. Proper maintenance will prevent this; the only point we are making here is that when tightening a fan **belt** you should remember that fan belts are

40.3 Setting the fanbelt tension - about right by the look of it

cheaper and easier to replace than alternators and water pumps (photo). We have not yet mentioned the crankcase breather, which should be given a new seal ring and bolted down with its single bolt. The crankcase ventilation system is considered in Chapter 3.

4 The pipe which runs along the side of the block from the water pump to the heater is clamped by two of the exhaust manifold fixing bolts and is shown in photographs 9.1c. Just to remind you about the sleeves on the exhaust ports we refer you to photograph 9.1d.

5 Fit as much of the carburation or fuel injection system as was on the engine when you took it out of the car. We suggest that you don't fit the distributor cap and plug leads at this stage; distributor caps are all too easily damaged.

6 We suggested that in the beginning the engine should be put back in the car with the gearbox attached. If you now fit the gearbox and bellhousing you are at least ready to re-unite the car and engine which by now you are probably beginning to think had been parted for far too long.

41 Engine replacement

1 You will find that replacing the engine is a simpler matter than taking it out. To start with, you will have had previous experience of balancing your engine on the hoisting gear, and the gearbox will not make a tremendous amount of difference. In any event, it will be an advantage for the engine to be tilted more when the gearbox is attached than it was when it came out without the box.

2 It is all too easy to trap the odd loose lead, hose or cable as the engine is being lowered. Get them out of the way as much as possible and keep a firm eye on stragglers.

3 Once the engine is in, go back to the lists of things you had to remove (Sections 5,6 and 7) and use these as a check when you are putting them all back again.

4 Finally check that the drain taps are closed, refill the cooling system with coolant and the engine with the specified oil. If you have been working on the gearbox, don't forget to fill that too with the specified oi. It is better to make sure of these points now than be forcibly reminded of them when the car is on the road.

42 Engine - initial start up after overhaul and major repair

1 Just have a quick look at the last item in the previous Section.

2 Make sure that your battery is fully charged - it may have to work hard before the engine starts.

3 If the fuel system has been dismantled, it will require quite a lot of engine revolutions to get the petrol up to the carburettors. With the fuel injection engine, of course, you don't have this problem. If you are a bit doubtful about your battery, take the plugs out and you will pump the petrol up with far less effort.

4 As soon as the engine fires and runs, keep it going at a fast tickover only (no faster) and bring it up to normal working temperature.

5 As the engine warms up, there will be odd smells and some smoke from parts getting hot and burning off oil deposits. Look for water or oil leaks which will be obvious if serious particularly as the engine is so nice and clean. Check also the clamp connection of the exhaust pipe to the manifold - these generally bed in a bit under vibration and you will need to tighten the clamp a bit more. Do this, of course, after the engine has cooled down.

6 When the engine running temperature has been reached, adjust the idling speed as described in Chapter 3.

7 Let the engine run at normal temperature for ten minutes. Then take off the rocker cover and tighten the cylinder head bolts to a torque of 61 - 68 lb ft (8.5 - 9.5 kg m).

8 Stop the engine and wait a few minutes to see if any lubricant or coolant drips out.

9 By now you will hardly be able to wait to get the car on the

road and check that the ignition timing is ocrrect and gives the necessary smoothness and power. Don't forget that even though you may be using the old pistons and crankshaft, you have fitted new bearing shells. Treat it as a new engine and run in at reduced revolutions for 500 miles (800 kms).

43 Decarbonisation

1 If this is to be carried out with the engine in the car, it starts with disconnection of the plug leads and removal of the inlet and exhaust manifolding (inlet ducting on fuel injection engines) as described and illustrated in Sections 6 and 7. The cylinder head is then removed as described in Section 9, paragraph 3.

2 Clean the carbon from pistons and the tops of the cylinder bores with a scraper or rotary wire brush. If the pistons are still in the cylinders, take care that no carbon gets into the bores because this can scratch the cylinder walls or cause damage to the piston and rings. You can prevent this by bringing the piston you are cleaning to top dead centre and stuffing the two bores where the pistons are at bottom dead centre with rag, or, better, sealing them off with paper and masking tape. The waterways and pushrod holes should be treated likewise to prevent particles of carbon entering the cooling system and damaging the water pump or entering the lubrication system and causing damage to a bearing surface.

3 Be careful not to score the pistons or the tops of the bores when cleaning them. If you use a screwdriver - and a broad screwdriver is an excellent tool to use for this purpose - round off its corners before you start.

4 If your engine is past its first youth and the oil consumption is not as low as it might be, leave a ring of carbon about an 1/8" (3 mm) wide round the edge of the piston. The carbon there is doing a useful job as an oil seal and that amount will make no difference to engine performance. The usual advice that instruction manuals give at this point is to put an old piston ring on top of the piston and so mask the edge, but what they never tell you is where to find the old piston ring. It is a good idea though, and you can get the same effect with a piece of plastic covered copper wire. This also ensures that you do not scratch the bores with your screwdriver.

5 If you don't want to leave a carbon ring, press a little grease into the gap between the cylinder wall and the piston you are working on. When all the carbon has been removed, clean away the grease which will have caught the carbon particles that might otherwise have found their way past the system.

6 Polish the top of the bore the crown and the piston with metal polish to assist prevention of carbon build-up.

7 Whether or not you intend to remove the valves from the cylinder head, clean the carbon off the combustion chamber and valve heads while the valves are still in place. This prevents any possibility of damage to the valve seats.

8 It makes sense to overhaul the cylinder head as described in Sections 35 and 36, but if you don't do this, clean as much carbon as you can out of the exhaust ports before replacing the head. Use a new gasket and new water pump seals and tighten the nuts to a torque of 58 lb ft (8.0 kg m). For further details see Section 35.

9 When all is reassembled, run the engine for ten minutes, allow it to cool and then give the cylinder head bolts their final tightening to a torque of 61 - 68 lb ft (8.5 - 9.5 kg m).

44 Removing the sump - engine in vehicle

This is only possible if you lower the complete front axle relative to the engine. This is the way you go about it:

1 Prop up the vehicle near the front jacking points so that both front wheels are well clear of the ground, and remove them. Make a good firm job of the propping. Naturally your back wheels will be chocked and your handbrake on.

2 Now there is plenty of room to do it, drain off the engine oil. Take out the dipstick so that it doesn't get in the way when the sump comes off.

3 Prop up the engine so that the weight is off the engine mountings. Remove the lower nuts from the engine mountings.

4 Disconnect the steering rods from the steering arms (see Fig.11.11).

5 Jack up the front axle member, being careful that you don't take too much weight away from your engine and vehicle props but nevertheless ensuring that the front axle member is secure.

6 Remove the rear bolts securing the front axle members to the two body members. The front axle is secured to each of the body members with two bolts, and you can see one of the front mounting bolts in the photograph. The corresponding rear bolt is directly behind it on the other side of the axle member. In their place put two UNC ½ - 13 x 114 bolts or any similar bolt about 4" (11 cms) long. Screw nuts onto the end of these bolts and let them dangle.

44.6 The front right hand mounting screw for the axle member is just to the left of the steering arm in this photo

7 Now remove the front mounting bolts and carefully lower the axle member with the jack. You will soon have it suspended on the two 4" bolts through the rear mounting holes.

8 You can now remove the reinforcing plate (see photo 9.16a) remembering that two bolts hold it to the gearbox bellhousing as well as the four which hold it to the crankcase) and the sump can then be removed.

45 Replacing sump in vehicle

Replacement is a straightforward reversal of the removal process. Ensure that the mating surfaces are thoroughly clean and free from all traces of old gasket, and assemble using a new gasket very lightly smeared with grease.

see next page for 'Fault diagnosis'

46 Fault diagnosis

When investigating starting and uneven running faults do not be tempted into snap diagnosis. Start from the beginning of the check procedure and follow it through. It will take less time in the long run. Poor performance from an engine in terms of power and economy is not normally diagnosed quickly. In any event the ignition and fuel systems must be checked first before assuming any further investigation needs to be made.

Symptom	Reason/s	Remedy
Engine will not turn over when starter switch is operated	Flat battery Bad battery connections Bad connections at solenoid switch and/or starter motor	Check that battery is fully charged and that all connections are clean and tight.
	Starter motor jammed	Rock car back and forth with a gear engaged. If ineffective remove starter.
	Defective solenoid	Remove starter and check solenoid.
	Starter motor defective	Remove starter and overhaul.
Engine turns over normally but fails to fire and run	No spark at plugs	Check ignition system according to procedures given in Chapter 4.
	No fuel reaching engine	Check fuel system according to procedures given in Chapter 3.
	Too much fuel reaching the engine (flooding)	For carburettor engines: Slowly depress accelerator pedal to floor and keep it there while operating starter motor until engine fires. Check fuel system if necessary as described in Chapter 3. For fuel injection engines: Flooding signifies malfunction of cold starting system - check cold start valve and thermal timer and their electrical connections.
Engine starts but runs unevenly and misfires	Ignition and/or fuel system faults	Check the ignition and fuel systems as though the engine had failed to start.
	Incorrect valve clearances	Check and reset clearances.
	Burnt out valves	Remove cylinder heads and examine and overhaul as necessary.
Lack of power	Ignition and/or fuel system faults	Check the ignition and fuel systems for correct ignition timing and carburettor settings.
	Incorrect valve clearances	Check and reset the clearances.
	Burnt out valves	Remove cylinder heads and examine and overhaul as necessary.
	Worn out piston or cylinder bores	Remove cylinder heads and examine pistons and cylinder bores. Overhaul as necessary.
Excessive oil consumption	Oil leaks from crankshaft oil seal, rocker cover gasket, oil pump, drain plug gasket, sump plug washer, oil cooler	Identify source of leak and repair as appropriate.
	Worn piston rings or cylinder bores resulting in oil being burnt by engine. Smoky exhaust is an indication	Fit new rings - or rebore cylinders and fit new pistons, depending on degree of wear.
	Worn valve guides and/or defective valve stem seals	Remove cylinder heads and recondition valve stem bores and valves and seals as necessary.
Excessive mechanical noise from engine	Wrong valve to rocker clearances	Adjust valve clearances.
	Worn crankshaft bearings Worn cylinders (piston slap)	Inspect and overhaul where necessary.
Unusual vibration	Misfiring on one or more cylinders	Check ignition system.
	Loose mounting bolts	Check tightness of bolts and condition of flexible mountings.

Chapter 2 Cooling system and heater

Contents

Specifications

Type	Sealed system with expansion tank
	B.18	B.20
Pressure valve opens at	4 - 5 lb/in^2 Approx. 10 lb/in^2
	(0.28 - 0.35 kg/cm^2) (0.7 kg/cm^2)
Capacity	Approx. 2.2 gallons (2.6 US gallons, 10 litres)

Thermostat

	Type 1	Type 2
Type	Wax	Wax
Marking	170	82°
Starts to open at	168 - 172° F	177 - 181° F
	(75 - 78° C)	(81 - 83° C)
Fully open at	192° F (89° C)	195° F (90° C)
Recommended coolant	50/50 water and ethylene glycol	

1 General description

1 A diagram of the cooling system is given in Fig.2.1 and our photograph shows the main components of the system. The expansion tank is shown in Fig.2.2.

2 The Volvo 140 series employs a sealed, water cooling system. A centrifugal water pump mounted on the cylinder block and carrying the fan blades pumps coolant into the top of the block. Within the block it circulates by thermo-syphon action; leaving the block by way of the thermostat which is situated on the top right-hand side of the block not very far from the water pump.

3 When the engine has reached its running temperature, the thermostat permits the coolant leaving the block to enter the top of the radiator. The water pump draws coolant from the bottom of the radiator and the liquid is cooled as it flows through.

4 The cooling system is of the sealed type, that is to say that it has no overflow into the outside air. The radiator has no header tank as normally understood but is connected to a separate expansion tank situated on the right-hand side of the engine compartment. This tank contains an air space to allow for the expansion of the coolant as it warms up.

5 We have done our best to talk about coolant instead of water (though we find it impossible to talk about a "coolant pump") because Volvo recommend a coolant mixture of 50% ethylene glycol and 50% water all the year round as a precaution against corrosion in the cooling system which may occur with weaker solutions.

1.1 Cooling system components: the top hose is detached from the thermostat housing and below it we see the fan attached to the water pump. The long thin pipe goes to the expansion tank illustrated in Fig.2.2

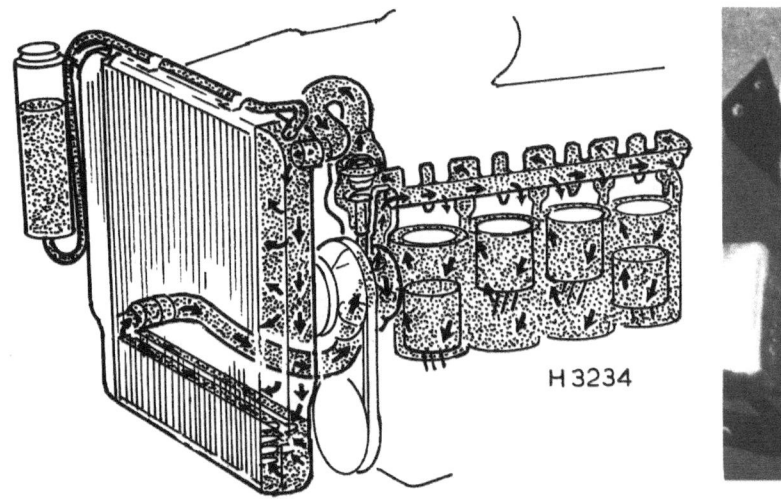

Fig. 2.1 The cooling system

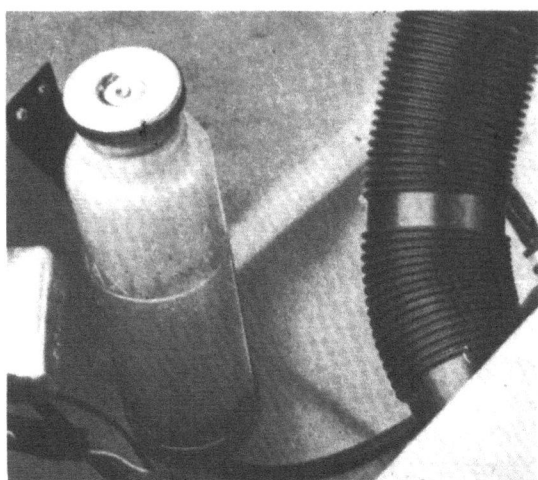

Fig. 2.2 The expansion tank

2 Draining and filling

1   To drain the system, start by removing the caps from the expansion tank and the radiator. Then disconnect the bottom radiator hose from the block, arranging a container to catch the coolant as it comes out. To drain the expansion tank, disconnect it from its mounting and hold it above the radiator; the coolant will then run down into the radiator and out through the bottom hose. Finally, drain the block through the tap just behind the oil filter on the right-hand side of the block (see Chapter 1, photograph 5.3a).

2   Before filling, flush the cooling system with clean water.

3   While refilling, the heater control valve should be set at maximum heat.

4   Fill the system with a 50% solution of water and ethylene glycol through the filler cap on top of the radiator. This cap is used only when refilling completely or as an air inlet when draining. When the radiator is completely full, replace the radiator cap and fill up through the expansion tank until the level reaches the 'Maximum' mark.

5   When you have filled the system, run the engine for several minutes at different speeds. If necessary, top up with more coolant after this and then fit the expansion tank cap.

6   After driving for a short time, check the coolant level again and if necessary top up with more coolant - it takes some time before the system is completely free of air.

3 Pressurising

1   The expansion cap filler tank is provided with a valve which opens at a pressure of 10 lb in^2 (0.7 kg cm^2) above atmospheric on B20 engines or 4-5 lb in^2 (0.28-0.35 kg cm^2) on B18 engines. This corresponds to a boiling point of 238°F (114°C) or 222-225°F (106-107°C).

2   If for any reason the water in the system approaches boiling point, air and possibly steam will be driven out through the cap. When the system cools down again another valve in the cap opens to relieve the partial vacuum that would otherwise occur.

3   If the coolant is very close to boiling point, it will certainly start to boil when the expansion chamber cap is removed and coolant may well be forced out and make a mess in the engine compartment which needs to be wiped up as the glycol has a corrosive action. For this reason you should be very careful about opening the cap when the temperature gauge needle is reading high. Put a rag over it, turn it slightly and allow the pressure to dissipate before you remove the cap entirely.

4 Cooling fan

1   On B18 engines a simple four-bladed fan is fitted, but on the B20 series a five-bladed fan with a slipping viscous drive coupling is used.

2   At low speeds, the blades revolve at the same speed as the water pump shaft to which it is attached, but as the water pump speed increases the fan speed levels off and for shaft speeds of over 4000 rpm it actually drops as shown in Fig.2.3.

3   Fig.2.4 gives a diagram of the fan coupling. The central hub is bolted to a flange which is in turn bolted to the front of the water pump pulley. The fan itself is bolted to the back of the coupling unit with four bolts.

4   The disc attached to the central hub is covered with friction material which causes it to drag against the viscous liquid with which the coupling is filled. Because of the energy dissipated the liquid gets quite hot - hence the cooling fins.

5   It is highly unlikely that this unit will give trouble unless due to wear or mechanical damage the oil leaks out. It is unlikely that this leakage would pass undetected. You can check that all is well with the fan by turning the blades by hand and noting the slight resistance produced in the coupling. If you want to be really fussy you can mark the fan pulley and the fan itself with chalk and check their speeds with a stroboscope for comparison with Fig.2.3.

6   If anything goes wrong with the fan coupling it is very unlikely that you will be able to repair it. The only remedy is replacement.

Fan speed

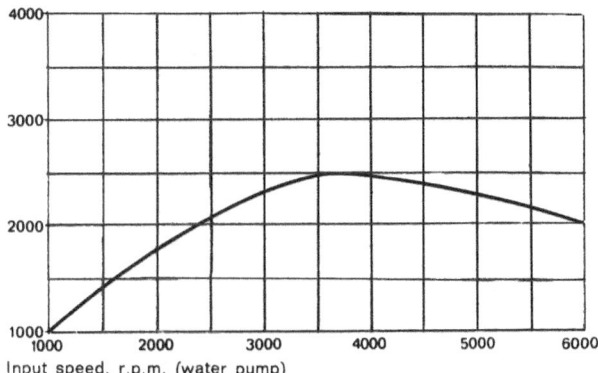

Input speed, r.p.m. (water pump)

Fig. 2.3 Speed graph for viscous fan coupling

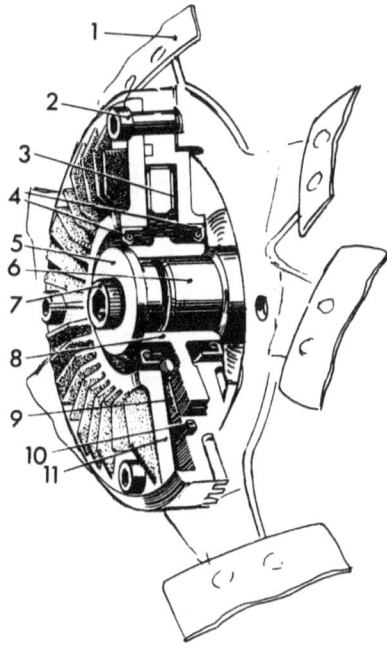

Fig. 2.4 Viscous slip coupling for fan

1	Fan blade	7	Centre bolt
2	Bolt	8	Hub
3	Oil	9	Friction material
4	Seals	10	Rubber ring
5	Washer	11	Shoulder casing
6	Flange, water pump		

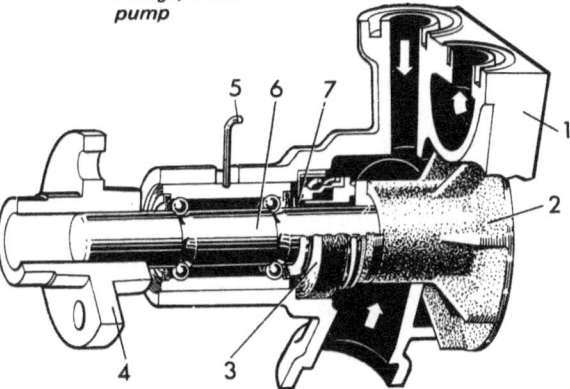

Fig. 2.5 Water pump

1	Housing	5	Lock spring
2	Impeller	6	Shaft with ball bearings (integral unit)
3	Seal ring	7	Wear ring
4	Flange		

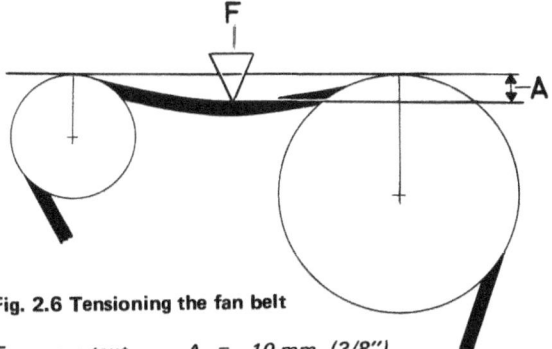

Fig. 2.6 Tensioning the fan belt

F — see text   A = 10 mm (3/8'')

5 Water pump

1 This important component of the system should be removed and checked occasionally. To get at it you have to remove the radiator as described in Chapter 1, Section 5. The fan belt must then be slackened by moving the alternator, after which the belt can be removed and the pump can be unbolted from the crankcase. Free the pump by pulling it downwards to release the seals.

2 Once the pump is on the bench, clean the exterior thoroughly and remove the fan. Thoroughly clean out the interior passages and the impeller blades and check the pump shaft for smooth rotation in its bearings and freedom from sideways play. A small amount of end play is permissible.

3 If there is an appreciable amount of play or the blades are severely corroded the pump should be replaced complete.

4 To reinstall the pump you will, of course, obtain new seals and gasket. Be sure you get the correct sealing rings for your particular model. Varying heights of rings are obtainable to allow for different thicknesses of cylinder head gasket. A trace of grease will hold the gasket against the cylinder block while you ease the upper sealing rings into place. Tighten the fan belt as described in the next Section.

6 Fan belt

1 Proper tensioning of the fan belt will ensure that it has a long and useful life. Volvo make a special belt tensioner tool, but they have not neglected those of us who press on the belt with our finger to judge its tightness.

2 They recommend that if the belt is depressed 3/8 '' (10 mm) as shown in Fig.2.6 the pressure applied at "F" should be 15.5 lbs (7.0 kg) for a belt which has had some use and been stretched a bit, and 22 lbs (10.0 kg) for a new one. These figures apply to left-hand drive vehicles; for right-hand drive the corresponding figures are 12 lbs (5.5 kg) and 15.5 lbs (7.0 kg) and for right-hand drive vehicles fitted with air conditioning, 22 lbs (10.0 kg) and 8.5 lbs (19 kg).

3 When tensioning a new belt, drive the car for 10 minutes or so before making the final tension adjustment.

7 Cooling system and thermostat

1 The action of the thermostat is shown in Figs.2.7a and 2.7b. Note the definate change-over action - when the water is allowed to flow through the main hose which is connected from the top of the thermostat casing to the radiator the circulation path to the water pump is closed up by the tongue on the bottom of the thermostat. For proper operation of the system, therefore, you should be careful not to bend or twist this tongue when removing or fitting the thermostat.

2 There are two types of thermostat, one marked 170° and the other marked 82°. As the specification shows, their performance is not very different because the 82° type is marked in degrees centrigrade. The two types are completely interchangeable.

3 To replace a faulty thermostat, lower the level of the coolant in the engine by draining it through the tap on the cylinder block until the tops of the cooling tubes are uncovered as viewed through the hole for the radiator filling cap. Collect the coolant in a clean container for using again.

4 Disconnect the upper radiator hose and unbolt the thermostat housing from the cylinder head. Extract the faulty thermostat, and then fit a new one in the identical position. Renew the gasket, replace the housing and hoses and refill the system through the expansion tank.

5 To check the performance of the thermostat, suspend it in a container of water which can be heated. As the water warms up, note the temperature at which the thermostat begins to open and also that at which the fully open position is reached. Compare these with the figures in the specifications at the

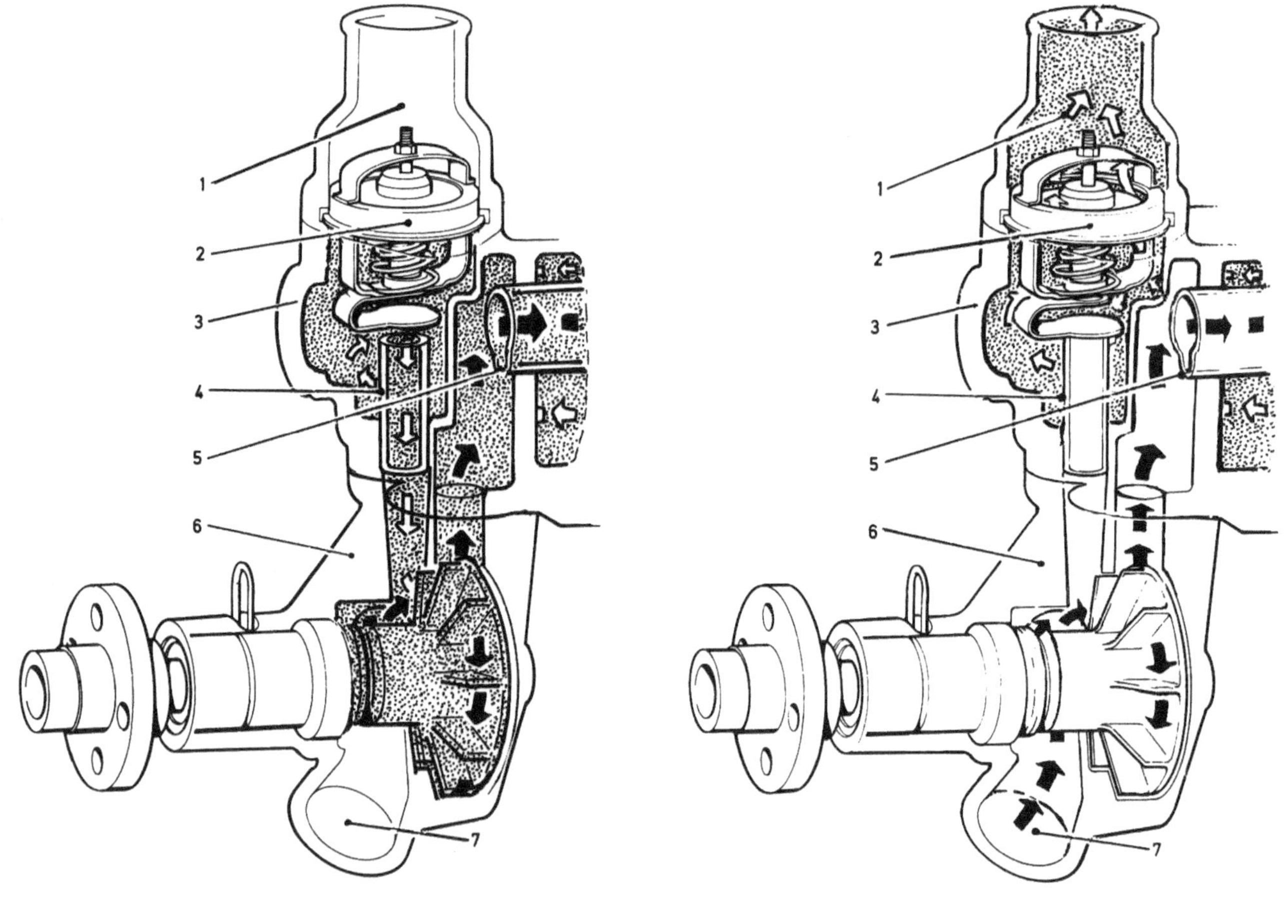

Fig. 2.7 Coolant path - (left) thermostat closed - (right) thermostat open

1 *To radiator*	3 *Cylinder head*	5 *Distributor pipe*	7 *From radiator*
2 *Thermostat*	4 *By-pass pipe*	6 *Water pump*	

beginning of the Chapter.

6   Generally speaking, when the thermostat fails it remains shut. This leads to overheating, and if for any reason you are unable to replace the thermostat you should remove it and run the car without it. In this situation the engine takes a long time to reach its correct operating temperature, and while it is running cool it uses more petrol. So do not regard this procedure as more than a temporary palliative.

8   Temperature gauge

1   The sensor for the coolant temperature gauge is a semi-conductor device whose electrical resistance varies with temperature. It is supplied with a constant voltage via the temperature indicator on the instrument panel (see Chapter 10, Section 33). The variations of resistance cause a varying current to pass through the sensor, and this current is registered on the indicator as a variation in temperature.

2   The sensor is located on top of the cylinder head at the rear right-hand corner close the fixing bolt (photo).

3   To remove it, drain the coolant through the tap in the cylinder block (removing the filler cap in the radiator) until the level has fallen to just below the top of the cylinder head. To check this, unscrew the sensor slightly and see if there is any tendency for coolant to leak out. When draining is sufficient, the sensor may be unscrewed for checking. The simplest way to do this is to attach temporary extension leads to the device (one from the tag on top to the lead in the cable harness the other from the metal part to the frame of the vehicle) and suspend it in a vessel of water (for example, an electric kettle) which is

then heated up to boiling point. You can check that the needle on the indicator rises smoothly as the water temperature rises, finishing well up in the red when the water starts to boil. Don't forget that the boiling point of water in free air is somewhat lower than the boiling point reached in the sealed system (see Section 3).

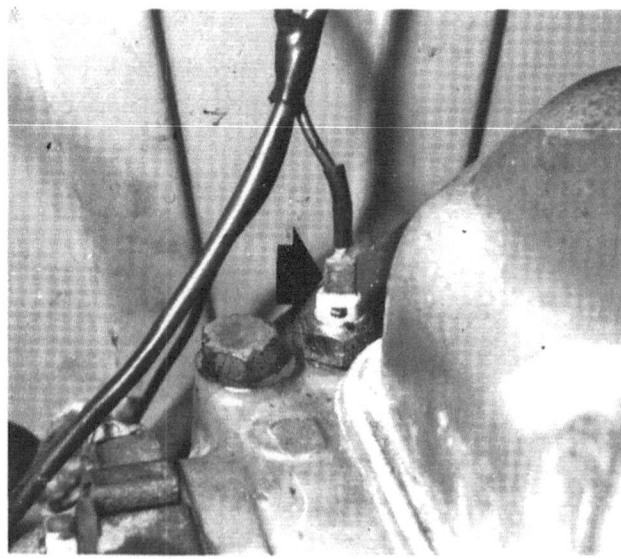

8.2 Temperator sensor (arrowed)

9 Flushing the cooling system

1 If the cooling system has been kept filled with 50/50 antifreeze solution and this solution has been changed every two years - as recommended by Volvo   it should never need descaling. If however, you have reason to believe that the system needs a good clean out (evidence for this would be consistent overheating for no apparent reason) it should be flushed as follows:

2 Having drained the system of coolant, open the cylinder block drain cock, remove the bottom hose, remove the radiator filler cap, set heater controls to maximum and then leave a hose running in the radiator filler hole for 15 minutes.

3 Reconnect the bottom hose, close the cylinder drain cock and fill the cooling system as described in Section 2 with water to which is added a proprietary cleaning compound. Run the engine for 15 minutes. All sediment and sludge should now have been loosened and may be removed by once more draining the system and refilling.

4 If this does not do the trick, try reverse flushing the radiator. This can be done either by hosing water from the bottom to the top - you have to make a reasonably watertight connection at the bottom hose inlet to achieve this - or more simply by taking the radiator out, turning it upside down and running water in at the bottom hose inlet which is now at the top. This can be followed by further treatment with a proprietary cleaner. However, a radiator this difficult to clear will probably be on its last legs even if you succeed in clearing it.

10 Radiator leaks

1 Leaks in the top and bottom tank of the radiator are usually easy to repair by soldering. The secret of success is to have the parts you want to solder thoroughly clean, use a good non-corrosive flux and have the parts you want to solder nice and warm - not so hot as to run the risk of melting the solder, but warm enough to make it easy for you to run the solder where you want it with a fair sized soldering iron.

2 If leaks appear in the small bore tubes for any other reason than direct mechanical damage this is a sign that the radiator is on its last legs. It signifies a fairly general state of deterioration of the tube walls, and if you manage to repair one leak it will be followed by another one in a very short space of time. The only sensible thing to do is to renew the radiator.

11 Cooling system - fault diagnosis

Symptom: excessive rise in coolant temperature
1 Broken or loose fan belt.
2 Low coolant level in system.
3 Faulty thermostat.
4 Ignition too far retarded.
5 The temperature rise may be only apparent - the fault may be in the temperature gauge.

Symptom: loss of coolant
1 Leaking hoses or joints.
2 Leaking drain cock,
3 Leak in cylinder head gasket. This may well happen soon after an engine overhaul if the proper procedure for tightening the cylinder head bolts has not been followed.

Note: Unlike an open cooling system, the sealed system loses little or no coolant unless there is a definite leak somewhere or overheating is so pronounced that it would be detected quite apart from its effect on the coolant.

12 Cooling system - maintenance

1 Every two years you should change the coolant, flushing the system out with water after you have emptied it. Refill it with new coolant.
2 Keep the radiator clean - hose it down well to rid it of dirt, dead flies etc.
3 Keep an eye on your hoses - replace any that show signs of deterioration.
4 Check your thermostat periodically - when you change the coolant is a good time.

13 Heating system

1 The heating system is a combined warm air/fresh air system. Incoming air is blown by a fan through the miniature radiator in the heater unit and out into the car. The fresh air can be heated and directed to the required area of the car by various controls.
2 The ducting system varies with the model and year, but all employ the same heating unit. A typical installation is shown in Fig.2.8.

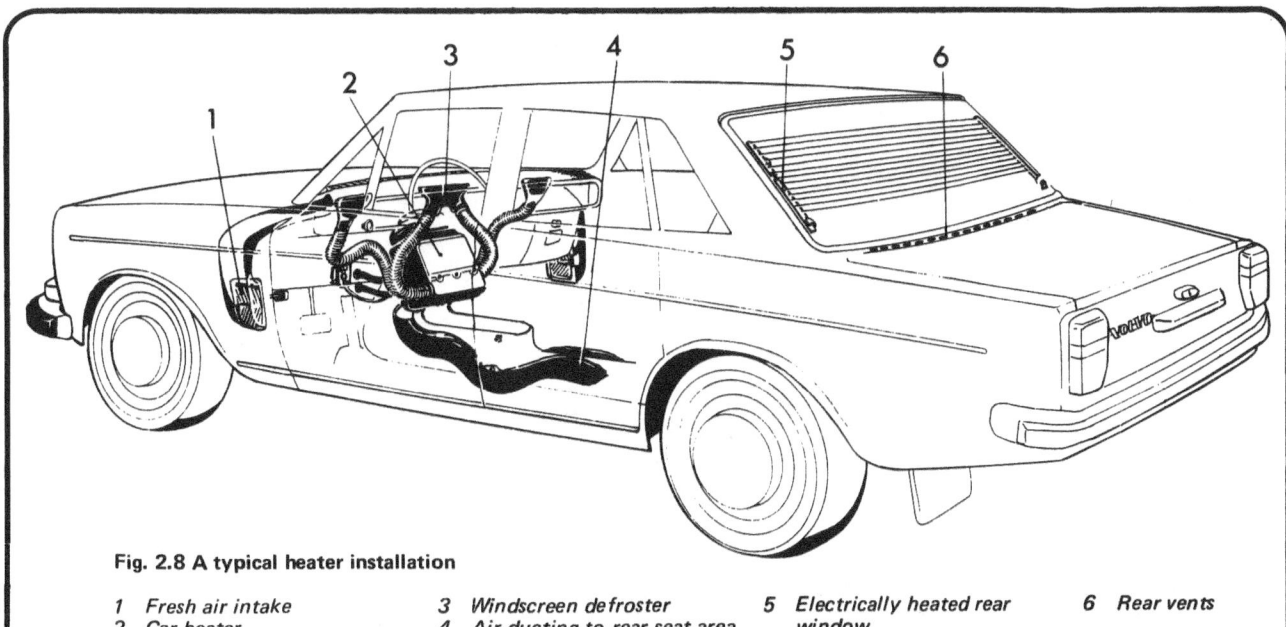

Fig. 2.8 A typical heater installation

1 Fresh air intake	3 Windscreen defroster	5 Electrically heated rear window
2 Car heater	4 Air ducting to rear seat area	6 Rear vents

3 The flow of coolant through the heater is regulated by a control valve employing a thermostat which is sensitive to the temperature within the vehicle.

4 The heater has two separately controlled outputs - floor ducts and defrosters. These are regulated by flaps which are connected by cables to the control unit fixed to the dashboard. A similar cable arrangement from this unit operates the heat control valve.

5 Fig.2.9 shows an exploded view of the heater.

14 Heater unit - removal, overhaul and replacement

1 Drain off the coolant and disconnect the positive battery lead.

2 Remove the combined instrument panel (see Chapter 10, Section 31).

3 Disconnect the hoses to the control valve, the defroster hoses and the control wires. Remove the switch for the fan and disconnect the cables to the fan motor.

4 Unbolt the fuse box from the heater, and then the control valve and the upper hose to the heater unit. Take great care with the control valve and the copper pipe attaching it to the heater as these are easily damaged.

5 Plug the outlets on the heater so that the remaining coolant does not run into the car - antifreeze is not good for paintwork. Disconnect the earthing cable from the right-hand bracket, remove the four screws which hold the heater unit to the brackets and free the drain hose. The heater unit and control valve can now be removed.

6 Replacement is a straightforward reversal of this procedure. Handle the control valve and its connecting pipe with care.

15 Heater overhaul

1 Remove the four rubber bushes on the sides of the heater unit. Mark the fan casing so that you don't have to worry which way round it goes when reassembling. Remove the spring clips

(Fig.2.10) which hold the heater together and separate the two halves. This exposes the radiator system with its thermostatic control and the fan motor.

2 Inspect the radiator for signs of leakage and check that all is well with the flap system. Give it a drop of oil here and there. The only other overhaul procedure is replacement of the motor should its bearing be worn. The mounting plate for the motor is attached to the fan casing by bent over tabs. Straighten these carefully, and remove the mounting plate from the casing. The motor can then be unscrewed from the mounting plate.

3 On reassembly, scrape off the old sealing compound at the various joints in the heater and replace this with a suitable soft sealing agent. On reassembly use new spring clips and replace the rubber bushings.

16 Heater control unit

1 The complete unit is fixed to the dashboard with three nuts. To remove it, first take out the panel below the dashboard and then free the cables from the heater unit and control valve.

2 Pull the illuminating lamp and holders out of the unit, leaving them suspended in the wiring, undo the nuts and lift out the unit.

3 Check that the wheels and cables are operating freely. Oil where necessary. Replace any damaged or worn parts.

17 Air conditioner

1 Fig. 2.11 shows a side view of the combined evaporator/ heater unit which forms part of the latest Volvo air conditioning system. Associated with it is a compressor, also illustrated, which is driven by the fan belt which it shares with the alternator. This system is available as an optional extra on the 140 Series.

2 There is little that can be done to it by way of maintenance apart from keeping one's eye on the electric motor which drives the two fans, only one of which is shown in the illustration.

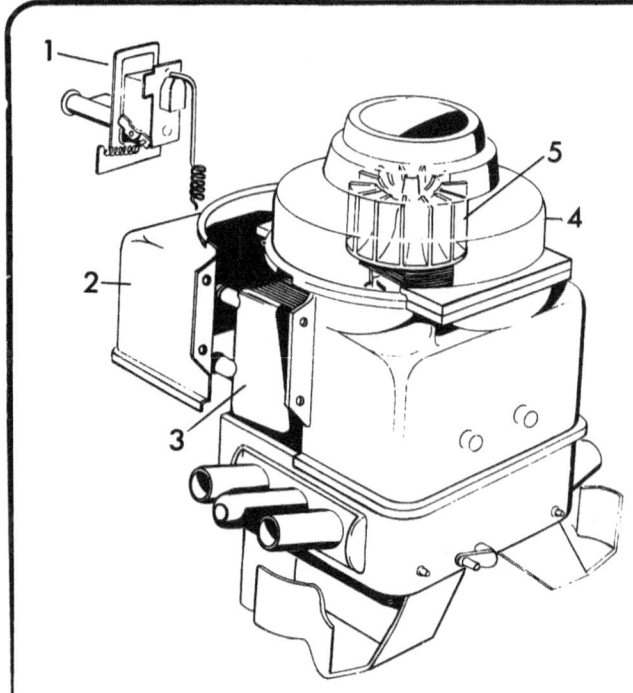

Fig. 2.9 Exploded diagram of heater unit

1	Heat control valve	4	Fan casing
2	Heater casing	5	Fan
3	Cell system		

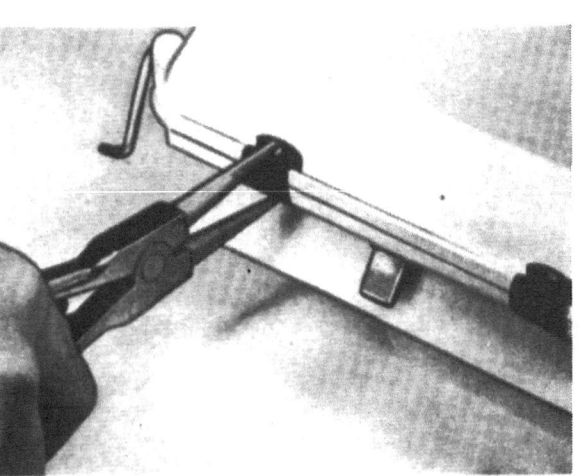

Fig. 2.10 Removing the spring clips on the heater (open the pliers to expand the clips)

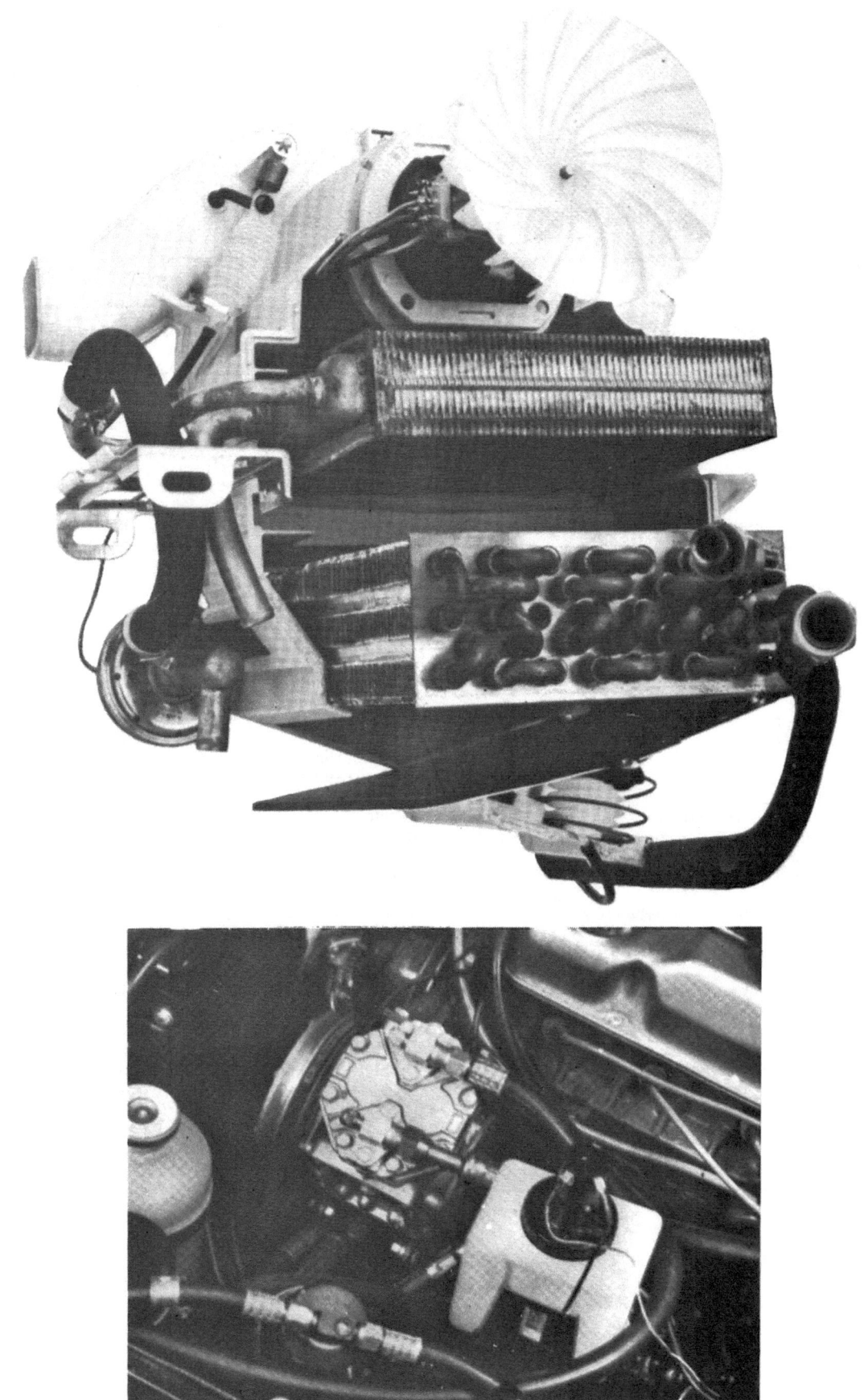

Fig. 2.11 Air conditioning - (top) Conditioner unit - (bottom) Compressor

Chapter 3 Fuel system

Contents

Specifications

Carburettor engines:

Fuel pump	Diaphragm type, AC -YD or Pierburg APG

Fuel pressure, measured at same level as pump

Min.	1.56 lb/in^2 (0.11 kg/cm^2)	1969/70 and after
Max.	3.55 lb/in^2 (0.25 kg/cm^2)	
Min.	1.42 lb/in^2 (0.10 kg/cm^2)	1968/69
Max.	3.55 lb/in^2 (0.25 kg/cm^2)	
Min.	2.0 lb/in^2 (0.14 kg/cm^2)	1967/68
Max.	3.55 lb/in^2 (0.25 kg/cm^2)	

Air intake diameter	1.63 in. (41.3 mm)
Idling speed	800 rpm (cars with manual transmission)
	700 rpm (cars with auto. transmission)

Oil for carburettor damping cylinders		Automatic transmission fluid, type A (Castrol)
CO-test		(Hot engine, idling speed) 2.5%

Carburettors and fuel needles

a	Zenith Stromberg 175-CD2-S
b	Zenith Stromberg 175-CD2-SE
c	SU HS6
d	SU HIF6

			Carburettor	Needle	Notes
B 18A	1968/69 ...	... ...	a	4F	
B 18B	1968/69 ...	... ...	cc	KD	
B 20A	1969/70 ...	... ...	b	B2AF	Same needle whether or not EEC fitted
B 20B	1969/70 ...	... ...	cc	KN	Standard EEC fitting
B 20B	1969/70 ...	... ...	bb	B1AN	USA/Canada EEC fitting
B 20A	1970/71 ...	... ...	c	BAH	Standard EEC fitting
B 20A	1970/71 ...	... ...	b	B1AN	USA/Canada EEC fitting
B 20B	1970/71 ...	... ...	cc	KN	Standard EEC fitting
B 20B	1970/71 ...	... ...	bb	B1AP	USA/Canada EEC fitting
B 20A	1971/72 on	... ...	b	B1AN	All B 20A installations
B 20B	1971/72 on	... ...	bb	B1BL	
B 20B	1971/72 on	... ...	dd	BBB	

Double letters indicate twin carburettors)

Electronic fuel injection engines:

Fuel filter

Type	Paper filter
Changing intervals	12000 miles (20000 km)

Fuel pump

Type	Rotor pump
Capacity	22 Imp. galls = 26 US galls/h at 28 p.s.i. (100 l/h at 2 kg/cm^2)
Current consumption	5 amps
Relief valve opens	Approx. 64 p.s.i. (4.5 kg/cm^2)

Pressure regulator

Setting value	28 p.s.i. (2.0 kg/cm^2)

Injectors

Resistance in magnetic winding	2.4 ohms at + 68° F (20° C)

Cold-start valve

Resistance in magnetic winding	4.2 ohms at + 68° F (20° C)

Auxiliary air regulator

Fully open at	−13° F (−25° C)
Fully closed at	+140°F (60°C)

Temperature sensor I (intake air)

Resistance	Approx. 300 ohms at + 68° F (20° C)

Temperature sensor II (coolant)

Resistance	Approx. 2500 ohms at + 68° F (20° C)

Pressure sensor

Resistance in primary winding (connections 7 and 15) ...	Approx. 90 ohms
Resistance in secondary winding (connections 8 and 10) ...	Approx. 350 ohms

Air cleaner

Changing intervals	25000 miles (40000 km)

CO-test

Hot engine, idling speed	1.0 − 1.5% (Automatic 0.5 − 1.0%)

Venting filter (only USA)

Changing intervals	25000 miles (40000 km)

PART 1 – CARBURETTOR ENGINES

1 General description

The basic fuel system comprises a single fuel tank at the back of the car from which petrol is pumped by a mechanical pump to a horizontally mounted single or twin carburettor system. The air filter is of the replaceable paper type, the element being circular in single carburettor engines and in earlier models with twin carburettors and rectangular on the B20B where one element filters the air for both carburettors.

In order to meet air pollution regulations in the United States and elsewhere, modifications and improvements to the basic fuel system have been introduced over the years. Positive crankcase ventilation and improved fuel utilisation during initial warm-up deal with pollution due to products of combustion, while a re-cycling system prevents petrol vapour from reaching the atmosphere.

2 Fuel pump - general description

1 Though the two types of fuel pump used in the 140 series differ in detail, their principle of operation is the same. The description that follows, together with a study of Figs.3.1 and 3.2, will enable you to see how they work.

2 The basic components of a mechanical petrol pump are:
A petrol chamber incorporating a filter
An inlet valve
An outlet valve
A diaphragm
A spring which pushes on the diaphragm
A lever which pulls the diaphragm
A small spring against which the lever operates
The inner end of the lever is linked to a rod attached to the diaphragm.

3 If there is no petrol in the pump the diaphragm is pushed up by the spring so that the space inside the fuel chamber is a minimum. In this case, the outer end of the lever is in its lowest position.

4 The lever is operated by a cam on the engine camshaft. The cam pushes the lever upwards, the diaphragm is drawn downwards, the space inside the fuel chamber increases and petrol is sucked in to fill the resulting vacuum. When the cam leaves the lever, the diaphragm returns to its original position, but the inlet valve stops the petrol from returning to the tank.

5 As this operation is repeated, the fuel chamber soon fills with petrol which passes through the outlet valve and outlet pipe to the carburettor float chamber. When the float chamber is full, the carburettor needle valve closes and no more petrol can pass along the pipe.

6 When this happens, the diaphragm cannot return to its original position. Soon the pump becomes full of petrol and the diaphragm is extended downwards, holding the lever away from the cam on the camshaft which operates it.

7 When the level in the carburettor float chamber drops, the needle valve opens and petrol can once more pass along the outlet pipe. The diaphragm moves upwards as it pushes the petrol out, the lever moves closer to the cam and the diaphragm is operated until the pump is again filled up.

3 Fuel pump - importance of efficient operation

1 Pumping takes place only when the pump is not full of petrol. The more effectively the pump is working, the less often the lever and diaphragm will have to move. If there is any fuel starvation, you can be sure that the pump is working much harder than it ought, and consequently wearing much faster. If the inefficiency is due to wear, that wear will progress at an ever increasing rate.

2 Any air leakage on the inlet side will cause the pump to take in air and so reduce its efficiency. Very often mechanical pumps

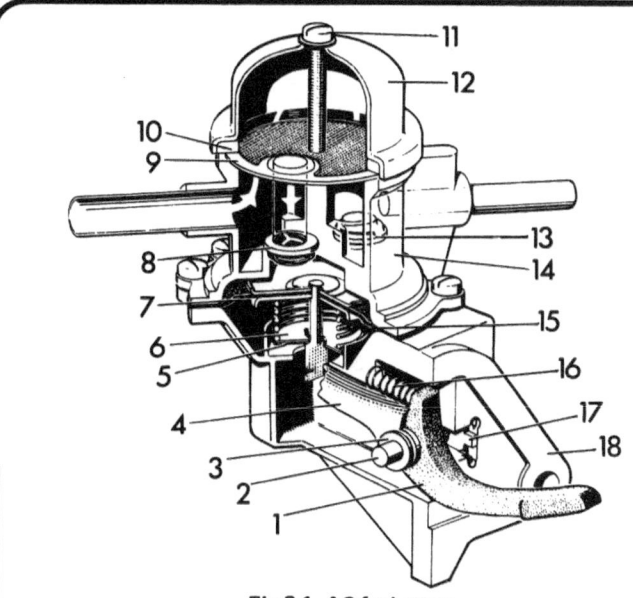

Fig.3.1. AC fuel pump

1	Rocker arm	11	Screw with washer
2	Shaft	12	Cover
3	Washer	13	Outlet valve
4	Lever	14	Upper pump housing
5	Rubber seal	15	Diaphragm spring
6	Washer	16	Return spring
7	Diaphragm	17	Shaft retainers (one each
8	Inlet valve		side)
9	Strainer	18	Lower pump housing
10	Gasket		

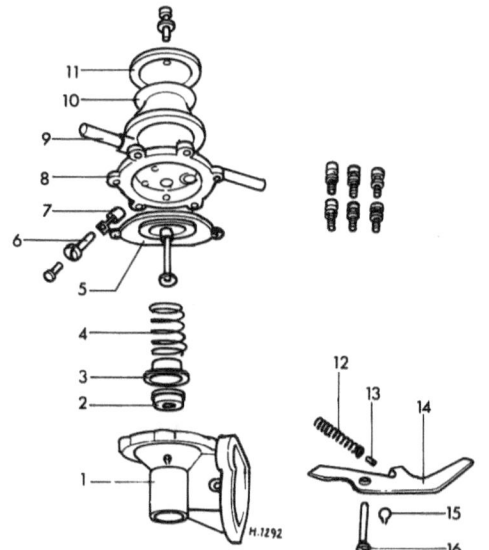

Fig.3.2. Pierburg fuel pump dismantled

1	Lower pump housing	9	Inlet pipe
2	Rubber seal	10	Strainer
3	Guides	11	Cover with gasket
4	Diaphragm spring	12	Return spring
5	Diaphragm	13	Spring holder
6	Stop arm	14	Lever
7	Spring	15	Circlip
8	Upper pump housing	16	Lever shaft

are fitted below the level of the petrol tank so that the inlet pipe does not empty back into the tank if there is air leakage. This means that you get no direct indication that leakage is occurring and causing the pump to work harder than it ought, so it is a good idea to check that all is well on the inlet side of the fuel pump from time to time.

4 Fuel pump - removal and replacement

1 Remove the fuel inlet and outlet connections from the fuel pump and plug the ends of the pipes to stop loss of fuel and the entrance of dirt.
2 Unscrew the bolts holding the pump body to the crankcase and lift it away (see Chapter 1, photo 9.5a).
3 Remove the fuel from the pump - by operating the lever a few times - before dismantling it.
4 Replacement is the reverse process to removal. Inspect the gaskets on either side of the insulating block and if they are damaged replace them with new ones.

5 Pierburg fuel pump

1 Thoroughly clean the outside of the pump with paraffin or a detergent such as Gunk and then dry. To ensure correct reassembly mark the upper and lower body flanges.
2 Take off the cover and remove the gasket and fuel strainer.
3 Undo the six screws joining the upper and lower pump housing and separate these, freeing the diaphragm which is sandwiched between them. Be very careful not to damage the diaphragm in the process - you may wish to use it again.
4 Remove the circlip from the lever shaft, push out the shaft, remove the lever and its return spring.
5 Remove the diaphragm with the spring, spring guide and rubber seal. The spring can be removed after the rubber seal has been levered over the nylon washer.
6 Remove the screw on the underside of the upper body section, take out the stop arm and the leaf spring inlet valve, (see Fig.3.3).

6 Pierburg fuel pump - inspection and reassembly

1 Thoroughly clean all parts in paraffin. Dry off and examine each part for signs of wear. As we have already pointed out, very little mechanical wear can be accepted. Look for it on the rocker arm pin or bearing holes, the face of the cam lever and the linkage between the cam lever and the diaphragm pull rod. Renew any part about which you are doubtful.
2 The diaphragm and pull rod (a single assembly) must be renewed if there are any signs of wear or cracking in the diaphragm.
3 Check that the seating surface for the inlet valve spring is clean and smooth and that the port edges are free from burrs. There is no provision for removing the outlet valve, but it never seems to give any trouble. Ensure that it is clean before you reassemble the pump.
4 To reassemble, first install the cam lever and its pivot pin in the lower body. Replace the lever return spring.
5 Assemble the diaphragm spring, seal and washer in the order in which they are dismantled and centre the diaphragm in the return spring. Engage the diaphragm pull rod with the lever and position the diaphragm so that the holes round its edge are exactly in line with those on the body flange. When all is correctly positioned, check that the pull rod is properly seated in the lever fork and that everything operates smoothly.
6 To fit the upper half of the body, hold the diaphragm against the flange by pushing on the lever while you place the upper body in position, with the alignment marks made on the two flanges coinciding. Insert the six screws and tighten them until the heads just engage with the spring washers. Check that the diaphragm is correctly centred and that it does not overlap the

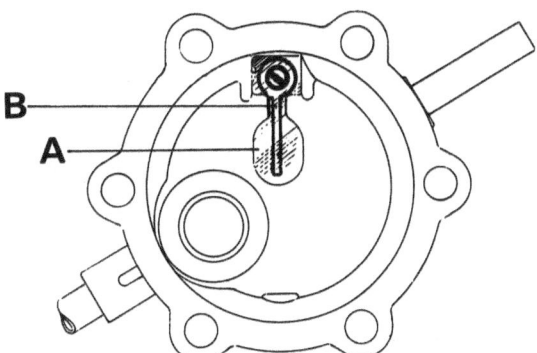

Fig.3.3. Pierburg fuel pump

A Inlet valve
B Stop arm

edge at any point. Then tighten the screws alternately until all are fully home.
7 Replace the filter gauze and refit the top cover using a new gasket. Do not overtighten the screw on the top cover or you may distort the cover and be troubled with leakage at the joint.

7 AC fuel pump - dismantling

1 Thoroughly clean the outside of the pump with paraffin or a detergent such as Gunk and then dry. To ensure correct reassembly mark the upper and lower body flanges.
2 Remove the cover retaining screw, lift away the cover, sealing ring and fuel filter.
3 Remove the screws holding the upper and lower halves of the body together. Lift off the upper half of the body, being careful not to damage the diaphragm in doing so - you may want to use it again later.
4 Free the diaphragm from the lower half of the body carefully, and rotate it a quarter of a turn to free the pullrod from the slot in the lever which operates it.
5 The spring can now be removed from the diaphragm by turning the slide washer until the slot in the washer will pass over the end of the pull rod.
6 The rocker arm shaft is secured by retainers which are slid into grooves in the main body and held there by peening the ends of the grooves. Remove the peening with a fine file or grindstone and remove the rocker-arm shaft, rocker arm and lever.

8 AC fuel pump - inspection and reassembly

1 Thoroughly clean all parts in paraffin. Dry off and examine each part for signs of wear. Very little wear can be accepted; look for it on the rocker arm shaft, its retainers and the faces of the cam lever and the rocker arm.
2 If the diaphragm shows any signs of wear or cracking, replace the diaphragm and pull rod assembly.
3 The valve body and valves must be thoroughly cleaned and the valves seating properly. If the valves are not satisfactory, lever them out of their seatings and insert new valves, making sure that you put them in the right way round. Be very careful to keep them square with the valve bore during fitment; a good way of going about it is to use a piece of tubing of suitable diameter pushed against the outer edge of the valve, tapping this gently if necessary.
4 Reassemble the cam lever and rocker arm into the body, over the grooves for the retainers as in the original assembly.
5 Reassemble the diaphragm, spring and washer with its rubber seal in the order in which they were dismantled and mount the assembly on the rocker arm, turning a quarter of a turn to secure it. Carefully align the holes in the diaphragm with the holes in

the body.

6 Refit the upper half, inserting the screws and tightening until the heads just engage with their spring washers. Check that the diaphragm is correctly centred and does not overlap the edge at any point and then tighten the screws alternately until all are fully home.

7 Replace the filter gauze and fit the top cover. Do not over-tighten the screw on this cover or you may have trouble with leakage at the joint caused by distortion of the cover.

9 Fuel pump - testing (either type)

Hold the pump steady in the protected jaws of a vice. Fit two short lengths of plastic tube to the inlet and outlet pipes and take the inlet tube to a container of paraffin (much safer than petrol) set a short distance away, with the paraffin level slightly above that of the pump. Insert the end of the outlet pump into a measuring jar set a little below the pump. Pump with the lever arm until paraffin is coming through without bubbles. Once pumping is established the pump should deliver not less than 1.75 fl oz (50 cc) in 10 strokes. If the delivery is below this, it indicates a faulty valve or weak diaphragm return spring. If bubbles appear continuously in the output, an air leak some-where in the chamber is the cause.

Empty the pump of paraffin and remove the plastic tubes. Push up the cam lever, cover the end of the inlet pipe with one finger and then release the cam lever - a distinct suction should be felt, the lever should return very slowly, and on removing the finger there should be an inrush of air as the lever springs back.

Installation of the fuel pump is a simple matter and has been dealt with in Chapter 1, Section 30 (see photo 30.2).

10 Carburettors - general description and basic principles

1 Two makes of carburettor are found on the 140 series - the SU and the Stromberg. Each of these has been altered since the beginning of this series to cope with the requirements of exhaust emission control regulations in the USA and elsewhere. In the case of the Stromberg, the original type 175-CD2 S was only modified in detail and became the 175-CD2 SE. The CD2 S was fitted to the B18A engine, the CD2 SE being used on the B20 series. The chief differences between the CD2 S and the CD2 SE are two: first, in the CD2 S the position of the jet relative to the carburettor needle can be adjusted by turning a nut underneath the carburettor, whereas in the CD2 SE there is no external adjustment; second, the CD2 SE is fitted with a temperature compensator consisting of an air valve regulated by the carburettor temperature which maintains the fuel-air mixture constant irrespective of the fuel temperature.

In an exploded view of this carburettor (Fig.3.4) we have shown a typical version of the CD2 SE (there are several) together with the jet assembly associated with the CD2 S. This figure, together with Fig. 3.5, will give a sufficient guide to the variations of the Stromberg carburettor as well as illustrating its working principles.

The SU HS6 carburettor was fitted to the B18B engines and to B20 engines up to late 1970. At this time the familiar SU body with its separate float chamber and the handy jet adjust-ment nut underneath disappeared from the Volvo scene and was replaced by the SU HIF6. This has its float chamber tucked underneath the main body of the carburettor, the jet adjustment nut has been replaced by a small adjusting screw and altogether it looks more like the Stromberg than the original SU HS6 from the outside. The exact jet position is controlled by a bi-metallic strip inside the float chamber and a special cold start device is fitted in place of the arrangements in the HS6 whereby the "choke" control moves the jet bodily downwards. Exploded views of the HS6 and HIF6 are given in Figs. 3.6 and 3.7 and typical examples are shown in Figs. 3.8, 3.9, 3.10 and 3.11.

2 A study of Figs. 3.5 to 3.11 will at once reveal the basic similarity of the two makes. They both work on the same

Fig.3.4. Stromberg carburettors - exploded view

1 Main body	49 Sealing washer
2 Jet (175-CD2 SE)	50 Lock washer (two items)
3 Throttle spindle	51 Fixing bolt - temperature
4 Throttle disc	compensator to main body
5 Fixing screws	(two items)
6 Seal	52 Idle adjustment screw
7 Return spring	53 Spring
8 Actuating lever	54 Needle valve
9 Bushing	55 Washer
10 Pick-up lever	56 Float
11 Washer	57 Float shaft
12 Lock washer	58 Float chamber
13 Nut	59 Gasket
14 Pick-up lever (rear	60 Fixing screw - float
carburettor)	chamber to main body
15 Secondary throttle	(four items)
operating lever	61 Fixing screw - float
16 Cam regulating secondary	chamber to main body
throttle	(two items)
17 Mock washer	62 Washer (six items)
18 Nut	63 Spring washer (six items)
19 Actuating lever (single	64 Plug with fuel passages
and rear)	(175-CD 2SE)
20 Fast idle adjusting screw	65 O-ring for 64
21 Lock nut	66 Piston
22 Throttle stop screw	67 Diaphragm
23 Spring	68 Retainer ring
24 Cold start device assembly	69 Retainer
25 Cold start device cover	70 Retainer fixing screw
26 Shaft	(four items)
27 Clip	70a Washer (four items)
28 Spring	71 Carburettor needle
29 Pierced disc	72 Needle lock screw
30 Channel disc	73 Return spring
31 Return spring	74 Upper half of body
32 Actuating lever	(suction chamber)
33 Choke cable clamp screw	75 Fixing bolts (two items)
34 Washer	76 Spring washers (two items)
35 Stop washer	77 Damper piston assembly
36 Nut	78 Sealing ring
37 Fixing screw (two items)	79 Adjustment screw - channel
38 Stop washer (two items)	to suction chamber
39-41 Clamp for choke control	80 Isolating ball
cable outer case	81 Locking screw
42 By-pass valve	82 Plug replacing 79, 80 and
43 Gasket	81 on later production
44 Spring washer (three items)	83 Adjustable jet assembly,175-CDS2
45 Fixing bolt - by-pass valve	84 Adjuster screw
to main body (three items)	85 Sealing ring
46 Fixing screw - by-pass	86 Plug holding jet and adjuster screw
valve cover (two items)	87 Jet
47a Temperature compensator	88 Sealing ring
device - cover	89 Spring
47b Cover fixing screw	90 Washer
(two items)	91 Sealing ring
48 Sealing ring	92 Bushing
	93 Washer

NOTE: Items in boxes labelled 'front' appear in positions shown on the front carburettor of a twin installation only, those in boxes marked 'rear' appear in these positions on the rear carburettor of a twin installation only and those marked 'single' appear in these positions in a single carburettor installation

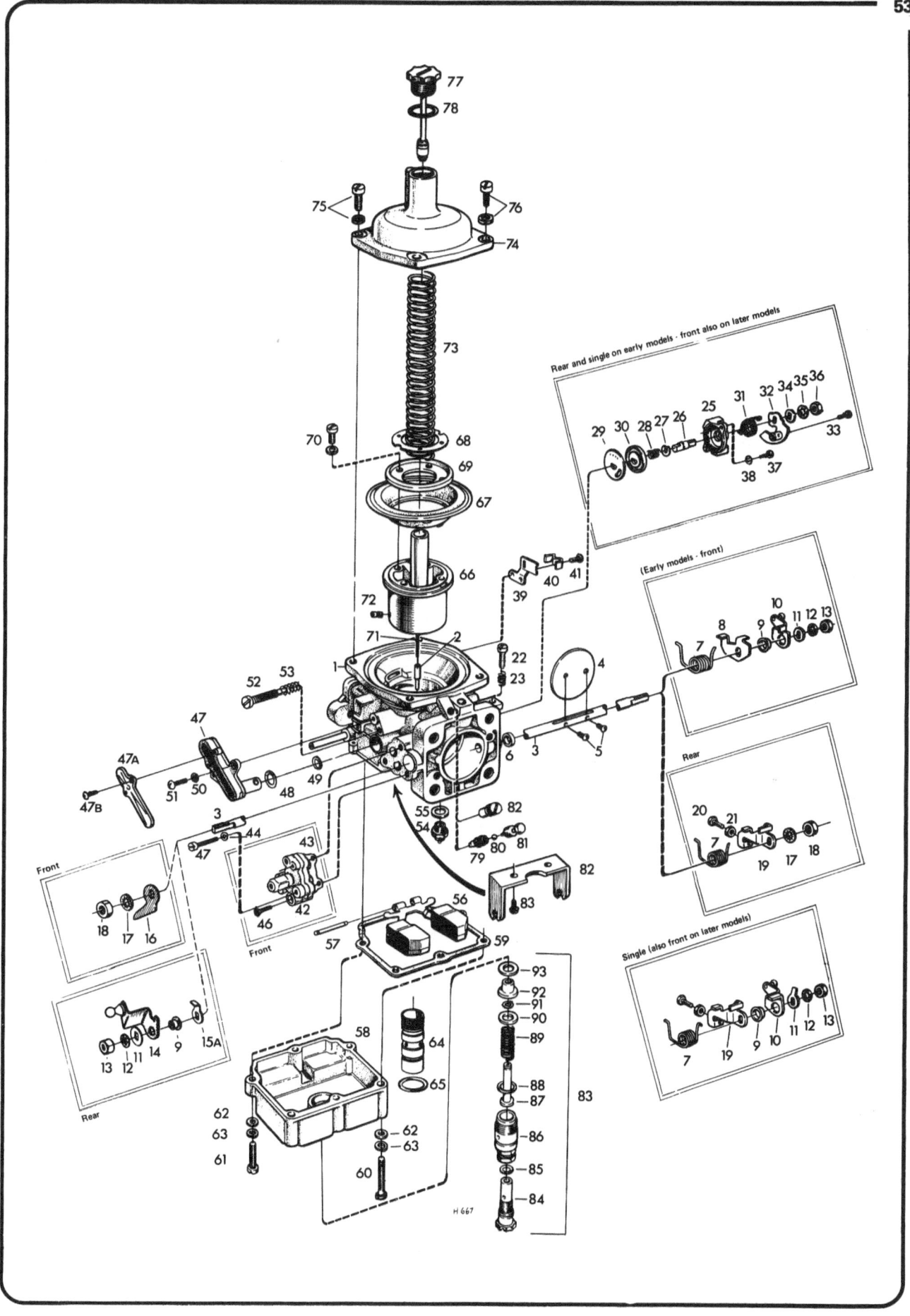

53

Rear and single on early models · front also on later models

(Early models · front)

Rear

Single (also front on later models)

Front

Rear

Front

H 667

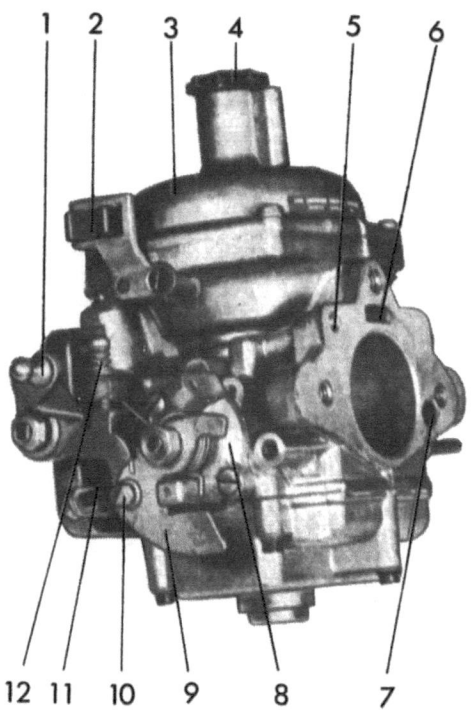
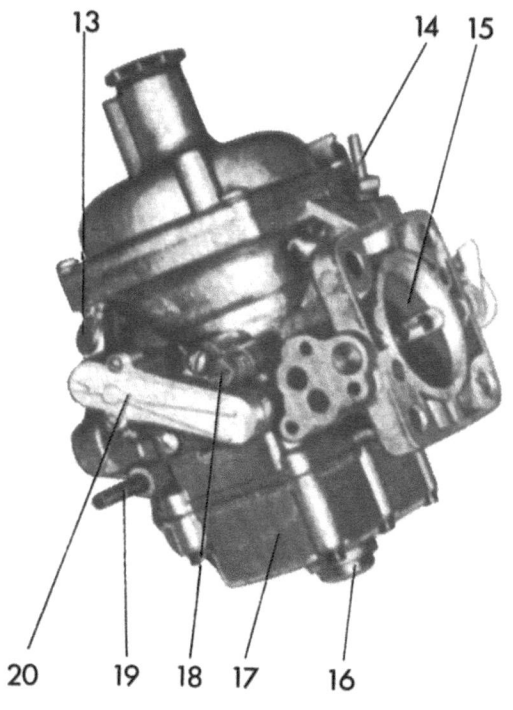

Fig.3.5. Stromberg CD2 SE carburettor as fitted to B20A engines

1	Throttle control pick-up lever	6	Drilling for air supply under diaphragm	10	Choke wire connection	16	Plug
2	Choke cable clamp	7	Drilling for air supply to temperature compensator and idle trimming screw	11	Fast idle stop screw	17	Float chamber
3	Suction chamber			12	Throttle stop screw	18	Idle trimming screw
4	Hydraulic damper	8	Cold start device	13	Sealed plug	19	Connection for fuel pipe
5	Vent drilling from float chamber	9	Fast idle cam	14	Connection for vacuum pipe to distributor	20	Temperature compensator
				15	Throttle		

Fig.3.6. SU HS6 carburettor - exploded view (single carburettor installation or rear carburettor of twin installation)

1	Spring for jet needle (later production)	23	Jet bearing	50	Retaining nut/return spring carrier
2	Guide for jet needle (later production)	24	Sealing washer	51	Lock washer
3	Key to locate piston	25	Jet locating nut	52	Throttle return spring
4	Fixing screw	26	Spring	53	Cam lever - fast idle
5	Piston lifting pin	27	Jet adjustment nut	54	Return spring - jet actuating lever
6	Spring	28	Float chamber		
7	Rubber washer	29	Distance piece/key	55	Return spring for 53
8	Washer	30	Float chamber fixing screw	56	Sleeve for choke control/fast idle assembly
9	Clip (6, 7, 8 and 9 are assembled to 5)	31	Washer		
		32	Spring washer	57	Fixing screw - fast idle assembly (also anchors spring 52)
10	Throttle stop screw	33	Float chamber cover		
11	Vacuum chamber with piston (supplied as matched pair)	34	Battle plate	58	Spring washer
		35	Needle valve and seat	59	Choke control linkage (including jet actuating lever)
12	Jet needle fixing screw	36	Gasket		
13	Spring	37	Fixing screw (three items)	60	Washer
14	Damper piston and cap	38	Spring washer (three items)	61	Screw fixing actuating lever to jet
15	Gasket	39	Float	62	Jet adjustment nut locking sleeve (fitted where unauthorised adjustment is forbidden by exhaust emission control regulations)
16	Jet needle	40	Float hinge pin		
16a	Jet needle (later production)	41	Throttle shaft		
17	Fixing screw (three items)	42	Throttle flap		
18	Jet assembly	42a	Over-run relief valve brackets		
19	Armering for feed pipe			63	Throttle control assembly for single installations
20	Gland nut	43	Fixing screw (two items)		
21	Washer	44	Throttle actuating lever	64	Return lever
22	Gland (NOTE: Items 20, 21 and 22 are threaded over the pipe and Item 22a) (if fitted) is threaded inside the pipe before assembly to the float chamber)	45	Pin fixing actuating lever to throttle spindle	65	Spacing piece (carrying 66)
		46	Throttle return lever/secondary throttle operating lever	66	Throttle return spring
				67	Throttle actuating lever
		47	Fast idle adjustment screw	68	Pick-up lever
		48	Spring	69	Bushing
		49	Spacing washer		

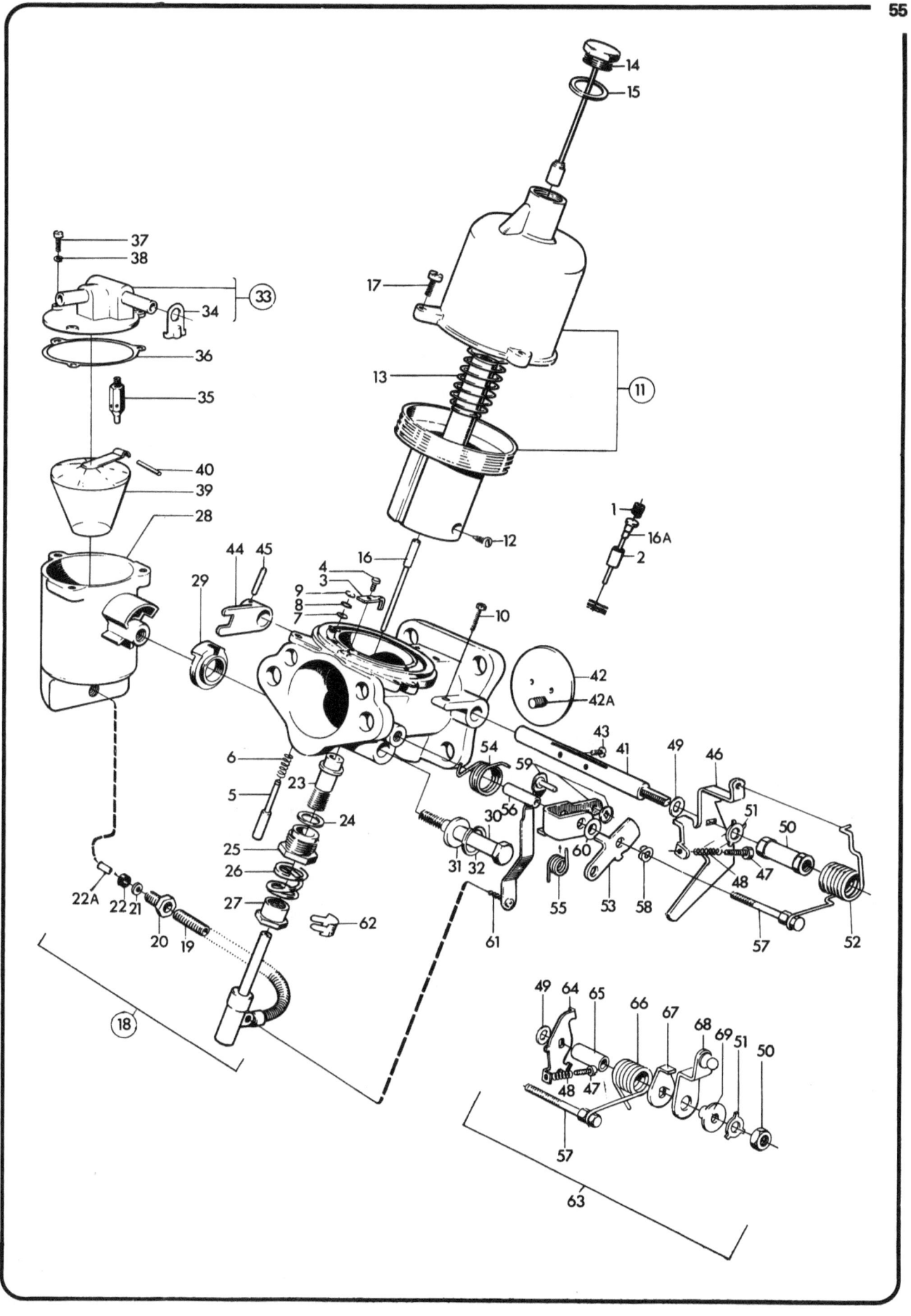

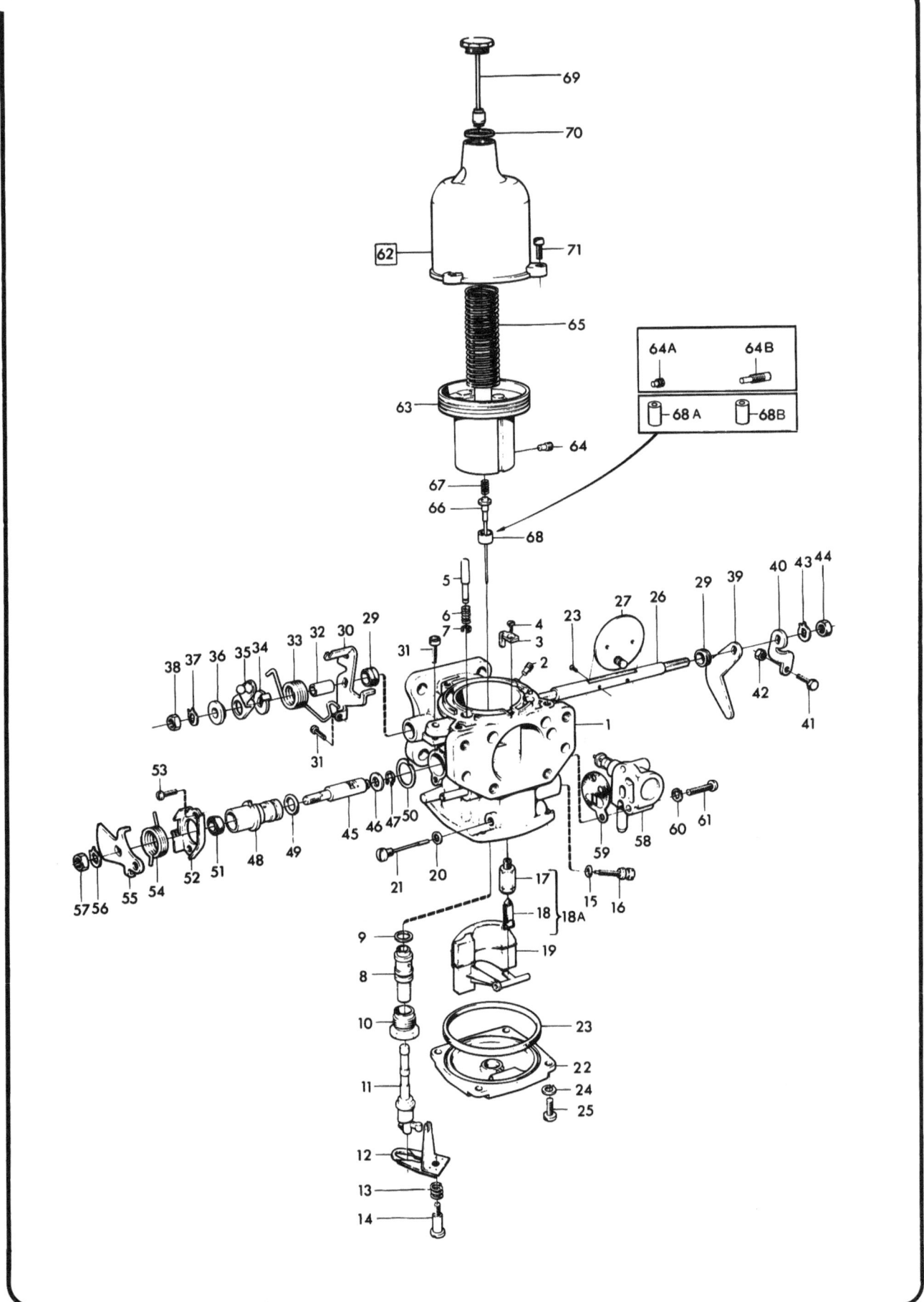

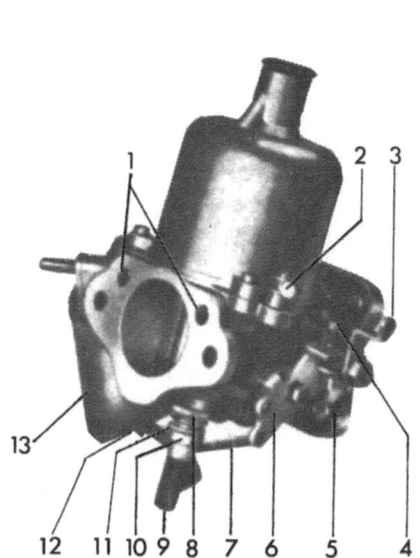  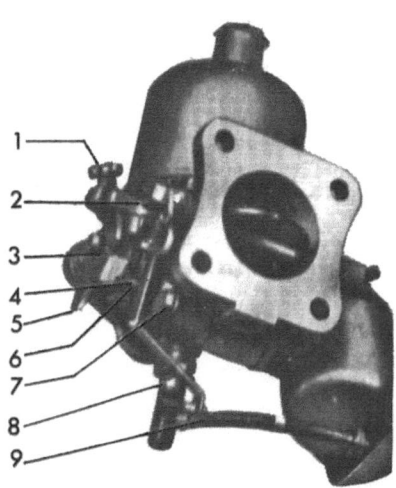

Fig.3.8. SU HS6 carburettor, single carburettor or front unit in twin installation
(viewed from right)

1   Ventilation holes
2   Attachment for choke control
3   Lever
4   Idling screw
5   Screw for fast idle
6   Lever
7   Link for jet
8   Lock nut
9   Jet
10 Adjusting nut
11 Spring
12 Fuel line
13 Float chamber

Fig.3.9. SU HS6 carburettor (viewed
from left)

1   Suction chamber
2   Screw for damper piston
3   Lifting pin
4   Float chamber cover
5   Ventilation hole
6   Fuel line
7   Lever
8   Throttle flap
9   Connecting flange

Fig.3.10. SU HS6 carburettor (other
components)
1   Attachment for choke control outer
    casing
2   Throttle flap spindle
3   Return spring
4   Return spring
5   Lever for fast idle
6   Lever for lowering jet
7   Bolt for float chamber
8   Link for lowering jet
9   Fuel line

Fig.3.7. SU HIF6 carburettor - exploded view (front carburettor in twin installations)

1   Main body
2   Plug
3   Locating key for piston
4   Fixing screw
5   Piston lift pin
6   Spring
7   Clip
8   Jet bearing
9   Sealing washer
10 Jet bearing retaining screw
11 Jet
12 Bi-metal assembly
13 Spring
14 Fixing screw
15 O-ring seal for jet adjuster screw
16 Jet adjuster screw
17 Needle valve seat
18 Needle valve
19 Float
20 Sealing washer
21 Float spindle (with threaded end
    and screw head)
22 Float chamber cover
23 Sealing ring
24 Spring washer (four items)
25 Fixing screw (four items)

26 Throttle spindle
27 Throttle disc (including over-run
    relief valve)
28 Fixing screws (two items)
29 Seal (two items)
30 Throttle return lever
31 Fast idle adjustment screw
32 Distance piece carrying 33
33 Throttle return spring
34 Throttle actuating lever
35 Throttle control pick-up lever
36 Bushing
37 Lock washer
38 Throttle spindle nut
39 Secondary throttle actuating lever
40 Hot start valve actuating lever
41 Adjustment screw
42 Nut
43 Lock washer
44 Throttle spindle nut
45 Cold start device - slotted shaft
46 Washer
47 Circlip
48 Housing
49 O-ring (sealing housing to
    main body)

50 Gasket
51 Rubber seal for spindle
52 Retainer and housing for 54
53 Fixing screw (two items)
54 Return spring
55 Fast idle cam
56 Lock washer
57 Securing nut
58 Hot start valve
59 Gasket
60 Spring washer (two items)
61 Fixing screw (two items)
62 Upper half of body (suction
    chamber)
63 Piston
64a Carburettor needle locking screw
    (early production)
65 Return spring
66 Carburettor needle
67 Spring
68a Needle guide (early production)
68b Needle guide (later production)
69 Damping piston assembly
70 Sealing washer
71 Fixing screws (three items)

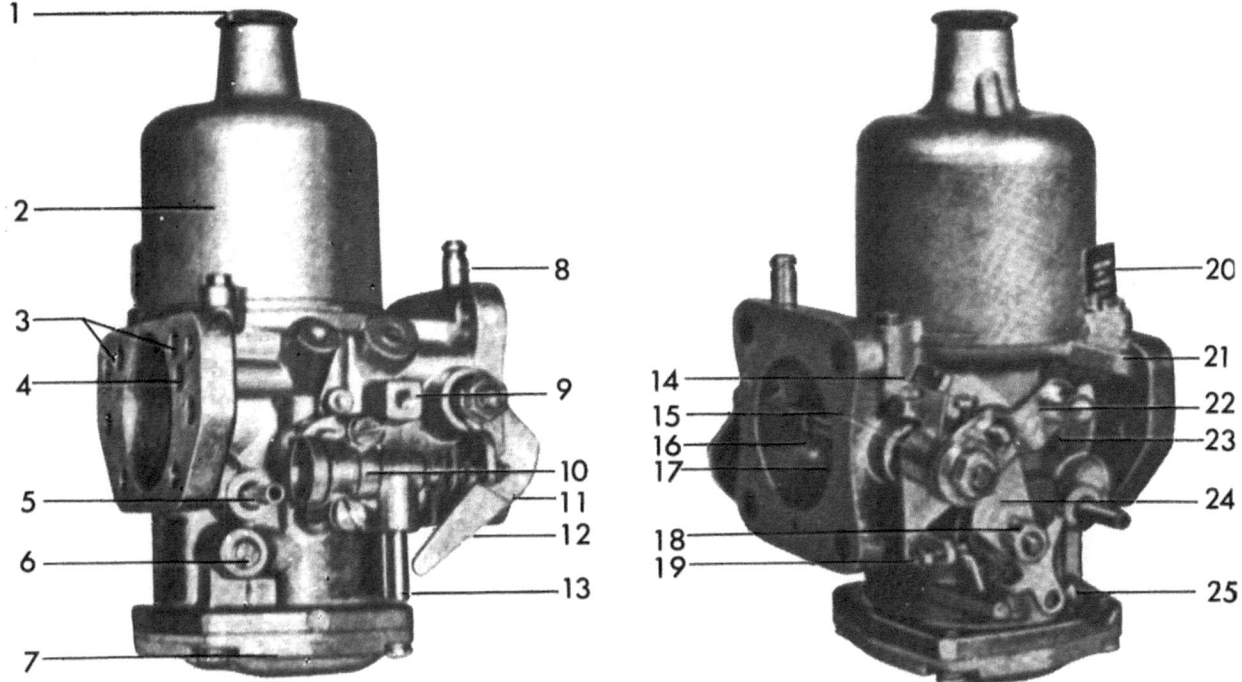

Fig.3.11. SU HIF6 carburettor as fitted in twin installations

1 Cap of hydraulic damper	8 Connection (positive) for	13 Outlet from float	19 Fast idle stop screw
2 Suction chamber	hose to venting filter	chamber (connection for	20 Designation plate
3 Drillings for air supply	9 Boss for guard	hose to venting filter)	21 Attachment for choke
under air valve	10 Hot start valve	14 Throttle stop screw	control
4 Vent holes and float chamber	11 Hot start valve adjusting	15 Return spring	22 Lever
5 Connection for fuel line	screw	16 Primary throttle	23 Lift pin
6 Jet adjusting screw	12 Lever actuating secondary	17 By-pass valve	24 Cam for fast idle
7 Float chamber cover	throttle	18 Cold start device	25 Screw head for float shaft

NOTE: In later installations, arrangements for operating the secondary throttle are different and lever 12 is not fitted

principle.

Air sucked through the carburettor by the engine draws petrol from the jet, so forming the petrol-air mixture. The amount of petrol drawn from the jet depends on the position of the tapered carburettor needle, which moves up and down the jet orifice in accordance with the state of the engine vacuum which acts on a piston (to which the needle is attached) which sits in the cylindrical upper part of the carburettor body. On top of this big piston is a tube, and inside this tube is a small piston which runs in oil and damps the motion of the large piston. This ensures that the changes in mixture are not too sudden and the engine responds smoothly to the throttle.

In the Stromberg, the piston is not in fact a piston in the strict sense of the word, in that it incorporates a rubber diaphragm to seal it off instead of relying on being a good fit in the body.

3 The level of petrol in the carburettor jet is determined by the level in the float chamber. When this level is correct, the float closes a needle valve which prevents further petrol from entering the carburettor. As the level drops, the valve opens and more petrol is pumped in until the level is restored. By this means the level is kept constant within close limits.

4 Generally speaking these carburettors are very trouble free. Because of the large size of the jet it is unusual for this to become blocked and usually any blockage can be cleared by revving up the engine and then releasing the throttle, producing the highest possible suction at the jet. There is no reason why the carburettor should lose tune and in fact what usually happens is that as the engine gets older and less efficient, more or less fruitless attempts are made to bring back performance by playing about with the carburettor. This is never very successful and in those parts of the world where exhaust emission is regulated by law it is inadvisable and indeed very often forbidden to alter curburettor settings without monitoring

exhaust emission with specialised apparatus.

5 The ultimate cause of most carburettor troubles is wear. Wear on the linkages prevents proper operation of the controls and wear on the needle will upset the mixture. In the SU carburettor which relies on accurate positioning of the piston and its associated components for its proper operation you may get trouble with pistons sticking. A drop of oil from time to time on the various linkages will ensure that they last for years without trouble, and should help to ensure that carburettor overhaul should be no more frequent than major engine overhaul.

11 Removing and refitting carburettors

1 Removing the carburettor(s) is basically a simple operation, with minor complications arising from the necessity to deal with various pipe connections and linkages associated with arrangements for exhaust emission control. We start with directions for dealing with a single carburettor fitting, and follow these with some notes on more complicated installations.

2 The photograph shows a typical single carburettor arrangement, the air filter being pulled slightly to one side to give a better view. With the air filter removed, only four external connections to the carburettor remain, all of which can be seen in the photograph: they are the throttle linkage (which has a photograph of its own), the choke control, the fuel pipe and the vacuum pipe to the distributor.

3 If you are not sure how to deal with the throttle linkage, see Chapter 1, Section 5, paragraph 13. When you remove vacuum pipes, close up their ends (particularly important in the case of the distributor pipe). If - as may well happen - there are more than one, notice which vacuum pipe goes to which connection on the carburettor - having them the wrong way round will affect your ignition timing and hence your engine performance.

11.2a B20A Carburettor installation - the feed pipe, middle right - ventilates the crankcase via the air cleaner

11.2b With the clip removed, the throttle link rod can be disconnected

Disconnection of the choke cable and the fuel pipe need no comment.

4   With the odds and ends out of the way, the fixing nuts can be undone and the carburettor removed. Put the insulation block (if fitted) and any guard plate arrangement on one side and don't forget them when refitting. Plug the manifold with rag and/or masking tape.

5   A final point to note with twin carburettor installations: When you have removed the carburettors, keep the front and rear carburettors strictly separate - particularly when you are dismantling them. By ensuring that you never get parts of the two mixed you will save yourself a lot of time and annoyance. Also it is always a sound principle during mechanical work to ensure that whatever is taken apart is put back in exactly the same position as it was before, even though many parts are interchangeable. If you get into the habit of doing this, mechanical work will be easier and more pleasant.

6   Throttle linkage arrangements for twin-carburettor install-ations are illustrated in Figs.3.12 and 3.13. Notice that on the twin SU installation the carburettors must be removed together, after which, they can be separated by undoing the links to the rod connecting their throttle controls.

7   In Stromberg installations the rear carburettor may carry an

extra lever which regulates the hot start valve fitted to the side of the air cleaner casing (Fig. 3.15). To avoid upsetting the adjustment of the hot start valve, detach this lever from the carburettor before removing it.

8   On earlier Stromberg installations, the rear carburettor only is fitted with a cold start "choke" device. On SU installations and later Stromberg installations both carburettors have cold start controls operated by independent cables branching from a single choke control.

9   On the B20B, as part of the exhaust emission control system, the inlet manifold is fitted with secondary throttles driven by cams on the throttle shafts of the carburettors. When refitting, see that the cam and lever are properly engaged.

10 A fuller description of the functioning of the devices mentioned above is given later in this Chapter, for the moment we are only concerned with their effect on the removal and refitment of carburettors.

11 Some of the points to be noted on refitting have already been given in the preceding paragraphs. Generally speaking, refitment is a simple reversal of the removal procedure. Be sure that the mating surfaces of the manifold and carburettor are completely clean, don't forget the insulation block and any guard plate arrangements, and finally, have a look at the photo associated

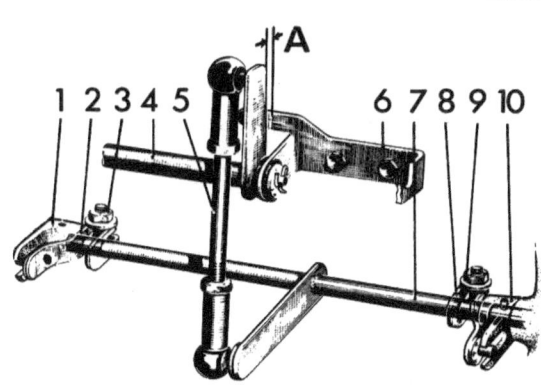

Fig.3.12. Throttle control - twin SU HS6 installation

1,10 Throttle levers
2,8 Adjustable levers
3,9 Lock nuts
4   Control rod
5   Adjustable link rod
6   Bracket
7   Intermediate shaft

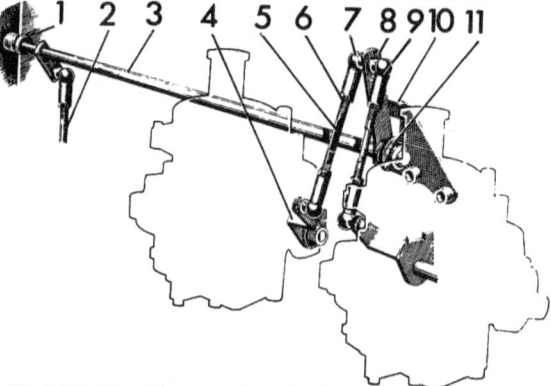

Fig.3.13. Throttle control - twin Stromberg installation Twin SU HIF6 is almost identical

1   Bush
2   Pedal link shaft
3   Control shaft
4   Throttle arm lever
5   Adjustable link rod
6   Lock nut
7   Ball joint
8   Control shaft lever
9   Locking clip
10 Bracket
11 Rubber mount

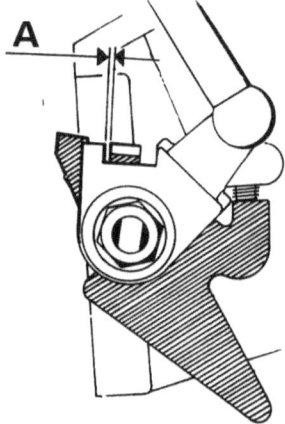

Fig.3.14. Stromberg carburettor - throttle lever clearance

A = 0.004" (0.1 mm)

11.11 Lubricate the throttle linkages

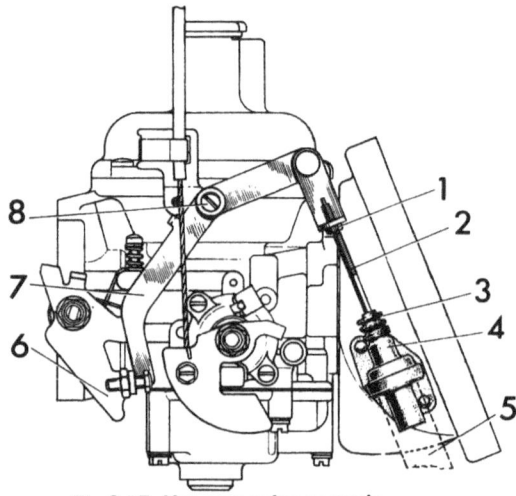

**Fig.3.15. Hot start valve controls -
twin Stromberg installation**

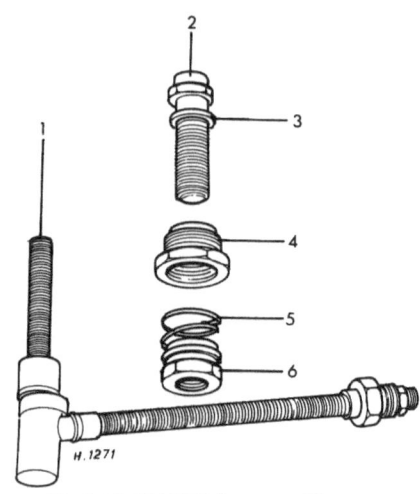

Fig.3.16. SU HS6 jet assembly

1 Lock nut	(only on vehicle with
2 Control rod	Evaporite unit)
3 Rubber seal	6 Adjusting screw
4 Hot start valve	7 Control lever
5 Venting filter hose	8 Fixing/pivot screw

1 Jet with fuel pipe		4 Lock nut	
2 Jet bearing		5 Spring	
3 Washer		6 Adjusting nut	

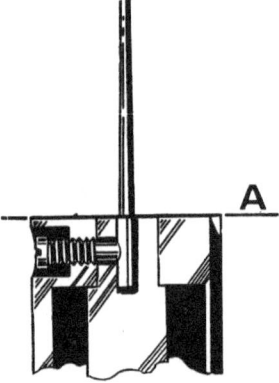

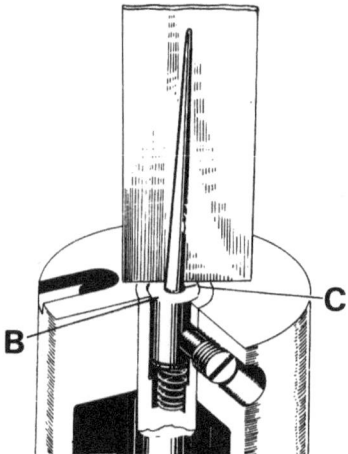

Fig.3.17. Fitting the fuel needle SU HS6 carburettors

(left) old type   (right) later type
*Shoulder of needle (A) or top of mounting (B) must be flush with piston face. With spring mounting, engraved line (C) must point
away from port in piston face and needle must lean in this direction*

with this paragraph. Linkage lubrication is essential just after reassembly when many of the linkages may be dry.

12 SU type HS6 carburettor - dismantling, inspection and overhaul

1 Assuming that you have the carburettor on the work bench, start by cleaning the exterior thoroughly with paraffin or a detergent such as Gunk, using a stiff brush where necessary.

2 Mark the position of the float chamber lid relative to the body and remove it by unscrewing the three screws holding it down. Empty out any fuel still in the float chamber.

3 Undo the cap at the top of the carburettor and withdraw it complete with small damper piston. Empty the oil from the dashpot.

4 The float chamber is secured to the body by a single bolt. Undo this bolt and detach the float chamber from the body, being very careful not to strain the flexible feed pipe. Unscrew the pipe union from the float chamber by holding it in a spanner and turning the float chamber anti-clockwise. Doing it this way will avoid placing any strain on the fuel pipe.

Withdraw the pin on which the float pivots, take out the float, float lever and unscrew the needle valve assembly, preferably with a small socket spanner.

5 Dismantle the throttle and choke levers and linkages, and then remove the adjusting nut, spring, locknut, seal, jet sleeve and jet from the body (see Fig. 3.16). Be sure you know how the linkages work before you take them off. It is an easy matter to sort this out before you take them apart but much more difficult when they are in bits.

6 Remove the uppermost of the carburettor body, marking the flanges so that you will know the correct position when replacing it. Remove the piston spring and piston with the jet needle attached. Put the piston somewhere safe - a good idea is to stand it in a narrow necked jar with the needle inside. If the piston is dropped you will be very lucky if it is still serviceable when picked up.

7 Undo the screws holding the throttle disc into its rod, being careful not to put too much pressure on the rod in the process (support it with the other hand). Withdraw the throttle shaft.

8 The piston lifting pin can be removed if necessary - usually it isn't - by pushing it upwards and removing its retaining clip. Watch the washer, seal and spring on the underside when you take it out, or they will roll under the bench. Dismantling is now completed.

9 Generally speaking the SU carburettor is very reliable, even so it may develop faults which may not be readily apparent unless a careful inspection is carried out. Before the inspection can begin each individual component will need to be thoroughly washed in paraffin.

10 Inspect the carburettor needle for ridging. If this is apparent it is usually a sign of incorrect fitting and you will probably find that the rim of the jet is damaged where the needle has been striking it. If the needle is ridged, it must be renewed - do not attempt to rub it down with abrasive paper as carburettor needles are made to very fine tolerances.

11 When replacing the needle locate it in the piston as shown in Figs. 3.17. The needle shoulder or (if spring mounted) the surrounding stub should be flush with the piston and the engraved line on the supporting stub should point directly away from the channel in the piston face.

In some cases the supporting stub for the needle has a flat on it which should engage with the locking screw.

12 Inspect the jet and the jet bearing for wear. Wear inside the jet will accompany wear on the needle. The outside of the jet may be worn due to movement up and down in the jet bearing when the choke control has been operated. The bearing may be worn for the same reason. Replacement is the only remedy.

13 Examine the float chamber needle valve and its seating for signs of ridging. If this is apparent, replace both.

14 Inspect the carburettor body carefully for signs that the piston has been in contact. When the carburettor is operating,

the piston should not come into contact with the carburettor body. The whole assembly is supported by the rod of the piston which slides in the centre guide tube, this rod being attached to the cap in the top of the carburettor body. It is possible for wear in the centre guide tube to allow the piston to touch the wall of the body. Check for this by assembling the small pistons in the carburettor body and sliding the large one up and down, rotating it about the centre guide tube at the same time. If contact occurs and the cause is worn parts, replace them. This contact is invariably the cause of piston sticking. In no circumstances try to correct piston sticking by altering the tension of the return spring, though very slight contact with the body may be cured - as a temporary measure - by polishing the offending portion of the body wall with metal polish or extremely fine emery cloth.

15 Check that the damper piston moves freely on its rod with an axial play of 0.04 - 0.07" (1.1 -1.9 mm) (see Fig. 18).

16 Check for wear on the throttle shaft and bushes through which it passes. Apart from the nuisance of a sticking throttle, excessive wear here can cause air leaks in the induction system adversely affecting engine performance. Worn bushes can be extracted and new bushes fitted if necessary.

17 Reassembly is a straightforward reversal of the dismantling process. If you leave the fitting of the float chamber until last you can carry out the jet centring procedure described in the next section (a must after the carburettor has been dismantled) without having to undo work you have already done.

18 After assembly, fill the dashpot with automatic transmission fluid A to within .25" (6 mm) of the top of the cylinder and reinsert the piston. Check operation of the piston by lifting it with the external lifting pin (see Fig. 3.9). There should be some resistance to lifting but practically none to the return, the piston contacting the bridge with an audible click.

13 SU HS6 carburettor - jet centring

1 This operation is always necessary if the carburettor has been dismantled, but to check if it is necessary on a carburettor in service, first screw up the check adjusting nut as far as it will go without forcing it and lift the piston with the lifting pin, letting it fall under its own weight. It should fall on to the bridge with a soft metallic click. Now repeat the procedure with the adjusting nut screwed right down. If the click is not audible in either of the two tests proceed as follows.

2 Disconnect the jet link from the bottom of the jet and the nylon flexible tube from the underside of the float chamber. Gently slide the jet and the nylon tube from the underside of the carburettor body. Next unscrew the jet adjusting nut and lift away the nut and the locking spring. Refit the adjusting nut without the locking spring and screw it up as far as possible without forcing it. Replace the jet and tube but without bothering to reconnect the tube to the float chamber.

3 Slacken the jet locking nut so that it may be rotated with the fingers only. Unscrew the top cap and lift away the piston damper. Gently press the piston down on to the bridge and

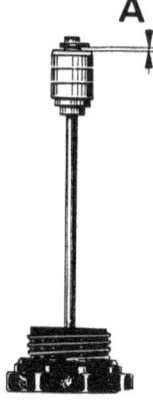

A

Fig.3.18. Damper piston clearance

A = 0.04 - 0.07" (1.1 - 1.9 mm)

tighten the locknut. Lift the piston using the lifting pin and
check that it is able to fall freely under its own weight. Now
lower the adjusting nut and check once again. If this time there
is a difference in the two metallic clicks repeat the centring
procedure until the sound is the same for both tests.
4   Gently move the jet and unscrew the adjusting nut. Refit the
locking spring and jet adjusting nut. Top up the dashpot with oil,
if necessary, and replace the damper. Connect the nylon flexible
tube to the underside of the float chamber and finally reconnect
the jet link.

14 SU HS6 carburettor - fuel level - checking and adjustment

1   This is best done with the carburettor in position on the
engine.
2   With the float chamber full of petrol, remove the top half of
the body with the piston and dashpot.
3   Check that the level of fuel in the jet is about 1/16" (1.6
mm) below the top of the jet. If the level is appreciably above or
below this, check the float level by inverting the float chamber
cover and measuring the distance between the rivet head on the
float arm and the ridge on the cover. This should be approximately 0.126" (3.2 mm) for early production models or 0.189"
(4.8 mm) for later models (see Fig. 19). If the float level is
appreciably different from the figures given above do not bend
the float arm, but replace the faulty part. No great precision is
required as the carburettor is relatively insensitive to variations
in the float level.

15 SU HS6 carburettor - tuning (single and twin installations)

1   Before tuning the carburettor(s), check that the valve
clearances, spark plugs and gaps, contact breaker settings and
ignition timing are all correct, that there is no air leakage on the
intake and that the vacuum advance tube is in place. Make the
final adjustments with the engine at its normal running temperature, and finish off by setting the throttle stops to give the
proper idling speed when you have replaced the air cleaner and
crankcase ventilation pipes, which should be removed before you
start.
2   With either carburettor installation, set the jet(s) to the basic
position by unscrewing the adjusting nut(s) in until the upper
end of the jet just touches the lower face of the piston when this
is as low as it will go: With the air filter removed you can check
the setting visually. Now turn back 15 flats of the nut(s) ie 2½
full turns.
3   On a twin carburettor installation, set the throttle stops on
both carburettors so that the throttle is fully closed in each case
and adjust the locknuts on the intermediate rod and the length
of the link rod so that when the throttles are on the verge of
being opened by the controls there is a gap of .02" (0.51 cms)
between the levers on the control rod and its stop (see Fig.3.12).
Now screw up the throttle stop screws on the carburettors by
1.5 turns, thus opening the throttle slightly. Make sure that the
two throttles open in synchronism with each other. For a single
carburettor adopt the same procedure adapted to the simpler
linkage.
4   For a single installation, run the engine until it is at
operational temperature and then adjust the speed to 700
revs/min with the throttle stop screw.
5   Adjust the jet until the maximum idling speed is obtained,
then screw the nut inwards until the speed begins to drop. This is
the correct setting.
6   Adjust the throttle stop screw until the idling speed is 800
revs/min (700 revs/min for automatic transmission).
7   For a twin installation, run the engine until it reaches
operational temperature and then adjust the speed to 700
revs/min with the throttle stop screws, ensuring as far as possible
that the air intake to each carburettor is the same. In the absence
of special test gear check that a slight movement of either
throttle stop screw has the same effect on idling speed; also

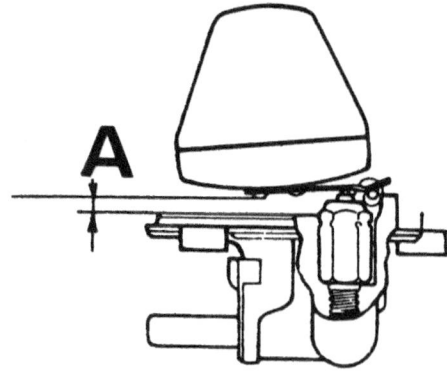

Fig.3.19. SU HS6 float level

A = approx 0.126 (3.2 mm) on early production
  or   0.189 (4.8 mm) on later production

listen to the hiss at the carburettor intakes. The air cleaner
should be removed during carburettor adjustment. Now adjust
the jets with the adjusting nuts until maximum idling speed is
obtained, then turn the nuts equally clockwise (ie screw them up
so that the jets rise in the body of the carburettors) until any
further turning of either nut causes the engine speed to drop.
This is the correct setting. Be sure that turning either nut has an
equal effect on engine speed.
     As a further check, lift the piston of one of the carburettors
with the lifting pin and check the fall-off in engine speed, which
should be approximately the same for either carburettor, 150 -
250 rpm. Finally, re-adjust the idling speed to 800 rpm or for
automatic transmission cars 700 rpm.
8   To adjust the choke and fast idle controls, first pull out the
choke control on the instrument panel by about 5/8" (15 mm)
and set the locking screw for the choke cable on the carburettor
so that the jet is just starting to move downwards at this point.
Adjust the fast idle screw so that at this stage the throttle is just
starting to open. In cold weather, it may sometimes be advisable
to adjust this screw so that it contacts the cam a little earlier
than this. Where two carburettors are involved, make sure that
both the carburettors respond to the choke control in exactly
the same way.
9   By following the above routine you can get excellent results
with a bit of care. Two points may be mentioned: first, if you
are able to get access to equipment for monitoring the air intake
to twin carburettors you can more easily adjust the throttle
controls so that the inputs are equal over a wide range of
settings; second, that jet adjustment should ideally (and in some
parts of the world it is a legal requirement) be set for minimum
CO emission using the appropriate test gear and then sealed. In
countries or states where stringent exhaust emission control laws
are in force, the foregoing tuning procedures must be regarded as
for information or emergency use only.

16 SU type HIF6 carburettor - dismantling, inspection and overhaul

1   Assuming that you have the carburettor on the work bench,
start by cleaning the exterior thoroughly with paraffin or a
detergent such as Gunk, using a stiff brush where necessary.
2   Undo the cap at the top of the carburettor and withdraw it
complete with the small damper piston. Empty the oil from the
dashpot.
3   Mark the position of the float chamber cover relative to the
body and remove it by unscrewing the four screws holding it
down. Empty out any fuel still in the fuel chamber.
4   The float is held to the body by a spindle having a screw head
on it (shown on Fig. 3.11). Unscrew and remove the spindle

with its sealing washer, remove the float, unscrew the needle valve socket and remove it and the needle.

5 Dismantle the various control linkages, being sure by studying Figs. 3.7, 3.11 and 3.13, that you know how they fit together. It is an easy matter to sort this out before you take them apart but much more difficult when they are in bits.

6 Remove the hot start valve which is held to the body by two screws (Fig. 3.11).

7 Unscrew the nut holding the fast idle cam - having first straightened its tab washer, take off the cam and its spring which is contained in a small housing behind it. Undo the two screws holding down this housing and pull on the spindle which held the fast idle cam and the whole cold start assembly will come out of the body. It is shown dismantled in Fig. 3.20.

8 On the opposite side of the carburettor will be found the hot start device. Undo the two screws connecting this to the body and remove it (see Fig. 3.21).

9 Undo the screws holding the throttle disc into its shaft, being careful not to put too much pressure on the shaft in the process (support it with the other hand). Remove the disc and withdraw the throttle shaft.

10 Mark the flanges and remove the top part of the body (suction chamber) and the piston. Be careful of the needle on the end of the piston - a good idea is to stand the piston on a narrow-necked jar with the needle hanging inside it.

11 Unscrew the jet adjusting screw and remove the bi-metal assembly holding the jet.

12 The carburettor is now sufficiently dismantled for inspection to be carried out. One or two adjusting screws and the like have been left in the body, but it is recommended that these are only removed when you are actually ensuring that the various channels are clear. Generally speaking, the SU carburettor is very reliable but even so it may develop faults which are not readily apparent unless a careful inspection is carried out, yet may nevertheless effect engine performance. So it is well worthwhile giving the carburettor a good look over when you have got it dismantled.

13 Inspect the carburettor needle for ridging. If this is apparent you will probably find corresponding wear on the inside of the jet. If the needle is ridged, it must be replaced. Do not attempt to rub it down with abrasive paper as carburettor needles are made to very fine tolerances.

14 When replacing the needle locate it in the piston as shown in Fig. 3.17. The supporting stubs should be flush with the piston and the engraved line should point directly away from the channel in the piston face. Note that this makes the needle incline in the direction of the carburettor air cleaner flange when the piston is fitted.

15 Inspect the jet for wear. Wear inside the jet will accompany wear on the needle. If any wear is apparent on the jet, replace it. It may be unhooked from the bi-metal spring and this may be used again (see Fig. 3.22).

16 Inspect the piston and the carburettor body (suction chamber) carefully for signs that these have been in contact. When the carburettor is operating the main piston should not come into contact with the carburettor body. The whole assembly is supported by the rod of the piston which slides in the centre guide tube, this rod being attached to the cap in the top of the carburettor body. It is possible for wear in the centre guide to allow the piston to touch the wall of the body. Check for this by assembling the small piston in the carburettor body and sliding the large one down, rotating it about the centre guide tube at the same time. If contact occurs and the cause is worn parts, replace them. In no circumstances try to correct piston sticking by altering the tension of the return spring, though very slight contact with the body may be cured - as a temporary measure - by polishing the offending portion of the body wall with metal polish or extremely fine emery cloth.

17 The fit of the piston in the suction chamber can be checked by plugging the air hole in the body and assembling the piston in the chamber without its return spring, fitting the damper piston without filling the dashpot with oil. If the assembly is now turned upside down as shown in Fig. 3.23 the piston should sink to the bottom in 5-7 seconds. If the time is appreciably less than this, the piston and suction chamber should both be replaced since they are matched to each other.

18 Check for wear on the throttle shaft and bushes through which it passes. Apart from the nuisance of a sticking throttle, excessive wear here can cause air leaks in the induction system adversely affecting engine performance. Worn bushes can be extracted and new bushes fitted if necessary. For inspection and overhaul of the cold start and hot start devices see Sections 17

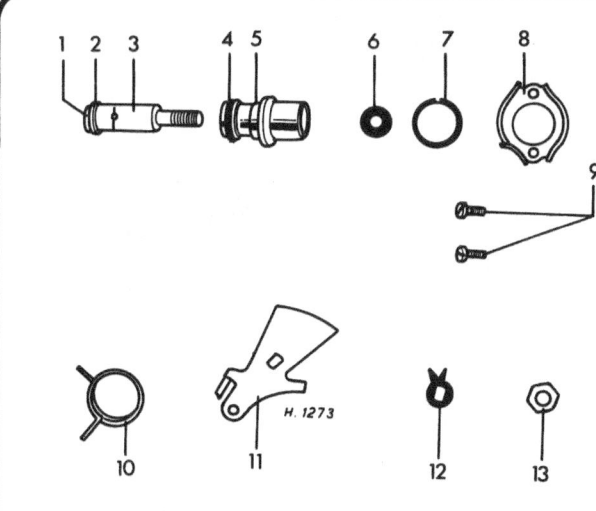

Fig.3.20. SU HIF6 carburettor - cold start device

1	Circlip	7	Gasket
2	Washer	8	Spring retainer
3	Spindle	9	Fixing screws
4	Rubber ring	10	Return spring
5	Housing	11	Fast idle cam
6	Rubber seal for	12	Tab washer
	spindle	13	Nut

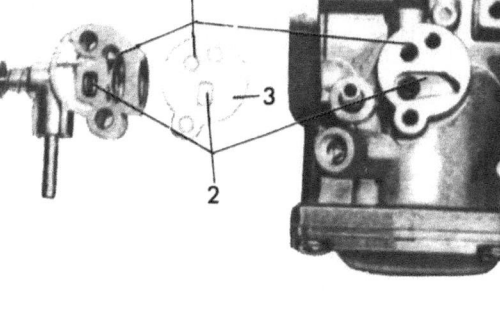

Fig.3.21. SU HIF6 hot start device

1 Channel to air cleaner
2 Channel to float chamber
3 Gasket

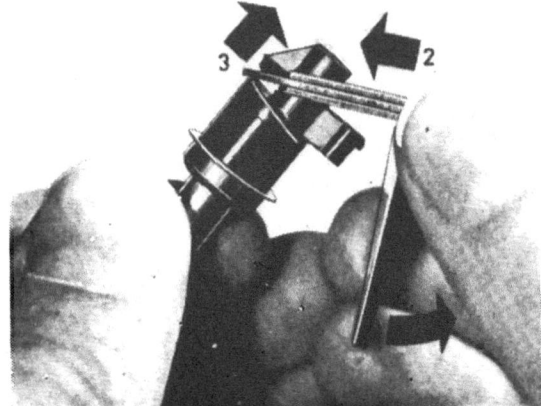

Fig.3.22. SU HIF6 removing bi-metal strip from jet

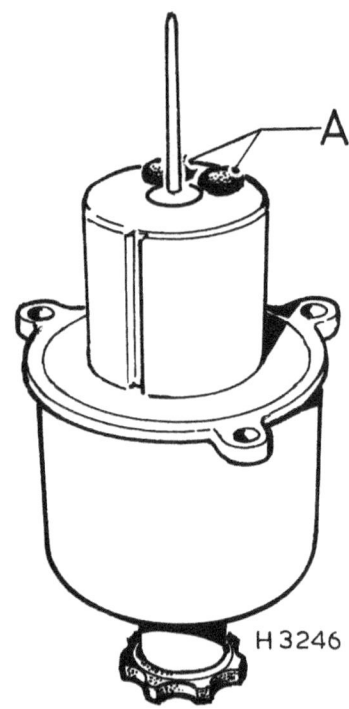

H 3246

Fig.3.23. Testing fit of piston in suction chamber

A = Plugs of rubber or cork

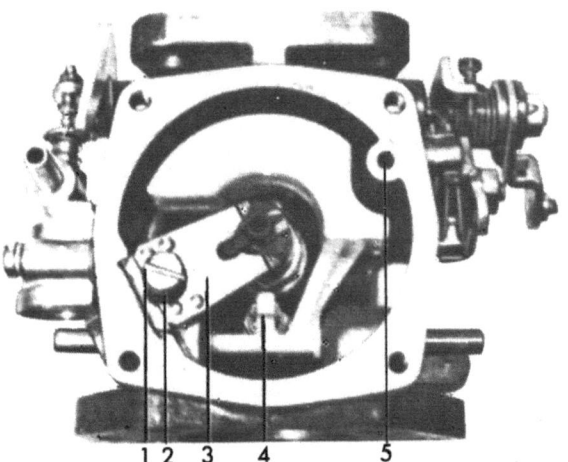

1 2 3 4 5

Fig.3.24. SU HIF6 jet and float assembly

1	Fixing screw for bi-metal assembly
2	Spring (under head of screw)
3	Bi-metal assembly
4	Float valve retainer
5	Drilling to cold start valve

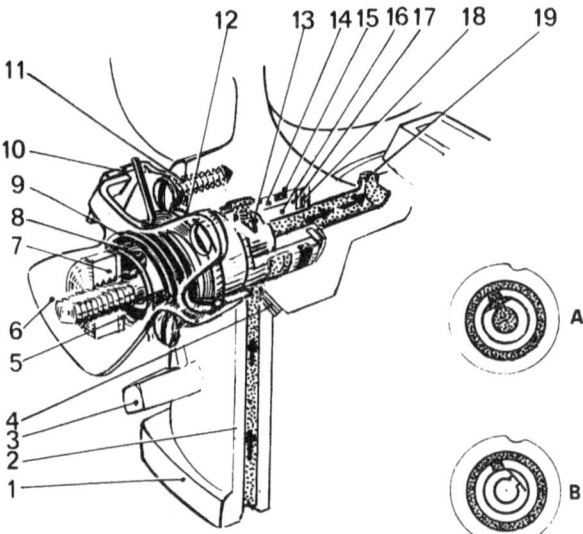

Fig.3.25. SU HIF6 cold start device

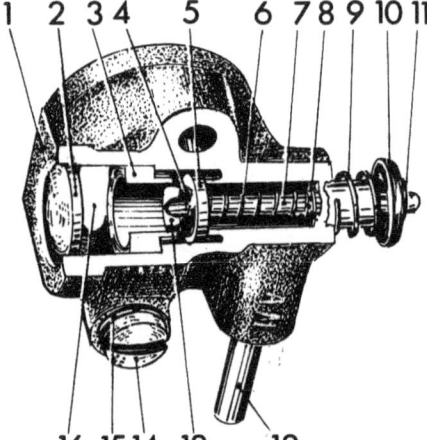

1 2 3 4 5 6 7 8 9 10 11

16 15 14 13 12

Fig.3.26. SU HS6 hot start device

1	Housing
2	Sealing washer
3	Valve seat
4	Circlip
5	Valve washer
6	Thrust spring
7	Control rod
8	Circlip
9	Thrust spring
10	Washer
11	Circlip
12	Hose connection (outlet)
13	Channel from float chamber
14	Fixing screw
15	Spring washer
16	Channel to air cleaner

A	Disengaged	10	Spring retainer
B	Engaged	11	Screw
1	Carburettor housing	12	Packing
2	Channel from float chamber	13	V-slot
3	Stop tab for lever	14	Valve housing
4	Channel for additional air	15	Rubber ring
5	Tab washer	16	Spindle
6	Cam for fast idle	17	Washer
7	Nut	18	Circlip
8	Sealing	19	Channel to carburettor throttle chamber
9	Return spring		

and 18.

19 Reassembly is a strightforward reversal of the dismantling process. During reassembly the float level can be checked and adjusted if necessary as described in Section 19. When assembling the jet, screw up the adjusting screw so that the upper edge of the jet comes level with the bridge, then turn it 2½ turns clockwise. This gives the initial position for jet adjustment. Fig. 3.24 shows the jet assembled on the bi-metallic strip in the main body and also indicates the correct positioning of the float valve retainer on the tab on the float arm.

20 When the carburettor is assembled, the dashpot should be filled with automatic transmission fluid A to within .25" (6 mm) of the top of the cylinder before re-inserting the damper piston. Check that the piston is operating properly by lifting it with the lifting pin and letting it fall. It should hit the bridge of the carburettor with an audible metallic click. If it does not, perhaps the needle is fouling the jet (it is supposed to touch it lightly). This should not occur with careful assembly; there is no provision for centring the jet but if it is properly assembled this is not necessary.

17 SU HIF6 carburettor - cold start device

1 The cold start device is shown assembled in Fig. 3.20 and a diagram is given in Fig. 3.25 from which it will be seen that as the spindle (which also carries the fast idle cam) revolves, a "V" shaped slot in the spindle progressively opens a channel between the float chamber and throttle chamber. At the same time a small air channel is opened so that a little air is mixed with the incoming vapour.

2 The fast idle cam operates the throttle by acting on a stop screw on a lever on the throttle shaft.

3 The whole device can be removed from the carburettor body (see Section 16, paragraph 7) and dismantled for cleaning and inspection. If kept oiled it should give no trouble. Should the spindle or the housing show signs of wear they should both be replaced.

18 SU HIF6 carburettor - hot start device

1 This device is shown in Fig. 3.26 and a functional diagram is given in Fig. 3.27. When the engine is idling, particularly in hot weather, the carburettor tends to fill with petrol vapour and the idling speed is affected, the tendency being to slow down the engine or even stop it. To prevent this, the hot start valve plunger is depressed when the engine is idling and a channel is opened between the float chamber and the outside atmosphere, the vapour being vented either to the atmosphere or to the evaporative control system. When the throttle is opened, the valve shuts off the outlet to the atmosphere and opens a channel to the inlet manifold.

2 The hot start valve is not intended to be taken apart. By way of overhaul it should be thoroughly cleaned to ensure that no particles of dirt prevent the valve disc from sealing.

3 Check the operation of the valve by blowing with the mouth into the pipe outlet connection with the control rod in the outer position. Don't blow too hard or you will lift the valve off the seating, but it should definitely seal for light pressure. Now depress the control rod and at the same time cover up the small retangular hole in the valve body. Again the valve should be sealed.

4 Check also that the control rod does not jam when moving. A drop of oil will ensure smooth operation.

5 When the valve is refitted, use a new gasket. Make sure that the gasket is the right way round, so that the rectangular hole in the body is aligned with its corresponding hole in the gasket (see Fig. 3.21).

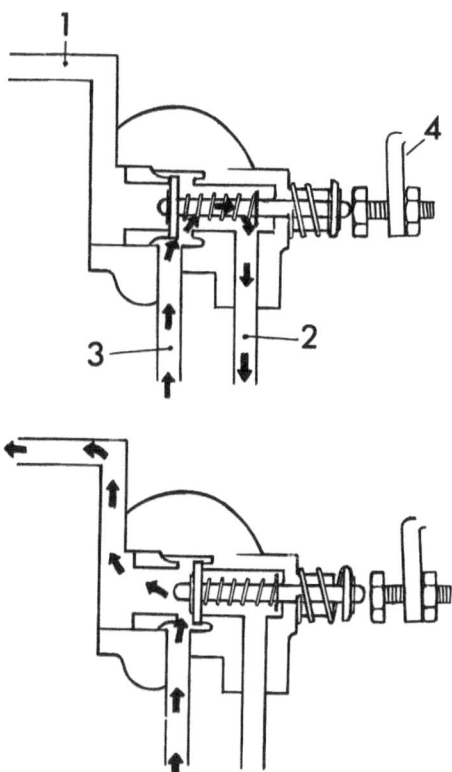

Fig.3.27. SU HIF6 hot start device - operating principles

Top Idling position
Bottom Running position
1 Channel to air cleaner
2 Channel to atmosphere or venting filter
3 Channel from float chamber
4 Lever connected to throttle spindle

19 SU HIF6 carburettor - checking the float level

1 This is best checked with the carburettor body upside-down. The float will then be resting on the needle valve. The lowest part of the float should then be just a little higher than the face of the carburettor body, as illustrated by Fig. 3.28.

2 The distance between the float and the flange (measurement A in Fig. 3.28) should be between 0.02 - 0.06" (0.5 - 1.5 mm).

3 The level can be adjusted by carefully bending the metal tab on the float arm. Do not attempt to bend the arm itself. If there is a plastic tab instead of metal one, no adjustment is possible, but it is unlikely to be needed.

4 There is no reason why you should not check this measurement with the carburettor in-situ, holding the float against the flange while you do it. It is awkard but possible.

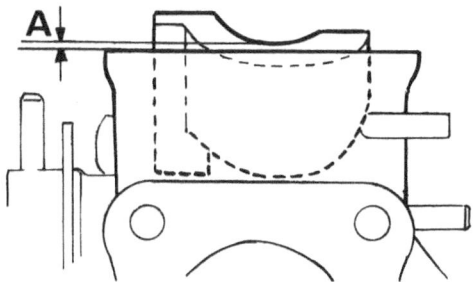

Fig.3.28. SU HIF6 float level

A = 0.02-0.06" (0.5-1.5 mm)

20 SU HIF6 carburettor - tuning

1 Before tuning the carburettors, (this type is only found in twin installations), check that the valve clearances, spark plugs and gaps, contact breaker settings and ignition timing are all correct, that there is no air leak on the intake and that the vacuum ignition advance tube is in place. Make the final adjustments with the engine at its normal running temperature, and finish off by setting the throttle stops to give the proper idling speed when you have replaced the air cleaner and crankcase ventilation pipes, which are removed when tuning so that you can check piston position etc. Do not allow the engine to get more than normally hot when setting the carburettor jets as these are temperature controlled and are best set for normal operating temperature.

2 Remove the tops of the carburettors and gently depress the piston until it touches the main body. Be certain that the jet is at a lower level than the piston when you do this - if necessary lower it by turning the adjusting screw (see Fig. 3.11) clockwise. Now turn the adjusting screw carefully anti-clockwise until the jet just touches the piston. Then lower the jet by turning the adjusting screw 2½ turns clockwise. This provides the basic jet setting if the carburettor temperature is about 68°F (20°C). You can compensate for temperature by further adjustment of the screw. If the temperature is higher than 68°F (20°C) turn the screw clockwise after making the initial setting and if lower turn the screw anti-clockwise. A quarter turn of the screw compensates for a temperature difference of about 68° F (20° C).

3 Set the throttle stop screws on both carburettors so that the throttle is just fully closed in each case and then adjust the link rods from the intermediate rod so that when the lever on this rod is hard against its stop there is a clearance of about 0.04" (1 mm) between the square hole on the throttle lever and the tonque that enters it from the throttle spindle (see Fig. 3.29). Now screw up the throttle stop screws 1½ turns so that the throttles are slightly open.

4 Run the engine until it reaches operational temperature and then adjust the speed to 700 revs/min with the throttle stop screws, ensuring as far as possible that the air intake of each carburettor is the same. In the absence of special test gear check that a slight movement of either throttle stop screw has the same effect on idling speed, also listen to the hiss at the carburettor intakes. The air cleaner should be removed during carburettor adjustment. Now adjust the jets with the adjusting screws until maximum idling speed is obtained, then turn the screws equally anti-clockwise until you reach the stage when any further turning of either screw causes the engine speed to drop (briefly race the engine a couple of times during adjustment). This is the correct setting. Be sure that turning either adjustment screw has an equal effect on engine speed. As a further check, lift the piston of one of the carburettors with the lifting pin and check the fall off in engine speed. Repeat the procedure with the other carburettor. The fall off in speed should be approximately 150-250 rpm in both cases. Readjust the idling speed to 800 rpm or for automatic transmission cars 700 rpm. Make further small adjustments if necessary to ensure that the pistons are at the same level in both carburettors over a wide range of running speeds.

5 Pull out the choke control on the instrument panel 0.8" (20 mm), set the cables operating the cold start controls so that the devices are just starting to be effective at this point. The corners of the fast idle cam should be opposite the fast idle adjustment screws. Set these screws for an idling speed of 1100-1600 rpm. Ensure that alteration of either fast idling screw has the same effect on fast idling speed. Note that in very cold conditions it may be desirable to set the idling speed slightly faster.

6 By carefully following the above routine you can get excellent results. If however you are able to get access to equipment for monitoring the air intake to the carburettor you can adjust the throttle control so that the inputs are equal over a wide range of throttle openings. Furthermore, in many parts of the world jet adjustment is subject to legal restrictions and

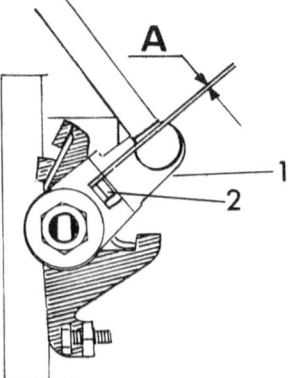

Fig.3.29. SU HIF6 clearance between control lever and actuating lever

A = 0.04" (1.0 mm approx)
1 Control lever
2 Actuating lever

should be carried out for minimum CO emission using the appropriate test gear and then sealed. In countries or states where stringent exhaust emission control laws exist, the foregoing tuning procedures must be regarded as for information or emergency use only.

21 Stromberg carburettors - dismantling, inspection and overhaul

1 As already noted, there is very little basic difference between the original Stromberg type 175-CD2 and the later type 175-CD 2S. The earlier type was fitted with an external adjusting screw for the jet. On the later type this was discontinued, and a temperature compensating attachment was fitted to the side of the body. In early twin Stromberg installations, only the rear carburettor carries a cold start device. In later fittings, this is present on both carburettors. The front carburettor carries a by-pass valve for exhaust emission control on idling. The working of these devices is described later. A further fitting on the rear carburettor is a lever worked by the throttle control which operates the hot start valve fitted in the air filter assembly. Single carburettor installations have the cold start device but not the by-pass valve.

2 Assuming that you have the carburettor on the work bench and removed from the car, start by cleaning the exterior thoroughly with paraffin or a detergent such as Gunk, using a stiff brush where necessary.

3 Mark the position of the float chamber lid relative to the body and remove it by unscrewing the six screws holding it down. It is sealed either to a blind plug which holds the jet in position or to the jet adjustment assembly. Ease it off carefully, turning it to-and-fro. Empty out any fuel still in the float chamber.

4 Carefully push out the pin on which the float is pivoted to the main body, take out the float and unscrew the needle valve assembly. The pin and the needle valve assembly are obviously designed to lose themselves easily, so put them in a safe place. The sealing washer for the needle valve should be replaced on reassembly.

5 Dismantle the various linkages on the body and remove the temperature compensating device, the by-pass valve, and the cold start device where fitted.

6 Undo the cap at the top of the body and remove it complete with the damper piston. Empty the oil from the dashpot. Remove the upper part of the carburettor body, marking the flanges so that you will not have to think twice about its position when replacing it. Remove and dismantle the piston, needle and diaphragm assembly (see photographs). Treat this

21.6a When the top is removed ...

21.6b ... the piston and diaphragm can be lifted out (note the lug on the diaphragm)

21.6c The diaphragm retainer is detached ...

21.6d ... and the diaphragm removed (note lug in middle of diaphragm)

21.6e Component parts of the piston assembly

assembly carefully - a good idea is to stand the piston in the top of a jar with the needle hanging down inside.

7   Where a jet adjustment assembly is fitted, remove this from the body and dismantle it, keeping a strict eye on the numerous bits and pieces shown in Fig.3.4. Where no adjustment is fitted, remove the blind plug from the main body, being careful not to damage the surface where it seals to the float chamber cover. Underneath it you will see a tube which is pressed into the main body and communicates with the jet. The jet itself is pressed into the body from the other end. Its removal and replacement is a matter for the specialist.

8   Undo the screws holding the throttle disc into its shaft, being careful not to put too much pressure on the shaft in the process (support it with the other hand). Remove the disc and withdraw the throttle shaft.

9   The carburettor is now sufficiently dismantled for inspection to take place. One or two adjusting screws still remain in the body, but these are best removed as you clean out the various airways and replaced immediately. Generally speaking the Stromberg carburettor is very reliable but even so it may develop faults which are not readily apparent unless a careful inspection is carried out, yet may nevertheless affect engine performance. So giving the carburettor a good looking over when dismantled,

is well worthwhile.

10 Start by cleaning the various parts, making sure that the air channels in the main body are completely clear. This is best achieved by blowing through them.

11 Inspect the carburettor needle for ridging. If the needle is ridged, it must be renewed - do not attempt to rub it down with abrasive paper as carburettor needles are made to very fine tolerances.

12 Where the jet is removable, inspect it for wear. Wear inside the jet may well accompany wear on the needle. If the jet is worn, replace it. Where the jet is pressed into the main body, it can be examined from above. Replacement, if worn, is a matter for the specialist.

13 Examine the diaphragm and replace it if it shows any sign of weakness or cracking. Examine the piston, in particular the dashpot cylinder on the top of it but unless there has been any maltreatment (such as dropping it) you are unlikely to find anything wrong. Check that the damper piston has a to and fro movement along its shaft of between 0.04-0.07" (1.1-1.9 mm) (see Fig. 3.18) and that it moves perfectly freely. This movement is essential for proper damping action. If there is any fault in the assembly, replace it complete.

14 Check for wear on the throttle shaft and the bushes through which it passes. Apart from the nuisance of a sticking throttle, excessive wear here can cause air leaks in the induction system (though this is less likely when the bushes are sealed) affecting the performance. Worn bushes can be extracted and new bushes fitted if necessary.

15 Reassembly is a straightforward repetition of the dismantling process. Where the jet is removable, replace it carefully and be sure that the needle moves up and down in it freely. Note when refitting the diaphragm that it has lugs on it which engage in slots on the body and on the piston. These are clearly shown in photos 21.6b and 21.6d.

16 The cold start device, temperature compensator and by-pass valve should be inspected as detailed in Sections 23,24 and 22 respectively which deal with them.

17 Reassembly is a straightforward reversal of the dismantling process; some reassembly points have already been noted in the preceding paragraphs. Where the jet is adjustable, ensure that the needle can move freely up and down in the jet over the whole adjustment range. Careful assembly should avoid any trouble here. Do not forget to fill the dashpot with transmission fluid type A to within ¼" (6 mm) of the top before inserting the damper piston.

22 Stromberg carburettor - by-pass valve

1 The purpose of this valve is to ensure that when the throttle is shut off with the engine running at high speed a certain amount of air still enters the engine, ensuring proper burning of the mixture and reducing noxious emissions from the exhaust. It is entirely self-contained, functioning automatically as the result of the high vacuum that occurs when the throttle is shut off under these conditions. In effect it slows up the rate at which the engine reduces speed when the throttle is closed. Once normal idling speed is reached, the valve ceases to operate.

2 The component parts of the by-pass valve are shown in Fig. 3.30 and a diagram in Fig. 3.31. In Fig. 3.31 we are looking downwards on the valve, as is shown by the foreshortened view of the throttle flap which is in the closed position, ie vertical in the normal placing of the carburettor. The valve itself of course is shown in section. The heart of the valve is a small diaphragm carrying a valve face. This is lifted when the vacuum behind it is great enough. The lifting force necessary is controlled by a spring acting on the diaphragm, this spring being tensioned by the adjusting screw. In Fig. 3.31 the diaphragm is shown lifted by the vacuum, allowing petrol/air mixture to find its way round the throttle even though this is closed. When engine speed falls and the vacuum decreases, the diaphragm will be pushed inwards by the spring and the valve face will sit on the entrance to the outlet channel, thus blocking this route

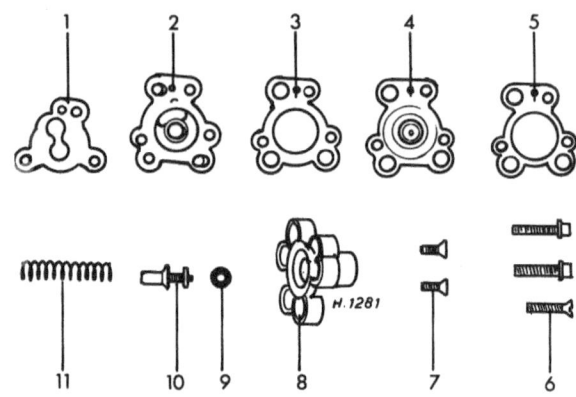

Fig.3.30. Stromberg by-pass valve dismantled

1	Gasket	7	Cover screw
2	Housing	8	Cover
3	Gasket	9	Rubber ring
4	Diaphragm	10	Adjusting screw
5	Gasket	11	Spring
6	Fixing screws		

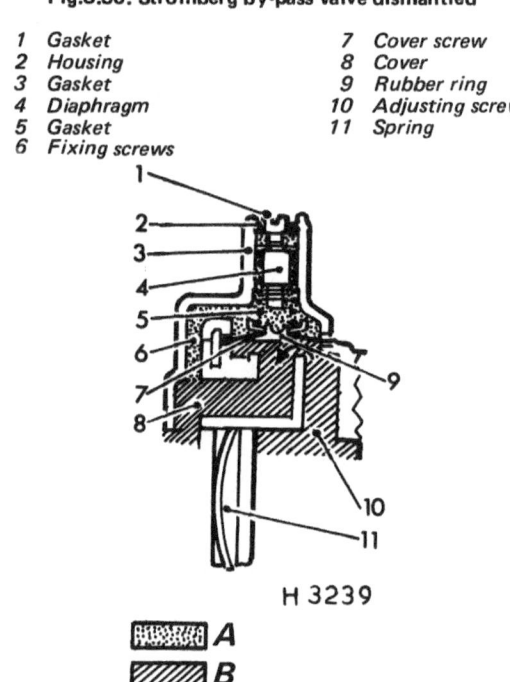

Fig.3.31. Stromberg by-pass valve - diagram

Shading A - Vacuum
        B - Fuel/air mixture

1	Adjusting screw	7	Diaphragm
2	Rubber ring	8	Outlet channel for
3	Cover		fuel/air fixing
4	Nut	9	Valve
5	Spring	10	Inlet channel for
6	Drilling to underside		fuel/air mixing
	of diaphragm	11	Flap

completely.

3 No maintenance is possible except to ensure that its channels are thoroughly clean. Its construction is simple and it can readily be dismantled (see Fig. 3.30). If however it does not respond to adjustment as detailed in the next three paragraphs, it should be replaced complete.

4 If the engine does not reduce speed as it should when the throttle is closed after fast running, turn the adjusting screw to the left until correct operation is obtained. This assumes, of course, that your throttle stop settings, fast idle adjustment etc., are correct. If however, this process is overdone, the valve will not open at all. This is indicated when, on closing the throttle after racing the engine, the piston of the front carburettor drops down at the same time as the piston of the rear carburettor (this can be seen by looking into the air intakes with the air filter removed). If this happens, turn the adjusting screw to the right until normal function is obtained.

5 There should be a range of adjustment over which speed reduction and delayed lowering of the front carburettor piston are both obtained. Find the centre position between these adjustments and then turn the screw a further half turn to the left.

6 When turning the screw, be careful not to press it inwards too hard or you will dislodge the little rubber ring which seals it to the valve body just under its head.

23 Stromberg carburettor - cold start device

1 A diagram of this device is given in Fig. 3.32. It consists of a pierced disc which is placed against the body of the carburettor and covers up two holes, one of which leads to the float chamber disc which is placed against the body of the carburettor and covers up two holes, one of whoch leads to the float chamber and one to the throttle chamber. Held against this by a spring is a channel disc which forms an airway between the holes and the slot on the pierced disc. As the spindle is turned, one or more of the small holes in the pierced disc come opposite the channel leading to the throttle chamber, admitting fuel vapour to it. As the disc is revolved, the number of holes opposite the channel increases and the amount of vapour available to the throttle chamber is correspondingly increased.

2 The device calls for no special maintenance apart from being kept clean and given a touch of oil. If necessary it can be dismantled. When fitting it to the carburettor, ensure that the mating surfaces are completely clean and smooth, there is no gasket. The outer end of the spindle carries a combined choke control lever and fast idling cam. The cam bears an engraved mark which should be set opposite the fast idle screw when the fast idling is adjusted.

24 Stromberg carburettor - temperature compensator

1 This device ensures efficient idling over a wide range of temperature variations and is thus a contribution to exhaust emission control. It is pictured in Fig.3.33.

2 It consists of a valve controlled by a bi-metallic strip which is so adjusted that it starts to open at a temperature of 70°-77°F (21°-22°C). When the valve is open a small amount of extra air is admitted to the throttle chamber, thus compensating for the increased amount of vapour appearing there because the fuel is warmer.

3 The operation of the bi-metalic strip can easily be checked by putting the device in water at the appropriate temperature. It is easier still to take the device into a room having a temperature of 70°-77°F (21°-22°C) and adjust it there until the valve is just on the point of opening. Adjustment is carried out by turning the nut which presses on the bi-metallic strip.

4 Check that the valve moves easily in its housing. If necessary it can be centred by slackening the cross-headed screw which holds the bi-metallic strip and adjusting its position.

25 Stromberg carburettor - float level adjustment

1 The adjustment is illustrated in Fig.3.34. It is achieved by bending the lug on the float arm which bears on the needle valve. With the carburettor body inverted, check the dimensions "A" and "B" in Fig.3.34 and bend as necessary. It is possible to carry out this adjustment with the carburettor in-situ by pressing the float lightly against the needle valve, but a great deal more awkward. Do not try to bend the arm between the float and the needle valve.

26 Stromberg carburettor - tuning - single carburettor installations

1 Before tuning the carburettor, check that the valve clearances, spark plugs and gaps, contact breaker settings and ignition timing are all correct, that there is no air leakage on the

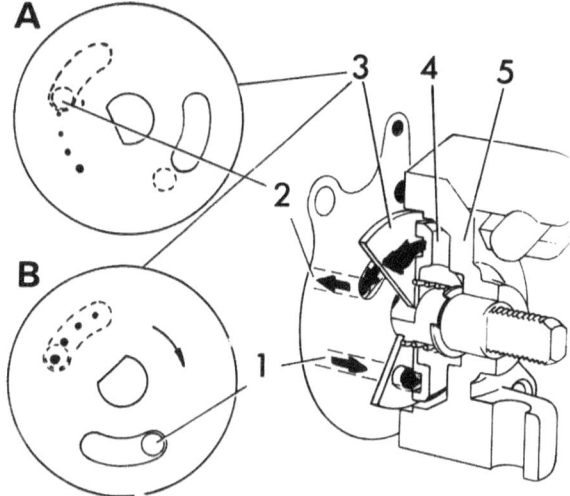

Fig.3.32. Stromberg cold start device - diagram

1 Passage from float chamber
2 Passage to throttle chamber
3 Pierced disc
4 Channel disc
5 Housing

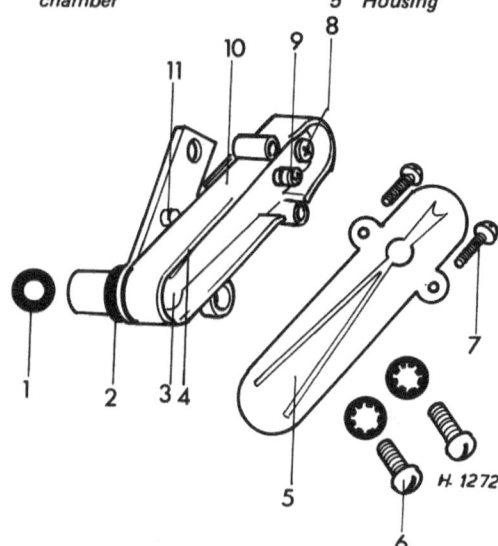

Fig.3.33. Temperature compensator

1	Rubber seal		ature compensator
2	Rubber seal	7	Screw for cover
3	Valve	8	Cross-slotted screw
4	Bi-metal spring	9	Adjustment nut
5	Cover	10	Housing
6	Screw for temper-	11	Identity label

Fig.3.34. Float level

A = 0.35 – 0.51" (9 – 13 mm)
B = 0.59 – 0.67" (15 – 17 mm)

intake and that the vacuum ignition advance tube is in place. Make the final adjustments with the engine at its normal running temperature, and finish off by setting the throttle stops to give the proper idling speed when you have replaced the air cleaner and crankcase ventilation pipes.

2   Where jet adjustment is provided on the carburettor (ie with the 175-CD 2S) make a preliminary adjustment by removing the top of the carburettor, pressing down the piston until it touches the bridge (if it touches the jet first, you will have to unscrew the jet adjusting screw) then, having slackened off the flanged nut holding the screw slightly where this is fitted, carefully screw up the adjusting screw until the jet just touches the piston. Then unscrew it 1½ turns. This gives the initial rough adjustment.

3   Set the throttle stop screw so that the throttle is just closed. Now adjust the length of the throttle pull rod so that there is about .02" (0.5 mm) gap between the throttle lever arm and its stop when the control is just about to operate the throttle. Then screw up the throttle stop screw 1½ turns, thus opening the throttle slightly.

4   Start the engine and run until it has reached operating temperature, then set the throttle stop to give a speed of 600-650 revs/min. Then unscrew the jet adjusting screw until the engine begins to run unevenly. Mark the position, then screw up the adjusting screw until the engine again begins to run unevenly. The optimum setting for the jet is midway between these two positions.

5   Re-adjust the throttle stops until the idling speed is again 650 revs/min.

6   Where no jet adjustment is fitted (ie on the B20A installation with the 175-CD2 SE carburettor) screw up the idling trimmer screw (see Fig. 3.5) as far as it will go and then undo it two full turns. Now run the engine until it has reached operational temperature, adjust the engine speed to 700 revs/min by means of the throttle stop screw and then adjust the idle trimmer to give smoothest engine running on idling and good pick up on acceleration. When adjusting this screw, should the idling speed increase, correct on the throttle stop screw.

7   Pull out the choke control on the instrument panel 0.9-1.0" (23-25 mm) and adjust the cable so that the mark on the fast idle cam comes opposite the centre line of the fast idle screw. On the 175-CD 2S carburettor, if the cam is not marked set it to the position shown in Fig. 3.5.

8   Finally, with the air cleaner and vacuum pipes reconnected, set the idling speed to 650 revs/min for the B18A, 700 revs/min for B20A with automatic transmission, or 800 revs/min for B20A with manual transmission.

27 Stromberg carburettor - tuning - twin installations

1   Read paragraph 1 of Section 3.26.

2   Disconnect the throttle linkage at the lower ball joints (see Fig. 3.13). Now screw in the idling screws on both carburettors as far as they will go and turn them both back two full turns. Set back the throttle stop screws until they only just touch the throttle cam plate and then turn each forward one full turn.

3   Start the engine and allow it to reach operating temperature. Adjust the throttle stop screws equally to give an idling speed of 800 revs/min (700 revs/min if the car has automatic transmission) and check that the valve piston, visible through the intakes in each carburettor with the air cleaner removed, is floating at the same height above the bridge.

4   Adjust the idle trimming screws on each carburettor equally to give the best idling speed, not more than half a turn in either direction, resetting the throttle stop screws as necessary.
   At the same time, ensure as far as possible by listening to the hiss of the carburettor inputs (the air filter being removed, of course) and observing the positions of the pistons, that each carburettor takes in the same amount of air.

5   Adjust the length of the link rods to the main throttle control rod so that when the links are fitted there is a clearance of about .004" (0.1 mm) between the lever worked by the linkage and the lever that actually operates the throttle spindle

(see Fig. 3.14).
   Make sure that the link rods are so adjusted that the two carburettor throttles operate in complete synchronism.

7   Pull out the choke control on the instrument panel 0.9-1.0" (23-25 mm), adjust the cable so that the mark on the fast idle cam comes opposite the fast idle screw, and set the screw to give an engine speed of 1100-1300 rpm.

28 Stromberg carburettor - special test equipment and exhaust emission control

1   By following the above routine you can get excellent results with a bit of care. If however you are able to get access to equipment for monitoring the air intake to the carburettors you can adjust the throttle controls of a twin installation so that the inputs are equal over a wide range of throttle settings.

2   Jet adjustment should ideally (and in some parts of the world, by legal enforcement) be set for minimum CO emission using the appropriate test gear and then sealed. In countries or states where stringent exhaust emission control laws exist the foregoing tuning procedures must be regarded as for information or emergency use only.

29 Stromberg carburettor - hot start system

1   On twin Stromberg installations a separate hot start valve is fitted to the air cleaner and operated by a lever attached to the rear carburettor and worked from the throttle control. Fig.3.35 gives a picture of the set-up.

2   During warm weather and when the engine is hot, fuel fumes develop in the carburettor float chamber and tend to give the engine too rich a mixture on starting, which makes starting difficult. The hot start valve vents the float chamber to the atmosphere (or the venting filter of the Evaporite control unit, if fitted) when the accelerator pedal is up, so relieving the situation. When the throttle pedal is depressed, the valve connects the float chamber to the air cleaner and any fumes that arise are sucked back into the inlet, their effect on the ingoing air being negligible.

3   Fig. 3.36 shows in diagrammatic form the operation of the valve. It is a simple change-over device, air entering it from the carburettor (represented by arrows pointing to the left) being routed to the atmosphere or back into the air cleaner according to the position of the plunger. Connections to the hot start valve are flexible pipes inside the air cleaner case. There is a drilling on the inlet face of the carburettor which connects with the float chamber and air from this drilling is channelled to the hot start valve.

4   The valve is not designed to come apart and no maintenance is called for. You can check its operation by attaching a tube to the outlet and removing the pipes from their connections to the carburettors. To check correct operation with the plunger down, blow through the pipe on the outlet and see that air comes out through the air cleaner pipe. Now pinch the end of this pipe and check that there is no appreciable leakage into the carburettor pipes. With the plunger up, blow through the air cleaner pipe, check that air comes out through the carburettor pipes, pinch the ends of these and check that there is negligible leakage into the outlet. Leakage may be caused by dirt lodging on the seatings or the piston faces, and if so this can probably be cleared by blowing air (or blowing hard yourself) through one or other of the pipes. If this fails, the only recommended action is replacement of the complete valve, though if you feel like taking it apart and seeing if you can rectify it, why not - it is a very simple device.

5   To set the control lever for correct operation of the valve, loosen the locknut on the plunger rod and rotate the rod so that the lever runs up or down on the screw thread (see Fig.3.35). Set it so that in the idling position the operating lever is just on the verge of being pushed by the lever on the carburettor.

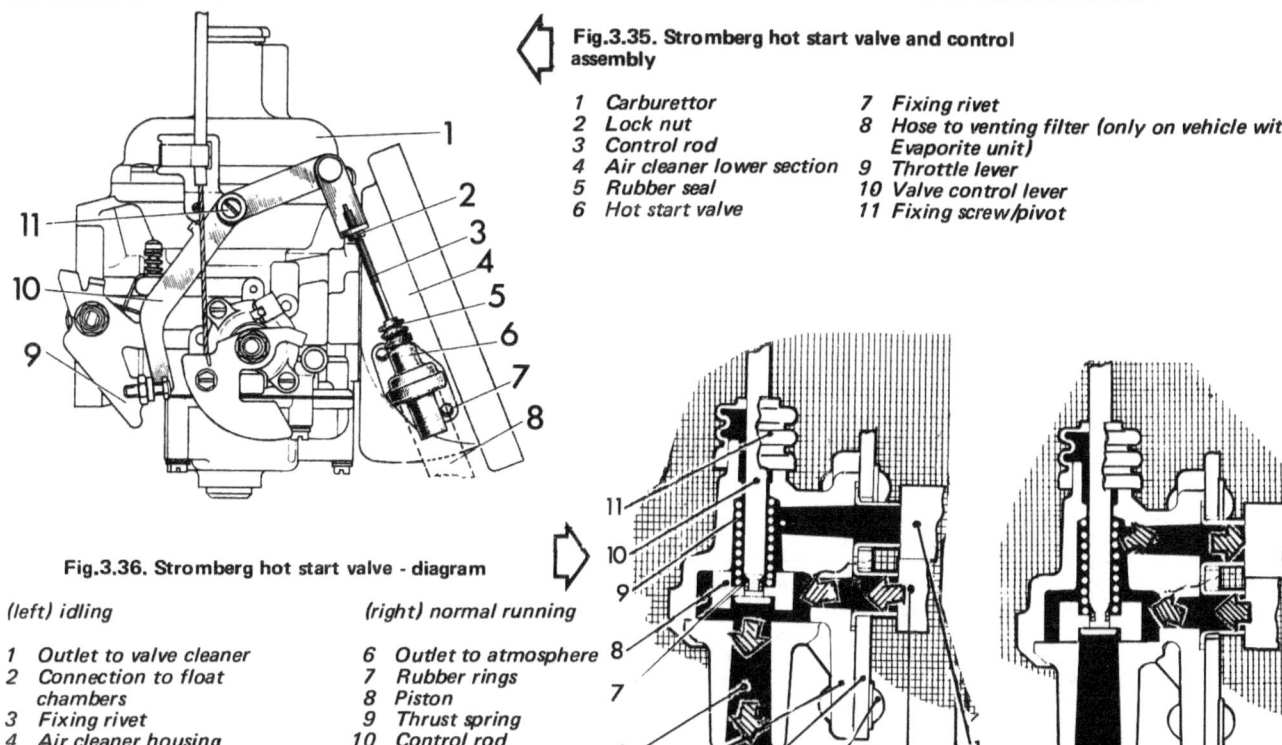

Fig.3.35. Stromberg hot start valve and control assembly

1 Carburettor
2 Lock nut
3 Control rod
4 Air cleaner lower section
5 Rubber seal
6 Hot start valve
7 Fixing rivet
8 Hose to venting filter (only on vehicle with Evaporite unit)
9 Throttle lever
10 Valve control lever
11 Fixing screw/pivot

Fig.3.36. Stromberg hot start valve - diagram

(left) idling   *(right) normal running*

1 Outlet to valve cleaner
2 Connection to float chambers
3 Fixing rivet
4 Air cleaner housing
5 Valve body
6 Outlet to atmosphere
7 Rubber rings
8 Piston
9 Thrust spring
10 Control rod
11 Rubber seal

30 Closed crankcase ventilation

1 For efficient engine operation it is necessary that pressure should not build up in the crankcase. In times past this has been taken care of by providing a simple breathing device (sometimes, but not always, fitted with an oil trap) which vented the crankcase to the atmosphere. Such a device is found on early B18A engines, but thereafter all Volvo engines have been fitted with a closed crankcase ventilation system in which the build-up of crankcase pressure is prevented without allowing it to breathe directly into the atmosphere.

2 Figs. 3.37 and 3.38 illustrate the two systems employed by Volvo-one on B18 engines and the other on the B20 series. In the B18 engine vapour from the breather in the side of the crankcase is drawn through a control valve via a short length of pipe into the oil filler cap via the air filter. The oil filler cap contains a simple flame trap to prevent any possibility of carburettor backfire reaching oil vapour in the valve chest. The purpose of the control valve (connected into the system close to the crankcase breather) is to restrict the intake of air into the inlet manifold, particularly at low throttle settings, thus preventing undue degrading of the fuel/air mixture coming from the carburettor. If, due to the restriction imposed by the control valve, pressure starts to build up in the crankcase the flow through the valve cover and filler cap reverses, the excess crankcase vapour is discharged into the inlet, where it is simply mixed with the air going into the

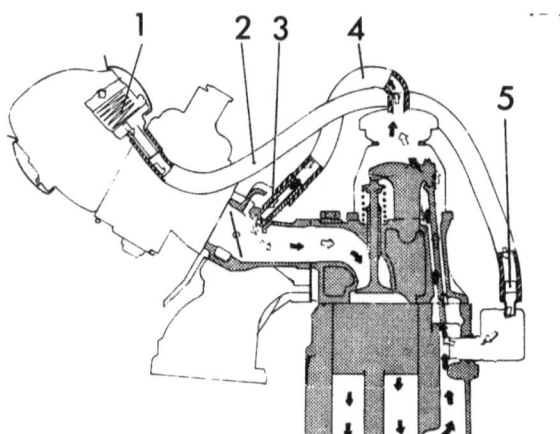

Fig.3.37. Closed crankcase ventilation - B18 engines

1 Pipe connection to air cleaner
2 Pipe connection to inlet manifold
3 Pipe from air cleaner to oil filler cap
4 Flame trap in oil filler cap
5 Pipe from crankcase oil trap to inlet manifold
6 Control valve
7 Pipe connection on oil trap
8 Oil trap

Fig.3.38. Closed crankcase ventilation - B20 engines

1 Cleaner insert
2 Pipe for fresh air supply to crankcase
3 Nipple
4 Pipe for crankcase gases
5 Flame guard

carburettors.

3   In the B20 fitting, the control valve is done away with and clean air from a subsidiary filter in the air cleaner assembly is drawn into the crankcase via a small flame trap in the crankcase breather. The oil filler cap is connected to the inlet manifold through a nipple which restricts the amount of air drawn into the manifold while at the same time causing pressure in the crankcase to be lower than atmospheric, thus ensuring that air is drawn in from the air intake. When the throttle is fairly wide open, the vacuum in the inlet manifold is less than that in the air cleaner, and vapour flows out of the crankcase along both routes. Much of this enters the air cleaner via the subsidiary insert where it is remixed with fuel vapour and again enters the engine.

4   The only attention that these systems require, is periodical cleaning of the nipple (B20) or checking of the control valve (B18). To ensure that pollution of the atmosphere is kept to a minimum, ensure that the flexible pipes and their clips are in good order and airtight.

31 Constant temperature air device

1   In order to ensure that the air entering the carburettor(s) of the B20 engine is rapidly raised to a temperature which thereafter remains constant, air at atmospheric temperature from an intake in the front of the car is mixed with air which has passed over a hot spot on the exhaust system in a box which incorporates a flap controlled by a thermostat. A view of this box with the hose connections removed is given in Fig. 3.39.

2   Inside the box is a flap which in one extreme position completely blanks off the warm air intake and in the other blanks off the cool air intake. Fig. 3.40 shows the small tab found on either side of the box indicating the position of the flap. When it points to "hot" the cold air intake is completely shut off and the warmest possible air is fed to the carburettor(s), the reverse happening when it points to "cold".

3   To check the operation of the thermostat, remove the unit from the car and test it in warm water. The flap should shut off the hot air intake (tab pointing to "cold") at a temperature of 95-105°F (35-41°C) and shut off the cold air intake at 70-77°F (27-31°C).

4   The device is very unlikely to go out of adjustment, but the thermostat may possibly cease to function properly. If so, the complete device should be replaced.

5   When fitting, note that the thermostat should be in the middle of the air flow and that any hose clamp screws should be on top of the housing; (in photograph 11.2a) the clamp is displaced.

32 Secondary throttle system - B20B engines

1   The B20B engine has a special inlet manifold incorporating a secondary throttle system which ensures that the fuel/air mixture entering the engine is thoroughly warmed when the engine is idling. This ensures efficient burning of the mixture and thus reduces atmospheric pollution by the exhaust.

2   Fig. 3.41 shows a diagram of the inlet manifold, showing on the left the path taken by the fuel/air mixture when the secondary throttles are closed. The air passes over heating fins warmed directly from the exhaust.

3   This tortuous path would put a severe limit on engine performance if it were followed all the time. However, when the main throttle is opened, a linked control lever opens up the secondary throttle and allows the intakes for each carburettor to operate in the more civilised manner shown on the right of Fig. 3.41. The carburettors are still connected to the pathways to the heating system, and because of this synchronising becomes somewhat easier, though it can be argued that some of the advantages of a truly twin carburettor system are lost. In practice, there is very little sacrifice of performance.

4   A drop of oil now and then on the throttle spindles is all the

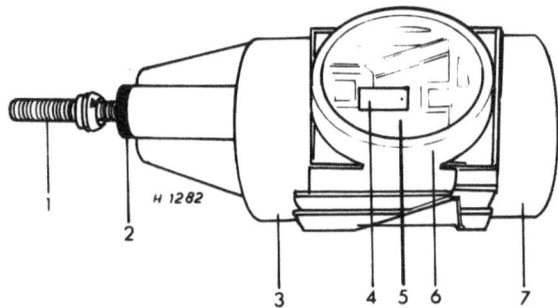

Fig.3.39. Constant air temperature device

1 Thermostat	5 Flaps
2 Lock nut	6 Warm air intake
3 Air feeler connection	7 Cold air intake
4 Flap control	

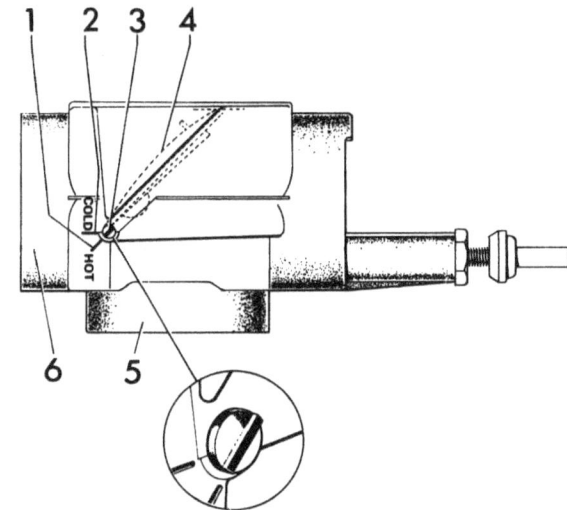

Fig.3.40. Constant air temperature device - diagram

1   Hot - open for warm air
2   Cold - open for cold air
3   Tab
4   Shutter
5   Warm air intake
6   Cold air intake

maintenance needed. Keep an eye on the rubber seal (Fig.3.42) - refit if a new one is necessary, ensuring that it fits so that the measurement shown in Fig. 3.42 lies between 0.18 - 0.20" (4.5-5.0 mm). Be careful not to damage the seal against sharp edges of the spindle when you are fitting it.

5   Adjust the control lever as shown in Fig. 3.43 so that the throttle actuating lever has to move through a distance of 0.11-0.17" (2.7-4.3 mm) before it starts to operate the secondary throttle. Later arrangements differ slightly from that shown in Fig. 3.43, but the adjustment is the same. It is not critical; all you require is that by the time the engine is running at normal road speed the main intake manifolds are completely open and at idling speed and a little over it is shut.

33 Evaporite fuel vapour control system - general description

1   In hot countries the problem of atmospheric pollution by evaporation of petrol from motor cars is a serious one. In California, it has been estimated that a car left out all day can lose as much as a gallon of fuel by evaporation. Even if the average figure is less than a hundredth of this, when one considers all the cars there are in California the fact that legislation has been introduced enforcing evaporation control is not surprising.

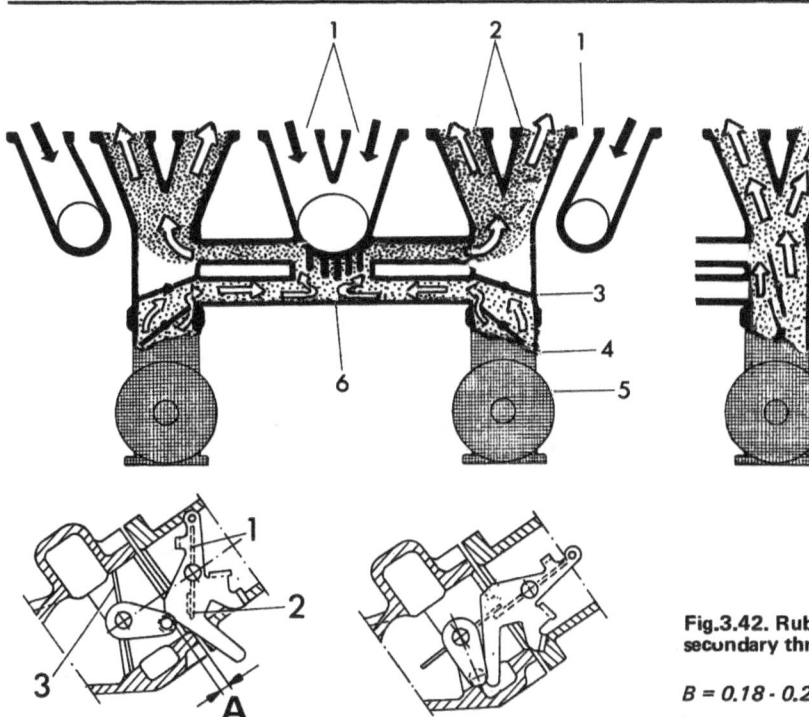

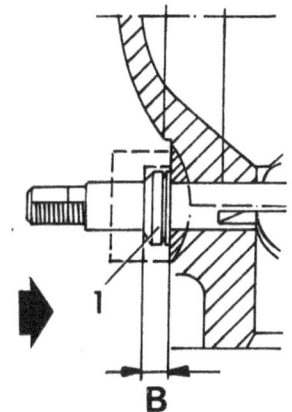

Fig.3.41. Secondary throttle system

(left) light load - pre-heating
(right) heavy load - direct inlet
1   Exhaust manifold
2   Intake manifold
3   Secondary throttle
4   Primary throttle
5   Carburettor
6   Pre-heating chamber

Fig.3.42. Rubber seal (1) on secondary throttle spindle

B = 0.18 - 0.20" (4.5 - 5.0 mm)

Fig.3.43. Setting-up the secondary throttle

(left) throttle position at low output
(right) throttle fully open
1   Primary throttle
2   Valve
3   Secondary throttle
A = 0.11 - 0.17" (2.7 - 4.3 mm)

2   The sources of evaporation are:-
a) the carburettor float chambers   b) the fuel tank
In the control system used by Volvo, when the engine is switched off or idling the vapour from these two sources is channelled into an absorptive element made up of active carbon granules which soak up the fumes like a sponge. When the engine is running, air is drawn through the active carbon element into the carburettor air intake, purging the element and drawing in vapour from the fuel tank as it is generated. At the same time the channel from the float chamber is diverted from the filter direct to the carburettor intake.

3   Figs. 3.44a and 3.44b show how the system operates. When the engine is idling or switched off, the hot start valve (which has already been described in Section 29) has its plunger in the up position and any petrol vapour coming from the float chamber is fed into the filter. At the same time the main fuel tank can evaporate into an expansion tank where a certain amount of condensation can occur, the remaining vapour being passed to the filter also. The air valve on top of the filter, which is operated by engine vacuum, is closed when the engine is idling and the filter is cut off from the air intake. This is the position shown in Fig. 3.44a.

4   When the engine is running normally the vacuum falls sufficiently to let the air valve open and at the same time the plunger of the hot start valve is lowered by its control lever. Vapour from the float chamber is now taken via the hot start valve into the air cleaner, while vapour from the circulation tank and the filter is sucked into the carburettor throttle chamber where it mixes with what is already being provided by the carburettor. The air drawn through the filter removes fuel fumes stored in the active carbon element (Fig. 3.44b).

34 Evaporite venting filter and expansion tank

1   Fig. 3.45 illustrates this filter with the air valve on top

Fig.3.44. Evaporite system
(a) engine idling (top) (b) engine running (bottom)

1 Fuel tank	7 Control rod (connected
2 Expansion tank	to throttle)
3 Venting filter	8 Air cleaner
4 Air valve	9 Carburettor
5 Diaphragm	10 Float chamber
6 Hot start valve	11 Intake manifold

as fitted in a typical installation, and Fig. 3.46 gives a diagrammatic representation of the filter with the air valve removed. No particular comment on its working is called for. The foam plastic filter element at the bottom (which is detachable) should be replaced every 25,000 miles (40,000 kms), but the rest of it, short of major disaster, is everlasting.

2   The air valve which normally fits on top of the filter is shown diagrammatically in Fig. 3.47. It is a simple matter to check this valve for sealing when the engine is switched off, and it can be removed from the top of the air filter to see whether or not it opens when the engine is running. Provided that it opens at a speed corresponding to fast idling or just a little faster and seals reasonably, all is well. If it does not function properly, it must be replaced complete.

3   Fig. 3.48 shows a photograph of this tank and its connections, which are fitted behind the protective wall board in the luggage compartment of saloons and on the right-hand side in the cargo space on the 145. We suspect that this piece of information will be the least used in the whole book.

35 Exhaust system - removal and refitting

1   Loosen the clamps then detach the intermediate pipe from the front silencer.

2   Using a screwdriver, carefully prise off the front silencer suspension rings; detach the front silencer from the front exhaust pipe.

3   Carefully prise off the rear suspension rings and remove the rear pipe, rear silencer and intermediate pipe as an assembly.

4   *Carburettor engines:* Remove the carburettor preheater shield.

5   *Engines with EGR:* Remove the air cleaner and battery, then disconnect the vacuum hose and remove the EGR valve. From the front pipe remove the lower pipe followed by the nipple and washer.

6   Detach the front pipe at the manifold and remove the clamp on the gearbox, then work the front pipe free.

7   Refitting is basically the reverse of the removal procedure, but the following points should be noted:

a   *Commence refitting working from the front end of the system*

b   *Allow approximately 1½ in (40 mm) of overlap of all joints*

c   *Ensure that replacement rear silencer of part nos 461356 or 460981 are fitted with the end marked IN towards the front silencer*

d   *Tighten the manifold flange nuts first, then progressively work rearwards ensuring that the system hangs satisfactorily*

e   *Renew any rubber suspension rings which have deteriorated or are damaged*

f   *When a round rear silencer is used, ensure that the bracket is mounted approximately 4° from the vertical*

g   *Where an oval rear silencer is used, ensure that it is set approximately 15° from the horizontal*

Fig.3.45. Venting filter

1   *Hose for rear carburettor hot start valve*
2   *Hose for front carburettor hot start valve*
3   *Hose from fuel tank via expansion tank*
4   *Hose for front carburettor vacuum connection*
5   *Hose for rear carburettor vacuum connection*
6   *Air valve*
7   *Venting filter*

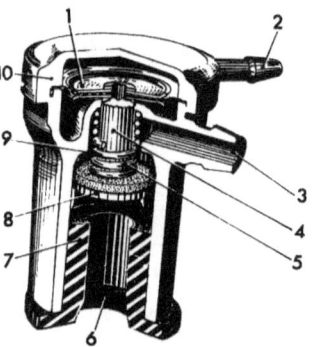

Fig.3.47. Air valve - diagram

1   *Diaphragm*
2   *Connection to rear carburettor*
3   *Connection to front carburettor*
4   *Valve rod*
5   *Thrust spring*
6   *Connection for venting filter*
7   *Rubber sleeve*
8   *Valve*
9   *Valve seat*
10 *Housing*

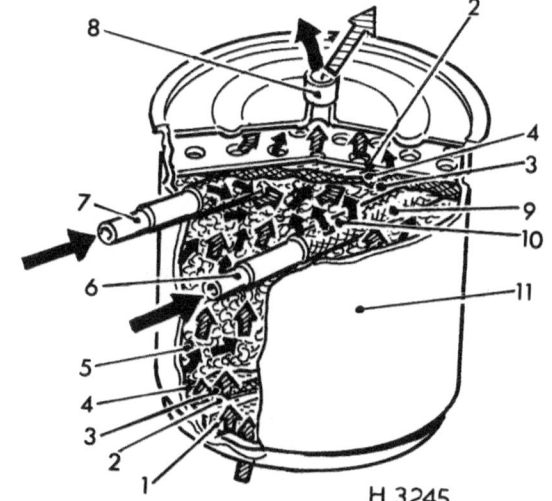

H 3245

Fig.3.46. Venting filter - diagram

1   *Foam plastic filter*
2   *Plate (perforated)*
3   *Wire net (gauze)*
4   *Felt*
5   *Active carbon*
6   *Connection to expansion tank*
7   *Connection to hot start valve*
8   *Connection to air valve*
9   *Gauze filter*
10 *Perforated pipe*
11 *Canister*

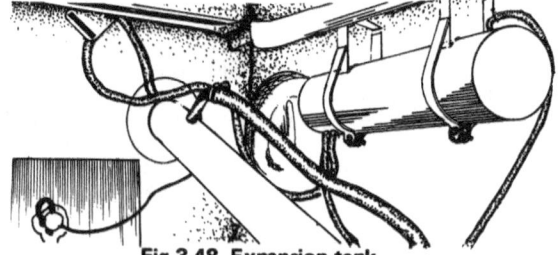

Fig.3.48. Expansion tank

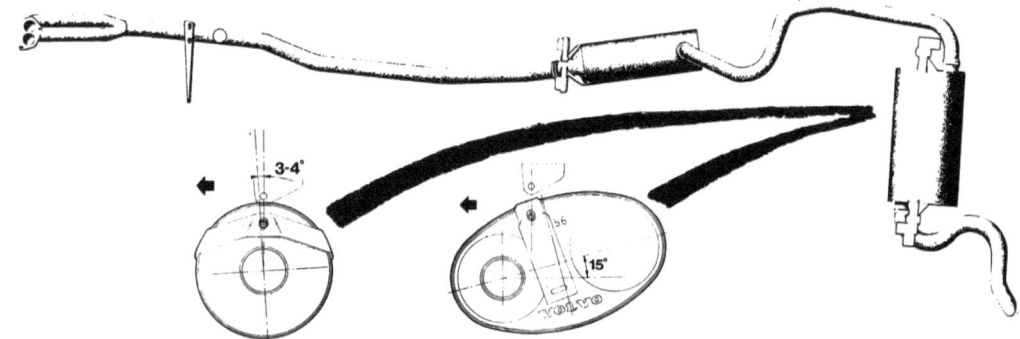

Fig. 3.48A Exhaust system arrangement (typical)

36 Carburettor faults and symptoms

We give in this section a table detailing a few of the symptoms of carburettor or fuel system trouble, possible causes and remedies. You should always bear in mind that it is very difficult to distinguish between ignition faults and carburettor faults in many cases. Your golden rule should be - before starting on the carburettor, make 100% certain of the ignition. Ignition faults are easy to check, ignition adjustments, when required, are easy to make, and furthermore when adjustment is required as a result of normal wear and tear this adjustment is much more likely to be in the ignition than in the carburettor. The following table, therefore assumes that all is in order in the ignition system.

Fault Finding Chart

Symptom	Reason	Remedy
Smell of petrol when engine is stopped	Leaking pipes or unions Leaking fuel tank	Repair or renew as necessary. Fill fuel tank to capacity and examine carefully at seams, unions and filler pipe connections. Repair as necessary.
Smell of petrol when engine is idling	Leaking fuel lines or unions between pump and carburettor Overflow of fuel from float chamber due to wrong level setting, ineffective needle valve or punctured float	Check lines and unions and tighten or repair. Check fuel level setting and condition of float and needle valve and renew if necessary.
Excessive fuel consumption for reaons not covered by leaks or float chamber faults	Worn needle and/or jet Sticking needle or piston	Replace. Check correct movement of needle and piston assembly, as detailed in this Chapter.
Difficult starting, uneven running, lack of power, cutting out	Blockages in carburettor Float chamber fuel level too low or needle valve sticking Fuel pump not delivering sufficient fuel Intake manifold gaskets leaking or manifold fractured	Clean out float chamber and body Dismantle and check fuel level and needle valve. Check pump delivery and clean or repair as required. Check for blockage in fuel pipes. Check tightness of mounting nuts and inspect manifold.
Difficulty in starting not associated with faults already given	Over-rich mixture entering cylinders as a result of too much use of choke control or depressing the accelerator pedal when starting	Keep your foot off the accelerator pedal until the engine fires. If 'over-choking' has already occurred, push the pedal right down to the floor and operate the starter. Usually this will clear the fault. It will clear itself in time anyway.
Engine does not respond properly to throttle pedal	Sticking piston or needle Damper piston not working properly Oil level in dashpot low	Check correct movement of piston Check free play or damper piston on its rod. Top up.
Engine idling speed drops markedly after a long period of idling, (in warm weather especially)	Defective temperature compensator (Stromberg Hot start valves sticking in run position	Adjust or replace as necessary. Determine cause, adjust or replace as necessary.
Engine does not take up proper idling speed when throttle released	Sticking controls Defective by-pass valve (Stromberg) or relief valve in throttle flap (SU)	Clean and oil as required. Correct defect or replace as necessary.

PART 2 — THE FUEL INJECTION SYSTEM

37 Fuel injection - general principles

1   The best way to an understanding of the working of the fuel injection engine is to consider the basic operation of the normal carburettor system.

Obviously, the more fuel an engine burns the more power it will give out. Notice that we say burns - fuel taken in and not burnt will add to your petrol consumption without doing anything to help you along.

To ensure that the fuel is properly burnt, it must be mixed with air in the right proportions. If the mixture is too rich, there will not be enough oxygen to support combustion, as every motorist who has ever used his choke too enthusiastically will realise. If it is too weak, the burning process is slow and irregular - sometimes it is still going on when the inlet valve opens and flames shoot through the carburettor/s as a result.

The basic function of the fuel system, then, is simply to provide the amount of fuel the engine needs at any given time, mixed with the amount of air required to ensure that it is properly burnt.

2   The modern carburettor solves this problem by reversing it. For a given throttle setting, the engine will suck in a certain amount of air per stroke. A measure of the amount of air going in is the amount of suck which occurs on the carburettor side of the throttle, ie the degree of vacuum set up there. This pressure drop causes the carburettor to release an amount of petrol vapour suitable to the amount of air going in.

This is not an easy problem to solve, as is obvious when one looks at the complexity of a modern carburettor. Quite apart from the initial case when the engine is cold and the vapour starts to condense before it ever enters the cylinders, we find devices for modifying apparent size of jet (the vacuum controlled piston and needle arrangement used by the carburettors described in this Manual) or various arrangements of subsidiary jets, tubes in which the petrol level rises and so on.

On top of this, we are faced with difficulties caused by temperature variations. The proportion of air to petrol varies with the temperature of the air being mixed in, basically because when air is warm the same weight of air occupies more space and it is weight of air to weight of fuel that we have to worry about, not volume to volume. Also, quite apart from this, the required mixture depends on the temperature inside the cylinder and generally speaking the carburettor has no way of knowing what this is. In an ordinary carburettor system, these problems are to some extent side-stepped because the engine temperature and the air temperature stabilise themselves after the engine has been running for a while. In the 140 series, in fact, quite elaborate arrangements are made for stabilising the temperature of the input air on carburettor engines; as we shall see, the problem is tackled in a different way in the fuel injection engine and the thermostatically operated flap and branch pipe to a hot spot on the exhaust system are conspicuous by their absence.

Cold starting is a problem on its own. The mixture is arbitrarily enriched so that in spite of condensation which may occur on the way there is a reasonable chance that some at least of the cylinders will receive mixture of a strength which will ignite when a spark appears. Where these devices are automatically controlled, they come off when the engine temperature has reached a certain level.

3   Over the years, the carburettor manufacturers have solved their various problems in different ways, all to some extent compromises, as is shown by the variety of carburettor designs. In the last few years, insistence on the reduction of atmospheric pollution has made the carburettor designers task more difficult. The electronic fuel injection system tackles these problems in an entirely different way from the traditional carburettor approach.

The first thing we must realise when considering this system is that the fuel is not injected into the cylinders as is the case with a diesel engine where the injectors are in fact small pumps operating against pressure. The fuel injection engine has the same arrangement of suction through the inlet valve - in fact it is the same engine - as the carburettor engine; the fuel is "injected" into the inlet manifold where it mixes with the air sucked in on the inlet stroke.

As with the carburettor engine, the basic regulation of engine power is carried out by opening or closing the throttle which allows the engine to suck in more or less air. The rate at which air is sucked in is indicated by the state of the vacuum in the inlet manifold. On each inlet stroke an accurately metered amount of fuel is sucked into the engine together with the air, this amount of fuel being injected into the inlet manifold by what is in effect a tap which is turned on for a controlled amount of time.

The tap is turned on by a short electrical impulse (its length varies between 2 and 10 milliseconds - a millisecond is 1/1000 part of a second - these impulses being generated by an electronic control unit.

To this unit is fed electrical impulses which inform it about all the factors that we have just been considering as having an effect on the required proportion of fuel to air. If you look at Fig. 3.49, you will see that the unit receives inputs from:

a) A pressure sensor (7) which indicates the vacuum in the inlet manifold.
b) A water temperature sensor (18) which tells it the running temperature of the engine.
c) An air temperature sensor (1) which enables it to allow for air temperature and thus does away with the necessity for stabilising this and
d) a contact arrangement on the distributor (14) which tells it when to turn on the taps and how fast the engine is running. In addition to these four main inputs it receives two further ones from a unit called the throttle valve switch (4). One of these inputs tells it that the driver has just put his foot down. It responds to this by giving an extra squirt or two of fuel from the injectors - this is just the same sort of thing as happens with the accelerator pump which is fitted to some types of carburettor (not in the Volvo 140 series). The other input tells it that the accelerator pedal is up, ie that the engine is idling (if the engine is switched off, of course, the unit is switched off too). In the idling position, the amount of fuel injected is adjusted by a screw on the side of the unit (this is of course an electrical control) which is set to give minimum CO content in the exhaust while idling.

As well as these six information inputs, the electonic brain receives power from a battery input and an earth return closes its circuit. It has three outputs. One of these controls is the fuel pump (13) when the engine is first switched on, the fuel pump is allowed to run for between 1 and 2 seconds, to ensure that the fuel system is primed. After that it only works when the engine is running or being turned over by the starter motor. The control unit knows when the engine is turning over because it gets impulses from the triggering contacts on the distributor. If some such precaution as this were not taken, a leaking injector or cold start valve would flood the engine with petrol if it were switched on for some time before the starter was pressed.

The two remaining outputs operate the injectors. At first sight it seems surprising that there are not four outputs for doing this, but what happens is that, for example, the injectors to cylinders one and three, are worked together and the fuel in number three inlet duct remains in stationary suspension for ¼ revolution of the engine before being sucked in to the cylinder.

In earlier installations the control unit also operated the cold start system, but later on this task was taken over by a device which worked directly from the engine temperature known as the thermal timer (17).

The electronic control unit is a wonderful device, but you do not need to think of it as being something fragile or easily put out of adjustment. It is robustly made and well engineered, and provided that it is not maltreated - and the only possible forms of maltreatment (other than physical damage or severe mechanical shock) are overheating and excess voltage - there is no reason to suppose that it should give trouble. In fact, by modern electronic standards it is quite a simple piece of apparatus - and perhaps that is the most remarkable thing of all.

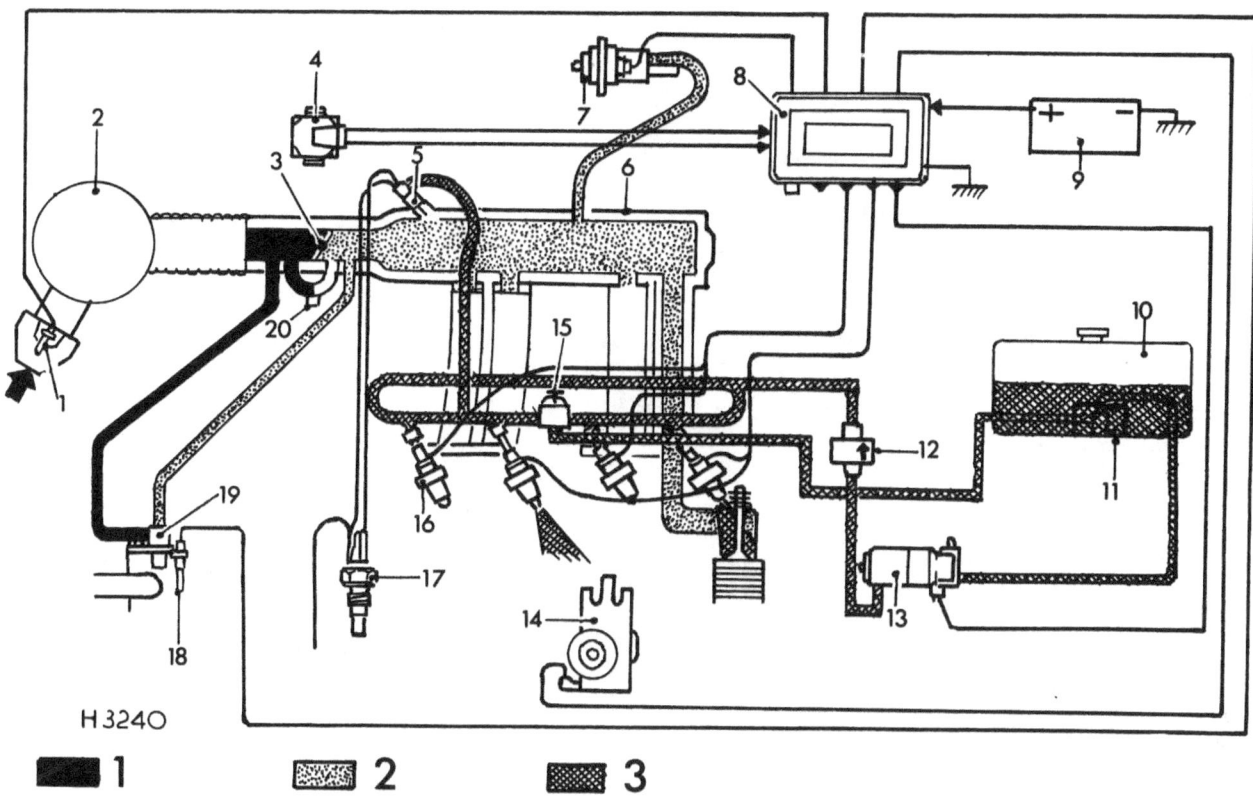

Fig.3.49 Fuel injection system

Shading 1 - air input to throttle/idling channel
Shading 2 - air after throttle/idling channel
Shading 3 - fuel circulation

1   Temperature sensor for
    induction air
2   Air cleaner
3   Throttle valve
4   Throttle valve switch
5   Cold start valve
6   Inlet duct
7   Pressure sensor
8   Control unit
9   Battery
10 Fuel tank
11 Fuel filter suction
    line
12 Fuel filter discharge
    line
13 Fuel pump
14 Distributor with
    triggering contact
15 Pressure regulator
16 Injectors
17 Thermal timer
18 Temperature sensor for
    coolant
19 Auxiliary air regulator
20 Idling adjustment
    screw

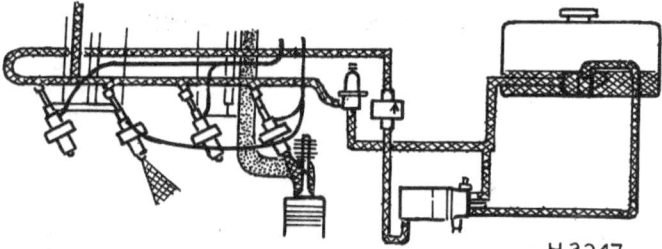

Fig.3.50. Alternative fuel distribution system as fitted on early installations

38 Control unit - description, removal and replacement

1   The control unit is located under the right-hand front seat as shown in Fig. 3.51. In order to remove it, first move the seat as far to the rear as possible.
2   Remove the bolt between the tubular framework and the link screw. Then move the seat to the front stop position and fold it backwards (see Fig. 3.53).
3   Undo the two screws which hold the control unit in position.
4   Remove the screw holding down the clamp over the cable harness entering the control unit. When this clamp is moved out of the way you can slide out the plastic cover and reveal the framework which holds the plug connecting the cable harness (see Figs. 3.54 and 3.55).
5   Make a puller on the lines of the one shown in Fig. 3.56, hook in this puller and pull out the framework holding the cable harness plug, carefully. The unit can now be removed.
6   Installation is a simple reversal of the removal procedure.

Fig.3.51. Control unit installation

Fig.3.52. B20E Fuel injection installation

1	Distribution pipe		start valve
2	Pressure regulator	9	Cold start valve
3	Retaining cap for	10	Channel for throttle
	injector		control cable
4	Electrical connection	11	Electrical connector to
	to injector		cold start valve
5	Pipe from fuel pump	12	Vacuum pipe to
6	Fuel connection to		distributor
	injector	13	Throttle valve
7	Hose to auxiliary		switch
	air regulator	14	Pressure sensor
8	Fuel pipe to cold	15	Inlet duct

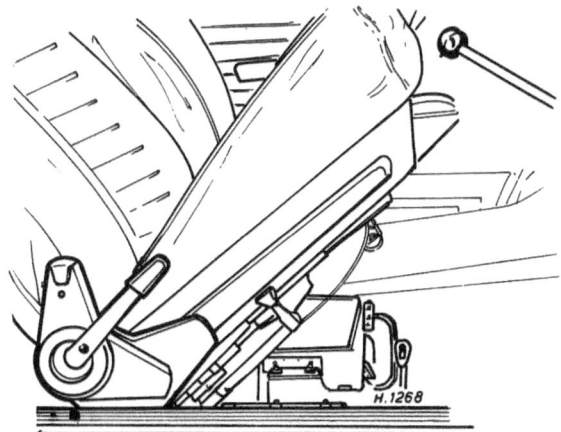

Fig.3.53. Removing the control unit

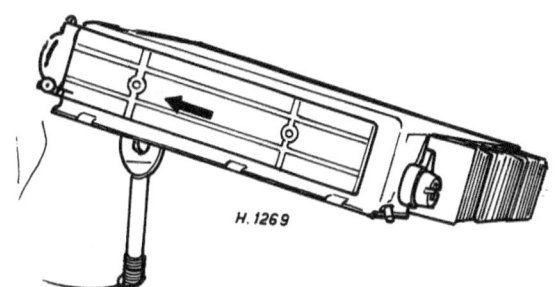

Fig.3.54. Removing the plastic cover

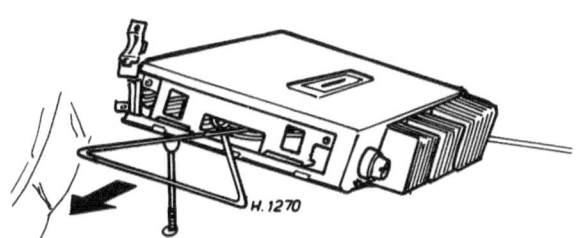

Fig.3.55. Taking out the cable harness connector

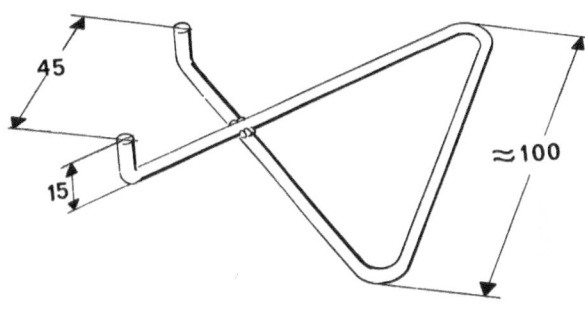

Fig.3.56. Puller for cable harness connector (material 5/64ths" (2 mm) welding wire or similar)

39 Control unit - maintenance

1   There is no special maintenance routine for the control unit. There are, however, a number of precautions which the user should observe if he wishes to be sure that it will never let him down.

2   The first of these is always to disconnect the battery positive lead while using a fast battery charger. This will ensure that no excessive voltage ever reaches the control unit. Such excessive voltages are quite capable of ruining it.

3   Never let the engine run with the battery disconnected. This again may put excessive voltages on the control unit.

4   Never use a high speed battery charger as a starting aid.

5   Under no circumstances must the control unit get hotter than 185°F (85°C), - even if it is switched off. It must not be switched on when the ambient temperature exceeds 158°F (70ᵁ C). You may think that the chances of this happening are remote, but there is one case in which this sort of heating is quite likely - if you are having the vehicle sprayed and it is stoved. So check up on this point if you have a respray and if necessary take the unit out of the vehicle.

6   Do not connect or disconnect the control unit with the ignition switched on.

7   Do not allow the cooling fins to become clogged up with the debris which so often accumulates under car seats. It is important that air should be able to circulate round them freely.

40 Control unit - testing

There is only one simple, certain test of the control unit. If you suspect that all is not well with it, take it out and replace it with a unit which is known to be good, or alternatively put it in another car where everything is known to be in working order. If the trouble disappears when a new unit is fitted, only to return when the old one is put back again, or alternatively if the trouble follows the unit when this is replaced in another vehicle, it is obvious where the fault lies. If the unit is faulty, there is no alternative to replacement. Repair of the units is a highly specialised job. Luckily it is rarely necessary.

41 Control relays

1   Two control relays - three in earlier installations form part of the system. A three relay set-up is illustrated in Fig. 3.57 where these relays are titled. They are situated on the right-hand side of the engine compartment, not very far from the bonnet hinge.

2   The cold start relay is operated by the control unit and switches the cold start valve on and off. In later installations this job is done by the thermal timer unit.

3   The pump relay, also operated by the control unit, switches the fuel pump on and off.

4   The main relay operates via the ignition switch, being in fact directly connected to the ignition coil through the cable harness. It incorporates a diode (fitted internally) which prevents it from being switched on if the battery is connected the wrong way round. This ensures that the control unit itself cannot be switched on if the battery connections are reversed - a proceeding which would probably prove fatal to it.

5   The three relays are identical except for the diode which is included in the main relay. This relay is marked with a blob of paint to distinguish it from the others.

6   Fig. 3.58 shows the terminal connections to these relays. Their operation can easily be checked by disconnecting the

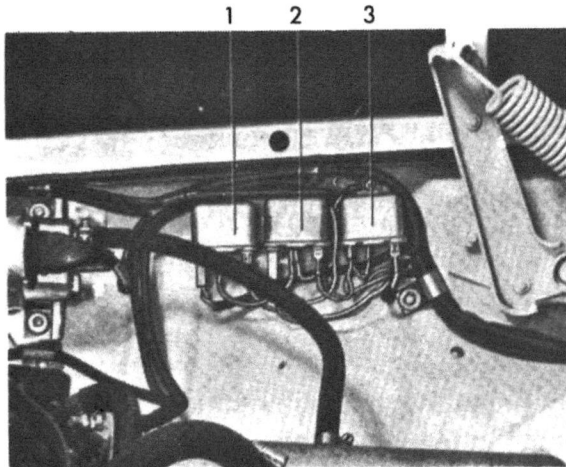

Fig.3.57. Control relays

1 Cold start relay
2 Pump relay
3 Main relay

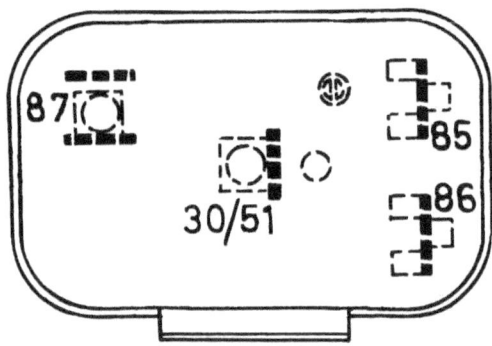

Fig.3.58. Control relay terminals

Fig.3.59. Coolant temperature sensor

Fig.3.60. Intake air temperature sensor

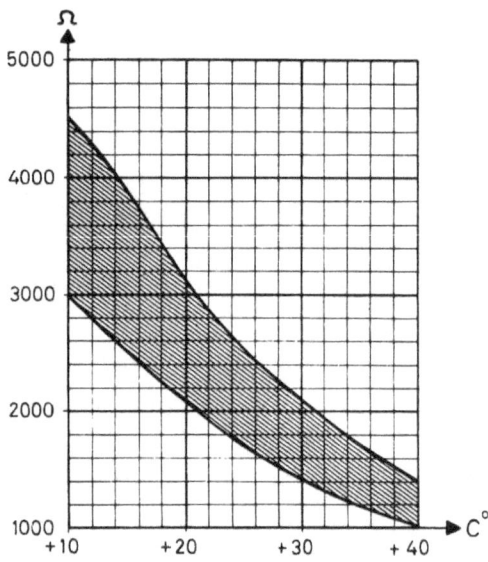

Fig.3.61. Coolant temperature sensor - resistance chart

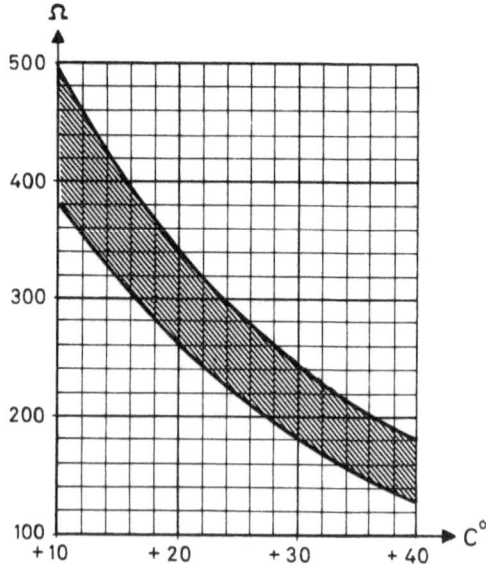

Fig.3.62. Air temperature sensor - resistance chart

various leads from the tags on the relay (this is important) and connecting the battery positive to terminal 86, battery negative (or earth) to terminal 85. This causes the relay to go over with a click, producing a short circuit between terminals 87 and 50/51. If the battery connections are reversed, the main relay should cease to operate. Reversal of connections on the other two relays has no effect.

42 Temperature sensors - description, removal and replacement

1 The system is fitted with two temperature sensors, one for coolant and one for intake air. They both work on the same principle, although they are not identical. They contain an electrical resistance element made of what is known as semi-conductor material whose resistance varies considerably with temperature. You can see from Figs. 3.61 and 3.62 how much this variation is. The control unit measures the resistance of these devices and thus receives information about air and water temperature.

2 The coolant temperature sensor is located at the front end of the cylinder head as shown in Fig. 3.59. The temperature sensor for the intake air is placed in front of the air cleaner as shown in Fig. 3.60.

3 To remove either of them, simply pull off its electrical connection and unscrew it. For the coolant sensor, you will have to drain off or make some arrangement for plugging up the hole quickly as soon as you have taken the device out. Replacing is straightforward. Don't forget the sealing ring when replacing the coolant sensor.

43 Temperature sensors - testing

This is easily carried out by putting the units in warm water and taking one or two resistance readings at various temperatures. If reading near each end of the scale and one in the middle come well within the shaded band shown in Figs. 3.61 and 3.62, all is well. It is not very likely that the temperature sensors themselves will give trouble. If they appear to be faulty, the cause will probably be found in electrical connections.

44 Pressure sensor - description, removal and replacement

1 The pressure sensor is located on the right-hand side of the engine compartment, not far from the control relays. It is connected to the inlet manifold by a short length of flexible pipe (see Fig. 3.63).

2 The only point to watch during removal and replacement is the possible entry of dirt into the unit when the pipe connecting it to the inlet manifold is removed. When you take this pipe off, plug up the hole immediately.

3 A diagram of the inlet is given in Fig. 3.64. Near the right-hand end there is a diaphragm which is vented to the atmosphere on its right-hand side as seen in the diaphragm, ie on the side remote from the main part of the unit. This diaphragm is connected to bellows which in turn are connected to an armature which can move to and fro in the middle of the windings (primary and secondary) of a transformer. The armature can move to and fro, acting against a spiral spring and being prevented from over-rapid vibration by a damping spring which is a friction fit on the spindle at the end of the armature. The movement of the armature is brought about by variations in engine vacuum communicated to the pressure sensor through the pipe from the inlet manifold.

4 The pressure moves the armature in two ways. Firstly, the whole of the unit on the left-hand side of the diaphragm, as seen in the diagram, ie the part containing the bellows, the transformer and the armature, is at reduced pressure caused by the engine vacuum and the diaphragm is thereby sucked to the left. This causes the armature to move. Secondly, the bellows (which are evacuated just like the bellows in an aneroid barometer), expand as the pressure is reduced and their expansion causes armature movement additional to that produced by the movement of the diaphragm. We see that initially as the pressure starts to drop the diaphragm and the bellows act together to move the armature, but below a certain pressure level the diaphragm comes up against a stop, after which the armature moves under the influence of the bellows only. This arrangement gives a relationship between armature movement and pressure drop which is well suited to the information requirement of the control unit.

5 The pressure in the inlet manifold is subject to small rapid fluctuations as the inlet valves open and close, and it is not desirable that these should influence the movement of the armature. To prevent this, the inlet to the pressure sensor is closed by a valve containing a small hole which only admits air at a very limited rate, thus damping out fluctuations. For sudden acceleration however, where the pressure suddenly rises (because the vacuum in the inlet duct suddenly decreases) the valve lifts off its seating and the pressure change is immediately

Fig.3.64. Diagram of pressure sensor

1	Damping spring	8	Diaphragm
2	Coil spring	9	Full load stop
3	Spring (suspension)	10	Part load stop
4	Secondary winding	11	Armature
5	Primary winding	12	Electrical connection
6	Spring (suspension)	13	Valve
7	Diaphragm bellows	14	Bellows connection

Fig.3.63. Pressure sensor

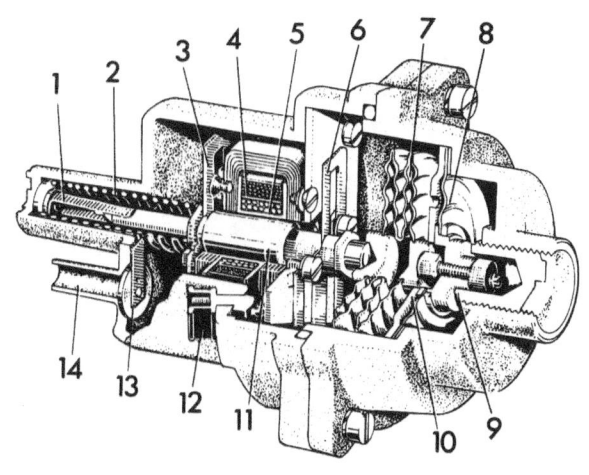

communicated to the diaphragm and bellows.

6 The transformer which surrounds the moving armature consists of two windings, primary and secondary. A small alternating current is introduced into the primary winding from the control unit and this produces a current in the secondary windings whose strength depends on the position of the armature. The control unit senses the secondary winding current and thus receives information as to the position of the armature and hence the state of the engine vacuum.

45 Pressure sensor - testing

1 There is only one certain test for this unit, and that is substitution - either the substitution of a unit known to be working in your own car or the substitution of your own unit in a car which is known to be alright. If the fault disappears when you fit a new unit, and even more certainly if the fault follows the unit to another car, you have your answer.

2 You can check the electrical resistance of the transformer windings with a multimeter or ohmmeter. The resistance should be approximately 90 ohms between terminals 7 and 15 (primary winding) and approximately 350 ohms between terminals 8 and 10 (secondary winding). All other combinations - including resistance between terminals and frame - should give an infinity reading. If the transformer passes these tests it is almost (but not 100%) certain to be alright. You can be quite certain, however, that readings differing significantly from the values given - and particularly readings well below the infinity mark for cross-connections or resistance to frame - signify that the unit is defective.

46 Throttle valve switch - description, removal and replacement

1 Fig. 3.65 gives a photograph of this switch, which is mounted on the inlet duct and connected to the throttle shaft which operates it. It has two functions, to emit impulses to the control unit to increase the fuel supply during acceleration and to switch on the CO control in the control unit when the engine is idling.

2 A working diagram is shown in Fig. 3.66. Two sliding contacts pass over thin copper strips, one of which is a zig-zag so that as the contacts rotate that particular part of the switch keeps going on and off. Current passing through the switch supplied by the control unit is, therefore, interrupted as the switch is rotated and

the speed and number of the interruptions depend on the rate and extent of the switch rotation, ie the extent and speed with which the driver puts his foot down.

3 When the throttle is being pushed down, and the switch is rotating anti-clockwise as seen in the diagram, the lever which pushes the sliding contacts round also closes another pair of contacts which are in series with the sliding contacts. When the driver lifts his foot, the switch rotates the other way and the lever - which is now pushing in the other direction - no longer closes these particular contacts; this means that the current supply to the sliding contacts from the control unit is interrupted and so they transmit no current pulses when the throttle is released.

4 Two further contacts form the switch for the CO control in the control unit. These are only closed when the throttle is closed or nearly so, ie when the switch spindle is in the extreme clockwise position as seen in the diagram.

5 To remove the switch, first of all note its position carefully. Make a mark on the inlet duct against the upper scale if no mark is there already. Pull out the electrical connector, undo the two fixing screws and the switch can be withdrawn from the inlet duct, it being simply keyed into the throttle shaft. When the switch is replaced it will need adjustment as described in Section 48.

47 Throttle valve switch - testing

1 Arrange an ohmmeter so that you can connect it to the terminals on the switch. Now turn the spindle of the switch fully anti-clockwise. You will now find that a pair of the switch terminals show a short circuit, all other combinations showing open circuit. If you do not, and you have really turned the spindle anti-clockwise and not, perhaps, clockwise the switch is defective.

2 With the switch still turned anti-clockwise, connect the ohmmeter to the other pair of terminals. Now rotate the spindle slowly clockwise and if all is well you will find that you get alternate short circuit and open circuit across these terminals. You should get 18 separate short circuits each lasting for 2° of spindle rotation, separated by open circuits also lasting for 2°.

3 When you have turned it as far as you can, turn it back again. You should not get any short circuits on the return rotation, because the extra pair of contacts referred to in Section 46, paragraph 3 should operate to prevent this.

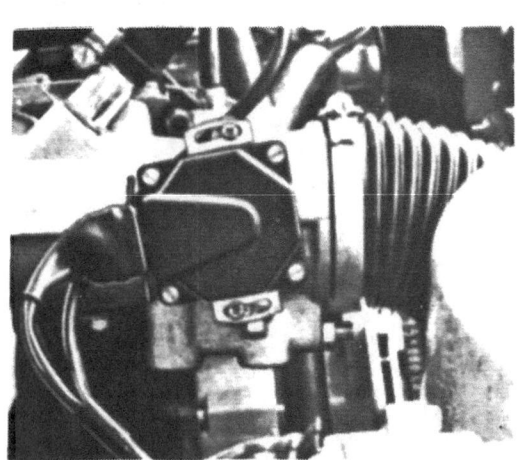

Fig.3.65. Throttle valve switch

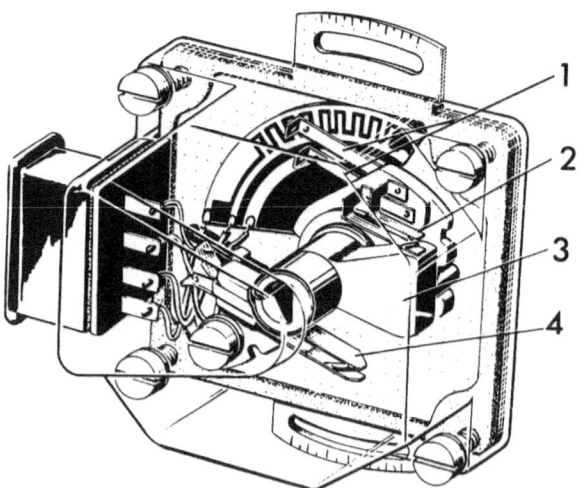

Fig.3.66. Throttle valve switch - diagram

1 *Sliding contacts*
2 *Switch contacts for accelerator function*
3 *Connection to the throttle spindle*
4 *Switch pair for CO-potentiometer*

48 Throttle valve switch - adjustment

1 The switch should be fitted so that with the throttle closed the sliding contacts are just coming up to the first of the short circuit positions.

2 To achieve this, slacken the screws holding the switch and turn the body of the switch as far as it will go clockwise. Connect an ohmmeter to the appropriate terminals of the switch socket as described in the previous section, and note that it indicates open circuit. Now turn the switch body slowly anti-clockwise until the ohmmeter goes over from infinity to zero. Now turn a further 1° (½ a division on the scale at the upper fixing screw) and tighten down the screws.

3 As an additional check, place a 0.02" (0.50 mm) feeler gauge between the stop screw and the stop on the throttle valve spindle. This should cause the ohmmeter to go over. Do the same thing with a 0.014" (0.30 mm) feeler gauge and the ohmmeter should not change.

49 Triggering contacts - description, removal, checking, replacement

1 The control unit receives information as to the firing time and the engine speed from a pair of contacts operated by a cam on the distributor shaft and fitted just below the governor in the distributor. These contacts are exactly the same sort of thing as normal points, being actuated by spring loaded levers lifted by the cam. They interrupt a small current supplied to them by the control unit and thus transmit impulses to it.

2 How they are removed and replaced is obvious from Fig. 3.67 which illustrates them.

3 Because the contacts only have to break small currents, they are unlikely to pit and burn like ordinary ignition contacts. However you should keep an eye on them for signs of wear on the cam followers and dirt on the contacts themselves. No provision is made for adjustment, and there is no need for special timing procedures. Put a smear of grease on the cam followers (Castrol LM is suitable) when you are replacing them. Make sure that the rubber seal between the assembly and the distributor case is intact; if in doubt replace it.

4 To check the opening of these contacts, wedge the cam followers by pushing something between them and the body of

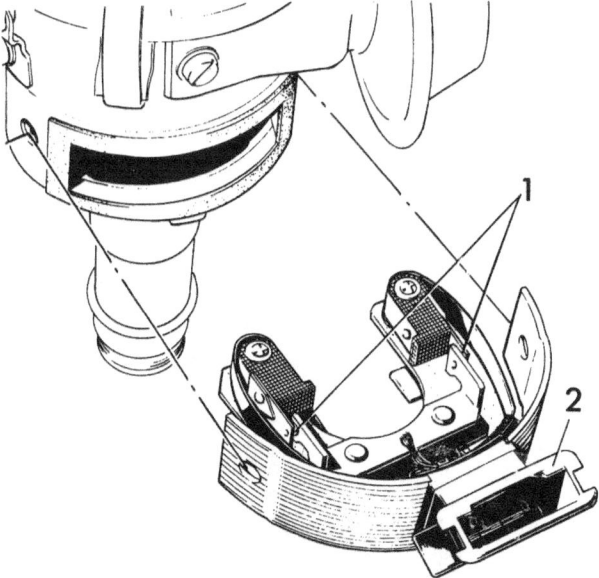

Fig.3.67. Trigger contacts

1 Triggering contacts
2 Electrical connection

the assembly (possibly a piece of razor blade or old feeler gauge) so that, once pushed over, they do not return under the action of their springs. This is easier said than done but not impossible. Once you have got your system acting reliably, temporarily refit the assembly to the distributor case and turn the engine over with the starter motor. Then remove it and measure the contact clearances.

50 Fuel supply arrangements - general description

It is essential for the proper operation of the injectors that they receive fuel at constant pressure. This is achieved by a system reminiscent of the normal oil circulation, where pressure exerted by the oil pump is limited by the action of a relief valve (see Fig. 3.49). Petrol is continuosly circulated by an electric fuel pump through a filter and from there to a pipe system leading to a pressure regulator which passes the fuel through it when the pressure exceeds 28 lb/in^2 (2.0 kg/cm^2). The pump itself maintains a pressure of about twice this amount, the result being that near the pressure regulator a constant pressure is maintained. The system appears in two different forms, but the principle is the same. For cold starting, fuel is injected into the inlet manifold not far from the throttle by a special valve, the cold start valve. This valve is electrically operated, being switched on and off by the control unit in earlier installations and by a switch controlled by engine temperature (known as the thermal timing unit) in later ones. This system corresponds to the cold start arrangement found on normal carburettors.

To match this extra amount of fuel, extra air is admitted to the manifold through a valve which by-passes the throttle. This valve, known as the auxiliary air regulator, is controlled by engine temperature. This set-up is analogous to the system whereby when the choke control is pulled out on a normal carburettor, the throttle is opened a little way to let in extra air.

For idling adjustment, instead of setting the throttle slightly open as is the usual practice with carburettors, a controlled amount of air is allowed to by-pass the closed throttle. The amount of air flowing through the by-pass loop is controlled by the idling adjustment screw.

51 Fuel pump - description

1 Fig. 3.68 shows how the fuel pump is installed under the vehicle on the right-hand side of the fuel tank. Close to the pump is the fuel filter.

2 The two patterns of fuel pump, which only differ from each other in their relief valve arrangements, are illustrated diagrammatically in Figs. 3.69a and 3.69b. The heart of the pump is a rotor which carries small pockets on the outside which open into the main body of the pump. These pockets scoop up petrol from the inlet and push it out - by centrifugal force into the main body. The whole of the main body of the pump - motor and all - becomes full of petrol and a considerable pressure is built up. The outlet is taken from the main body and includes a ball valve so that when the pump is turned off the pressure built up in the fuel distribution system is maintained.

3 When the pressure in the main body of the pump exceeds 64 lb/in^2 (4.5 kg/cm^2) a ball valve incorporated in the pump opens. In the earlier type of pump (Fig. 69a) the opening of this valve permits petrol to pass along an overflow outlet and back to the main fuel tank. In the later pattern, the petrol flows back into the inlet side and thence back into the pump again - which is just what happened with the earlier design except that then it returned to the pump via the fuel tank instead of going round and round locally.

4 This valve limits the pressure that can be built up in the pump should some fault in the pressure regulator or blockage in the fuel line stop the circulation of fuel to 64 lb/in^2 (4.5 kg/cm^2). In normal operation, the pressure exerted by the pump is about 28 lb/in^2 (2.0 kg/cm^2), this being determined by the pressure regulator.

52 Fuel pump - checking

1   The pump should be capable of delivering 22 gallons per hour (25.6 US gallons or 100 litres) at a pressure of 28 lb/in^2 (2.0 kg/cm^2). At this load, current consumption should be 5.0 amps.

2   This can easily be checked on the vehicle. Disconnect the flexible pipe from the outlet on the underside of the pressure regulator and arrange a temporary pipe to lead into a calibrated container. We suggest that you make your container big enough for the pump to half fill it in half a minute - in other words, it should be capable of holding 1/60th of the quoted figures.

3   When this is organised, take the lead off terminal 87 of the pump relay and connect this to the negative terminal of an ammeter scaled to read 0-10 amps (to be on the safe side) and when you are ready to run fit the positive terminal of the ammeter to the battery.

4   The pump should now operate and pump petrol into your container. Let it run for half a minute, meanwhile reading the current on the ammeter.

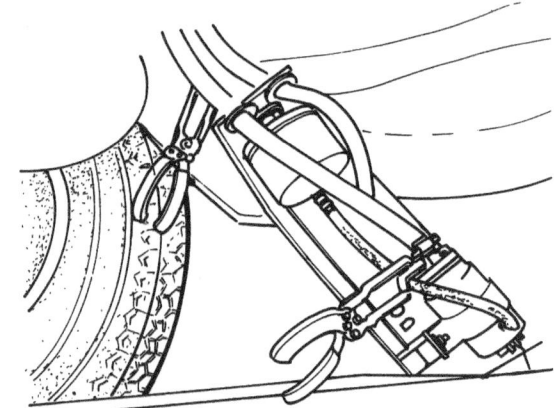

Fig.3.68. Fuel pump and fuel filter - tray on underside of vehicle detached for removal of fuel filter

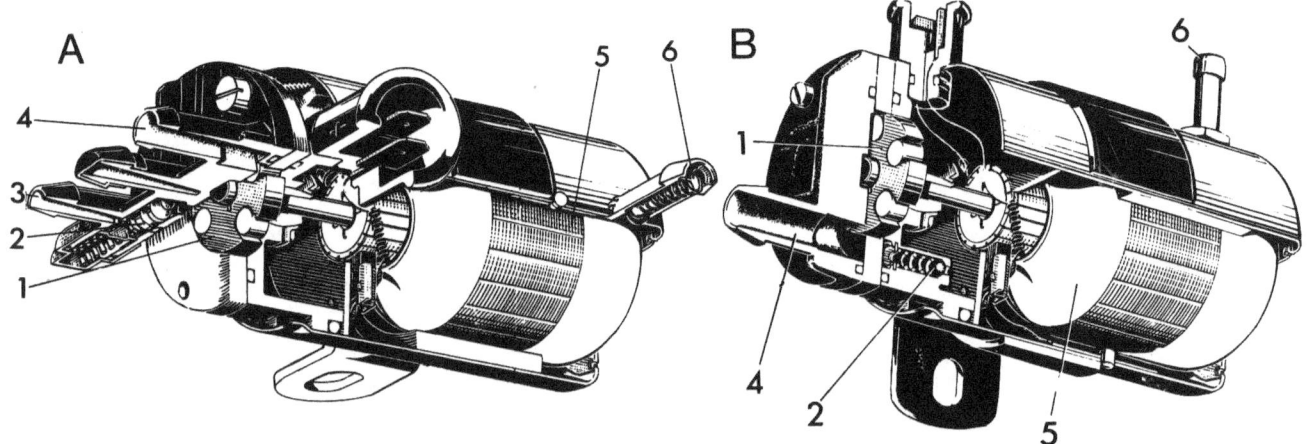

Fig.3.69. Fuel pump

(a) early type (left)   (b) later type (right)

1 Pump rotor	3 Overflow channel (old type only)	5 Rotor for electric motor
2 Overflow valve	4 Inlet	6 Outlet

Fig.3.70. Pressure regulator

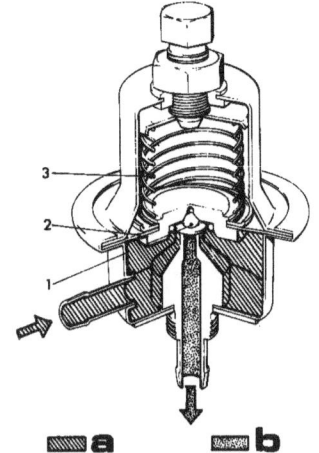

Fig.3.71. Pressure regulator (diagram)

1   Valve, 2   Diaphragm, 3   Spring

Shading a) - fuel at 28 lb/in^2 (2 kg/cm^2)
Shading b) - fuel returned to tank

5 If your pressure regulator is correctly set, you should get 1/120th of the quoted figures per hour in your container. If the level is a little low, do not worry unduly, as there is some pressure drop in the pipes and the pressure at the pump is consequently a little higher than the 28 lb/in^2 (2 kg/cm^2) that you get at the pressure regulator. A higher yield of petrol is nothing to worry about if you are sure that your pressure regulator is correctly set. It is as well to be certain of this before you start your test anyway. Checking the pressure regulator is dealt with in Section 3.56.

53 Fuel pump - removal and replacement

1 Disconnect the cable harness plug from the petrol pump, undo the two screws holding the tray carrying the pump and filter in place, and withdraw the tray.
2 Remove the plastic clamp holding the hoses together. Clean round the pump hose connections so that when you remove the hoses no dirt will go into the pump.
3 Pinch the hoses leading from the pump to the fuel tank (two of these in earlier installations, one only in later ones) and the hose from the fuel pump to the circulating system to avoid fuel leakage when you disconnect them from the pump. The mole wrench or vise-grip do this job excellently.
4 Remove the screws holding the pump and take it out.
5 Replacement is the reverse of the removal process.
6 When all is reassembled, let the pump run and check that none of the hose connections is leaking.

54 Fuel filter (discharge line) removal and replacement

1 Carry out all the preliminaries described in the previous Section for removing the petrol pump, nipping up the hose between the petrol pump and the filter and the hose between the filter and the main circulation system. Clean round the filter hose connections.
2 Removal of the old filter and fitting a new one is now simple (Fig. 3.68). Make sure that the new filter is fitted with the arrow pointing in the flow direction. Don't forget to run the pump and check for leaks after the refitting is complete.

55 Pressure regulator - description

1 The pressure regulator is located either on a bracket mounted on the fire wall (bulkhead) or on the distbution pipe, between the second and third injector (see Fig. 3.70). It is a purely mechanical device. A diagram illustrating its working is given in Fig. 3.71. When the fuel pressure lifts the diaphragm against the pressure of the spring the entrance to the return outlet is opened and fuel flows through this, thus reducing the pressure.
2 Its removal and replacement need no special comment.

56 Pressure regulator - checking and adjusting

1 To check the pressure regulator you need a pressure gauge with a short length of metal pipe connected to it to which you can clamp the pipe which normally goes to the cold start valve. An old oil gauge would do, washed out with paraffin - all you need to know is exactly what it reads when the pressure applied to it is 28 lb/in^2 (2.0 kg/cm^2). A tyre inflation air line would do the job.
2 Disconnect the flexible pipe from the cold start valve and clamp it to your pressure gauge.
3 Disconnect the lead from terminal 87 of the pump relay and temporarily connect the lead to the battery positive terminal. The pump will now run and you can read the pressure on your pressure gauge.
4 If this does not read 28 lb/in^2 (2.0 kg/cm^2) slacken off the locknut on top of the pressure regulator and turn the screw

clockwise to increase the pressure or anti-clockwise to decrease it. When the reading is correct, tighten up the lock nut. If the pressure cannot be brought to the correct value by adjustment, the pressure regulator must be replaced.

57 Injectors - description

1 Fuel is injected into the intake ports in the cylinder head via the inlet ducts by four injectors, one for each port. The injectors are mounted in holders fitted on the cylinder head (Fig. 3.74).
2 The injectors are triggered off in pairs, and the fuel is injected while the inlet valves are closed. Fuel stays in the inlet duct until the inlet valve opens.
3 Fig. 3.72 shows a sketch of an injector and Fig. 3.73 a diagram of how it works. The injector is in fact no more than a solenoid acting on an accurately made needle valve. The armature and the needle are all one piece, the top of the armature being pushed down by the return spring situated more or less in the middle of the injector.
   When the magnetic winding is energised, the needle is lifted about 0.002 (0.5 mm) from the seat and fuel is able to pass. Since the needle and opening in the valve are accurately calibrated and the fuel pressure is maintained constant by the pressure regulator, only the time that the needle is lifted will determine the amount of fuel injected. This can vary from 2-10 milliseconds ie 0.002-0.01 seconds.

58 Injectors - removal and replacing

1 The injector is held in its holder on the cylinder head by a retaining ring in a bayonet fitting. If you turn this ring anti-clockwise it comes away and the injector is simply lifted out (see Fig. 3.74).
2 The simplest approach is to take them all out at once, still attached to the distributor pipe. Fig. 3.75 shows this for the later type of installation, but it works just as well for the earlier type.
3 If you wish to examine any particular injector, simply undo the hose connection between it and the distribution pipe.

59 Injectors - checking

1 Do not try to test an injector by connecting it across the battery. The maximum operating voltage is 3 volts.
2 The resistance between the two terminals in the socket can be measured with an ordinary multi-meter. It should be 2.40 ohms at 70°F (20°C). If you are within 10% of this you have no worry.

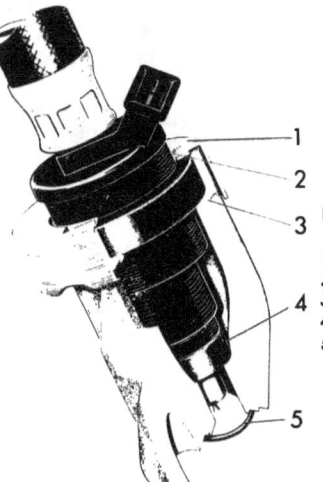

Fig.3.72. Injector with holder

1 Circlip
2 Steel washer
3 Rubber seal
4 Rubber seal
5 O-ring

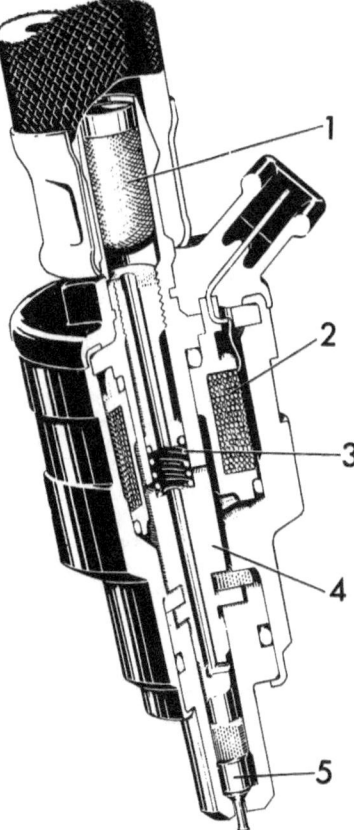

Fig.3.73. Injector - diagram

1   Filter
2   Magnetic winding
3   Return spring
4   Magnetic armature
5   Sealing needle

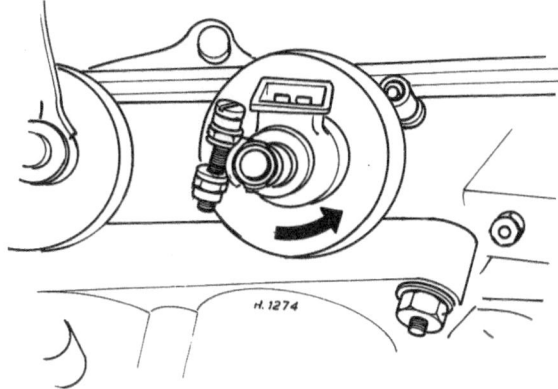

Fig.3.74. Removing an injector

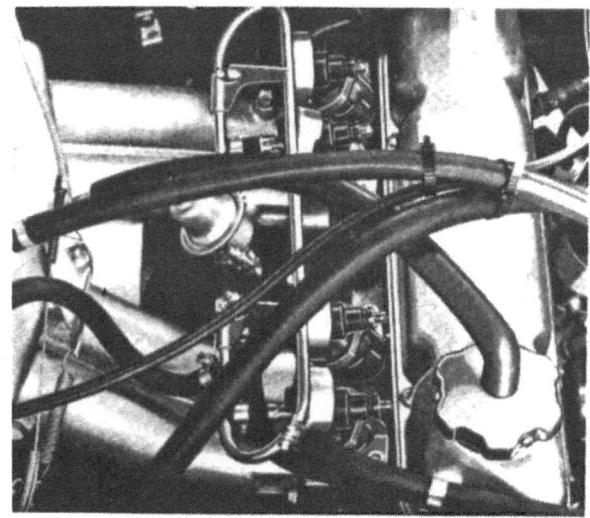

Fig.3.75. Injectors removed while connected to distribution pipe

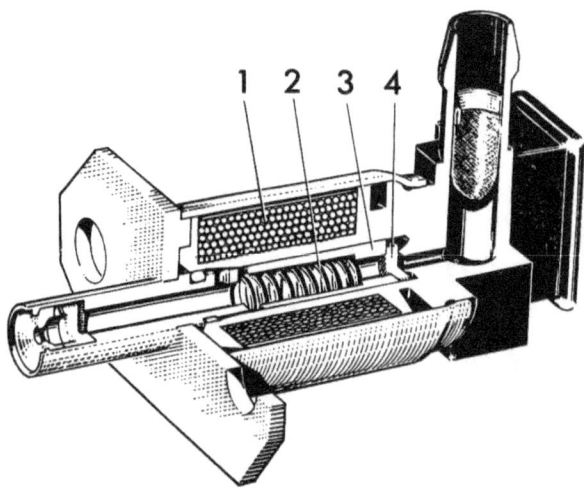

Fig.3.76. Cold start valve

1   Magnetic winding   3   Magnetic armature
2   Return spring   4   Packing

60.1 Cold start valve

3   A limited amount of leakage from the injectors is permissible. It can simply be checked for all injectors at once by having them out of the engine and still connected to the distribution pipe as described in the previous section, and running the pump by making a temporary connection as described in Section 52. Maximum permitted leakage for an injector is five drops per minute at 28 psi (2.0 kg/cm^2) ie under normal running conditions.

4   If a single injector is suspected of being faulty, for example because of some irregularity in engine firing find out which cylinder is actually producing the symptoms. Irregular firing on one cylinder, for example, can be isolated by disconnecting or short circuiting each plug in turn. Once the troublesome cylinder has been identified, exchange its injector with that supplying a different cylinder. If the fault follows the injector, you have your answer.

60 Cold start valve - description, removal and replacement

1   The cold start valve is mounted in the inlet duct just after the throttle. It is an electrically controlled valve which simply admits extra fuel to the inlet manifold when it is switched on. A diagram showing its working is given in Fig. 3.76. In the unlikely event of its being defective, repair or adjustment is not possible and it has to be replaced. (photo).

2   It is switched on for a time governed by the thermal timer in later installations or the control unit in earlier ones, but only when the starter motor is running. When the engine is running and the starter motor has been shut off the valve ceases injecting regardless of the state of the thermal timer or control unit.

3   Removal and replacement is simple. Pinch the fuel pipe leading to it to prevent leakage, disconnect the pipe and plug contact, unscrew the screws holding the valve to the inlet duct and remove it. Don't forget its gasket when you replace it.

61 Cold start valve - checking

1   When the engine is cold, take the valve out of the inlet manifold, leaving the fuel and electrical supply connections attached. If you now switch on the ignition and turn the engine over with the self starter, you should be able to see it emitting fuel.

2   If no fuel appears, remove the plug and check that when the starter motor is turning 12 volts appears across the socket terminations. If it does, the valve must be faulty and will have to be replaced.

62 Thermal timer - description, removal and replacement

1   Basically the thermal timer is a pair of contacts controlled by a bi-metallic strip which bends when it is sufficiently warm and breaks the contact. The bi-metallic strip is warmed by the engine and also by a small heating element. If the engine is very cold, the heating element has to operate for perhaps as long as 12 seconds before the strip is warm enough to break the contact, but on the other hand if the engine is warmer than 95°F (35°C) contact is broken without any assistance from the heating element.

2   The timer is supplied with 12 volts to warm up the element while the starter motor is running, one of the two green cables connected to the heater terminal going direct to the starter motor solenoid control. The other green cable is taken to the cold start valve, so this, too, is only supplied with power when the starter motor is running.

3   The other terminal is also connected to the cold start valve, and when the bi-metallic strip is cool this terminal is earthed through the contacts inside the thermal timer, thus completing the circuit through the cold start valve and allowing it to operate.

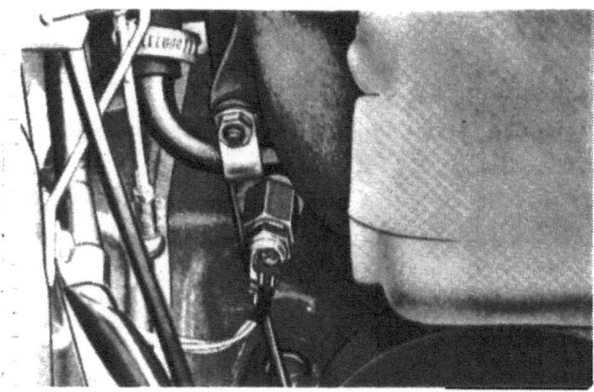

Fig.3.77. Thermal timer

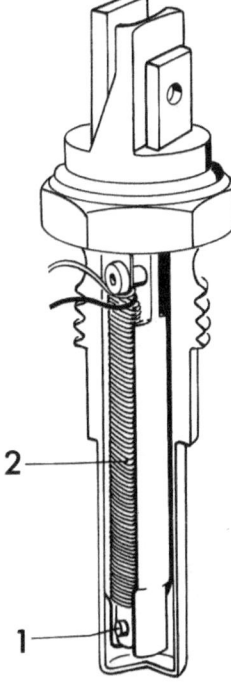

Fig.3.78. Thermal timer - diagram

1   Contacts
2   Heating element enclosing bi-metal spring

4   A photograph of the thermal timer is shown in Fig. 3.77 and a diagram in Fig. 3.78.

5   Removing and replacing the timer is a simple matter, but as it is in direct connection with the coolant you will either have to drain the coolant or have a small cork handy which you can quickly put in the hole when you take the timer out.

63 Thermal timer - checking

1   The thermal timer has no specification laid down for it. The resistance of this sort of device varies greatly with temperature and the timing intervals are probably not very precise. If you are doubtful about it, you can carry out some simple checks by putting it in water and seeing how long the contacts take to break (shown when an ohmmeter between the contact terminal and the case switches over from zero to infinity). As you approach 95°F (35°C) the time should become very short, and above this temperature you will soon find that the contacts remain permanently open. At this other end of the scale, the device is supposed to take 12 seconds to operate at - 4°F (-20°C), so that at around about 50°F (10°C) you would expect it to take 5 seconds or so. If it is somewhat outside this figure there is no need to worry - all you are really concerned with is that the contacts should stay closed for as long as you press the starter motor unless the engine is really warm.

64 Auxiliary air regulator - description, removal and replacement

1   A photograph of the auxiliary air regulator is shown in Fig. 3.79 and a cut-away diagram in Fig. 3.80.

2   It consists of an expanding element (probably vapour filled bellows) which pushes a piston against the action spring and so cuts off an air path which exists through it when it is cold. Thus, when the engine is cold, extra air is provided through this path to mix with the fuel injected at this time from the cold start valve.

3   Removal and replacement is a simple matter involving two bolts and a gasket, but if you do not want to drain the coolant you must have a bung handy for filling up the hole when the regulator comes out.

65 Auxiliary air regulator - checking

1   It is probably enough to be sure that the element passes air when the engine is cold and blocks it when the engine is hot. It should completely close off the air path at a water temperature of 140°F (60°C). At the other end of the scale, it is fully opened at -13°F (-25°C). The only thing likely to happen to the regulator in service is failure of the expansion element, and if this occurs the air path will be open all the time.

66 Fuel injection system - tuning and adjustment

1   Some may regret that the electronic fuel injection system gives very little scope to the man who feels that by careful attention to jet settings, choke opening relative to fast idle, ignition timing, careful setting of carburettor float level and so forth he can be sure of getting the last ounce of performance and economy out of his motor. However, there are a few points in favour of a system in which mixture control is determined by an electronic device which takes the factors of engine speed, engine temperature, air temperature and engine vacuum into account far more thoroughly than the normal carburettor can hope to do.

2   We should also consider why adjustment becomes necessary. By and large, the reason is wear: wear in the carburettor controls and linkages which has to be taken up, and later in the life of the engine, poor compression caused by leaking valves or worn cylinders, ineffective operation of ignition advance mechanism and so on. Very often, in an attempt to bring back lost engine performance, carburettor jet settings are altered, idling settings adjusted and ignition timing changed. The improvement in performance arising from these activities is at best limited and at worst illusory. In most cases it is better to accept that your engine has lost some of its youthful zest and to plan the day when you can put it all back again with a thorough engine overhaul.

3   Be that as it may, there are adjustments that can be made in the fuel injection system, and though once these are made they are unlikely to need alteration it is as well to check that they are correct - particularly after some fault investigation or repair work has been carried out.

67 Adjusting the throttle valve

1   Slacken the locknut for the stop screw on the throttle spindle (see Fig. 3.81) and unscrew the screw a couple of turns so that it does not lie against the stop on the throttle valve spindle. Check to make sure that the throttle is completely closed.

2   Screw in the screw until it touches the stop on the spindle, and then screw it ¼ - 1/3 turn more and tighten the locknut. Check that the throttle does not jam or stick in the closed position.

3   After carrying out this adjustment, adjust the throttle valve switch as described in Section 3.48.

Fig.3.79. Auxiliary air regulator

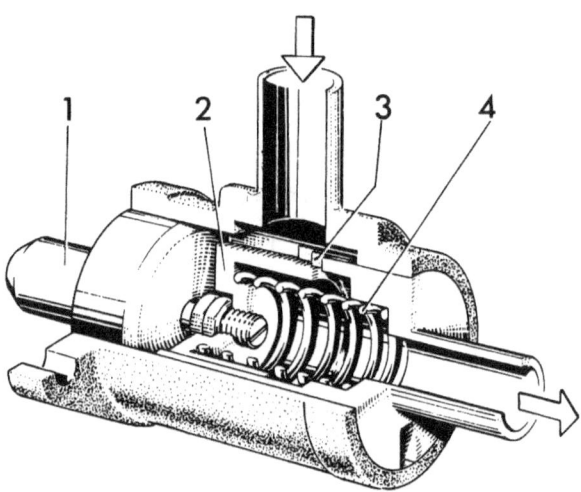

Fig.3.80. Auxiliary air regulator - diagram

1 Expanding element	3 Auxiliary air pipe
2 Regulator	4 Return spring

Fig.3.81. Throttle stop screw

(Note: this is not the idle adjustment screw)

1 Locknut	3 Stop on throttle valve
2 Stop screw	spindle

67.5 Bracket holding throttle cable (actual cable fixing nut not visible)

67.6 Rod from throttle pedal acting on throttle cable

68.3 Idling adjustment screw

4 Note particularly that idling must not be adjusted with this screw.

5 Check that the wire operating the throttle is slack enough for you to be sure that the throttle rests against the stop and is not restricted by the cable. Adjust for this by releasing the locknut where the cable case screws into the bracket on the inlet duct (see photo).

6 Adjust the length of the throttle control rod which actuates the throttle cable through a linkage on the fire wall (see photo), so that the lever rests against the bracket when the cable is slightly slack. You may have to repeat these operations until you get the ideal state: throttle stop screw resting on stop, actuating lever resting on bracket, cable very slightly slack.

68 Idling adjustment

1 Run the engine until it is thoroughly warm (approximately 176°F (80°C).

2 Check that the auxiliary air regulator is completely closed by pulling off the hose connecting it to the inlet duct between the air cleaner and the throttle and covering the end of this hose with the hand. If this causes the engine speed to drop, the auxiliary air regulator is not operating correctly - either the engine is not warm enough or the regulator is faulty. You can carry on the adjustment regardless of a faulty regulator if you

plug the end of the hose with a well fitting cork. Naturally, if you do this, when you refit the regulator hose the idling speed will go up, and the only way to stop this is to replace the regulator.

3 Adjust the idling speed to 900 rpm with the throttle closed by turning the idle adjustment screw (photo). If the speed cannot be lowered sufficiently, the throttle valve must be slightly open (check its setting as described in the previous section) or there must be some air leakage on the engine side of the throttle.

69 Evaporite control system - fuel injection engines

1 The evaporite fuel vapour control system fitted to fuel injection engines is a slightly simplified version of that fitted to carburettor engines. It does not have the arrangements for sealing the venting filter off from the air intake, the filter being connected to the inlet duct between the air cleaner and the throttle. Apart from this modification, which is reflected in a slightly different appearance to the venting filter in most installations, the location of the various components and the working of the system is as described in Section 33. Fig. 3.82 shows the venting filter as installed in fuel injection engines, and Fig. 3.83 gives a diagram of the system and incidentally illustrates how the pattern of venting filter used in carburettor engines is sometimes adapted for use with fuel injection.

Fig.3.82. Venting filter, B20E engine

1 Connection to inlet duct

2 Connection from expansion tank

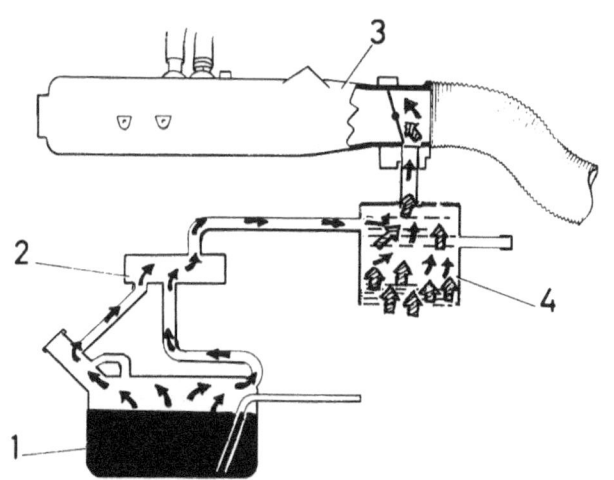

Fig.3.83. Evaporite system, B20E engine

1 Fuel tank
2 Expansion tank

3 Inlet duct
4 Venting filter

70 Fuel injection system - faults and symptoms

We give in this Section a table detailing a few of the symptoms of fuel system trouble, possible causes and remedies. You should always bear in mind that it is very difficult to distinguish between ignition faults and fuel system faults in many cases. Your golden rule should be - before starting on the fuel system - make 100% certain of the ignition. Ignition faults are easy to check, ignition adjustments, when required, are easy to make, and furthermore when adjustment is required as a result of normal wear and tear this adjustment is much more likely to be in the ignition than in the fuel system The following table assumes that all is in order in the ignition department.

Symptom	Reason	Remedy
Smell of petrol when engine is stopped	Leaking fuel pipes or unions Leaking fuel tank	Repair or renew as necessary. Fill fuel tank to capacity and examine carefully at seams, unions and fuel pipe connections. Repair as necessary.
Smell of petrol when engine is idling	Leaking fuel lines or unions in fuel distribution system	Check lines and unions and tighten or repair.
Excessive fuel consumption, not accounted for by leaks	Leaking injectors Leaking or sticking cold start valve	Check and replace where necessary. Check and replace if necessary.
Uneven running, lack of power, cutting out (trouble distributed evenly over all cylinders)	Fuel starvation Air leaks on engine side of throttle	Check pump delivery. Check for blockage in fuel pipes. Check gaskets and tightness of mounting nuts.
As previous symptom but confined to two cylinders (one-three or two-four)	Faulty connection between control unit and pair of injectors Fault in control unit	Check connection and repair as necessary. Check control unit and replace as necessary.
As previous but on one cylinder only	Faulty electrical connection to injector Faulty injector	Check and repair as necessary. Check by exchanging with another injector, if fault follows injector replace.
Difficulty in starting not associated with faults already given	Auxiliary air regulator not working Cold start valve not working	Check and replace as necessary. Check and replace as necessary.
Engine does not respond properly to throttle pedal	Throttle switch not working properly	Check and replace if necessary.
Engine does not take up proper idling speed when throttle released	Sticking control Thermal timer contacts permanently open	Clean and oil as required. Check for proper operation and replace if necessary.
Performance short-comings normally associated with over-rich or over-lean mixture where causes are not revealed by checks already given	Faulty air temperature sensor Faulty engine temperature sensor Faulty pressure sensor, (this will have a more disastrous effect on performance than the previous two) Faulty control unit	Check and replace if necessary. Check and replace if necessary. Check by replacing with a sensor known to be working. If faults disappear, replace. Check by substituting another control unit, replace if necessary.
Intermittent failure or short-comings in performance	Faulty trigger contacts on distributor	Check and replace as necessary.

Note: that very similar symptoms are produced by ignition trouble e.g., dirty points, points not opening properly etc.

Poor performance not covered by above checks	Faulty control unit	Check by substitution, replace if necessary. Before doing this make quite sure that the pressure sensor is not to blame.

71 Cable harness

A final point for the home mechanic - treat the cable harness with care. When removing plugs, lift back the rubber shrouds by their attached tongues and ease the plugs out of their sockets. Always hold the plugs, never pull on the wire. When putting the plugs back in again, locate them properly and push them in gently, though firmly. These two precautions will prevent the occurrence of that electrician's nightmare - the intermittent fault (caused by broken ends of wires just touching each other or pins and contacts not connecting properly) which is never there when you are looking for it but appears again as soon as you have reassembled the equipment.

A diagram of the cable harness is given in Fig. 3.84 together with a list of connections.

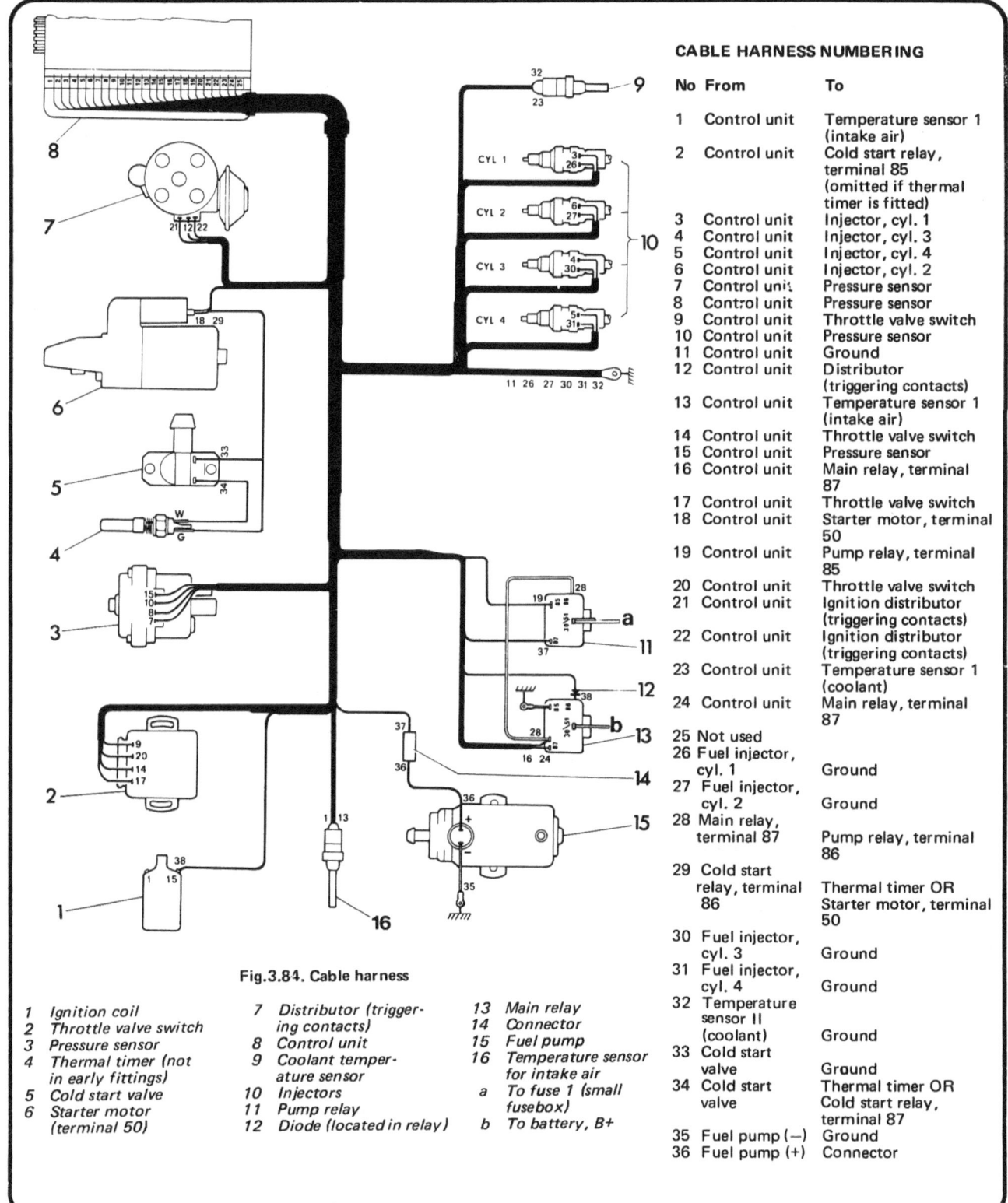

Fig.3.84. Cable harness

1	Ignition coil	7	Distributor (trigger-ing contacts)	13	Main relay
2	Throttle valve switch	8	Control unit	14	Connector
3	Pressure sensor	9	Coolant temper-ature sensor	15	Fuel pump
4	Thermal timer (not in early fittings)	10	Injectors	16	Temperature sensor for intake air
5	Cold start valve	11	Pump relay	a	To fuse 1 (small fusebox)
6	Starter motor (terminal 50)	12	Diode (located in relay)	b	To battery, B+

CABLE HARNESS NUMBERING

No	From	To
1	Control unit	Temperature sensor 1 (intake air)
2	Control unit	Cold start relay, terminal 85 (omitted if thermal timer is fitted)
3	Control unit	Injector, cyl. 1
4	Control unit	Injector, cyl. 3
5	Control unit	Injector, cyl. 4
6	Control unit	Injector, cyl. 2
7	Control unit	Pressure sensor
8	Control unit	Pressure sensor
9	Control unit	Throttle valve switch
10	Control unit	Pressure sensor
11	Control unit	Ground
12	Control unit	Distributor (triggering contacts)
13	Control unit	Temperature sensor 1 (intake air)
14	Control unit	Throttle valve switch
15	Control unit	Pressure sensor
16	Control unit	Main relay, terminal 87
17	Control unit	Throttle valve switch
18	Control unit	Starter motor, terminal 50
19	Control unit	Pump relay, terminal 85
20	Control unit	Throttle valve switch
21	Control unit	Ignition distributor (triggering contacts)
22	Control unit	Ignition distributor (triggering contacts)
23	Control unit	Temperature sensor 1 (coolant)
24	Control unit	Main relay, terminal 87
25	Not used	
26	Fuel injector, cyl. 1	Ground
27	Fuel injector, cyl. 2	Ground
28	Main relay, terminal 87	Pump relay, terminal 86
29	Cold start relay, terminal 86	Thermal timer OR Starter motor, terminal 50
30	Fuel injector, cyl. 3	Ground
31	Fuel injector, cyl. 4	Ground
32	Temperature sensor II (coolant)	Ground
33	Cold start valve	Ground
34	Cold start valve	Thermal timer OR Cold start relay, terminal 87
35	Fuel pump (−)	Ground
36	Fuel pump (+)	Connector

Chapter 4 Ignition system

Contents

Specifications

Spark plugs

B18A	Bosch W175 T35
B18B	Bosch W200 T35
B20A	Bosch W175 T35 or W200 T35
B20B	Bosch W200 T35 or W225 T35 (use W225 T35 if engine is driven hard)
B20E	Bosch W240 T35
B20F	Bosch W225 T35
Tightening torque	25.3 to 29.0 lb ft (3.5 to 4.0 kg m)
Gap ... (B18A 1967)	0.028 in (0.7 mm)
... (Other B18 engine)	0.025 in (0.65 mm)
Firing order	1 3 4 2

Distributor

B18 engines 1967	Bosch JFR4
Other B18 engines	Bosch 0231 153 003
B20, A, B	Bosch JFUR4
B20, E, F	Bosch JFURX4
Dwell angle	59° to 65° (1967 - 61° to 66°)
Gap	0.016 to 0.020 in (0.4 to 0.5 mm)
Condenser capacities	0.23 - 0.32 mF

Ignition coil

Type	Bosch 12V
Current consumption (engine not running)	Approx 4.5 to 5.0A at 13.5V

Ignition timing (stroboscope with vacuum unit disconnected)

B18A	21 - 23° BTDC at 1500 rpm
B18B	17 - 19° BTDC at 1500 rpm
B20A	14° BTDC at 600 - 800 rpm
B20B, E and F	10° BTDC at 600 - 800 rpm

Centrifugal advance

B18A to 1967	Start ...	2° 800 - 1000 rpm
		10° 1300 - 1850 rpm
	Finish ...	19° - 25° 2800 - 3300 rpm
B18A post 1967	Start ...	600 - 1000 rpm
		11° 1700 - 2000 rpm
	Finish ...	23° - 29° 4800 rpm
B18B	Start ...	600 - 1000 rpm
		11° 1700 - 2000 rpm
	Finish ...	23° - 29° 4800 rpm
B20A	Start ...	300 - 500 rpm
		5° 750 - 950 rpm
		10° 1220 - 1750 rpm (1210 - 1750 up to 1970)
	Finish ...	12° - 14° 2400 rpm

B20B to 1970	...	...	...	...	...	Start ...	500 - 600 RPM
							5° 675 - 775 RPM
							10° 1430 - 2100 RPM
						Finish	13.5° - 14.5° 2400 RPM
B20B post 1970	...	...	...	...	...	Start ...	500 - 600 RPM
							5° 625 - 720 RPM
							9° 1110 - 1630 RPM
						Finish	9.75° - 11.25° 1825 RPM
B20E, F	...	...	...	...	...	Start ...	375 - 550 RPM
							5° 610 - 800 RPM
							7° 970 - 1140 RPM
							9° 1200 - 1375 RPM
							11° 1300 - 1450 RPM
						Finish	11° - 13° 1500 RPM

Vacuum advance/retard (Inches and millimetres refer to vacuum measured on a mercury scale)

B18A (Advance)	...	...	...	...	...	Start ...	4 in. (100 mm)
						Finish	7° - 13° 5.12 in. (130 mm)
B20A (Advance)	...	...	...	...	...	Start ...	2.36 - 3.96 in. (60 - 100 mm)
							3° 4.13 - 5.71 in. (105 - 145 mm)
						Finish	4° - 6° 5.91 - 6.30 in. (150 - 160 mm)
B20B (Retard)	...	...	...	...	...	Start ...	6.30 - 9.45 in. (160 - 240 mm)
							2° 9.06 - 12.0 in. (230 - 305 mm)
						Finish	4.5° - 5.50° 11.0 - 12.6 in. (280 - 320 mm)
B20E, F (Retard)	...	...	...	...	...	Start ...	1.18 - 4.33 in. (30 - 110 mm)
							3° 3.15 - 4.92 in. (80 - 125 mm)
						Finish	4° - 6° 5.12 in. (130 mm)

1 General description

1 The ignition system on the Volvo 140 series comprises a coil which is connected to the battery via the ignition switch; a contact breaker which interrupts the supply to the coil at suitable moments; a condenser (often known as capacitor) connected across the contact breaker, and a distributor which ensures that the spark is channelled to the right spark plug. The distributor consists of a rotor arm which revolves at one half of the crankshaft speed. The rotor arm is surrounded by four terminals, each of which is connected to a spark plug. The end of the arm does not actually touch the plug terminals but the spark easily jumps over the small gap that is present when the arm is aligned with the terminal and appears at the selected plug. Thus during one revolution of the rotor arm (corresponding to two revolutions of the crankshaft) each of the plugs is selected once.

2 The rotor arm sits in a shaft which carries a four lobed cam. This cam operates the contact breaker which opens four times in one revolution of the rotor arm, ie twice per engine revolution.

3 The coil consists of two windings known as the primary or low tension (LT) winding and the secondary or high tension (HT) winding. These windings surround a core of a laminated magnetic material. The secondary winding contains many more turns than the primary winding, and most people envisage the coil as a sort of transformer which sets up a kind of alternating voltage produced at the primary by the contact breaker to produce 8000-10000 v at the HT terminal. This is only part of the story.

4 When current is flowing in the primary winding, the core becomes magnetized and in doing so stores a certain amount of energy - rather like the energy stored in a revolving flywheel. When the contact breaker opens and the path between the battery and the coil is interrupted, this stored energy keeps the current flowing in the circuit for a short time, and this current flows into the capacitor, producing a surprisingly high voltage across it - two or three hundred volts in fact. The capacitor is no more than two sheets of foil separated by a thin layer of insulating material, the foil area and the insulator thickness determining how much electrical charge it can absorb for a given rise in voltage, The measure of its ability to do this is known as its capacitance. The condenser (capacitor) must possess sufficient capacitance to ensure that the voltage does not build up too rapidly. When the contacts open, there is a little sparking

at first but they separate faster than the voltage builds up so the spark soon goes out and the electrical energy is stored in the condenser instead of being dissipated as a spark.

Thus when the contact breaker opens a comparatively high voltage builds up at the condenser end of the primary winding. The other end is held at the battery voltage, so the voltage change across the primary is the same as the voltage build up across the condenser. This voltage change gives rise to a stepped-up voltage change across the secondary. When the secondary voltage reaches a sufficiently high value, it produces a spark at the plug electrodes and this spark (which needs a much higher voltage to start it than to maintain it), dissipates most of the energy stored in the condenser.

5 To sum up, energy stored in the magnetization of the core of the coil when the contacts are closed is transferred to the condenser when the contacts are open, giving rise to a rapid increase of voltage across the primary which gives rise to a corresponding stepped-up voltage across the secondary. This voltage produces the spark which finally dissipates the stored energy. For the ignition system to give of its best, the initial storage must be as great as possible and as much as possible of the stored energy must be transferred to the spark. Initial energy storage depends on the square of the current flowing in the coil; if this is down to 70% of what it ought to be you only store half the energy. The current is directly proportional to battery voltage, which may be well down when a feeble battery is driving the starter. It also depends on the state of the contact breaker points - a good reason for having these clean and correctly gapped. The condenser can affect things in two ways; it can possess a partial short circuit across which the charge leaks away or it can possess insufficient capacitance (generally caused by an open circuit lead in which case it has no capacitance at all to speak of) in which case, as we have seen, energy is dissipated in sparking across the contact breaker. Finally, energy may be dissipated on the secondary side through electrical leakages - across damp surfaces for example, or due to tracking in the distributor cap. Leakage across damp surfaces is easy to get rid of, but leakage due to electrical breakdown, once started, usually necessitates the replacement of the part concerned.

6 The possibility of electrical breakdown is reduced, the effect of leakage due to damp is kept down, and energy transfer is improved if the plugs are kept in good condition and their gaps correctly set. This ensures that the secondary voltage needed to initiate the spark is low enough to avoid undue electrical stress in

the high tension circuits, the coil and the condenser. Don't be tempted, however, to close your plug gaps to below the recommended value. If your ignition system won't work properly unless this is done, there is something wrong with it which ought to be put right.

2 Contact breaker points - adjustment

1 Most people are familiar with the fixed contact which slides about when a locking screw is slackened off, allowing the gap between this contact and the moving contact (held up by one of the lobes on the cam) to be set to a specification width. We give some photographs showing this being carried out. There is a small notch on the outside edge of the contact and you can use a small screwdriver in this notch to give delicate control over the movement of the fixed contact.

2 The contact breaker (points) gap is specified as 0.016 - 0.020" (0.4 - 0.5 mm) for B18 and B20A engines and simply as 0.014" (0.35 mm) for B20B, E and F engines. We suggest that you deal with the first of these by setting so that a 0.018" (0.45 mm) feeler gauge will enter it and a 0.020" (0.5 mm) will not. For the other, choose 0.013" (0.32 mm) and 0.015" (0.38 mm) as your go/no-go values.

3 All this assumes that your contacts are in good condition. If

they are dirty or pitted, take them out and carefully clean them up or replace them.

3 Contact breaker points - removal, overhaul and replacement

1 Details of the contact breaker arrangements vary according to the model of the car, but the basic removal procedure is the same for all of them. The moving contact sits on a spindle from which it is insulated by bushes. It is held in position by a spring clip. A lead attached to this contact goes to a terminal which is connected to the ignition coil. The condenser is connected between this terminal and earth.

2 Having lifted off the rotor arm, the terminal just mentioned must be dismantled and the lead to the contact freed. The contact can then be detached from its spindle and removed complete with the spring which holds it inwards. The fixed contact simply needs detaching from the bracket plate to which it is screwed.

3 The surface of the contact breaker points should be flat, smooth and greyish in colour. If they fall short of the ideal, a limited amount of cleaning up can be done with a very fine file. You will probably find that the special metal of the contact surface does not extend right the way through the contact, so beware of filing too much, Be careful that when you have

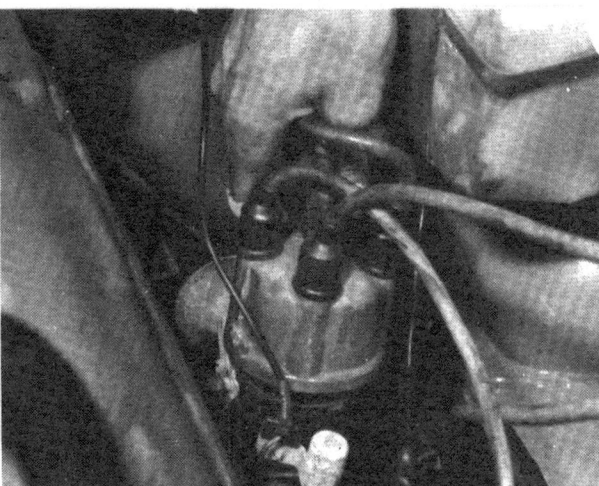

2.1a Removing the distributor cap ...

2.1b ... reveals the rotor arm and contact breaker points. Note that the LT lead has been taken off in this photo

2.1c The rotor arm is lifted off and the gap is adjusted

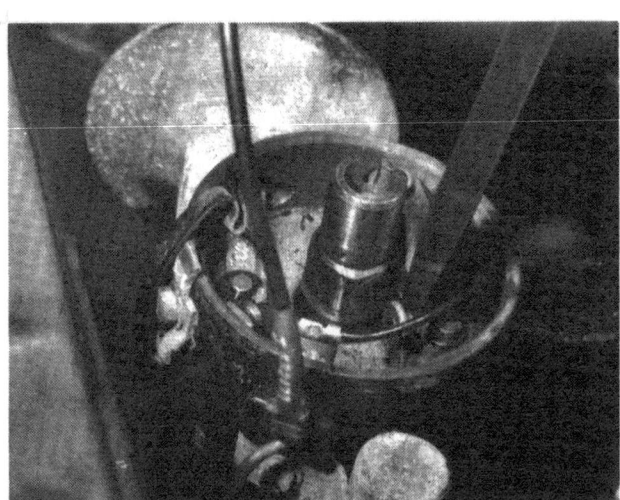

2.1d Checking the gap

finished the contact faces are flat and perpendicular to their axes so that when the contacts meet they touch over a large area.

4 If the contacts are in such a state that they cannot be restored by a moderate amount of filing, they should be replaced. Fitting new or cleaned up contacts must be followed by setting the gap as described in the previous section.

4 Condenser - removal, testing and replacement

1 The function of the condenser has already been considered in Section 1. It fails less often than is commonly supposed, but nevertheless it does sometimes deteriorate in a way that is not easy to detect directly. If you get excessive sparking at the contacts - perhaps accompanied by signs of burning on the breaker points - and your plugs are in good condition with correctly set gaps, the condenser may well have lost capacitance or become entirely open circuit. If your condenser is short circuiting, you will get no spark at the contacts or anywhere else. If it is partly short circuited, you may get a rather feeble spark.

2 There is only one reliable test that you can carry out without special equipment - substitution by a condenser known to be good. It does not have to be exactly the same pattern, but the suspected condenser must be disconnected from the terminal before the substitute is (temporarily) connected up.

5 Distributor - lubrication

1 It is important that the distributor is lubricated every 6000 miles (10000 km). There are three lubricating operations.

2 To lubricate the distributor shaft, fill the oil cup (clearly shown in Fig. 4.2) with engine oil.

3 Give the contact surface of the cam and the cam follower a thin coating of grease (Castrol LM). Do the same for the triggering contact cam followers and their cam (20, Fig. 4.4) where fitted.

4 To lubricate the ignition advance mechanism, remove the distributor arm and put two or three drops of light oil (Castrol Everyman) on the wick at the top of the distributor shaft.

5 Be careful not to use too much lubricant, because if any gets on to the contact breaker points it will produce burning and misfiring.

6 Distributor - removal and replacement

1 Presumably you are not going to turn the engine when the distributor is removed. Unless you are dismantling the engine set it to a known position, eg 'top-dead-centre' on compression stroke in No 1 cylinder, before taking out the distributor. To do this take out the spark plugs so that you can turn the engine over easily by hauling on the fan belt. Remove the distributor cap and turn the engine until the timing marks on the crankshaft pulley indicate 'top-dead-centre' (see Chapter 1, Section 9, photograph 9.7) and at the same time the rotor arm is pointing to the distributor cap segment which is connected to No 1 spark plug (or would be if the cap was on and the spark plug was in).

2 Mark the distributor so that you know the exact position of the rotor arm and the exact position that the distributor case occupies in its clamp.

3 Disconnect the battery lead from the terminal on the side of the distributor.

4 Undo the bolts holding down the distributor clamp and lift out the clamp and distributor assembly as a unit (see Chapter 1, Section 7, photograph 7.11a).

7 Distributor - dismantling

1 Figs. 4.3 and 4.4 between them give a pretty good idea of the bits and pieces that go to make up the distributor mechanism. In B18 engines, the vacuum advance/retard unit is not fitted. Before you start taking things apart, give the outside case a good clean with paraffin.

2 Pull off the distributor arm or if necessary lever it off gently with a screwdriver. Remove the circlip for the pull rod from the vacuum unit and take off the unit (Fig. 4.1).

3 Mark the location of the spring clips for the distributor cap (to save trouble on reassembly) and remove them. Remove the terminal for the low tension lead and the capacitor. Your distributor may possibly be different from that shown in the illustration, but the principle is the same. The terminal is screwed through to the breaker plate and must be removed before this can be released.

4 With the LT terminal removed, the breaker plate can be lifted out, revealing the centrifugal advance mechanism.

Fig. 4.1 Removing the vacuum regulator

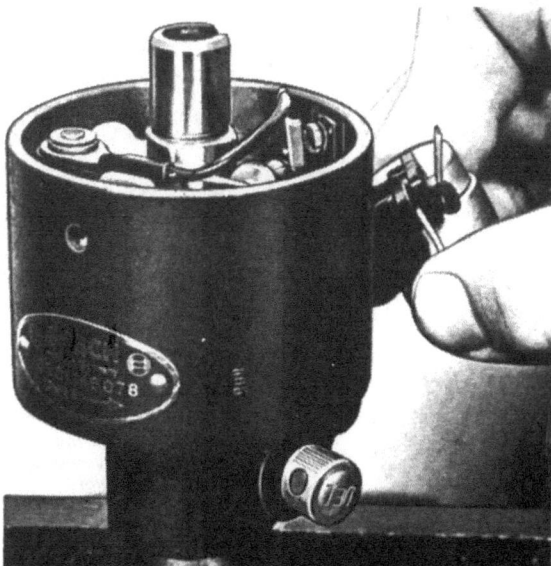

Fig. 4.2 Removing the low tension terminal and condenser

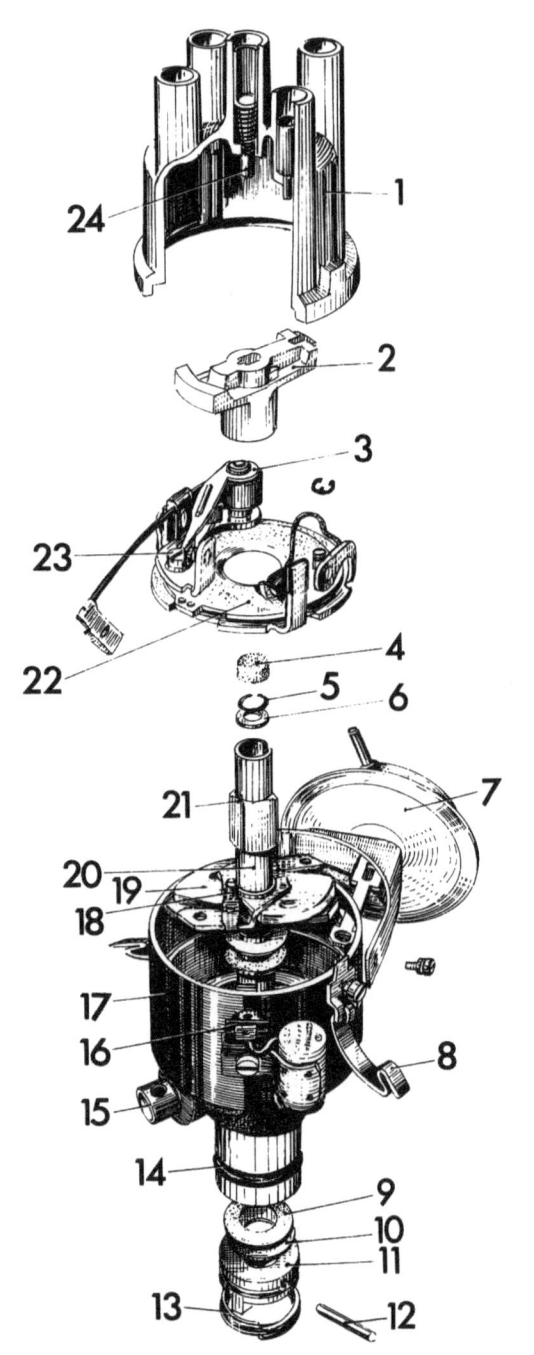

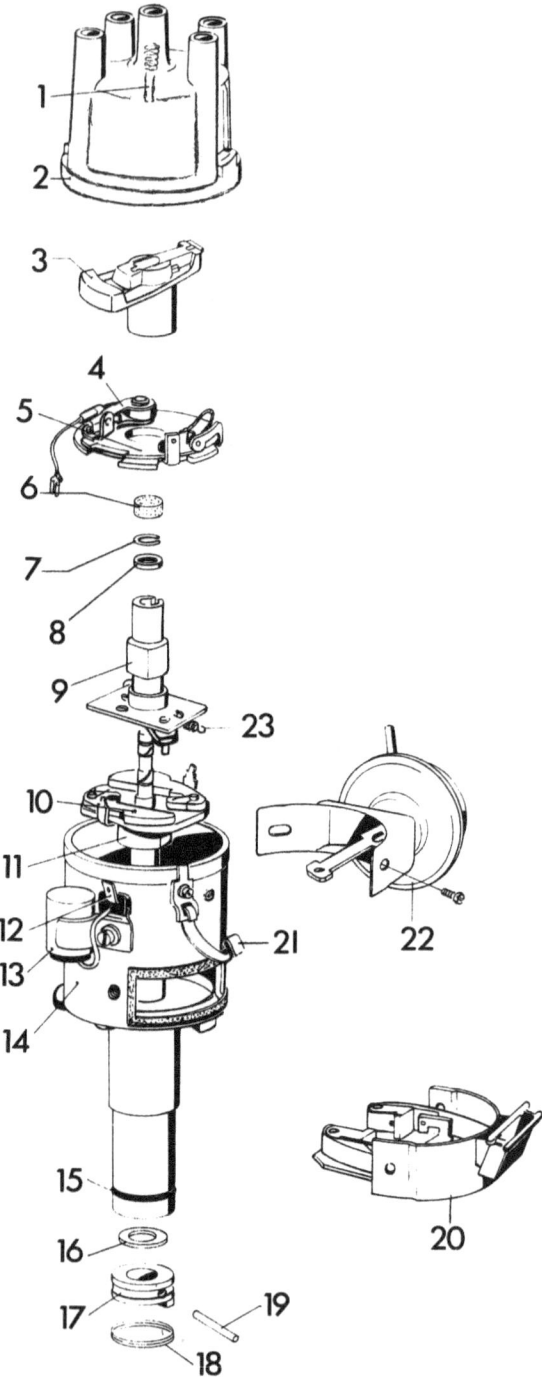

Fig. 4.3 Distributor - B20 carburettor engines
(vacuum regulator not fitted on some B18 engines)

1 Distributor cap	13 Resilient ring
2 Distributor arm	14 Rubber seal
3 Contact breaker	15 Lubricator
4 Lubricating felt	16 Primary connection
5 Circlip	17 Distributor housing
6 Washer	18 Centrifugal governor spring
7 Vacuum regulator	19 Centrifugal weight
8 Cap clasp	20 Breaker camshaft
9 Fibre washer	21 Breaker cam
10 Steel washer	22 Breaker plate
11 Driving collar	23 Lock screw for breaker
12 Lock pin	contacts
	24 Rod brush (carbon)

Fig. 4.4 Distributor - B20 fuel injection engines

1 Rod brush (carbon)	13 Capacitor
2 Distributor cap	14 Distributor body
3 Distributor arm	15 Rubber seal
4 Contact breaker	16 Washers
5 Breaker plate	17 Driving collar
6 Lubricating felt	18 Resilient ring
7 Circlip	19 Lock pin
8 Washer	20 Contact device
9 Breaker cam	21 Lock clasp for distr. cap
10 Centrifugal weight	22 Vacuum regulator
11 Cam for triggering contacts	23 Centrifugal governor spring
12 Primary terminal	

5 Looking at this, you will see that the breaker cam is free to move relative to the distributor drive shaft. It has a plate integral with it with projections which engage with two small weights attached to the top of the distributor shaft. These weights and the top of the distributor shaft are clearly shown in Fig.4.5. When the weights move outwards under centrifugal force as the distributor shaft rotates they move the distributor cam round and so advance the ignition. A pair of small, but important, springs (23, Fig. 4.4) provide opposition for the weights to push against; upon these springs the proper working of the mechanism depends and you should be careful not to distort them in any way when you remove them. In a number of cases they are not identical, so watch for this and note which spring goes where, marking the distributor if necessary to ensure that they go back in the right place. If you have to replace them, be sure that you get the right ones for your particular distributor.

6 With these springs removed, mark the cam and distributor shaft so that on reassembly the cam goes back in the correct position. Now hold the cam in a vice with protected jaws as shown in Fig.4.6 and tap the distributor housing with a hide mallet or similar to release the breaker cam which is held in position by a clip. Draw the cam off the shaft, bringing with it the lubricating wick, the clip and a washer (7, 8 and 9, Fig. 4.4).

7 Undo the screws and remove the contact device (20, Fig. 4.4), where this is fitted.

8 Remove the resilient ring (18, Fig. 4.4) and mark the shaft and driving collar to ensure that when you put the collar back it is the correct way round. Drive out the pin (19, Fig. 4.4) and take the collar off the shaft.

9 Take the shaft out of the housing, being careful not to lose any of the spacing washers on the shaft.

10 Remove the spring clips which hold the centrifugal weights to the shaft and take off the weights (Fig.4.5).

Fig. 4.5 Distributor drive shafts and weights (the cam and the governor springs have been removed)

Fig. 4.6 Tapping the housing releases the circlip holding the cam to the drive shaft

---

8 Distributor - inspection and repair

1 Thoroughly wash all mechanical parts in petrol or paraffin and wipe dry using a clean non-fluffy rag.

2 Check the contact breaker points as described in Section 3.

3 Check the distributor cap for signs of tracking, indicated by a thin black line between segments. Replace the cap if this is evident. Check that the carbon brush moves freely in the centre of the distributor cap and replace it if it is worn or in bad condition.

4 If the metal portion of the rotor arm is badly burned or loose, renew the arm. Slight burning can be cleaned up with a fine file.

5 Examine the fit of the contact breaker plate on the base plate and also check the breaker arm pivot for looseness or wear. If necessary replace the plate.

6 Examine the centrifugal weights and pivot pins for wear in particular, the holes in the centrifugal weights should not be oval or deformed in any other way. The importance of the springs has already been mentioned and these should be checked and renewed (if spare parts are available) if necessary.

7 Check the fit of the breaker cam on the distributor shaft. Play between the distributor shaft and the breaker cam must not exceed 0.004'' (0.1 mm). If the breaker cam itself shows signs of wear or scoring, replace it.

8 The play between the distributor housing and the drive shaft should not exceed 0.008'' (0.2 mm). If the play is excessive, replace the bushes and, if this is insufficient, also the shaft.

9 Fig.4.7 shows the assembly of bushes and washers on the drive shaft. Replacement of the old bushes is a matter of driving or pulling them out and pressing or gently tapping the new ones in, one from each end with the felt lubricator between them. The lubricator and the bushes should be soaked in oil for at least half an hour before fitting. The fibre washers at each end of the shaft should be next to the housing. The end play in the shaft should lie between 0.004 - 0.010'' (0.1 - 0.25 mm). If necessary this can be adjusted by altering the number of spacing washers on the distributor shaft.

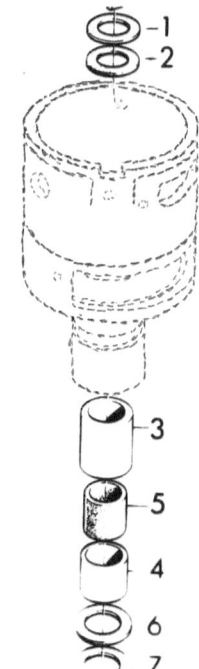

Fig. 4.7 Spacing washers and bushes for the drive shaft

1 Spacing washer
2 Fibre washer
3 Bush
4 Bush
5 Lubricating felt
6 Fibre washer
7 Spacing washer

Extra spacing washers may be used to adjust clearance

9 Distributor - reassembly

1 Assemble the driving shaft into the housing as described in the previous paragraph (Section 8, paragraph 9).

2 One of the most important aspects of reassembly is lubrication. The cam lobes and the cam followers should all be lightly coated with grease (Castrol LM) and so should the weights (Castrol LM). A touch of grease should also be applied where the pull rod from the vacuum regulator is attached to the breaker plate. Do not be too free with grease in this area - otherwise it may end up on the breaker contacts.

3 Assembly generally is a straightforward reversal of the dismantling procedure. To assemble the breaker cam on the driveshaft, slide the washer and circlip down the inside of the cam (using a suitable sleeve or two thin metal strips) until the circlip clicks into position. If you have replaced some of the parts whose position you marked when you were taking the distributor apart, be particularly careful about getting the new ones in the right position - you can easily be sure of this by checking with the old parts which you marked.

4 Check the action of the weights in the fully advanced and fully retarded positions and ensure that there is no binding.

5 Finally set the contact breaker points as described in Section 2.

10 Ignition timing

1 The ignition timing is varied with engine speed and loading on B20 engines by a centrifugal advance mechanism whose workings have already been considered (see Section 7, paragraph 5) and by a vacuum diaphragm which, as we have seen, moves the breaker plate to and fro by means of a push rod. The centrifugal system advances the ignition as engine speed increases, and the vacuum system advances the ignition with increase of engine vacuum for all engines where it is fitted except B20E and B20F unless exhaust emission control is fitted. In this case it is arranged to retard the system as the vacuum is increased, and is connected to a point between the throttle and the engine. In this case the ignition is retarded when the throttle is closed while the engine is running instead of being advanced when the throttle is open as is the usual case. On B18B engines vacuum advance/retard is not fitted.

2 It is not easy to check that these devices are operating to specification, but if they have been properly maintained it is a fairly safe bet that if they are working at all, they are working within specification. The only point to watch in the mechanical system is the strength of the springs; if you are in doubt about these you can replace them - being sure you get the right springs for the particular model.

3 It is quite easy to check that the vacuum regulator is working properly. Disconnect its pushrod from the breaker plate and detach the unit from the housing by undoing its two fixing screws. To avoid the possibility of straining the vacuum pipe connection, do not attempt to remove the unit with the pipe connected. When it is removed, reconnect the pipe and run the engine, opening and closing the throttle, when you will be able to see the pushrod moving in and out as the vacuum varies.

4 To set the basic timing, take out the plugs and turn the engine by means of the fan belt until No 1 cylinder is at 'top-dead-centre' on its compression stroke, unless of course you had already put the engine in this position before you took the distributor off as described in Section 6, paragraph 1. If necessary you can easily identify the compression stroke by putting your thumb over the plug hole of No 1 cylinder as you turn the engine and feeling the air being driven out. Having identified the position, turn the engine backwards and then forwards again until it comes up to 12° BTDC - B18A to 1967; 15° BTDC - B18A post 1967; 11° BTDC - B18B; 5° BTDC for other models, as observed on the crankshaft pulley timing scale (see Chapter 1, photograph 9.7). Now loosen the clamp holding

the distributor housing and turn this housing until the contact is just opening. The simplest way to check that the contact is opening is to connect a 12 v bulb between the low tension terminal on the distributor and earth; with the ignition switched on this bulb will light up when the contacts are open.

5 Setting the timing in this way will certainly enable you to start the engine and run it, but because of the characteristics of the centrifugal and vacuum controls it cannot give you the final answer. This can only be got by checking the ignition timing using a stroboscopic test lamp, and if available, a tachometer.

6 To do this, connect a stroboscopic test lamp in accordance with the manufacturer's instructions. Disconnect the vacuum line from the distributor (On B20 engines this must be temporarily plugged). Run the engine at the speed given in the Specifications and point the stroboscopic lamp at the timing marks on the crankshaft pulley. Alter the position of the distributor to obtain the correct timing for the particular engine.

7 On completion disconnect the test lamp and tachometer (if used).

11 Spark plugs and HT leads

1 The correct functioning of the spark plugs is vital for the proper running and efficient operation of the engine.

2 At intervals of 6000 miles (10000 km) the plugs should be removed, examined, cleaned and if worn excessively, renewed. The condition of the spark plug can tell much about the general condition of the engine (Fig. 4.8).

3 If the insulator nose of the spark plug is clean and white, with no deposits, this is indicative of a weak mixture, or too hot a plug (a hot plug transfers heat away from the electrodes slowly - a cold plug transfers heat away quickly).

4 If the insulator nose is covered with hard black looking deposits, then this is indicative that the mixture is too rich. Should the plug be black and oily then it is likely that the engine is fairly worn as well as the mixture being too rich.

5 If the insulator nose is covered with light tan to greyish brown deposits, then the mixture is correct, and it is likely that the engine is in good condition.

6 If there are any traces of long brown tapering stains on the outside of the white portion of the plug, then the plug will have to be renewed, as this shows that there is a faulty joint between the plug body and the insulator, and compression is being allowed to leak away.

7 Plugs should be cleaned by a sand blasting machine, which will free them from carbon more completely than cleaning by hand. The machine will also test the condition of the plugs under compression. Any plug that fails to spark at the recommended pressure should be renewed.

8 The spark plug gap is of considerable importance, as, if it is too large or too small the size of the spark and its efficiency will be seriously impaired. The spark plug gap should be set to 0.028 - 0.032" (0.7 - 0.8 mm) (See Fig. 4.8).

9 To set it, measure the gap with a feeler gauge, and then bend open, or close, the outer plug electrode until the correct gap is achieved. The centre electrode should never be bent as this may crack the insulation and cause plug failure, if nothing worse.

10 When replacing the plugs, remember to use new washers and replace the leads from the distributor cap in the correct firing order which is 1,3,4,2 No 1 cylinder being the one nearest the fan.

11 The plug leads require no maintenance other than being kept clean and wiped over regularly. At intervals of 6000 miles (10000 km) however, pull each lead off the plug in turn and remove it from the distributor cap. Water can seep down these joints giving rise to a white corrosive deposit which must be carefully removed from the end of each cable. At the same time, check that the suppressor connections are in good condition. If cracked or damaged they should be replaced.

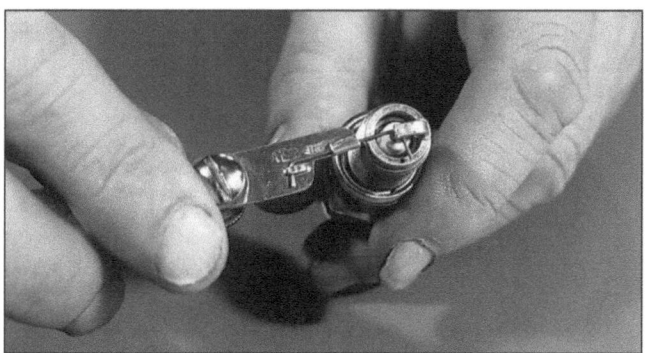

Electrode gap check – use a wire type gauge for best results.

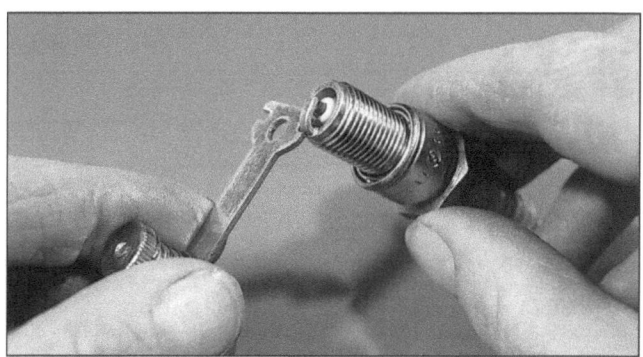

Electrode gap adjustment – bend the side electrode using the correct tool.

Normal condition – A brown, tan or grey firing end indicates that the engine is in good condition and that the plug type is correct.

Ash deposits – Light brown deposits encrusted on the electrodes and insulator, leading to misfire and hesitation. Caused by excessive amounts of oil in the combustion chamber or poor quality fuel/oil.

Carbon fouling – Dry, black sooty deposits leading to misfire and weak spark. Caused by an over-rich fuel/air mixture, faulty choke operation or blocked air filter.

Oil fouling – Wet oily deposits leading to misfire and weak spark. Caused by oil leakage past piston rings or valve guides (4-stroke engine), or excess lubricant (2-stroke engine).

Overheating – A blistered white insulator and glazed electrodes. Caused by ignition system fault, incorrect fuel, or cooling system fault.

Worn plug – Worn electrodes will cause poor starting in damp or cold conditions and will also waste fuel.

12 Ignition system - fault symptoms

There are two general symptoms of ignition faults. Either the engine will not fire, or the engine is difficult to start and misfires. If it is a regular misfire, ie the engine is only running on two or three cylinders, the fault is almost sure to be in the high tension circuit, If the misfiring is intermittent, the fault could be in either the high or low tension circuits. If the engine stops suddenly, or will not start at all, it is likely that the fault is in the low tension circuit. Loss of power and overheating, apart from faulty carburettor settings, are normally due to faults in the distributor, or incorrect ignition timing.

13 Fault diagnosis - engine fails to start

1   If the engine fails to start and it was running normally when it was last used, first check that there is fuel in the petrol tank. If the engine turns over normally on the starter motor and the battery is evidently well charged, then the fault may be in either the high or low tension circuits. First check the HT circuit.
Note: If the battery is known to be fully charged, the ignition comes on, and the starter motor fails to turn the engine, **Check the tightness of the leads on the battery terminals** and also the secureness of the earth lead to the **connection to the body.** It is quite common for the leads to have worked loose, even if they look and feel secure. If one of the battery terminal posts gets very hot when trying to operate the starter motor this is a sure indication of a faulty connection to that terminal.
2   One of the commonest reasons for bad starting is wet or damp spark plug leads and distributor. Remove the distributor cap. If the condensation is visible, internally dry the cap with a rag and wipe over the leads. Replace the cap.
3   If the engine still fails to start, check that current is reaching the plugs by disconnecting each plug lead in turn at the spark plug ends and holding the end of the cable about 3/16 inch (4.7 mm) away from the cylinder block. Spin the engine on the starter motor. For automatic transmission models a second person should operate the ignition/starter switch.
4   Sparking between the end of the cable and the block should be fairly strong with a regular blue spark (hold the lead with rubber to avoid electric shocks). If current is reaching the spark plugs, then remove them and clean and regap them to 0.028''-0.032'' (0.7-0.8 mm). The engine should now start.
5   If it is still difficult to start or misfires, disconnect the HT lead from the centre terminal of the distributor and hold it close to the block as you did with the plug leads, and spin the engine as before, when a rapid succession of blue sparks between the end of the lead and the block indicate that the coil is in order, and that either the distributor cap is cracked, the carbon brush is stuck or worn, the rotor arm is faulty, or the contact points are burnt, pitted or dirty. If the parts are in bad shape, clean and reset them as described in Section 3.
6   If there are no sparks from the end of the lead from the coil, then check the connections of the lead to the coil and distributor cap, and if they are in order, check out the low tension circuit starting with the battery.
7   Switch on the ignition and turn the crankshaft so that the contact breaker points have fully opened. Then, with either a 20 volt voltmeter or bulb and length of wire, check that current from the battery is reaching terminal 50 on the starter solenoid switch. No reading indicates that there is a fault in the cable to the switch or in the connections at the switch or at the battery terminals. Alternatively, the battery earth lead may not be properly earthed to the body.

8   If in order, then check that current is reaching the ignition switch by connecting the voltmeter to the ignition switch input terminal (terminal 50, blue/yellow cable) and earth. No reading indicates a break in the wire or a faulty connection at the switch or solenoid.
9   If the correct reading (approximately 12 volts) is obtained check the output terminal on the ignition switch (the one with the yellow cable) no reading means that the ignition switch is broken. Replace with a new unit and start the car.
10 If current is reaching the ignition switch output terminal, then check link between fuses 3 and 4 on the fuse unit with the voltmeter. No reading indicates a break in the wire or loose connections between the link and the terminal. Remedy and the car should now start.
11 Check the switch terminal on the coil. No reading indicates loose connections or a broken wire from the terminal on the fuse unit. If this proves to be at fault, remedy and start the car.
12 Check the contact breaker terminal on the coil (the lead to the distributor is connected to it). If no reading is recorded on the voltmeter then the coil is broken and must be replaced. The car should start when a new coil has been fitted.
13 If a reading is obtained at the - terminal then check the wire from the coil for loose connections etc. The final check on the low tension circuit is across the contact breaker points which must be open for this test. No reading indicates a faulty condenser, which when replaced will enable the car to finally start.

14 Fault diagnosis - engine misfires

1   If the engine misfires regularly, run it at a fast idling speed, and short out each of the spark plugs in turn by placing an insulated screwdriver across the plug terminal to the cylinder block.
2   No difference in engine running will be noticed when the plug in the defective cylinder is short circuited. Short circuiting the working plugs will accentuate the misfire.
3   Remove the plug lead from the end of the defective plug and hold it about 3/16 in (4.7 mm) away from the block. Restart the engine. If sparking is fairly strong and regular the fault must lie in the spark plug.
4   The plug may be loose, the insulation may be cracked or the electrodes may have burnt away giving too wide a gap for the spark to jump across. Worse still, the earth electrode may have broken off. Either renew the plug, or clean it, reset the gap and then test it.
5   If there is no spark at the end of the plug lead, or if it is weak and intermittent, check the ignition lead from the distrbutor to the plug. If the insulation is cracked or damaged, renew the lead. Check the connections at the distributor cap.
6   If there is still no spark, examine the distributor cap carefully for signs of tracking. This can be recognised by a very thin black line running between two or more segments, or between a segment and some other part of the distributor. These lines are paths which now conduct electricity across the cap thus letting it run to earth. The only answer is to fit a new distrbutor cap.
7   Apart from the ignition timing being incorrect, other causes of misfiring have already been dealt with under the section dealing with failure of the engine to start.
8   If the ignition timing is too far retarded, it should be noted that the engine will tend to overheat, and there will be quite a noticeable drop in power. If the engine is overheating and power is down, and the ignition is correct, then the carburettor should be checked, as it is likely that this is where the fault lies. See Chapter 3 for details.

Chapter 5 Clutch

Contents

Specifications

Clutch type	Single dry plate, diaphragm sprung
Manufacturer	Fichtel and Sachs or Borg and Beck
Size	8½ in. (20.3 cm)
Total friction area	68 sq. in. (440 cm^2)
Clutch pedal travel	4.91 - 5.12 in. (125 - 130 mm)
Throw-out yoke travel	0.12 in. (3 mm)

1 General description

1 The Volvo 140 series (other than those with automatic transmission) are fitted with an 8½" diameter diaphragm spring clutch operated by a cable which is directly connected to the clutch pedal. An overall picture is given in Fig. 5.2, and the two types of clutch fitted, which are interchangeable, are shown in Fig. 5.1.

2 A steel cover dowelled and bolted to the rear face of the flywheel has attached to it a pressure plate which (when the clutch is engaged) clamps a disc covered with high friction lining material to the flywheel. This disc has a central hub which engages with splines on the gearbox input shaft (first motion shaft). Thus when the clutch is engaged, the flywheel drives the gearbox through the disc and the whole assembly rotates at engine speed.

3 The gearbox input shaft is kept in alignment with the crankshaft because the end of it is held in a small bearing which is set in the end of the crankshaft. This bearing is known as the pilot bearing.

4 The pressure holding this sandwich together is exerted by a diaphragm spring fitted to the clutch cover. A diagram of this spring is given in Fig. 5.3 and you can see the central part of it quite clearly in the photograph.

In order to disengage the clutch, pressure is applied to the central part of the spring by a thrust bearing actuated by a lever attached to the flywheel housing. A look at Fig.5.3 shows how this pressure acts to draw back the outer edge of the spring, so withdrawing the pressure plate. When the pressure plate is drawn back, the friction disc is no longer sandwiched between the flywheel and the pressure plate and ceases to be driven by the

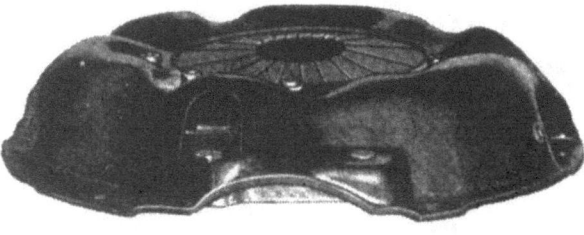
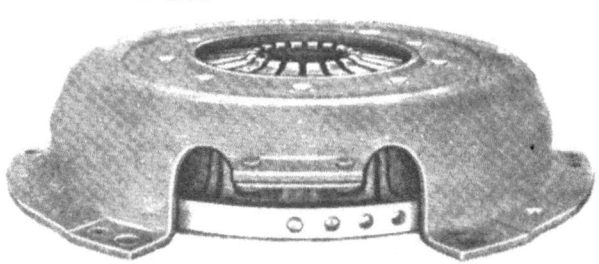

Fig. 5.1 Two types of clutch. Complete assemblies are interchangeable, but not individual parts or friction discs.

1.4 This view of the clutch in the car clearly shows the segmented diaphragm spring

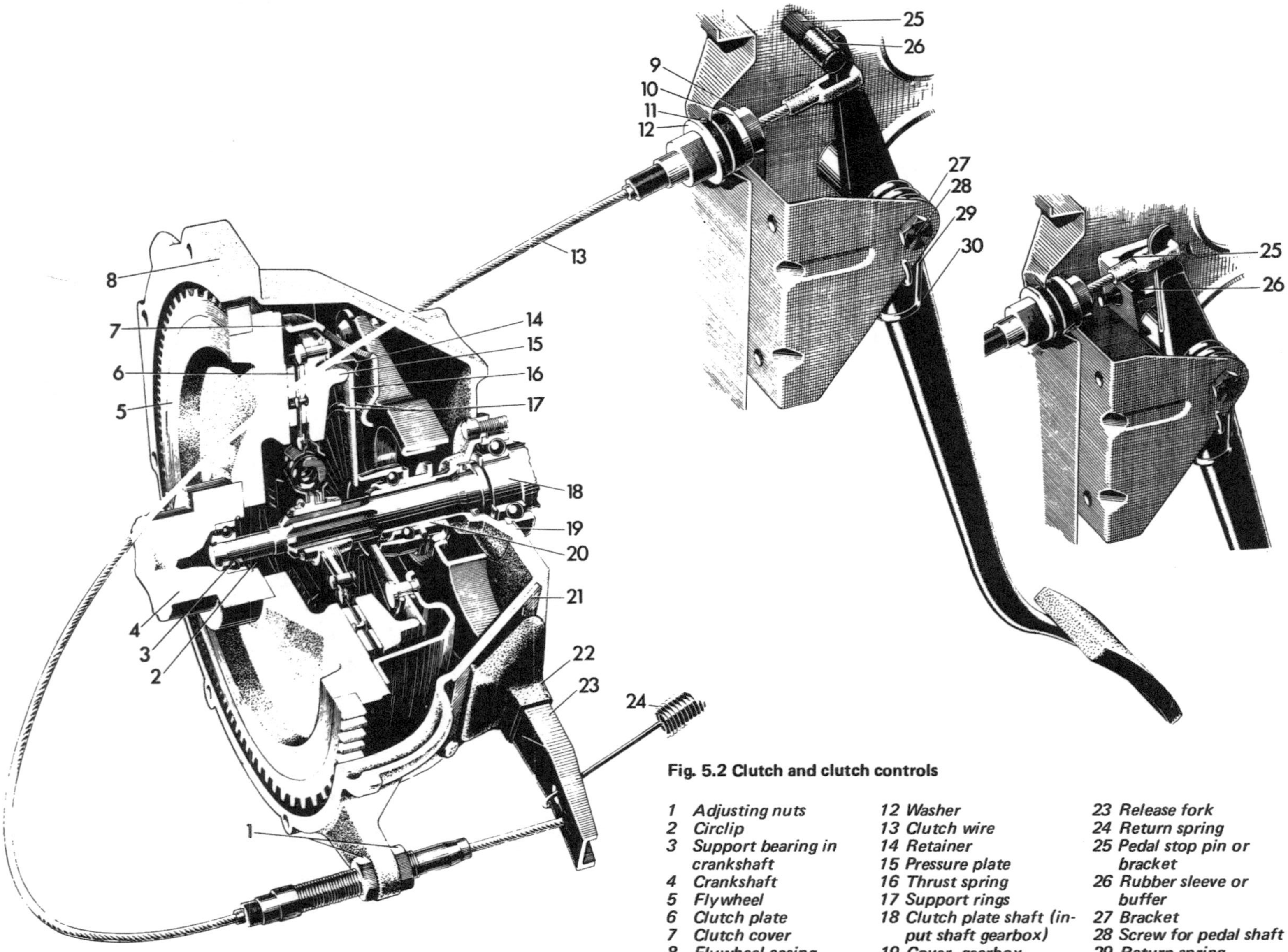

Fig. 5.2 Clutch and clutch controls

1 Adjusting nuts
2 Circlip
3 Support bearing in crankshaft
4 Crankshaft
5 Flywheel
6 Clutch plate
7 Clutch cover
8 Flywheel casing
9 Nut
10 Washer
11 Rubber bush
12 Washer
13 Clutch wire
14 Retainer
15 Pressure plate
16 Thrust spring
17 Support rings
18 Clutch plate shaft (input shaft gearbox)
19 Cover, gearbox
20 Release bearing
21 Holding plate
22 Dust cover
23 Release fork
24 Return spring
25 Pedal stop pin or bracket
26 Rubber sleeve or buffer
27 Bracket
28 Screw for pedal shaft
29 Return spring
30 Clutch pedal

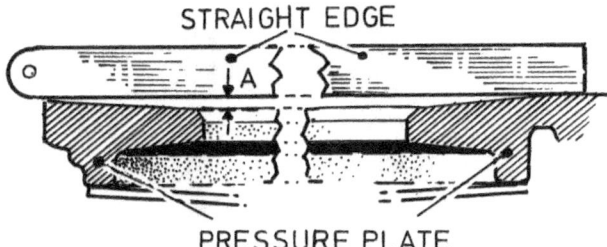

STRAIGHT EDGE

A

PRESSURE PLATE

Fig. 5.3 Diagrammatic section through clutch assembly. Dimension "A", representing deviation from flat on driving face, must not exceed 0.0012" (0.03 mm).

flywheel.

5   The thrust bearing is concentric with the gearbox input shaft, but in no way connected to it; the front part of the bearing revolves when it is in contact with the spring but the back part is stationary being attached to the release arm which is also stationary. When the clutch is engaged, the front of the bearing is not in contact with the spring and so does not revolve.

6   The central hub of the clutch friction disc is sprung in order to absorb transmission shocks and to help ensure a smooth take-off.

2   Clutch adjustment

1   Engagement and disengagement of the clutch depends on the movement of the clutch lever which is actuated by the clutch cable. When the lever is pulled back, the clutch is disengaged, and when the lever is allowed to go forwards the bearing on the other end of it will move backwards and the centre part of the spring will also move backwards until the disc is firmly sandwiched between the plate and the flywheel. Once this has happened, the spring will cease to follow further movement of the bearing which will continue to move backward until the clutch cable is taut. It is obviously desirable that there should be some clearance between the spring and the bearing when the clutch is engaged.

2   The friction disc will wear in use and become thinner. When this has happened, the pressure plate will move a little closer to the flywheel when the clutch is engaged. The centre part of the spring will correspondingly move a little further backwards and the clearance between the spring and the thrust bearing will be reduced.

3   The clearance is restored by adjusting the position of the clutch operating cable in the bracket on the flywheel housing where it is held by two fixing nuts (photo). There should be 0.12" (3 mm) free travel between the ball on the operating cable and the clutch release lever when the lever is pulled back against the action of the return spring until the thrust bearing meets the clutch diaphragm spring. This free travel will be felt as free play movement of the clutch pedal. It is most important that this free play is always present. If you get to the stage where you cannot obtain it by bringing the cable further through the bracket it is high time you replaced the friction disc.

3   Clutch cable - removal and replacement

1   Unhook the return spring for the release lever (photo).

2   Slacken off the nuts connecting the cable to the flywheel housing and disconnect the cable from the lever (photo).

3   Remove the panel under the dashboard covering the pedal mounting. Take off the bearing bolt for the clutch pedal and unhook the pedal from the cable (see Fig.5.4)

4   Undo the nut fastening the cable casing to the body near the pedal mounting.

2.3 These fixing nuts provide for clutch clearance adjustment

3.1 Return spring for clutch release lever

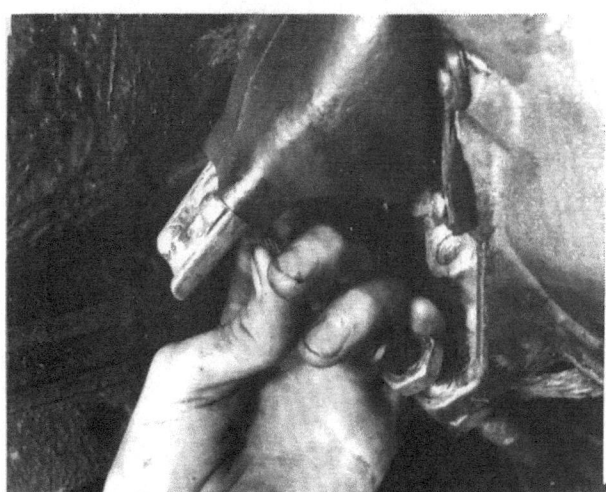

3.2 It's difficult to unhitch the clutch cable unless you slacken off the fixing nuts first

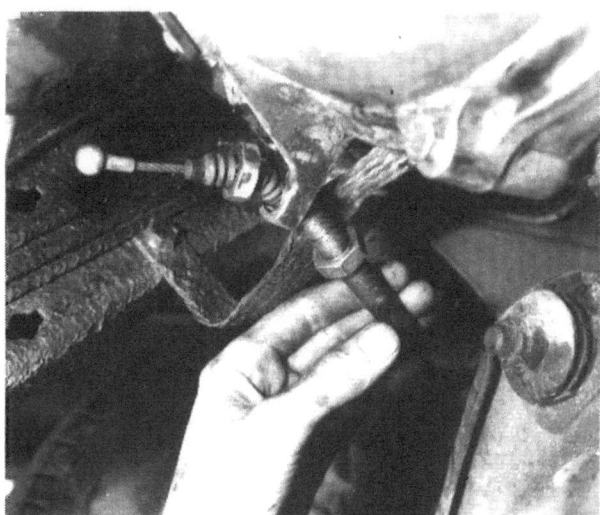

3.6 Removing the clutch cable

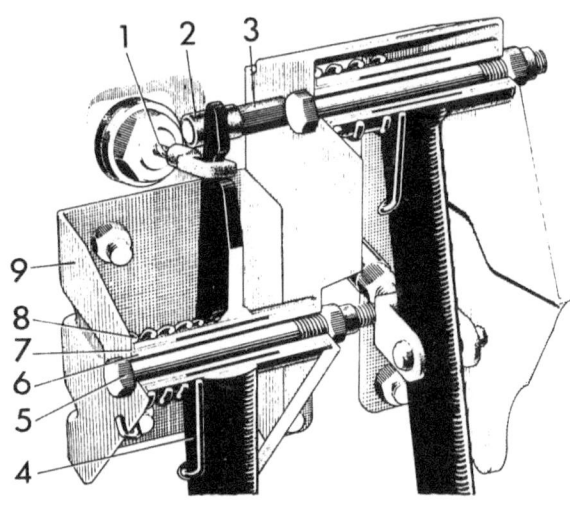

Fig. 5.4 Clutch pedal mounting details.

1 Clutch wire
2 Rubber sleeve
3 Pedal stop
4 Clutch pedal
5 Bolt
6 Shaft
7 Bush
8 Return spring
9 Bracket

5.3 Clutch release lever and thrust bearing

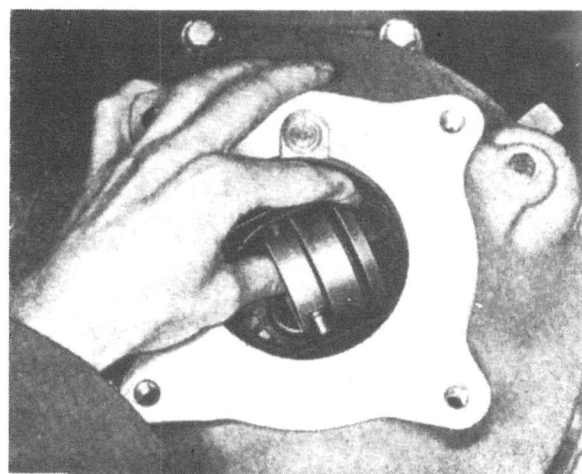

Fig. 5.5 Removing the thrust bearing

7.1 This friction disc is in excellent condition (notice which way round it fits)

Fig. 5.6 Removing the clutch

5 Starting from where the pedal emerges from the far wall under the bonnet, trace its route through the engine compartment to the bracket on the flywheel housing, releasing the various clamps you will find along the way. If you have a left-hand drive car, you will think that this instruction is ridiculous, but in a car with right-hand drive the cable enters the bonnet on the opposite side of the engine and comes right round the front of the engine on its way to the flywheel housing, being clamped at four different points.

6 With the cable now free to move about, it is a simple matter to release it from the bracket on the flywheel housing (see photo) and remove it from the car.

4 Clutch pedal and mounting - overhaul

1 Remove the panel under the dashboard which covers the pedal mounting. Details of the clutch pedal mounting are shown in Fig. 5.4.

2 Unhook the return spring for the pedal, slacken the nut and remove the pedal pivot bolt. Disconnect the pedal from the wire and remove the pedal.

3 The pedal runs on bushes bearing on a hollow shaft through which the bearing bolt passes. Take this shaft out, give the whole assembly a good clean and inspect for signs of wear and excessive play between the pedal and the shaft.

4 If necessary, drive out the bushes and replace them.

5 Inspect the tubular shaft for signs of wear (it is not very likely that you will find any) and replace if necessary.

6 Replace the return spring unless you are perfectly sure that it is all right. It is most annoying if you have to do the work all over again because a silly little spring breaks, only weeks after you have had an assembly like this to pieces.

7 Grease the shaft, bushes and spring generously and reassemble. Remember to hook the cable on to the pedal before you bolt it to the mounting.

8 If the pedal stop is mounted on an adjustable bracket, set this bracket so that there is between ½" and 5/8" (1.25 - 1.41 cms) of free play on the pedal corresponding to the free play in the cable. No adjustment is provided on the pedal stop where this consists simply of a pin; you should get around ½" (1.25 cms).

5 Clutch release thrust bearing - removal, inspection and replacement

1 The classic symptom of wear in the clutch release bearing - and it is one which should not be disregarded - is clutch squeal, heard when you depress the clutch pedal. Before getting to this stage, you may hear a whirring noise when you have the clutch pedal down.

2 The thrust bearing only has to perform when your foot is on the clutch pedal. If you use the clutch pedal as a foot-rest the thrust bearing may well be revolving even though there is no clutch slip; this is a temptation which it is well worthwhile to resist.

3 To remove the thrust bearing, detach the gearbox from the bell housing as described in Chapter 6. You can now get at the thrust bearing through the hole at the back of the bell housing and get the thrust bearing away from the clutch release lever by turning it and sliding it towards the cable end of the lever as shown in Fig. 5.5. If you look at the photograph you will see how the bearing sits in the lever where it is retained by two pegs. You can see one of these pegs quite clearly in Fig. 5.5. When the gearbox is assembled to the bell housing, the sleeve on the front of it holds the thrust bearing in position; the pegs are simply there for preliminary location of the thrust bearing in the lever.

4 Check the bearing by placing it on the bench and rotating it under light pressure. The bearing should turn easily with no suspicion of binding and there should be no suspicion of play when it is under pressure. If you are in any doubt about it, replace it. The whole assembly is replaced; there is no question of dismantling it and fitting a new bearing inside. Be sure when

getting hold of a replacement to specify the clutch type as the thrust bearings are not the same.

6 Removing the clutch

1 Remove the gearbox complete with the bell housing as described in Chapter 6. This will give you a view of the flywheel and clutch shown in photograph 1.4.

2 Undo the screws attaching the clutch housing to the flywheel cross-wise a couple of turns at a time to prevent possible warping of the clutch housing. Remove the clutch as shown in Fig. 5.6. The disc is not attached to anything at this stage, hence the thumb in the hole to keep hold of it.

7 Clutch inspection and overhaul

1 The view of the friction disc in the photograph shows what this should look like when it is good condition. Inspect the friction disc for wear and contamination by oil.

2 Wear on the linings is gauged by the depth of the rivet heads below the surface of the friction material. If this is less than 0.025" (0.6mm) the linings are worn enough to justify renewal.

3 When one considers how easy it is to slip on a polished floor, it is not surprising that the highly polished surfaces of the clutch are able to generate so much friction. This is the case because there is - or should be - a complete absence of any form of lubricant between the mating surfaces. Under these conditions, the smoother the surface the better the contact and consequently the surface of the friction gears should have the appearance of smoothly finished wood - the grain of the material being clearly seen. It should be quite light in colour. If oil has penetrated to this surface, it will have been burnt off and it will darken the face. If however, the polish of the facing remains such that the grain of the material can still be distinguished clearly this will have little effect on clutch performance. Naturally, if you feel that oil is - or has been - present in the clutch you will take good care to find out how it got there and put a stop to it. Refer to Section 28 of Chapter 1 if the crankshaft rear seal is to be renewed. If a more severe degree of oil contamination has occurred, the surface may be affected in two ways depending upon the nature of the oil.

a) The oil may burn off and leave a carbon deposit on the surface of the facings which become highly glazed and have a definite tendency to slip. In this condition the surfaces have the appearance of varnished wood and in general the grain of the material is hidden.

b) Oil may partially burn and leave a resinous deposit on the facings. This has a tendency to produce a fierce clutch and may also cause clutch spin due to the tendency of the face linings to stick to the surface of the flywheel or pressure plate.

4 If there are signs of severe over-heating - brought about as a result of clutch slip - it is as well to replace the disc complete. It may be distorted or the temper of the shock absorbing springs may have been affected. If only the friction lining is affected, it is quite practicable to replace this oneself rather than buy a complete replacement disc assembly. Most people feel it is hardly worth doing and we would be inclined to agree with this school. Nevertheless, the linings and rivets are available as Volvo spares if you wish to have a go.

5 To replace the facings, first drill out the old rivets with 0.14" (3.5 mm) drill. Then check the clutch plate. The indentations on the tongues should be even. The clutch plate must not be warped. The clutch springs and rivets in the hub should fit securely and not show any signs of looseness. Check to make sure that there are no cracks. If the plate does not pass all these tests with flying colours, replace it.

6 Rivet on the new facings (preferably in a rivet press). The rivets should be inserted from the side on which the facing lies and rivetted up from the opposite direction against the disc. Use alternate holes in the facing, - the holes not occupied by rivets fixing one facing will contain the rivets for the other. After rivetting - the faces should be quite flat and spaced from each

other by the indentations on to the clutch disc. This spacing is most important in order to achieve smooth engagement of the clutch. Be sure that during these operations the clutch facings are kept absolutely free from oil.

7 The pressure plate assembly should be replaced complete if faulty. Check the pressure plate for damage by heat, cracks, scoring or other damage on the friction surface. Check the curvature of the pressure plate with a 9½" (240 mm) steel straight edge placed diagonally across the friction surface. It is permitted for the plate to be very slightly concave, i.e. the centre of the plate lies below the straight edge. The distance between the plate and the straight edge must not exceed 0.0012" (0.03 mm), check this with feeler gauges. If the plate is convex, i.e. the centre is higher than the edges, replace the assembly. Check the pressure spring carefully; if cracked or damaged in any way, the assembly should be replaced.

8 Pilot bearing

1 This bearing is not all that easy to remove without damaging it. For this reason we recommend that you wash it out and inspect it while it is still in the crankshaft. This way you only have to remove it if you have already decided to replace it and your problems are simpler. Its removal is considered in Chapter 1, Section 19.

2 Don't forget that the flywheel surface is an important component of the clutch. If the surface of the flywheel in contact with the clutch friction disc is uneven or burnt it should be reground. This is a job for the specialist. We suggest that if this is necessary, you take the flywheel and clutch assembly to the firm who is to do the grinding and have them balanced as a unit after the grinding has been carried out.

9 Clutch reassembly

1 Before you start, be sure that the clutch assembly and friction disc are completely free from oil. If necessary, wash in petrol and dry off with a clean rag.

2 Organise things so that you will be able to hold the clutch assembly against the flywheel with one hand while putting in one or two screws with the other. Position the disc in the pressure plate assembly with the part of the hub that sticks out facing backwards (see photograph 7.1).

3 Keeping the pressure plate as central as possible with a finger or thumb through the central hole as in Fig. 5.6, offer the assembly to the dowels on the flywheel, taking note of any position marks.

4 Insert two or three bolts and tighten them up just enough to be sure that the friction disc will not slip about when you let go of the assembly.

5 Now you have both hands free, put in the remainder of the screws and tighten them just enough for the friction disc to be free to move about when pushed but stays put when left alone. As far as possible have the bolts evently tightened all round.

6 The friction disc must now be centralised so that the gearbox input shaft can pass through the spline hub and into the pilot bearing. Quicker than making up some temporary centreing device is to take the gearbox off the bell housing and use that. If you do it this way you can at least be 100% sure that you are going to be able to get the gearbox back.

7 When the centering is complete, screw up the fixing bolts for the flywheel housing cross-wise and evenly - one or at most two turns at a time - until the housing is screwed down tight. Volvo do not specify a tightening torque for the clutch housing fixing bolts; we suggest 18 lb ft. (2.5 Kg. m.).

8 All that now remains is to refit the bell housing and gearbox, being careful when inserting the input shaft into the clutch not to put any strain on the clutch assembly. This work is dealt with in detail in Chapter 6.

9 Finally, adjust the clutch cable as detailed in Section 2.

10 Fault diagnosis

Symptom	Reason/s	Remedy
Judder when taking up drive	Loose engine/gearbox mountings or over flexible mountings	Check and tighten all mounting bolts and replace any 'soft' or broken mountings.
	Badly worn friction surfaces or friction plate contaminated with oil deposits	Remove engine and replace clutch parts as required. Rectify any oil leakage points which may have caused contamination.
	Worn splines in the friction plate hub or on the gearbox input shaft	Renew friction plate and/or input shaft.
	Badly worn pilot bearing	Renew pilot bearing.
Clutch spin (failure to disengage) so that gears cannot be meshed	Clutch actuating cable clearance too great	Adjust clearance.
	Clutch friction disc sticking because of rust on lining or splines (usually apparent after standing idle for some length of time)	As temporary remedy engage top gear, apply handbrake, depress clutch and start engine. (If very badly stuck engine will not turn). When running rev up engine and slip clutch until disengagement is normally possible. Renew friction plate at earliest opportunity.
	Damaged or misaligned pressure plate assembly	Replace pressure plate assembly.
Clutch slip - (increase in engine speed does not result in increase in vehicle speed - especially on hills)	Clutch pedal free play too little or non-existant resulting in partially disengaged clutch at all times	Adjust clearances.
	Clutch friction surfaces worn out (beyond further adjustment of operating cable) or clutch surfaces oil soaked	Replace friction plate and remedy source of oil leakage.
Clutch squeal when clutch is disengaged	Worn clutch release thrust bearing	Replace thrust bearing

Chapter 6 Gearbox
overdrive and automatic transmission

Contents

Specifications

M 40 (Manual gearbox)

Type designation	M 40
Reduction ratios:	
1st speed	3.13 : 1
2nd speed	1.99 : 1
	1.36 : 1
4th speed	1 : 1
Reverse	3.25 : 1
Lubricant, see under 'Lubrication'	
Oil capacity	0.75 litre (1.32 Imp. pints = 1.58 US pints)

Tightening torque

Nut for driving flange	9.5 - 10.5 kg m (65 - 75 lb ft.)

M 41 (Gearbox M 40 with overdrive)

Reduction ratio, overdrive	0.797 : 1 (B20) 0.756 : 1 (B18)
Clearance, piston-cylinder in oil pump	0.005 - 0.040 mm (0.0002 - 0.0016 in.)
Oil pressure, direct drive	Approx. 1.5 kp/cm^2 (21 p.s.i.)
overdrive	32 - 35 kp/cm^2 (455 - 500 p.s.i.)
Lubricant, see under 'Lubrication'	
Oil capacity, gearbox and overdrive	1.6 litres (2.81 Imp. pints = 3.38 US pints)

Tightening torque

Nut for driving flange	11.0 - 14.0 kg m (80 - 10 lb ft.)

Automatic transmission

Make and type	Borg-Warner, type 35	
Reduction ratios:		
1st gear	2.31 : 1)	
2nd gear	1.45 : 1)	X Converter ratios
3rd gear	1 : 1)	
Reverse	2.09 : 1	

Number of teeth, front sun gear	...	...	...	...	...	32	
	rear sun gear	...	...	...	...	...	28	
	planet gear, short	...	...	...	...	16	
	planet gear, long	...	...	...	...	17	
	ring gear ...	...	...	...	...	67	
Size of converter	...	...	...	...	...	9½ in. (24 cm)	
Torque ratio in converter	...	...	...	...	...	2 : 1 - 1 : 1	
Normal stall speed, B20A engine	...	...	...	...	2200 rpm	
	B20B engine	...	...	...	...	2100 rpm	
	B20E engine	...	...	...	...	2550 rpm	
	B20F engine	...	...	...	...	2450 rpm	

Weights:

						Kg	lb
Gearbox	...	...	...	...	...	37.2	82
Converter case	...	...	...	...	...	3.0	6.6
Converter	...	...	...	...	...	10.9	24
Total, without fluid	...	...	...	...	51.1	112
Weight of fluid	...	...	...	...	...	6.0	13.25
Total with fluid	...	...	...	...	57.1	126

Fluid, type	...	...	...	...	...	...	Automatic Transmission Fluid, Type F
Fluid capacity	...	...	...	...	...	...	6.2 litres (11.0 Imp. pints = 13.0 US pints)
Normal operating temperature of fluid	...	...	...	...	Approx. 212 - 240º F (110 - 115º C)

Approximate shift speeds

Car	Engine	Throttle position	1 — 2 shift		2 — 3 shift		3 — 2 shift		3 — 1 shift	
			km.ph	m.p.h.	km.p.h.	m.p.h.	km.p.h.	m.p.h.	km.p.h.	m.p.h.
142, 144	B20A	Full throttle	43	27	70	43				
		Kick-down	60	37	95	59	86	53	52	32
	B20B	Full throttle	47	29	77	48				
		Kick-down	66	41	105	65	95	59	57	35
	B20E	Full throttle	45	28	80	49				
	& B20F	Kick-down	65	40	112	70	100	62	55	34

Torque wrench settings

						lb ft.	kg m
Torque converter - drive plate	...	...	...	...	25 to 30	3.5 to 4.1
Transmission case - converter housing	...	...	...	...	8 to 13	1.1 to 1.8
Extension housing - transmission case	...	...	...	...	30 to 55	4.1 to 7.6
Oil pan - transmission case	...	...	...	...	8 to 13	1.1 to 1.8
Outer lever - manual valve shaft	...	...	...	...	7 to 9	1.0 to 1.2
Pressure point	...	...	...	...	...	4 to 5	0.6 to 0.7
Oil pan drain plug	...	...	...	...	...	8 to 10	1.1 to 1.4

Special threaded parts

					lb ft.	kg m
Starter inhibitor switch locknut	...	...	...	4 to 6	0.6 to 0.8
Downshift valve cable adaptor - transmission case	...	...	8 to 9	1.1 to 1.2
Coupling flange - driven shaft	...	...	...	...	35 to 50	4.8 to 6.9

1 Gearbox - general description

1 Fig.6.1 illustrates the gearbox employed in the 140 series which has remained basically the same throughout, though there have been various detail modifications, so when you order spares be sure to quote the gearbox number. There are three gear lever arrangements - mounted directly on top of the box, mounted on an extension at the rear of the box, and mounted on the steering column from where it operates the gearbox through a linkage. Corresponding to each of these arrangements in a separate design of the gearbox top cover, but below the cover you find the same gearbox in every case.

2 The gearbox has four forward speeds and reverse, with synchromesh on all forward gears. Its design is conventional and the problems associated with dismantling, inspection and assembly are in no way atypical. Coping with these problems is well within the scope of the intelligent owner mechanic, even though he may never have tackled a gearbox before. If your experience is limited, (and after all, the average gearbox doesn't go wrong all that often) we suggest that you give a little thought to the working of your gearbox before starting to take it apart.

3 Start by taking a look at Fig.6.2. Ignoring for the moment the arrow we see two clusters of gears, and looking more closely at these we see that four pairs of gears are actually in mesh. Another pair of gears doesn't quite make it, and indeed they are not even exactly in line. We know better than to suppose that by

now you haven't looked at Figs.6.3, 6.4, 6.5 and 6.6 as well, and you will have ssen that the upper one of this particular pair of gears can move to-and-fro and gets linked up with its opposite number by a subsidiary gear to provide reserve.

4 If we now consider the arrow in Fig.6.2 which shows the way the drive is transmitted in bottom gear we at once realise that the two shaft ends at the top of the figure must belong to different shafts, because they are rotating at different speeds. The shaft on the left which we will call the input shaft is quite short; it only carries one of the gears and fits into the other shaft about mid-way betweeen the gear pair on the left and the gear pair next to it. The shaft on the right, which we will call the output shaft, or mainshaft, carries the three other gears of the upper set, any one of which can be locked to it as described later. The gear on the input shaft is integral with it. (photo).

5 The lower set of gears is all one piece. This assembly is known as the layshaft. In practice the assembly has a hole through the middle of it and revolves on needle bearings on a spindle as shown in Fig. 6.1 (photo).

   The left-hand gear is driven by the gear on the input shaft, causing the whole layshaft to rotate with a speed that always bears the same ratio to the engine speed.

6 Although the various layshaft gears are all revolving at the same speed, the gears they drive on the mainshaft all revolve at different speeds because each one is a different size and consequently has a different ratio to its opposite number on the layshaft. Gearbox ratios are selected by locking one or other of

Fig. 6.1 Gearbox - Type M.40

1 Gear lever, upper section with knob
2 Rubber bushes
3 Gear lever, lower section
4 Washer
5 Spring
6 Cover
7 Lock spring
8 Bush
9 Protective cover.
10 Gearbox cover.
11 End casing
12 Rear cover
13 Ball bearing
14 Striker (x-ray)
15 Bush
16 Gear shifter rod

17 Circlip
18 Selector fork, 1st and 2nd speeds
19 Gate
20 Sliding plate
21 Sleeve (reverse catch)
22 Spring
23 Sleeve
24 Spring
25 Insert
26 Engaging sleeve and gear wheel for reverse
27 Synchronising cone
28 Needle bearings
29 Gear wheel for 2nd speed

30 Push plate for overdrive switch (only M.41)
31 Overdrive switch (only M.41)
32 Thrust washer
33 Circlip
34 Thrust washer
35 Gear wheel for 3rd speed
36 Needle bearings
37 Mainshaft (output shaft)
38 Spring
39 Interlock ball
40 Synchronising hub
41 Insert

42 Selector rail for 3rd and 4th speeds
43 Selector rail for 1st and 2nd speeds
44 Selector rail for reverse
45 Engaging sleeve
46 Spring
47 Synchronising cone
48 Ball bearing
49 Roller bearing
50 Sealing ring
51 Cover
52 Input shaft
53 Spacer washer
54 Thrust washer
55 Housing

56 Needle bearing
57 Spacer washer
58 Layshaft spindle
59 Layshaft
60 Reverse shaft
61 Reverse gear
62 Bush
63 Striker lever (x-ray)
64 Needle bearings
65 Gear wheel for 1st speed
66 Thrust washer
67 Speedometer worm gear
68 Bleeder nipple
69 Oil seal
70 Flange

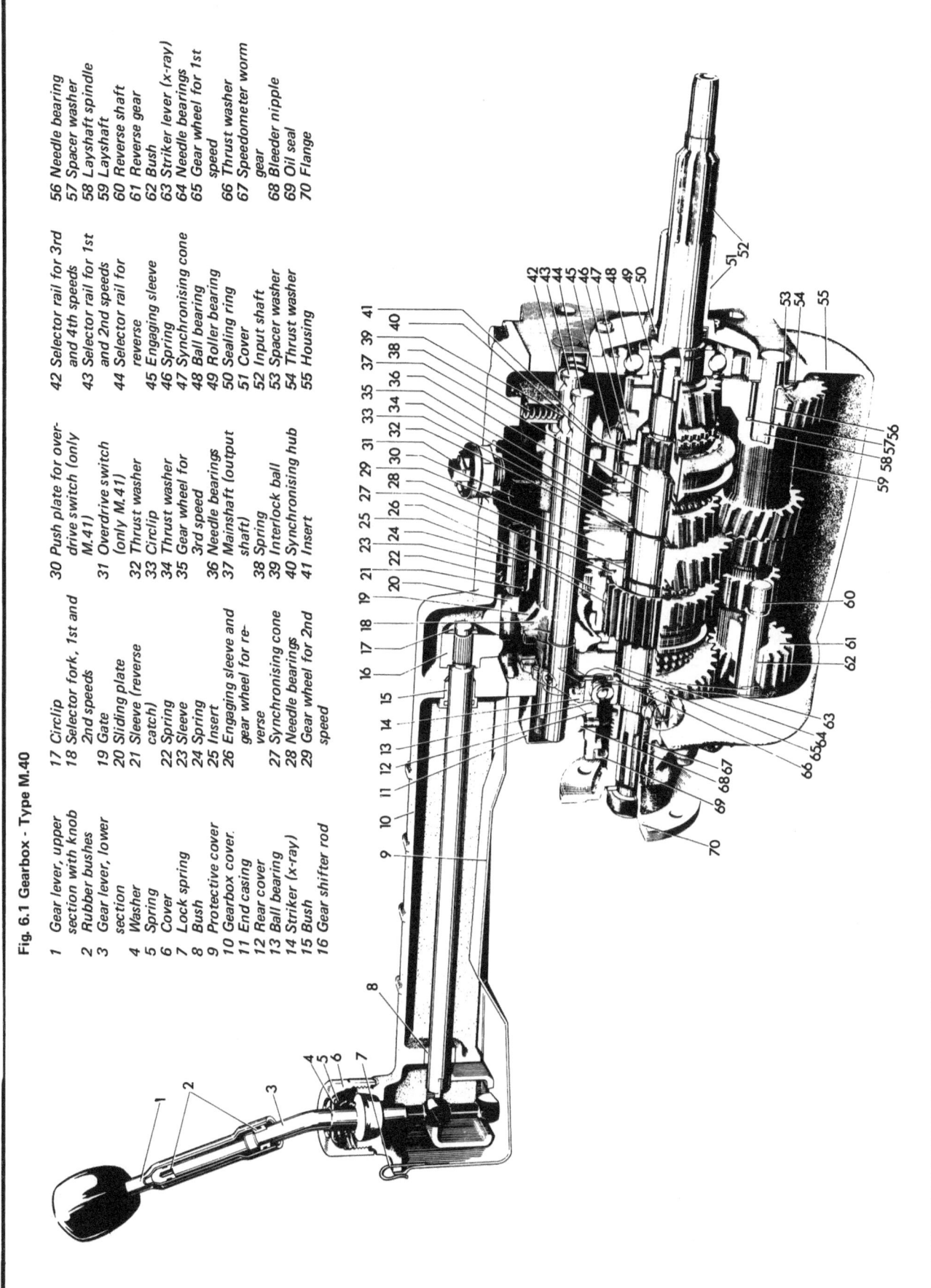

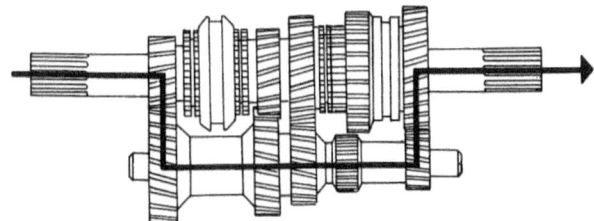

Fig. 6.2 Power path - first speed

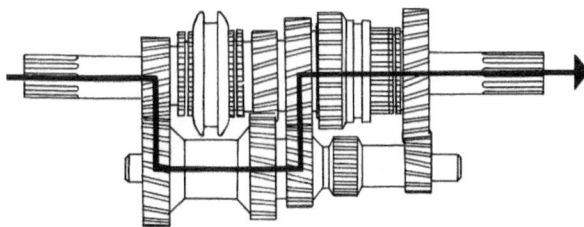

Fig. 6.3 Power path - second speed

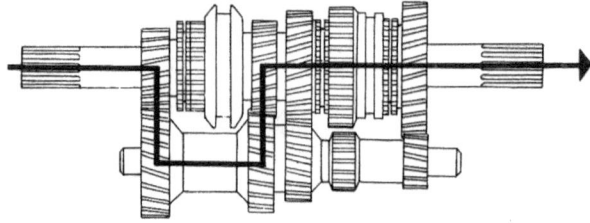

Fig. 6.4 Power path - third speed

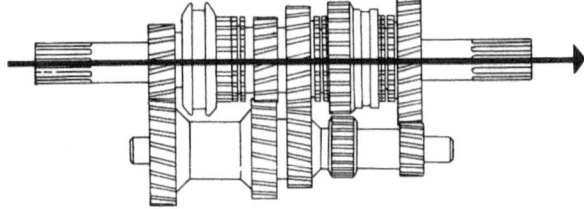

Fig. 6.5 Power path - fourth speed

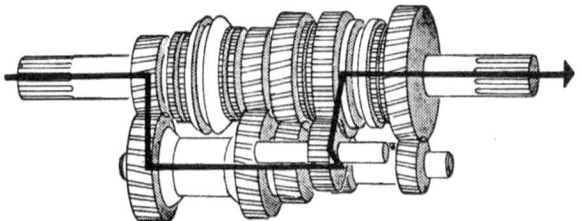

Fig. 6.6 Power path - reverse

1.4 Gears on input shaft and main shaft (output shaft). Compare this with Figs.6.2 - 6.6

1.5 The lay shaft

these gears to the mainshaft.

7   Details of the locking mechanism are considered later. At this stage it is sufficient to say that the locking is achieved by sliding operating sleeves along the mainshaft. If we look at Fig. 6.1, we see that there are two of these sleeves on the mainshaft. The one on the right is pushed over as far as it will go to the right and when it is in this position it locks the right-hand gear to the mainshaft. This gear now drives the mainshaft and we get the power transmission path indicated by the arrow. This particular gear is bigger than the other two, which means that its opposite number on the layshaft has got to be smaller than those driving its companions. Hence, this pair of gears has a larger reduction ratio than the others and gives us 'bottom gear'. In Fig.6.3 we see the right-hand operating sleeve slid along the shaft as far as it will go to the left, in which position it locks the centre one of the three driven gears which is intermediate in size between the other two and gives us a reduced reduction ratio corresponding to 'second gear'. In Fig. 6.4 the right-hand operating sleeve is positioned mid-way between the two gears associated with it and in that position locks neither of them. The left-hand sleeve, however, has been moved over until it is close to the gear on its right, which it locks to the shaft. This is smaller than the other two driven gears and consequently gives less reduction - ie, 'third

gear'. Fig. 6.5 shows the state of things for top gear. The left-hand sleeve is slid as far over to the left as it will go, and in this position it locks the input shaft direct to the output shaft. They operate as one shaft, not being driven through any gear train, hence the silence of top gear operation however rough the gearbox may be. Fig. 6.6 shows the set-up for reverse gear, Two gears set opposite each other on the mainshaft and the layshaft which do not engage directly are coupled together by a small pinion which is pushed into position when 'reverse' is selected. There is no particular significance in the fact that a driven gear for reverse forms part of an operating sleeve; this is simply a matter of engineering convenience. The sleeve is of course keyed to the shaft though it can slide along it freely.

8 The operating sleeves are pushed along the shafts by selector forks which are attached to selector rods. These rods carry dogs which are engaged by the gear lever. A simple interlock (described in Section 5, Paragraph 3) prevents more than one selector rod being moved at a time. One selector rod is associated with each of the engaging sleeves and a third rod operates the lever that engages the reverse pinion (photo).

9 Associated with the operating sleeves is the synchromesh mechanism which ensures that when a driven gear is about to be locked to the mainshaft — gear and mainshaft are rotating at the same speed. This is described in the next section.

2 Synchromesh mechanism

1 We have already seen that when a gear is engaged, the gear wheel concerned is locked to the mainshaft by the engaging sleeve. Splines inside the engaging sleeve mesh with teeth on the hub of the gear wheel and simultaneously with the 'synchronising hub' on the mainshaft. In Fig. 6.2 the left-hand engaging sleeve is not locked to either of the gears on each side of it, but the right-hand sleeve is engaged with the gear on its right. You can see the synchronising hub on which it slides quite clearly on the left of it.

2 The purpose of the synchromesh is to provide an obstacle to travel of the engaging sleeve when the mainshaft (and hence the sleeve itself) is revolving at a different rate from the gear which it is desired to engage. The speed of this gear is determined by the engine speed via the layshaft. This obstacle is provided by the synchronising cone, which has teeth round its edge which get in the way of the synchronising hub when this is rotating faster or slower than the desired gear.

Photograph 6.5a gives a better idea of the mechanism than any drawing can. On the left we see the first speed gear (this photograph is the other way round to Figs.6.2 - 6.6 which show the first speed gear on the right). It is displaced along the shaft -

it would normally be running on the larger diameter portion. The hub of this gear has a taper on it and also carries the engaging teeth which do not show up well in this photograph but may be seen quite clearly in photograph 6.5b where this gear appears in the foreground. Returning to photo 6.5a, it is easy to see that if the gear and the engaging sleeve are pressed together with the synchromesh cone between them the engaging sleeve will not get past the synchromesh cone unless the teeth on the cone line up with the splines inside the sleeve. If we now glance at Fig. 6.7 we see that the engaging sleeve has assembled inside it three detents which are held in position by two circular springs. Two of these detents are clearly visible in photograph 6.5a, the one nearer the camera showing up very well as it has caught the light. Opposite this detent we can see a notch in the synchronising cone in which the detent engages. If the cone is so positioned that one or other of the ends of the slot are touching the detent the teeth on the cone get in the way of the splines on the engaging sleeve and this sleeve cannot get past it. If the gear wheel revolves faster or slower than the engaging sleeve, friction between the tapered part of the gear hub and the cone will push it one way or the other until it comes to rest against the detent. If the relationship reverses, the cone will start to move relative to the engaging sleeve in the other direction and the time will come when the sleeve can slip past it. As soon as this happens the splines on the engaging sleeve pick up the engaging teeth on the gear and the synchromesh cone just sits between them while they revolve as one unit.

3 Gearbox - removal and replacement

1 If the gearbox is fitted with overdrive, read Section 21 of this Chapter before you go any further.

2 Unlike most, the gearbox in the Volvo 140 series is detachable from the clutch bell housing. We recommend, however, that you remove the gearbox with the bellhousing as a unit.

The four Allen screws fixing the gearbox to the bell housing are difficult to get at (in fact Volvo make a special tool for undoing them) and easily damaged.

Start by removing the gear lever before your hands get dirty. Our photos show the procedure for models where the lever is directly on top of the gearbox. Fig.6.1 shows the alternative mounting on an extended gearbox cover. The lever is attached in exactly the same way and the same procedure applies; undo the fixing screws for the cowling surrounding the lever and move it out of the way, pull back the rubber boot, unscrew the retaining socket from the gearbox and remove the lever (photos). Plug the hole with a piece of rag.

3 Undo the drain plug and catch the oil in a clean container. It

1.8 The reverse pinion

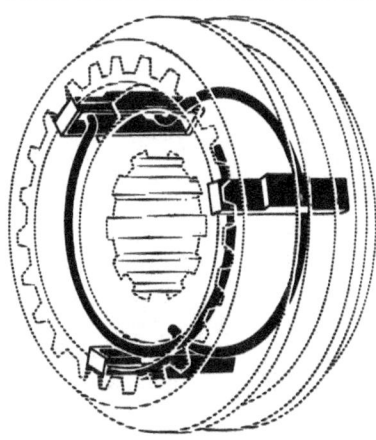
Fig. 6.7 Synchroniser pall and spring assembly

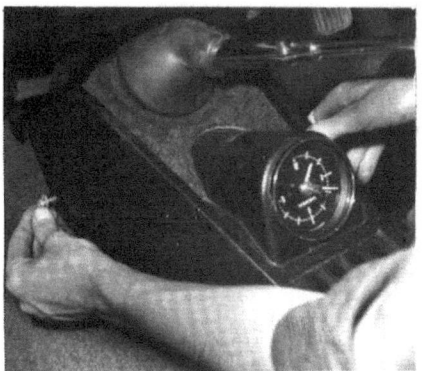
3.2a Removing the cowling

3.2b Taking out the gear lever

3.3 Drain and filler plugs

3.5a Disconnect the speedometer cable ...

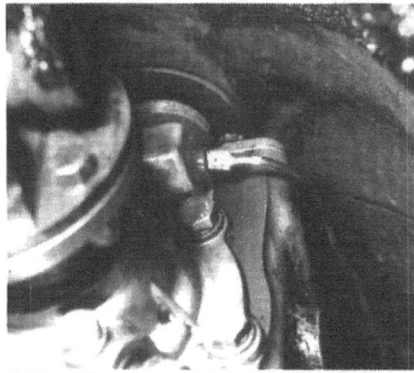
3.5b ... the reverse light switch contact...

3.5c ... and the earth lead

3.6 Taking out the gearbox support member.

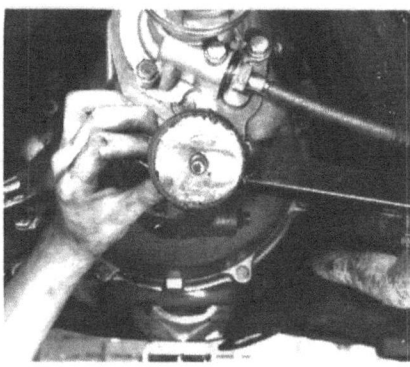
3.7 Removing the support stay

3.10a All ready for removal of the gearbox

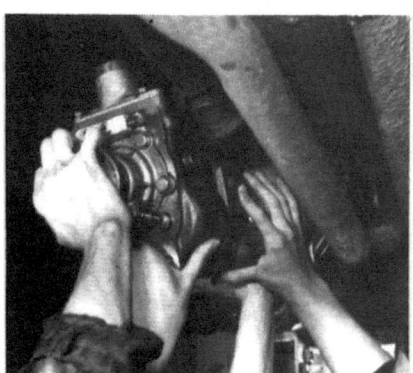
3.10b The gearbox comes out

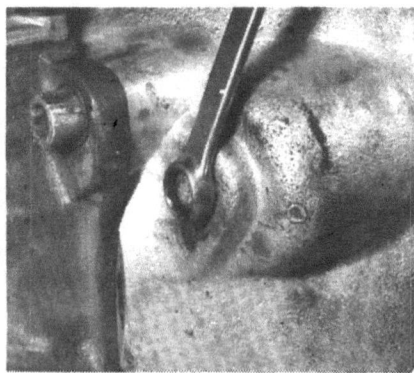
5.2a This screw holds the clutch with drawal fork ...

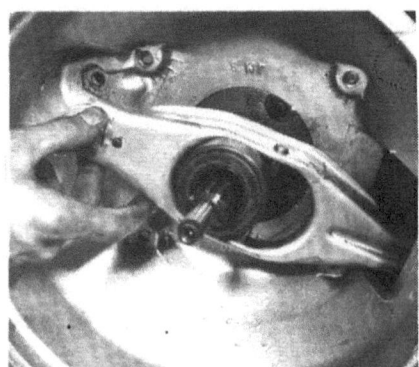
5.2b ... which is easily removed when the screw has been undone

may be worth using again. The drain plug is on the bottom right-hand side of the gearbox where it joins onto the bell housing (photo).

4   While the oil is draining, remove the starter motor. A look at Chapter 1, Section 5, Paragraph 9 and Section 9, Paragraph 2 and the illustrations that go with them will give you any guidance you need.

5   Disconnect the speedometer cable, the connection for the reversing light, and the earth lead (photos).

6   Take the weight of the gearbox on a jack. Remove the nut in the centre of the cross member just behind the gearbox, unscrew the four bolts which hold this member to the main frame and remove it (photo).

7   This reveals a further supporting stay which is removed together with the rear engine mounting (photo).

8   Disconnect the flange at the rear of the gearbox from the front universal joint of the propeller shaft. Tie the propeller shaft up with a piece of wire or stout string to keep it out of the way. You can see the propeller shaft sitting up against the exhaust pipe in photo 3.10b which shows the gearbox being lifted out, and if you look very hard you can see the wire which is tying it up.

9   Disconnect the clutch cable as described and illustrated in Chapter 5, Section 3, Paragraphs 1 and 2.

10 We are now in the state shown in the photograph for a gearbox without overdrive. If overdrive is fitted, disconnect the battery lead and lower the engine enough to let you get at the upper fixing nuts holding the overdrive unit to the spacing flange. You can now remove the unit, leaving the spacing flange on the gearbox, where it will do a useful job protecting the extra long output shaft. Having dealt with the overdrive, if fitted, all that remains is to undo the bolts holding the bell housing to the engine and remove the gearbox, being careful not to let it hang on its input shaft which goes into the clutch. An extra pair of hands makes this job a lot easier. (photo).

11 Replacement is simply a reversal of the removal procedure.

12 Don't forget to refill the gearbox with oil! The easiest way to do this is through the top of the box before you put the gear lever on. The gearbox should be filled to the level of the filler plug. Naturally you take the plug out to check this if you are filling through the gear lever mounting.

---

4   Gearbox - removal by separation from bell housing

In the previous Section we stated our reasons for preferring the method there described for removing the gearbox and bell housing as a unit. If the gearbox is separated from the bell housing, the preliminary work is slightly reduced because there is no need to remove the starter motor, earth braiding or clutch cable. This saving will count for nothing, however, if you have trouble with the four Allen screws attaching the gearbox to the bell housing; and in our experience it is easier to cope with these screws on the bench than from underneath the car. If you decide to remove the gearbox this way, carry out the operations described in Section 3 apart from those we have just mentioned until you reach the stage of removing the gearbox, which of course you now do by undoing the Allen screws instead of undoing the bolts around the bell housing.

---

5   Gearbox - dismantling

1   Give the whole exterior a thorough clean with paraffin or a detergent such as Gunk. As well as making the job more pleasant it is the only way to be certain that you will not get dirt inside the gearbox at some stage in the proceedings.

2   If the gearbox has been dismantled complete with the bell housing, the clutch thrust bearing and its withdrawal fork are easily removed for inspection. The withdrawal fork is attached to the bell housing by a bolt which threads into a captive bush on the fork. There is no locking mechanism on the fork itself; the bolt simply being screwed tight into the housing with a lock

washer under its head. As the lever cannot be rotated round the bolt cannot come off (photos).

3   Start by taking off the cover. On the underside of the cover you will see the interlock plate with square bosses, these lock all selectors except the selector that is being operated so that only that particular selector can move - this also ensures that the gear lever is properly positioned over the selector you want because if it isn't you won't be able to move the selector. A look at the photograph of the selectors as seen from the top of the box will show you at once how the system fits together. The action of the spring on the interlock plate make the gear lever return to the right-hand side of the box. When you select reverse, you have to give an extra push to make the interlock plate overcome the resistance of the plunger which is backed by a fairly strong spring.

4   Remove the three springs (normally held in by the lid) which press on locating balls for the selector rods (see photo). The balls can be left in the holes for the time being if you keep an eye on them.

5   Engage two gears at once by pushing both the forward speed selector rods as far in one direction as they will go. This locks the gearbox and enables you to undo the nut holding the flange on the mainshaft with difficulty. Pull the flange off the shaft with a puller if it will not respond to very gentle taps with a hammer (photos). Now is a good time as any to remove the speedometer drive pinion by undoing the screw that retains it (photo). Follow this by removing the screws which hold the mainshaft bearing housing - this gives the shaft freedom of movement at this stage and makes subsequent dismantling a little easier. Note the sealing washers on these screws which go right through into the gearbox.

6   Remove the cap covering the ends of the selector rods, take out the locking screws holding the selector fork and the engaging dogs to the two outer rods (this will release the lever actuating the reverse pinion as well) and withdraw the rods. Be careful in your choice of screwdriver for undoing these screws - choose one that is a good fit in the slot. These screws are screwed in tightly because a lot depends on them (photos).

Go easy when you take the rods out; keep the dogs and selectors parallel with the shaft as they may jam if they get slightly askew.

7   The dog on the centre shaft is held in by a roll pin because a screw would get in the way of the gear lever (photo). Move the selector as close as you can to the side of the gearbox (i.e put it in the 'first speed' position). Drive the pin out a little way, but not so far as to foul the teeth of the first speed gear on the layshaft which is underneath it. (photo). Having started the pin on its way, take the selector back past the first speed gear when you have enough room to drive it out. Having done this, you can withdraw the rod (photo). With the rods out of the way you can take out the dogs and selector forks (photos).

8   Remove the bell housing, which until now will have been serving as a most useful stand, being careful to use a correctly fitting key for the Allen screws - which hold it to the gearbox. These screws should be done up tightly and trying to unscrew them with a key which isn't quite right will almost certainly damage them (photo).

9   Removal of the bell housing reveals one end of the layshaft spindle. The other end is normally half concealed by the mainshaft housing at the other end of the gearbox. If you turn this housing slightly there is nothing to stop you from driving the spindle straight out, but don't do it for a moment - remember what was said in Section 1, Paragraph 5 and have a look at the photos. It would be nice if we could drive out that spindle without having 48 (or in some cases 42) needles scattered all over the place. The difficulty arises because we have got to drive out the spindle and allow the layshaft to fall to the bottom of the gearbox before we can remove the mainshaft.

The ideal solution to the problem is to have a shaft or tube 1 - 1¼ inches (2.5 - 3.1 cms.) shorter than the layshaft spindle, i.e. a bit shorter than the layshaft itself, and having a diameter equal or slightly less than that of the spindle. If this shaft were driven into the middle of the layshaft, the layshaft spindle being

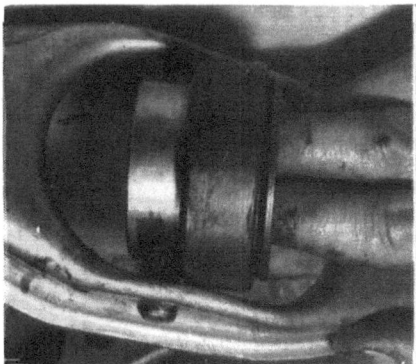

5.2c Pegs in the fork retain the thrust bearing, which is easily removed when the input shaft of the gearbox is out of the way

5.3a Taking off the cover reveals the springs which push down the locating balls for the selector rods

5.3b The locking plate, its return spring and the plunger that loads the reverse position

5.3c The selector rods, showing the dogs that engage with the gear lever. Note the lever that operates the reverse pinion in the lower right hand corner of the gearbox

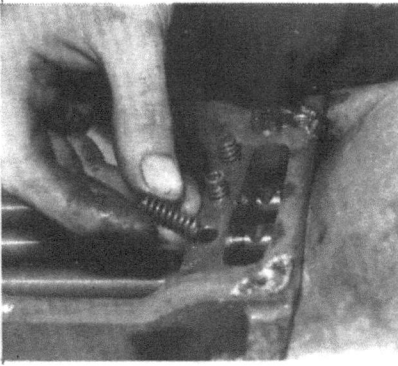

5.4 Removing the springs that hold down the locating balls

5.5a Removing the flange nut ...

5.5b ... the flange ...

5.5c ... the speedometer drive pinion ...

5.5d ... and the fixing screws for the mainshaft bearing housing

5.6a The cap covering the ends of the selector rods with the reversing switch on the near end.

5.6b Release the set screw holding the engaging dog ...

5.6c ... and the selector fork, and pull out the rod

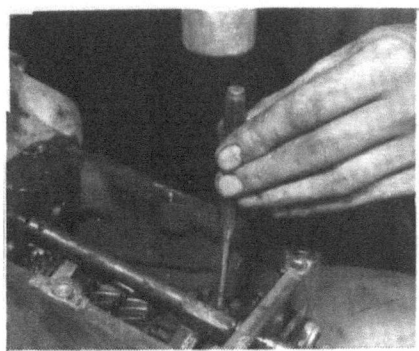

5.7a Drive out the roll pin ...

5.7b ... (this is what it looks like) ...

5.7c ... and pull out the selector rod

5.7d Out comes the fourth/third speed selector fork

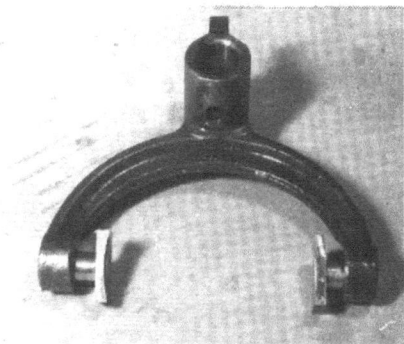

5.7e The second/first speed selector fork has brass engaging pieces fitted

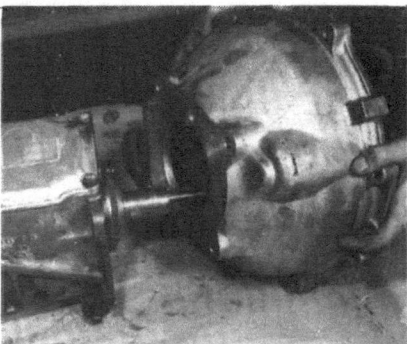

5.8 The bell housing comes away

5.9a The layshaft, layshaft spindle and needle roller bearings

5.9b When the mainshaft bearing housing is turned round, the layshaft spindle can be pushed out

5.10a Removing the Allen screws holding the input shaft bearing housing

removed, the layshaft would fall to the bottom of the gearbox with the substitute spindle inside it retaining the needle bearings in position. Volvo have produced such a rod (Tool no. SVO 2907) and if you can borrow it from a Volvo agent that's fine, but if you are faced with making something we suggest that you don't bother at this stage, but just push out the spindle and allow the whole lot to drop to the bottom of the gearbox. It will be much easier to devise something to use during reassembly (where it is almost essential) when you have the layshaft and bearings available to try out your system and see if it works. This is what we did, and in Section 13 we describe how we went about it.

Whatever you do about retaining the bearings at this stage, you will have to push out the layshaft spindle and let the layshaft drop to the bottom of the gearbox before you can deal

with the mainshaft.

10 Undo the three Allen screws which hold the input shaft housing (note their O-ring seals - these screws go right through to the inside of the gearbox) take off the housing and withdraw the input shaft with its bearing. The inner end of this shaft contains 14 rollers on which the mainshaft runs - watch out for them (photos). There is a synchromesh cone associated with this shaft - keep corresponding cones and gears together so that when you inspect the components you know which is associated with what (photo).

11 Take out the mainshaft assembly complete with its bearing housing. With the mainshaft out of the way, you can remove the layshaft. Check that you have got all those needle rollers that go inside it. Most gearboxes have 48; some - like the one used for our photographs - have 42 (photos).

5.10b The allen screws and their O-rings

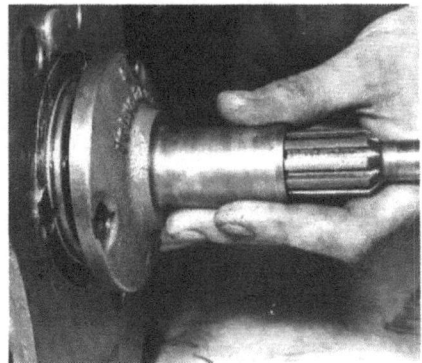

5.10c The bearing housing is removed ...

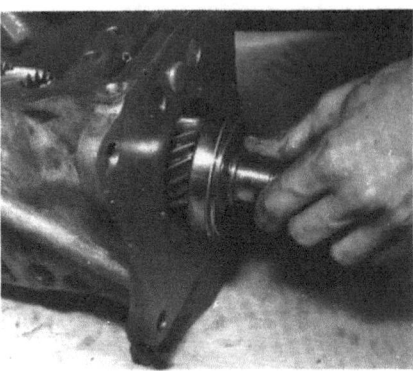

5.10d ... followed by the input shaft

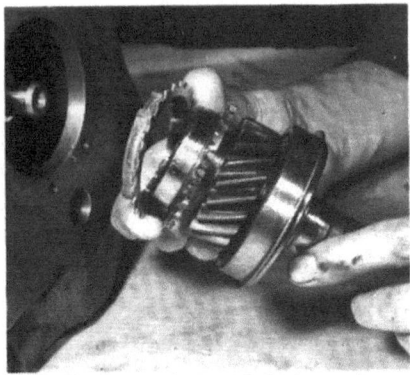

5.10e The input shaft with its integral fourth speed gear and engaging teeth, and their associated synchromesh cone.

5.10f The needle bearing in the input shaft which supports the end of the mainshaft

5.11a The mainshaft assembly being removed

5.11b The layshaft coming out with most - if not all - of its needle roller bearings. Note right hand thumb (on left of photo) and left hand forefinger

6.1 Mainshaft assembly

6.2a Remove the circlip retaining the synchromesh hub ...

6.2b ... and slide off the hub and the engaging sleeve as a unit

6.2c Then take off the synchronising cone ...

6.2d ... the third speed gear and the spacer ring behind it ...

6 Mainshaft - dismantling

1   The photograph shows a view of the mainshaft and its associated components. The right-hand end enters the input shaft and the engaging sleeve picks up the engaging teeth on this shaft in top gear. The left-hand end (sticking out of the housing) normally carries a flange which engages with the propeller shaft. Where overdrive is fitted, the left-hand end of the mainshaft is a lot longer and carries an eccentric for operating the overdrive oil pump. The bearing housing is different because it does not have to carry the speedometer drive. The bearing housing and rear end of this mainshaft are shown in Fig.6.8. The eccentric for operating the pump is keyed on to the shaft just behind the shoulder. Once this is removed, the remainder of the instructions in this and the next Section apply equally to both types of shaft.

2   Remove the circlip at the end of the shaft remote from the bearing housing and slide off the synchronising hub and engaging sleeve as a single unit, then the synchronising cone and third speed gear (photos). If the hub is a tight fit on the shaft, use a puller with its ends tucked behind the third speed gear as shown in Fig.6.9. You know this is the third speed gear because it is the smallest of the three forward gears and so gives the least reduction ratio apart from the direct drive for top gear.

3   Slide off the synchronising cone, the second speed gear and the spacing ring behind it (photos). This brings you to the circlip retaining the second speed gear.

Remove this circlip and spacing ring that lies between it and the second speed gear, and slide off the gear.

4   Slide off the synchronising cone and the engaging sleeve which also serves as a member of the reverse gear train. In this case you cannot take the synchronising hub with it as with the fourth speed/third speed engaging sleeve (paragraph 3) because the hub is in one piece with the shaft. When you pull it off, watch for the detents and spring which will fall out.

5   Using the first speed gear as a support, drive or push out the mainshaft from the bearing housing. Fig. 6.27 shows this being done for the overdrive version of the mainshaft in a press; a hide mallet carefully applied will do the trick or you can use a suitable puller or a home-made substitute.

The spacing ring and first speed gear can now be slid off the shaft, followed by the first speed synchronising cone. (photos)

6   Remove the circlip from the mainshaft bearing housing and lift out the bearing. This reveals the speedometer pinion unless you have the overdrive version in which the speedometer is naturally driven from the overdrive unit. Notice the way the friction drive spring for the pinion is fitted (photos).

7   Remove the oil seal from the other side of the bearing housing.

7 Input shaft - dismantling

The input shaft bearing is held on by a circlip and removal calls for no special comment. Note that this circlip comes in alternative thicknesses and is selected to be a snug fit in the groove. Bear this in mind if you have to renew the shaft or circlip.

8 Gearbox - examination

1   If the gearbox has been stripped because some specific fault such as failure to stay in a selected gear, difficulty in engaging gear, or the sort of noise which can no longer be ignored, the cause of the fault will usually be pretty obvious (see also Fault Diagnosis, Section 17). A not so obvious cause of noise and trouble is bearing wear, which it is well worthwhile to rectify by replacing the bearings concerned before things get to such a state that you have to replace a shaft.

2   If you can detect slop in the bearings when they are still full of oil they are obvious candidates for the scrap heap, but otherwise you should give them a good wash in paraffin or

Fig. 6.8 Mainshaft of gearbox used with overdrive. The shaft is being pressed out of its bearing in the bearing housing.

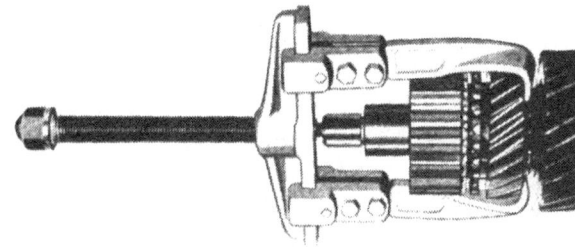

Fig. 6.9 Pulling off the front synchroniser.

cleaning fluid with a final rinse in White Spirit. You can then examine them for signs of wear, scoring, blueing or excessive play - i.e. any play that you can actually feel. If you are in any doubt at all, replace them. In fact there is a lot to be said for replacing the bearings as a matter of course.

3   If the synchromesh cones show signs of wear or have a battered look around the slots that engage with the detents, they should be replaced. Once again, it is a good idea to replace them as a matter of routine - they are not expensive.

4   Examine the teeth of all gears for signs of uneven/excessive wear and chipping. If a gear is in a bad state have a good look at the gear it engages with - you may have to replace this too, a nuisance if it happens to be on the layshaft which will then have to be replaced complete.

5   All the gears should be a good running fit on the shaft with no signs of rocking. The fourth/third speed synchronising hub should not be a sloppy fit on the shaft splines.

6   All parts of the selector mechanism should be examined for wear. This includes the selector forks - Volvo have thoughtfully fitted engaging pins on the first/second speed selector fork so that you don't have to replace the whole lot if these get worn, (photo 5.7e).

7   We think it is false economy not to renew the oil seals, but

6.3a ... revealing the circlip holding the second speed gear

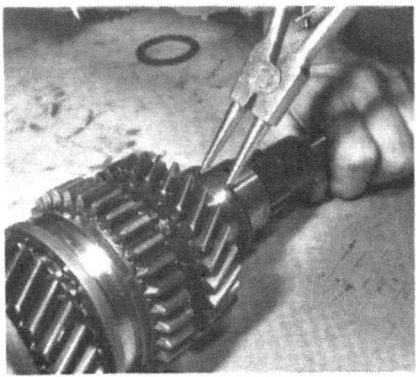

6.3b Remove the circlip and the spacing ring behind it

6.3c Slide off the second speed gear

6.5a The first gear and its synchronising cone coming off the mainshaft (Note: the engaging sleeve is still in position).

6.5b Mainshaft components (engaging sleeves assembled on synchronising hubs)

6.6a Remove the circlip from the bearing housing ...

6.6b ... which, is then, easily pushed out

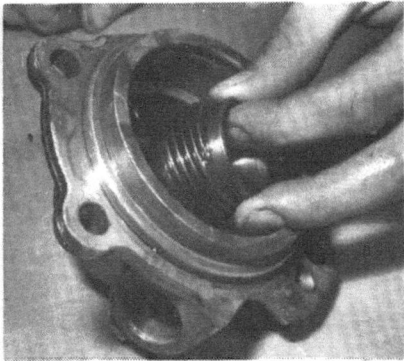

6.6c Removing the speedometer drive pinion ...

6.6d ... and its friction drive spring

10.4a The detents are inserted between the engaging sleeve and the synchronising hub ...

10.4b ... backed by a spring at each end (see Fig.6.7)

10.4c Select circlips which fit snuggly in their grooves; they are supplied in different thicknesses

if you intend to use the old ones again check that they are in perfect condition.

9 Gearbox - reassembly

1 Assembling the gearbox is a slightly tricky business, but there is nothing really to worry about. It is not the sort of job in which, if you make a mistake, you find out about it disastrously some months later. It is more like a jigsaw puzzle - once you have done it you know it is right. The chief precaution you need to take if you haven't worked on a gearbox before is to allow yourself a lot more time than you think you can possibly need.
2 You may also like to give yourself a revision course on gearbox design before you start. Take a look first at Fig.6.5. This shows the input shaft locked to the mainshaft by the synchronising sleeve on the left which is pushed over to the left as far as it will go. This is of course the forward end of the gearbox. Obviously as we change from fourth speed to third speed this is the synchronising hub that moves, so we know at once that the third speed gear is at the front end of the mainshaft, near where it joins the input shaft. The next two gears must be second and first, with the reverse gear forming part of the synchronising hub which slides between them. The gear stick comes backwards to engage second speed and forwards to engage first speed, so we know that the synchronising sleeve moves forwards to engage second speed and backwards to engage first speed, just as the other synchronising sleeve moves forwards to engage fourth speed and backwards to engage third speed. This means that the first speed gear (the biggest one, having the most reduction) must be at the back end of the mainshaft.
3 With the biggest gear at the back, naturally we have to have the smallest gear on the layshaft also at the back. So now we know which way round and in what order you have to put the various gears. Obviously the cone surfaces on each pair of gears have to face each other so we know which way round on the mainshaft the gears have to go. A look at the layshaft reveals that the reverse gear is close to the second speed gear; this tells you that the reverse gear teeth on the synchronising hub on the mainshaft must be near the second speed gear, ie they must face the front. Once you have the logic of the thing in mind, you won't need to keep referring to Fig. 6.5 or any other figure to see which way round and where the various gears have to go.

10 Mainshaft - reassembly

1 Where applicable, assemble the speedometer drive gear into the bearing housing (see photographs 6.6c and 6.6d).
2 Using a suitable drift, press the mainshaft bearing into the housing (see Fig.6.10). You can easily make a substitute for the Volvo drift shown in the Figure and use your vice as a press. Smear the bearing and housing with oil and be sure that the bearing goes in perfectly straight.
3 Smear the oil seal with oil and fit it the correct way round, ie the thin end towards the gearbox.
4 Before fitting the bearing housing to the shaft, assemble the first speed/second speed engaging sleeve with its detents and springs over the synchroniser hub on the shaft (photo and Fig.6.7) The groove on the synchroniser faces the rear of the shaft, ie the flange end or, if overdrive is fitted, the long splined end. Then slip the first gear and its synchronising cone on to the shaft (both gear and synchronising sleeve, of course, must have their tapered ends facing the synchronising hub), assemble the housing on to the shaft and fit the circlip. Assemble the second and third speed gears and the third/fourth speed synchroniser on to the shaft, using the dismantling photo sequence 6.2, 6.3 and 6.5 in reverse order as guidance. The parts should be well smeared with oil before assembly. There is nothing particular to watch unless you are fitting new circlips, when you should be sure that these are selected to be a snug fit in the grooves; they are supplied in different thicknesses. (photos).

11 Input shaft - reassembly

1 Press the bearing on to the input shaft, having smeared both with oil using a suitable substitute for the tool shown in Fig. 6.11.
2 Grease the 14 mainshaft bearing rollers and assemble these in the input shaft (see photo 5.10e). From now on the input shaft must be handled with a steady hand in order that the rollers do not get jolted out of place.

12 Reverse pinion - reassembly

1 If you have removed it, reassemble the idler pinion for the reverse train with its shaft into the casing (photo). Note that the shaft end must protrude 0.28 - 0.30" (7.0 - 7.6 mm) outside the housing (see Fig. 6.12).

13 Layshaft assembly

1 Whatever you did on dismantling, you will have to have some sort of retainer for the needle bearings inside the layshaft which you can rely on to hold them in place while you fiddle about with it during reassembly of the gearbox. We used a tube of

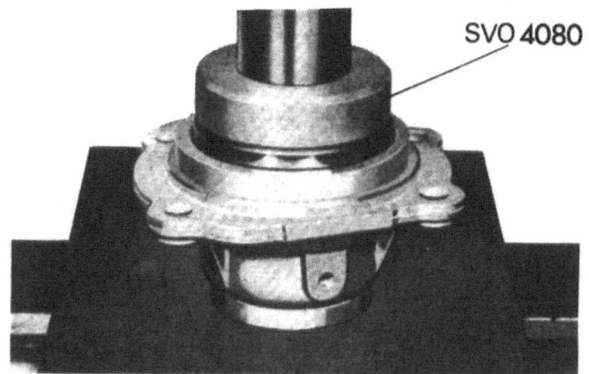

Fig. 6.10 Fitting the mainshaft bearing into its housing.

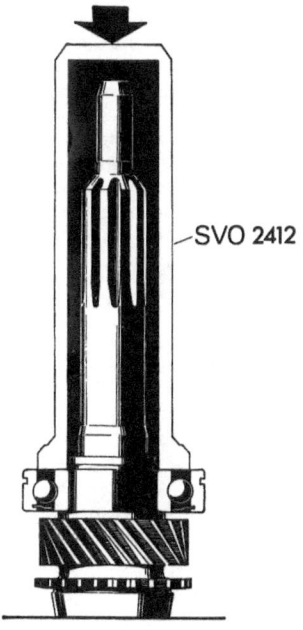

Fig. 6.11 Fitting the input shaft bearing on the shaft.

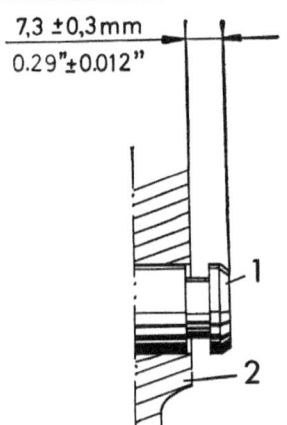

7,3 ±0,3mm
0.29"±0.012"

1

2

Fig. 6.12 Fitting reverse pinion shaft (note clearance).

slightly smaller diameter than the layshaft spindle; slotting its ends and opening them out until they were a good fit inside the needle bearing assembly (photo).

2   Using the layshaft spindle as a steady, fit the spacing washers and bearing needles into the layshaft, using plenty of grease to anchor them (photos). The grease will stick better if the layshaft is really clean and dry. Then slide the retainer in, letting it push the layshaft spindle out of the layshaft (photo).

14 Assembling components into gear case

1   Press the input shaft bearing into the gear case as far as it will go (ie until its retaining clip touches the case). Now stick the thrust washers for the layshafts to the inside of the case with grease. If the case and washers are clean and dry they will stick all right. (photo 13.2f).

2   Now comes the bit where a steady hand and deliberate movement is all important. Give things a jolt now, and they will come unstuck - literally. With the case standing upright on the bench, position the layshaft on the bottom of the case centrally and the right way round, ie with the larger gears at the input shaft end.

3   Check that the rollers in the input shaft are properly in place and that the thrust washers are aligned with the holes for the layshaft spindle. Slip the synchronising cone over the input shaft, and then pass the mainshaft through the hole in the end of the case (don't forget its gasket!) and gently engage it with the input shaft, pushing the housing into the hole in the casing as far as it will go.

4   Now comes the most ticklish bit. If it doesn't come off first time the penalty isn't very severe - you will simply have to remove the mainshaft, reposition the thrust washers and if you are very unlucky take out the layshaft and reposition some of its rollers. To avoid this irritating frustration, proceed deliberately

and gently. Get hold of the gear case, positioning your forefingers in the holes for the layshaft spindle so that if necessary you can prevent the thrust washers from sliding right over the holes. Gently turn the case upside down so that the layshaft comes to rest on the mainshaft with its ends more or less opposite the holes for the layshaft spindle. The photograph shows the state of things when this has been successfully completed. If the thrust washers have moved slightly, align them with the holes and then insert the layshaft spindle (photo). Push the spindle through the layshaft, letting it drive out the retaining tube (photo). When the end of the the spindle appears in the hole at the far end of the case, you have won.

5   Do not be tempted to pick up the gearbox from the bench until you have fixed the mainshaft bearing housing in its correct position - and for the overdrive gearbox this involves fitting the spacing flange for the overdrive unit with its gasket and the tab washers (new of course) for the bottom pair of fixing bolts. Do not forget the sealing washers for the fixing bolts. (photo).

6   Slide the circular gasket over the input shaft, making sure that it is the proper way round - there is a hole in the gearbox casing which must be lined up with the hole in the gasket. This provides a path for oil to reach the input shaft bearing. Push the housing over the shaft and fasten to the gear case with its three fixing bolts, not forgetting their O-ring seals (photo).

7   Replace the speedometer drive pinion in the bearing housing where applicable (photo).

15 Selector assembly

1   Place the two selector forks in their correct positions (the photo shows which way round they ought to go) before you insert any of the selector rods.

2   Insert the centre rod and drive in the roll pin which anchors the selector fork to it.

3   Insert the first/second speed rod, fitting the dog to it so that when positioned on the shaft by its grub screw it slopes towards the dog on the centre shaft. Tighten the grub screws for the fork and the dog with a screwdriver that adequately fills (without strain) the slots on the grub screws (photo).

4   Fit the remaining selector rod whose dog operates the lever which moves the reverse idler gear. We have now reached the state of assembly shown in photo 5.2c.

5   If you have removed the caps at the front of the case which cover the ends of the selector rods, be sure that they are replaced as shown in photograph 5.10c, with the centre cap projecting about 5/32" (4 mm) outside the face of the housing.

6   Place the interlock balls and springs in position and fit on the gearbox cover. Check that all the gears engage and disengage freely. (photos).

7   Fit the cover over the ends of the selector rods as illustrated in photo 5.6a.

8   For a gearbox without overdrive, engage two gears at once, thus locking the output shaft and fit the flange. For a gearbox with overdrive, fit the eccentric which operates the oil pump on

12.1 The reverse pinion and lever fitted into the gearbox casing

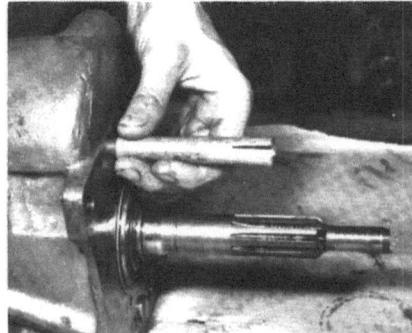

13.1 A piece of copper tube with the ends flared out a little made a successful needle roller bearing retainer for the layshaft

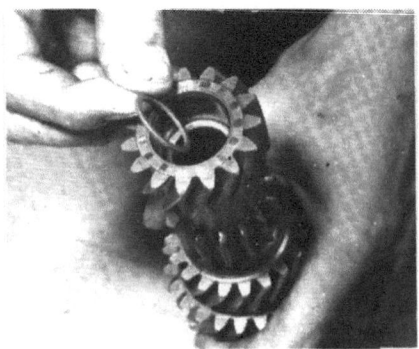

13.2a To reassemble the layshaft needle bearings, first insert a spacing ring ...

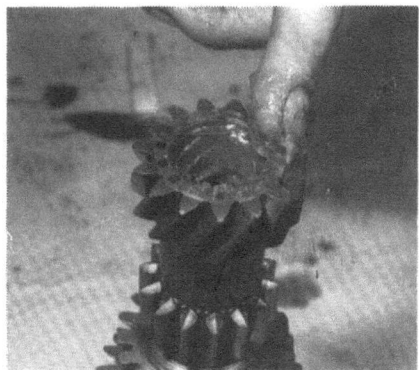

13.2b ... then, using plenty of grease ...

13.2c ... and the layshaft spindle as a steady, insert the needle roller bearings in the layshaft ...

13.2d ... followed by the second spacer

13.2e Then insert the retainer, letting it push the spindle through the layshaft

13.2f/14.4a Here is a view (taken during reassembly of the gearbox) of the layshaft with the retainer inside it, ready to receive the spindle

14.4b The layshaft spindle inserted

14.4c The bearing retainer comes out as the spindle is pushed in

14.5 Fixing the mainshaft bearing housing

14.6 Don't cover up this hole when fitting the gasket for the input shaft housing

14.7 Inserting the speedometer drive

15.1 Be sure the selector forks are in place before you put the rods back

15.3 Use a suitable screwdriver for this important tightening operation

15.6a Don't forget these locking bolts ...

15.6b ... or these springs ...

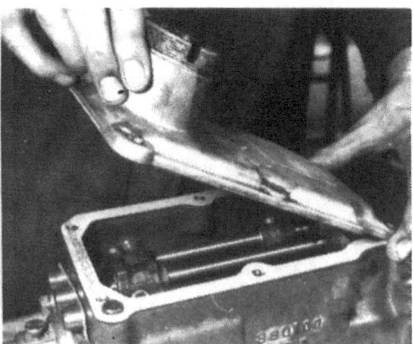

15.6c ... or the new gasket for the gearbox cover

the mainshaft, using a circlip which fits snugly into the groove (they are supplied in different thicknesses).

9   Do not forget to fill the gearbox with oil. It holds 1.32 Imperial pints or 1.56 US pints (0.75 litres); in practical terms this means 1 1/3 Imperial pints; 1½ US pints plus a little, or ¾ litre. The best time to put the oil in is just before replacing the gear lever when the gearbox is back in the car. Simply pour a measured amount of oil in through the gear lever hole - doing it this way you do not even have to bother to undo the level plug. We mention it here because we would hate you to forget it.

10   Plug the hole where the gear lever enters the box with non-fluffy rag. This will stop dirt or even the odd nut or screw falling into the gearbox, and removing the plug to fit the gear lever will remind you that you have still got to fill the box with oil.

11   Assemble the bell housing to the gearbox together with the clutch release lever and thrust bearing.

16 Gearbox - re-fitting in vehicle

This calls for no special comment, being simply a reversal of the removal procedure which has already been described. Don't forget the electrical connection to the overdrive unit if fitted and the reversing light. Above all, when you remove the plug from the gear lever socket - don't forget the oil!

17 Manual gearbox - Fault diagnosis

Symptom	Reason/s	Remedy
WEAK OR INEFFECTIVE SYNCHROMESH		
General wear	Synchronising cones worn, split or damaged	Dismantle and overhaul gearbox. Fit new gear wheels and synchronising cones.
	Synchromesh dogs worn, or damaged	Dismantle and overhaul gearbox.
JUMPS OUT OF GEAR		
General wear or damage	Broken gearchange fork rod spring	Dismantle and replace spring.
	Gearbox coupling dogs badly worn	Dismantle gearbox. Fit new coupling dogs.
	Selector fork rod groove badly worn	Fit new selector fork rod.
EXCESSIVE NOISE		
Lack of maintenance	Incorrect grade of oil in gearbox or oil level too low	Drain, refill, or top up gearbox with correct grade of oil.
	Bush or needle roller bearings worn or damaged	Dismantle and overhaul gearbox. Renew bearings.
	Gearteeth excessively worn or damaged	Dismantle and overhaul gearbox. Renew gear wheels.
	Laygear thrust washers worn allowing excessive end play	Dismantle and overhaul gearbox. Renew thrust washers.
EXCESSIVE DIFFICULTY IN ENGAGING GEAR		
Clutch not fully disengaging	Clutch pedal adjustment incorrect	Adjust clutch pedal correctly.

18 Overdrive - general description

1   The overdrive is essentially an extra gearbox, automatically controlled, driven by the output shaft of the main gearbox and producing on its own output shaft a step-up ratio of 0.756 : 1 for B18 engines or 0.797 : 1 for B20 engines. The 'gear change' is controlled hydraulically, the hydraulic control valve being operated by a solenoid. The electrical connections to the solenoid are taken through a switch on the cover of the main gearbox which ensures that overdrive can only be brought into

operation when the car is in top gear.

2   Cutaway pictures of the overdrive units fitted to B18 and B20 engine (which differ somewhat in detail although not in principle) are shown in Figs. 6.13 and 6.14 while Figs. 6.15 and 6.16 are exploded views of the units fitted to B20 engines and B18 engine respectively.

3   The heart of the overdrive is the epicyclic gear system whose components are shown in Fig. 6.15 Nos. 73-75, 84-88, and 110. These parts are assembled on the elongated mainshaft which extends from the main gearbox. Two of these parts, the planet carrier and the unidirectional clutch, are splined to the mainshaft

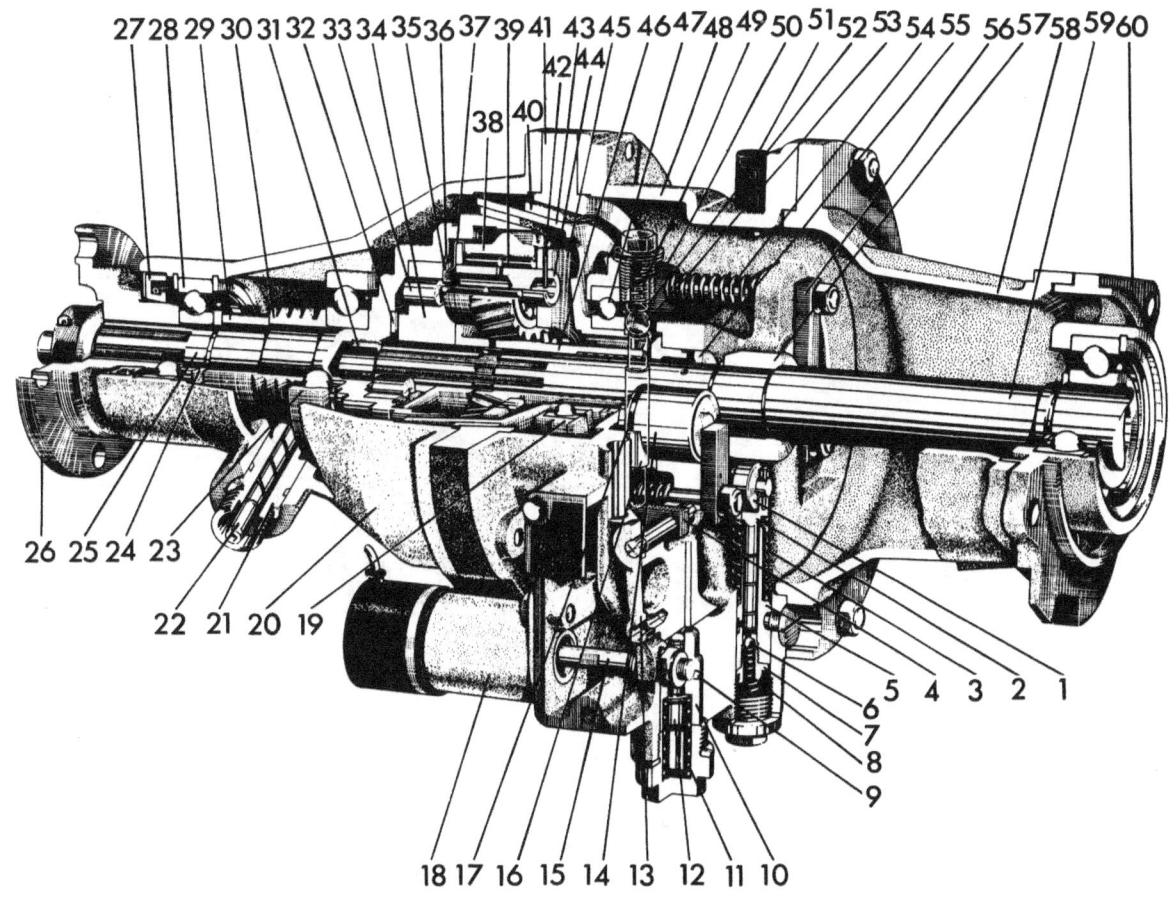

Fig. 6.13 Overdrive fitted to B18 engined cars

1	Roller	17	Plunger seal
2	Pump plunger	18	Solenoid
3	Spring	19	Thrust bearing retainer
4	Lever	20	Housing, rear part
5	Pump cylinder	21	Bush
6	Ball	22	Speedometer gear, driven
7	Valve seating	23	Ball bearing
8	Spring	24	Thrust washer
9	O-ring	25	Output shaft
10	Valve seating	26	Coupling flange
11	Spring	27	Sealing ring
12	Valve plunger	28	Ball bearing
13	Lever	29	Spacing sleeve
14	Piston	30	Speedometer gear, drive
15	Armature for solenoid	31	Needle bearing
16	Valve rod ('X-ray' view)	32	Thrust washer

33	Rollers for uni-directional clutch	48	Housing, front part
34	Clutch hub	49	Spring ('X-ray' view)
35	Oil deflector plate	50	Pressure plate
36	Circlip	51	Breather nipple
37	Oil catcher	52	Tappet ('X-ray' view)
38	Planet gear	53	Ball ('X-ray' view)
39	Needle bearing	54	Spring
40	Friction lining	55	Bush
41	Brake ring	56	Bridge piece
42	Locking pin	57	Cam for pump
43	Outer cage	58	Extension piece
44	Shaft	59	Input shaft
45	Planet gear carrier	60	Rear cover, gearbox
46	Sunwheel		
47	Ball bearing		

and always revolve, therefore, at mainshaft speed. The uni-directional clutch sits inside the output shaft and ensures that if nothing else is driving the output shaft it will be driven by the gearbox mainshaft. In this manner of course we get the 1 : 1 ratio. When this occurs, the planet carrier and the annulus on the output shaft are revolving at the same speed so the planet gears within the planet carrier are not being driven forwards or backwards and remain stationary on their spindles. This means that the sun wheel must also be revolving at the same speed as the planet carrier and the annulus. The sun wheel is splined to the sliding clutch member (75) and this too is revolving at the mainshaft speed. In practice the sliding clutch member is held against the tapered extension of the mainshaft when the 1 : 1 ratio is required and the whole gear system is locked together. If we look at diagram 1, Fig. 6.17 we can see this depicted.

4   To obtain the step-up ratio, the sliding clutch member is drawn away from the output shaft annulus and comes up against the outer casing of the gearbox which holds it stationary. It is still splined to the sun wheel so this, too, is prevented from turning. This is shown in Fig.6.17 Diagram 2. The planet carrier continues to revolve at mainshaft speed, but because the sun wheel is stationary the planet wheels turn around their spindles in the planet carrier. This means that the outer teeth of the planet wheel (which mesh with the annulus) are moving relative to the planet carrier, and this makes the annulus move faster than the planet carrier.

5   All we have to do to 'change gear', therefore, is to slide the clutch member (75) along the mainshaft. If we look at Figs. 6.13 and 6.14 we can see that this member is pushed forwards by four coil springs anchored by bridge pieces (for example, No. 56, Fig. 6.13) through a thrust bearing assembly. When the hydraulic system is actuated, two pistons (for example No. 14 in Fig. 6.13) push on the bridge pieces and draw the sliding member along the shaft until it comes up against the outer case. This changes the

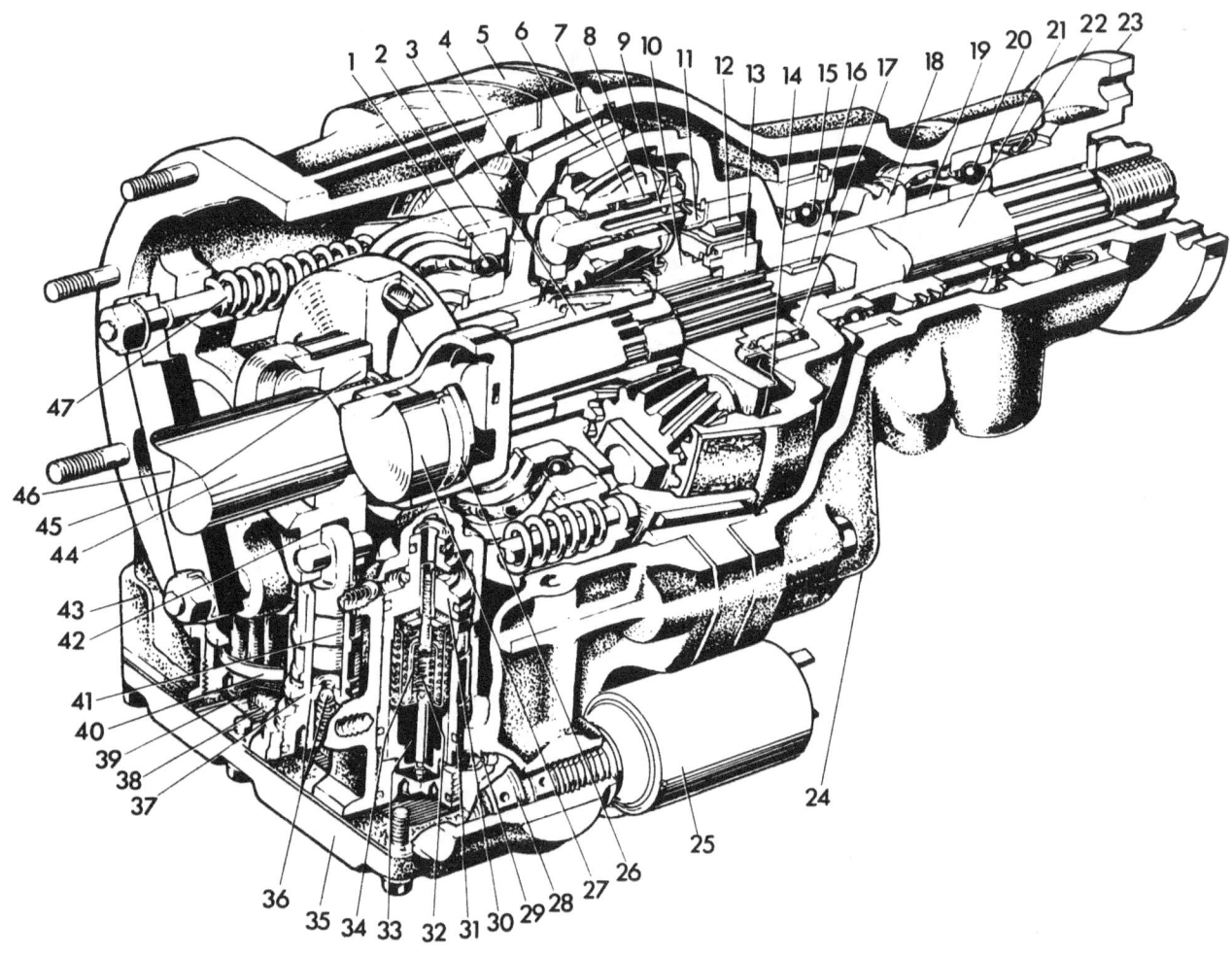

**Fig. 6.14 Overdrive fitted to
B20 engined cars**

1 Thrust bearing	13 Uni-directional clutch	25 Solenoid	37 Pump cylinder
2 Thrust bearing retainer	14 Oil trap	26 Piston seal	38 Magnet
3 Sunwheel	15 Ball bearing	27 Piston	39 Pre-filter
4 Clutch sliding member	16 Bush	28 Operating valve	40 Fine filter
5 Brake ring	17 Thrust washer	29 Orifice nozzle	41 Pump plunger
6 Clutch member linings	18 Speedometer driving gear	30 Cylinder top	42 Connecting rod
7 Planet gear	19 Spacer	31 Cylinder	43 Front casing
8 Needle bearing	20 Ball bearing	32 Spring	44 Input shaft (gear-box mainshaft)
9 Shaft	21 Output shaft	33 Large piston	45 Eccentric
10 Planet carrier	22 Oil seal	34 Small piston	46 Bridge piece
11 Oil thrower	23 Coupling flange	35 Base plate	47 Spring
12 Uni-directional clutch rollers	24 Rear casing	36 Check valve for oil pump	

drive ratio as already described.

6 We have already seen that the sliding member is bolted to bridge pieces. Behind these bridge pieces are hydraulically operated pistons which are able to push the bridge pieces away from the case against the action of the clutch return springs when the hydraulic pressure is great enough. This means that changing gear is simply a matter of raising the oil pressure

applied to the pistons. The oil pressure is generated in the first instance by a piston pump which is driven by an eccentric connected to the gearbox mainshaft. The pressure is limited by a release valve which gives either a low pressure or a high pressure according to whether the solenoid is energised or not, (details of how this is done is given in Sections 6.19 and 6,20). The oil reaches the pistons through oilways in the casing.

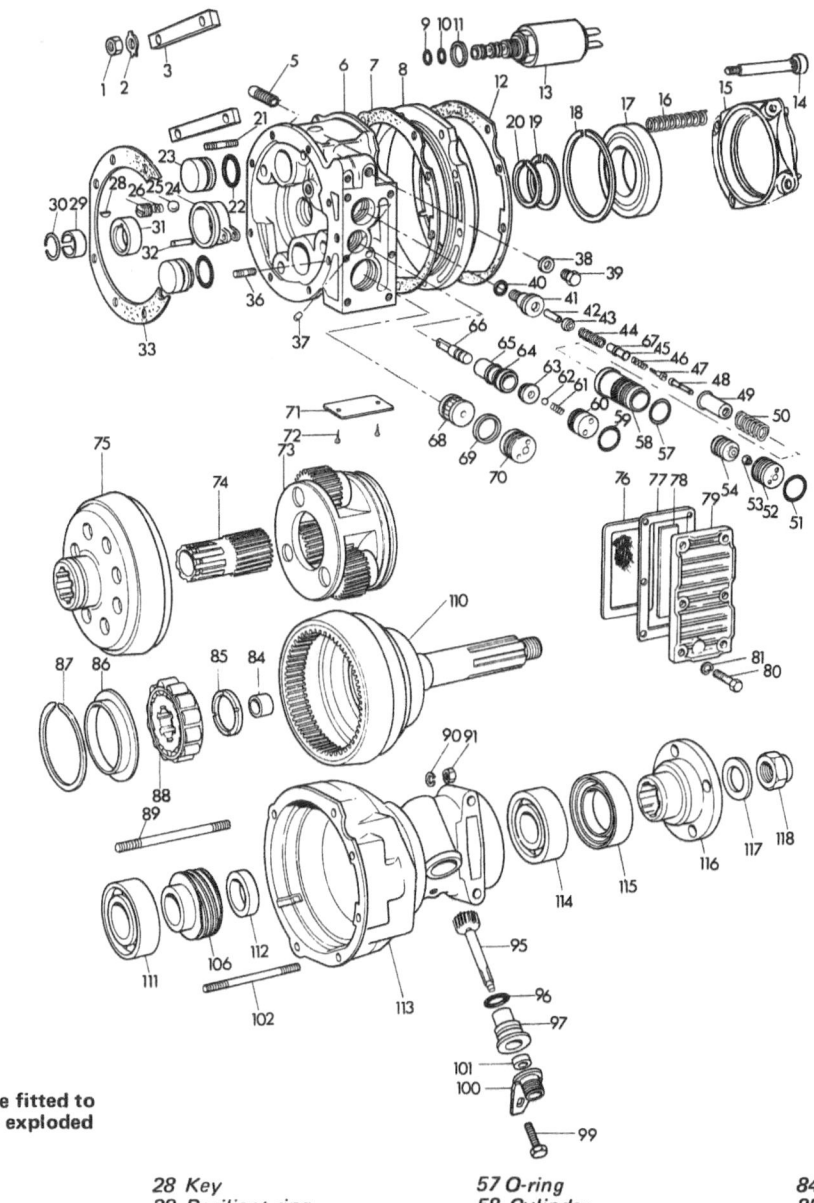

Fig. 6.15 Overdrive fitted to B20 engined cars - exploded view

1 Nut
2 Lock washer
3 Bridge piece
5 Breather
6 Front casing
7 Gasket
8 Brake ring
9 O-ring
10 O-ring
11 Seal
12 Gasket
13 Solenoid
14 Bolt
15 Thrust bearing retainer
16 Spring
17 Thrust bearing
18 Circlip
19 Circlip
20 Circlip
21 Stud
22 Piston seal
23 Piston
24 Connecting rod
25 Non-return ball
26 Non-return valve spring
27 Plug

28 Key
29 Resilient ring
30 Circlip
31 Eccentric
32 Piston pin
33 Gasket
36 Stud
37 Orifice nozzle
38 Seal
39 Plug
40 O-ring
41 End piece
42 Piston
43 Washer
44 Spring
45 Retainer
46 Spring
47 Screw
48 Screw
49 Holder
50 Spring
51 O-ring
52 Plug
53 Nut
54 Piston

57 O-ring
58 Cylinder
59 O-ring
60 Plug
61 Spring
62 Ball
63 Non-return body
64 O-ring
65 Pump body
66 Pump plunger
67 Washer
68 Fine filter
69 Seal
70 Plug
71 Data plate
72 Screw
73 Planet gear and carrier
74 Sunwheel
75 Clutch sliding member
76 Pre-filter
77 Gasket
78 Magnet
79 Base plate
80 Bolt
81 Resilient washer

84 Bush
85 Thrust washer
86 Oil thrower
87 Circlip
88 Uni-directional clutch
89 Stud
90 Resilient washer
91 Nut
95 Speedometer pinion
96 O-ring
97 Bush
99 Bolt
100 Retainer
101 Oil seal
102 Stud
106 Speedometer driving gear
110 Output shaft
111 Ball bearing
112 Spacer
113 Rear casing
114 Ball bearing
115 Oil seal
116 Flange
117 Washer
118 Nut

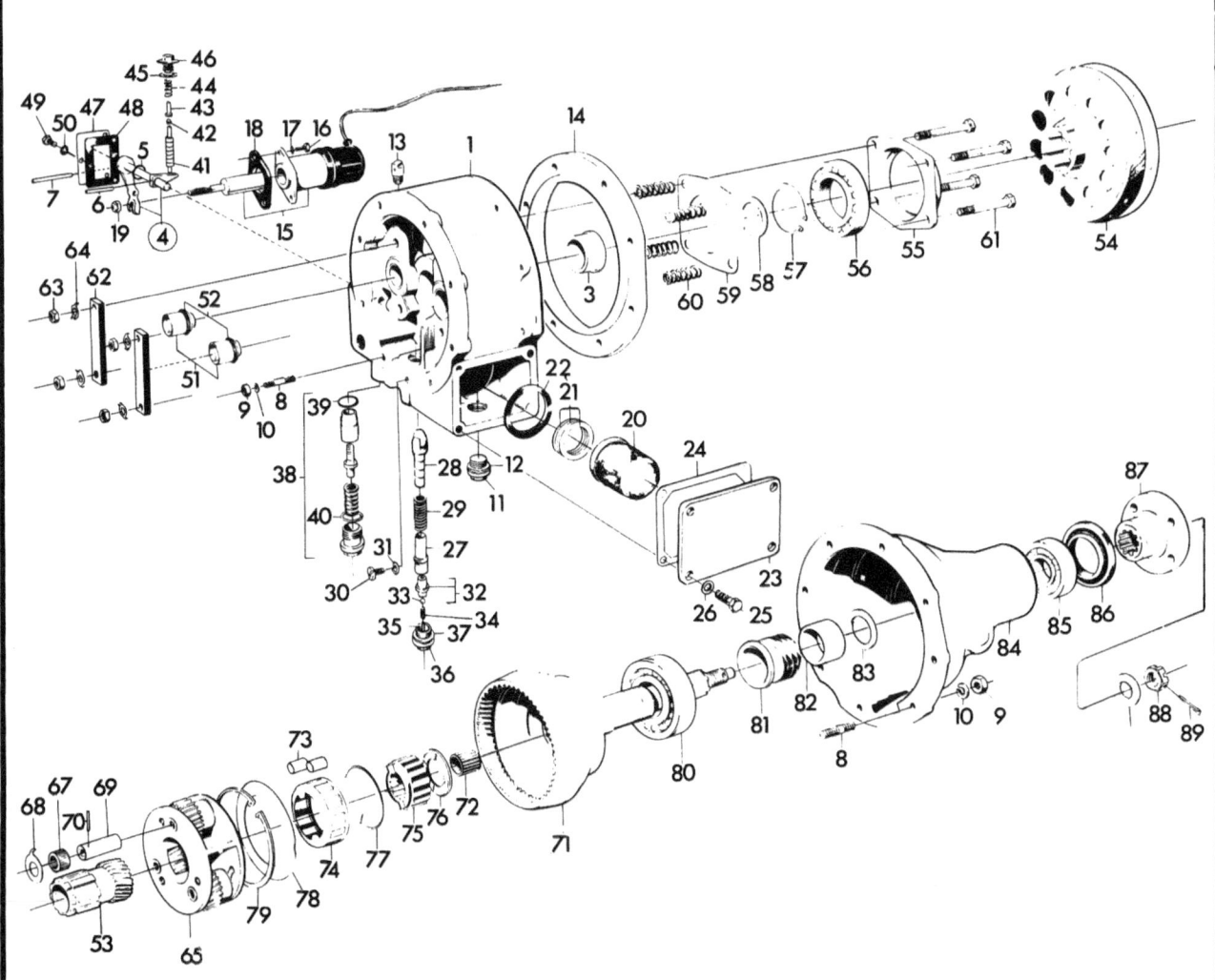

Fig. 6.16 Overdrive fitted to B18 engined cars - exploded view

1 Housing	22 Gasket	45 Spring	69 Bearing pin) gear
3 Bushing	23 Cover	46 Packing	70 Lock pin) assembly
4 Lever	24 Gasket	47 Cover	71 Shaft
5 O-ring	25 Screw (4 items)	48 Gasket	72 Needle bearing
6 Lock pin	26 Lock washer (4 items)	49 Screw (3 items)	73 Roller kit
7 Lock pin	27 Sleeve	50 Lock washer (3 items)	74 Retainer
8 Stud	28 Piston	51 Piston (2 items)	75 Bearing cone
Stud (7 items)	29 Spring	52 O-ring	76 Thrust washer
Stud (2 items)	30 Lock screw	53 Sun wheel	77 Clamping ring
Stud (6 items)	31 Washer	54 Clutch disc	78 Lock disc
9 Nut (16 items)	32 Sleeve	55 Bearing cage	79 Circlip
10 Spring washer (16 items)	33 Ball	56 Ball bearing	80 Ball bearing
11 Plug	34 Spring	57 Circlip	81 Speedometer gear
12 Packing	35 Guide pin	58 Circlip	82 Spacer sleeve
13 Air-venting nipple	36 Plug	59 Lock plate	83 Spacer washer
14 Brake drum	37 Packing	60 Spring (4 items)	84 Housing
15 Solenoid	38 Relief valve	61 Screw	85 Ball bearing
16 Screw (2 items)	39 O-ring	62 Bridge piece (2 items)	86 Seal ring
17 Lock washer (2 items)	40 Packing	63 Nut (4 items)	87 Companion flange
18 Packing	41 Operating valve	64 Lock washer (4 items)	88 Nut
19 Adjuster nut	42 Ball	65 Planetary gear assembly	89 Split pin
20 Oil strainer	43 Pin	67 Needle bearing) part of	
21 Plastic washer kit	44 Spring	68 Pressure washer) planet	

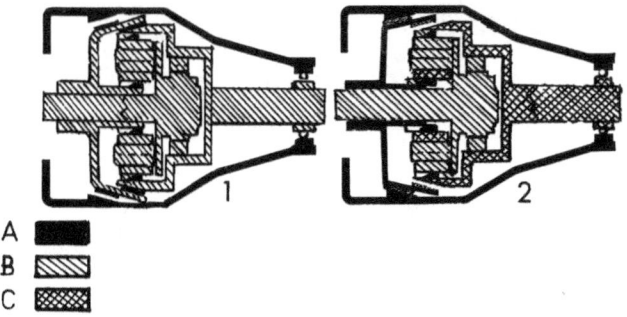

Fig. 6.17 Working principle of overdrive -

1 Direct drive   2 Overdrive
*Shading A - Non-rotating parts, Shading B - Parts
rotating at a higher speed than the input shaft, Shading C
Parts rotating at the same speed as the input shaft.*

A
B
C

19 Hydraulic pressure control - B20 overdrive

1 Fig. 6.18 is a diagram of the hydraulic circuit used on the
B20 overdrive. Although the various components in the diagram
are a good representation of the actual bits and pieces, the
connections between them are purely diagrammatic and do not
look much like the oilways in the overdrive casing which they
represent. For example, the orifice nozzle (No. 1 in Fig. 6.18
and No. 29 in Fig. 6.14) sits actually in a short channel not
much longer than itself.
2 The solenoid operated control valve is a simple double-ended
affair which is sprung against a seating and blocks off the oil
inlet to the valves when the solenoid is not energised. When
voltage is applied to the solenoid, the valve is pushed against its
spring until it comes up against a lower seating, allowing oil to
flow through the control valve and into the relief valve via the
orifice nozzle. To see how this affects the relief valve take a look
at Fig. 6.19.
3 The key to this Figure is the small piston (9) which when
pushed down by oil pressure building up in the inlet channel (6)
uncovers drillings in the body (8) which allows oil to flow into
channel (7) and also to the relief valve (5) which sets a limit on
the pressure that can build up. This cylinder acts against a
complex arrangement of dashpots and springs which eventually
all push against a large piston (1), at the bottom of the valve.
When oil is admitted into the lower input channel (15) by the
action of the control valve, this piston is pushed upwards

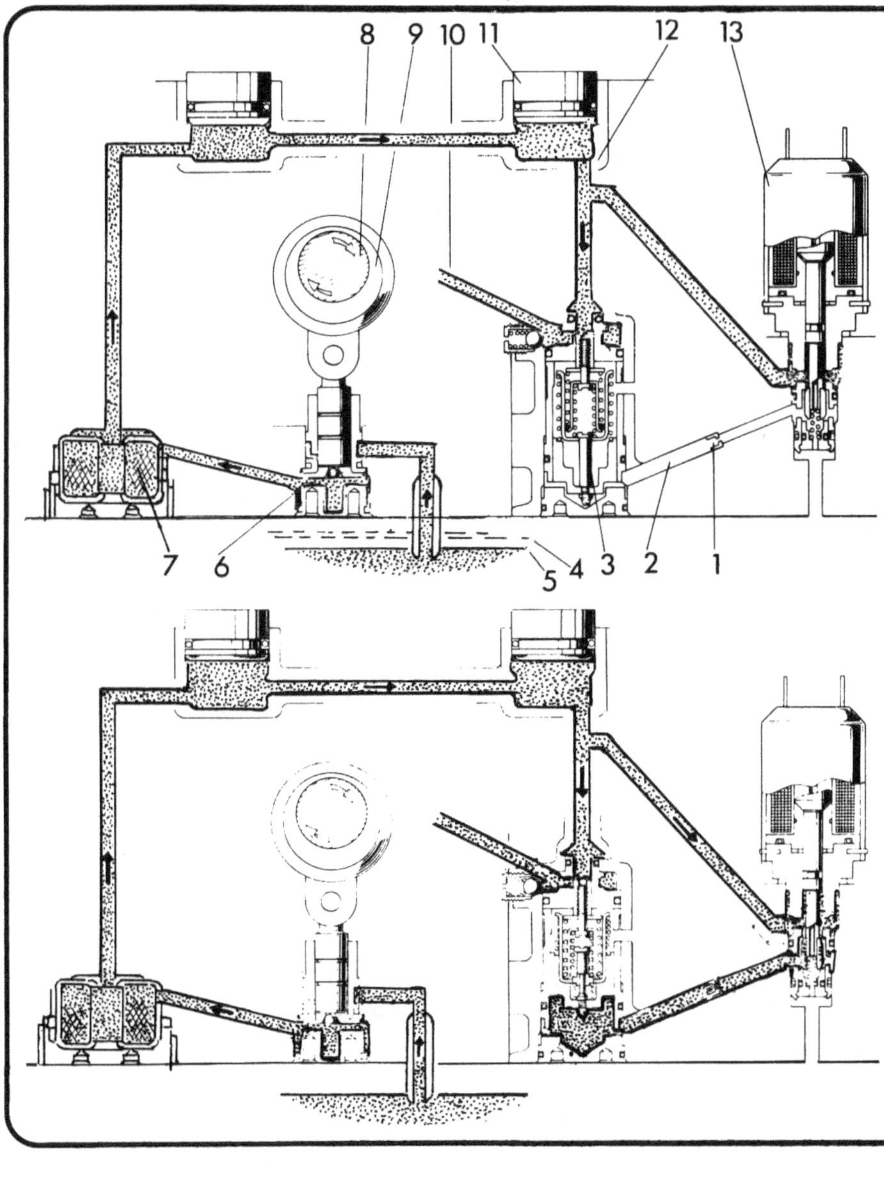

**Fig. 6.18 Hydraulic system - overdrive
fitted to B20 engined cars.**

(Top) direct drive   (Bottom) Overdrive

*1 Nozzle
2 Channel, control valve - relief valve
3 Relief valve
4 Pre-filter
5 Oil sump
6 Oil pump
7 Fine filter
8 Gearbox mainshaft
9 Eccentric
10 Channel relief valve - mainshaft
11 Piston
12 Channel, oil pump - hydraulic cylin-
     der - control and relief valves
13 Control valve and solenoid*

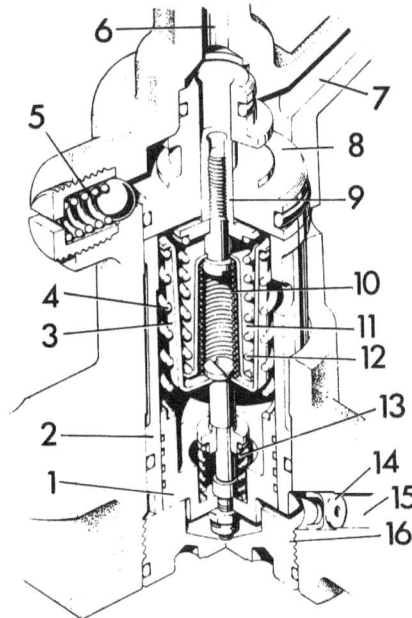

Fig. 6.19 Relief valve cutaway - overdrive fitted to B20 engines

1	Dashpot piston	9	Relief valve spindle
2	Dashpot sleeve	10	Residual spring
3	Dashpot spring cup	11	Relief valve spring cup
4	Dashpot spring	12	Relief valve spring
5	Relief valve for lubricating oil pressure	13	Double dashpot spring
6	Drilling from oil pump	14	Restrictor plug
7	Drilling to mainshaft	15	Drilling from operating valve
8	Relief valve body	16	Dashpot plug

Note - lower dashpot and item 13 are omitted in later models

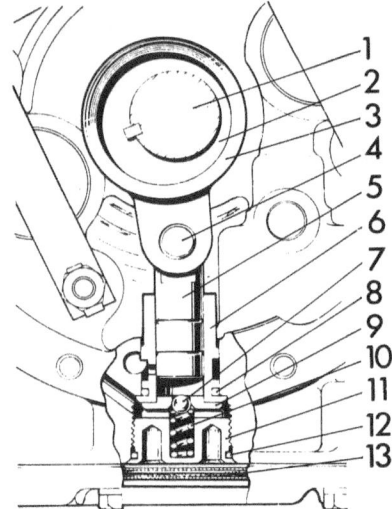

Fig. 6.20 Oil pump cutaway - overdrive fitted to B20 engines

1	Mainshaft	8	O-ring
2	Eccentric	9	Valve seat
3	Connecting rod	10	Spring
4	Gudgeon pin	11	Plug
5	Piston	12	O-ring
6	Cylinder	13	Pre-filter
7	Ball		

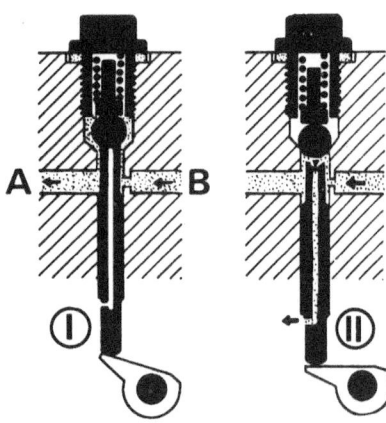

Fig. 6.21 Control valve cutaway - overdrive on B18 engines

SVO 2834

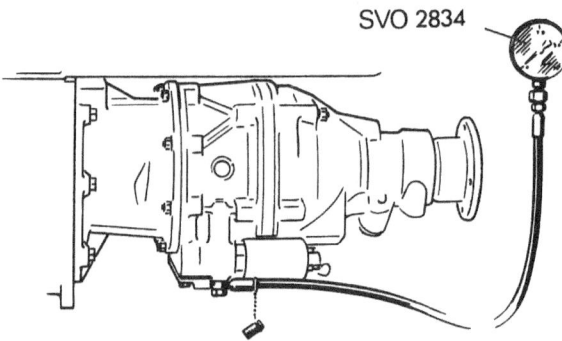

Fig. 6.22 Checking oil pressure

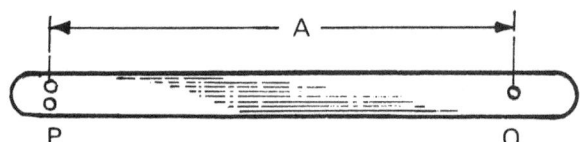

Fig. 6.23 Tool for applying correct torque when refitting plugs: To obtain correct tightening torque - connect spring balance to 'Q', keeping it at right angles to tool

'Q' Balance hole   P Pegs for holes in plugs A = 12" (30 cm). Balance reading of 16 lbs (7.33 gm) = 16 lbs. ft (2.2 kg. m) of torque.

Fig. 6.24 Three plugs under the base plate and pre-filter hold the fine filter (shown dismantled), the relief valve and the oil pump.

1   Filter
2   Seal
3   Plug

compressing the springs and thus making it harder for the small piston to be pushed down. The oil pressure builds up until this piston eventually moves against the increased spring pressure and a new state of equilibrium is reached.

4 The oil pump (shown in Fig. 6.20) is simple in principle, oil being drawn in on the up stroke of the plunger and pushed past the ball valve into the outlet channel on the down stroke. It draws oil from the bottom of the case which acts as a sump and the system incorporates a filter, just like the oil system in a car engine.

5 As well as supplying the hydraulic system, the oil pump provides pressure lubrication via a drilling in the gearbox mainshaft which connects with channel (10), Fig. 6.18. The oil finds its way through the unidirectional clutch, and via the planet gear back to the bottom of the overdrive case.

20 Differences between B18 and B20 fittings

1 The overdrive fitted to the B18 series differs in a number of details from that fitted to the B20 series, but the description above applies to both with the exception of those parts relating to the control valve and relief valve. The mechanism for obtaining different pressures in the earlier models is very much simpler than that just described.

2 Fig. 6.21 shows details of the B18 control valve. This is a relief valve in which a ball is seated on the end of a drilled rod which can be moved up and down by a lever which is operated by the solenoid. The solenoid plunger pulls on a fork on the same spindle as the lever, turning this spindle and pushing the seating rod upwards when the solenoid is energised. The mechanism is quite obvious from an examination of Fig. 6.16 where it is shown in the top left-hand corner. The valve and its rod are shown in Fig. 6.13 (parts Nos. 16,53 and 54 are the vital bits)

3 When the solenoid is energised and the control valve spring is compressed, the valve does not normally open. Pressure in the system is determined by the relief valve which is a somewhat simpler version of its counterpart in the B20 model (simpler because it is not operated by hydraulic control but simply limits the pressure). In both systems the pressure relief valve is complicated because it incorporates dashpot devices which control its opening and closing to ensure a smooth change-over from direct drive to overdrive and vice-versa.

21 Overdrive unit - removal and replacement

1 It is helpful if, before removing the overdrive, you drive the car and engage and disengage the overdrive with the clutch pedal depressed. This will avoid leaving any residual torque in the mainshaft, planet carrier and unidirectional clutch. If you have not done this, disconnect the propeller shaft and you can then of course achieve the same object without moving the car.

2 To remove the overdrive unit follow the procedure for removing the gearbox given in Section 3, paragraphs 2,6,8 and 10 until you reach the point where the overdrive is separated from the intermediate flange.

3 Refitting to the gearbox is dealt with in Section 27.

22 Overhaul - preliminaries

1 Overhauling an overdrive presents special problems to the owner mechanic whose workshop facilities are limited. These arise from the fact that the unit incorporates a hydraulic mechanism which depends for its operation on the same oil that lubricates the gears. Absolute cleanliness is therefore essential. We recommend that for anything other than the simplest check the unit is removed from the vehicle, thoroughly cleaned, and then taken to a work place where scrupulous cleanliness can be maintained throughout the whole time that the unit is dismantled. Any lower standard than this is asking for trouble. Another set of problems is posed by the multiplicity of small

parts in the hydraulic units. The best - almost the only - way to cope with these is to lay out the bits and pieces in order as they are dis-assembled, on a clean surface (a table covered with newspaper for example) where they can be covered over and left undisturbed. Putting them in small separate containers is very much a second best; if you do this you will almost certainly waste a lot of time during reassembly making sure that everything is in the right place and the right way round.

2 Dismantling and reassembling the mechanical bits and pieces presents no special problem apart from the requirement for extreme cleanliness. Have the outside spotlessly clean before you start - this is more than just a good idea - it is essential. Smear all parts with oil as you assemble them.

3 If you think we are trying to discourage you from light-heartedly stripping down your overdrive, you are right. It is a job which needs better working conditions than the average owner has available and every bit of care and thoroughness that he can muster. This being said, we would not wish to imply that it is beyond the capabilities of the average intelligent man who has some feel for engineering.

4 If the overdrive is in working order prior to overhaul, it is worthwhile to check the oil pressure. Volvo recommend that this is done while the car is being driven and their Agents have a special pressure gauge with suitable adaptors to fit to the different models of overdrive unit. For the B20 model, the pressure gauge is fitted as shown in Fig. 6.22 to a plug underneath the solenoid-controlled operating valve and on B18 model the adaptor for the pressure gauge takes the place of the plug under the relief valve. When driving on direct drive at about 25 mph (40 kmph) the pressure should be about $21/lb.in^2$ (1.5 $kg.cm^2$). When the overdrive is engaged, the pressure should rise to 455 - 500/lb. in^2 (32-35 $kg.cm^2$). When the overdrive is disengaged, the pressure should drop to about $21/lb.in.^2$ ($1.5/kg.cm.^2$) within three seconds.

23 Solenoid, oil pump, hydraulic valves - dismantling

1 Dealing first with the B20 overdrive, remove the base plate and the pre-filter and drain the oil into a perfectly clean container if you are proposing to use it again.
Warning: If the overdrive has been running just before you drain it, the oil may be hot enough to scald you.

2 Remove the solenoid, using a 1" (25 mm) open-ended spanner on the hexagon. The solenoid and operating valve form an integral unit which cannot be dismantled further and must be replaced complete if faulty.

3 Removing the base plate and pre-filter will have revealed three plugs which retain the fine filter, petrol pump and relief valve (see Fig. 6.24). To make a suitable tool for removing these plugs, get hold of two small bolts whose heads fit into the holes in the plugs and screw these into a pair of holes in a length of metal strip. If the surface of your strip rests against the plugs and the bolt heads are a reasonable fit in the holes you will be able to remove the plugs quite easily without trouble or damage (see Fig. 6.23). It is well worthwhile taking the trouble to make something like this rather than simply pushing bolts into the holes in the plugs - a method which will certainly lead to loss of time and loss of temper.

4 Remove the fine filter and its seal which are under the largest of the three plugs. Then turn your attention to the awe-inspiring assortment of bits and pieces which go to make up the relief valve. Check each part as it comes out against the exploded view in Fig. 6.15 and the cut-away view in Fig. 6.19 (the secondary dashpot is not present in later models). We strongly recommend that you lay the pieces out somewhere where they will not be disturbed or get dirty. Draw out the body of the relief valve as shown in Fig. 6.25 which also illustrates the seating at the top of the valve for the small piston and the positioning of the ball valve which limits the pressure that can build up in the relief valve. The pump plunger can now be detached from it actuator and withdrawn through the pump body, which can then be withdrawn itself using a wire hook if necessary.

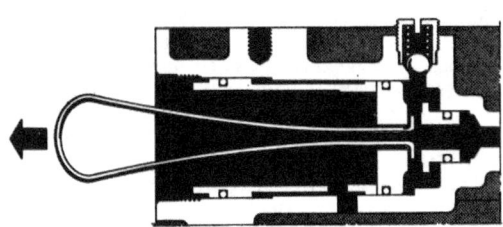

Fig. 6.25 Removing the relief valve with a wire hook

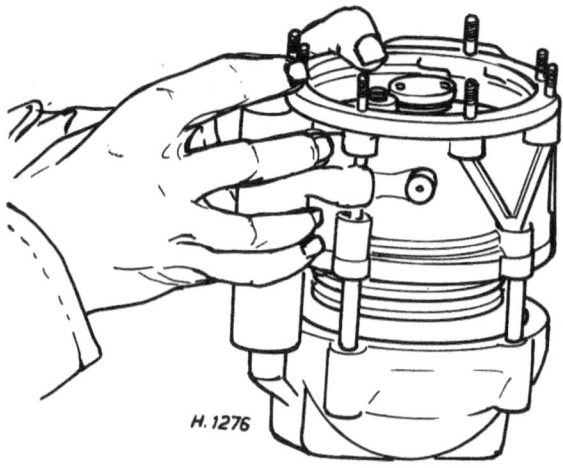

H. 1276

Fig. 6.26 Dismantling the overdrive

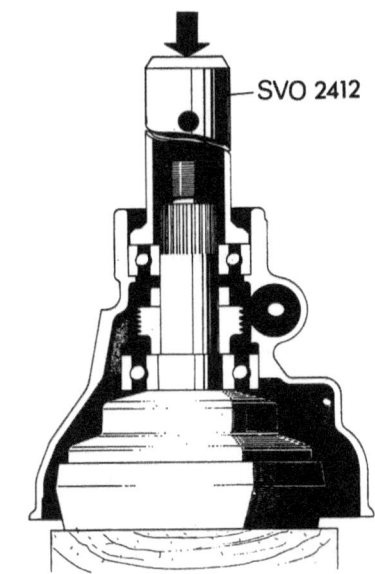

SVO 2412

Fig. 6.27 Pressing the output shaft and its bearings into the rear casing

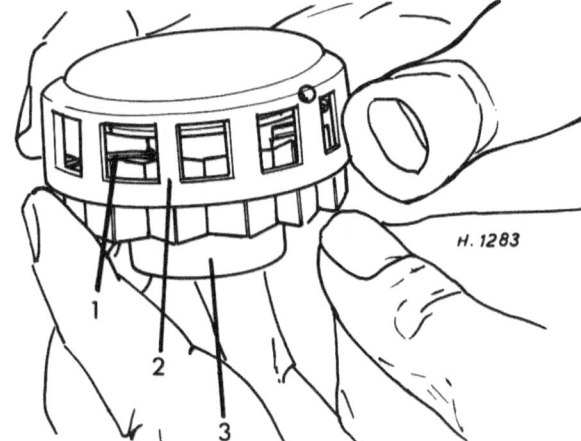

H. 1283

Fig. 6.28 Uni-directional clutch assembly

1 Spring
2 Cage
3 Hub

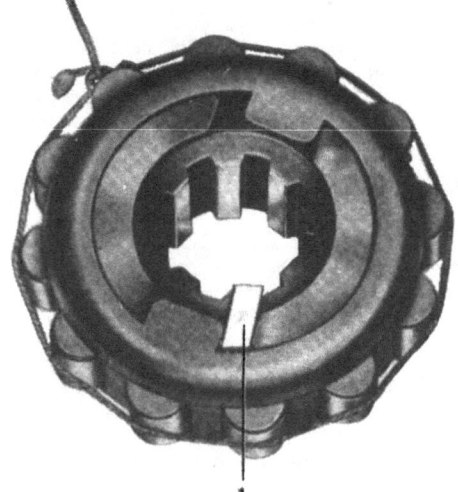

Fig. 6.29 Assembling the uni-directional clutch

1 Wedge

5   As a glance at Fig. 6.16 will show, the arrangements for the B18 overdrive are somewhat different. Drain the oil by removing the plug in the base of the casing. Then remove the side plate and withdraw the filter, the magnetic/plastic washer assembly and the gasket.

6   Now remove the plates on the other side, exposing the mechanism whereby the solenoid controls the operating valve. Detach the solenoid plunger from the small fork and remove the solenoid. Undo the plug retaining the ball valve spring (see Fig.6.21 and the exploded view in Fig. 6.16), remove the fork and lever assembly and push the piston of the valve up its drilling in the casing, expelling the spring, the pin on which the pin sits and the ball. A bit of copper wire will be helpful here. Finally, withdraw the piston itself by the same route.

7   The relief valve and the plunger for the oil pump are retained by hexagon headed plugs screwed into the base of the casing and can be withdrawn when these are removed. The oil pump plunger is drawn out upwards.

8   We strongly recommend that the considerable array of bits and pieces are carefully laid out somewhere where they will not be disturbed or get dirty.

24 Overdrive mechanical components - dismantling

1   A study of Figs. 6.13 and 6.14 will show that the two types

of overdrive are very similar mechanically, differing only in detail, for example, in the different design of the planet wheels and their bearings and the extra oil catching/oil slinging arrangements on the B20 model. The numbers in brackets in this Section refer to Fig. 6.15 which is a drawing of the B20 overdrive, but anyone dismantling a B18 overdrive will have no difficulty in following these instructions.

2 Mount the unit vertically in a vice with wooden or copper jaw inserts, front end upwards. It is assumed that at this stage the solenoid and intermediate flange have been removed.

3 Straighten the locking tabs and unscrew the nuts for the piston bridge pieces (1,2,3) and remove the bridge pieces.

4 Unscrew the nuts holding together the front and rear sections of the casing (6,113) which have the brake ring (8) sandwiched between them. These should be slackened off gradually all round in case there is a difference in tension in the clutch sliding member return springs (16). The front casing and brake ring can now be lifted off the studs in the back case as shown in Fig. 6.26.

5 If necessary, use a copper drift to help free the brake ring from the casing.

6 Remove the clutch sliding member return springs and lift this member out complete with thrust bearing and sun wheel.

7 Lift out the planet carrier complete.

8 Removal of the pistons (23) from the front casing is best done with a small sucker (you can cut down one that is too big), unless you have compressed air available, when you can blow it out.

9 From the front casing remove the pump connecting rod (24) or in the B18 model the pump plunger with its cam follower.

10 To dismantle the clutch sliding member assembly, first remove circlip (20) and pull out the sun wheel. Then remove the circlip (19) and separate the bearing (17) and its housing (15) from the clutch sliding member. Finally, remove circlip (18) and press the bearing out of its housing.

11 Turning now to the rear casing, remove the bolt (99) and pull out the speedometer pinion and its associated bits and pieces.

12 Remove the flange nut and pull the flange off the shaft. Be sure that the centre part of your puller does not damage the thread at the end of the shaft - particularly if you are using a home-made device.

13 Have a look at Fig. 6.28 which gives a good picture of the assembly of the output shaft in the rear casing. To dis-assemble this, you must first press the output shaft out of the casing, then extract the inner bearing, freeing the speedometer pinion and spacer, then press out the rear bearing. These operations may make a bigger demand on the owners workshop facilities than he is able to meet. We suggest, therefore, that having removed the oil seal (115) you check the assembly for lateral play after having washed all the oil out with paraffin followed by white spirit and if you find all is well leave it assembled; if not, have the bearings renewed at a local garage or workshop equipped for the job.

14 Remove circlip (87), take off oil thrower (86) and remove the unidirectional clutch from the annulus. Be doubly careful with the unidirectional clutch - make quite sure which way round it goes and mark it in some way to ensure that it goes back correctly, and watch the rollers as the clutch comes out - they are not attached in any way and like all such objects they have a wonderful instinct for concealment. Having got them all safely, have a good look at the way the spring and the cage are assembled in the outer frame of the unidirectional clutch. Compare the actual device with Fig. 6.28, which by itself may not be very revealing but will certainly serve as a reminder when you have seen the real thing.

15 Examine the bush (84) in the middle of the annulus before deciding to remove it, check that it is free from scores. Fit the output shaft to the gearbox mainshaft and check that there is no undue slop. We are sorry if you have got to trail out to the garage, but we think it is worth it. If you are dubious, remove the bush and fit a new one. Be careful when fitting that it goes in straight and is not distorted, or you will find yourself with a reaming job on your hands.

25 Overdrive - inspection

1 No one will dismantle an overdrive unless he is certain that there is something wrong with it - excessive noise, failure to engage or disengage properly, or something of that sort. The nature of its shortcomings will have given a clue as to what to look for on dismantling and it may well be that the fault will be revealed before dismantling is complete. If this does happen, it still makes good sense to dismantle completely and give the whole thing a thorough inspection.

2 First of all, wash out all the passages in the casings and make sure that they are clean and dry. Two common domestic objects go a long way towards substituting for the compressed air so freely mentioned in service manuals and so rarely found in owner's workshops; the ordinary hair drier and an empty plastic washing-up liquid container. This latter with its small rounded nozzle is a most useful device so long as it is clean and dry.

3 Give all the hydraulic bits and pieces a good wash and a good look over. Examine the seatings of all valves for possible scoring. Check the control valve mechanism in the B18 overdrive for wear and replace as necessary.

4 Wash the various bearings and the unidirectional clutch pieces in white spirit, dry them thoroughly with lint-free rag and inspect for excessive play and signs of wear.

5 Examine the various gears for signs of wear and damage. Make sure that the bush on the sun wheel is not worn. If it needs replacement, get a new sun wheel complete with bush - the bush must be concentric with the gear wheel and to achieve this is a factory job.

6 Check the pistons which act on the bridge pieces for signs of wear. Replace them if they are not perfect.

7 Check the brake ring for abrasion, cracks or wear.

8 Check the linings on the clutch sliding member for burning or wear.

9 Check the solenoid with a 12 volt battery and an ammeter. Current consumption should be about 2 amps and there should of course be no hesitation about its operation when it is disconnected from the unit. This should be checked again when the solenoid-operated control valve or control valve mechanism has been reassembled.

26 Overdrive - reassembly

1 Use new gaskets, O-rings, tab washers and oil seals when reassembling. If you are in any doubt about the filters, renew these too. The cost of these items is a small price to pay for peace of mind.

2 Absolute cleanliness is, of course, even more important during reassembly than during dismantling. Give every part a quick cleanliness check and smear it with oil as you reassemble. it.

3 To assemble the rear casing and output shaft, press the front bearing on to the output shaft, followed by the speedometer spacers. Press the rear bearing into the rear casing using a drift similar to that shown in Fig. 6.27. Support the output shaft on a wooden block and then press the rear casing onto the shaft by pushing on the rear bearing with the same drift. Fig. 6.27 shows this process almost completed. As mentioned in Section 24 paragraph 13, this pressing operation may prove difficult for the average owner and it may be a good idea to have it done by a specialist.

4 Press in the oil seal, lubricating it well first. Get it the right way round - see Fig. 6.15 or 6.16.

5 Fit the coupling flange, washer and nut. Tighten the nut to a torque of 80-100 lb.ft. -(11—14 kg.m).

6 Assemble the unidirectional clutch cage on the hub with the spring as shown in Fig. 6.28, so that when viewed as in Fig. 6.29 the cage is sprung anti-clockwise. Rotate the cage clockwise as far as it will go and lock it in this position with a temporary wedge as shown in Fig. 6.29. Position the rollers in the cage and

tie them in with string.

7   Insert the thrust washer and follow this by the clutch in the centre of the output shaft, easing the string off the rollers when they are held by the mainshaft and removing the temporary wedge (see Fig.6.30). Fit the oil thrower and circlip.

8   Reassemble the speedometer pinion and bush in the casing.

9   Position the planet gear assembly in the output shaft annulus. Note that when the overdrive is fitted to the gearbox the splines in the planet carrier will have to line up with those in the uni--directional clutch - both these items being splined to the gearbox mainshaft. Volvo make a special splined tool for ensuring this and you may care to make something that will do the same thing - perhaps either a wooden dowl with one or more 'splines' made of metal strip - but it can be done without as there is no centering problem - it is simply a matter of getting the splines lined up. You could do this at the last minute with a thin screwdriver pushed up the middle of the assembly.

10 Turning now to the clutch unit, first press the ball bearing into its retainer and fit the circlip (Fig. 6.15 Nos. 15,17, 18 - numbers in brackets in the following paragraphs also refer to this figure).

11 Put the bolts (14) through their holes on the retainer and press the bearing with retainer on to the clutch sliding member. Fit the circlip (19). Fit the sun wheel and its circlip (20).

12 Insert the sun wheel into the planet cluster and fit the four thrust springs (16) on to the bolts. The clutch/output shaft assembly is now complete.

13 Now is a good time to consider exactly how you are going to ensure that those splines are lined up. It is better to solve this problem on the bench than underneath the car.

14 Assembly of the hydraulic components in the front case calls for no particular comment, being simply a reversal of the dismantling process. Don't forget a light smear of oil on everything. Put the actuating pistons (23) back in the case before assembling the valves and pump to avoid possible trouble with air pressure behind them. For the B18 model, do not assemble the oil pump completely at this stage; simply put the plunger into the casing and assemble the rest of the pump after the overdrive has been fitted to the gearbox. Otherwise you will have trouble with the pump plunger interferring with the cam on the gearbox mainshaft when you offer the overdrive unit to the gearbox.

15 Install the brake ring on the front casing and reassemble the front and rear casings with the brake ring between them exactly as they were taken apart (see Fig. 6.26). Tighten the fixing nuts evenly, a little at a time all round to avoid any possibility of distortion by the tension in the clutch springs. Note that the two upper fixing nuts have copper washers. Don't forget the tag washers on the nuts for the bridge pieces.

16 Finally, fit the solenoid and check its operation, adjusting the linkage as necessary on the B18 version.

27 Overdrive - refitting to gearbox

1   It is as important to preserve cleanliness during this operation (carried out underneath the car in all probability) as it is when you are assembling the overdrive unit on your specially cleaned work bench. When working underneath the car it is easy to accidentally dislodge dirt from the subframe; this dirt then rains down - and could enter the overdrive unit if precautions are not taken during refitment. To avoid this problem, we suggest that you stick newspaper above the gearbox area so that at least the fall-out doesn't descend all over the overdrive. If the car is well jacked up you will have more room to work and that's a help.

2   Don't forget the gasket.

3   A look at Fig. 6.14 will show that when you offer the overdrive unit to the gearbox the splines on the mainshaft will enter the unidirectional clutch at much the same time as the eccentric enters the connecting rod for the pump. However, thanks to the generous chamfer provided on this component it will pull itself into line if it is not exactly right to start with. The secret of success is to arrange matters by lining up the mainshaft

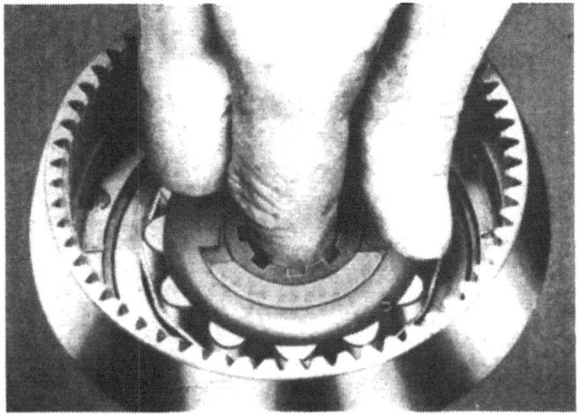

Fig. 6.30 Fitting the uni-directional clutch into the ouput shaft

splines, their opposite numbers on the unidirectional clutch and the planet gear cage and the pump connecting rod so that you can slide the unit straight on to the intermediate flange (attached to the gearbox) and pick up the holes on the flange with the studs - all this without having to turn the overdrive unit. Careful alignment before you start and a small amount of rocking just as the studs enter the intermediate flange should do the trick. If it doesn't, the best thing to do is to withdraw the unit and do the lining up again.

4   On the B18 overdrive, you still have the oil pump to install.

5   The rest of the installation is a simple reversal of the removal procedure.

6   Finally, don't forget to fill the unit with oil until level with the bottom of the filler plug hole in the side of the case. Check the oil after the car has been driven 6-9 miles (10-15 kms).

28 Overdrive - fault diagnosis

We list below the commonest troubles experienced with overdrive and some possible causes. Start at the top of the list when looking for a fault and work your way through it. The overdrive is a well tried and well proven mechanism and - as the list reveals - trouble is more often due to causes outside the overdrive unit itself than within it.

Overdrive will not engage
1   Faulty solenoid.
2   Fault in electric wiring.
3   Faulty gearbox switch.
4   Faulty overdrive selector switch.
5   Faulty relay (if fitted).
6   Low oil level in overdrive unit.
7   Faulty non-return valve in oil pump.
8   Blocked oil filter.

Overdrive will not release
NOTE: This fault should be attended to immediately. Above all, do not reverse when overdrive is engaged as this will cause considerable damage.
1   Fault in electrical wiring, (voltage permanently on solenoid).
2   Control valve (integral with solenoid on B20 models all mechanically operated by solenoid on B18 models) sticking.
3   Mechanical damage in overdrive (note that when found this may be the result of the trouble and not its original cause).
4   Sticking uni-directional clutch.

Clutch slip in overdrive
1   Low oil level in overdrive unit.
2   Control valve incorrectly adjusted or not operating properly.
3   Worn linings on clutch sliding member.

Noise

As the overdrive ages, normal wear may give rise to a certain amount of noise when the unit is in overdrive. Regard any harsh noise with the utmost suspicion. The only way you can be reasonably certain that the noise in your unit is significant or not is to consult someone who has the experience necessary to judge it.

29 Automatic transmission unit - general description

The Borg Warner Model 35 automatic transmission system fitted to the Volvo 140 series comprises two main components - a three element hydrokinetic torque converter coupling capable of torque multiplication at an infinitely variable ratio between 2 : 1 and 1 : 1 and a hydraulically operated epicyclic gearbox providing three forward ratios and reverse.

The automatic transmission is connected to an oil cooler which is housed in the bottom of the radiator. On some earlier models the oil cooler may not be fitted.

The control lever (which may be mounted on the steering column or the floor) has six positions in later models, five in earlier ones. Position 'P' locks the transmission for parking; 'R' is reverse; 'N' is neutral; 'D' is the normal driving position; '2' stops the gearbox from engaging its third gear; '1' keeps the gear-box in first gear. In earlier models, instead of positions '1' '2'.

An overall view of the automatic transmission unit is shown in Fig. 6.31. Fig. 6.32 shows diagramatically how the oil cooler is connected and Fig. 6.33 illustrates the position of the oil cooler connectors on the unit.

30 Automatic transmission - repair and maintenance

Because of the complexity of this unit, we do not recommend that the owner should attempt to dismantle it himself. If performance is not up to standard or some failure occurs, your Volvo Agent should be called in. He will have special equipment for accurate fault diagnosis and rectification. Bear in mind that many tests of the unit are best carried out when it is still in the car, so if you have (or suspect) trouble, do not remove the unit from the car before placing it in the hands of the repairer.

The following Sections, therefore, confine themselves to adjustments and servicing information. Instruction for removal is given because this is an essential preliminary to removing the engine. Tightening torques are given in the specifications at the beginning of this Chapter.

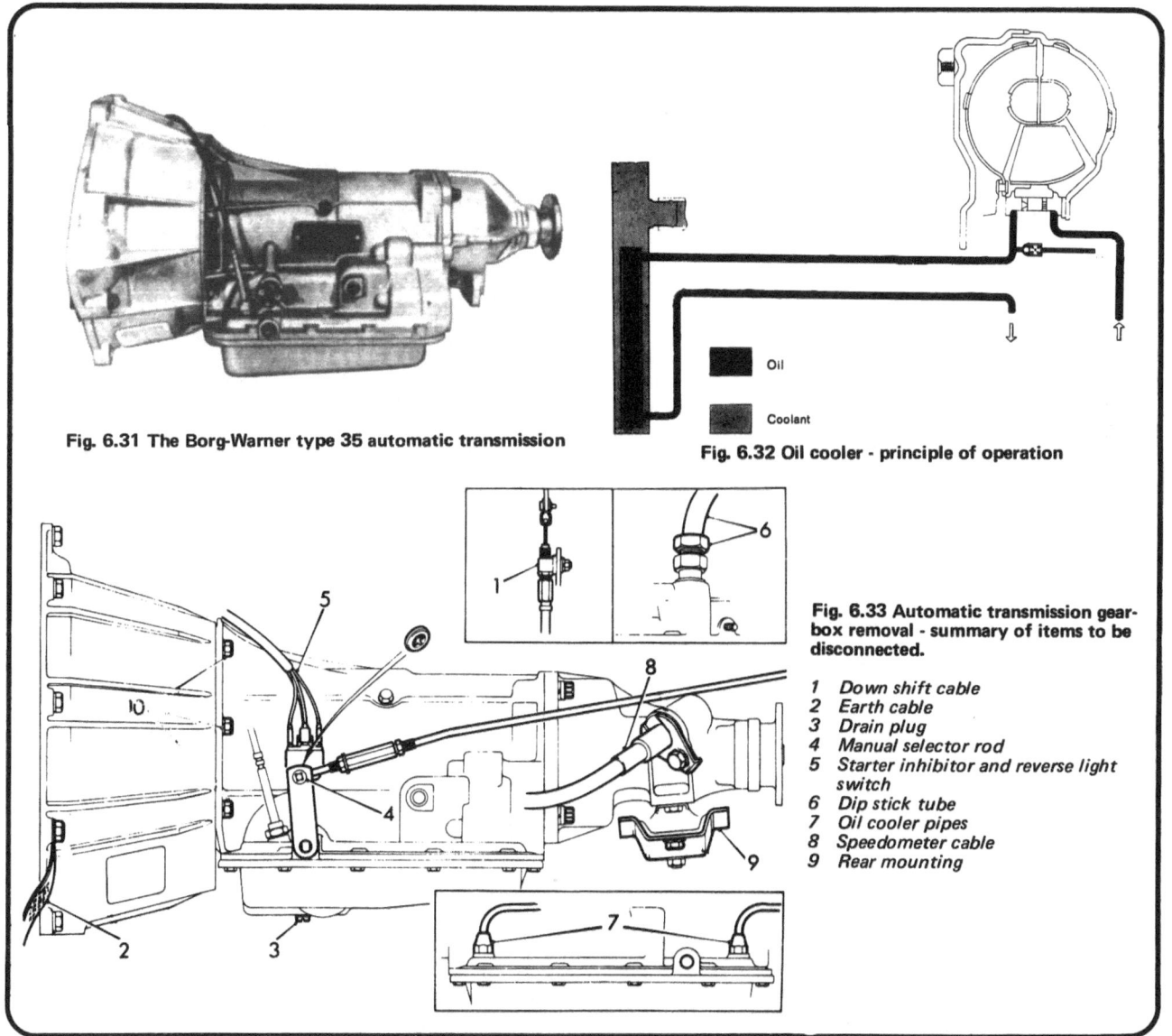

Fig. 6.31 The Borg-Warner type 35 automatic transmission

Fig. 6.32 Oil cooler - principle of operation

Oil

Coolant

Fig. 6.33 Automatic transmission gear-box removal - summary of items to be disconnected.

1 Down shift cable
2 Earth cable
3 Drain plug
4 Manual selector rod
5 Starter inhibitor and reverse light switch
6 Dip stick tube
7 Oil cooler pipes
8 Speedometer cable
9 Rear mounting

31 Automatic transmission fluid

It is important that the transmission fluid is manufactured to the correct specification. Castrol TQF is ideal. The capacity of the unit is approximately 9½ Imperial pints (11.4 U.S. pints; 5.4 litres), the oil cooler taking a further 1½ Imperial pints (1.7 U.S. pints; 0.8 litres). If the unit is drained, 3½ Imperial pints (4.2 U.S. pints; 2.4 litres) will remain in the converter so that you will need that much less oil to refill it. Full information on checking the oil level will be found in the routine maintenance Section at the beginning of this Manual.

32 Automatic transmission - removal and replacement

1 Think twice before removing the unit if it is faulty. Much fault diagnosis is best carried out with the unit still in the car, and the best thing is to take the car with the unit still in it to a specialist repairer.
2 The unit is best removed in two parts - gearbox and converter housing. To remove the gearbox, first get the car well off the ground as the unit is fairly heavy and you will want room to manoeuvre. Use ramps if possible, or, failing that, high axle stands.
3 Disconnect the battery lead (to avoid possible strain on it when you lower the engine) and items 1-9 shown in Fig.6.33.
4 Support the transmission unit with a jack underneath the oil pan; use a wooden pad to spread the weight. Arrange things so that later on you will be able to lower the engine about 1" (2.5 cms). Raise the engine and gearbox sufficiently to enable you to remove the crossmember supporting the rear end of the transmission unit.
5 Drain the oil from the transmission unit.
   WARNING: If the unit has been running just before it is drained, the oil can be hot enough to scald you.
6 Disconnect the exhaust pipe from its flange at the engine. Disconnect the battery lead in case it gets strained when the engine is lowered.
7 Disconnect the propeller shaft from the transmission unit flange.
8 Now lower the engine about ¾" (20 mm) and position a jack under it to take most of the weight. This will enable you to unscrew the bolts (No.10 in Fig. 6.33) holding the gearbox to the converter. Ease the gearbox backwards and remove it when it is free.
9 Unbolt and remove the starter motor and than take off the converter housing. The converter itself is fastened to the flywheel via a special adaptor plate with four bolts, see Fig.6.34. Mark the converter, plate and flywheel to ensure that you can re-fit them in the same relative positions, undo the four bolts and remove the converter. It will have quite a lot of oil in it - be prepared for this.
10 Replacement is a straightforward reversal of the removal process. Use new tab washers when fixing the converter to the flywheel and tighten the bolts a little at a time all round to a torque of 25-30 lb.ft. (3.4-4.1 Kg.m.).
11 When replacing the gearbox, carefully align the converter and front pump driving dogs and slots - also the input shaft and drive dogs. You should then be able to assemble the gearbox to the housing without difficulty. Tighten the six securing bolts to a torque of 8-13 lb.ft. (1.1-1.8 kg.m.).
12 The rest of the reassembly needs no special comment.

33 Starter inhibitor/reverse light switch - check and adjustment

1 Firmly chock all wheels and apply the handbrake.
2 Make a note of the electrical cable connections to the switch and then detach the terminals. The starter terminals are narrow and the reverse terminals wide.
3 Connect a test lamp and battery to the starter inhibitor terminals and unscrew the switch until the test lamp comes on

(don't bother to do this, of course, if the lamp is on already) then screw in the switch until the lamp goes out. Mark this position on the housing and gearbox. (Fig.6.35).
7 Connect the test lamp to the reversing light terminals and follow the same procedure, finishing with another pencil mark on the switch housing to indicate where the lamp is on the verge of coming on. Now set the switch midway between these positions. Lock with the locknut, connect the leads, put back the selector lever if necessary, and finally check that the switch is behaving properly when the entire system is reconnected to the vehicle.
8 If the switch is to be renewed, always apply a little liquid sealer to the threads of the new switch to preclude any possibility of oil leaks.

34 Down shift cable - adjustment

1 Be sure before you adjust the down shift cable that it really needs adjustment and there is not some other fault. During the production of the car the adjustment is set by a crimped stop on the carburettor end of the inner cable. It is unusual for this setting to change except after high mileages when the inner cable can stretch. If difficulty is experienced in obtaining 2:1 down shift in the 'kick-down' position at just below 31 m.p.h. (48 km.p.h.) it is an indication that the outer cable is too short. If there is a bumpy or delayed shift at low throttle opening it is an indication that the outer cable is too long. To check and adjust proceed as follows:
a) Apply the handbrake firmly and chock the front wheel.
b) Run the engine until it reaches normal operating temperature. Put the selector in the "D" position and adjust the engine idle speed to 700 - 750 rpm.
c) Stop the engine and with an open spanner slacken the locknut (4, Fig.6.36) at the carburettor end of the cable. Adjust the threaded sleeve until it almost touches the stop crimped on the cable in the case of single carburettor or fuel injection engines or is 1/32 in. (1 mm) away from the stop for twin carburettor engines.
d) If this is not possible, you will have to carry on with the next part of the procedure. If all is well however, set the selector to "N" and reset the engine idle to 700 rpm.
e) Where the above procedure has not done the trick, you will have to remove the oil pan and work at this end of the cable. Before doing this, thoroughly clean around the drain plug (so as not to get dirt in the oil when it comes out), undo the plug and drain the oil into a perfectly clean container of at least 8 Imperial pints (9½ U.S. pints, 4½ litres) capacity.
f) Undo and remove the 15 oil pan retaining bolts and spring washers. Take care not to damage the joint between the transmission casing and the pan.
g) With the engine idle speed correctly set and the throttle pedal released, the heel of the cam should contact the full diameter of the down shift valve with all the slack on the inner cable taken up (see 'Idle' position, Fig.6.36). If necessary, alter the position of the crimped stop on the cable so that this can be achieved with a fairly central setting of the threaded adjustment sleeve.
h) When this has been done, check that with the accelerator pedal fully depressed and the carburettor lever at the full open stop, the constant radius area of the cam makes contact with the down shift valve (see 'Kick-down' position, Fig 6.36).
i) Refit the oil pan, tightening the bolts in a diagonal pattern.
j) Refill the transmission with the fluid you drained out of it. Top up if necessary with Castrol TQF.

35 Selector linkage - adjustment

1 Basically, this is very simple, irrespective of the selector mechanism employed. Fig. 6.37 shows the relationship between the lever positions on the gearbox and the setting of the floor

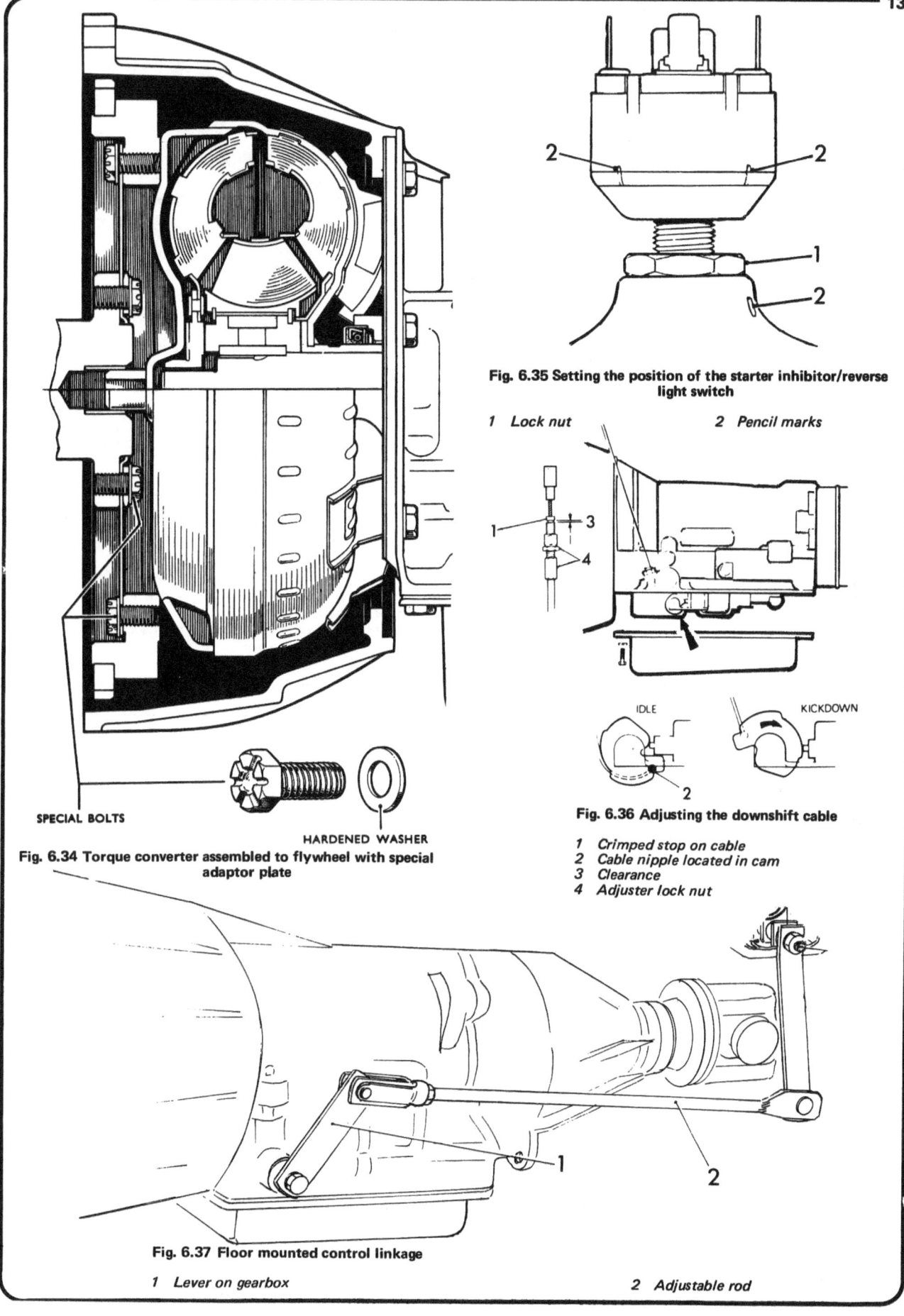

SPECIAL BOLTS

HARDENED WASHER

Fig. 6.34 Torque converter assembled to flywheel with special adaptor plate

Fig. 6.35 Setting the position of the starter inhibitor/reverse light switch

1   Lock nut   2   Pencil marks

Fig. 6.36 Adjusting the downshift cable

1   Crimped stop on cable
2   Cable nipple located in cam
3   Clearance
4   Adjuster lock nut

IDLE   KICKDOWN

Fig. 6.37 Floor mounted control linkage

1   Lever on gearbox   *2   Adjustable rod*

mounted selector. The gearbox lever clicks into position and the selector rod length should be adjusted by the turn buckle so that the lever clicks into place under the control of its detent for every setting of the selector. Note that in some models where 'L' takes the place of '2' and '1' there are nevertheless six click positions on the gearbox lever. To avoid any confusion due to this, check your settings starting with the 'Park' or 'P' position.

2 For the steering column selector, carry out the same procedure on the selector rod illustrated in Fig. 6.38. In this case you remove the top end of the rod from the ball joint and adjust its length by screwing up or unscrewing the ball socket on the rod.

36 Automatic transmission - fault diagnosis and rectification

1 The test procedure with its accompanying diagnosis and rectification instructions given in Section 58 will enable the owner to decide for himself whether or not the automatic transmission unit is faulty and, if faults are present, whether he himself will be able to rectify them or whether the fault must be corrected by a Volvo Agent.

2 Test No. 3 in this procedure is described in a little more detail in the remainder of this Section.

3 Before carrying out a stall test, make sure that the engine is developing full power and is properly adjusted. An engine which is not developing full power will affect the stall test reading.

4 Allow the engine and transmission to reach correct working temperatures.

5 Connect a tachometer to the vehicle.

6 Chock the wheels and apply the handbrake and foot brake (devise some means of clamping the foot brake pedal).

7 Select position 'L' or 'I' and run the engine with the accelerator pedal fully depressed. Check the engine speed against the figures specified at the beginning of the Chapter. Repeat the procedure with the selector in position 'L'. The implications of speed readings outside the specification and other possible symptoms are discussed in Section 58, Test 3.

8 Do not carry out a stall test for a longer period than 10 seconds, otherwise the transmission will overheat.

37 Converter fault diagnosis

1 Inability to start on steep gradients, combined with poor acceleration from rest and low speed, indicate that the converter stator unidirectional clutch is slipping. This permits the stator to rotate in an opposite direction to the impeller and turbine and torque multiplication cannot occur.

2 Poor acceleration in third gear above 30 m.p.h. (48 km.p.h.) indicates that the stator unidirectional clutch has seized. The

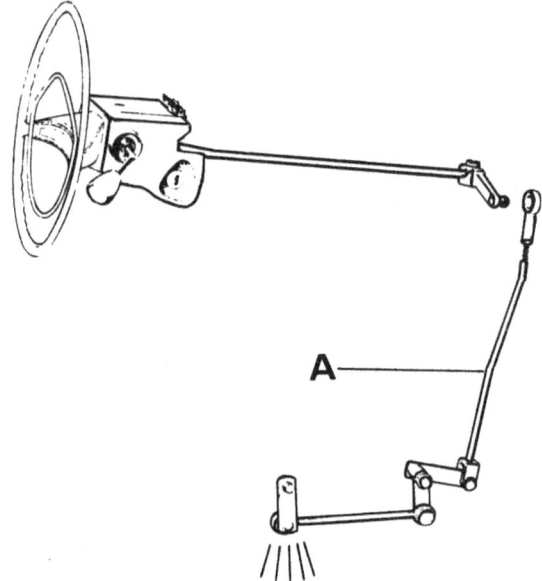

stator will not rotate with the turbine and impeller and the 'fluid flywheel' phase cannot occur. This condition will also be indicated by excessive overheating of the transmission although the stall speed may be correct.

Fig. 6.38 Steering column control linkage A - Adjustable rod

38 Road test procedure

The following test procedure may well be carried out periodically by the owner who is concerned with ensuring that his automatic transmission remains in tip-top condition. It will indicate the necessity for adjustment and may well reveal faults at an early stage, before they make themselves obvious by producing catastrophic failure.

We recommend that, even if you think you have found the cause of any trouble, you carry the tests through completely once you have started. One fault may give rise to another and it is as well to be sure that you know the full extent of the trouble; if any.

The test procedure follows.

ROAD TEST	FAULT DIAGNOSIS	RECTIFICATION (See table overleaf)
1. Check that the starter will operate only with the selector lever in 'P' and 'N' and that the reverse light operates only in 'R'	Starter will not operate in 'P' or 'N' Starter operates in all selector positions	19 20
2. Apply the hand and foot brakes and with the engine idling select 'N–D', 'N–2', 'N–1' (or 'N–L') and 'N–R'. Gearbox engagement should be felt in each position	Excessive bump on engagement of 'D', '2', 'I' or 'R'	4, 3
3. Check the stall speed in 'I' (or 'L') and 'R' Do not stall for more than 10 seconds or transmission will overheat	High stall speed: a) With slip and squawk in 'I' or 'L' b) With slip and squawk in 'R' Low stall speed: more than 600 rpm below that specified at start of Chapter Low stall speed: less than 600 rpm below that specified at start of Chapter	 1, 2, 3, 13a, c, f, 11 1, 2, 3, 13a, c, f, e, 12 21 23

4. With transmission at normal running temperature, select 'D' release the brakes and accelerate with minimum throttle. Check for 1—2 and 2—3 shifts. Confirm that third gear has been obtained by selecting '2' (or 'L') when a 3—2 shift should be felt	No drive in 'D' '2' or 'I' No drive in 'D', drive in 'I' No drive in 'D', '2', 'I' (or 'L') or 'R' Delayed or no 1—2 shift Slip on 1—2 shift Delayed or no 2—3 shift (if normal drive in 'R', omit 12)	1, 2, 3, 13a, 11, 16 1, 2, 3, 16 1, 2, 3, 13a, 11, 16, 17 3, 14, 13a, 5, 6 2, 3, 5, 6, 7, 13c, f 3, 14, 13g, h, c, d, 5, 6, 12
NOTE: A feature of this transmission is that a slight increase in throttle depression between 15 and 30 mph (25 and 48 kmph) may produce a 3—2 down-shift (part throttle down-shift)	Slip or engine run-up on 2—3 shift Bumpy gear-shifts Drag in 'D' and '2' Drag or binding on 2—3 shift	2, 3, 5, 13a, c, 12 3 8 5, 6
5. From a standing start, accelerate using 'kick-down'. Check for 1—2 and 2—3 shifts at speeds specified at start of Chapter	Slip and squawk or judder on full throttle take-off in 'D' Loss of performance and overheating in third gear Other possible faults are as given in test No. 4	1, 2, 3, 13a, c, 11 21 Continue as in test 4

6a. At 40 mph (65 kmph) in top gear release the accelerator and select '2' or 'L'. Check for 3—2 shift and engine braking
    Check for 2—1 roll out
b. At 15 mph (25 kmph) in second gear release the accelerator and select 'I'
    Check for 2—1 shift
	No 3—2 down-shift or engine braking
	
	No 2—1 down-shift and engine braking
		1, 5, 6, 7, 12
		
		8, 9, 10

7a. At the speed specified for 3—2 shift, in 3rd gear, depress the accelerator to kick-down, when the gearbox should down-shift to second gear b. At the speed specified for 3—1 shift, in second gear, depress the accelerator to kick-down when the gearbox should down-shift to first gear	Transmission will not down-shift Transmission will not down-shift	3, 13f, g, 14 3, 13f, g, 14
8a. Stop, engage 'I' or 'L' and accelerate to 20 mph (30 kmph). Check for clutch slip or breakaway noise (squawk) and that no up-shift occurs b. Stop, engage 'R' and reverse the vehicle using full throttle if possible. Check for clutch or breakaway noise (squawk)	Slip, squawk or judder on take-off in 'L' Transmission up-shifts Slip, squawk or judder on take-off in 'R' As above, with engine braking available in 'I' Slip but no judder on take-off in 'R'. No engine braking available in 'I' Drag in 'R' No drive in 'R', no engine braking in 'I' As above, with engine braking in 'I'	1, 2, 3, 13, 11 1 1, 2, 3, 13b, c, e, f, g, 12 1, 2, 3 1, 2, 3, 8, 9, 10 5 1, 2, 3, 8, 13e, f, g, 9, 10, 12 1, 2, 3, 13e, 12
9. Stop the vehicle facing downhill, apply the brakes and select 'P'. Release the brakes and check that the pawl holds. Re-apply the brakes before disengaging 'P'. Repeat facing uphill	Parking pawl inoperative Miscellaneous: Screech or whine increasing with engine speed Grinding or grating noise from gearbox Knocking noise from torque converter area At high speeds in 'D' transmission down-shifts to second ratio and immediately up-shifts back to third ratio	1, 15 17 18 22 12

RECTIFICATION CHART

X 1 Check manual linkage adjustment
X 2 Recheck fluid level
X 3 Check adjustment of down-shift valve cable
X 4 Reduce engine idle speed
   5 Check adjustment of front band
   6 Check front servo seals and fit of tubes
   7 Check front band for wear
   8 Check adjustment of rear band
   9 Check rear servo seal and fit of tubes
  10 Check rear band for wear
  11 Examine front clutch, check ball valve and seals, also
      forward sun gear shaft sealing rings. Verify that cup
      plug in driven shaft is not leaking or dislodged
  12 Examine rear clutch, check ball valve and seals
      Verify that rear clutch spring seat inner lip is not
      proud. Check fit of tubes

  13 Strip valve bodies and clean, checking:
      a. Primary regulator valve sticking
      b. Secondary regulator valve sticking
      c. Throttle valve sticking
      d. Modulator valve sticking
      e. Servo orifice control valve sticking
      f. 1 to 2 shift valve sticking
      g. 2 to 3 shift valve sticking
      h. 2 to 3 shift valve plunger sticking
  14 Strip governor valve and clean
  15 Examine parking pawl, gear, and internal linkage
  16 Examine one-way clutch
  17 Strip and examine pump and drive tangs
  18 Strip and examine gear train
X 19 Adjust starter inhibitor switch inwards
X 20 Adjust starter inhibitor switch outwards
X 21 Replace torque converter
X 22 Examine torque converter drive plate for cracks or fracture
X 23 Check engine performance

Items marked thus X can be carried out by the owner as they do not involve stripping down the unit.

Chapter 7 Propeller shaft

Contents

1 General description

1 The propeller shaft couples two rotating parts which move independently of each other. The engine moves a comparatively small amount in its mountings, while the rear axle has a considerable degree of fore and aft displacement. Hence the universally accepted arrangement of universal joints and sliding splines. Because the propeller shaft rotates without being rigidly clamped anywhere, it has to be very carefully balanced or it will vibrate. This balance is lost if the shaft is distorted and runs out of true. Wear in the universal joints will allow it to rotate off centre and this too will produce vibration.

2 The Volvo propeller shaft is made in two parts (Fig.7.1). The front part is coupled by a universal joint to a flange on the gear box or, if fitted, the overdrive unit, and is supported at its other end by a ball bearing in a flexible rubber housing. This arrangement takes care of engine movement. (Fig.7.2).

3 The rear half has two universal joints. At one end it terminates in a flange which is connected to the rear axle and at the other end the universal joint is connected to a splined shaft which slides into the front part. The spline allows for the fore and aft movement of the rear axle.

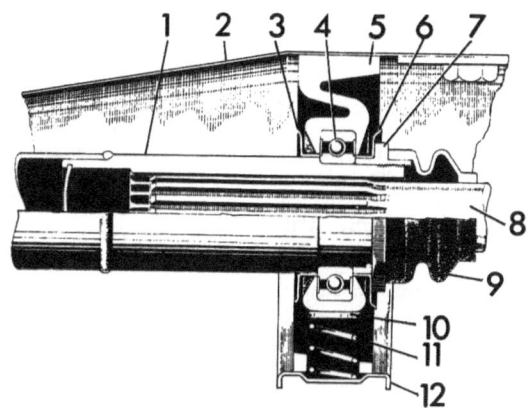

Fig. 7.2 Propeller shaft support bearing

1 Front section of propeller shaft
2 Floor tunnel
3 Dust cover
4 Ball bearing
5 Rubber housing
6 Dust cover
7 Nut
8 Rear section of propeller shaft
9 Rubber cover
10 Washer
11 Suspension spring
12 Cover

(Note: earlier types differ slightly in detail)

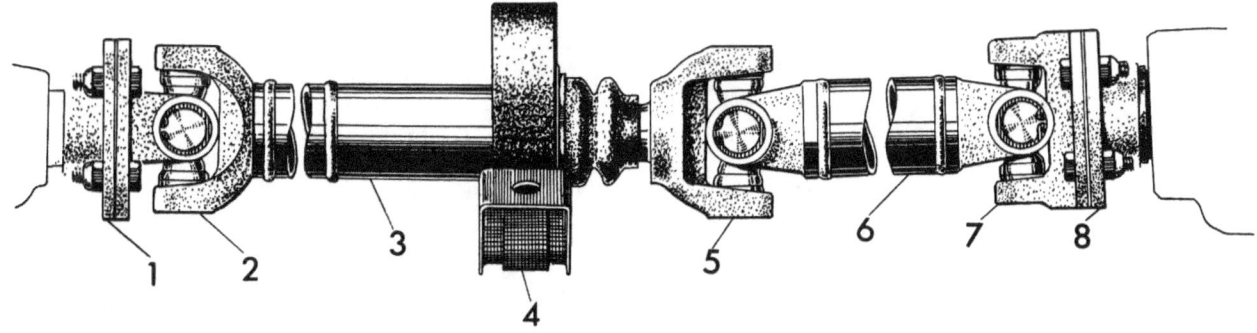

Fig. 7.1 Propeller shaft and support bearing

1 Flange on gearbox
2 Front universal joint
3 Front section of propeller shaft
4 Support bearing
5 Intermediate universal joint
6 Rear propeller shaft section
7 Rear universal joint
8 Flange on rear axle

2 Faults and their symptoms

1 The usual indication that wear or damage has occurred in the propeller shaft system is vibration. If caused by wear, it appears gradually and at first you may not suspect its source. It may only happen at certain speeds.

2 The only other fault symptom is a 'clunk' when drive from the engine comes on or goes off. When this occurs you have probably been having vibration previously but decided to ignore it. If you hear 'clunks', ignoring should cease.

3 Propeller shaft - removal

1 The easiest way is to remove the two parts separately. Start by removing the bolts between the universal joint and the rear axle flange, lowering the shaft and withdrawing it to the rear. The splined part will pull straight out of the centre bearing.

2 Remove the nuts and bolts joining the gearbox or overdrive flange to the universal joint. Put a couple of bolts back in the holes to take the weight while you undo the two screws fixing the support bearing housing to the chassis (photos).

3 Remove the front half of the propeller shaft with the bearing housing attached.

4 Support bearing - removal

1 Bend back the tab washer and unscrew the nut on the end of the propeller shaft. The bearing and its housing can now be withdrawn from the shaft.

2 Dismantle the housing and take the bearing out. The bearing housing assembly is shown in Fig.7.3.

5 Universal joints - dismantling

1 Remove the circlips which retain the bearings for the spiders. (Fig. 7.4).

2 Support one yoke of the joint in a vice. Take care when doing this not to distort the shaft which is hollow.

3 Drive the spider as far as it will go in one direction; this will make the bearing stick out of the yoke. (Fig. 7.5).

4 Repeat the process in the opposite direction. You will now find that the spider can be taken out of the yoke. (Fig. 7.6).

5 Drift the bearings out of the yoke.

6 Propeller shaft - inspection

1 The approved test is to mount the shaft between centres and check for run-out along the whole length. If it is more than 0.010 inches (0.25 mm) out of true it should be replaced. If, like most owners, you don't have measuring equipment of this sort of accuracy, get someone to do it for you if you have any suspicion of vibration. This small tolerance emphasises the importance of correct balancing.

2 It also shows that even minor damage can be a source of trouble. Inspect the shaft for this and replace if necessary.

7 Support bearing - checking

Examine the support bearing by pressing the bearing races against each other by hand and turning them in opposite directions. The bearing should run easily without binding at any point. If it does not. replace it.

8 Universal joints - inspection and assembly

1 Wash out the needle bearings thoroughly, finishing off with white spirit to remove all traces of cleaning fluid and grease. Check for signs of wear, rust or blueing. Check that their rubber seals are undamaged.

2 Check spiders for signs of wear.

3 If as in paragraphs 1 and 2 any imperfection is revealed replace the spiders and the bearings.

4 If the yokes are damaged or the bearings are a loose fit in them, replace the shaft concerned. The yokes cannot be removed from the shaft.

5 To reassemble universal joints, fill the bearings half-full of grease. Push the spider over to the side of the yoke on which you are fitting a bearing so that you can be sure that the bearing slides on to the shaft when you fit it (Fig. 7.7). Drive the bearing home gently with a drift just less than a bearing diameter and put in the circlip. Do the same on the other end.

9 Propeller shaft assembly

1 Assembly can be a straightforward reversal of the removal described above.

2 Alternatively though it is more awkward, there is something to be said for assembling both halves of the propeller shaft with the centre bearing housing into a single unit before putting it back on the vehicle. This will ensure that the splines and centre bearing do not collect any dirt in the process. The splines should be lubricated with molybdenum disulphide grease (Castrol MS3 Grease) before assembling.

3.2a Disconnecting the propeller shaft flange from the gearbox

3.2b Propeller shaft and gearbox flanges

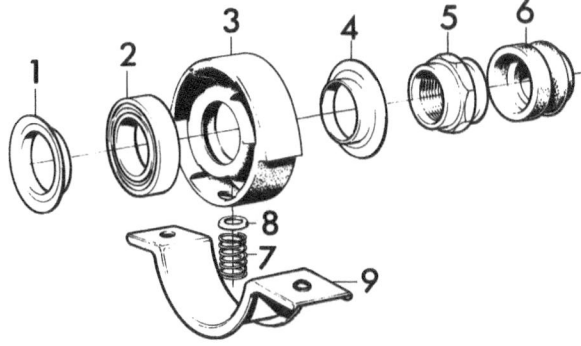

Fig. 7.3 Propeller shaft support bearing and housing assembly

1 Dust cover - front
2 Ball bearing
3 Rubber housing
4 Dust cover - rear
5 Nut
6 Rubber boot
7 Spring
8 Washer
9 Cap

Note: Detail variations occur between models. There are two types of bearing and three types of rubber housing.

Fig. 7.4 Removing circlips which retain bearings

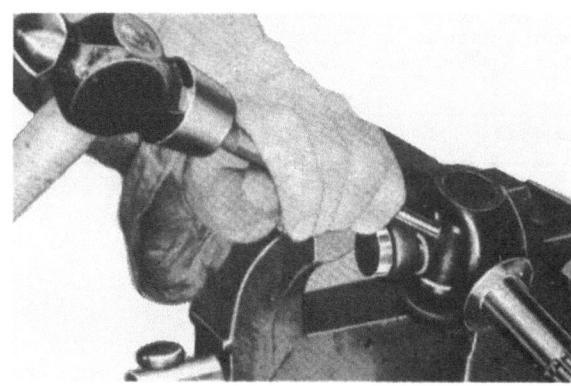

Fig. 7.5 Driving bearings through yoke. The bearing on left has already been driven through

Fig. 7.6 When both bearings have been driven through, the yoke will come away

Fig. 7.7 Push the spider as far through the yoke as possible and slide the bearing over it when reassembling

Chapter 8 Rear axle and rear suspension

Contents

Specifications

Rear springs	142 - 144	
	Standard	Optional
Type	Helical spring	Helical spring
Wire diameter	12.1 mm (0.48 in.)	12.64 mm (0.50 in.)
External diameter	127.1 mm (5.0 in.)	127.60 mm (5.0 in.)
Number of effective turns	8.9	8½
Test values:		
Loading (for a compression of 1 cm = 0.4 in.)	15.8 - 16.8 kg (35 - 37 lb.)	19.9 - 20.9 kg (44 - 46.0 lb.)
within a spring length of	272 - 322 mm (10.7 - 12.7 in.)	258 - 308 mm (10.15 - 12.12 in.)
Length, fully compressed	max. 114.9 mm (4.52 in.)	max. 116 mm (4.6 in.)
Load/spring length	211 -225 kg/97 mm (464 - 495 lb/11.7 in.)	217 - 232 kg/283 mm (477 - 510 lb/11.0 in.)
Rear springs	Standard	Optional
Type	Helical spring	Helical spring
Wire diameter	12.85 mm (0.51 in.)	13.10 mm (0.52 in.)
External diameter	127.9 mm (5.1 in.)	127.0 mm (5.0 in.)
Number of effective turns	9.0	8.6
Test values:		
Loading (for a compression of 1 cm = 0.4 in.)	19.6 - 21.1 kg (43 - 47 lb.)	23.1 - 24.7 kg (51 - 54 lb.)
within a spring length of	270 - 320 mm (10.6 - 12.6 in.)	280 - 330 mm (11.0 - 13.0 in.)
Length, fully compressed	max. 127 mm (5.0 in.)	max. 121 mm (4.8 in.)
Load/spring length	242 - 257 kg /295 mm (532 - 565 lb/11.6 in.)	236 - 250 kg /305 mm (519 - 550 lb/12.0 in.)
Shock absorbers		
Type	Double acting, hydraulic, telescopic	
Rear axle		
Rear axle, type	Semi-floating	
Track	1350 mm (53.15 in.)	
Final drive		
Type	Spiral bevel (hypoid)	
Reduction ratio	4.10 : 1 (10/41) or 4.30 : 1 (10/43)	
Warp, crown wheel	max. 0.08 mm (0.0032 in.)	
Backlash	0.15 - 0.20 mm (0.003 - 0.008 in.)	
Pre-loading on pinion bearings, new bearings	11 - 23 kgcm (9.55 - 20 lb. in.)	
run-in bearings ...	6 - 11 kgcm (5.21 - 9.55 lb. in.)	
Pre-loading on differential bearings	0.13 - 0.20 mm (0.005 - 0.008 in.)	

Lubricant, see under 'Lubrication'
Oil capacity ...   .   2.3 Imp. pints (1.3 litres, 2.7 US pints)

Torque wrench settings

			kg m	lb ft
Flange	... ...		28 - 30	200 - 220
Caps ...	... ...		5.0 - 7.0	35 - 50
Crownwheel	... ...		6.5 - 9.0	45 - 65
Wheel nuts ...	... ...		10 - 14	70 - 100

Wheels

Wheel rims:
Type ...   .   Disc
Designation: 142, 144 de luxe and grand luxe   ...   .   5 J x 15 L
                    145 de luxe   ...   .   5 J x 15 H
                    142, 144   ...   .   4.5 J x 15 L
                    145   ...   .   4.5 J x 15 H
Radial throw   ...   .   max. 1.6 mm (0.063 in.)
Warp ...   .   max. 1.6 mm (0.063 in.)
Imbalance, complete wheel   ...   .   900 gcm (7.8 lb. in.)
Tightening torque for wheel nuts ...   .   10 - 14 kgm (72 - 101 lb. ft.)

Tyres

Type ...   .   Tubeless
Size, 142, 144   ...   .   165 SR 15-4-PR
        145   ...   .   165 S 15-8-PR, 165 SR 15-4-PR
        USA   ...   .   6.85 S 15-8-PR
Pressures:
    Front   ...   .   1.8 kgf/cm^2 (26 psi)
    Rear   ...   .   1.9 kgf/cm^2 (27 psi)

1   Rear suspension - general description

1   A diagram of the rear suspension is given in Fig.8.1 (see also photos). The rear axle assembly is supported on two arms pivoted to the chassis and sprung against it by coil springs. It is steadied by torque rods attached to the same brackets on the chassis as the swinging arms but taken to points nearer the middle of the rear axle assembly. Hydraulic shock absorbers are attached between the body and the swinging arms, and a single tie or "Panhard" rod extends from an anchorage on the axle casing to a bracket on the opposite side of the body.

2   The shock absorbers are of exactly the same pattern as the front shock absorbers (though not interchangeable with them)

and for further comment see Chapter 11, Section 16.

2   Shock absorbers and springs - removal

1   Jack up the axle and remove the wheel.

2   With the spring under compression (ie with the axle jacked up after you have removed the wheel) you can remove the shock absorber. If you are only concerned with removing the spring, it is sufficient to let go one end of the shock absorber.

3   To remove the spring, undo the top and bottom attachments while it is still under compression and then take the compression off by jacking up the body and if necessary letting down the axle, until you are able to take out the spring and its spacers.

1.1a Rear suspension, showing support arm, torque rod and the transverse track rod attached to the rear axle at one end and the body at the other

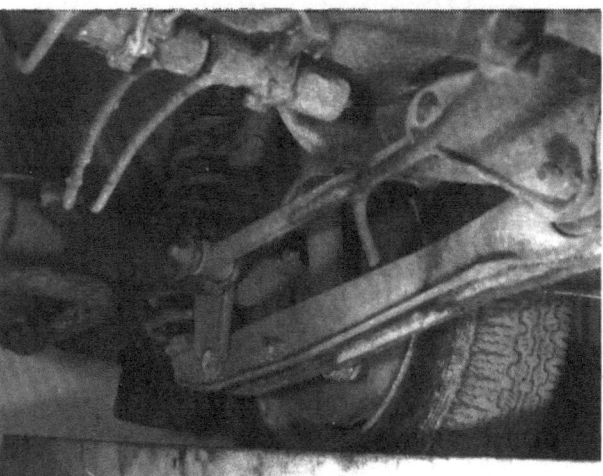

1.1b Here you can see the shock absorber which doesn't show in 1a. It looks as if someone has used the support arm as a jacking point - not a good idea

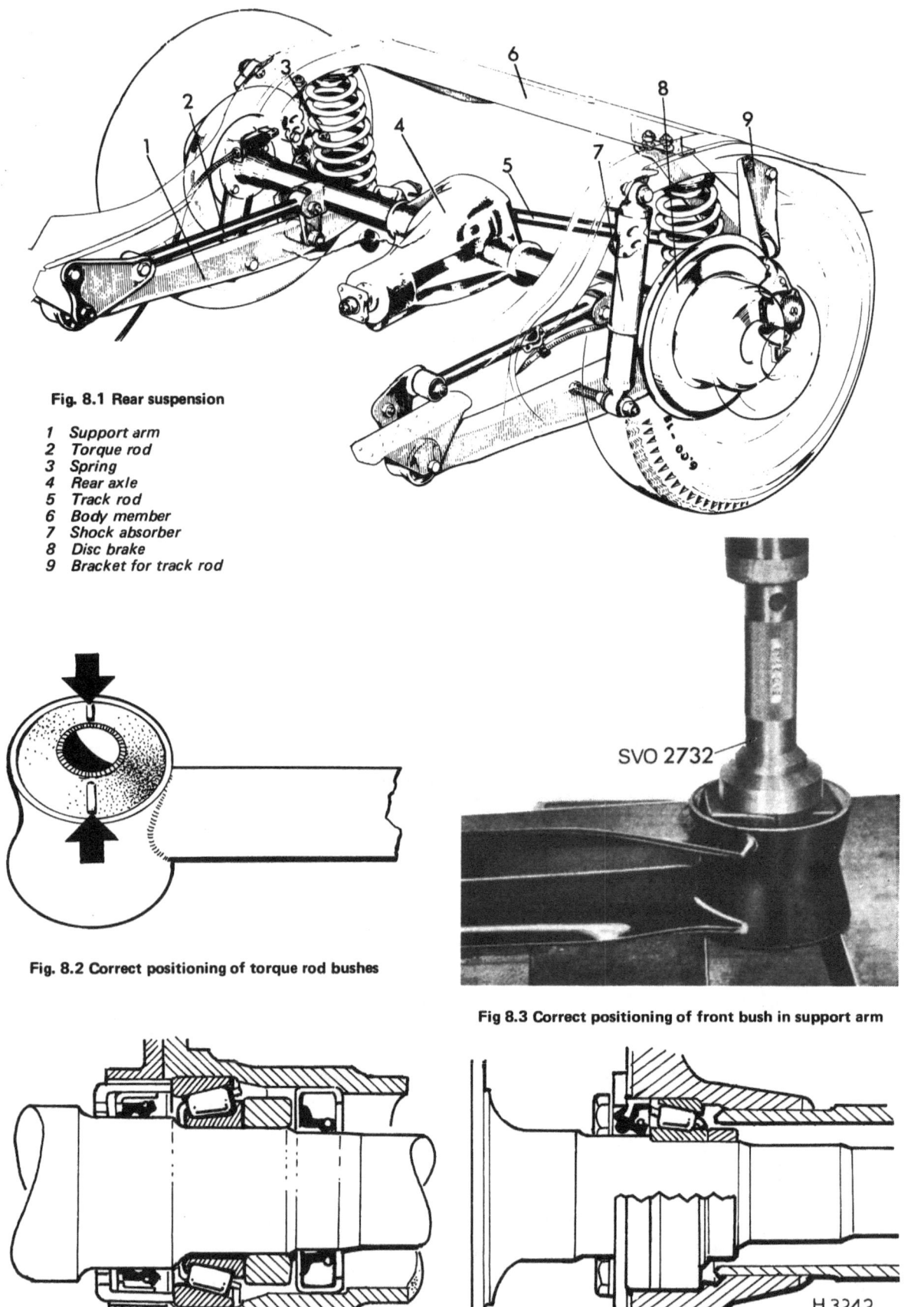

Fig. 8.1 Rear suspension

1 Support arm
2 Torque rod
3 Spring
4 Rear axle
5 Track rod
6 Body member
7 Shock absorber
8 Disc brake
9 Bracket for track rod

Fig. 8.2 Correct positioning of torque rod bushes

SVO 2732

Fig 8.3 Correct positioning of front bush in support arm

H 3242

Fig. 8.4 Half-shaft bearing assemblies pre-1970 (left) and 1970 onwards (right)

3 Shock absorbers and springs - checking and replacement

1 Shock absorbers may be checked as described in Chapter 11, Section 16. No maintenance or repair is possible.
2 If you replace a spring, be sure to replace its opposite number even if there is nothing apparently wrong with it. Springs should be obtained in matched pairs.

4 Rubber bushes - replacement

1 Generally speaking, replacement of any of the numerous rubber bushes in the rear suspension is a straightforward business. Press out the old one, give the new one a generous coating of oil, press it in. Two bushes need further comment.
2 Bushes for the torque rods are marked and the marks should be placed at right angles to the rod, (see Fig.8.2).
3 The front bushes for the support arms have flats on them. Fit these so that a flat side is at right angles to the length of the support arm (Fig.8.3).

5 Rear axle - general description

1 The rear axle is entirely conventional, of the hypoid type with the pinion below the centre line of the crown wheel. Some models incorporate a limited slip ("anti-spin") device which is described in detail in Section 14.
2 The half shafts are supported at their outer ends in taper roller bearings, grease packed and sealed.
3 The bearing arrangements for the half shafts were changed at the end of 1969 ie after the first year production of cars with B20 engines. They are shown in Fig.8.4.

6 Half shaft removal

1 Jack up the car and remove the wheel. If you are removing the half shafts as a preliminary to dismantling the back axle, note the remarks on jacking in Section 11, paragraph 1.
2 Unbolt and remove the brake calipers and brake disc (see Chapter 9).
3 Remove the parking brake shoes and their associated mechanism (Chapter 9).
4 Remove the bolts securing the brake backing plate to the back axle casing. You can get at these through holes in the half shaft flange.
5 The half shaft is now free to be withdrawn, bringing with it its bearing and the retaining plate which was bolted to the rear axle casing. A little judicious tapping with a hammer on a drift applied behind the flange may be necessary to start it off, but generally it presents no difficulty.

7 Broken half shafts

1 If the half shaft is broken, the splined end will of course remain inside the axle when the outer end is withdrawn. With the normal differential this can be done without dismantling the rear axle or removing it from the car.
2 Remove the cover to the differential housing, being careful not to get any dirt into the differential as you do so.
3 With a piece of stiff wire or something similar, push the broken end of the half shaft (which will still be engaged with the side gear) into the axle casing.
4 When you have got it well clear of the side gear, you will be able to fish it out with a hooked wire inserted at the outside end of the casing.
5 With the limited slip differential, the side gears are totally enclosed and you cannot get at the broken end of the half shaft without removing the other half shaft and partial dismantling.

8 Half shaft bearing and oil seals - replacement

1 If half shaft removal is part of a general overhaul of the rear axle, all oil seals should be replaced. This means that the taper bearing must be removed and replaced, even though it may be entirely satisfactory. If you have no facilities for pressing off the bearing and its locking ring, you can remove the locking ring by drilling and splitting (see Fig.8.5). Use a ¼ inch (6 mm) drill and be careful you don't drill right through to the half shaft.
2 Press or gently drive the shaft out of the bearing.
3 Remove the seal, adjusting nut (old pattern) or retaining nut (new pattern) and back plate. From the early pattern axle casing, extract the interior oil seal.
4 Clean the bearing, giving it a final wash in white spirit to remove every trace of old grease and cleaning fluid. Examine for signs of wear or blueing. Replace if necessary.
5 Reassemble with new oil seals and (if necessary) a new bearing.
6 Even if the old locking ring is intact, it must be renewed.
7 Press or drive on the locking ring, making sure that the whole assembly is as close up as possible to the shoulder on the half shaft.

9 Half shaft inspection

Clean and examine the half shafts thoroughly. The splines must be clean and sharp and there must be no trace of twist or warp.

10 Half shaft reassembly

1 Fill the taper bearing and its housing with multi purpose ball bearing grease (Castrol LM Grease).
2 Pass the half shafts into the axle casing. Mind you don't damage the inner oil seal on the earlier pattern. Feel for the mating spline on the side gear in the differential and gently engage with it.
3 Fit the bolts securing the back plate and retaining ring, tightening them to a torque of 36 lb ft (5 kg m).
4 The old pattern of bearing assembly must have its end play adjusted. To do this, first slacken back the adjusting nut a turn and hammer gently on the back of the flange to ease it out of the casing.
5 Check the end play and adjust it to between .002" and .005" (.050 - .012 mm) by tightening the adjusting nut. The play can easily be estimated by putting a metal block behind the flange and using feeler gauges.
6 Finally, lock the adjusting nut with its tab washer.
7 The new pattern has no provision for adjustment.

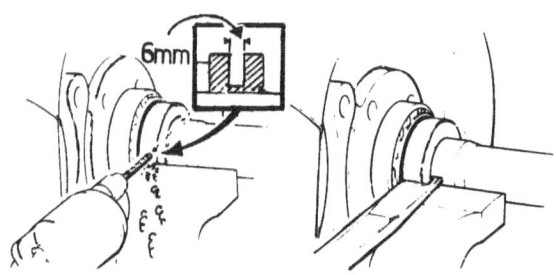

Fig. 8.5 Removing half shaft bearing locking ring by drilling and splitting

11 Rear axle - removal

1 Operations more extensive than half shaft removal and outer bearing replacement mean that you must remove the rear axle from the car. This presents one or two problems which, though not difficult, you should solve before you start, namely how you are going to support it as it comes out. Axle supports on the sides are not enough because the axle will tend to roll about them when it is released. If you had a third support just behind the flange attaching the propeller shaft, this would be fine, but then you have the problem of lowering three supports at once. If you settle for three point support, a very good way is to support the axle just behind the flange hammock-wise with a rope with ends tied to the garage walls or whatever is suitable, but arrange things so that you can easily raise it and lower it. Another approach is to rest the axle on fixed supports close to the ground when you have removed wheels and propeller shaft, and then raise the car high enough for the axle to come clear with a block and tackle. Be sure you chock the front wheels when you do this.

2 When you are sure that you can carry out paragraph 7 of this Section without having everything fall over, make a start by removing the half shafts as described in Section 6.

3 Undo the bolts securing the rear parts of the propeller shaft to the flange on the rear axle, withdraw the propeller shaft from the centre bearing (see Chapter 7) and put it on one side out of harms way. It is all too easy to damage the propeller shaft if you leave it lying about under the car still attached to the main bearing.

4 Loosen the front pivot bolts on the support arms one turn to enable them to swing freely without damaging their bushes.

5 Release lower ends of spring and shock absorbers.

6 Remove the track rod at the rear of the axle.

7 Lower the rear axle and/or raise the car until the support arms are free of the rear springs. Remove the pivot bolts attaching support bars and torque rods to the rear axle and lower these until they are clear of their associated lugs.

8 The axle assembly is now free of the car.

12 Pinion shaft oil seal - replacement

1 This can be done without removing the rear axle from the vehicle. Two simple press tools are needed to remove and refit the flange on the pinion shaft. The special Volvo tools are illustrated, and enough information given to enable you to produce adequate substitutes, in Figures 8.6 and 8.7.

2 Disconnect the rear section of the propeller shaft from the flange on the pinion.

3 Take the opportunity of checking the pinion shaft for looseness. If there is any appreciable play, particularly if the differential is noisy, you should be thinking about a complete overhaul.

4 If all is well, prevent the flange from turning while removing the nut from the shaft.

5 Pull the flange off the shaft.

6 Take off the dust cover and oil slinger and extract the oil seal.

7 Coat the new oil seal generously with grease, particularly all round the coil spring. This will prevent any tendency for the coil spring to come off the seal while you are fitting it. (Fig.8.8).

8 Fit the oil seal, replace the dust cover and oil slinger, press the flange on to the shaft and tighten the nut to a torque of 200-220 lb ft. (28-30 kg m).

13 Differential - general description

1 The vast majority of Volvo cars are fitted with the normal type of differential illustrated in Fig.8.9. Two pinions which are completely free to turn independently of one another are contained in a cage which is attached to the crownwheel. In the Figure, one of these pinions is in full view and you can just get a

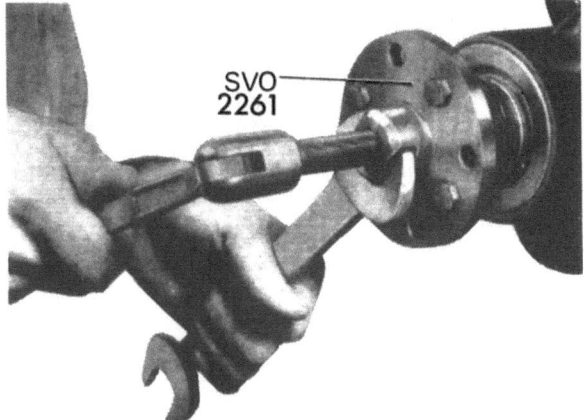

Fig. 8.6 Pulling off the flange. SVO 2261 is a plate bolted to the flange with a screw threaded into its centre

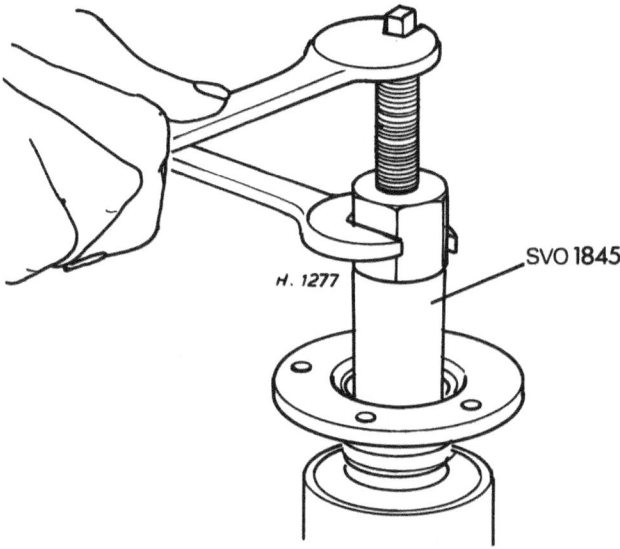

Fig. 8.7 Pressing on the flange - SVO 1845 is a bolt screwed into the shaft with a tube pushed down it as the nut is turned.

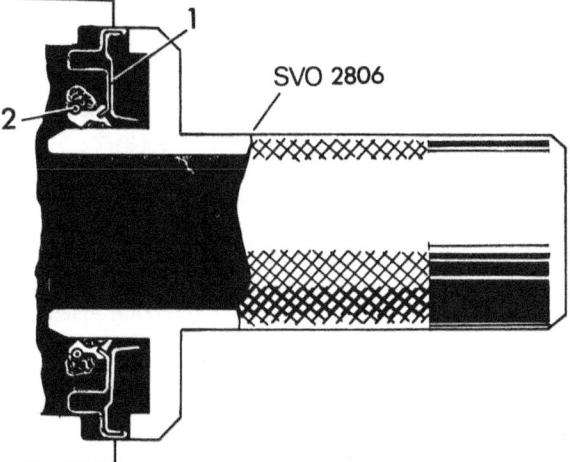

Fig. 8.8 Fitting pinion shaft oil seal (SVO 2806 is handy but not essential

1   Oil seal
2   Coil spring well covered with grease

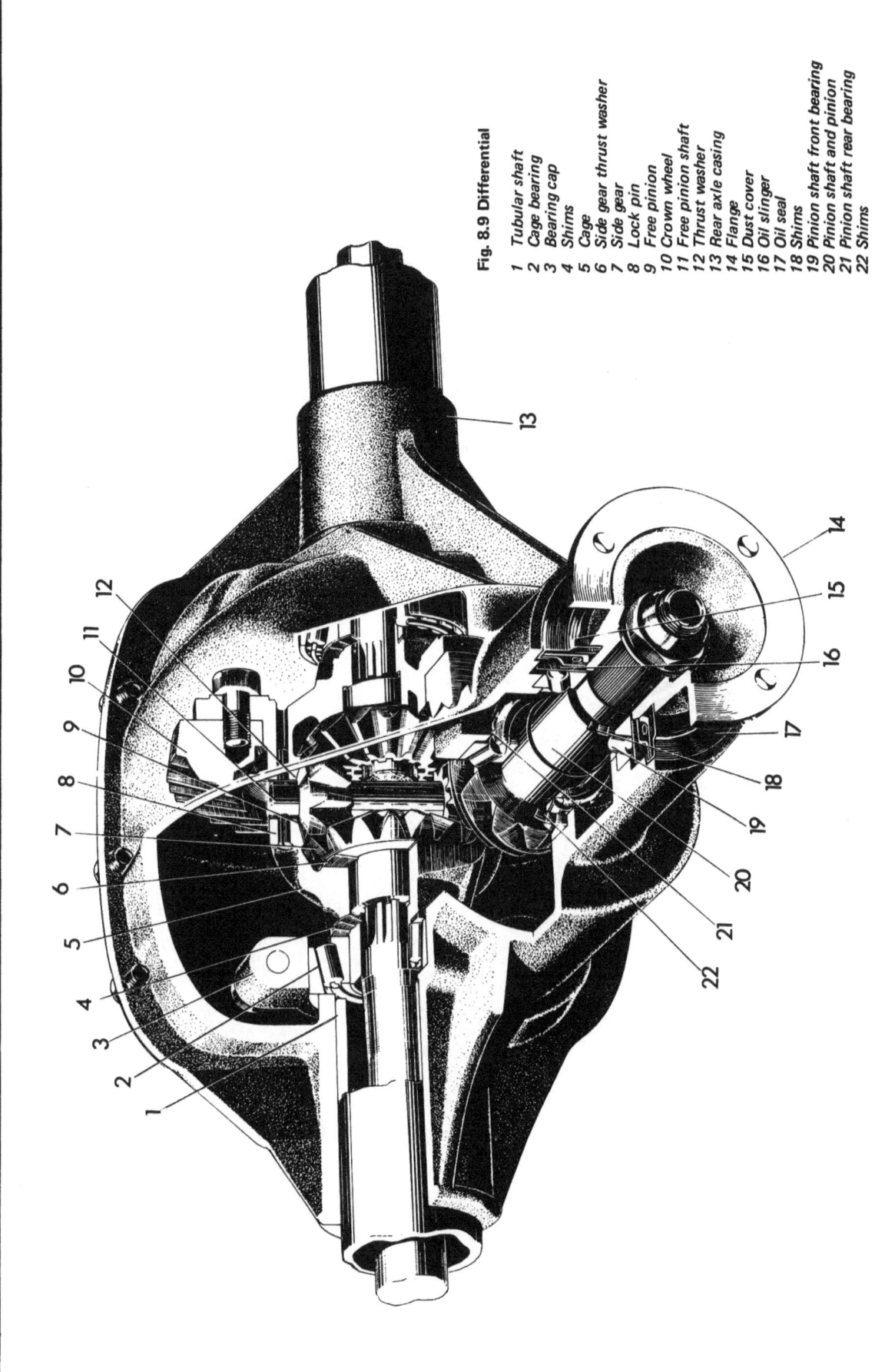

Fig. 8.9 Differential

1 Tubular shaft
2 Cage bearing
3 Bearing cap
4 Shims
5 Cage
6 Side gear thrust washer
7 Side gear
8 Lock pin
9 Free pinion
10 Crown wheel
11 Free pinion shaft
12 Thrust washer
13 Rear axle casing
14 Flange
15 Dust cover
16 Oil slinger
17 Oil seal
18 Shims
19 Pinion shaft front bearing
20 Pinion shaft and pinion
21 Pinion shaft rear bearing
22 Shims

glimpse of the other one at the other end of the shaft. The crownwheel is driven by a pinion connected to the propeller shaft flanges and when it revolves, taking the cage and free pinions with it, these pinions push on the side gears into which the half shafts are splined.

2 When it is running, the system sorts itself out so that equal torques are applied to each of the half shafts, even though they may be running at different speeds. If (as is the normal case when the car is running straight forward) the half shafts are revolving at the same speed, the teeth on the side gears keep the same position relative to each other and the pinions which lie between them do not revolve. In this case there is no relative motion between the side gears and the cage.

14 Limited slip differential - general description

1 The normal differential suffers from the well-known disadvantage that if one of the wheels spins there can be very little torque on the other one because of the torque equalisation principle. This can be overcome to some extent by arranging for the side gears to be a friction fit against the cage. When this is done, there is always a certain amount of torque on a side gear even if the

wheel it drives is spinning, and this torque is, as we have seen, equally available to the wheel which is not spinning. In the limited slip differential fitted to Volvo cars, this friction is provided by devices similar to small multi-plate clutches fitted in the cage, which has a completely different appearance from the normal type of cage shown in Fig. 8.9.

2 As already mentioned, in normal running there is no relative motion between the side gears and the cage, so the presence of the friction device has no effect, nor does it tend to wear out. It only comes into use on corners or when wheel spin occurs.

3 Fig. 8.10 gives a diagrammatic representation of the system used by Volvo. The side gears have outside splines which engage with friction discs. These discs are sandwiched between thin steel plates carrying lugs which engage with grooves in the cylindrical housing. The sandwiches include dished steel plates which act as springs and maintain them in compression.

4 The housing carries two pairs of free pinions on crossed shafts linked at their centres. These shafts are capable of a limited amount of sideways movement, and have specially shaped ends which engage in V-shaped slots in the housing. As drive torque is increased, the shafts rise up in these slots and the pinions push the side gears outwards, increasing the compression in the friction disc assemblies and so increasing the friction.

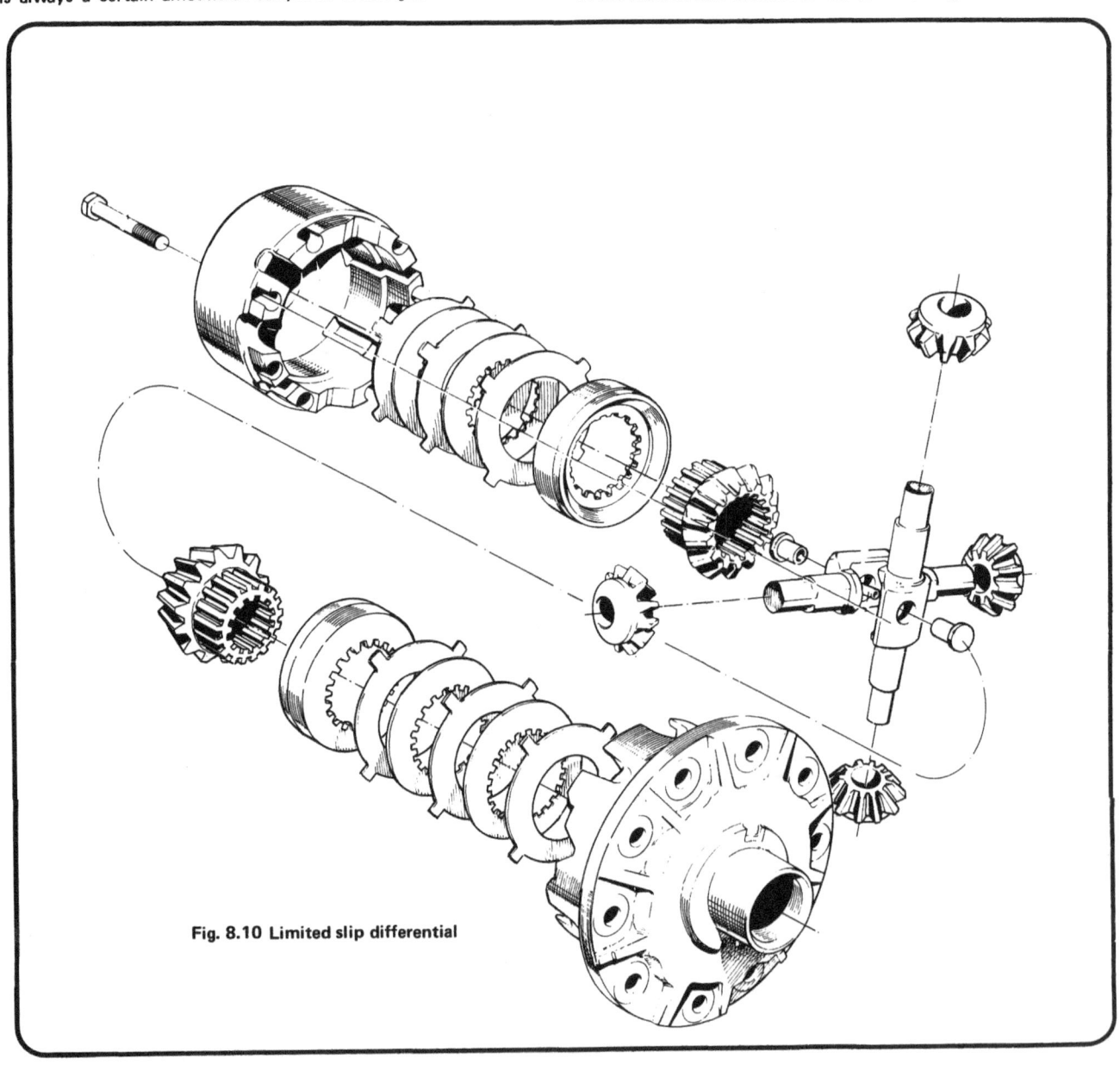

Fig. 8.10 Limited slip differential

15 Overhauling the differential

1 The first sign of wear in the differential is that well-known transmission whine which all cars past their first youth emit to some degree. If the differential is stripped down and overhauled as described here before the noise has become excessive, the odds are that you can get away without having to replace gears - and gears are expensive.

2 Confident assessment of the state of the transmission from the noise it makes can only come from experience. Consult a friendly and expert professional, and be guided by what he says. Remember that it is particularly true in this field that "a stitch in time saves nine".

3 The differential is full of teeth. The object of overhauling the differential is to ensure that those teeth are in good condition and correctly meshed.

4 If they are not in good condition, there is only one remedy - replacement.

5 Meshing is controlled by shims which take up manufacturing tolerances. Selection of correct shims is one of the principal tasks facing the repairer.

6 In the garage or factory this is done by the use of accurate measuring equipment and special jigs. These are very unlikely to be available to the ordinary owner who has to proceed by trial and error. This takes longer but care and patience will produce perfectly satisfactory results.

7 One special tool you will have to have - the Volvo expander SVO 2394 and its clips SVO 2601. It is a rugged hunk of metal, so your Volvo Agent need have no fear that you will damage it if he lends it to you. Its purpose is to stretch the axle housing slightly; unless you do this you cannot remove the differential assembly. **Do not try to do without it unless you can get hold or make a really adequate substitute.** A Volvo differential is an expensive item to experiment on.

8 Because reassembly is a trial and error process, you will be faced with the problems of removing bearings from shafts and casings without damaging them. Your experience in the dismantling stage will tell you whether your tools and methods are adequate to do this. Make certain before reassembling that you have an adequate armoury of pullers and drifts. It is worth while spending some time in getting their essential dimensions (eg diameters of discs used as drifts or of tubes used with bolts for pulling) right.

9 Before you start to reassemble, stock up with shims. These come in kits from your Volvo agent. A micrometer for checking shim thickness is essential. Shim thicknesses available are:-

Side gears: (thrust washers)	0.031	0.032	0.034	0.035	0.037	in.
	0.78	0.28	0.86	0.90	0.94	mm.
Cage bearings:	0.003	0.005	0.010	0.030		in.
	0.08	0.13	0.25	0.75		mm.
Pinion shaft front:	0.003	0.005	0.010	0.030		in.
	0.08	0.13	0.25	0.75		mm.
Pinion shaft rear:	0.003	0.005	0.010			in.
	0.08	0.13	0.25			mm.

10 For reassembly, you will also need a new set of bolts for fixing the crownwheel to the differential and a new nut for holding the flange to the pinion shaft, even though the originals may seem perfectly all right. The nut is a lock nut and is less efficient when used a second time, while the screws have been tightened to an extent which effects their elastic properties and because of this should not be used a second time.

16 Differential (ordinary pattern) - dismantling and inspection

1 Remove the rear axle from the vehicle as described in Section 11.

2 Take off the cover and look for alignment marks on the bearing caps and case which will tell you exactly where and which way round the bearing caps have to go (Fig.8.12).

3 At this stage it may be a good idea to check the meshing of the crownwheel and pinion as described in Section 17, paragraph 7. This might give some fault indication which could be helpful later.

4 Remove the bearing caps.

5 Fit the expansion tool SVO 2394 in the position shown in Fig.8.11, adjusting the screw until the pegs enter the holes on the axle casing. Then screw up the bolt three and a half turns. This will stretch the axle housing enough to enable the crownwheel and differential assembly to be lifted out.

6 Wash the interior of the housing with paraffin or cleaning fluid.

7 Undo the nut on the centre of the pinion shaft and pull off the coupling flange. (Fig.8.6).

8 Extract the dust cover, oil slinger and oil seal.

9 Drive out the shaft and pinion. The outer ring of the rear bearing and the whole of the front bearing remain in the housing.

10 Between the rear bearing and housing will be found shims.

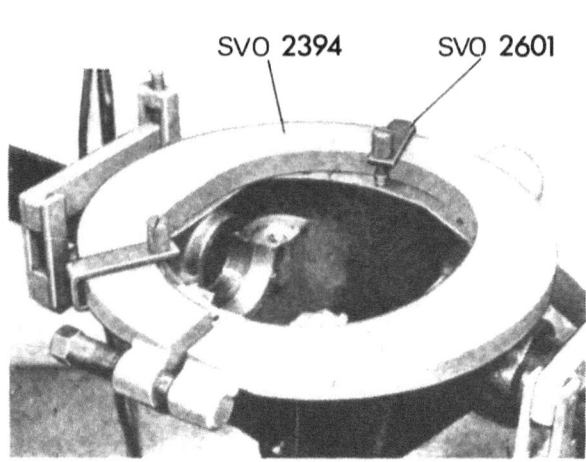

Fig. 8.11 Expansion tool and clips fitted to casing. Pegs on the underside engage with the fixing holes in the casing.

Fig. 8.12 Be sure your alignment marks tell you where, and which way round the caps have to go

These determine how far the pinion extends inside the case and hence control the meshing of the pinion with the crownwheel.

11 Between the front bearing and the housing will be found another set of shims. These shims fit against the shoulder on the pinion shaft and take up end play in the shaft.

12 Drive out the front bearing, using a drift just small enough to pass through the rear bearing ring. This need be no more than a disc backed up by a suitable length of rod. Clean the shims and put them on one side, making sure that you will know where they came from when you are reassembling.

13 Drive out the rear bearing ring and treat its shims likewise.

14 Mark the crownwheel and cage, take out the securing bolts and remove the cage from the crownwheel.

15 Knock out the locking pin (Fig.8.13) and remove the axle passing through the free pinions. Hold one of the side gears still and turn the other until the free pinions are opposite the holes in the cage.

16 Remove the free pinions and their dished washers.

17 Take out the side gears and their thrust washers, Mark and put on one side so that they can be refitted in the places they came from.

18 Pull the bearings off the ends of the cage. Store them in such a way that you will know on reassembly which bearing and which shims went on which end of the cage.

19 Thoroughly clean all parts. Check all the bearing races and bearings. The races, rollers or roller containers must not be scratched or damaged, and assembled bearings must have no detectable play.

20 Check the crown wheel and pinion tooth damage. Slight scuff marks may not mean that replacement is necessary; consult an expert. The cause may be incorrect running-in, wrong oil, insufficient clearance or faulty tooth contact.

21 Check the teeth and splines of the side gears for damage.

17 Reassembling the differential

1 Start by assembling the cage, side gears and free pinions. Whether the parts are new or old, they should be clean and dry so that you can check the thickness and loading tolerances accurately. Assemble the side gears in the cage, using the original shims in their original positions even if you are putting in new gears. Insert the free pinions and their washers (see Fig.8.14) and their axle. Do not lock this axle permanently for the moment.

2 Check the side play of the side gears with feeler gauges, and if this is greater than .0024 inches, take it up by increasing the thickness of the thrust washers on both sides by the same amount. The ideal condition is when a slight torque is needed to turn the side gears, Use a torque wrench working on something pushed into the splines (a piece of wood would do) and check that this torque does not exceed 7lb ft (1 kg m). Use marker blue to check that the meshing of each of the side gears with the free pinions is the same. If it is not, transfer side washer thickness from one side to the other by increasing one side washer and decreasing the other by the same amount. When all is well, lock in the shaft with the locking pin. Make sure that the locking pin is firm in the cage.

3 Fit the crown wheel. If this is a tight fit, heat it in the oven to about 200°C. It should then go on quite easily. Draw it down with the fixing bolts, and if it has been heated allow it to cool. Finally, tighten the fixing bolts to 47-72 lb ft (6.5 - 8.5 kg m).

4 We now turn to the rear pinion. If you are using the original, assemble it with the original shims between the back bearing and the pinion. Be sure the bearing is pressed well home. If it is a new one, observe the marking code. If it is the same as the old one (very unlikely) use the same shims as before. If not, the shim thickness must be altered in accordance with the markings on the pinions.

Notice first of all that there are two types of marking. In one system (used on units made by Volvo themselves) the figures are shown without plus (+) or minus (-) signs and indicate hundredths of a millimetre, and in the other (used on units made for Volvo by outside manufacturers) the figures are preceded by + or - and indicate thousandths of an inch. The markings are used to indicate shim thickness alteration as follows:-

Old pinion mark	New pinion mark	Increase by	Decrease by
+ M	+ N	M − N	N − M
+ M	− N	M + N	
− M	− N	N − M	M − N
− M	+ N		M + N
M	N	M − N	N − M

Where alternatives are given, the choice depends on the relative sizes of M and N, eg old pinion marked +5, new one marked +8, decrease by 0.003", or if old pinion is marked 7, new one 5, increase by 0.02 mm.

Fig. 8.13 Knocking out the locking pin

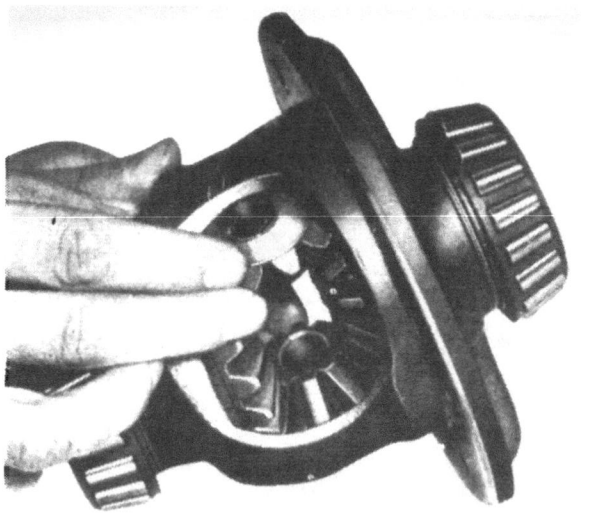

Fig. 8.14 Fitting the free pinions and their thrust washers into the cage

5   Having fitted the shims and back bearing on the pinion shaft, assemble it in the case, using only the back bearing for the time being. Now put the bearings on the cage without any shims, put the crownwheel and cage assembly in the case and temporarily screw down the bearing caps. **Do not** fit the expansion tool SVO 2394 at this stage. Get the crownwheel meshing with the pinion, and using marker blue observe the pattern made on the crown-wheel by the pinion. Fig.8.15 shows what this should look like and how to tell whether your pinion is set too near or too far from the centre of the crownwheel. You can get the areas of the patterns approximately equal by moving the cage assembly slightly from side to side (ultimately the shims fitted behind the bearings will sort this out), but at this stage you are simply concerned with getting them evenly spaced. If they are not, you will have to drive out the pinion shaft and alter the shims until you get it right. Check the patterns at three points on the crown wheel in case it is warped.

6   When these shims are correct, put back the original front shim thickness altered by the same amount as you have altered the back shim thickness. Fit the front bearing and the flange. Do

not bother about the oil seal, or slinger and dust cover at this stage as this is only a trial run. Use the original fixing nut, and tighten it carefully. If there is a tendency for the pinion to bind before the nut is fully tightened, remove the nut, remove the flange, and drive out the pinion as described in Section 14, paragraphs 9.12. Increase the shim thickness and try again. If on the other hand you get end play, estimate as best you can (eg by using feeler gauges between the pinion and case) how much end play there is, take out the pinion, remove the front bearing ring and increase the shim thickness. You should aim to get a very slight stiffness, which can be measured by the bar and weight method shown in Fig.8.16 and should be not less than 5.2 lb in and not more than 9.5 lb in (6-11 kg cm) unless you have fitted new bearings, in which case it should lie between 9.5-20 lb in (11-23 kg cm). If the stiffness is too great, of course, you will have to reduce the shim thickness. If you are unlucky, you may have to have two or three tries, but there is one consolation - when you have got through this stage you are over the worst of it.

7   When the shims are correct, take off the flange again and fit

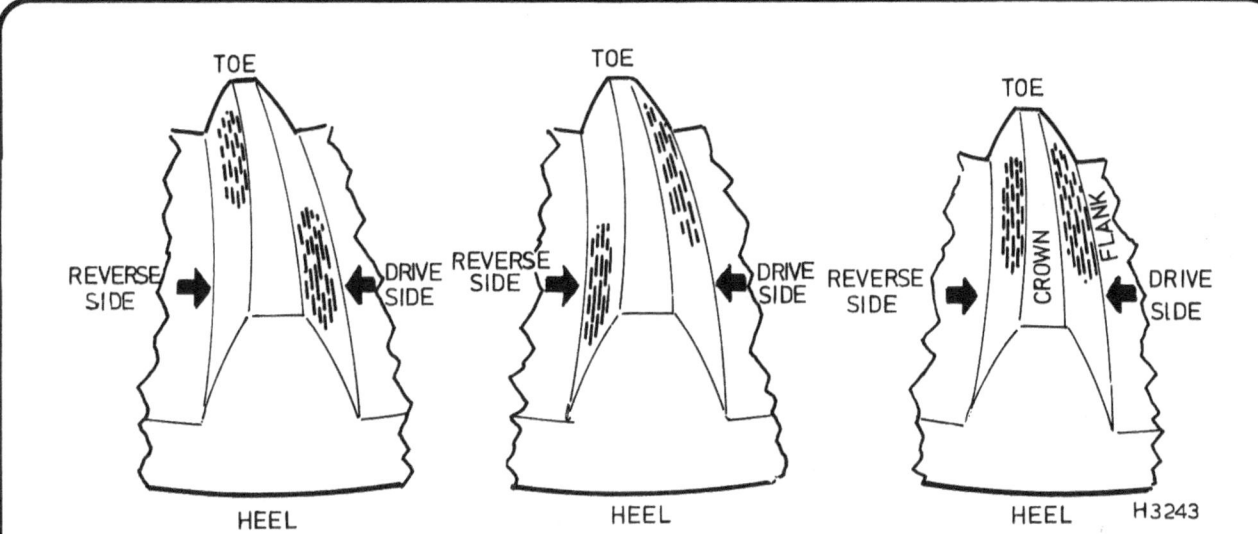

Fig. 8.15 (left) Pinion too far from centre of crown wheel - increase shims (centre) Pinion too near centre of crown wheel - decrease shims (right) Pinion distance correctly set.   Note:- Unequal contact areas when pinion is correctly set indicate wrong positioning of cage assembly.

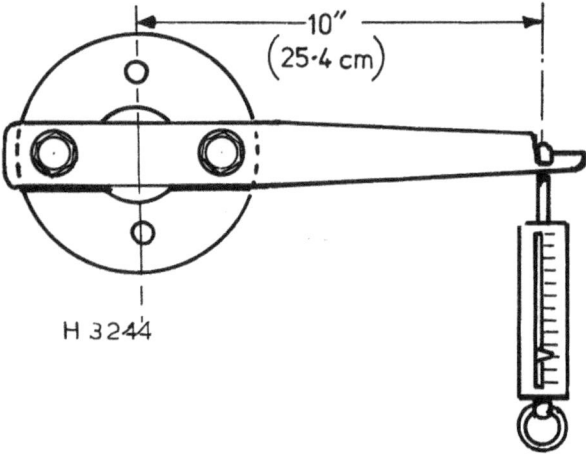

Fig. 8.16 Measuring torque on bearing shaft with a spring balance and bar bolted to flange. Balance reading should be between 0.52 - 0.95 lb. (0.24 - 0.44 kg)

the oil seal, oil slinger and dust cover as described in Section 12, paragraphs 7 and 8. This time fix the flange to the shaft with a new fixing nut and tighten to 200-220 lb ft (28-30 kg m).

8 It now remains to adjust the play and centring of the crown wheel/cage assembly. Start off by choosing a shim thickness .003" (.076 mm) less than the original shim thickness on each side, putting the appropriate shims behind the bearings and pushing the bearings well home. If, having done this, the assembly will not go into the case, reduce the shim thickness by another .002" (.05 mm). We suggest that you try this rather than taking out .005" straight away because there is quite a chance that the .003" reduction will give the right answer.

9 Check the end play in each direction, and use marker blue to observe the meshing patterns of the pinion and crown wheel as described in paragraph 5, but this time you are after equality of area. If necessary, alter shim thickness from one side to the other to get the desired result.

10 Once you have got the shims correct, remove the assembly from the casing and add a further .003 ins (.076 mm) to each side. Then reassemble, using the expansion tool to stretch the case and enable the assembly to go in. Three or four turns on the screw of the expansion tool should be sufficient.

11 Fit the bearing caps, but don't at this stage tighten the bolts more than finger tight.

12 Remove the expansion tool, tighten the cap bolts to a torque of 36-50 lb ft (5.0 - 7.0 kg m).

13 Fit inspection cover with new gasket, bolt down evenly all round.

14 Reinstall the half shafts as described in Section 8 and the rear axle is ready to be refitted to the vehicle.

18 Installing rear axle

1 If you have not already done so, fill it with oil to the correct level.

2 Installation is a straightforward reversal of the procedures involved in taking it off, but added to this there will of course be such items as bleeding and adjusting the brakes. Remember this when assessing how long it will take you to put the axle back by comparison with the time it took you to take it off.

19 Limited slip differential - overhaul

1 The only difference between the limited slip differential and the normal is in the housing containing the free pinions and side gears. The crown wheel and pinion are the same, and so is the rear axle housing which contains the whole assembly. In fact it is possible to replace the limited slip assembly by a normal cage. This means that all the overhaul instructions previously given apart from those specifically dealing with the cage and the free pinions apply equally to the limited slip differential. The following instructions, therefore, deal only with the special housing.

2 Mark the two halves of the housing and the axles carrying the free pinions so that on reassembly these go together exactly as they came apart. Remove the screws holding the two parts together, separate them and dismantle the unit, making sure that all washers, shims etc., are kept in the same order and the same way round as they were in the assembly so that if necessary the whole can be assembled in exactly the same way as it came apart.

3 Clean the parts thoroughly. Examine the pinions and side gears for signs of wear. If signs of wear are such as to merit replacement, **the whole housing must be replaced as a unit.**

4 If any of the friction discs and steel plates look other than in first class condition, replace **all of them.**

5 These sweeping replacements are called for because the unit has no built-in means of taking up wear. However, it is quite likely that none of them will be necessary.

6 Remember that the oil specified for rear axles with limited slip differentials is different from that for ordinary differentials. It contains molybdenum disulphide, the correct Castrol grade being Castrol Hypoy LS.

20 Wheels

Basic information about the wheels fitted by Volvo is given in the specifications at the beginning of this Chapter. Front hubs are dealt with in Chapter 11.

Be careful if you have to replace a wheel stud. It is easy to distort brake discs by careless removal of studs. Volvo replacement studs are supplied oversize and should be pressed into the hole left by the old stud without any preliminary enlargement of the hole. If the new stud is not a tight fit in the hole, the offending shaft or hub must be replaced.

Chapter 9 Braking system

Contents

Specifications

Front wheel brakes

Type	Disc brakes
Brake discs:	
Outside diameter	272.2 mm (10.7 in.)
Thickness new, B20E	14.28 - 14.4 mm (0.562 - 0.567 in.)
other engines	12.7 - 12.8 mm (0.500 - 0.504 in.)
reconditioned, B20E	min. 13.14 mm (0.557 in.)
other engines	min. 11.6 mm (0.457 in.)
Warp	max. 0.10 mm (0.004 in.)
Brake linings:	
Thickness, new	10 mm (0.394 in.)
Effective area, 142 and 144	150 cm^2 (23 sq. in.)
145	145 cm^2 (22.5 sq.in.)
Wheel unit cylinders:	
Area, 142 and 144	10.25 cm^2 (1.6 sq in.)
145	10.17 cm^2 (1.5 sq. in.)

Rear wheel brakes

Type	Disc brakes
Brake discs:	
Outside diameter	295.5 mm (11.63 in.)
Thickness, new	9.6 mm (0.378 in.)
reconditioned	min. 8.4 mm (0.331 in.)
Warp	max. 0.15 mm (0.006 in.)
Brake linings:	
Thickness, new	10 mm (0.394 in.)
Effective area, 142 and 144	100 cm^2 (15.5 sq. in.)
145	105 cm^2 (16.3 sq. in.)
Wheel unit cylinders:	
Area, 142 and 144	11.43 cm^2 (1.8 sq. in.)
145	11.33 cm^2 (1.7 sq. in.)

Master cylinder

Nominal diameter	7/8 in. (22.2 mm)
Bore	max. 22.40 mm (0.882 in.)
Piston diameter	min. 22.05 mm (0.868 in.)

Brake valve

Operating pressure, 142 and 144	34 $\pm$ 2 kg/cm^2 (484 $\pm$ 28.4 p.s.i.)
Operating pressure, 145	50 $\pm$ 2 kg/cm^2 (711 $\pm$ 28.4 p.s.i.)

Servo cylinder

Type	Direct operating
Make	Girling
Designation	FD type 50
Ratio	1 : 3

Handbrake

Brake drum:

Diameter	Max. 178.33 mm (7.0 in.)
Radial throw	Max. 0.15 mm (0.006 in.)
Out-of-round	Max. 0.2 mm (0.008 in.)
Brake linings, effective area	175 cm^2 (27 sq. in.)

Torque wrench settings

	lb ft	kg m
Attaching bolts, front brake caliper	65 to 70	9 to 10
Attaching bolts, rear brake caliper	45 to 50	6 to 7
Wheel nuts	70 to 100	10 to 14
Stop screw, master cylinder	9.5	1.3
Attaching nuts, master cylinder	17	2.4
Bleeder nipples	3 to 4.5	0.4 to 0.6
Brake hose, front brake caliper	12 to 15	1.6 to 2.0
Warning valve, switch	10 to 15	1.4 to 2.0
Brake pipes	8 to 11	1.1 to 1.5
Plug, brake valve	70 to 85	10 to 12
Locknut, brake valve	18 to 25	2.5 to 3.5

1 General description

1 The 140 is fitted with two independent braking systems. One of these, the footbrake system, is controlled by the brake pedal and operates on all four wheels hydraulically. The other, controlled by the handbrake lever, operates mechanically on both the rear wheels.

2 Fig.9.1 shows the arrangement of the footbrake system which has disc brakes all round. The hydraulic part has two separate circuits, operated by a tandem type master cylinder. One of the circuits operates the lower cylinders of the front wheel brake units together with the right-hand rear wheel, while the other circuit takes care of the upper cylinders of the front wheel brake units and the left-hand rear wheel. Thus, failure anywhere in the hydraulic system except in the master cylinder itself can only put one rear brake out of action, leaving the rest of the system intact. Such failure will be immediately obvious because of the pulling caused by uneven braking at the rear and possibly the locking of the rear wheel whose brake is

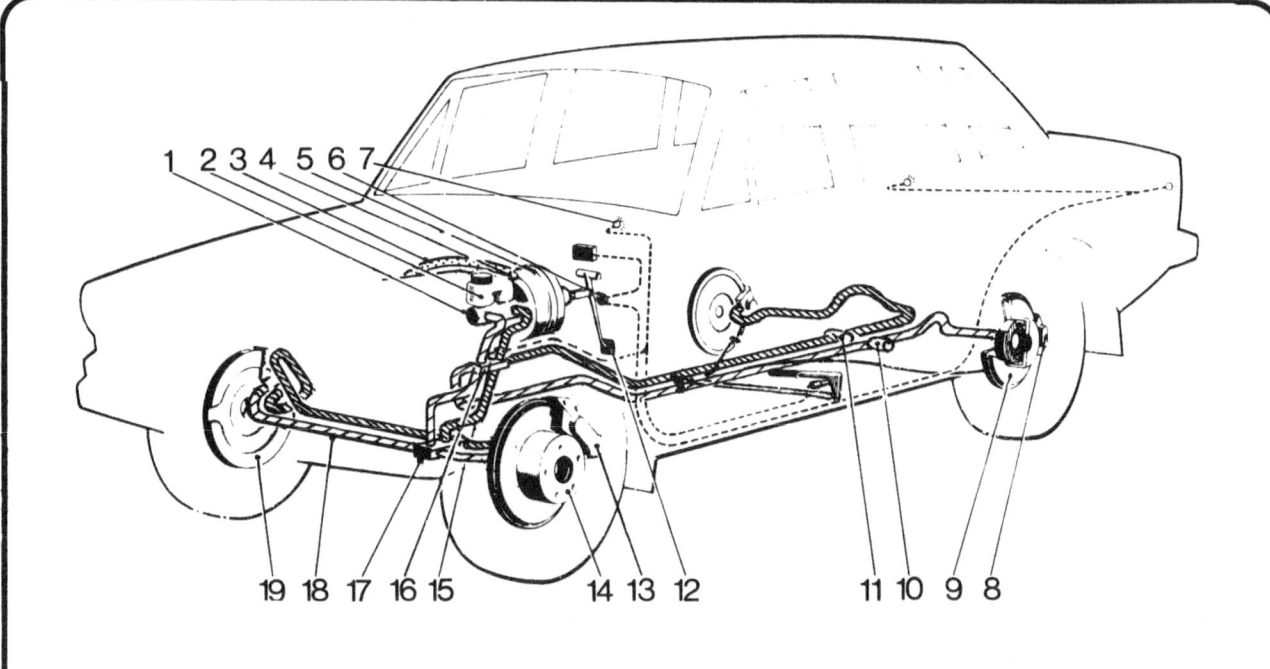

Fig. 9.1 Footbrake system

1 Tandem master cylinder	6 Brake switch	11 Brake valve, primary circuit	16 Warning valve
2 Brake fluid container	7 Warning lamp	12 Brake pedal	17 6-branch union,
3 Vacuum line	8 Rear brake caliper	13 Front brake caliper	(double 3-branch union)
4 Check valve	9 Brake disc with drum	14 Brake disc	18 Brake pipe
5 Servo cylinder	10 Brake valve, secondary circuit	15 Warning switch	19 Cover plate

still working.

3 The brake pedal operates the master cylinder through a servo unit which is operated by engine vacuum. This unit gives a pressure boost of up to three times the normal pressure when the engine is running.

4 The rear brakes are worked through valves which progressively increase the pressure difference between the rear brakes and the front brakes as the overall brake pressure is increased. This makes for an even distribution of braking power between the front and rear wheels.

5 Associated with the braking system is a warning lamp which lights up when the handbrake is on (in which case it is earthed by a switch operated by the handbrake lever (see Fig.9.2) or alternatively when there is an appreciable difference in pressure between the two hydraulic circuits, such as would result if one of them were faulty. In this case the lamp is operated by a valve receiving an input from each of the hydraulic circuits which earths the lead from the lamp when there is a pressure difference between the two inputs. This lamp is supplied with current through the ignition switch and only operates when this switch is on.

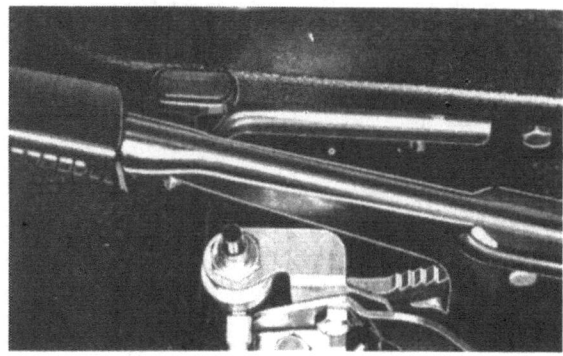

Fig. 9.2 Handbrake warning light switch

2 Bleeding the hydraulic system

1 Whenever the hydraulic system has been overhauled, a part renewed or the level in the reservoir has become too low, air will have entered the system. This will cause some or all of the pedal travel to be used up in compressing air rather than pushing fluid against brake pistons. If only a little air is present the pedal will have a 'spongy' feel, but if an appreciable amount has entered, the pedal will not offer any appreciable resistance to the foot and the brakes will hardly work at all.

2 To overcome this, brake fluid must be pumped through the hydraulic system until all the air has been passed out in the form of bubbles in the fluid. If only one rear brake caliper has been removed and little brake fluid run out, you may get away with bleeding this brake only, but otherwise you should bleed the whole system whenever you have worked on it.

3 The system should be bled in the order shown in Fig.9.3.

4 One or two points should be watched when bleeding the brakes:

a) Before you start, depress the brake pedal several times in order to even out pressure in the servo cylinder.

b) Make sure that the bleed nipples and their immediate surroundings are thoroughly clean. Dirt is the deadly enemy of hydraulic systems.

c) Remove the switch from the warning valve (see Fig.9.24 and Section 10, paragraph 2 where the reason for doing this is given).

d) Clean round the cap on the brake fluid container and clean the cap itself, making sure that the vent hole of the cap is clean. You are going to have to take the cap on and off to top the reservoir up when you are bleeding the brakes. If you leave the cap off all the time dirt may enter the system. You can see the fluid level perfectly well through the translucent container even when the cap is on.

5 Have a look at Fig.9.4. This shows a transparent tube fitted over one of the bleed nipples and fed into a bottle containing brake fluid, the end of the tube dipping below the brake fluid. This is essential to avoid air being sucked back into the system as the bleeding procedure is carried out. There is a good sketch of a bleed nipple in Fig.9.5 and a corresponding photograph showing the nipple with its end covered by a rubber sealing cap in Fig.9.9. This nipple is unscrewed half a turn anti-clockwise which enables brake fluid to pass through it from the brake cylinder. Use a 5/16 AF spanner to slacken the nipple. The indefatigably thorough Volvo organisation have produced what is, in essence, a hollow tubular spanner with provision for fitting the plastic tube over the end as depicted in Fig.9.4 - surely, the perfect Christmas present for the Volvo owner-mechanic.

6 When all is set up, fill the master cylinder reservoir with

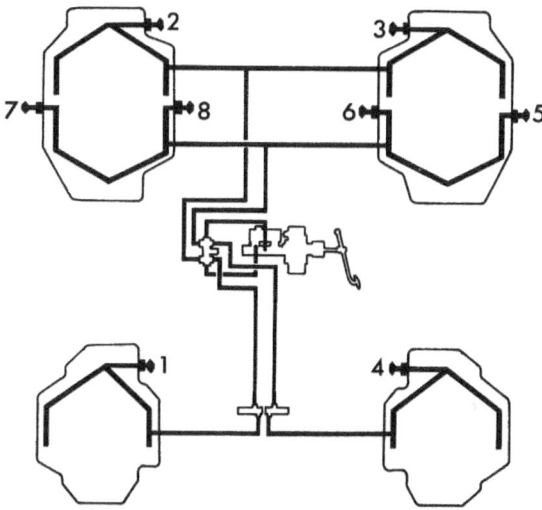

Fig. 9.3 Bleeding sequence

1 Left rear wheel
2 Left front wheel, upper, inner
3 Right front wheel, upper, inner
4 Right rear wheel
5 Right front wheel, outer
6 Right front wheel, lower inner
7 Left front wheel, outer
8 Left front wheel, lower, inner

Fig. 9.4 Bleeding a front wheel brake unit

brake fluid up to the "Max" mark (see photo) and have an assistant pump the brake pedal up and down; this will pump fluid through the system and into the bottle. Once you have an inch or so of brake fluid in the bleeding jar, it is essential that the end of the bleed tube remains immersed until the bleed nipple is retightened. Keep the reservoir topped up as the level falls - never let it get as low as the "Min" mark or air will re-enter the system. The correct method of pumping is to press the brake pedal slowly as far down as it will go, pause a little and then quickly release it.

7 At first, air bubbles will be present in the liquid passing through the tube, but after a while it will be completely free of them. When this is so, pass the pedal to the bottom and screw up the bleed nipple. Don't forget to refit the rubber cap on the nipple when you take off the tube and spanner. Recommended tightening torque for the nipple is 12 - 15 lb ft (1.6 - 2.0 kg m). Generally it is only necessary to go round the whole car once, but if at the end of this, the brake pedal still feels 'spongy', the process should be repeated until all is well.

8 Finally, fill the brake fluid reservoir up to the "Max" mark and refit the warning switch, tightening it to a torque of 10-15 lb ft (1.4-2.0 Kg m).

9 Two final points about the brake fluid itself:
a) Don't let the fluid come in contact with friction surfaces or linings or with paintwork.
b) Do not return any of the fluid pumped out during bleeding to the system.

3 Disc brake calipers - construction and function

1 Fig.9.5 shows a diagram of the front wheel brake caliper. This caliper consists of a housing in two halves - referred to as the inner and outer half, Nos 6 and 14 in Fig.9.5 - bolted together and located on either side of the brake disc. Each half contains two cylinders and pistons. In the diagram the outer half is cut away to show the cylinder and piston assembly.

2 The cut away portion carries a bleed nipple which is additional to those illustrated in the diagram. It is shown in Fig.9.9.

3 The two upper cylinders are connected together and fed from one of the hydraulic circuits, while the two lower cylinders are fed from the other one.

4 The sealing rings (1) Fig.9.5 as well as preventing brake fluid from oozing out act as return springs for the pistons. When hydraulic pressure is released these rings, which distort as the piston moves past them, return to their natural shape and in so doing pull back the piston slightly. The amount of withdrawal of the piston is always the same, so that the system automatically

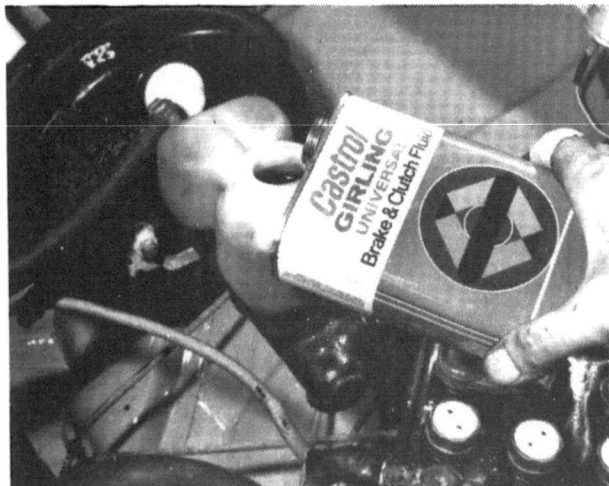

2.6 Topping up the brake reservoir

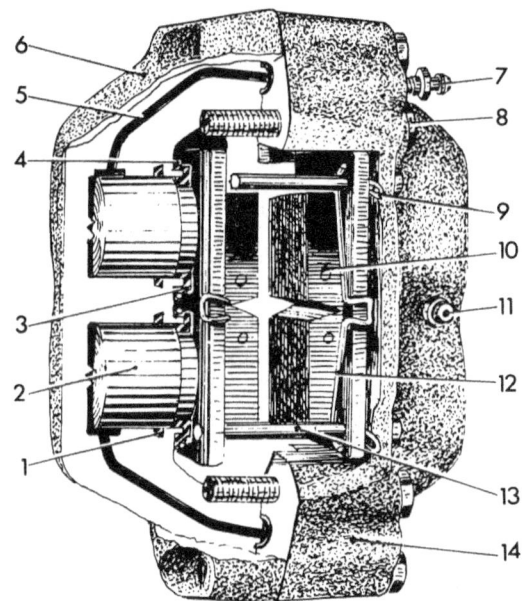

Fig. 9.5 Front brake caliper assembly

1 Sealing ring	8 Bolt
2 Piston	9 Retaining clip
3 Rubber dust cover	10 Brake pad
4 Retaining ring	11 Lower bleeder nipple
5 Channel	12 Damping spring
6 Outer half	13 Retaining pin
7 Upper bleeder nipple	14 Inner half

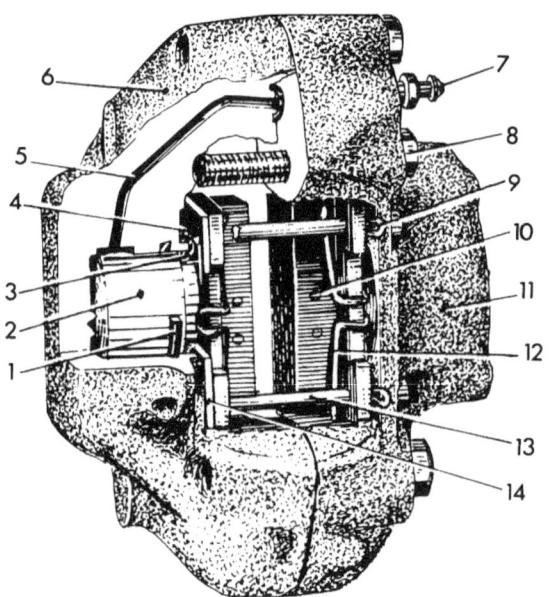

Fig. 9.6 Rear brake caliper assembly

1 Sealing ring	8 Bolt
2 Piston	9 Retaining clip
3 Rubber dust cover	10 Brake pad
4 Retaining ring	11 Inner half
5 Channel	12 Damping spring
6 Outer half	13 Retaining pin
7 Bleeder nipple	14 Washer

compensates for wear in the brake pads and needs no adjustment.

5 Fig.9.6 shows a diagram of the rear brake calipers, which operate in just the same manner as the front ones except that they only have one cylinder each. Each rear cylinder is fed by a different hydraulic circuit, so that if one circuit fails half the rear braking effort is still present.

4 Brake pads - removal and replacement

1 The brake pads should be replaced when about 1/8'' (3 mm) of the lining thickness remains. On no account may the linings be worn down to below 1/16'' (1.5 mm).

2 Start by jacking up the car and removing the wheel concerned.

3 For brakes of the pattern shown in Figs.9.5, 9.6 and the photos accompanying this paragraph, remove the locking clips holding the guide pins in position, pull out one of the lock pins while holding the damper springs in place, take out the springs and then remove the remaining lock pin.

4 Now extract the pads and - in the case of the rear brakes - the backing plates, with a pair of thin nosed pliers.

5 If it is intended to use the pads again, mark them so that you know which brake they came from and what position they

4.3a Removing the brake pads: Remove the locking clips holding the guide pins in ...

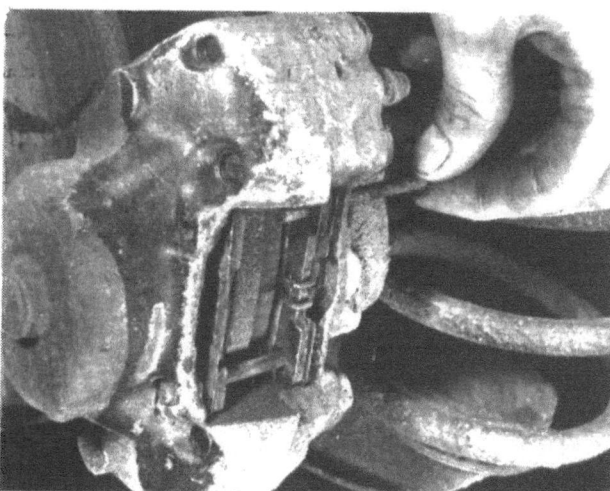

4.3b ... and take out one of the pins

4.3c With the pin out of the way the damper springs (indicated by the screwdriver) can be taken out

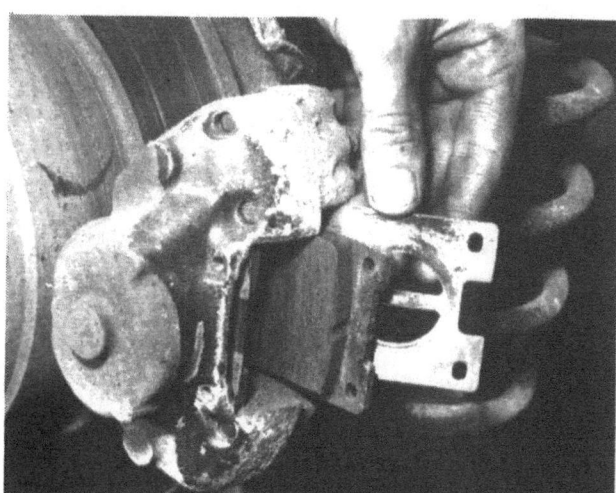

4.3d After removing the springs the other pin is taken out, freeing the pads for removal. Note the support plate found in the rear calipers

4.3e The front pads are flexible in the centre, being acted on by two pistons

occupied.

6   Clean the inside faces of the housings and examine the dust covers protecting the cylinders. Replace any dust covers that are damaged. They are held on to the housing by clip rings and are easily removed.

7   To make room for the new pads, push the pistons down into the cylinders with a screwdriver or the like, taking great care not to damage the dust covers while you do so.

8   Fitting new pads or refitting the old ones is simply a reversal of the removal procedure.

9   On the 145, a slightly different pattern of brake may be found. This is shown in Fig.9.7. The guide pins may be removed by drifting them out as shown in Fig.9.8, but they should be gently tapped in with a hammer as shown in Fig.9.9 otherwise they may be damaged. On reassembly it is simplest to replace one guide pin, slip the tensioning spring under it, and hold this in position while inserting the other pin. It is recommended that the tensioning springs are renewed when brake pads are replaced. Note that the rubber dust seals are different from those in the other type of brake and do not have retaining clips.

10 Before replacing the wheel, check that the brake is functioning properly. For the first 200-300 miles try to avoid violent braking. This will give the brake pads a chance to bed in and acquire a hard smooth surface, resulting in better braking and a longer life.

Fig. 9.7 Rear brake caliper, 145 series

5   Front calipers - removal and refitting

1   Jack up the front end of the car and support it on the front axle by placing blocks under the front jack attachment. It is

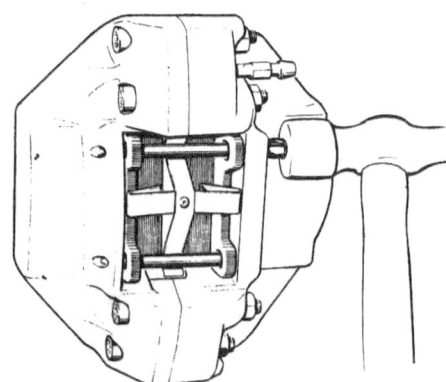

Fig. 9.9 Replacing the guide pins, 145 brake caliper

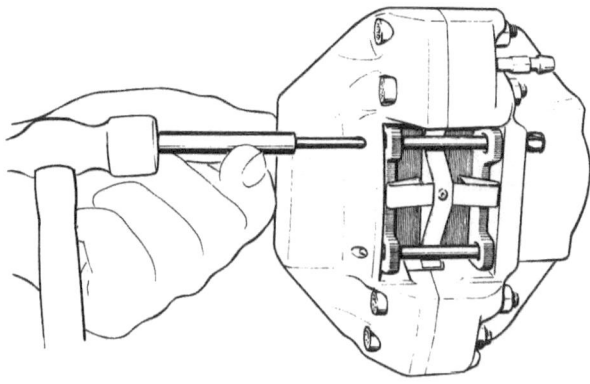

Fig. 9.8 Drifting out the guide pins, 145 brake caliper

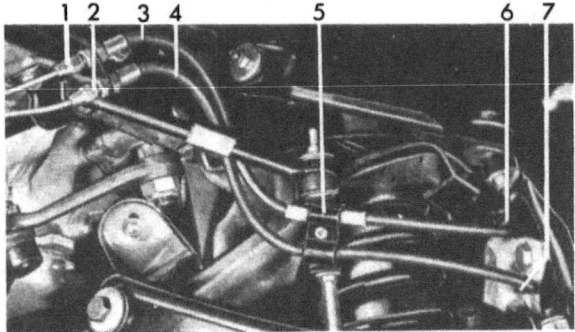

Fig. 9.10 Front wheel brake hose connections

1 Connection for the primary circuit	5 Clip
2 Connection for the secondary circuit	6 Connection for lower wheel unit cylinder
3 Upper brake hose	7 Connection for upper wheel unit cylinder
4 Lower brake hose	

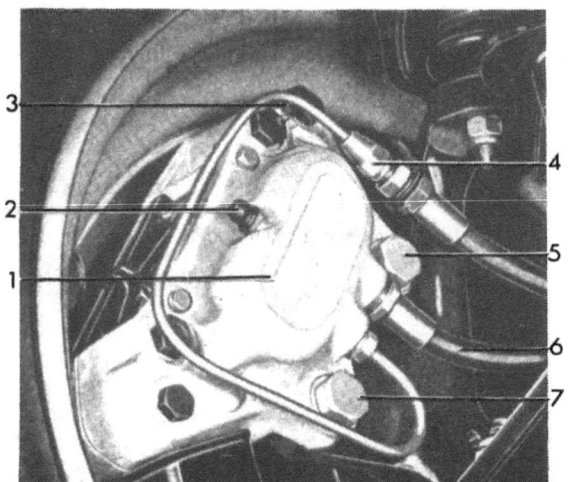

Fig. 9.11 Front wheel brake unit

1 Front wheel brake caliper	5 Attaching bolt
2 Lower bleeder nipple	6 Connection for upper wheel unit cylinder
3 Upper bleeder nipple	7 Attaching bolt
4 Connection for lower wheel unit cylinder	

important to do this so that when the hoses are refitted they are free from torsion under normal conditions.

2 Remove the clip that retains the hoses (see Fig. 9.10).

3 Block up the vent hole in the brake fluid container. This will greatly reduce leakage from the junctions when the brake hoses are disconnected. Disconnect the brake hoses from their junctions (1 and 2 in Fig. 9.10) plug the ends of the junctions to prevent unnecessary leakage, being very careful not to get dirt into the hydraulic fluid.

4 Undo the two fixing bolts (see Fig. 9.11) and remove the caliper.

5 Replacement is in the main simply a reversal of the removal procedure, but it should be done with care. Check that the contact surfaces of the caliper and frame are clean and undamaged.

6 The brake disc should be central in the caliper and parallel to it. This can be checked by measuring the distances between the bosses at the top and bottom of the caliper and the disc with spacers and feeler gauges. The difference between these distances should not exceed 0.010" (0.25 mm). The location of the caliper can be adjusted with shims which are available in thickness of .008" and 0.016" (0.2 - 0.4 mm). Coat the fixing bolts with a couple of drops of Loctite, Type AV.

7 When all is finished, do not forget to open the hole in the brake fluid container cover which you blocked up to reduce leakage.

8 Naturally, the brake system will need bleeding as described in Section 2.

6 Rear brake calipers - removal and refitting

1 The procedure for rear calipers is basically the same as for the front. The car should be jacked up and supported on its rear axle to ensure that when the hoses are fitted they are not in torsion under normal load conditions. Figs. 9.12 and 9.13 show the caliper fitted in position and being removed.

7 Brake calipers - overhaul

1 As with all hydraulic equipment, absolute cleanliness is essential when dismantling and reassembling these units. Clean the outside thoroughly before you start. Before dismantling rear brake calipers of the pattern shown in Fig. 9.7, mark the pistons so that you can refit them in the same position (see paragraph 7).

2 Remove the dust cover retaining rings (if fitted) and the dust covers themselves. Place a piece of wood about ½" (12.5 mm) thick between the pistons and apply compressed air to one of the hoses connected to the caliper to push the pistons out (see Fig. 9.14). A good source of compressed air for this job is a flexible bottle (for example the sort used for washing up liquid - but be sure that the bottle has been thoroughly cleaned out). If by any chance the piston is jammed in the housing and will not yield to this treatment, a local garage may be able to apply a high pressure air line for you.

3 Remove the inner sealing rings with a small screwdriver, being very careful not to scratch the bore or damage the groove. It is a good idea to round off the corners of screwdrivers used for this sort of thing.

4 Unscrew the bleed nipples, hose connections etc., from the unit but do not attempt to separate the two halves as reassembling them is a factory job needing specialised equipment.

5 Give the various parts and connecting paths a thorough clean with methylated spirit - about the only fluid which you can guarantee will not affect the rubber seals. Dry the various bits and pieces with a lint-free rag - a hair drier is very useful for the fluid pathways, to make sure - as you must - that all methylated spirit is removed.

6 Thoroughly inspect the various parts. If any of the cylinders is scored or scratched the entire cylinder housing must be replaced complete. Replace any other damaged or worn parts. If

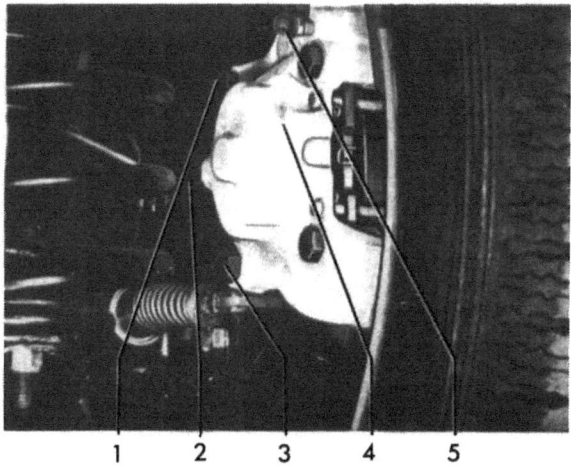

Fig. 9.12 Rear brake caliper in position

1 *Attaching bolt*
2 *Brake line*
3 *Attaching bolt*
4 *Rear wheel brake caliper*
5 *Bleeder nipple*

Fig. 9.13 Removing rear caliper

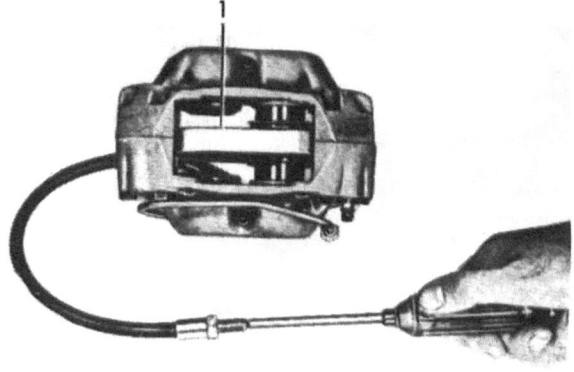

Fig. 9.14 Removing pistons using compressed air (note wooden spacer (1)

the caliper is of the pattern shown in Fig.9.7, the tensioning springs should invariably be replaced on reassembly.

7 Reassembly is straightforward. Coat the various parts with brake fluid before assembling them. Fit the inner sealing rings into their grooves, making sure they are the right way round (see Fig.9.5). Fit the pistons with the large ends inside the housings. In the case of rear brakes of the pattern shown in Fig.9.7, the outer end of the piston is not perpendicular to its axis and should incline 20° along a line determined by the template SVO 2919. You will not need this template if you marked the piston before dismantling as recommended in paragraph 1. If you are replacing the piston with a new one, compare new with old and mark the new one in the same place.

8 Master cylinder - removal, overhaul and replacement

1 Fig.9.15 shows a diagram of the master cylinder and our photograph (2.6) shows it in position with the fluid reservoir on the top being topped up with fluid we recommend. When topping-up the reservoir be sure you don't let brake fluid drip on your bodywork as it is a very effective paint remover.

2 The basic principle on which the cylinder works is perfectly simple. There are two pistons in tandem, the primary piston and the secondary piston. There is no difference in function - and there is certainly no difference in importance - between primary and secondary pistons and the circuits connected to them; the primary piston is so called because it is the one that gets pushed first. If all is working properly, pressure building up in front of the primary piston pushes forward the secondary piston and the same hydraulic pressure is exerted in both primary and secondary circuits. If the primary circuit develops a leak the primary piston is simply carried on until it meets the secondary piston and pushes it forward physically. If there is a leak in the secondary circuit, the secondary piston will carry on until it hits the end of the master cylinder, but pressure will be maintained in front of the primary cylinder and in the primary circuit.

3 To remove the master cylinder, first lift off the brake fluid container as shown in Fig.9.16. Nothing has to be unscrewed first - it simply sits on top of two rubber seals. If you put your fingers over the bottom holes quickly you will lose very little fluid. Rag placed underneath the cylinder will help to prevent what you do lose from dripping on to places where it is not wanted.

4 Remove the brake lines from the master cylinder and plug them with plastic plugs. Undo the fixing nuts and remove the cylinder.

5 Clean the outside of the cylinder thoroughly, dismantle it into the component parts shown in Fig.9.17, and clean the inside of the cylinder and the various parts thoroughly with methylated spirit.

6 Inspect carefully for wear and/or damage. Naturally you will replace all the rubber parts before reassembling. If the inside of the cylinder is scored or scratched it should be replaced. Small amounts of rust or very slight scratches can be removed by honing the cylinder, and it may be cheaper to have this done than to buy a new one. The upper limit for the inside diameter is 0.881'' (22.40 mm) as opposed to the nominal diameter of 7/8'' (22.2 mm) so the usefulness of this procedure is limited. In addition to replacing the rubber parts, Volvo recommend that during master cylinder overhaul you should replace the primary piston assembly complete (9, Fig.9.17) the stop screw (18) and its washer (17) and the circlip (12).

7 Reassembly is straightforward. Be sure that the secondary piston seals are assembled the right way round - there are two patterns of piston, see Figs.9.18 and 9.19.

8 Coat the cylinder with brake fluid and dip the piston and seals in brake fluid before fitting. Fit the secondary piston (see Fig.10.19) and follow this with the primary piston (Fig.9.20) and then follow this with the washer (11,Fig.9.17).

9 Check that the hole for the stop screw is clear and fit this with its sealing washer, tightening it to a torque of 7 - 9 lbft. (1-1.2 kg m).

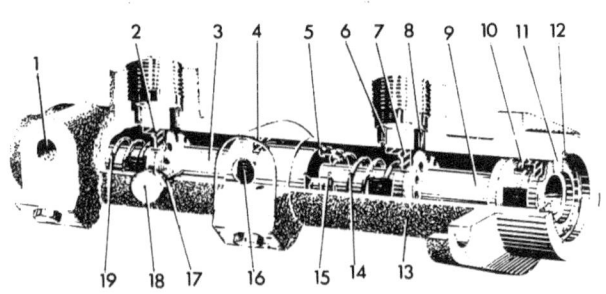

Fig. 9.15 Master cylinder

1　Connection for secondary circuit	12　Circlip
2　Piston seal	13　Cylinder
3　Secondary seal	14　Return spring for primary piston
4　Piston seal	15　Circlip
5　Spring guide	16　Connection for primary circuit
6　Equalising hole	
7　Piston seal	17　Sealing washer
8　Overflow hole	18　Stop screw
9　Primary piston	19　Return spring for secondary piston
10　Piston seal	
11　Thrust washer	

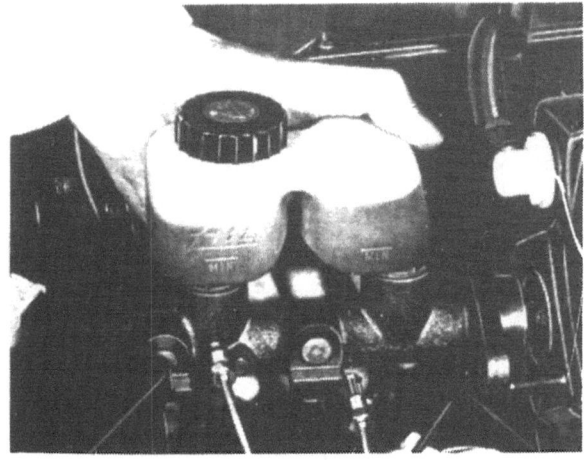

Fig. 9.16 Removing the fluid reservoir

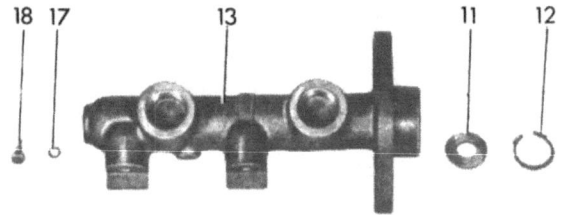

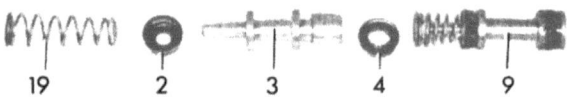

Fig. 9.17 Master cylinder dismantled

2　Piston seal	12　Circlip
3　Secondary piston	13　Cylinder housing
4　Piston seal	17　Sealing washer
9　Primary piston (assembled)	18　Stop screw
11　Thrust washer	19　Return spring

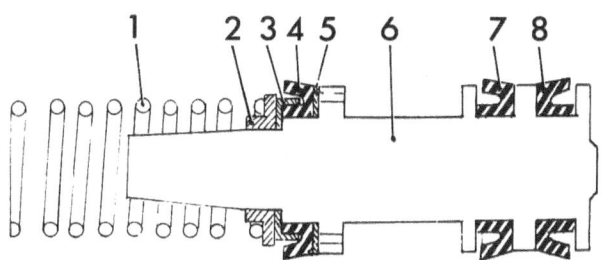

Fig. 9.18 Secondary piston

1	Spring	5	Washer
2	Spring plate	6	Piston
3	Back-up ring	7	Piston seal
4	Piston seal	8	Piston seal

Fig. 9.19 Fitting the secondary piston (alternative pattern to that shown in Fig. 9.18)

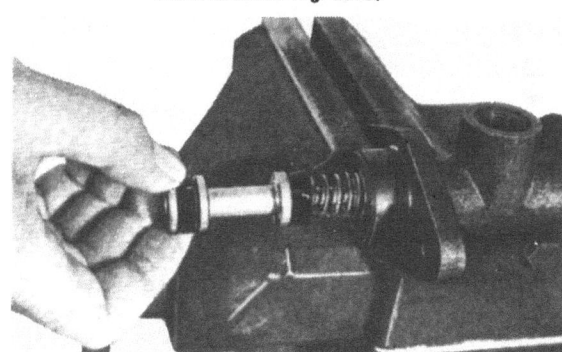

Fig. 9.20 Fitting the primary piston

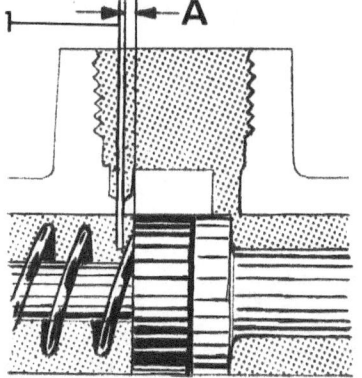

Fig. 9.21 Checking clearance of equalising hole

1 - 0.5 mm (25 SWG) soft copper wire
A = approx. 0.020'' (0.5 mm)

10 Check that the assembly is correct by pushing a piece of 0.5 mm (25 SWG) soft copper wire through the equalising holes in the container mounts (Fig.9.21). These holes should be clear of the pistons as shown. If they are not, you have done something wrong.

11 Fit the rubber seals on which the fluid container sits, together with their nuts and washers and refit the container.

12 The master cylinder is operated by a plunger rod which protrudes from the servo cylinder and there must be a definite clearance (Volvo recommend between 0.004-0.04 (0.1-1.0 mm) and this is set by turning the adjuster screw in the end of the thrust rod. Setting a clearance which you cannot get at to measure presents a slight problem; we think the easiest way is to aim for a clearance of 0.02 (0.5 mm) by measuring dimension "A", Fig.9.22 and adjusting dimension "B" to be 0.02 (0.5 mm) less than this. The master cylinder can now be fitted and the fixing nuts tightened to 17 lb ft (2.4 kg m). It now only remains to reconnect the pipes and bleed the entire brake system.

9 Warning valve

1 Fig.9.23 gives a diagram of this valve and Fig.9.24 shows where it is located. The valve contains a piston one end of which

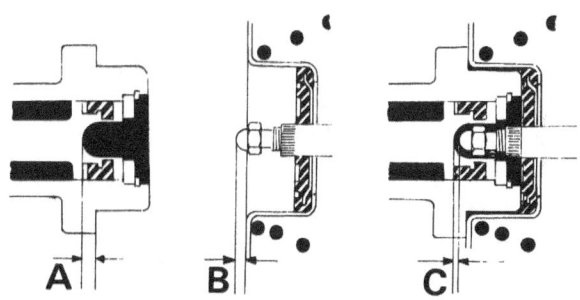

Fig. 9.22 Adjusting the thrust rod

C = 0.004 − 0.04'' (0.1 − 1.0 mm)

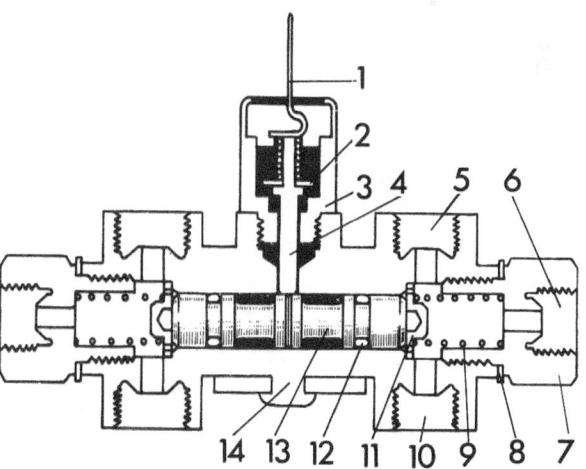

Fig. 9.23 Brake warning valve

1	Electrical connection	7	End piece
2	Switch washer	8	Sealing washer
3	Switch housing	9	Spring
4	Guide pin	10	Connection, front wheel brakes
5	Connection, rear wheel brakes	11	Thrust washer
6	Connection, master cylinder	12	O-ring
		13	Piston
		14	Housing

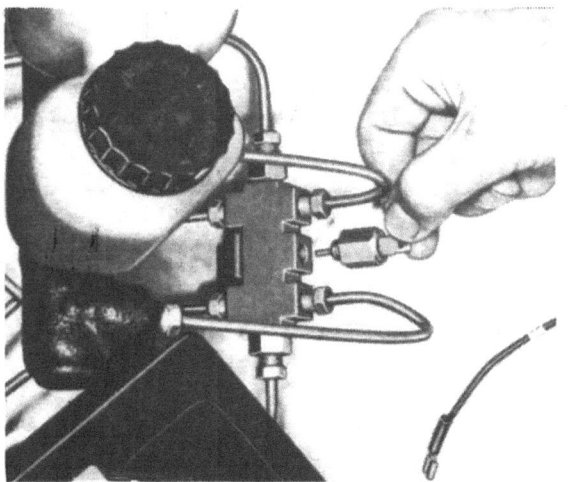

Fig. 9.24 Removing switch element from brake warning valve

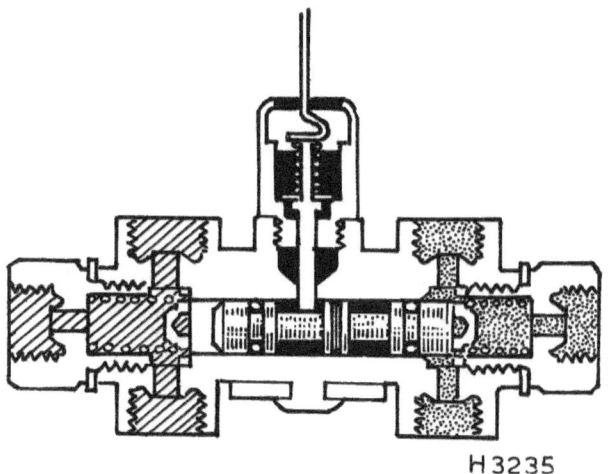

H 3235

Fig. 9.25 Operation of brake warning valve. Loss of pressure on right has caused the piston to move over and the switch plunger has descended

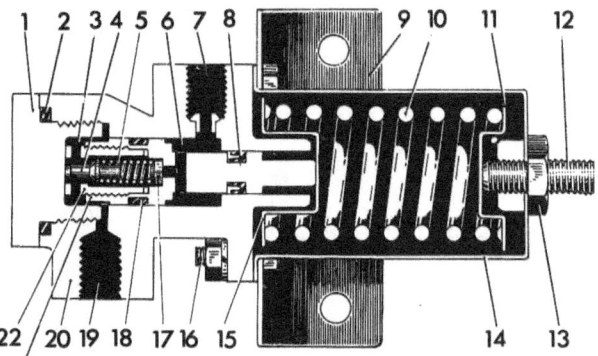

Fig. 9.26 Brake valve

1	Plug	12	Adjusting screw
2	O-ring	13	Locknut
3	Cylinder	14	Spring housing
4	Valve	15	Retainer
5	Valve spring	16	Screw
6	Cylinder	17	Equalising valve
7	Connection to master cylinder	18	O-ring
		19	Connection to rear brake cylinders
8	Piston seal	20	Housing
9	Bracket	21	Piston
10	Spring	22	Valve housing
11	Retainer		

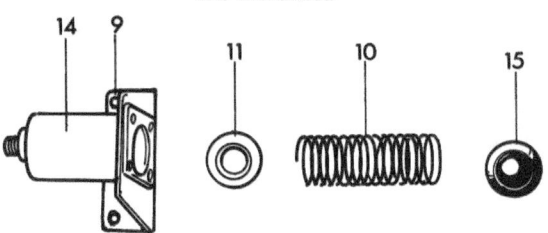

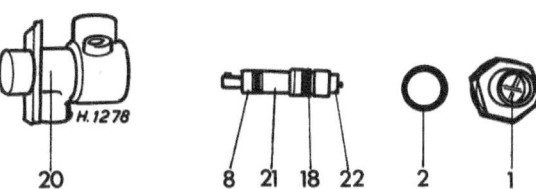

Fig. 9.27 Brake valve, dismantled

1	Plug	14	Spring housing
2	O-ring	15	Retainer
8	Piston seal	18	O-ring
9	Bracket	20	Housing
10	Spring	21	Piston
11	Retainer	22	Valve housing

10.1a The rear brake pressure limiting valves ...

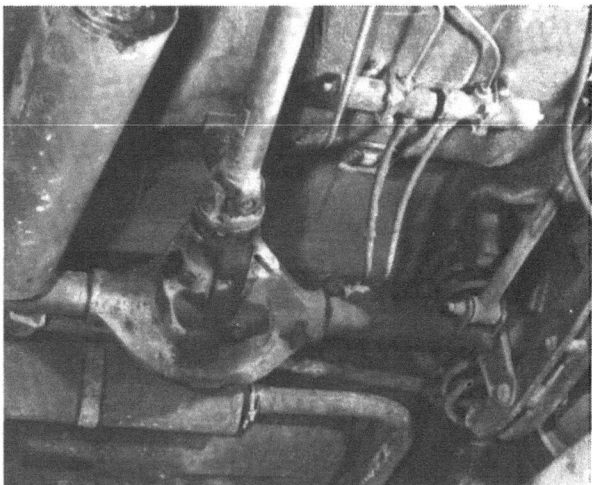

10.1b ... and where you find them

is connected to the primary hydraulic circuit and the other end to the secondary; if there is an appreciable pressure difference between the two the piston moves towards the low pressure end and allows the guide pin to fall as shown in Fig.9.25, earthing the cable termination and thus allowing the brake warning light to come on.

2 Once the piston has moved over, it cannot return until the switch element is removed (see Fig.9.24) when, if there is no pressure on either side, the piston will return to its central position. When the brake system is being bled, it is quite possible for pressure to be applied to, for example, the right-hand end of the piston in Fig.9.25 while no pressure is applied to the other end, thus putting a stress on the guide pin with some risk of damage. For this reason it is important to remove the switch element from the valve when bleeding the brakes.

3 It can easily be checked, if required, by undoing one of the rear brake bleeder nipples half a turn and applying the brakes. The lamp should then light. Screw up the nipple, reset the valve, and if desired repeat the process with the other rear brake.

4 The diagram gives sufficient guidance to dismantling if this is necessary, overhaul being simply a matter of cleaning, replacing rubber seals and O-rings, reassembly (coat the piston and inside of the cylinder with brake fluid) and refitting.

10 Rear brake valves

1 Hydraulic fluid in each of the rear brakes is taken through a valve whose function is to reduce the proportion of pressure fed to the rear brakes relative to the pressure in the master cylinder, which is applied directly to the front brakes. This reduces the tendency of the rear wheels to lock under heavy braking conditions. Fig.9.26 gives a diagram of the valve, Fig.9.27 shows its main components (the numbers correspond with those used in Fig.9.26) and the photographs show what the valves look like and where they are positioned in the car.

2 The piston assembly shown in Fig.9.27 can be identified in Fig.9.26 (where it is pointing the other way round) by the sealing rings 8 and 18 which it carries. At low pressure the hydraulic fluid entering from the master cylinder at connection 7 (Fig.9.26) passes through a path in the piston assembly, past the equalising valve (17) and the valve (4) which is held open because the end of it is touching the plug (1) and so passes with unreduced pressure to the rear brake through connection (19). When the hydraulic pressure approaches 484 lb in^2 (34 kg cm^2) or on the 145, 711 lb in^2 (50 kg cm^2) the piston assembly (21) overcomes the pressure of the large spring (10) and moves to the right. This permits the valve (4) to close, and once it does close the supply of fluid to connection (19) is cut off and pressure there cannot rise any further.

3 When this happens, there is a tendency for the piston (21) to be pushed back again to the left by the spring pressure, but this causes the pressure in (19) to increase again so the system stabilises itself with the valve (4) just about to open or just about to close, rather on the lines of a voltage regulator where a contact is on the verge of making or breaking the whole time. The valve is not designed to put an immediate upper limit on the pressure applied to the rear brake, but it cuts down the rate of increase of pressure on the rear brake when pressure on the front brake is increased.

4 Dismantling and inspecting this valve is a simple matter, but two points are of the utmost importance: the springs (5 and 10, Fig.9.26) must not be distorted in any way and the adjusting screw must not be touched. Separate the spring housing from the hydraulic part by moving the four screws (16, Fig.9.26). Shake out the spring and retainer. Then unscrew the plug (1) and push out the piston assembly complete. If, as Volvo recommend, you are going to replace the piston assembly regardless of its condition you do not need to bother with it further. Otherwise, dismantle it for cleaning. Clean all parts thoroughly with methylated spirit and inspect them.

5 If the cylinder surfaces are scratched or damaged by rust, the valve should be replaced complete. If however, the cylinder

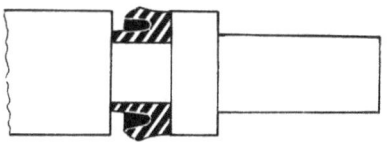

Fig. 9.28 Correct fitting of brake valve piston seal

surfaces are all right, you are recommended to replace the piston assembly even if there appears to be nothing wrong with it. When doing so, check that the seal is positioned as shown in Fig.9.28. Volvo supply a repair kit which includes a piston assembly, and all necessary seals and gaskets.

6 Coat all parts with brake fluid before reassembly. Fit the piston and screw in the plug (1), not forgetting its O-ring (2). Tightening torque is 70-85 lb ft (10-12 kg m).

7 The remainder of the reassembly is perfectly straightforward - be sure you get the spring retainers in their correct position in the housing as shown in Fig.9.26.

11 Rear brake valve - checking operation

1 Unfortunately, checking the performance of the brake valve needs apparatus which the average owner is unlikely to possess, ie equipment for generating and monitoring hydraulic pressure. This means that you have either got to have someone else check them for you, or accept that their performance is adequate on a basis of the performance of your braking system. It is unlikely that both the rear brake valves would be faulty at the same time unless the car has a long history of neglect (always a possibility, unfortunately, in a secondhand vehicle) so by and large if both your rear brakes are equally efficient and there is no great tendency for one wheel to lock rather than the other it is a pretty safe bet that the valves are functioning properly. If this is so, carrying out the reconditioning process just outlined will ensure that they will continue to do so for a long time ahead.

2 If, however, you suspect that all is not well with one or both of the valves, you should have them checked by a Volvo agent who has the specialised equipment necessary. If a fault is revealed, have them overhauled by him or replaced with new ones.

12 Servo cylinder

1 The servo cylinder (which is shown in our photograph 2.6) contains a diaphragm to which is attached the pushrod which operates the brake master cylinder. This diaphragm is itself pushed forward by another rod which enters the back of the servo unit. When no push is applied to the diaphragm, arrangements within the cylinder are such that engine vacuum (applied to the cylinder via the check valve which is clearly seen in photograph 2.6) appears equally on either side of the diaphragm. If however the diaphragm is pushed forward air is allowed to enter the cylinder at the back of the diaphragm and the resulting pressure difference tends to pull the diaphragm forwards, producing an extra push on the out going pushrod. The amount of air that enters is proportional to the displacement of the diaphragm, the nett result being that the pushrod operates on the master cylinder with a force up to three times greater than the force applied to the ingoing pushrod by the brake pedal linkage.

2 You cannot get at the inside if anything goes wrong with the cylinder, but by proper maintenance you can make pretty certain that nothing ever will. There are three basic maintenance requirements.

3 The first of these is concerned with the check valve and its connecting hose. You will not get much of a vacuum - and nor will your engine function as it should - if the hose is leaking. The moral is obvious. The check valve ensures that when suction

from the engine ceases a vacuum remains in the cylinder. It clips into the servo cylinder and can easily be removed with two screwdrivers. You should find it easy to suck through the hose connection end but impossible to suck through the end that enters the cylinder. With the replacement valve comes a new gasket and a supply of special grease for coating the inside of the gasket. When fitting the valve, ensure that the highest point of the vacuum hose is at the attachment to the valve. Our photo 2.6 shows valve and hose correctly positioned.

4   Since the cylinder takes in air at the entrance of the ingoing thrust rod, this rod passes through a filter assembly. This is incorporated in a rubber casing surrounding the pushrod and the complete assembly should be checked from time to time and replaced if necessary.

5   Finally, the pushrod for the master cylinder operates through a seal which keeps out dirt and ensures the proper maintenance of the vacuum. This seal should be replaced from time to time.

6   There are two versions of the servo cylinder, and we have shown outlines of these and their repair kits in Fig.9.29.

7   To replace the front sealing ring the master cylinder must be removed as described in Section 8. Be careful not to damage the thrust rod when you remove the sealing ring. Wipe the thrust rod and recess clean and lubricate them and the new sealing ring with a suitable grease. Fit the new sealing ring with the flange facing outwards.

8   Before the rear sealing and filter assembly can be fitted the servo cylinder must be removed. Removal is self-explanatory once the master cylinder has been removed (Section 9) and the brake pedal has been disconnected from the servo pushrod (Section 13). Typical filter details are shown in Fig. 9.30; although the precise arrangement may vary according to model, the principle remains the same.

9   For the later version, the assembly is shown in 9.31. Lubricate the new sealing ring, valve housing and sealing area of the new rubber cover with a suitable grease. Fit a new guide, sealing ring and lock washer as shown in the Figure, with the sealing lip and the guide level facing outwards. Carefully press the lock washer ring on until it just bottoms against the sealing ring all round. Fit the rubber cover and filter, making sure that they are not distorted or folded under in any way.

10 The very latest types of servo have no provision for servicing the pushrod seal. Additionally, the check valve may be fitted in the vacuum hose between the servo and the manifold, rather than in the servo body itself. Fit a new valve of this type with the arrow pointing in the direction of air flow, ie towards the manifold.

13 Brake pedal and brake switch

1   Fig.9.31 shows details of the brake pedal suspension. To replace the pedal or its bushes, first remove the split pin bolt (10, Fig.9.31) then lever off the return spring (6). Unscrew the nut (4) and pull out the screw (2) lift the pedal forwards.

2   Press out the bearing sleeve (1) and the bushes (3). Clean the parts. If the bearing sleeve is worn, replace it.

3   Press the new bushes (3) into position in the pedal and lubricate them with a thin layer of grease. Fit the bearing sleeve (1) and the return spring (6), place the pedal in position and fit the screw (2) and the nut (4). Fit on the return spring. Fit the split pin bolt (10) and split pin.

4   Fig.9.32 illustrates the brake switch assembly. The distance between the released brake pedal and the threaded brass hub on the switch (dimension 'A', Fig. 9.32) should be 0.16" ± 0.08" (4 ± 2 mm). This can be adjusted by slackening the fixing screws for the bracket and moving it until the distance is right.

14 Handbrake - description and adjustment

1   The handbrake operates on two small drums on the rear wheels. Fig.9.33 shows the layout adopted before and after 1970. Apart from the different placing of the operating levers the two systems are virtually identical. The brake lever operates a rod running underneath the body and connected to a stirrup

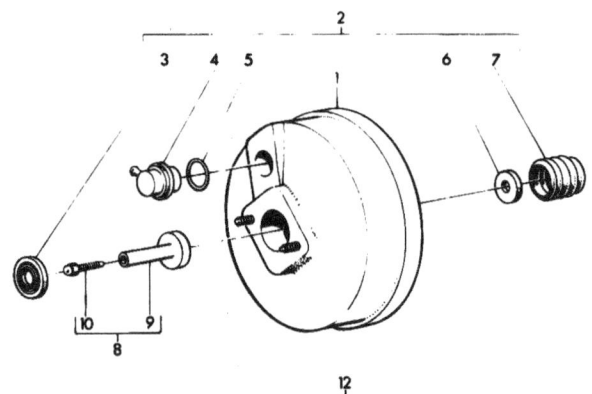
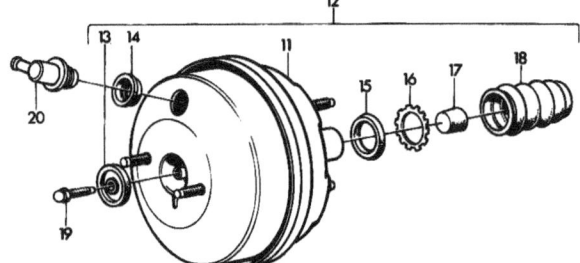

Fig. 9.29 Repair kits for brake servos

1 Vacuum brake cylinder, earlier type	11 Vacuum brake cylinder, later type
2 Repair kit	12 Repair kit
3 Seal	13 Seal
4 Check valve	14 Packing
5 O-ring	15 Seal ring
6 Filter	16 Circlip
7 Rubber casing	17 Filter
8 Repair kit	18 Rubber casing
9 Push rod	19 Adjuster screw
10 Adjuster screw	20 Check valve

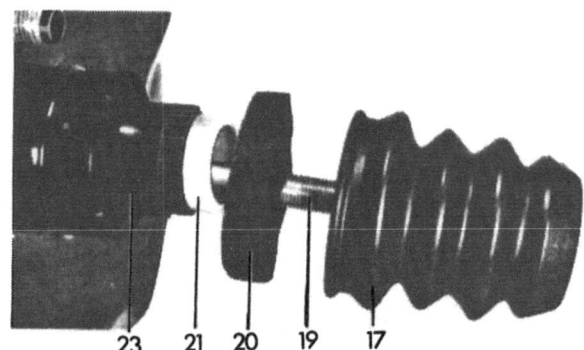

Fig. 9.30 Brake servo filter parts

17 Rubber cover	21 Plastic
19 Ingoing thrust rod	23 Valve housing
20 Filter	

carrying a pulley round which a cable runs which terminates at the brake levers (photos). A feature of the system is the spring between the brake rod and the stirrup which makes for a degree of progessive braking with application of the lever - a typical Volvo detail. In early models the stirrup was of a different pattern and did not incorporate a pulley.

2   When correctly adjusted the handbrake should give its full

effect on the third or fourth notch of the lever ratchet. To achieve this, first adjust the brakes.

3 To carry out this adjustment support the car with the rear wheels clear of the ground and remove them. Disconnect the brake cable from the levers.

4 Turn one of the drums until the adjustment hole coincides with the serrations on the adjustment screw (17, Fig.9.33).

5 Turn the screw until the shoes come up against the brake drum. You will feel the serrations clicking against the brake spring. When you have turned the screw as far as it will reasonably go (do not be too violent about it or you run the risk of damaging the serrations) the drum should be very stiff to turn against the friction of the brake shoes. Now turn the screw back four or five clicks and check that the drum turns with very little drag. If the drag is appreciable, turn the screw back a further two or three serrations.

6 Be sure while you are doing this that the disc brake pads are not rubbing on the disc and preventing it from rotating freely. As for deciding which way to turn the screw, we always find that the quickest method is to start turning, and if we get to an end stop without having the shoes jam against the drum we turn the other way.

7 Having done one wheel, treat the other in exactly the same way - that is, screw up the adjustment screw until the shoes come up against the drum applying the same pressure as you did on the other wheel and then turn it back by the same number of serrations. Check that it is rotating reasonably freely.

8 Connect up the brake cable ends again and see if the handbrake is operating on the third or fourth notch. Check too, that the braking effect is approximately equal on both wheels. If it is not, try the effect of altering one of the adjusters by a click or two checking that the altered one still rotates freely when the brake is off.

9 When you have got a reasonable balance, get the brake working on the third or fourth notch by adjusting the position of the stirrup on the brake rod (photo 14.1b).

15 Handbrake - brake drums and brake shoes

1 In order to remove the brake drum, the disc brake caliper must first be removed since the disc and the drum are all in one piece. Removing the caliper is described in Section 6. The wheel, of course, must be removed before you start, and it is a good idea to slacken off the brake adjuster as far as it will go.

2 Removal of the brake drum reveals the brake shoes assembly. Dismantling and reassembling these assemblies is a fiddling and sometimes a confusing business, and we suggest that unless you are pretty experienced at it you get both the brake drums off

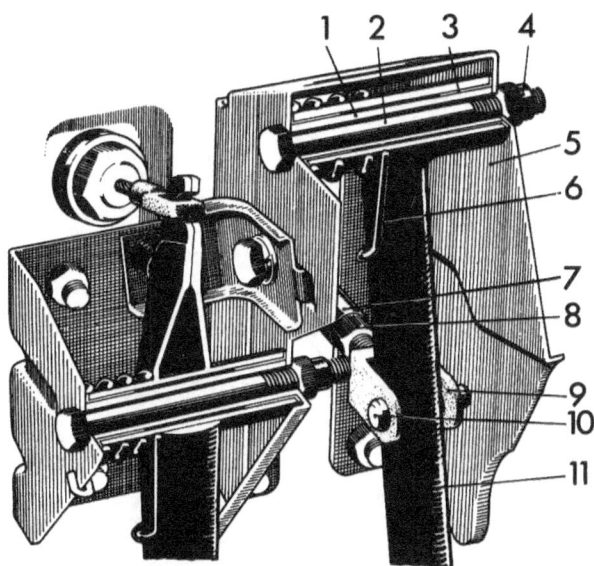

Fig. 9.31 Brake pedal suspension

1 Bearing sleeve	7 Thrust rod
2 Screw	8 Locknut
3 Nylon bush	9 Fork
4 Nut	10 Split pin bolt
5 Bracket	11 Brake pedal
6 Return spring	

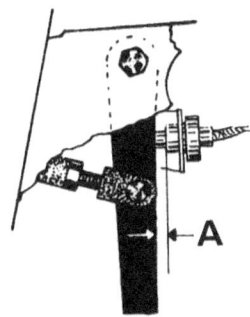

Fig. 9.32 Footbrake switch adjustment

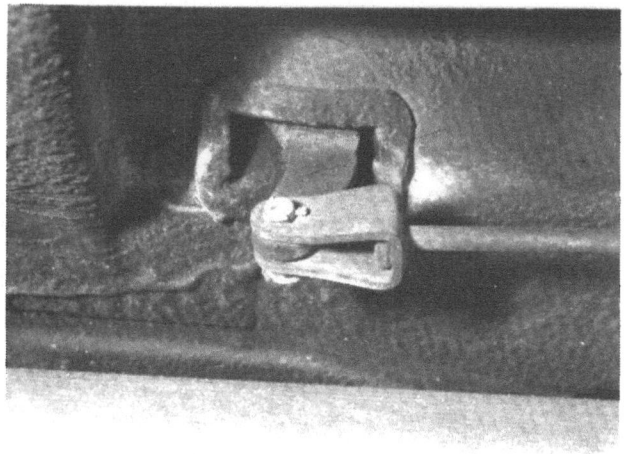

14.1a The handbrake lever operates a rod ...

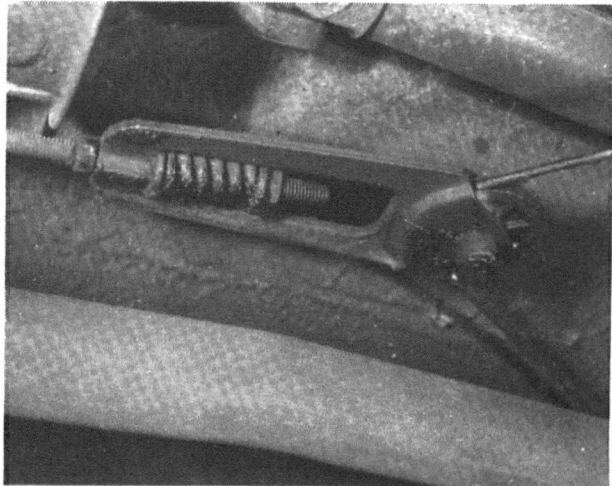

14.1b/14.9 ... which is connected to a stirrup acting on the brake cable. Note adjustment nuts and the spring which makes for smoother braking

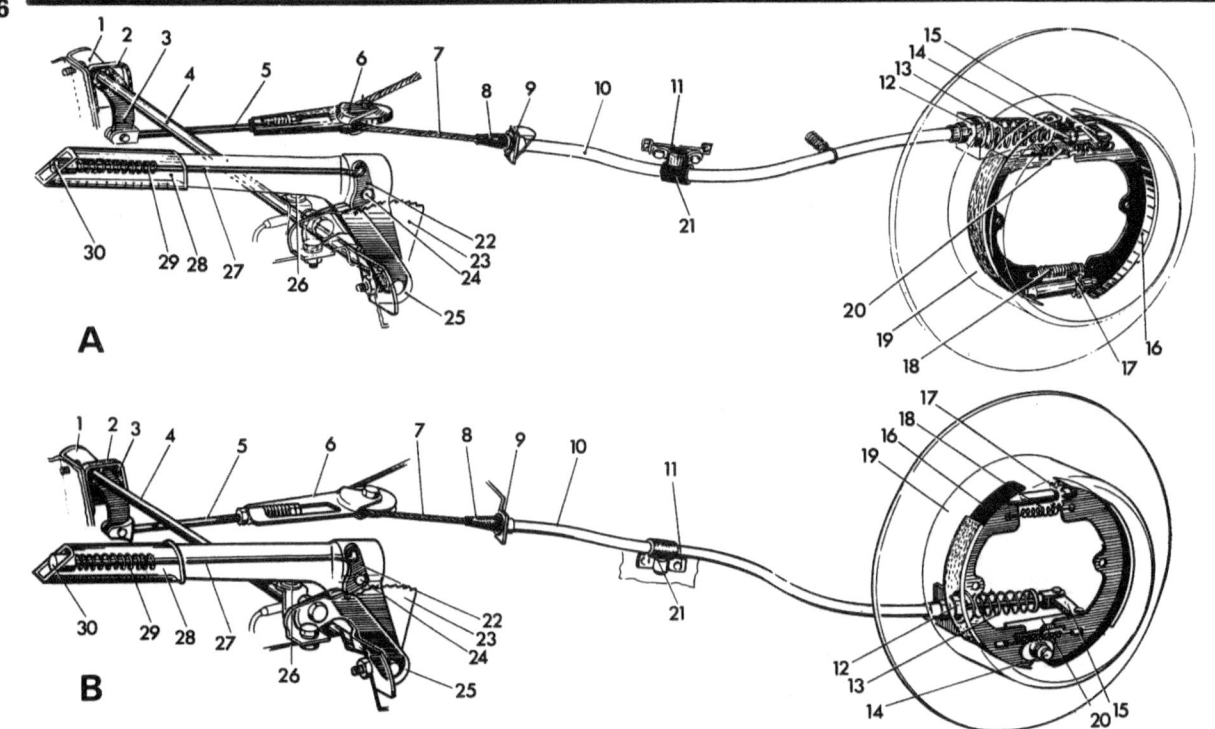

Fig. 9.33 Handbrake arrangements (a) before 1970 (b) 1970 and after

Fig. 9.34 Lever, fulcrum bar, anchor bolt and guide pins

KEY to Figs. 9.33 - 9.36

1	Inner support bracket	16b	Rear)
2	Rubber cover	17	Brake adjuster
3	Crank	18	Hold-on springs
4	Operating shaft	18a	Spring
5	Pullrod	18b	Washer
6	Stirrup	19	Brake drum
7	Brake cable	20	Fulcrum bar
8	Rubber cover	21	Sleeve
9	Fulcrum bar	22	Pawl and
10	Cable sleeve	23	ratchet
11	Centre sleeve bracket	24	Pawl pin
12	Rear sleeve bracket	25	Outer support bracket
13	Pull-off spring	26	Warning light switch
14	Anchor bolt	27	Pawl release rod
14a	Nut	28	Handbrake handle
14b	Washer	29	Pawl hold-on spring
15	Brake lever and clevis	30	Release button
16	Brake shoe	31	Guide pins
(16a	Front,	R	shoe retainer

Fig. 9.35 Earlier anchor bolt arrangement

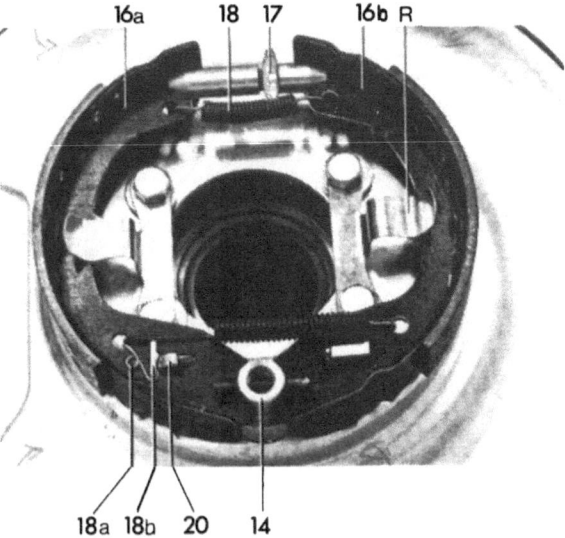

Fig. 9.36 Rear brake assembled

and then completely strip and reassemble one of the brakes before you touch the other one - this way you always have a complete correct assembly for comparsion.

3 To dismantle, remove both the return springs and take out the adjusting device which sits between the shoes. Disengage the shoes from their retaining linkages and remove them, marking shoes and backing plate so that you know which shoe went where if you are going to refit them.

4 Before doing anything else check that there is no oil leakage. If there is, you will have to replace the halfshaft oil seals as described in Chapter 8. Having checked for leakage, clean all the parts except the brake linings. Examine the various parts for wear and in particular check that the lever joint does not chafe.

5 If the brake linings are oily or worn almost down to the rivets, replace the brake shoes.

6 Volvo recommend that the brake drum should be replaced if its friction surface is concave or if it is more than 0.08″ (0.2 mm) out of round.

7 On reassembling, if you are fitting new linings or drums, be sure that the adjustment device is screwed right in so that it is as short as possible. This will save a struggle when you put on the drum. Coat the six guide lips on the backing plate as well as the lever joint and adjusting screw with heat resistant graphite grease intended for this purpose. Check that the lever, fulcrum bar and anchor bolt (15, 14 and 20, Fig.9.33) are correctly assembled and generally speaking that the assembly is the same as for the unit that has not been dismantled. When the brake shoes are fitted, the shorter sleeve on the adjusting device should be turned forwards on the right-hand side and backwards on the left hand side (see Fig.9.36). The rest of the assembly is straight-forward.

8 Refit the caliper as described in Section 9.5.

---

16 Handbrake lever - replacing pawl and ratchet

1 To dismantle the handbrake lever assembly, start by removing the pin holding the pull rod to the lever underneath the vehicle (photo 14.1a).

2 Loosen the three attachments for the frame of the seat slide rails and lift the whole seat forwards.

3 Removing the rubber cover now reveals the ratchet segment which is incorporated in the support arrangements for the lever (see Fig.9.37 and 9.33).

4 The dismantling procedure is straightforward. The lever comes away complete with the push rod and pawl. The release button unscrews from the push rod, allowing the pawl hold-on-spring to be removed (see Fig.9.33). After this the rivet holding the pawl can be removed and the pawl replaced.

5 Reassembly (replacing the ratchet if required) is straight-forward. Lubricate the bushes with a thin coat of ballbearing grease.

---

17 Brake discs

1 From time to time the brake disc should be examined and its friction surfaces and runout checked.

2 Small marks on the friction surface or linings are of minor importance, but radial scratches reduce the braking effect and increase wear on the linings.

3 The runout must not exceed 0.004″ (0.1 mm) for the front brakes and 0.006″ (0.15 mm) for the rear brakes at the outer edge of the disc. This is easy to measure if you have the right apparatus (see Fig.9.38) but otherwise it is difficult and we suggest that you get a garage to check this for you.

4 Removing a disc is simple, once the caliper has been taken off. Undo the two fixing bolts and draw the disc off over the wheel studs. When removing the rear discs, be sure that the brake shoes are not binding on them. Slacken off the brake adjustment if necessary. If it does not want to come off, tap it lightly with a hide mallet or similar.

5 If for some reason a new brake disc is not available, the old

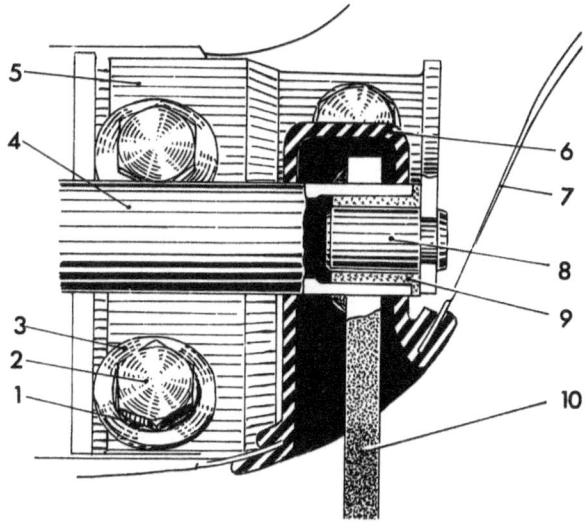

Fig. 9.37 Handbrake lever support arrangement

1 Spring washer
2 Attachment bolt
3 Flat washer
4 Shaft
5 Inner support attachment
6 Rubber cover
7 Floor
8 Support pin
9 Bush
10 Lever

Fig. 9.38 Checking brake disc run-out with a dial gauge

one can be machined - a specialist job. The minimum thickness for reconditioned discs is given in the specifications at the beginning of the Chapter. The surface finish should be 3 microns maximum measured on an arbitrary diameter and 5 microns maximum measured radially. The throw of a reconditioned disc may not exceed 0.004″ (0.1 mm) and the thickness may not vary more than 0.0012″ (0.03 mm).

19 Fault diagnosis (Items marked * refer to handbrake system)

Symptom	Reason/s	Remedy
EXCESSIVE TRAVEL IN BRAKE PEDAL OR HANDBRAKE LEVER		
Leaks and air bubbles in hydraulic system	Brake fluid level too low	Top up master cylinder reservoir. Check for leaks.
	Caliper leaking	Dismantle caliper, clean, fit new rubbers and bleed brakes.
	Master cylinder leaking (bubbles in master cylinder fluid)	Dismantle master cylinder, clean, and fit new rubbers. Bleed brakes.
	Brake flexible hose leaking	Examine and fit new hose if old hose leaking. Bleed brakes.
	Brake line fractured	Replace with new brake pipe. Bleed brakes.
	Brake system unions loose	Check all unions in brake system and tighten as necessary. Bleed brakes.
Normal wear	*Linings over 75% worn	*Fit replacement shoes and brake linings.
	*Cable stretched	*Replace or adjust as necessary.
BRAKE PEDAL FEELS SPRINGY		
Brake lining renewal	New linings not yet bedded-in	Use brakes gently until springy pedal feeling leaves.
	Brake discs badly worn and weak or cracked	Fit new discs.
BRAKE PEDAL FEELS SPONGY AND SOGGY		
Leaks or bubbles in hydraulic system	Caliper leaking	Dismantle caliper, clean, fit new rubbers, and bleed brakes.
	Master cylinder leaking (bubbles in master cylinder reservoir)	Dismantle master cylinder, clean, and fit new rubbers and bleed brakes. Replace cylinder if internal walls scored.
	Brake pipe line or flexible hose leaking	Fit new pipe line or hose.
	Unions in brake system loose	Examine for leaks, tighten as necessary.
BRAKES UNEVEN AND PULLING TO ONE SIDE		
Oil or grease leaks	Linings and brake drums* or discs contaminated with oil, grease, or hydraulic fluid	Ascertain and rectify source of leak, clean brake drums*, fit new linings.
	Tyre pressures unequal	Check and inflate as necessary.
	Brake backplate, caliper or disc loose	Tighten backplate, caliper or disc securing nuts and bolts.
	Brake shoes or pads fitted incorrectly	Remove and fit shoes or pads correct way round.
	Different type of linings fitted at each wheel	Fit the linings specified all round.
	Anchorages for front or rear suspension loose	Tighten front and rear suspension pick-up points including spring locations.
	Brake drums* or discs badly worn, cracked or distorted	Fit new brake drums* or discs.
BRAKES TEND TO BIND, DRAG, OR LOCK-ON		
Incorrect adjustment	*Brake shoes adjusted too tightly	*Slacken off rear brake shoe adjusters two clicks.
	*Handbrake cable over-tightened	*Slacken off handbrake cable adjustment.
	Master cylinder pushrod out of adjustment giving too little brake pedal free movement	Reset.
Wear or dirt in hydraulic system or incorrect fluid	Reservoir vent hole in cap blocked with dirt	Clean and blow through hole.
	Master cylinder by-pass port restricted - brakes seize in 'on' position	Dismantle, clean, and overhaul master cylinder. Bleed brakes.
	Caliper seizes in 'on' position	Dismantle, clean and overhaul caliper. Bleed brakes.
Mechanical wear	*Drum brake shoe pull-off springs broken stretched or loose	*Examine springs and replace, if worn or loose.
Incorrect brake assembly	*Drum brake shoe pull-off springs fitted wrong way round, omitted, or wrong type used	*Examine, and rectify as appropriate.

Chapter 10 Electrical system

Contents

Specifications

Battery

Type	Tudor 6 EX 3 op or equivalent
Grounded	Negative terminal
System voltage	12V
Battery, capacity, standard	60 Ah
Specific gravity of electrolyte:	
Fully charged battery	1.28
When recharging is necessary	1.21
Recommended charging current	5.5A

Generator (1968 only)

Type	Bosch G14 V30A
Nominal volts	12
Maximum output	420W
Rotation	Clockwise
Drive ratio, crankshaft to pulley	1.8 : 1
Regulator	Bosch VA 14V 30A

Alternator

S.E.V. Motorola 14V - 71270202

Output	490 W
Max. amperage	35 A
Max. speed	15000 rpm
Direction of rotation	Optional
Ratio: engine - alternator	1 : 2
Min. length, brushes	5 mm (0.2 in.)
Tightening torque: Attaching screws	0.28 - 0.30 kgm (2.0 - 2.2 lb ft.)
Nut for pulley	4 kpm (29 lb ft.)
Test values:	
Field winding resistance	5.2 ± 0.2 ohm
Voltage drop across isolated diode	0.8 - 0.9 V
Output test	30 A (min. at 3000 rpm and approx. 13 V)

S.E.V. Motorola 14V - 34833 (14 V 55 A)

Output	770 W
Max. amperage	55 A
Max. speed	15,000 rpm
Direction of rotation	Optional
Min. length, brushes	5 mm (0.2 in.)
Tightening torque: Attaching screws	0.28 - 0.30 kgm (2.0 - 2.2 lb ft.)
Nut for pulley	4 kgm (29 lb ft.)

Test values:

Field winding resistance	3.7 ohms
Voltage drop across isolating diode	0.8 - 0.9 V
Output test	48 A (min. at 3000 rpm and approx. 14 V)

Bosch K1 - 14V 35 A 20

Output	490 W
Max. amperage	35 A
Max. speed	12,000 rpm
Direction of rotation	Clockwise
Ratio, engine - alternator	1 : 2
Min. diameter of slip rings	31.5 mm (1.24 in.)
Max. permissible radial throw on, slip rings	0.03 mm (0.0012 in.)
rotor body	0.05 mm (0.0020 in.)
Min. length of brushes	8 mm (0.31 in.)
Brush pressure	0.3 - 0.4 kg (6.6 - 8.8 lb)
Tightening torque for pulley	3.5 - 4.0 kgm (25 - 29 lb ft.)

Test values:

Resistance in, stator	0.26 + 0.03 ohm
rotor	4.0 + 0.4 ohm
Output test	35 A (min. at 6000 rpm and 14 V)

Voltage regulator
S.E.V. Motorola 14V - 33525

Control voltage, cold regulator	13.1 - 14.4 V
after driving 45 minutes	13.85 - 14.25 V

S.E.V. Motorola 14V - 33544

Control voltage, cold regulator	13.1 - 14.4 V
after driving 45 minutes	13.85 - 14.25 V

Bosch AD - 14V

Control voltage at 4000 alternator rpm, cold regulator, read off within 30 seconds (lower two contacts)	14.0 - 15.0 V
Load current, lower two contacts	28 - 30 A
Control range (between two upper and lower contacts) ...	0 - 0.3 V
Load current, upper two contacts	3 - 8 A

Starter motor

Type	Bosch GF 12 V 1 PS
Voltage	12 V
Grounded	Negative terminal
Direction of rotation	Clockwise
Output	Approx. 1 h.p.
Brushes, number	4

Test values:
Mechanical

Armature end float	0.05 - 0.30 mm (0.002 - 0.12 in.)
Brush spring tension	1.15 - 1.3 kg (2.53 - 2.86 lb.)
Distance from pinion to ring gear	1.2 - 4.4 mm (0.047 - 0.173 in.)
Frictional torque of rotor brake	2.5 - 4.0 kgcm (2.17 - 3.81 lb in.)
Pinion idling torque	1.3 - 1.8 kgcm (1.13 - 1.56 lb in.)
Backlash	0.35 - 0.60 mm (0.014 - 0.024 in.)
Min. diameter of commutator	33 mm (1.29 in.)
Min. length of brushes	14 mm (0.55 in.)

Electrical

Unloaded starter motor:	
12.0 volts and 40-50 amp	6900 - 8100 rpm
Loaded starter motor:	
9 volts and 185 - 220 amp	1050 - 1350 rpm
Locked starter motor:	
6 volts and 300 - 350 amp	0 rpm

Control solenoid

Cut-in voltage	Min. 8 V	

Lamp bulbs

	Power	Socket
Headlights	45/40 W	P 45 t
Fog lights 142 GL, 144 GL	55 W	Pk 22 s
Parking lights, front	5 W	S 8
rear	5 W (4 cp)	Ba 15 s
Flashers, front and rear	32 cp	Ba 15 s
Stop lights	25 W (32 cp)	Ba 15 s
Reversing lights	15 W (32 cp)	Ba 15 s
Side marker lamps	5 W	Ba 15 s
Number plate light	5 W	S 8
Interior lighting	10 W	S 8
Glove compartment light	2 W	Ba 9 s
Instrumenting lighting, combined instrument	3 W	W 2.2 d
clock	2 W	Ba 7 s
Lighting, heater controls	1.2 W	W 1.8 d
Warning lamp, charging	1.2 W	W 1.8 d
turn indicators	1.2 W	W 1.8 d
handbrake	1.2 W	W 1.8 d
headlights	1.2 W	W 1.8 d
oil pressure	1.2 W	W 1.8 d
electrically heated rear window 142, 144 ...	1.2 W	W 1.8 d
145 ...	2 W	Ba 7 s
hazard warning signal flasher	1.2 W	W 1.8 d
overdrive	1.2 W	W 1.8 d
choke	1.2 W	W 1.8 d

1 General description

1 The electrical system is of the 12 volt type with negative earth. The battery (capacity 60 amps/r. at the 20 r discharge rate) is charged by a 2-brush generator with voltage regulator and cut-out on early models, but the vast majority employ an alternator with integral silicon diode rectifiers and vibrating contact regulator.

2 Although negative earth is undoubtedly the modern trend, many electrical accessories are made on the assumption that the earth will be positive; these need some small conversion procedure to make them suitable for negative earth. Where such devices contain transistors or silicon diodes they will probably be damaged if connected to an earth of the wrong polarity. Such items are, for example: radios, tape recorder players, electronic tachometers, automatic dipping, light sensitive parking lamps and anti-dazzle mirrors.

2 Battery - removal, maintenance, inspection and replacement

1 The battery is fitted on a shelf in the engine compartment (to the left of the radiator) and is held in position by a bar and clamp. When removing it, first disconnect the negative (earth) lead and then the positive lead. This way you avoid any possibility of damage through shorted circuits. The leads are fastened to the battery either by clamps (the normal Volvo practice) or by caps which are screwed to tapped holes in the battery terminals; this type of fitting may be found as a replacement for the original clamps. Removal of the battery is simply a matter of undoing the nuts holding the retaining bar, removing this and lifting the battery out.

2 Every three months the battery should be removed and cleaned - brush it down and give it a rinse with clean luke warm water. At the same time clean the battery shelf and the terminals, wire brushing these if necessary to remove corrosion.

3 Weekly maintenance consists of checking the electrolyte level in the cells to ensure that the separators are covered by ¼" (6 mm) of electrolyte. If the level has fallen, top up with distilled water only. Do not overfill. If you find it difficult to judge the correct level of electrolyte, you can buy battery fillers which automatically get it right for you, employing a simple valve or cut away in the spout. If the battery is overfilled or any electrolyte spilled, wipe away the electrolyte immediately as it attacks and corrodes any metal it comes into contact with very quickly.

4 Inspect the retaining bar, securing nuts, tray and battery leads for corrosion (white fluffy deposits on the metal which are brittle to touch). If any corrosion is found, clean off the deposit with ammonia and paint over the clean metal with an anti-rust/anti-acid paint.

5 Keep an eye on the battery case for cracks. It is possible to clean and plug these with proprietary compounds made for this purpose. If an appreciable amount of electrolyte has leaked away through a crack or if electrolyte has been spilt out of the battery it should be replaced with fresh electrolyte; otherwise all topping up should be done with distilled water.

6 If topping up becomes excessive and there is no leakage from the case, the battery is being overcharged and the voltage regulator will have to be checked and reset.

7 As part of the three-monthly check, measure the specific gravity of the electrolyte with a hydrometer. A table of specific gravity is given later in this section. There should be very little variation between different cells. If a variation greater than 0.025 is present, the cause must either be spillage or leakage - which has been topped up with distilled water, or an internal short circuit in the cell - an indication that the battery will soon need renewal.

8 To check a suspect cell, discharge the battery completely (for example, by leaving the headlights on). Recheck the specific gravities and if the dubious cell is still lower than the others remove some of the electrolyte if necessary and top it up with a mixture of one part sulphuric acid to 2.5 parts of water, repeating this process until the specific gravity comes up to standard. If it is too high to start with, of course, you will top it up with distilled water after removing the electrolyte, but in practice this never seems to happen.

9 Now recharge the battery at about 5 amps until the specific gravity of the electrolyte in the good cells has remained constant for about four hours. It will take you about 18 hours in all. It does not matter if you charge at a lesser rate, but it will take proportionately longer. You can save time by charging at up to 10 amps but do not be tempted to use a rapid charger which claims to restore the power of the battery in one or two hours. They can be dangerous devices to use with batteries that are past their best.

10 In all probability the suspect cell will now have the same

specific gravity as the others. Replace the battery in the car and keep a particular eye on this cell. If in a week or two the specific gravity has again dropped below the level of the others, you can resign yourself to the thought that very soon you will have to renew the battery.

11 When mixing sulphuric acid and water **never add water to sulphuric acid** - always pour the acid slowly on to the water in a glass container. **If water is added to sulphuric acid it will explode.**

12 Replacement is a direct reversal of the removal procedure. Connect the positive lead before the negative lead and smear the terminals with petroleum jelly such as "Vaseline" to prevent corrosion. Never use an ordinary grease as applied to other parts of the car.

13 In winter time when a heavy demand is placed on the battery it is a good idea to give the battery an occasional charge at about 5 amps. Ideally you should charge at this rate until the specific gravity has remained constant for four hours. We are usually content to observe the vigorous bubbling from the electrolyte which indicates that the battery is fully charged and let this go on for three or four hours.

14 A final hint - in very cold weather, top your battery up just before you start a run. Distilled water is lighter than electrolyte and may float on top of it instead of mixing with it if the car is cold and stationary. In this case it can easily freeze and may ruin your battery by cracking the case.

SPECIFIC GRAVITY TABLE

Specific gravity - fully discharged

1.098 at 100°F or 38°C electrolyte temperature
1.102 at 90°F or 32°C electrolyte temperature
1.106 at 80°F or 27°C electrolyte temperature
1.110 at 70°F or 21°C electrolyte temperature
1.114 at 60°F or 16°C electrolyte temperature
1.118 at 50°F or 10°C electrolyte temperature
1.122 at 40°F or 4°C electrolyte temperature
1.126 at 30°F or -1.5°C electrolyte temperature

Specific gravity - battery fully charged

1.268 at 100°F or 38°C electrolyte temperature
1.272 at 90°F or 32°C electrolyte temperature
1.276 at 80°F or 27°C electrolyte temperature
1.280 at 70°F or 21°C electrolyte temperature
1.284 at 60°F or 16°C electrolyte temperature
1.288 at 50°F or 10°C electrolyte temperature
1.292 at 40°F or 4°C electrolyte temperature
1.296 at 30°F or -1.5°C electrolyte temperature

3 Generator - general description

1 Fig.10.1 shows a sectional diagram of the direct current generator fitted to early models. The generator fitted to the B18 engine and having "028" as the last three figures of its type number has a ball race in the end bearing for the armature, whereas that fitted to the B18A has a plain bearing with lubricating felt and cup. Its type number ends in "036".

4 Generator - removal, servicing and replacement

1 Before starting work on the generator, disconnect the battery positive lead. Then remove the connections to the generator, marking them so that you can be sure you will put them back in the same positions.

2 Disconnect the tensioning stay, slacken off the bolts holding the generator and remove the fan belt.

3 Take out the securing bolts and lift the generator away.

4 Before dismantling the generator, clean the outside thoroughly with paraffin, drying off with a clean rag.

5 Take off the cover band which shelters the commutator, disconnect the brush leads, lift up the springs and take out the brushes. Take out the screw linking the brush holder to the positive terminal. Take out the screws whose heads you see at the commutator end of the generator - these screws go right through the body and hold the whole thing together.

6 With these screws out of the way, you can ease the end cap clear of the body of the generator and push out the end plate at the other end with the armature still in position.

7 Grip the armature in the protected jaws of a vice, remove the pulley nut and lock washer and draw the pulley from the shaft with a suitable puller. Watch for the key holding the pulley - if you don't it may fly out and become lost.

8 Tap gently on the end of the armature shaft and drive it backwards through the end plate. The ball race will stay on the shaft as will the race on the other end of the shaft (where one is fitted).

9 Brush away any carbon dust or dirt from the armature and the generator body, and wash the ball races free of oil and grease, giving them a final clean with White Spirit. You can do this without taking them off the armature shaft. This only becomes necessary if you find signs of wear, scoring, blueing or excessive play in the race.

10 The commutator itself should be free from ridging or signs of burning (such as evidence of melted solder where the wires from the armature join the copper strips). The surface should be dark metallic brown in colour and free from ridging. Light scores can be removed with fine sand paper or blue-back paper. It will of course look a lot shinier when you have done this, but there is no need to polish it up in this way unless you are removing scoring.

11 If heavily ridged, the commutator will need skimming down. The insulation between the strips will then have to be cut back. Unless you are experienced in this sort of work you should leave it to specialists.

12 Signs of burning on the commutator strips normally mean that the armature winding is defective. Have it checked and if necessary rewound by a specialist.

13 Worn brushes must be replaced by new ones of the same type. This is important because the electrical resistance of the brushes has an effect on the voltage output of the generator.

14 Do not attempt to remove the pole pieces. This is only necessary if the field windings are burnt out or open circuited, and in this case it is better to replace the generator or have it repaired by a specialist.

15 Reassembly and installation in the car is a straightforward reversal of the removal/dismantling procedure. Adjusting the fan belt tension is dealt with in Chapter 1, Section 40 (photograph 40.3).

16 Where a new generator is being installed, and sometimes after an old one has been overhauled it is necessary to polarise the field. To do this, run the engine with the D and F connections removed from the generator, and with a short length of wire connected to the battery positive terminal flick the generator F terminal a few times to pass a current of the correct polarity through it. After this treatment the generator will produce correctly polarised voltage ie the output terminal will show a positive voltage. It is a good idea to do this as a matter of course when refitting a generator which has been dismantled.

5 Voltage regulator for generator - general description

The regulator used with this generator is a two element sealed unit, one element being the cut-out and the other a voltage regulator. The voltage regulator works in the usual manner by reducing the field current when the voltage across its coil increases, but in addition to this it carries a subsidiary winding through which current is arranged to flow when the generator output current exceeds a certain figure. This is achieved by a "zener diode" which permits the flow of current when the voltage across it exceeds a certain figure, this voltage being proportional to the generator output current. Thus, the voltage

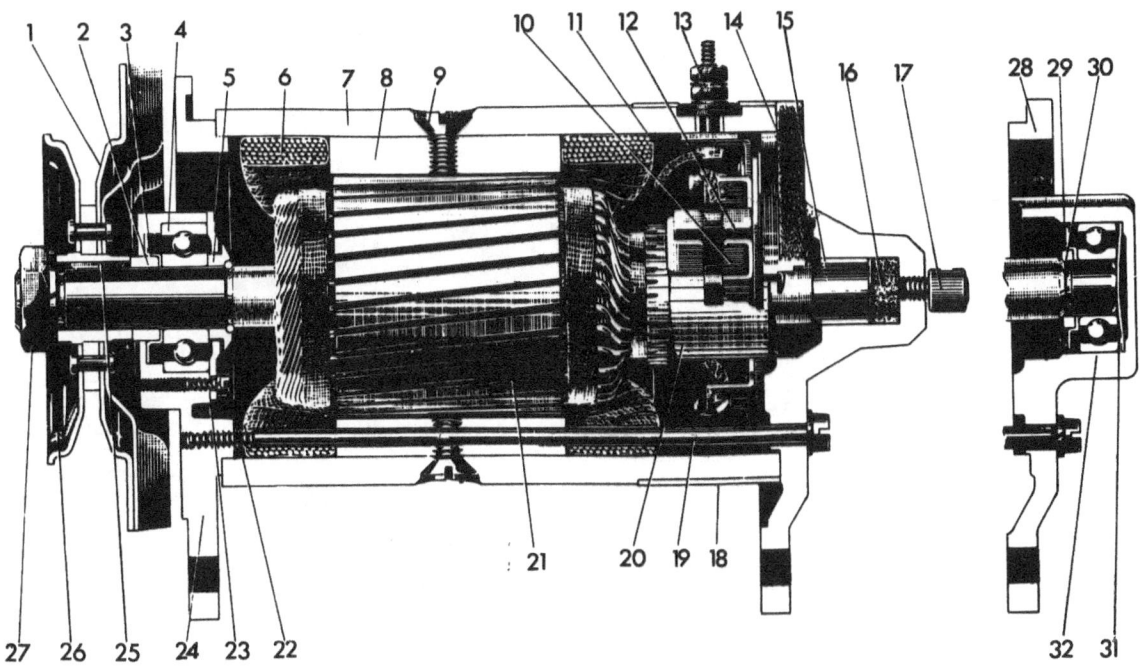

Fig.10.1. Direct current generator - sectional view

1	Belt pulley	9 Pole screw	17 Lubricating cup (type 036)	25 Key
2	Spacing ring	10 Brush holder	18 Protecting band	26 Spring washer
3	Oil seal washer	11 Brush spring	19 Screw	27 Nut
4	Ball bearing	12 Brush	20 Commutator	28 End shield (type 028)
5	Spacing ring	13 Terminal screw	21 Rotor	29 Oil spacer washer (type 028)
6	Field winding	14 End shield (type 036)	22 Screw	30 Spacing ring (type 028)
7	Stator	15 Bush (type 036)	23 Sealing washer	31 Spring ring (type 028)
8	Pole shoe	16 Lubricating felt (type 036)	24 End shield	32 Ball bearing (type 028)

regulator operates to limit the maximum current output as well as the maximum voltage of the generator.

The other element in the regulator unit is the normal cut-out which isolates the generator from the battery until the generator output voltage exceeds the battery voltage. The ignition warning light is connected across the contacts of the cut-out in the conventional manner.

Adjustment of the regulator is a skilled operation, and the best way to deal with a troublesome regulator is to exchange it for a new one.

6   Alternator - general description

1   In an ordinary generator the armature rotates between what are, in effect, the poles of a magnet or may be several sets of these poles. The magnetism is maintained by the field coils. As the position of the armature relative to the magnetic poles varies, the magentic field passing through the armature changes and it is this change of magnetism which produces current in the armature coils. It is only when the magnetic field is changing that current is produced, (when the armature is not rotating no current appears) and this current, like the changing field that produces it, is changing all the time. In fact, if it were not for the commutator which acts as a reversing switch operated in time with the changing current, the output of the ordinary generator would be alternating current and not direct current.

2   The alternator differs from the ordinary DC generator in that the armature is stationary and the field coils with their magnetic pole pieces rotate. The output from the armature is alternating current because there is now no rotating commutator to keep

changing it over, but the current passes through a system of diodes so arranged that whichever way the current is flowing when it leaves the armature it is always flowing in the same direction at the output terminals. It is easy to get an idea of how these diodes operate by looking at the circuit diagrams (Figs.10.2 and 10.3) and remembering that the electric current only passes through the diodes in the direction indicated by the arrows, so that it is only possible for current to enter and leave the output terminals in the direction shown, whatever is happening in the alternator coils.

3   There is nothing particularly novel about this idea, but it has only become practicable in the last few years because of a technological break through in rectifier design - the development of materials known as semi-conductors. It brings with it some very considerable design advantages. The first of these is that the brushes now only pass the field current - a matter of two or three amps - instead of the total output current of 30-50 amps, and this current needs no commutation but is simply passed into the field coil via slip rings. Because of this the size of the brushes can be greatly reduced and sparking becomes negligible.

4   In a normal generator, excessive current produces overheating of the brushes and commutator leading to complete breakdown of the armature. Because of this the current output has to be limited by an external regulator. With the alternator, provided that the armature is wound with thick enough wire, and in practice this is quite easy, the output current is limited to a safe value by reason of the magnetic effect it produces which cancels out the magnetism produced by the field coil. Because of this, only voltage regulation is needed with an alternator; the current can be allowed to look after itself.

5   Three different alternators are found in the 140 series. Two

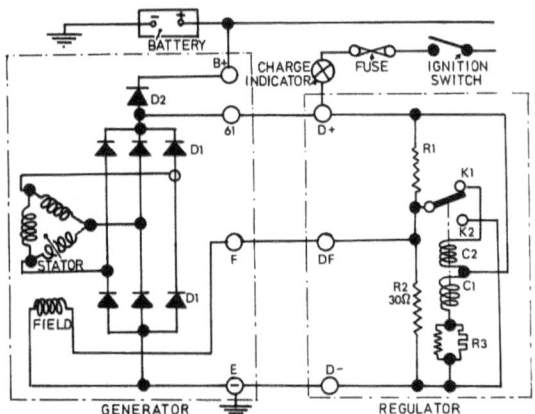

Fig.10.2. Motorola alternator and regulator circuit diagram

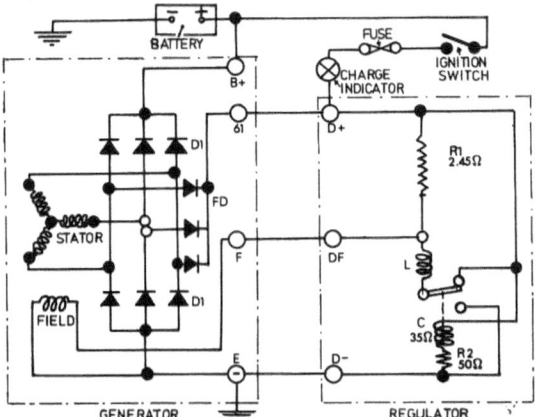

Fig.10.3. Bosch alternator and regulator circuit diagram

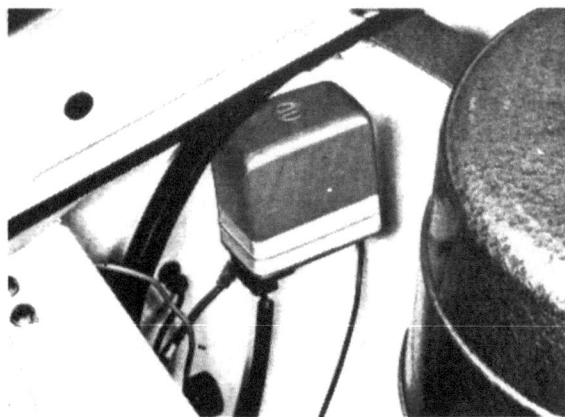

Fig.10.4. Bosch voltage regulator

of these, the Motorola 71270202 and the Motorola 34833 are almost identical, the second providing a larger current output and being fitted with two isolation diodes connected in parallel instead of one. The third type, made by Bosch, has slightly different electrical and mechanical arrangements but works on exactly the same principle.

6 The photograph (8.1) showing a Motorola generator being removed gives a good idea of its location, size and weight.

7 The voltage regulator for the alternator is located on the right-hand wheel housing close to the headlamp. Fig. 10.4 shows the Bosch regulator; the Motorola regulator looks very similar.

8.1 Removing the alternator

7 Alternator equipment - special precautions

1 The diodes used in alternator equipment are very sensitive to voltages and currents greater than they are designed to withstand, and in particular they are easily damaged by excessive reverse voltages. To avoid any risk of diode failure or shortened life, take the precautions outlined in the next few paragraphs.

2 When replacing or reconnecting the battery, make sure that it is connected with correct polarity. ie negative earth.

3 Never run the alternator unless the regulator is connected. If the battery is disconnected, be sure that there is some external load - headlamps, for example - connected across the output terminal.

4 No attempt should be made to polarise the alternator. This is not necessary.

5 When charging the battery while installed in the car, the negative battery lead should be disconnected.

6 A rapid charger should not be used as an aid in starting.

7 When using an extra battery as a starting aid, always connect it in parallel.

8 When carrying out electric welding on the vehicle, disconnect the negative battery lead as well as all the alternator leads. The welder should always be connected as near as possible to where the welding is carried out.

8 Alternators - removal and dismantling

1 Disconnect the battery negative, slacken the belt tensioner, remove the fan belt, disconnect the leads to the alternator, then undo the fixing bolts and remove the alternator from the engine (photo).

2 Give the alternator a good clean before starting to take it apart, using paraffin or a detergent such as "Gunk".

3 Figs. 10.5a and 10.5b give exploded views of Motorola and Bosch alternators respectively. The Motorola alternator shown is "Type 34833" - the differences between this and "71270202" are very slight.

4 Remove the screws attaching the brush holder and take off the holder.

5 Using the fan belt as protection, hold the live pulley in a vice with soft jaws as shown in Fig.10.6. Undo the fixing nut, lift off the pulley, key (watch this - its powers of concealment would do credit to a chameleon) spacing washer or washers (note the order of assembly) and fan.

6 Remove the two bolts holding together the alternator and

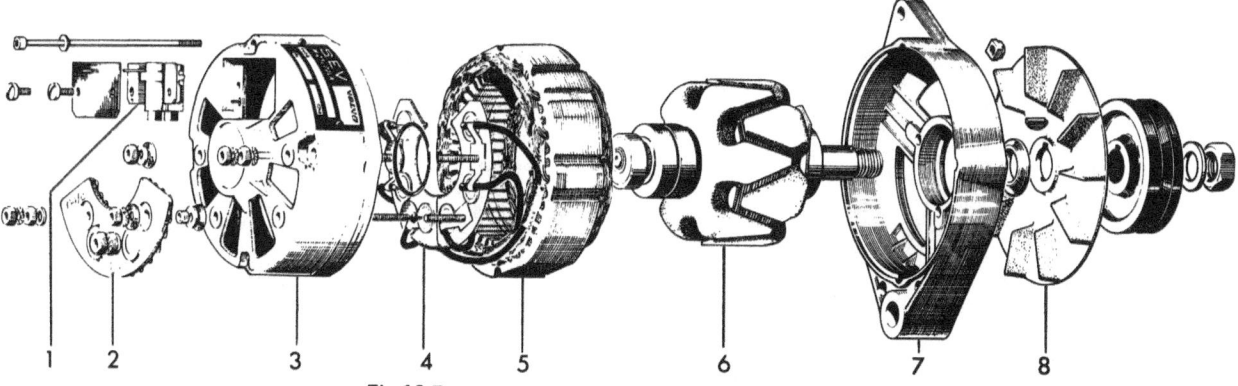

Fig.10.5a. Motorola alternator - exploded view

1 Brush holder   3 Slip ring end shield   5 Stator   7 Drive end shield
2 Isolation diodes with holder   4 Rectifier (silicon diodes) 6 Rotor   8 Fan

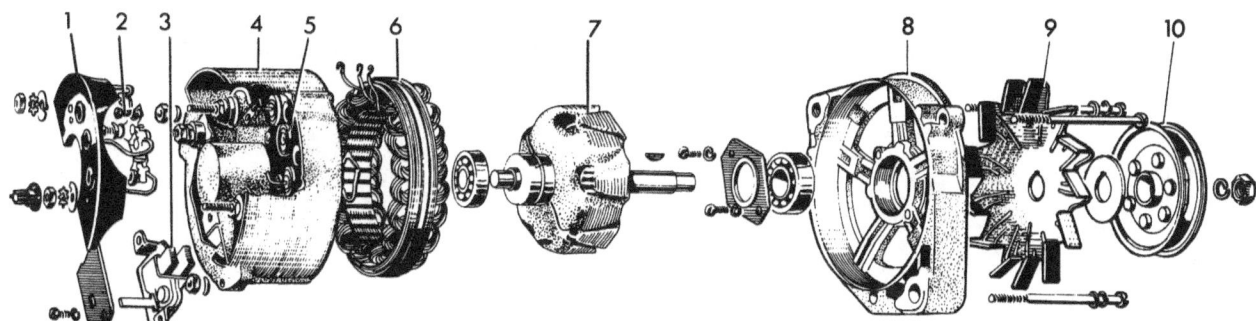

Fig.10.5b. Bosch alternator - exploded view

1 Rectifier (plus diode   3 Brush holder   6 Stator   9 Fan
   plate)   4 Slip ring end shield   7 Rotor   10 Pulley
2 Magnetizing rectifier   5 Rectifier (negative diodes) 8 Drive end shield

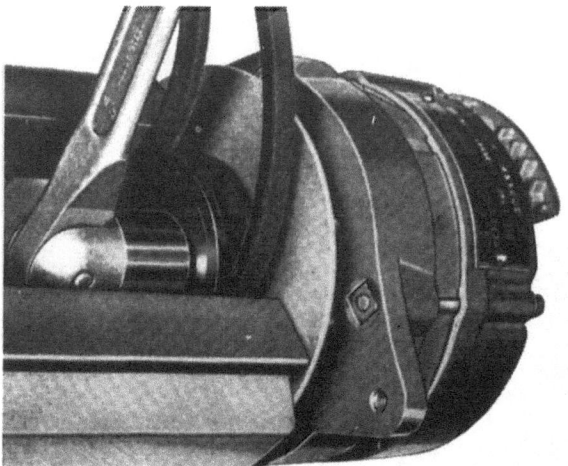

Fig.10.6. Undoing the pulley nut

Fig.10.7. Prising the end shield off the alternator (Bosch)

take off the drive end shield holding the alternator in a vice by the drive shaft as shown in Fig.10.7. Be careful when using screwdrivers to part the alternator - do not insert them further than 1/16" (2 mm) or you may damage the stator winding.

7 Remove the retaining plate which holds the rotor bearing in the drive end shield and knock out the bearing by gently tapping on the rotor shaft with a hide mallet or a piece of wood

(Fig.10.8).

8 In the Motorola alternator detach the isolation diode holder by removing the nuts and washers on terminal "61" and the corresponding ones on the other side of the isolation diode. This being done, it is a simple matter to detach the rectifier assembly from the slip ring end shield and withdraw the stator winding with the rectifier assembly still connected to it as shown in

Fig.10.8. Knocking out the rotor shaft

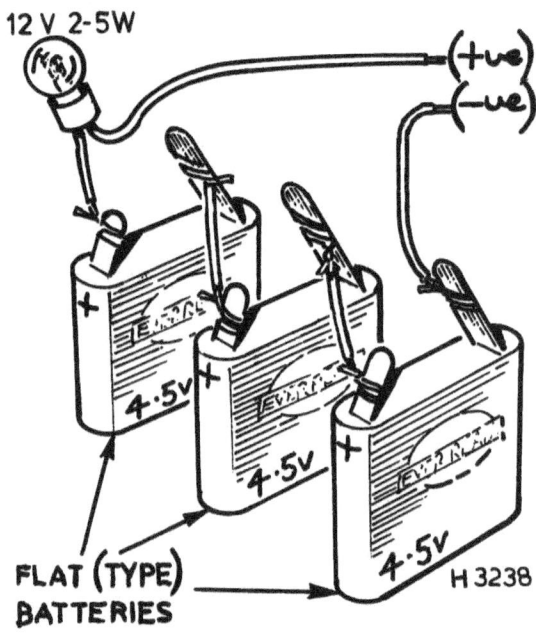

12 V 2-5W

(+ve)
(-ve)

FLAT (TYPE) BATTERIES

4·5v

4·5v

4·5v

H 3238

Fig.10.11. Dry batteries and bulb assembled for alternator testing

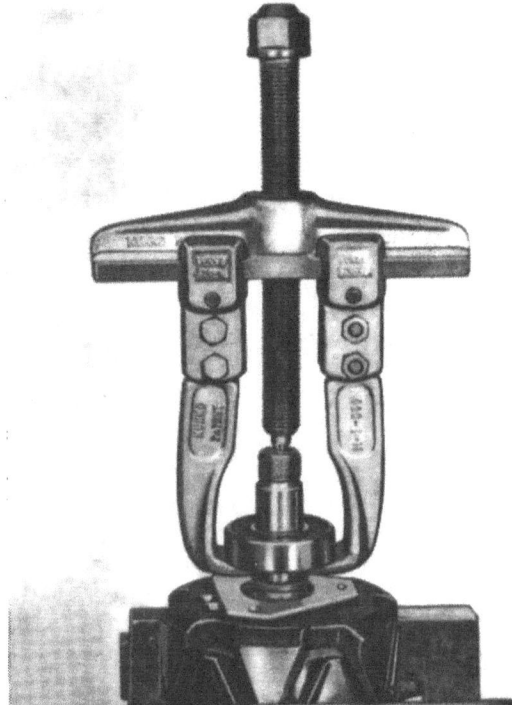

Fig.10.9. Drawing bearing off rotor shaft (Motorola)

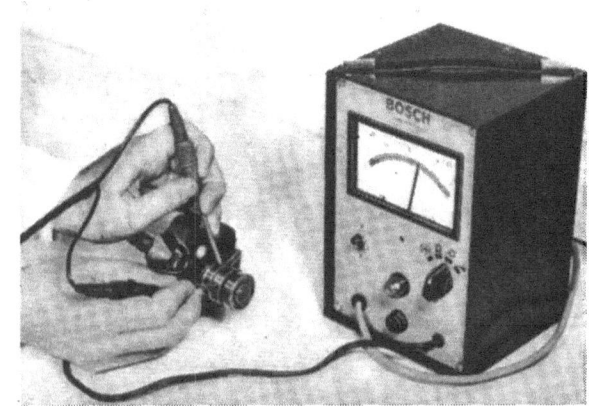

Fig.10.12. Checking rotor resistance

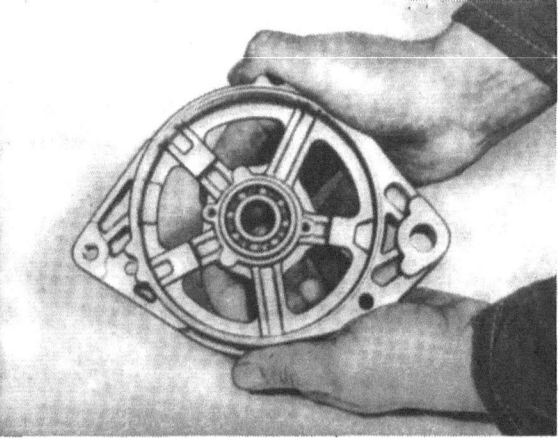

Fig.10.10. Removing bearing from end shield (Bosch)

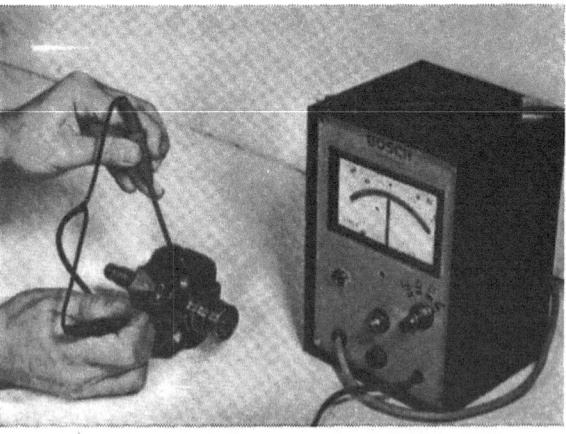

Fig.10.13. Rotor insulation can be checked with the test lamp arrangement of Fig.10.11 in place of the ohmmeter shown

Fig. 10.5a. The end shield may then be detached.

9   For the Bosch alternator, unsolder the stator winding leads from the terminals on the slip ring end shield, marking the leads and terminals so that you know which goes to which. The stator winding can then be withdrawn from the shield. Remove the positive diode assembly, the magnetizing rectifier assembly and the negative diode assembly from the slip ring end shield, which can then be separated from the stator.

9   Alternator bearings

1   Generally speaking the bearings for the rotor will stay on the rotor shaft when the alternator is dismantled, though sometimes they may remain in the end shields. Where these bearings are of the open type, they should be removed from the end shield or shaft (Figs.10.9 and 10.10), thoroughly cleaned in White Spirit and examined carefully for signs of scoring, scuffing, wear or blueing. If such signs are present or there is appreciable play in the bearing it should be replaced. Otherwise, pack the bearing with a suitable grease such as Castrol LM for further use.
2   If the bearings are of the sealed type, check them for play and smoothness of operation and replace them if you are in any doubt about their condition.

10 Brushes and slip rings

1   Using a 12 v 2-5 w bulb connected to a suitable source (see Fig.10.11 - three 4½ volt flat flash lamp batteries are very handy) check that the brushes are isolated from each other (ie the lamp must not light when connected between the brushes). Check that the connection between the brushes and their respective terminals on the holder are good - ie the test lamp should light when connected between a brush and its terminal.
2   The minimum length of the brush protruding from the holder should be 0.2" (5 mm) for Motorola alternators and 0.31" (8 mm) for Bosch.
3   The surface of the slip rings should be smooth. You may give them a polish with very fine sand paper (not emery paper), being careful to remove all traces of the sand paper when you have finished. If the slip rings are burnt or damaged in any other way, there is no reason why they should not be skimmed in a lathe, but a glance at the specifications for run-out given for the Bosch alternator will show that this is a specialist operation. You should resist the temptation to hold the rotor in an electric drill and take a file to the slip rings.

11 Checking the rotor

1   Check the slip rings as described in the previous Section.
2   Examine the winding for breakage or damaged insulation.
3   Check the isolation between the winding and the frame by connecting a test lamp and battery (see Fig. 10.11) between the frame and one of the slip rings. The lamp should not light.
4   Measure the resistance between the slip rings with an ohmmeter or multi-meter (see Fig. 10.12). It should be 5.2 ± 0.2 ohms for "Motorola 71270202", 3.7 ohms $\pm$ 10% for "Motorola 34833" and 4.0 ohms $\pm$ 10% for "Bosch".

12 Alternator - checking stator

1   Examine the winding carefully for signs of burning. If this is found, it means that there is a short circuit in the rotor winding and the rotor should be replaced or rewound.
2   Connect a test lamp (see Fig.10.11) between one of the winding terminations and the frame (see Fig.10.13) the lamp should not light. If there is the smallest glow, the stator should be replaced.
3   Using an ohmmeter or multi-meter, measure the resistance between each pair of winding terminations (in the case of the Bosch alternator, these are the leads that are connected to the diodes - not the star point which has three wires going to it). The presence of the diodes on the Motorola rotor windings will not affect these measurements unless the diodes are defective. The three different measurements should give the same value of resistance - certainly within 2%. For the Bosch alternator the resistance value should lie within 0.26 ± 0.03 ohms.

13 Alternator - checking diodes

1   The diode is simply a device which will allow electric current to pass through it one way and not the other way. In diagrams such as Figs.10.2 and 10.3 the direction in which current is able to flow through the diode is indicated by the black arrowhead. Electric current flows from positive to negative, so if you connect a positive voltage (for example, the positive lead of your battery/test bulb combination) to the broad end of the arrow and the negative lead to the other end, current will flow and the lamp will light. If you reverse the connections, the lamp will not light. Normally, you do not have to worry about which way round you connect your lamp, because if the lamp lights when connected one way round and does not light when connected the other way round, the diode must be all right. A faulty diode either lights the lamp both ways or not at all. Note that the positive voltage on a rectifier diode appears at the pointed end of the arrow. The diodes are made up to produce positive voltage at the casing or at the centre lead as required; both types are used in the alternator.
2   Unless specialised apparatus is available, it is necessary to unsolder the leads from the Motorola alternator to the diodes mounted on it in order to check them. To someone not experienced in working with electronic equipment, this soldering is a tricky business and best left to a specialist. There is no reason why the local radio shop should not do this for you. Check the diodes as just described with the test lamp and voltage source described in Fig. 10.11. In no circumstances should the test voltage exceed 14 v. If any defective diodes are found, re-place the relevant assembly or have a diode fitted to the existing plate by a specialist. In the Bosch alternator, the diode plate is disconnected from the stator winding when the alternator is dismantled and there is no need to unsolder the diodes themselves. The battery and lamp can be connected across each diode in turn.

14 Alternator - reassembly and installation

1   Reassembly in the main is a reversal of the dismantling process and presents no special problems. In the Bosch alter-nator, fit the bearing and retaining plate to the drive end bearing shield before assembling this to the rotor. Coat the slip ring end shield bearing seat with a light layer of "Molycote" paste or similar and assemble the alternator. Do not forget the spring ring, on the slip ring end shield bearing seat. Fixing screws and nuts should be tightened to a torque of 3.6-4.3 lb ft (0.50-0.60 kg m).
2   For the Motorola alternator, the fixing screws should be tightened to a torque of 2.0-2.2 lb ft (0.28-0.30 kg m).
3   Be sure that the isolation diode holder on the Motorola alternator is fitted with the full complement of plastic tube and isolation washers on its fixing screws.
4   Fit the spacer washer, key, fan, pulley, washer and finally the pulley nut in the order in which you took them off. Tightening torque for the pulley nut is 4 kg m for both Motorola and Bosch alternators.
5   When refitting the alternator in the car, disconnect the positive lead to the battery before you start and do not reconnect it again until you are sure that all is correct. Tightening the fan belt is dealt with in Chapter 1, Section 40, paragraph 3 and its accompanying photograph.

15 Alternator regulator checks

1 The Motorola regulator does not depend on spring tension, contact clearances etc for its correct operation, being controlled by a voltage sensitive resistor element (R3, Fig.10.2). No means of adjustment is available and if it does not meet the checking procedure which follows it should be replaced.

2 To check the Motorola regulator, start up the engine and run the alternator at about 5000 rpm (engine speed 2500 rpm) for 15 seconds. Switch everything off except the ignition and read the voltage between B+ and D- on the alternator. This should lie within the shaded area of Fig.10.14. Note that the temperature referred to is the air temperature, not the temperature of the regulator itself. The reading should change very little when the alternator is loaded with, for example, full beam headlights. Now drive the vehicle for 45 minutes and repeat the procedure. The readings should now be within the shaded area of Fig.10.15. If they are not, you will either have to live with it or replace the regulator.

3 To check the Bosch regulator, you will need to load the alternator with 28-30 amps ie full beam headlights plus as much again - another pair of bulbs, for example. The check must be carried out quickly, before the regulator has a chance to get really warm. Run the alternator to a speed of 4000 rpm (engine speed 2000 rpm) rapidly lower it to about 1000 rpm (ie idling speed), raise the speed again to 4000 rpm and read the voltage between B+ and D- on the alternator. This should be 14-15 v. Reduce the load on the alternator to 3-8 amps (ie one dipped headlight equivalent) and read the voltage again. It should now be between 0 and 0.3 v less than the first reading. If the voltage is outside specification - particularly if it is too high - the regulator should be adjusted by a specialist or replaced.

16 Starter motor - general description

1 The starter motor is of the pre-engaged type, in which the pinion is mechanically engaged with the flywheel ring gear before the motor is switched on, a roller clutch drive in the pinion assembly allowing the pinion to free-wheel when the engine starts. The mechanical engagement is driven by a solenoid which operates the starter motor switch after it has pushed the pinion into position. The operation is clear from Figs.10.16a and 10.16b.

2 If properly lubricated before assembly, the self-lubricating bearings of the starter motor will last as long as the engine.

17 Starter motor - servicing

1 All the servicing generally needed is a clean up of the exterior and a brief look at the brushes, solenoid contacts and pinion teeth at 12000 mile (20000 km) intervals. The solenoid contacts can easily be got at by taking off the cap carrying their terminals which is fastened to the front end of the solenoid cover by two screws.

2 The starter pinion can, of course, be inspected without taking the motor apart, but replacement entails a fair amount of dismantling, as does replacement of the brushes. We advise that should your checks reveal the necessity for this work, you have the motor repaired by a specialist or - simpler and quicker - get an exchange replacement.

18 Starter motor - testing on engine

1 If the starter motor fails to operate, first check the condition of the battery by turning on the headlamps. If they shine brightly for several seconds and then gradually dim, the battery needs charging.

2 If the headlights remain bright and it is obvious that the battery is in good condition, check the connections between the

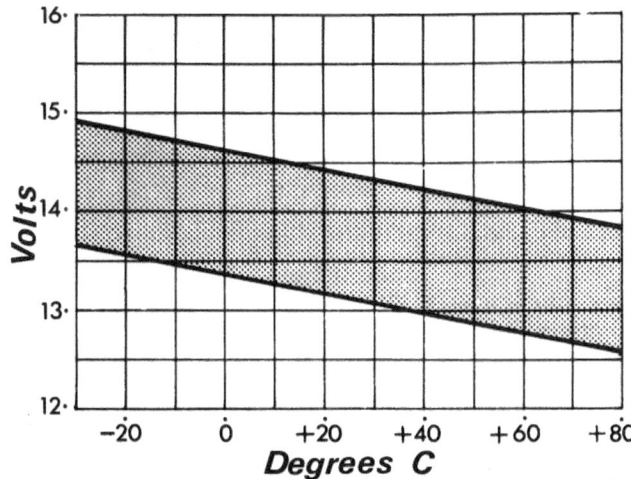

Fig.10.14. Voltage - temperature diagram, cold regulator (Motorola)

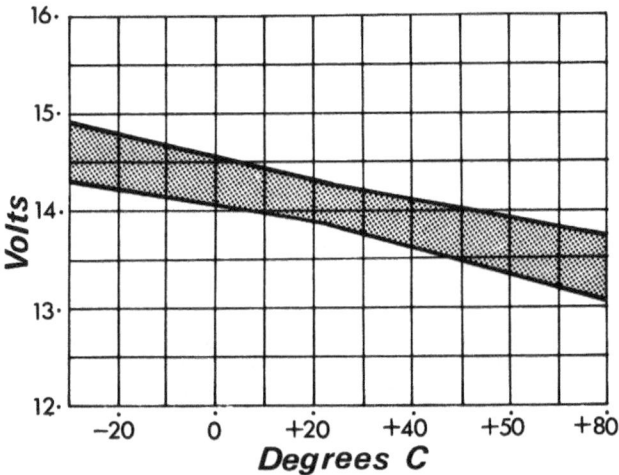

Fig.10.15. Voltage - temperature diagram, worm regulator (Motorola)

battery and the starter - this includes the earth lead from the battery terminal to the bodyframe.

3 If the wiring is in order, check that the starter pinion has not jammed in mesh with the flywheel. If this has happened - not a very likely event with this type of starter - the only method of disengagement is to engage a low gear and rock the car to and fro. There is no extension of the armature shaft available for turning with a spanner in the time-honoured fashion. If rocking does not do the trick, you will have to take the starter off the car. This is not a bad thing because jamming is a sign that something is wrong - worn teeth on the pinion or ring, for example, or defective mechanism in the starter - and should not be allowed to continue unchecked.

19 Exterior lights - general description

1 The lighting consists of two full - and dipped beam headlights, parking lamps, rear lamps, number plate light, side marker lights (USA only) and fog lights (140 GL, all markets except USA).

2 Switching is conventional, except that headlight dipping is operated by a relay which is energised via a switch by the direction indicator lever on the steering wheel. This relay is shown in Fig.10.37.

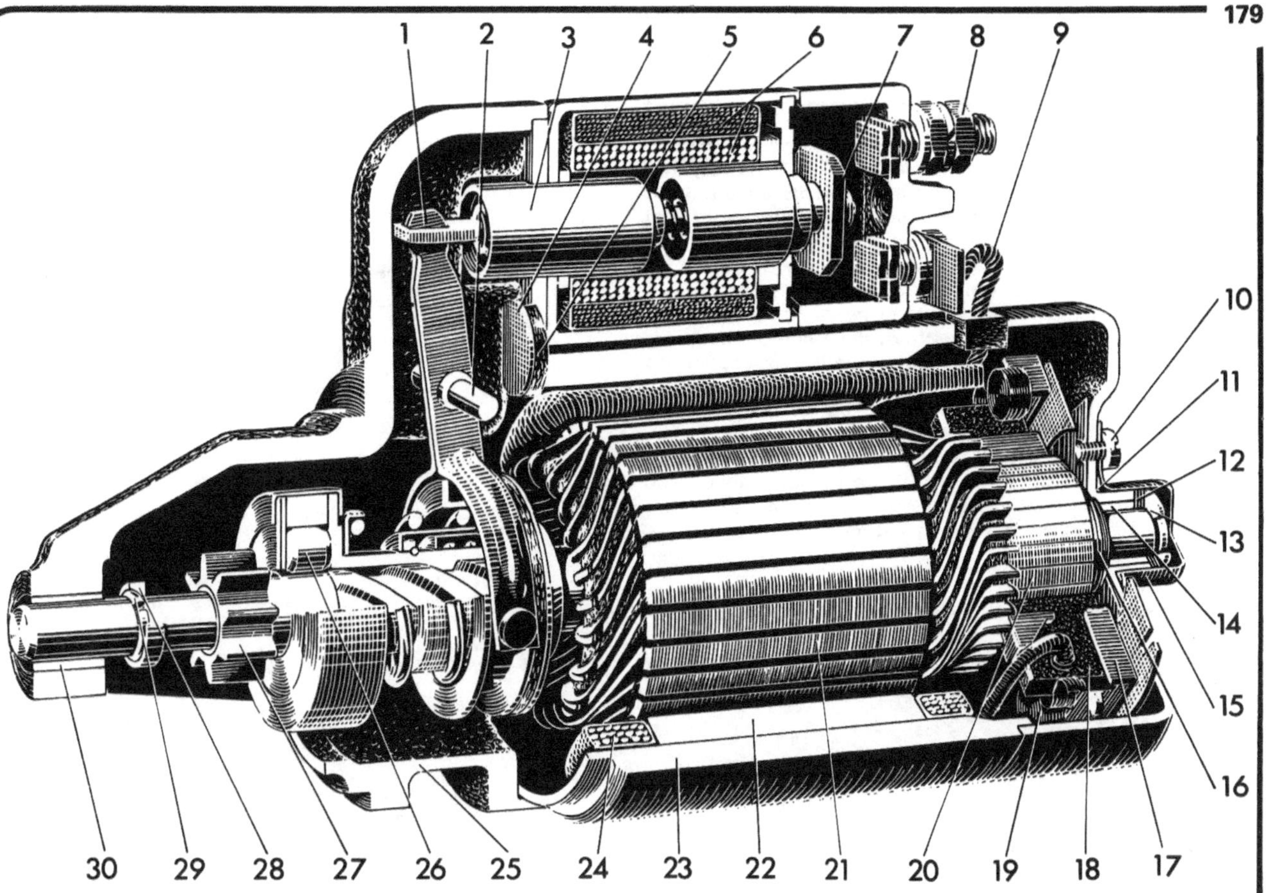

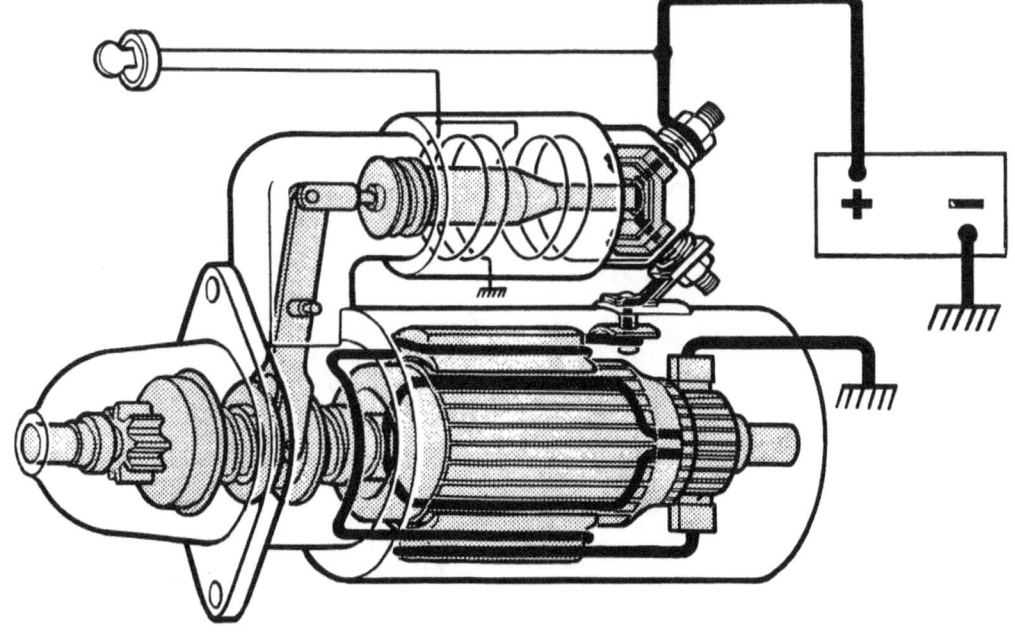

Fig.10.16a. Starter motor - exploded view

1	Shift lever	9	Connection lead to field	17	Brush holder	25	Drive end frame
2	Pivot pin (bearing screw)	10	Screw	18	Brush	26	One-way clutch
3	Plunger	11	Rubber gasket	19	Brush spring	27	Pinion
4	Steel washer	12	Shims	20	Commutator	28	Stop ring
5	Rubber washer	13	Snap ring	21	Armature	29	Snap ring
6	Winding	14	Bush	22	Pole shoe	30	Bush
7	Contact plate	15	Commutator end frame	23	Stator		
8	Terminal for battery lead	16	Adjusting washers	24	Field winding		

Fig.10.16b. Starter motor - general arrangement

20 Headlights

1   The exploded view of the headlamp in Fig.10.17 together with our photographs show clearly how to replace the bulb or the reflector insert and how to adjust the beam height and direction. They should be set so that the high beam is slightly below parallel with a level road surface. It is perfectly easy to set them up yourself if you can find a wall on a piece of level ground on which you can shine the car headlights at a distance of 10 or 20 feet (3-7 m). If the height of the beams on the wall is exactly the same as the height of the car headlamps, your beams are parallel with the ground. There is nothing particularly magical about the equipment that garages use for this work; it is handy to use in a workshop and saves them a lot of time.

2   Keep an eye on your headlight bulbs for discolouration (caused by evaporation from the filament). After about 200 hours operation the light loss is considerable - it is not a bad idea to change your headlight bulbs every autumn.

21 Fog lights

Fig.10.18 shows a view of the fog light which shows how to get at the bulb for replacement. The outer ring is a snap fit in the

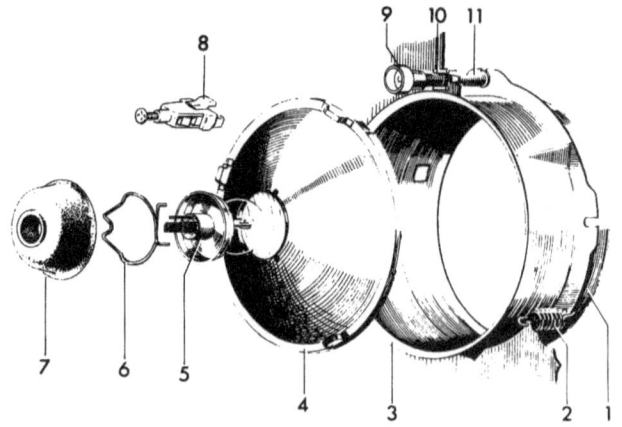

Fig.10.17. Headlight - exploded view

1	Ring	7	Rubber cover
2	Spring	8	Plastic holder
3	Retainer	9	Adjusting knob
4	Insert	10	Nut
5	Bulb	11	Screw
6	Bulb holder spring		

20.1a Rear view of the headlamp

20.1b The cover and connectors pull off, revealing a bulb holder clipped in place ...

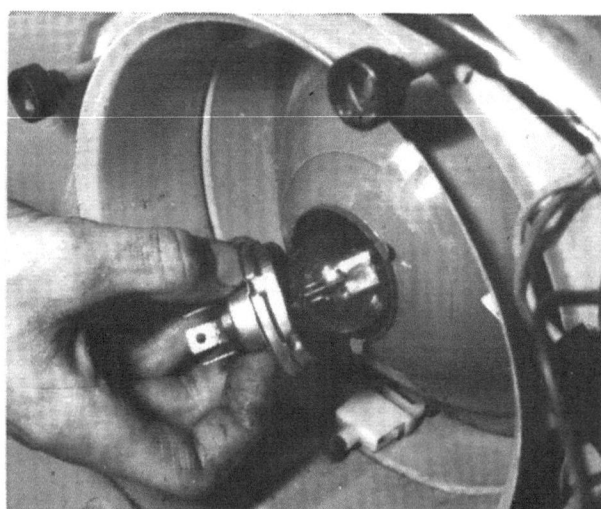

20.1c ... which is easily removed

20.1d This adjusting screw lowers and raises the beam; the other one (lower left) points it in the right direction

casing and is released by inserting a screwdriver at the top and turning. The fog lights may be checked as described for headlights.

22 Rear lights

1 To change the bulbs, remove the lens assembly by undoing the cross-head screws holding it to the lamp (photos).
2 The rear light can be removed from the body as a complete unit by unscrewing two screws whose heads are accessible inside the luggage boot. Removal of the unit gives access to the leads (see Fig.10.19).

23 Number plate light

1 On the 142 and 144 the bulbs in the number plate lights are changed by removing the cover which is held to the lamp by a single screw (photo).
2 The complete lamp is fixed to the body by three screws which are accessible from inside the luggage boot.
3 On the 145 the number plate lights are a clip-on fit to the tailgate. They can be removed with a screwdriver inserted on the

left-hand side of the housing (see Fig. 10.20) after which the cover can be unclipped from the housing and the bulb renewed. It is important to check that the rubber gasket is correctly positioned and that the clips are pushed home.

24 Parking lights and direction indicators

1 As our photo shows, if you undo the two screws holding the cover to the parking light the bulb holder can be withdrawn for changing the bulb and if necessary seeing that all is well with the leads.
2 The direction indicator, though differently shaped (see photos) has a similar construction.
3 Side marker lights are fitted to some models sold in the USA (see Fig.10.21). They may be found either at the front or the rear of the vehicle, and once again changing the bulb or getting at the leads is simply a matter of removing the two screws holding down the cover.

25 Direction indicator system - general description

1 The direction indicator system consists of a thermal type

Fig.10.18. Foglight assembly

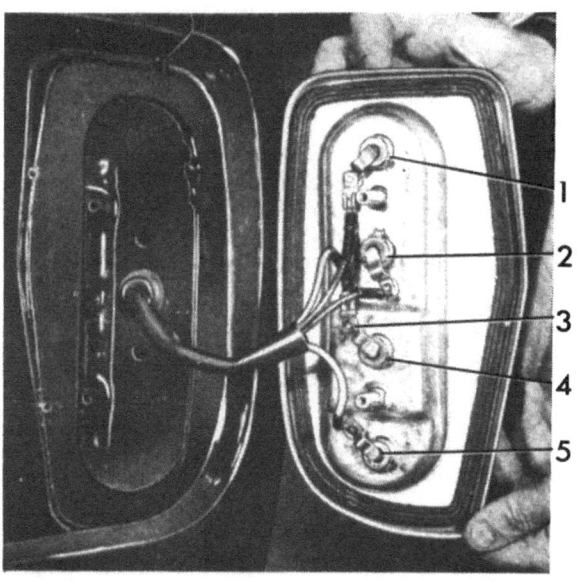

Fig.10.19. Rear light cable connections

1	Directional indicator light	3	Brake light
2	Reversing light	4	Brake light
		5	Rear light

22.1a Undoing two screws releases the rear lamp cover ...

22.1b ... revealing the bulbs

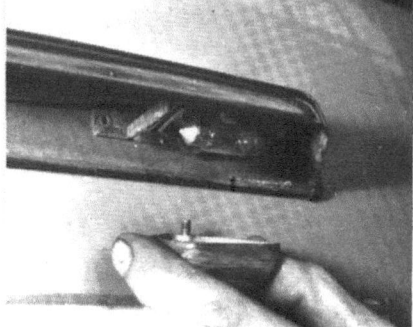

23.1 A single screw holds the number plate lamp cover (142/144)

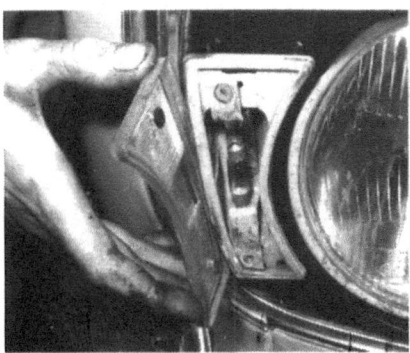

24.1 Two screws keep the side lamp cover in place ...

24.2a ... and the direction indicator cover is fixed in the same way

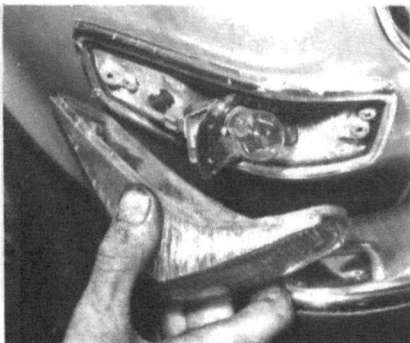

24.2b Removing it discloses the bulb

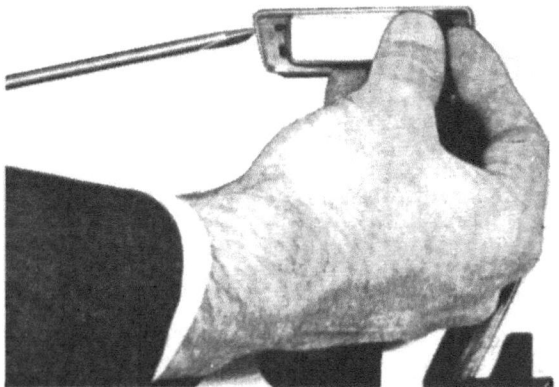

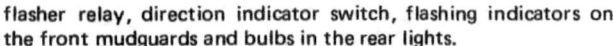

Fig.10.20. Removing cover from tailgate number plate light

Fig.10.21. Side marker light (centre) and direction indicator

flasher relay, direction indicator switch, flashing indicators on the front mudguards and bulbs in the rear lights.

2 In many models the direction indicators can be used as simultaneous emergency warning flashers at the push of a switch. In models with the ribbon type speedometer this switch will be found, if fitted, above and between the cigarette lighter and the fan switch. Incorporated with the switch is the flasher relay and the whole assembly is a click fit in the dashboard, removable from the rear.

3 Where the switch is not fitted, the flasher relay will be found clipped to the dashboard in much the same position. In the newer models with circular speedometers and a very different dashboard arrangement, the switch is fitted as one of a group of four just below the two central air intakes on the dashboard.

4 The flashing indicators have already been dealt with in Sections 19 and 24 of this Chapter, and all that remains to be considered is the lever switch. This is easily got at by removing the underside of the housing surrounding the steering column, and it is pictured in Fig.11.23 in the next Chapter.

5 If the switch is defective in any way, it should be replaced, It is tempting to try to repair this type of switch but only in an emergency is it worthwhile. These fiddly mechanisms only operate properly when their parts are unworn and undistorted and a repairer attempting to compensate for wear by introducing distortion can never hope to achieve more that a partial success.

6 Partial success means having the switch working until the time comes when you are absolutely dependent on it and miles away from a possible replacement, at which time it usually packs up for good.

26 Ignition switch and warning system - general description

1 As Fig.11.23 shows, the ignition switch is mounted on the steering column lock close to the direction indicator switch.

Where a warning buzzer is fitted, the leads to the buzzer (which are taken via a switch in the driver's door) are connected as shown in Fig.11.23b.

2 If this switch is defective, we refer you to paragraphs 5 and 6 of the previous Section.

3 If the buzzer does not operate, check the door switch and the buzzer itself before condemning the ignition switch.

4 The purpose of this buzzer is to make a noise when the driver opens his door while the ignition key is still in the ignition switch, ie the steering column is not locked; it thus reminds him to remove the key and thus lock the steering wheel before leaving the car. Generally speaking it is only fitted to cars intended for the USA.

27 Horns and horn ring

1 Twin horns are fitted, mounted to the left of the radiator behind the grille. The 12 v supply is taken to the horns via a fuse on a blue or brown wire, the black wire also connected to the horns going to the horn ring contact and so to earth when the horn ring is pressed.

2 If the horn does not operate, check that 12 v is present at the terminal connected to the blue or brown lead and if it is, earth the other terminal to the frame. If the horn now sounds the fault must lie between the terminal and the horn ring contact or in the contact itself.

3 The 12 v supply comes through a fuse which should be identified from the appropriate circuit diagram given at the end of the Chapter and checked if the voltage is not present.

4 If these tests reveal that a horn is defective, the only sensible remedy is replacement. If you want to economise, spend the time you would have taken to repair (or fail to repair) the faulty horn, taking a trip to the nearest scrap yard where you can pick up a perfectly good one which will cost you very much less than

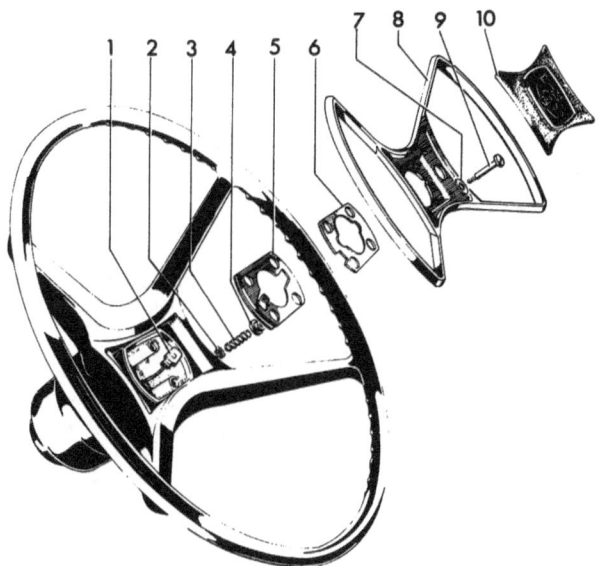

Fig.10.22. Horn ring assembly

1	Horn cable	6	Insulating washer
2	Tab washer	7	Washer
3	Spring	8	Horn ring
4	Bush	9	Stop screw
5	Contact washer	10	Shock guard

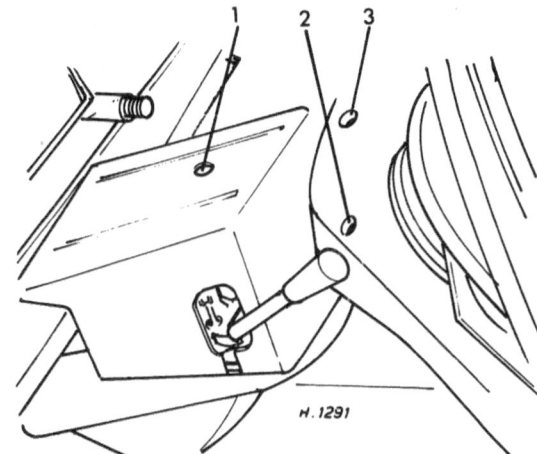

Fig.10.24. Horn ring assembly - removing screws

1 Fixing screw for upper housing
2 Securing screws, horn ring assembly)
3)

a new one.

5 The horn ring assembly, an exploded view of which, is shown in Fig.10.22 (it is also pictured in Fig.11.21a in the next chapter) is easily dismantled by inserting a screwdriver under the shock guard and levering it off the steering wheel. The four fixing screws can then be undone and the ring will lift off, revealing the contact plate to which the cable from the horns is connected.

6 Earlier models have a somewhat different horn ring assembly, an exploded view of which is shown in Fig.10.23. This assembly is retained in the steering column by two screws (shown in Fig. 10.24) and may be removed by taking out these screws, turning the ring through about 30° and pulling it out of the steering wheel.

7 The working principle of both these assemblies is the same though their design is different. The contact plate to which the horn cable is connected is held away from an earthed surface by

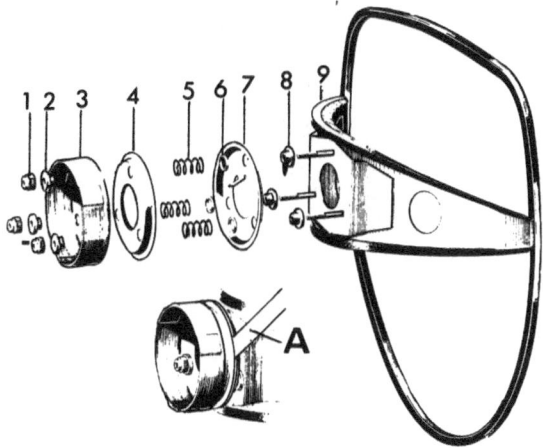

Fig.10.23. Horn ring assembly - earlier type

1	Nut	6	Washer
2	Bush	7	Contact plate
3	Retainer	8	Bush
4	Plate	9	Horn ring
5	Spring		

'A' = .016 - .024" (0.4 - 0.6 mm)

springs which are isolated from the plate by bushes. When the horn ring is pushed, one or more of these springs is compressed sufficiently to allow the plate to touch the earth surface and complete the circuit through the horns.

8 If the system does not work, first check that the cable to the contact plate is making a good connection (it may possibly be broken at the connecting tag) and if all is well with the cable see that the contact plate and its corresponding earth surface are clean. The system may be adjusted by screwing up the fixing nuts or screws until the springs are compressed to such a degree that light pressure anywhere on the horn ring will cause the horn to sound.

28 Windscreen wiper

1 The windscreen wiper system consists of a two-speed permanent magnet electric motor (the speeds are chosen by selection of one of two positive brushes) which drives a spindle through a gear housing. The spindle is connected to the wiper blades by linkages.

2 As so often is the case with windscreen wipers, removal is an awkward business entailing a fair amount of dismantling. In cars fitted with the ribbon speedometer, this has to come out as well as the intermediate defroster nozzle and its hoses before the wiper motor can be released by undoing its three fixing bolts. An exploded view of the wiper motor is shown in Fig.10.25.

3 The motor and the gear housing combined with it are easy to dismantle with the guidance of this Figure. When pulling the rotor out of the end containing the brushes, be careful of these as the rotor bearing has a larger diameter than the commutator. The motor should be checked electrically by examining the brushes for wear, the commutator for scoring or signs of burning, the windings for signs of overheating (indicating short circuited turns in the windings) and the bearings (washed in white spirit) for signs of scoring, blueing or scuffing and its play should be checked. The gear housing and its contents should be thoroughly cleaned and checked for signs of wear. Note on reassembly that the axial play for the plastic gear wheel can be adjusted by setting a screw in the cover.

4 The wiring diagram in Fig.10.26 illustrates the selection of the two motor speeds and the parking arrangement. The switch terminal marked "P" connects battery positive to the screen

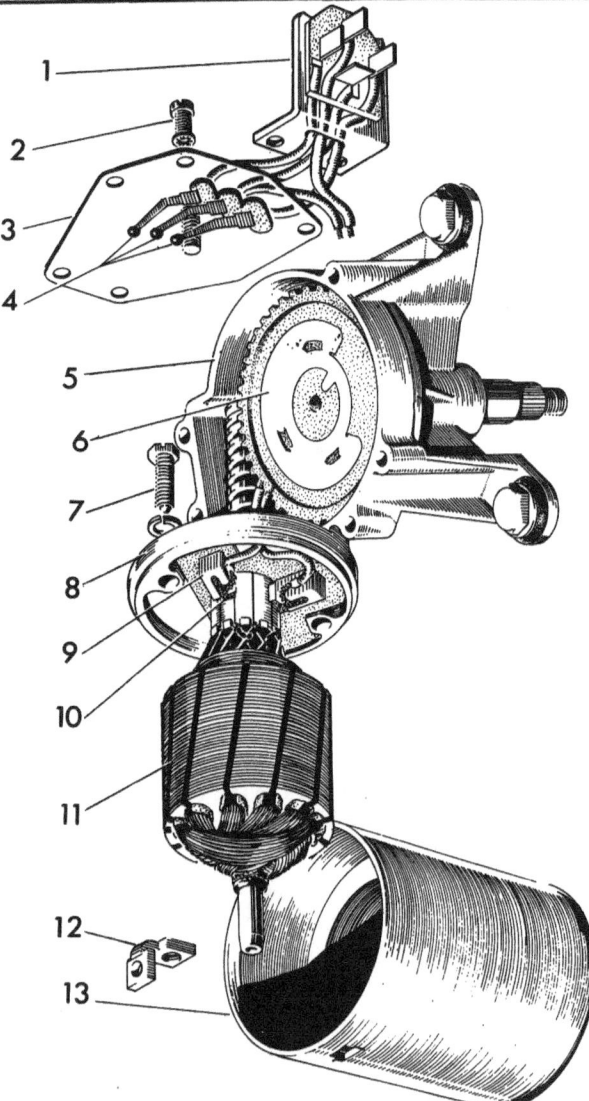

Fig.10.25. Windscreen wiper motor - exploded view

1 Terminal contact	8 End
2 Screw	9 Brush holder
3 Cover	10 Brush
4 Contacts	11 Rotor
5 Housing	12 Nut
6 Gear	13 Stator
7 Screw	

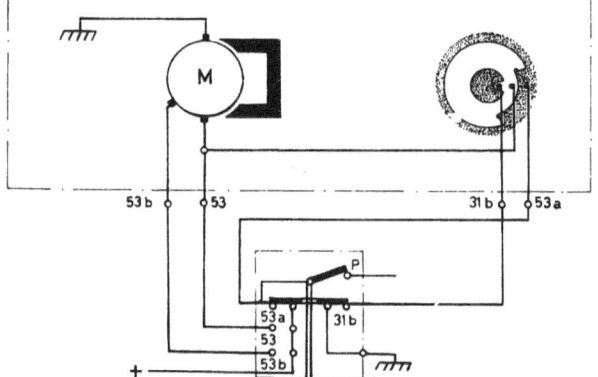

Fig.10.26. Windscreen wiper wiring diagram

P - Connection to windscreen washer

washer when the knob of the wiper switch is pushed in. Turning the knob connects battery positive to terminal "53B" for slow speed, "53" for fast speed and "53A" for parking. At the same time that battery positive is connected to terminal "53A", terminal "31B" is earthed. This is the switch position shown in the diagram.

5   Parking is controlled by three contacts which bear on a metal strip attached to the plastic gear in the gear housing. In the diagram the contact strip is shown in the parked position. In this case the metal strip is earthed via terminal 31B and this earths the high speed brush. If the gear wheel were in a different position, the contact plate would be disconnected from earth but connected to battery positive via terminal "53A". In this case the motor would run until the contact "53A" came off the plate, removing the positive voltage from the brush, Its inertia would then allow it to continue until the brush was shorted to earth as shown in the diagram. Earthing this brush produces a braking effect on the motor which brings it to rest immediately.

29 Tailgate window wiper - 145

1   The tailgate window wiper is operated by a single speed permanent magnet electric motor. It is connected to the wiper blade by a link arm.

2   The wiper is removed by taking off the panel on the inside of the tailgate and unscrewing the screws securing the reinforcing plate under the wiper motor which are found under this panel. The battery positive lead should be disconnected before you start as you will have to unscrew leads from terminals on the motor. These leads should of course be marked before removal. When the link arm has been disconnected and the reinforcing plate pushed to one side, the motor can be removed.

3   Dismantling and inspecting the motor and gear housing is a simple matter with the guidance of Figs.10.27, 10.28 and 10.29. Clean all the parts and check them for wear and mechanical damage. Check the armature for short circuiting between commutator and frame and also for short circuiting between and breakage in the winding coils. This is usually indicated by signs of overheating in the armature. Signs of burning on the commutator, on the other hand, indicate open circuit armature windings. If you are dubious about the armature, have it tested by a specialist.

4   On reassembly the drive housing should be well greased (use Castrol LM). The armature shaft and its bush should be very lightly oiled. Replace the brushes if they are worn.

5   The wiring diagram (Fig.10.30) illustrates the switching and parking arrangements which are quite different from those for the windscreen wiper. The tailgate wiper switch has three positions - park, wiper operating, wiper and washer operating. The connection "A" in the diagram takes battery positive to the window washer. When the switch is in the parking position (as shown in the diagram) the wiper motor continues to run until the changeover contact connected to the brush which is not permanently earthed switches over from 12 v positive to earth (reached via the switch) and this exerts a braking action on the motor which immediately comes to rest. The normal position of the contact, of course, connects battery positive to the motor brush.

6   When the switch is in one of the running positions, battery positive is connected to terminals "31B" and "53A". In this case, when the contact is actually changing over the current from the battery flows via "31B" through the diode to the motor so that there is no interruption in the supply while the contacts are actually changing over - a comparatively slow process. When the switch is in the parking position but before the contacts change over, the diode is connected between the motor and earth but does not present a short circuit to the battery because it does not permit current flow in the direction opposite to that indicated by the black arrow head.

7   Failure of this diode would be indicated by some hesitancy in leaving the parking position when the wiper is operating, but in all probability more noticeably by clicks in the car radio each

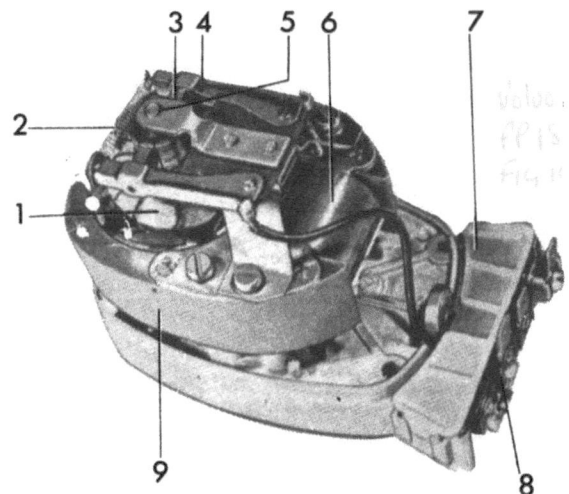

Fig.10.27. Tailgate window wiper motor

1 Rotor	6 Permanent magnet
2 Brush spring	7 Parking switch
3 Brush	8 Diode
4 Brush holder	9 Pole shoe
5 Stop tab for rotor	

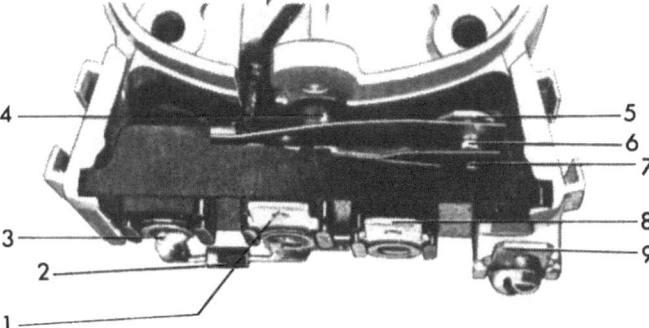

Fig.10.29. Tailgate window wiper - parking switch

1 Connection 31b	6 Contacts (2) 53
2 Diode	7 Contact 31b
3 Connection 53	8 Connection 53a
4 Lift tab	9 Connection 31
5 Contact 53a	

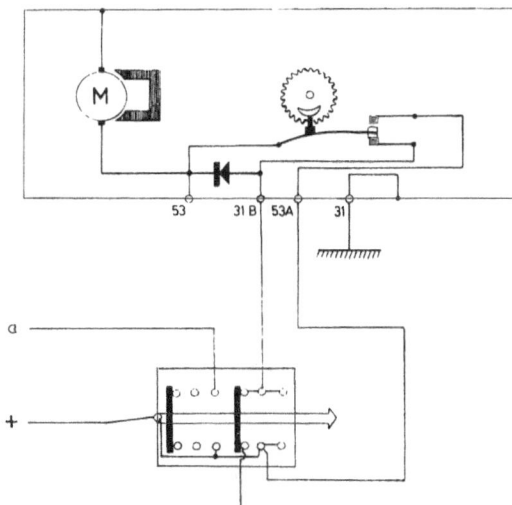

Fig.10.30. Tailgate window wiper wiring diagram

a - connection to window washer

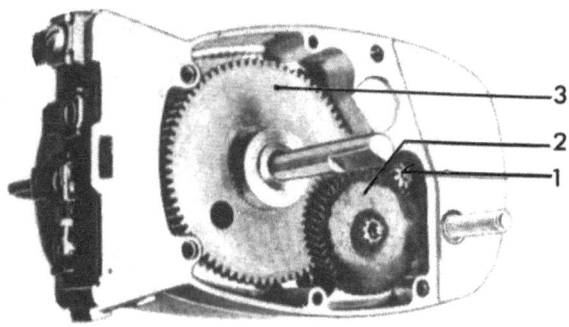

Fig.10.28. Tailgate window wiper drive housing

1 Drive on output shaft
2 Intermediate drive, fibre
3 Rotor shaft drive

time the wiper passes through this position. This assumes that the diode goes open circuit when it fails; if it goes short circuit it will either burn itself out very quickly (thus going open circuit) or blow the supply fuse.

30 Windscreen and tailgate window washers

1 Both these washers are of the same type. There are two versions, shown in Figs.10.31 and 10.32. They consist of a centrifugal pump driven by a small permanent magnetic motor. They need little maintenance apart from an occasional clean out of the system and repair of the motor is not a practicable proposition.

2 The windscreen washer is located on the right-hand wheel housing, where its position is very obvious. The tailgate window washer is placed in a cavity to the right under the floor of the cargo space (see Fig.10.33).

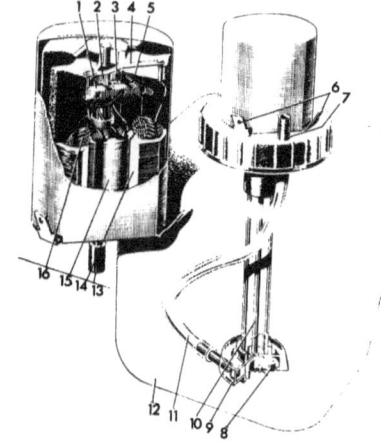

Fig.10.31. Screen washer

1 Brush holder	9 Pump housing
2 Commutator	10 Shaft
3 Brush	11 Hose
4 Thermal fusing	12 Container
5 Spring	13 Flange
6 Terminal pin	14 Stator
7 Water outlet	15 Rotor
8 Pump impeller	16 Field winding

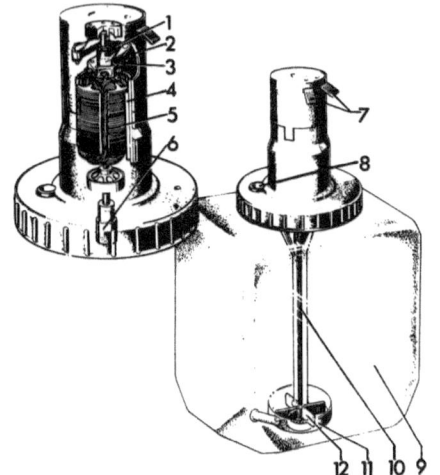

Fig.10.32. Screen washer - alternative version

1	Commutator	7	Connecting lip
2	Brush	8	Wiper fluid hose hole
3	Spring	9	Container
4	Permanent magnet	10	Shaft
5	Rotor	11	Pump housing
6	Flange	12	Pump impeller

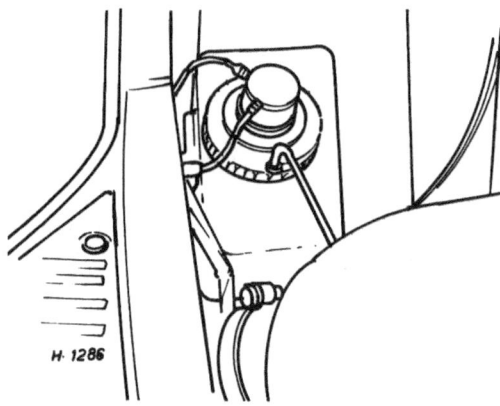

Fig.10.33. Tailgate window washer in position

31 Instrument panel

1   The instrument panel shown in Fig.10.34, long familiar to Volvo owners, has recently been replaced by a new version with a circular speedometer as shown in Fig.10.35. The instruments are of the same type though differently detailed and arranged. On some later models a tachometer, operated by electrical signals from the ignition coil, is fitted in the centre of the later type instrument panel.

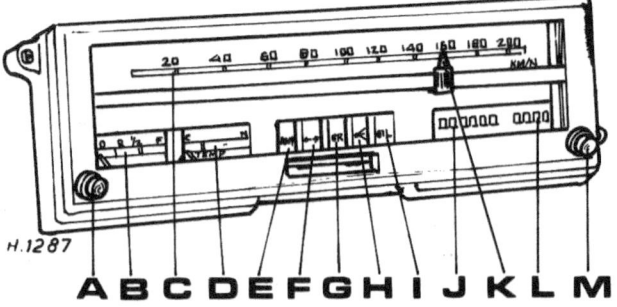

Fig.10.34. Instrument panel

A	Panel light switch		light (functions also as
B	Fuel gauge		warning light for both
C	Speedometer		service brake circuits)
D	Coolant temperature gauge	H	Main beam control light
E	Warning light, charging	I	Oil pressure warning light
F	Direction indicator control light	J	Milometer
		K	Speed warning indicator
G	Handbrake warning light (functions also as warning	L	Trip meter
		M	Trip reset knob

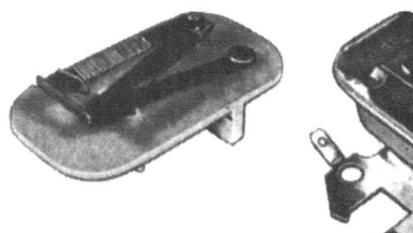

Fig.10.36. Voltage stabiliser, instrument panel

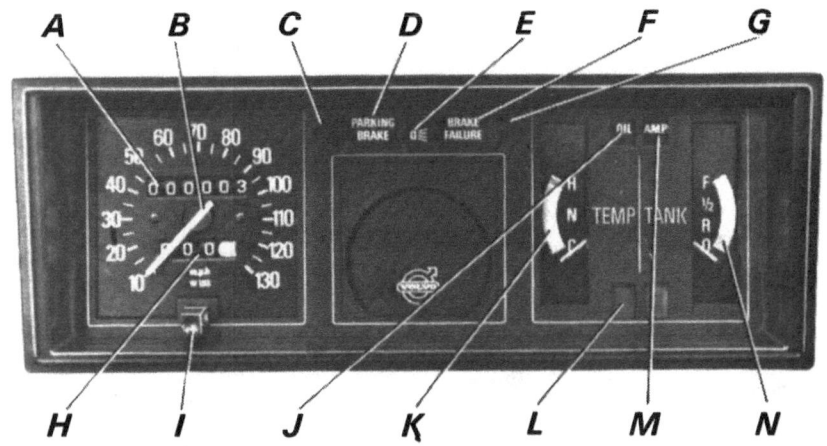

Fig.10.35. Instrument panel, later models

A   Odometer
B   Speedometer
C   Turn signal light
D   Warning light, parking brake and brake circuit failure
E   Main beam warning light
F   Warning light, parking brake and brake circuit failure
G   Turn signal light
H   Trip odometer
I   Trip odometer reset knob
J   Warning light, oil pressure
K   Temperature gauge
L   Warning light, overdrive
M   Warning light, battery charging
N   Fuel gauge

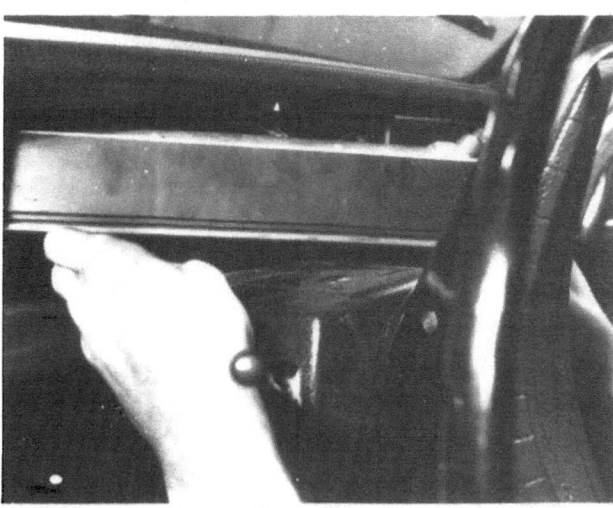

31.6a Manoeuvre the panel forwards ...

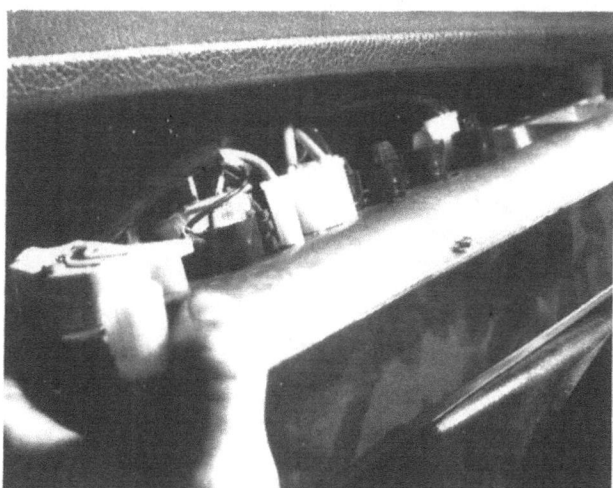

31.6b ... to gain access to the electrical connectors

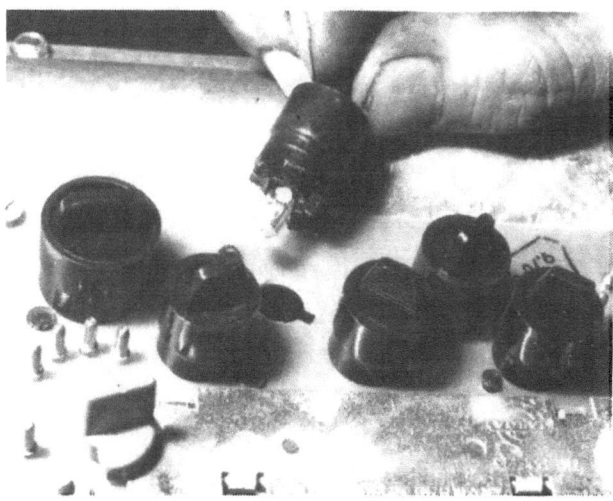

31.7 Warning light bulbs are a push fit in their holders

2 Disconnect the battery earth lead before commencing removal. First remove the steering column casings, then remove the bracket securing screw and allow the bracket to move towards the steering column.

3 The two screws securing the instrument panel can now be removed.

4 Reach behind the panel and disconnect the speedometer cable.

5 Still reaching behind the instrument panel, press the speedometer upwards and inwards to disengage the retaining lug(s).

6 It should now be possible to manoeuvre the panel forwards far enough to unplug the electrical connectors (photos). Label the connectors if you think you may forget their locations.

7 The panel can now be withdrawn from the dashboard. If it is wished to renew any warning light bulbs, they are a simple push fit in their holders (photo).

8 Refitting is the reverse of the removal procedure. Do not use force when refitting, or the bulb holders may be dislodged, or the bulbs themselves may fall from the holders.

32 Speedometer and speedometer cable

1 It is most important that the speedometer cable is correctly fitted if the speedometer is to function without trouble. It is vitally important that the cable is not bent too sharply. At no point must the radius of the bend be less than 4" (100 m). If the bending radius is less than this, vibration and noises can occur in the instrument. The drive couplings must run true in the outer casing of the cable.

2 This being said, fitting is not difficult. We suggest that you start at the speedometer end, because this is the cleanest. Withdraw the old cable as you go and fit the new one.

3 If a speedometer starts giving trouble, it should be replaced. Faulty operation is almost always the result of wear which cannot really be compensated by adjustment.

33 Temperature and fuel gauges

1 These gauges contain bi-metal strips heated by windings which are in series with the control rheostats operated by petrol level or water temperature. They are driven from a small voltage stabilizer (see Fig.10.36) which gives a constant output.

2 If both the fuel and temperature gauges give consistently high or low readings, the voltage stabiliser must be suspect. Checking the stabiliser requires a thermal voltmeter, equipment not normally available in the home mechanic's workshop, and the simplest test is by substitution.

3 Do not check the instruments by earthing their pick-up leads. This will cause an excessive current to pass through the instrument and damage it. Connect the lead to the chassis via a 10 ohm resistor.

4 As a further check, the resistance of the instruments should be approximately 12.5 ohms.

5 The water temperature gauge should indicate temperature as follows:-

Beginning of green (at "C")	105°F (40°C)
At dividing line between green areas	(70°C) 158°F
At dividing line between green and red areas	(100°C) 212°F

At room temperature the temperature sensor should have a resistance of approximately 200 ohms.

6   The fuel level gauge is illustrated in Fig. 10.38, and Fig. 10.39 shows a suitable tool for removing it. It is got at by removing the carpet and floor board in the luggage boot. At its upper stop the pick-up should have a resistance of approximately 10 ohms and at the lower, approximately 60-85 ohms. Movement of the float arm should not result in breaks in the resistance reading.

34 Fuses

1   The fuse compartment is sited centrally underneath the dashboard. In the newest models the cover of the compartment has been made into an auxiliary panel carrying the controls for the air conditioner and various other switches and warning lights, depending on the model.
2   The front cover of the compartment pulls out to reveal nine fuses, each in a holder with the fuse number as shown in the circuit diagram and the functions controlled engraved clearly on it. Where no lead is taken to the terminal associated with a fuse, that terminal is internally connected to one of its next door neighbours (photos).
3   The 140 GL is fitted with a small auxiliary fusebox controlling the fuel injection system and foglights (see Fig.10.37).
4   If a fuse blows, temporarily connect a headlamp bulb (main beam) across the fuse holder. If this bulb glows at full strength, you have a complete short circuit. This is certain to be caused by

Fig.10.37. Control relays and subsidiary fusebox

1   *Reversing light relay (or start relay for vehicles with automatic transmission)*
2   *Control relay for rear window defroster*
3   *Step relay for dipped, full-beams switching*
4   *Control relay for foglights (140 GL)*
5   *Fusebox for foglights and fuel injection system (140 GL)*

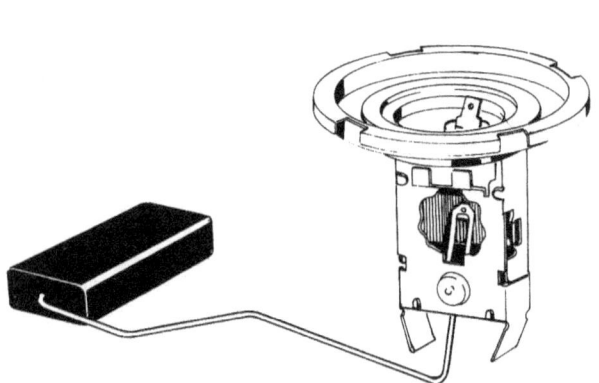

Fig.10.38. Pick-up for fuel gauge

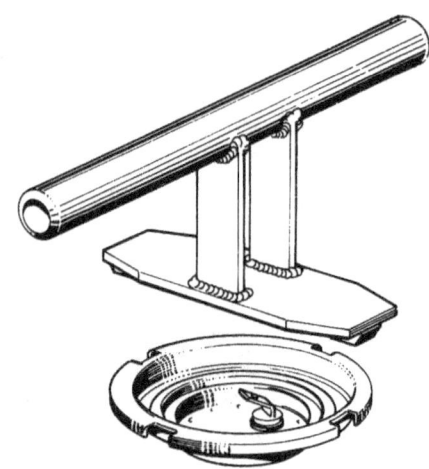

Fig.10.39. Tool for removing pick-up

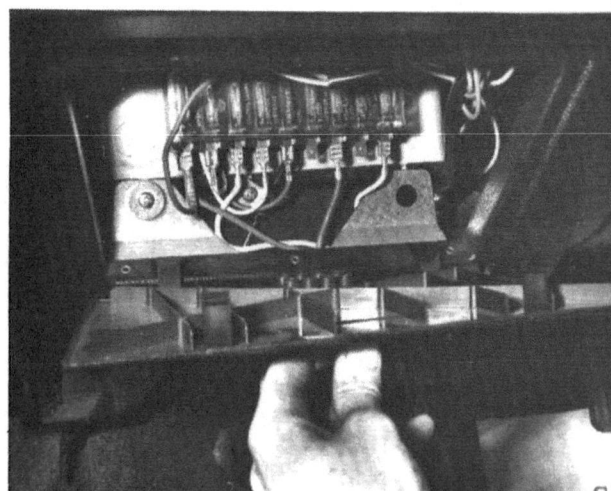

34.2a The fuse box cover is pulled off ...

34.2b ... to reveal the fuses, each with the functions it controls, engraved on its cover

a nipped wire, a broken connection with one end of the wire touching metal, or a connector being bent over to touch metal. If the bulb glows faintly, it may be replaced by an ammeter which will indicate how much the overload current is.

Do not leave the ammeter connected for any length of time in case the cause of the overload suffers damage from which it has been protected by the blowing of the fuse.

5 Tracing the cause of a blown fuse is a matter of logic and perseverance. Disconnect each of the switches, lamps etc fed by the fuse in turn until the overload disappears, thus revealing the culprit. If all the items fed by the fuse are dismantled and you are still getting trouble, the fault must lie in the wiring.

Intermittent short-circuits are almost invariably due to wiring and connector faults. These are often difficult to trace as they always seem to disappear when you are looking for them, but patience and thoroughness will lead you to them in the end.

6 Always use fuses having the values depicted on the appropriate circuit diagram. This way you can be sure of adequate protection without unnecessary replacement.

35 Control relays

1 Cars in the 140 series are fitted as standard with three control relays: a step relay for full-beam and dipped headlights, a control relay for the reverse lights and a control relay for the rear window defroster. Vehicles with automatic transmission are fitted with a start relay instead of a reverse light switch relay.

2 The 140 GL is fitted with a fourth relay for controlling the foglights where these are present.

3 All the control relays are placed on a bracket on the left-hand wheel housing as shown in Fig.10.37.

36 Fault - finding

1 Electrical faults fall into three classes:
a) Failure to generate.
b) Failure to start and;
c) Failure of instrument, accessories or lighting to function properly in an otherwise satisfactory electrical system.

2 Faults in the first two classes are dealt with in the table that follows. This table concludes with an example of a fault in the third class; this part of the table may be adapted to deal with almost any accessory, and certainly the first two or three possible reasons or remedies are of almost universal application, especially if we take the words "faulty control switch" to include faulty control relays where applicable.

37 Fault finding table

Symptom	Reason/s	Remedy
STARTER MOTOR TURNS ENGINE VERY SLOWLY		
Electrical defects	Battery in discharged condition	Charge battery.
	Starter brushes badly worn, sticking, or brush wires loose	Examine brushes, replace as necessary, tighten down brush wires.
	Loose wires in starter motor circuit	Check wiring and tighten as necessary.
Mechanical defect	Worn bearing bushes in starter motor	Replace starter motor.
STARTER MOTOR OPERATES WITHOUT TURNING ENGINE		
Mechanical damage	One-way clutch slipping	Clean clutch thoroughly - If this does not prove successful, replace motor.
	Pinion or ring gear teeth broken or worn	Fit new gear ring, and new pinion to starter motor drive.
STARTER MOTOR NOISY OR EXCESSIVELY ROUGH ENGAGEMENT		
Lack of attention or mechanical damage	Pinion or ring gear teeth broken or worn	Fit new ring gear, or new pinion to starter motor drive.
	Starter drive main spring broken	Dismantle and fit new main spring.
	Starter motor retaining bolts loose	Tighten starter motor securing bolts. Fit new spring washer if necessary.
	Worn bearing bushes	Replace starter motor
BATTERY WILL NOT HOLD CHARGE FOR MORE THAN A FEW DAYS		
Wear or damage	Battery defective internally	Remove and fit new battery.
	Electrolyte level too low or electrolyte too weak due to leakage	Top up electrolyte level to just above plates.
	Plate separators no longer fully effective	Remove and fit new battery.
	Battery plates severely sulphated	Remove and fit new battery.
	Drive belt slipping	Check belt for wear, replace if necessary, and tighten.
	Battery terminal connections loose or corroded	Check terminals for tightness, and remove all corrosion.
	Short in lighting circuit causing continual battery drain	Trace and rectify.
	Regulator unit not working correctly	Check setting, adjust where possible, replace if defective.
	Faults listed under next heading may also apply	

Symptom	Reason/s	Remedy
IGNITION LIGHT FAILS TO GO OUT, BATTERY RUNS FLAT IN A FEW DAYS		
Dynamo or alternator not charging	Drive belt loose and slipping, or broken	Check, replace, and tighten as necessary.
	Brushes worn, sticking, broken or dirty	Examine, clean, or replace brushes as necessary.
	Brush springs weak or broken	Examine and test. Replace as necessary.
	Commutator or slip rings dirty, greasy, worn, or burnt	Clean commutator and undercut segment seperators; in alternator, clean slip rings. ʲs
	Armature/rotor badly worn or shaft bent	Fit new or reconditioned armature/rotor.
	Faulty regulator unit or isolation diode	Check, replace.
WIPERS		
Wiper motor fails to work	Blown fuse	Check and replace fuse if necessary.
	Faulty control switch	Replace
	Wire connections loose, disconnected, or broken	Check wiper wiring. Tighten loose connections.
	Brushes badly worn	Remove and fit new brushes.
	Armature worn or faulty	If electricity at wiper motor remove and overhaul and fit replacement armature.
	Field coils faulty	Purchase reconditioned wiper motor.
Wiper motor works very slow and takes excessive current	Commutator dirty, greasy, or burnt	Clean commutator thoroughly.
	Drive to wheelboxes too bent or unlubricated	Examine drive and straighten out severe curvature. Lubricate.
	Wheelbox spindle binding or damaged	Remove, overhaul, or fit replacement.
	Armature bearings dry or unaligned	Replace with new bearings correctly aligned.
	Armature badly worn or faulty	Remove, overhaul, or fit replacement armature.
Wiper motor works slowly and takes little current	Brushes badly worn	Remove and fit new brushes.
	Commutator dirty, greasy, or burnt	Clean commutator thoroughly.
	Armature badly worn or faulty	Remove and overhaul armature or fit replacement.
Wiper motor works but wiper blades remain static	Driving cable rack disengaged or faulty	Examine and if faulty, replace.
	Wheelbox gear and spindle damaged or worn	Examine and if faulty, replace.
	Wiper motor gearbox parts badly worn	Overhaul or fit new gearbox.

Key to wiring diagrams D1, D2, D3 and D4
(letter references to 1968 and 1969 diagrams are shown in brackets)

1 (A)	Direction indicators	
2 (B)	Sidelights	
3 (C)	Headlamps (dipped)	
4 (D)	Headlamps (main beam)	
5 (E)	Horn	
6 (F)	Distributor	
7 (G)	Ignition coil	
8 (H)	Battery	
9 (J)	Starter	
10 (K)	Reversing light switch	
11 (L)	Main beam indicator	
12 (M)	Headlamp relay	
13 (N)	Horn ring	
14 (O)	Alternator or generator	
15 (P)	Reversing light relay or starter relay on automatic gearbox	
16 (Q)	Fusebox	

17 (R)	Regulator
18 (S)	Handbrake switch
19 (T)	Flasher unit
20 (U)	Handbrake on, indicator
21 (V)	Low oil pressure indicator
22 (X)	Charging indicator
23 (Y)	Connector
24 (Z)	Glove compartment light
25 (A)	Overdrive indicator
26 (A)	Column lights switch
27 (O)	Fuel gauge
28 (AA)	Voltage stabilizer
29 (BA)	Temperature gauge
30 (CA)	Oil pressure transducer
31 (DA)	Overdrive switch
32 (EA)	Direction indicator repeater
33 (FA)	Panel lighting

34 (GA)	Water temperature transmitter
35 (HA)	Heater control panel lights
36 (JA)	Blower
37 (KA)	Windscreen wiper
38 (LA)	Windscreen washer
39 (MA)	Overdrive solenoid
40 (NA)	Interior lighting
41 (OA)	Glove compartment switch
42 (PA)	Wiper and washer switch
43 (QA)	Dimmer
44 (RA)	Lighting switch
45 (SA)	Ignition switch
46 (TA)	Cigar lighter
47 (VA)	Door contact
48 (VA)	Switch on handbrake
49 (XA)	Fuel level transmitter
50 (ZA)	Reversing light

51 (AA)	Stop light
52 (AA)	Tail light
53 (OA)	Number plate light
54 (AB)	Overdrive control switch
55 (BB)	Brake failure warning
56 (K)	Starter/reversing light switch on automatic gearbox
57	Rear window heater (1970 only)
58	Switch for 58
59	Sidelights repeater (USA only)
60	Relay for 58
61	Instrument panel connectors
62	Ignition lock warning buzzer (USA only)
63	
64 (VA)	Driver's door switch

Cable Colour Code

SB (Svart) = Black W (Vit) = White Y (Gul) = Yellow GN (Gron) = Green GR (Gra) = Grey
BL (Blu) = Blue R (Rod) = Red BR (Brun) = Brown

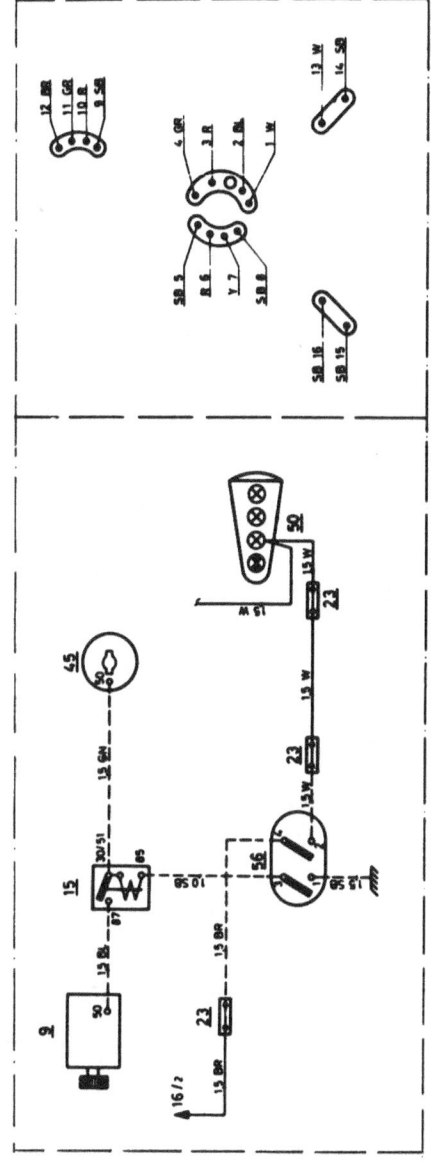

D1 - Connections on Borg-Warner gearbox (left) and to combined instrument panel (right) (1968 - 1970)

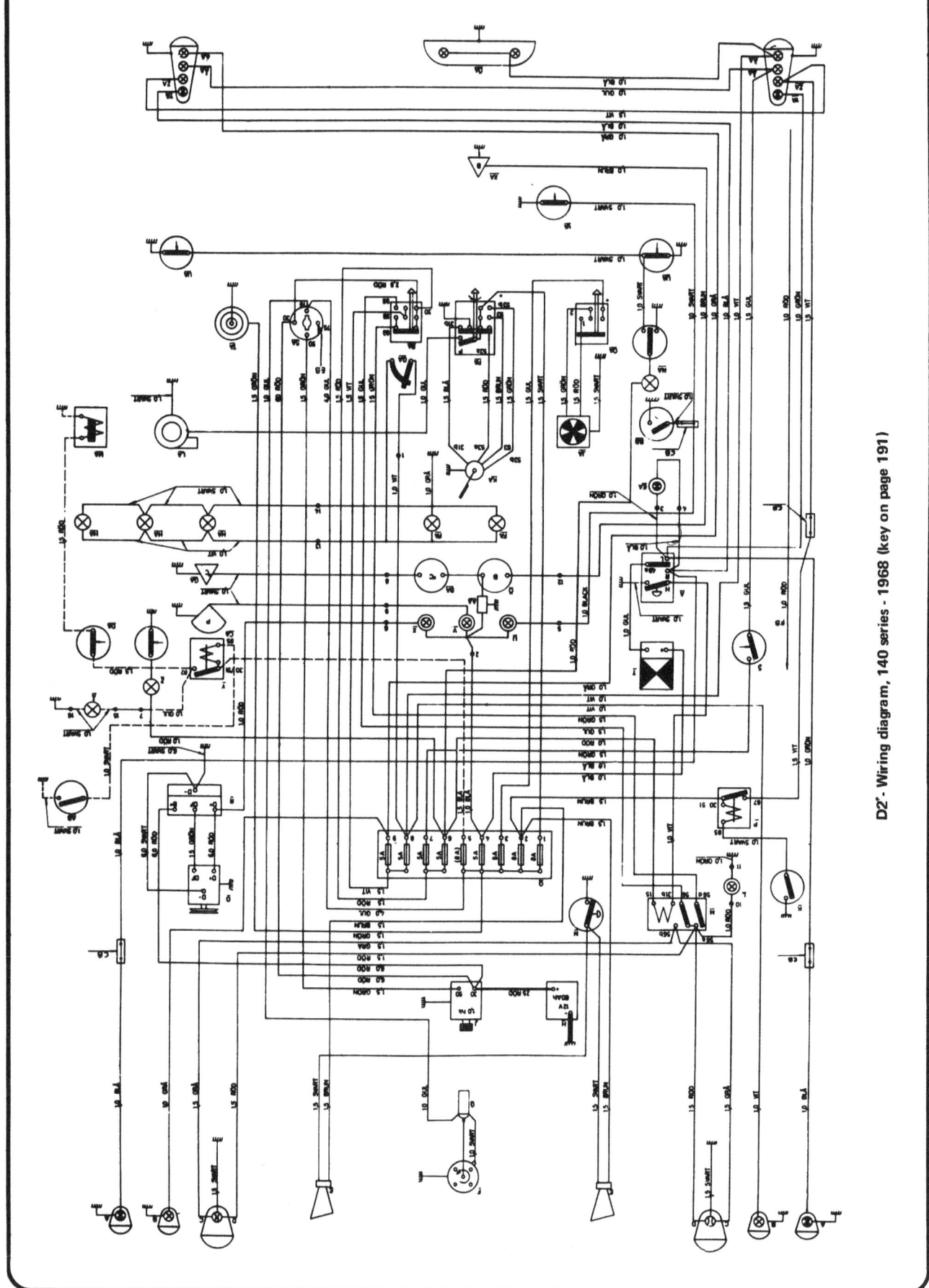

D2² - Wiring diagram, 140 series - 1968 (key on page 191)

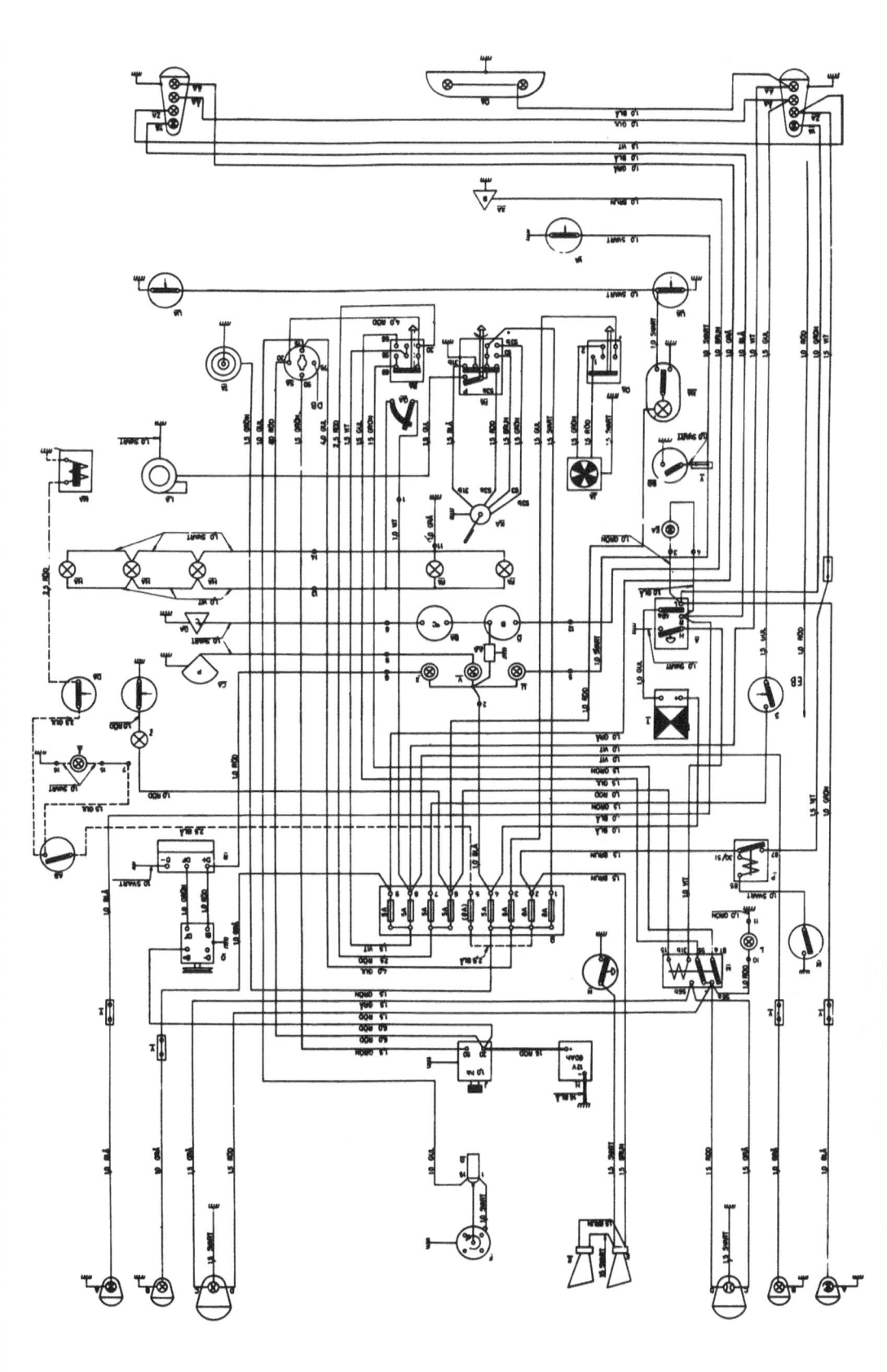

D3 - Wiring diagram, 140 series - 1969 (key on page 191)

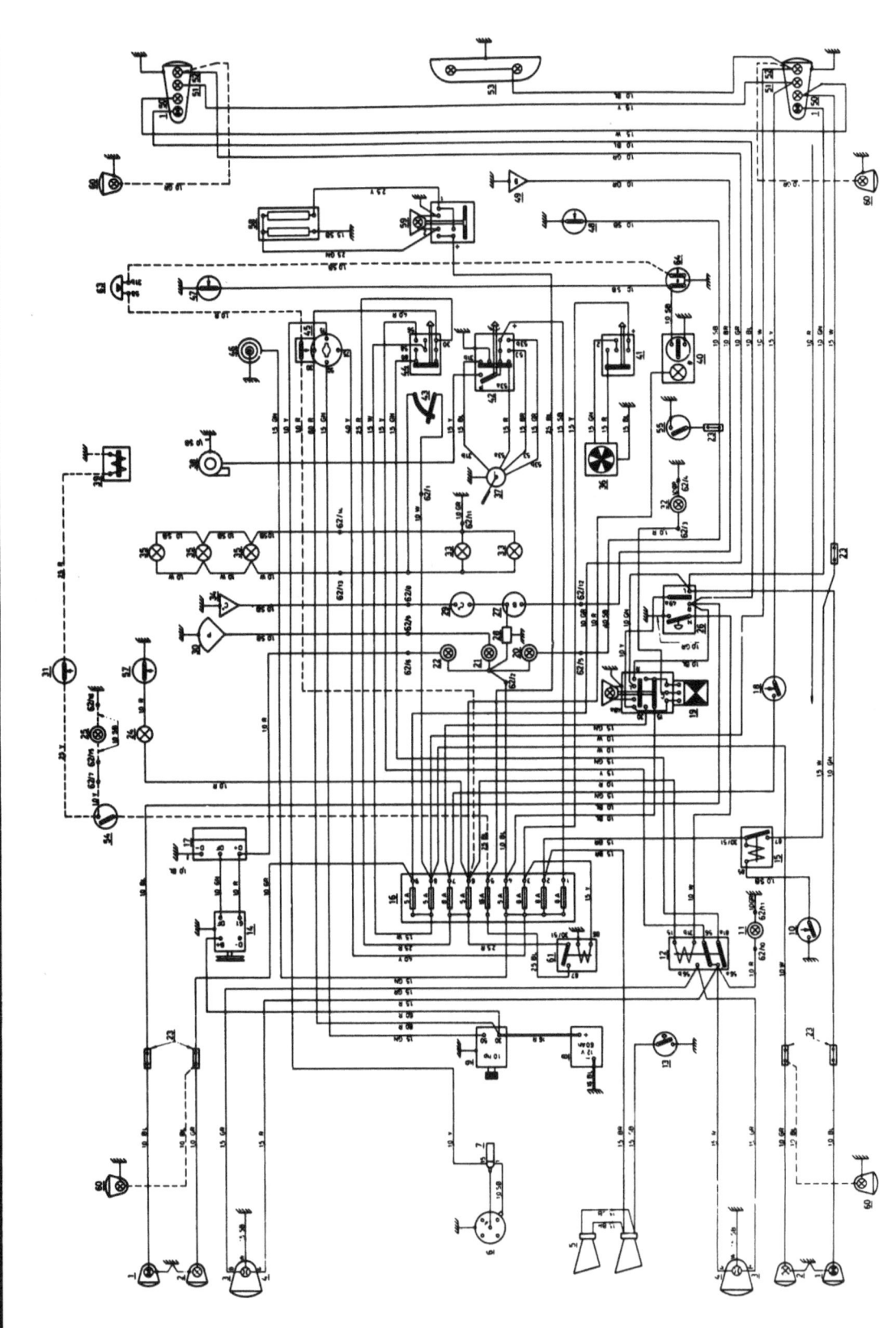

D4 - Wiring diagram, 140 series - 1970 (key on page 191)

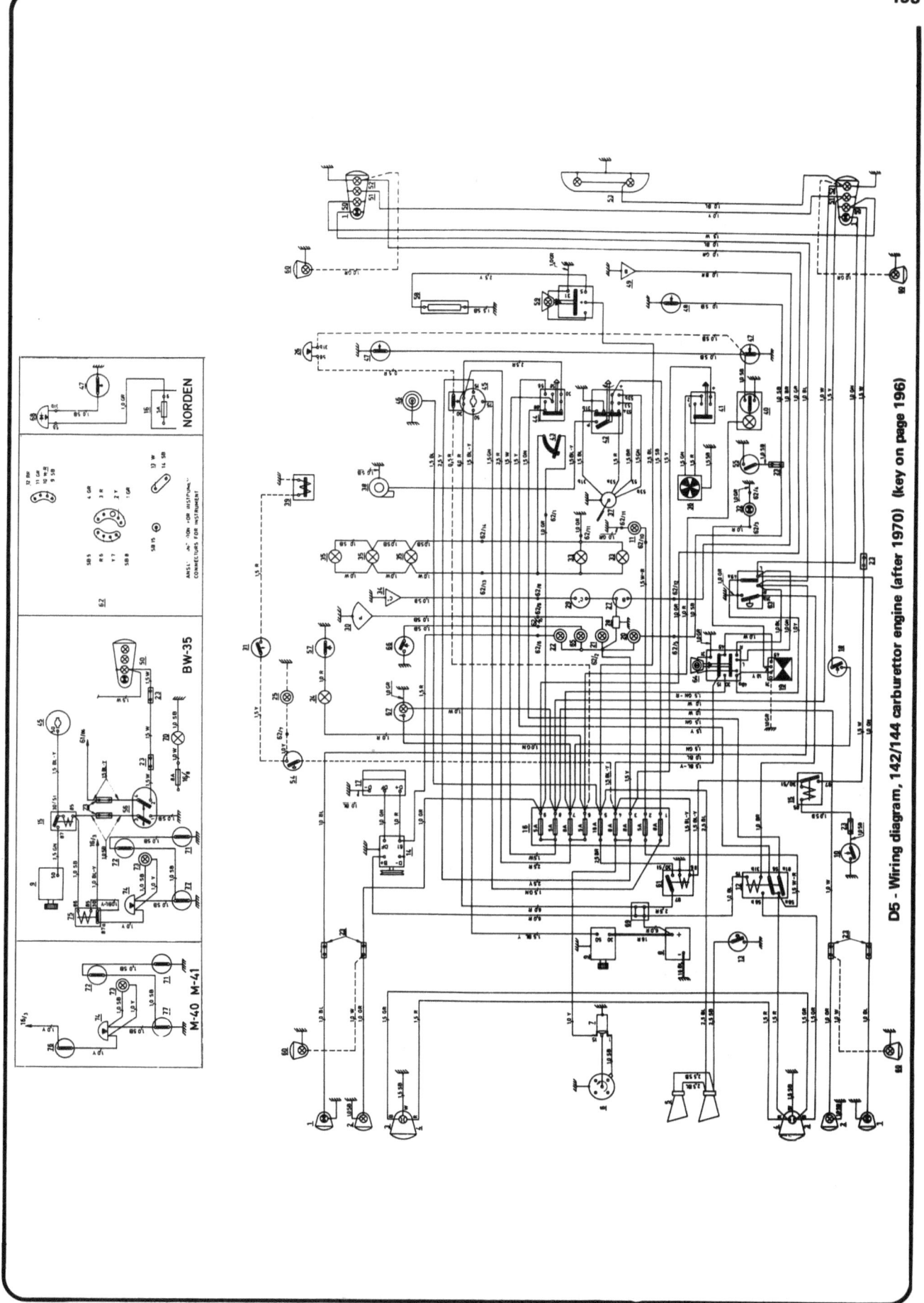

D5 - Wiring diagram, 142/144 carburettor engine (after 1970) (key on page 196)

Key to wiring diagram D5

Pos.	Title	Data
1	Dir. ind. flashers	32 CP
2	Parking lights	5 W
3	Headlight dipped beams	40 W
4	Headlight main beams	45 W
5	Horn	
6	Distributor firing order	1-3-4-2
7	Ignition coil	
8	Battery	12V 60 Ah
9	Starter motor	1.0 hp
10	Contact for reverse light (M40 and M41 only)	
11	Main beam warning lamp	
12	Step relay for main and dipped beams and headlight flashers	1.2 W
13	Horn ring	
14	Alternator	12V 35A
15	Relay for reverse light on M40, M41 and starter relay on BW 35	
16	Fusebox	
17	Charging regulator	
18	Brake contact	
19	Flasher unit	
20	Brake warning lamp	1.2 W
21	Oil pressure warning lamp	1.2 W
22	Battery charging warning lamp	
23	Connector	1.2 W
24	Glove locker light	2 W
25	Overdrive warning lamp M41	1.2 W
26	Warning buzzer, ignition key	
27	Fuel gauge	
28	Voltage stabilizer	
29	Temperature gauge	
30	Oil pressure sender	
31	Contact for overdrive on M41 gearbox	
32	Flashers warning lamp	1.2 W
33	Instrument lighting	2x3 W
34	Temperature gauge sensor	
35	Heater control light	3x1.2 W
36	Heater	
37	Windshield wipers	
38	Windshield washers	
39	Solenoid for overdrive on M41 gearbox	
40	Interior light 10 W	
41	Switch for heater	
42	Switch for windshield wipers and washers	
43	Panel light rheostat	
44	Light switch	
45	Ignition switch	
46	Cigarette lighter	
47	Door switch	
48	Switch for parking brake control	
49	Fuel gauge tank unit	
50	Reverse lights	15 W
51	Brake stoplights	25 W
52	Tail lights	5 W
53	License plate light	2x5 W
54	Switch for overdrive M41	
55	Brake warning switch	
56	Contact on gearbox BW 35	
57	Switch glove locker light	
58	Elec. heated rear window	
59	Switch, elec. heated rear window	
60	Side marker lights (USA only)	5 W
61	Main relay, starter switch	
62	Terminal at instrument	
63	Switch for dir. ind. and headlight flashers	
64	Switch for hazard warning flasher	
65	Choke warning lamp	
66	Choke control contact	
67	Clock	
68	Warning buzzer, headlights	
69	Connector	
70	Shift positions light	
71	Switch, seat buckle, passenger	
72	Switch, passenger seat	
73	Warning lamp, seat belts	
74	Buzzer, seat belts	
75	Relay, seat belts	
76	Contact, M40, M41 gearboxes	
77	Switch, seat buckle, driver	

Key to wiring diagram D6

Pos.	Title	Data
1	Dir. ind. flashers	32 CP
2	Parking lights	5 W
3	Headlight dipped beams	40 W
4	Headlight main beams	45 W
5	Horn	
6	Distributor firing order	1-3-4-2
7	Ignition coil	
8	Battery	12V 60 Ah
9	Starter motor	1.0 hp
10	Contact for reverse light (M40 and M41 only)	
11	Main beam warning lamp	
12	Step relay for main and dipped beams and headlight flashers	1.2 W
13	Horn ring	
14	Alternator	12V 55A
15	Relay for reverse light on M40, M41 and starter relay on BW 35	
16	Fusebox	
17	Charging regulator	
18	Brake contact	
19	Flasher unit	
20	Brake warning lamp	1.2 W
21	Oil pressure warning lamp	1.2 W
22	Battery charging warning lamp	
23	Connector	1.2 W
24	Glove locker light	2 W
25	Overdrive warning lamp M41	1.2 W
26	Switch for dir. ind. and headlights flashers	
27	Fuel gauge	
28	Voltage stabilizer	
29	Temperature gauge	
30	Oil pressure sender	
31	Contact for overdrive on M41 gearbox	
32	Flashers warning lamp	1.2 W
33	Instrument lighting	2x3 W
34	Temperature gauge sensor	
35	Heater control light	3x1.2 W
36	Heater	
37	Windshield wipers	
38	Windshield washers	
39	Solenoid for overdrive on M41 gearbox	
40	Interior light 10 W	
41	Switch for heater	
42	Switch for windshield wipers and washers	
43	Panel light rheostat	
44	Light switch	
45	Ignition switch	
46	Cigarette lighter	
47	Door switch	
48	Switch for parking brake control	
49	Fuel gauge tank unit	
50	Reverse lights	32 CP
51	Brake stoplights	32 CP
52	Tail lights	5 W
53	License plate light	2x5 W
54	Switch for overdrive M41	
55	Brake warning switch	
56	Contact on gearbox BW 35	
57	Switch glove locker light	
58	Elec. heated rear window	
59	Switch, elec. heated rear window	
60	Side marker lights (USA only)	5 W
61	Main relay, starter switch	
62	Terminal at instrument	
63	Warning buzzer, ignition key	
64	Door switch on driver's side	
65	Connector	
66	Clock	
67	Tailgate window wiper	
68	Tailgate window washer	
69	Warning buzzer, headlights	
70	Switch for tailgate window wiper	
71	Switch for hazard warning flasher	
72	Shift positions light	
73	Choke warning lamp	
74	Choke control contact	
75	Diode	
76	Switch, seat buckle, passenger	
77	Switch, passenger seat	
78	Warning lamp, seat belts	
79	Buzzer, seat belts	
80	Relay, seat belts	
81	Contact, M40 - 41 gearbox	
82	Switch, seat buckle, driver	

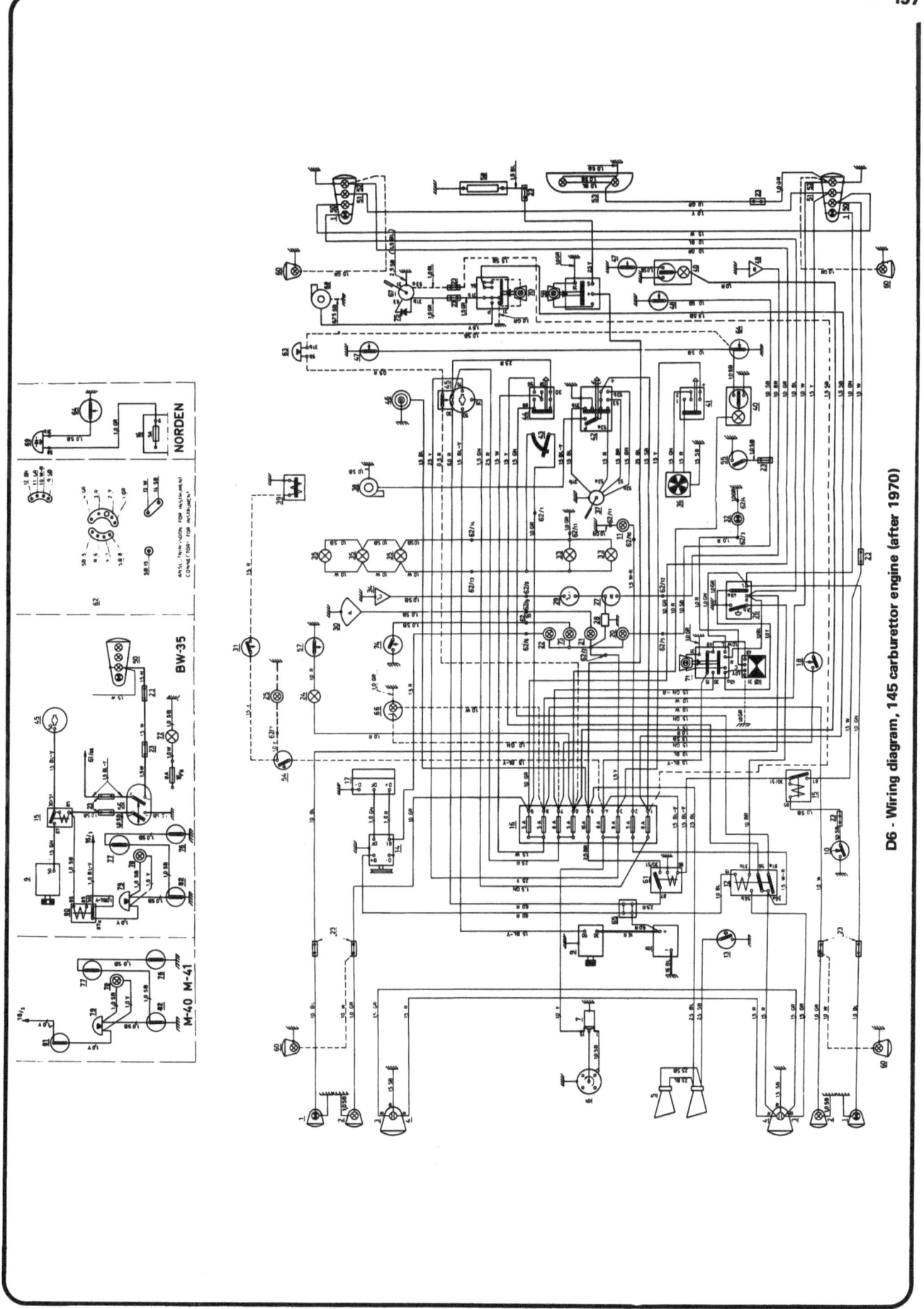

D6 - Wiring diagram, 145 carburettor engine (after 1970)

Key to wiring diagram - D7

Pos.	Title	Data
1	Dir. ind flashers	32 CP
2	Parking lights	5 W
3	Headlight dipped beams	40 W
4	Headlight main beams	45 W
5	Horn	
6	Distributor firing order	1-3-4-2
7	Ignition coil	
8	Battery	12V 60 Ah
9	Starter motor	1.0 hp
10	Contact for reverse light (M40 and M41 only)	
11	Main beam warning lamp	1.2 W
12	Step relay for main and dipped beams and headlight flashers	
13	Horn ring	
14	Alternator	12V 55 A
15	Relay for reverse light on M40, M41 and starter relay on BW 35	
16	Fusebox	
17	Charging regulator	
18	Brake switch	
19	Flasher unit	
20	Brake warning lamp	1.2 W
21	Oil pressure warning lamp	1.2 W
22	Battery charging warning lamp	1.2 W
23	Connector	
24	Glove locker light	2 W
25	Overdrive warning lamp M41	1.2 W
26	Warning buzzer, ignition key	
27	Fuel gauge	
28	Voltage stabilizer	
29	Temperature gauge	
30	Oil pressure switch	

Pos.	Title	Data
31	Switch for overdrive on M41 gearbox	
32	Headlight flashers warning lamp	1.2 W
33	Instrument lighting	2 x 3 W
34	Temperature gauge sensor	
35	Heater controls light	3 x 1.2 W
36	Heater	
37	Windshield wipers	
38	Windshield washers	
39	Solenoid for overdrive on M41 gearbox	10 W
40	Interior light	
41	Switch for heater	
42	Switch for windshield wipers and washers	
43	Instrument panel light rheostat	
44	Light switch	
45	Ignition switch	
46	Cigarette lighter	
47	Door switch	
48	Switch for parking brake control	
49	Fuel gauge tank unit	
50	Reverse light	15 W
51	Brake stop lights	25 W
52	Tail lights	5 W
53	License plate light	2 x 5 W
54	Switch for overdrive M41	
55	Brake warning switch	
56	Contact on transmission BW 35	
57	Switch glove locker light	
58	Elec. heated rear window	
59	Switch, elec. heated rear window	
60	Side marker lights (USA only)	
61	Main relay, starter switch, rear window	
62	Terminal at instrument panel	
63	Switch for dir. ind. and headlight flashers	

Pos.	Title	Data
64	Switch for hazard warning flashers	
65	Choke warning lamp	1.2 W
66	Choke control contact	
67	Clock	
68	Warning buzzer, headlights	
69	Connector	
70	Thermal timer contact	
71	Fuel pump	
72	Main relay for fuel injection	
73	Relay for fuel pump	
74	Pressure sensor	
75	Throttle valve switch	
76	Start valve	
77	Temperature sensor I	
78	Temperature sensor II	
79	Injection valves	
80	Triggering contacts	
81	Electronic control unit	
82	Spark plugs	
83	Fusebox	
84	Foglights	2 x 55 W
85	Relay for foglights	
86	Switch for foglights	
87	Shift positions light, aut. trans.	
88	Switch, seat buckle, passenger	
89	Switch, passenger seat	
90	Seat belts warning lamp	
91	Warning buzzer, seat belts	
92	Relay, seat belts	
93	Switch, M40, 41 gearbox	
94	Switch, seat buckle, driver	

Colour Code

SB Black, W White, Y Yellow, GN Green, GR Grey, BL Blue, R Red, BR Brown, BL-Y Blue-yellow, W-R White-red, GN-R Green-red

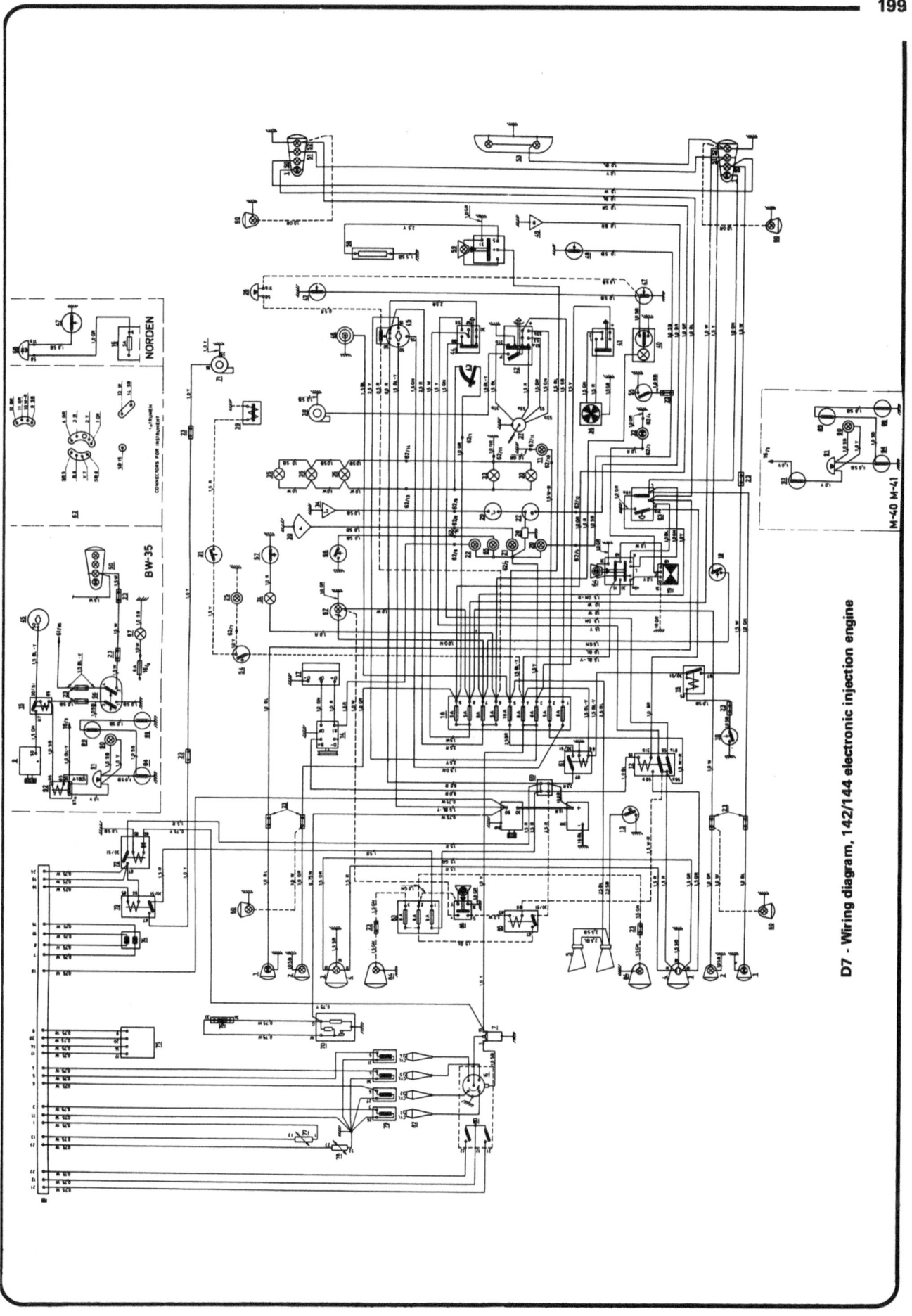

D7 - Wiring diagram, 142/144 electronic injection engine

Key to Wiring diagram - D8

Pos.	Title	Data
1	Battery	12 V 60 Ah
2	Connection box	
3	Ignition switch	
4	Ignition coil	
5	Distributor, firing sequence	1 - 3 - 4 - 2
6	Starter motor	
7	Alternator	
8	Charging regulator	
9	Fusebox	
10	Light switch	
11	Dip relay for main and dipped beams	
12	Headlights	45 W
13	Dipped beams	40 W
14	Position light	5 W
15	Rear lights	5 W
16	Side marking lights	5 W
17	Plate light	2 × 5 W
18	Brake stoplight contact	
19	Brake stoplights	32 cp
20	Connection at instrument	
21	Contact on gearbox M 40, M 41	
22	Reverse lights	32 cp
23	Flasher unit	
24	Direction indicator switch	
25	Switch, emergency warning flashers	
26	Flasher lights	32 cp
27	Part of 6-pole connection block	
28	Rev counter	
29	Thermometer	
30	Fuel gauge	
31	Voltage stabilizer	
32	Flasher light warning lamp	1.2 W
33	Diode	

Pos.	Title	Data
34	Warning lamp for main beams	1.2 W
35	Warning lamp for battery charging	1.2 W
36	Parking brake warning lamp	1.2 W
37	Choke warning lamp	1.2 W
38	Oil pressure warning lamp	1.2 W
39	Brake warning lamp	1.2 W
40	Vacant warning lamp	
41	Parking brake contact	
42	Choke control contact	
43	Temperature sensor	
44	Oil pressure sensor	
45	Brake warning contact	
46	Brake level sender	
47	Horn	
48	Horn ring	
49	Switch, windshield wipers/washer	
50	Windshield wipers	
51	Windshield washer	
52	Switch, fan	
53	Fan	
54	Switch, elec. heated rear window	
55	Elec. heated rear window	
56	Clock	
57	Cigarette lighter	
58	Rheostat for instrument panel lighting	
59	Instrument panel lighting	3 × 2 W
60	Lighting for control panel	3 × 1.2 W
61	Shift positions light, aut. trans.	1.2 W
62	Glove locker contact	
63	Glove locker lamp	
64	Interior lamp	
65	Door switch on left side	
66	Door switch on right side	

Pos.	Title	Data
67	Reminder buzzer for ignition key	
68	Joint	
69	Connection at instrument	
70	Passenger seat contact	
71	Reminder buzzer for seat belt	
72	Seat belt warning lamp	1.2 W
73	Contact for seat belt	
74	Switch for overdrive M 41	
75	Contact for overdrive on gearbox M 41	
76	Solenoid for overdrive on gearbox M 41	
77	Overdrive warning lamp	1.2 W
78	Contact on automatic transmission BW 35	
79	Reminder buzzer for lights	
80	Switch for elec. heated tailgate window	
81	Tailgate window wiper	
82	Tailgate window washer	
83	Rear roof light	10 W
84	Control unit	
85	Throttle valve switch	
86	Pressure sensor	
87	Relay for fuel pump	
88	Main relay for fuel injection	
89	Thermal timer contact	
90	Start valve	
91	Temperature sensor I	
92	Temperature sensor II	
93	Injection valves	
94	Trip contact	
95	Spark plug	
96	Fuse box	
97	Fuel pump	
98	Connection at instrument	
99	Connection at instrument	

Colour code

SB	Black	Bl-R	Blue-Red	W-R	White-Red
Y	Yellow	Gn-R	Green-Red	W	White
Bl	Blue	R	Red	Br	Brown
Bl-Y	Blue-Yellow	Gn	Green	Gr	Grey

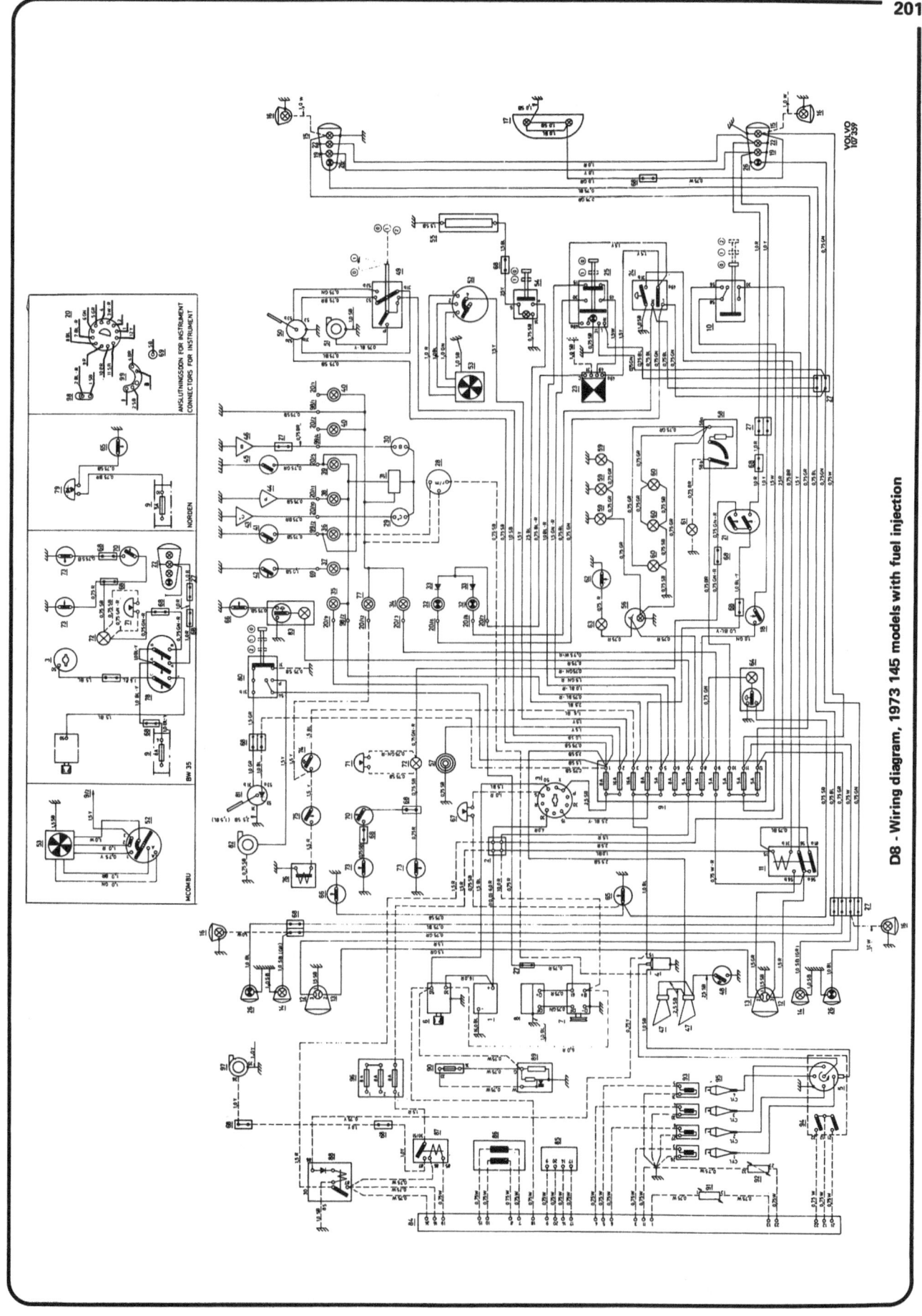

D8 - Wiring diagram, 1973 145 models with fuel injection

Chapter 11 Front suspension and steering

Contents

Specifications

Front springs

Type	Helical spring
Wire thickness	15.0 mm (0.59 in.)
Outer diameter	126.0 mm (4.96 in.)
Total number of turns	8.7
Test values:	
Loading for a compression of 1 cm (25/64 in.) (measured within a spring length of 185.5 - 205.5 mm = (7.3 - 8.1 in.)	52.7 - 56.7 kg (115 - 125 lb.)
Length, fully compressed	max. 125 mm (4.9 in.)
Length when loaded with 540 - 570 kg (1188 - 1254 lb.) ...	195.5 mm (7.7 in.)

Steering gear

Number of turns from lock to lock	4.15
Steering gear reduction ration	17.5 : 1
Lubricant, see under 'Lubrication'	
Oil capacity	Approx. 0.25 litre (0.4 Imp. pint, 0.5 US pint)

Wheel alignment (unloaded vehicle)

Caster	0 to +1°
Camber	0 to +0.5°
King pin inclination at a camber of 0°	7.5°
Toe-in	2 to 5 mm (0.08 - 0.20 in.)
Turning angles:	
At a 20° turn of the outer wheel the inner wheel should be turned 21.5° to 23.5°	
Shims, thickness	0.15 mm (0.006 in.)
	0.50 mm (0.020 in.)
	1.0 mm (0.039 in.)
	3.0 mm (0.118 in.)
	6.0 mm (0.236 in.)

Torque wrench settings

	kg m	lb. ft.
Nut, engine mounting	2.1 - 2.5	15 - 18
Nut, steering knuckle	7	50
Nut, upper control arm shaft	5.5 - 6.2	40 - 45
Nut, lower control arm shaft	14 - 18	100 - 130
Bolt for upper control arm shaft	5.5 - 7	40 - 50
Nut, upper ball joint	8.5 - 10	60 - 70

Nut, lower ball joint	...	...	...	...	...	...	10 - 12		75 - 90
Steering wheel nut	...	...	...	...	...	...	2.8 - 4		20 - 30
Bolt, steering box flange	...	...	...	...	...	...	3.5 - 4		25 - 30
Nut for pitman arm	...	...	...	...	...	...	17 - 20		125 - 145
Attaching nut, steering box and idler arm shaft	...	...	...	3.5 - 4		25 - 30
Locknut for tie rod	...	...	...	...	...	...	7.5 - 9		55 - 65
Nut for steering rod and tie rod	M 10	...	...	...	...	3.2 - 3.7		23 - 27
	3/8 - 24 UNF		...	...	3.2 - 3.7		23 - 27
	7/16 - 20 UNF		...	...	4.8 - 6.2		35 - 45
Wheel nut	...	...	...	...	...	...	...	10 - 14		70 - 100

1 Front suspension - general description

1 This is quite conventional in design (Fig.11.1). The suspension comprises upper and lower wishbones which are attached to steering knuckles by ball and socket joints. The shafts pivoting the lower wishbones pass through holes in the front axle member and their position is fixed. The upper wishbone shafts are bolted to the axle member and their distance from it can be adjusted by shims. By this means the top of the steering knuckle can be moved relative to the bottom to adjust castor and camber (photo).

2 The wishbones act against coil springs, and inside these springs are mounted telescopic shock absorbers. (photo).

3 This simple but effective suspension is completed by an anti-roll bar. This bar passes through bushes to the main body of the vehicle, and its ends are attached by long bolts and spacers to lugs on the lower wishbone. If, for example, the right-hand wheel is suddenly raised, the anti-roll bar will pivot on its bushes and tend to raise the left-hand wheel too, thus reducing the tendency to roll.

4 The front hubs are carried on their stub axles by taper roller bearings. Note that the stub axles are integral with the steering knuckles, as are the steering arms, so that whether the text refers to stub axles, steering arm or steering knuckle it is talking about the same piece.

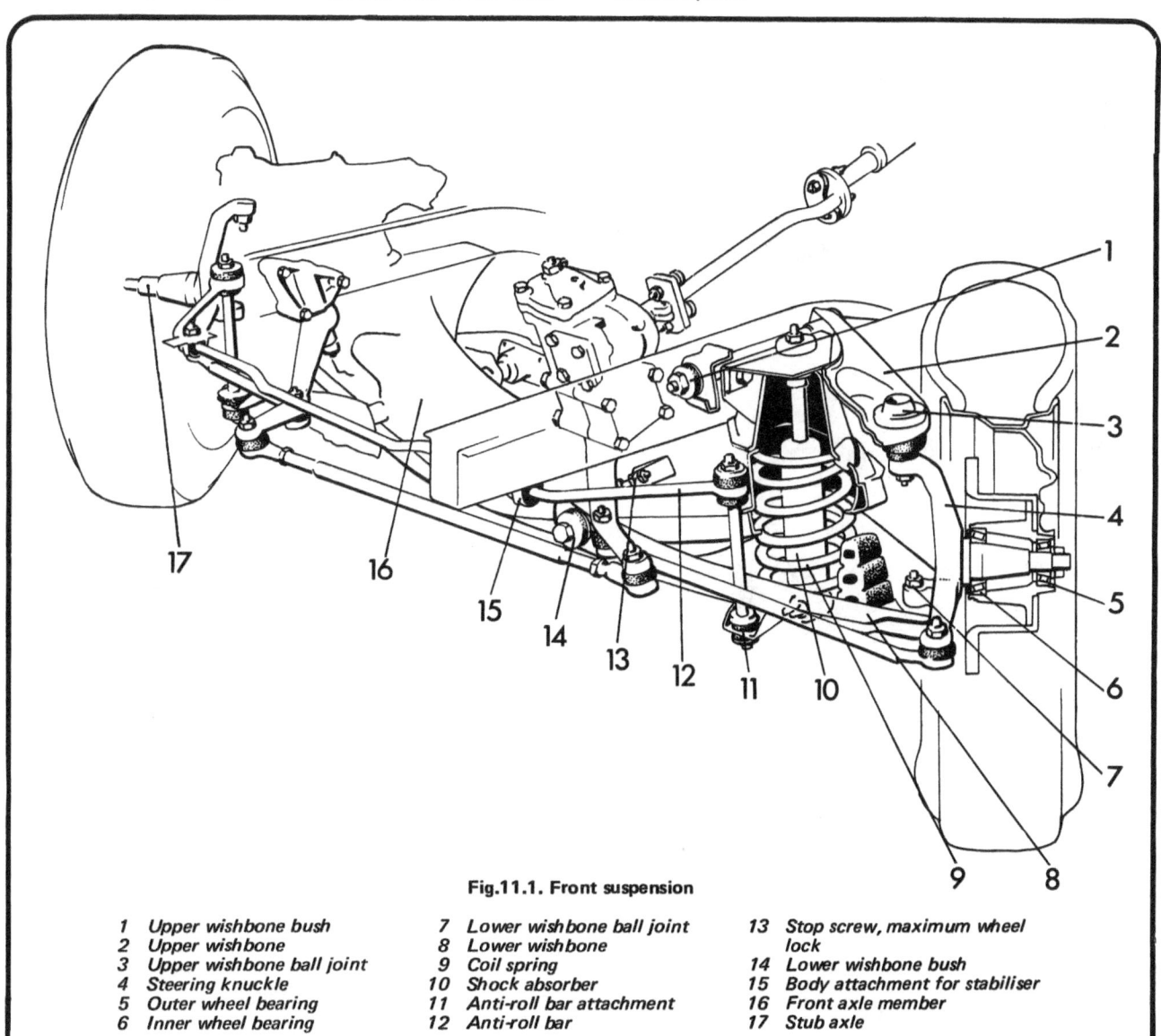

Fig.11.1. Front suspension

1	Upper wishbone bush	7	Lower wishbone ball joint	13	Stop screw, maximum wheel lock
2	Upper wishbone	8	Lower wishbone		
3	Upper wishbone ball joint	9	Coil spring	14	Lower wishbone bush
4	Steering knuckle	10	Shock absorber	15	Body attachment for stabiliser
5	Outer wheel bearing	11	Anti-roll bar attachment	16	Front axle member
6	Inner wheel bearing	12	Anti-roll bar	17	Stub axle

1.1 Steering linkages - rhd. 1 Drop arm. 2 Steering box. 3 Lower wishbone. 4 Rod fixed at top to anti-roll bar. 5 Steering rod fixed to knuckle and drop arm. 6 Tie rod (other end fixed to relay arm)

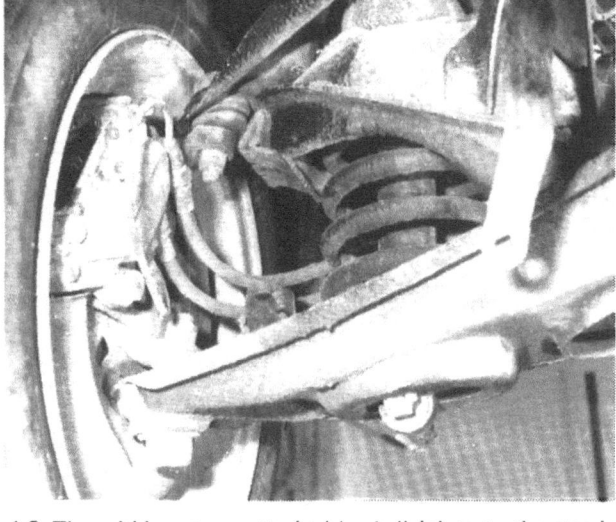

1.2 The wishbones are attached by ball joints to the steering knuckles. Clearly shown is the coil spring with the shock absorber inside it

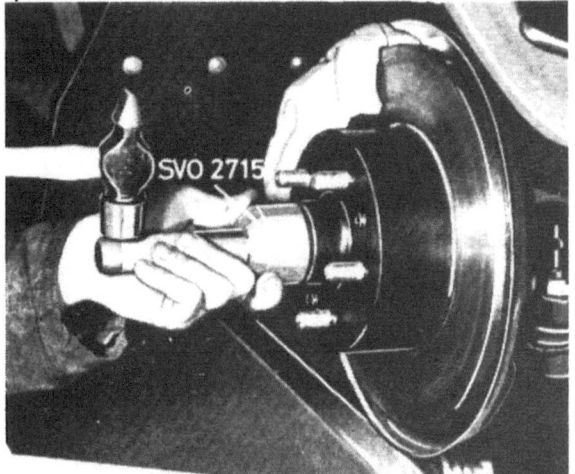

Fig.11.2. Removing grease cap

Fig.11.3. Pulling off the hub

2   Front hubs - stripping

1   Jack up the front of the car and transfer the weight to a block under the lower wishbone. This will ensure that everything is rigid for the rest of the operation.
2   Take off the wheel. Remove front brake unit as described in Chapter 9.
3   Clean all round the hub. Remember that dirt is death to bearings.
4   Remove the grease cap. Fig.11.2 shows this being done with the Volvo special tool, but a Mole or Vise-grip wrench carefully used is an adequate substitute.
5   Remove the split pin, castle nut and washer.
6   Pull off the hub with a suitable puller. It is easy to knock-up a substitute for the Volvo tool shown in Fig.11.3.
7   The inner hub bearing will most likely remain on the stub axle, though it may come off with the hub. Remove it if necessary using a puller like the one shown in Fig.11.4.

3   Front hub overhaul

1   Drift the rear bearings and the oil seal out of the hub if they

Fig.11.4. The expansion sleeve puller designed by Volvo for removing the inner hub bearing

are still in it.

2 Wash the grease away from the stub axle, hub and bearings, giving the bearings a final clean with white spirit to get rid of every trace of old grease and cleaning fluid.

3 It is essential that the bearings are completely clean and dry, but this drying should be carried out with clean lint-free rags, and certainly not with compressed air which often contains water and dust particles.

4 Check that the rollers are bright and shiny.

5 Check that the outer and inner races are without blemish.

6 If there is any sign of rust, blueing or scoring, the offending components must be replaced.

7 Drifting out the bearing races is shown in Fig.11.5. Notice how, in removing the inner race, you solve the problem of getting a large drift through a small hole.

4 Front hub reassembly and adjustment

1 If new bearings are being fitted, smear them with grease before pressing them into the hub.

2 Line the hub with grease.

3 Grease the inner bearing thoroughly, working grease well into the rollers. Insert it into the hub, making sure it is the right way round.

4 Press the oil seal into the hub. The felt ring should be well coated with light engine oil.

5 Smear the stub axle with grease, and thread the hub on to the axle, carefully centring it so that the felt ring on the oil seal does not get damaged.

6 Push the front bearing over the stub axle and into the hub - right way round of course.

7 Fill the assembly with grease up to the outer end of the outer bearing.

8 Thread on the washer and screw up the castle nut. Rotate the hub to and fro as you tighten the nut to make sure that everything beds down properly.

9 Tighten the castle nut to a torque of 50 lb ft (6.9 kg m). Do not exceed this torque. Now slacken the nut off a third of a turn.

10 If you can now get the pins through the hole in the stub axle, do so, otherwise slacken off the nut until the pin can be fitted. Check that the wheel turns easily without play.

11 Fill the grease cap half full of grease and gently tap it home

with a hide mallet or similar.

5 Upper ball joints - checking for wear

1 Jack up the lower wishbone until the wheel is clear of the ground.

2 Try to rock the wheel in and out vertically, holding it at its highest and lowest points. If this shows up any clearance in the upper ball joint, it should be replaced.

3 Be quite sure you do not mistake play in the wheel bearings for wear in the ball joints. If you are not sure, get someone to keep the brakes on while you check.

6 Lower ball joints - checking wear

1 For this check the vehicle should be standing on the ground with the wheels pointing forwards.

2 Make a single gauge like the one shown in Fig.11.6. Its dimensions will depend on which of two possible types of ball joint you have - the difference between types is shown in the Figure and is quite obvious. Type 1 has been superseded by Type 2.

3 If the gauge can be fitted over the ball joint as shown in the Figure, all is well, but if not the ball joint should be replaced.

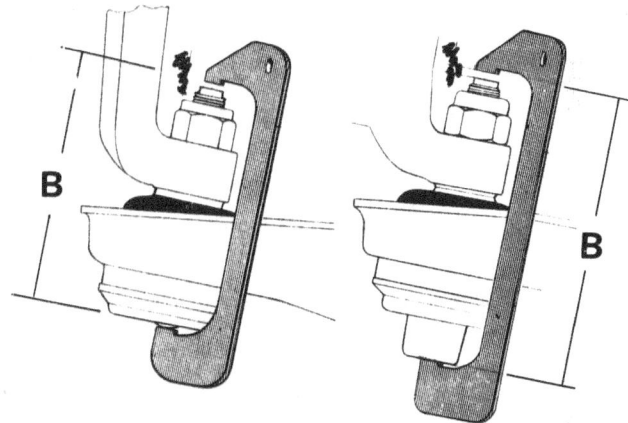

Fig.11.6. Test gauges for lower wishbone ball joints

Type 1 'B' = 3.91" (99.3 mm)
Type 2 'B' = 4.5" (113.0 mm)

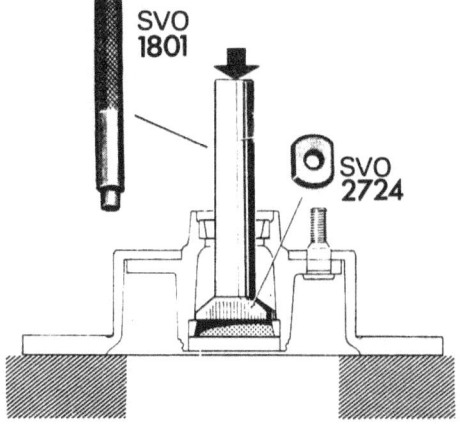

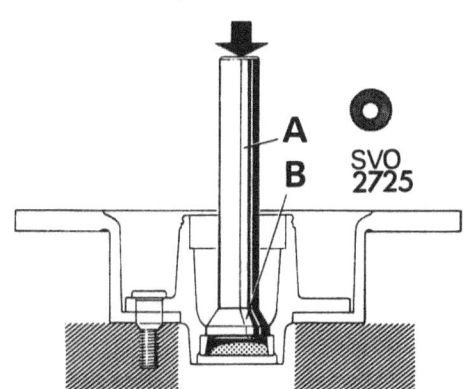

Fig.11.5. Drifting out the hub bearing rings

7   Ball joints - removal

1   This is one of those jobs where having suitable tools saves an enormous amount of time and trouble. Illustrations show the press tools and assortment of sleeves used in Volvo garages, and you can see from these the sort of thing that is wanted. If you are using makeshift devices out of bits of tubing and long bolts you may well find it easier to remove the wishbones and have them on the work bench where you can get at them more easily. Removal of the wishbone is described in Sections 11 and 12.

2   If your tools are adequate, then without doubt the simplest way is to remove the joints with the wishbones still in the vehicle as described.

8   Upper ball joint - removal

1   Jack up the front end of the vehicle and remove the wheels.

2   Slacken, but do not remove, the nut for the upper ball joint.

3   Tap off steering knuckle with a hammer round where the ball joint pin enters it, holding something heavy, such as another hammer, against the side of the knuckle opposite where you are tapping. This will loosen the pin.

4   Slacken the upper wishbone shaft nuts by half a turn. This prevents damage to the rubber bushes when the wishbone is rotated. Remove the nut from the ball joint pin, raise the wishbone clear of the steering knuckle and press out the ball joint (see Fig.11.7). Don't let the upper wishbone hang down and strain the brake hoses. Tie it up with a bit of wire or string.

9   Upper ball joint - installing

1   Before fitting the ball joint check that the rubber cover is filled with grease. Bend the pin end over the slot and check that the grease forces its way out. If necessary top up with Castrol LM Grease or similar grease.

2   Press the ball joint into the wishbone, making sure that the slot lies along the longitudinal centre line of the wishbone within plus or minus 8°, ie that it points directly inwards or directly outwards (Fig. 11.70) as the pin has maximum movement along this line. If the ball joint goes in crooked, turn the press tool half a turn and continue pressing.

3   Bring down the wishbone and let the ball joint pin enter its hole on the steering knuckle. Tighten wishbone shaft nuts.

4   Thread the nut on to the ball joint pin (no washer here - the nut is a self-locking one) and tighten it up against the steering knuckle. Don't let the ball joint rotate in the wishbone while doing this. If necessary, use a clamp (see Fig.11.8).

10   Lower ball joint - removal

1   Start off as though you were going to remove the upper ball joint as described above, but before freeing the upper wishbone, carry out paragraphs 2 and 3 below.

2   Disconnect the steering rod from the steering arm and disconnect the brake lines from the stabiliser bolt.

3   Loosen the nuts from the lower ball joint and tap round the pin as described for the upper ball joint until it loosens.

4   Raise the lower wishbone with a jack, remove the nut from the upper ball joint pin and free the upper wishbone as previously described.

5   Remove the nut from the lower ball joint pin and lift away the steering knuckle/stub axle/brake unit assembly.

6   Press the ball joint out of the lower control arm (see Fig.11,9a).

11   Lower ball joint - installing

1   The procedure for this is exactly as for the upper ball joint

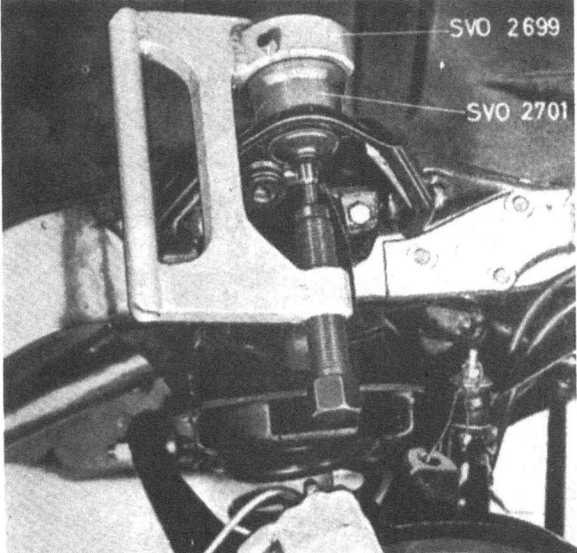

Fig.11.7a. Pressing out the upper ball joint.....

Fig.11.7b.... and fitting its replacement, making certain.....

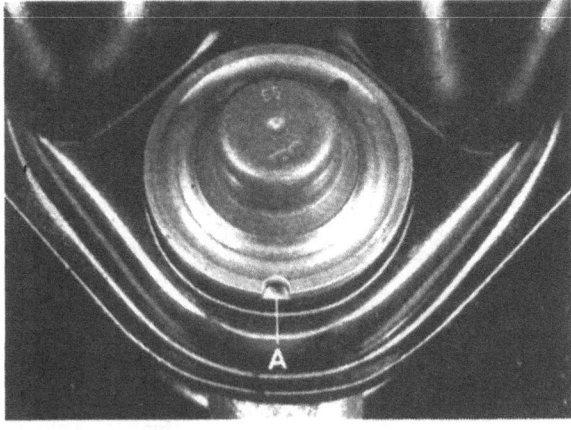

Fig.11.7c..... that it is correctly located (A = slot)

Fig.11.8. Clamping the upper ball joint

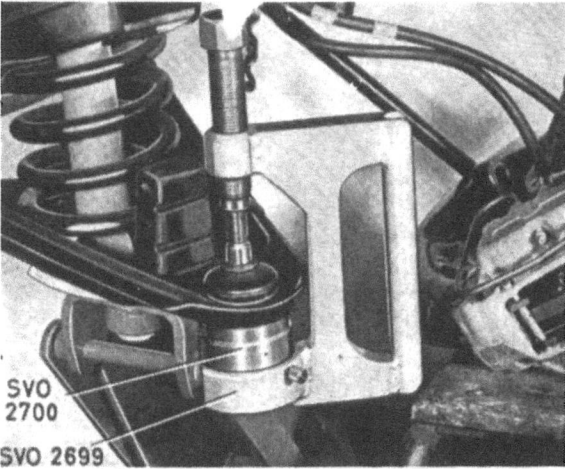

Fig.11.9a. Pressing out the lower ball joint .....

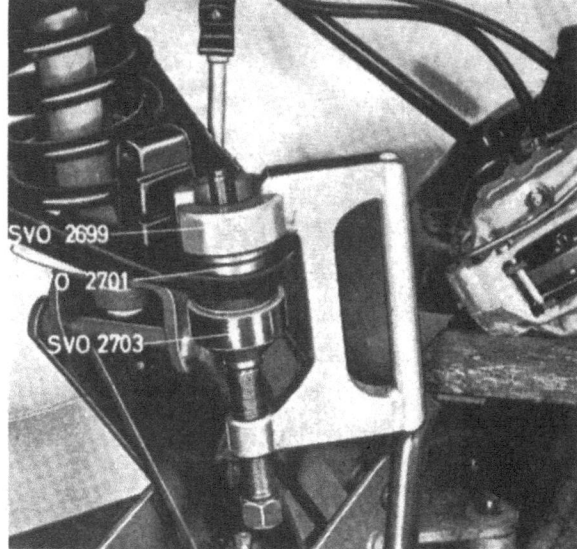

Fig.11.9b. ....and pressing in a new one

except that there is no slot to be positioned. As before, check that the rubber cover is filled with grease by forcing the pin to one side, when grease should be forced out. If this does not happen, then fill the rubber cover with grease.

2 Fit the lower ball joint exactly as described for the upper ball joint, clamping if necessary (Fig.11.9b).

3 After refitting the steering rod, remove the jack from under the lower wishbone, point the steering straight ahead and fasten the brake hoses to the stabiliser bolt.

4 All that now remains is to refit the wheel, tightening its nuts of course after you have lowered the vehicle to the ground.

12 Upper wishbone - removal

1 Start off as though you were going to remove the upper ball joint (Section 11.8). Be careful not to strain the brake hoses.

2 Having removed the ball joint pin from the steering knuckle, remove the screws for the control arm shaft as shown in Fig. 11.10. These are so awkward to get at that Volvo provide their garages with a special tool for the job. You may be successful with a crank ring spanner, but what you really need is a socket spanner kit with a universal joint.

3 Remove the screws attaching the control arm shaft to the main member. Mark the shims so that you know which are the front and which are the back ones. It is essential that when the arm is replaced these shims are put back in the same position as they were originally, because they affect the wheel geometry.

13 Lower wishbone - removal

1 Jack up the vehicle at the front jack attachments. Remove the wheels.

2 Remove the shock absorber as described in Section 16.

3 Disconnect the steering rod from the steering arm by pressing out the threaded pin (unscrewing the nut first of course), as shown in Fig. 11.11. Don't be tempted to use a hammer - or if you do, don't blame us for distorted steering arms!

4 Loosen the clamps for the brake hoses and remove the screw holding the anti-roll bar.

5 Jack up the lower control arm, loosen the nuts for the ball joints and tap round with a hammer until the ball joints loosen from the steering knuckle. Remove the nuts, lower the jack, remove the steering knuckle and front brake assembly.

6 Lower the jack and remove the spring.

7 Remove the nuts from the wishbone shaft and pull this out. It will help you if you move the wishbone about while you are doing this. The wishbone can now be taken away.

Fig.11.10. Removing the screws on the upper wishbone shaft. Note the shims (A) used for adjusting castor and camber

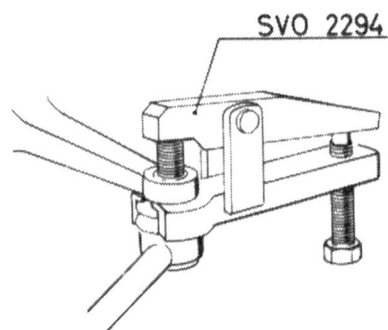

Fig.11.11. Pressing out the steering rod ball joint from the steering arm

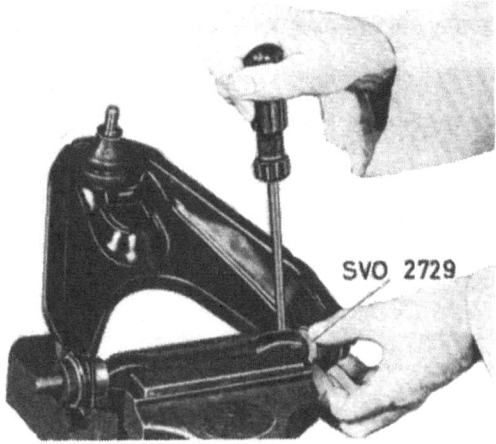

Fig.11.12a. Inset is a Volvo tool, but you can make one yourself out of a washer. It fits between the upper wishbone shaft and its bush and makes driving out the bush a lot easier

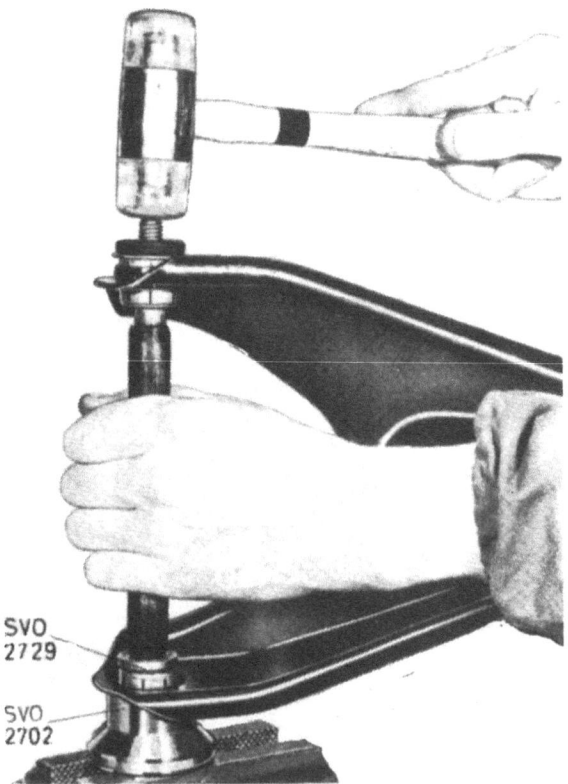

Fig.11.12b. Here it is doing its stuff

14 Removing and replacing wishbone bushes

1   The official Volvo instructions make this seem terribly difficult but it is all a matter of simple common sense. The Fig. 11.12 shows you what is involved.

2   In the upper wishbone, the flange of both bushes are on the outside, ie the flange of the front bush faces forwards and the flange of the back bush faces the rear. Don't forget to insert the wishbone shaft before you drive in the second bush!

3   In the lower wishbone the flanges of both the bushes face the rear of the vehicle ie the flange of the front bush is on the inside of the wishbone and the flange of the back bush is on the outside.

4   For the lower wishbone only, you need different bushes for cars fitted with radial tyres than for cross-ply. The Fig.11.13 shows what a radial ply bush looks like and tells you what position the lowest recess should occupy.

15 Refitting the wishbones

1   Generally speaking this is simply a reversal of the removal procedures. Some points to note follow.

2   For the upper wishbone, naturally you will assemble the nuts and washers on the ends of the shafts before fitting, but tightening to the correct torque of 40/45 lb ft (5.5/6.2 kg m) is more easily done after the wishbone has been fitted on the vehicle. Be sure that you have refitted the shims in the positions they occupied previously.

3   Note that the screws attaching the wishbone shaft to the vehicle contain nylon locking plugs. If you are in any doubt about the effectiveness of these they should be renewed. Faced with this sort of instruction and bearing in mind that lives might depend on these two screws, they should be renewed regardless.

4   For the lower wishbone, thread the washer and rubber spacer ring on to the shaft and insert this at the front. Don't forget that there is another washer facing the flange of the front bush (Fig. 11.14 makes this clear) and finally a washer over the flange of the rear bush. Tighten the nut to a torque of 40/45 lb ft (5.5/6.2 kg m).

5   When tightening the nuts on the upper and lower wishbone shafts, see that the wishbones are approximately horizontal.

6   For refitting the shock absorber and spring see Section 16.

16 Front shock absorbers and springs

1   **The front shock absorbers** are completely sealed, require no maintenance and cannot be dismantled. There is not much point therefore in giving a detailed description of the design, so all we will say here is that they are hydraulic and depend for their action on simple valves in a piston which moves up and down in a cylinder filled with hydraulic fluid. When they are in working order it is three times as hard to pull them out as it is to push them in, and they operate with complete smoothness in both directions.

2   **Shock absorbers - checking** The time-honoured method of rocking the car up and down will reveal any significant difference between the shock absorbers which will indicate that one of them is faulty. Noticeable leakage of fluid would, of course. be a danger signal but this happens so rarely that Volvo do not think it worth mentioning. It is safe to say that if there is no obvious difference in the operation of the two shock absorbers, all is well. The method of attaching the front shock absorbers is shown in Fig. 11.15, and in Fig. 11.16. To remove, undo the nut at the top. Take off the washer and the upper bush. Undo the two screws at the lower end, and withdraw the shock absorber downwards through the spring. Installation is a straightforward reversal of this process. Don't forget to put back the spacing piece between the bushes at the top.

3   **Front springs - removal** With the shock absorber removed, proceed as though you were going to remove the lower

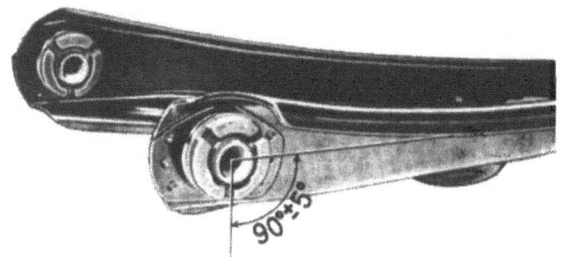

Fig.11.13. Lower wishbone - correct placing of bushes for radial tyres

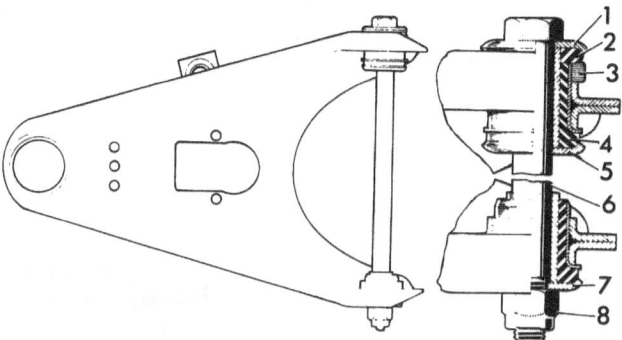

Fig.11.14. Lower wishbone showing shaft assembly

1 Washer
2 Rubber rings
3 Spacer ring
4 Bush
5 Washer
6 Wishbone shaft
7 Washer
8 Nut

Fig.11.15. Lower attachment, front shock absorber

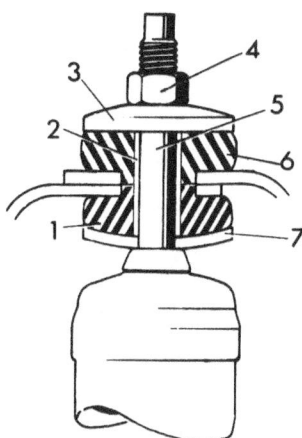

Fig.11.16. Upper attach-
ment, front shock
absorber

1 Rubber bush
2 Spacing sleeve
3 Washer
4 Nut
5 Spindle
6 Rubber bush
7 Washer

wishbone, except that you do not actually have to remove the wishbone. When the wishbone is lowered, the spring can be taken out.

4 Front springs - installation The only point to watch is the spacer at the top of the spring. Some models have a single rubber spacer and others have a metal spacer as well; left-hand and right-hand spacers may be different. Bear this in mind if you are replacing them. It is best to take the originals to your spares stockist and to quote the model and chassis number.

5 If you are replacing a faulty front spring, always replace its opposite number even if it has nothing wrong with it. Springs should be supplied in pairs matched for load and spring length. Earlier models were fitted with a slightly different spring than that specified in this Manual, but replacement with the later type is quite in order.

17 Steering gear - general description

1 The layout of the steering is shown in Fig.11.17. To each steering knuckle is connected a steering rod. The right-hand steering rod goes to the relay arm which in turn is connected to the tie-rod, this being connected to the drop arm. The left-hand steering rod goes direct from its knuckle to the drop arm.

2 The ball joints of the steering rods are plastic lined, which makes maintenance lubrication unnecessary. To replace these the steering rods are replaced complete.

3 The relay arm is bushed to the sub-axle held by a bracket on the right-hand side of the car.

4 This description refers to cars with left-hand drive. For right-hand drive cars, read "left" for "right" and vice versa. For a view of the layout for right-hand drive, see photo 25.7.

5 The working of the steering box is obvious from Fig.11.18 except for the method of adjusting the clearance between the drop arm shaft roller and the steering worm. The centre line of the roller is slightly above the centre line of the worm, and as the drop arm shaft is pushed down by the adjusting screw the two centre lines get closer together.

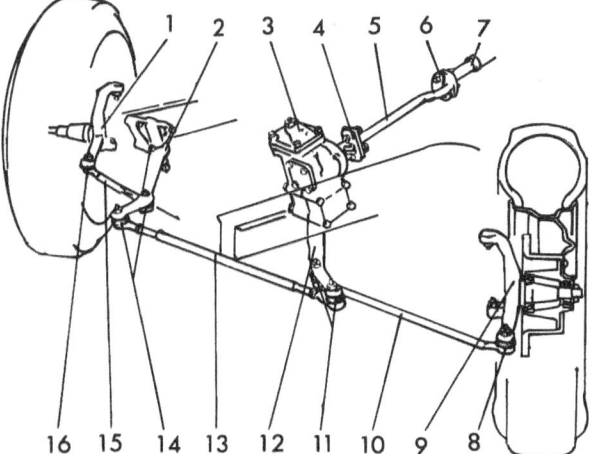

Fig.11.17. Steering gear (left-hand drive)

1 Steering knuckle, right
2 Relay arm
3 Steering box
4 Lower steering column flange
5 Lower steering column section
6 Upper steering column flange
7 Upper steering column section
8 Ball joint
9 Steering knuckle, left
10 Steering rod, left
11 Ball joint
12 Drop arm
13 Tie rod
14 Ball joint
15 Steering rod, right
16 Ball joint

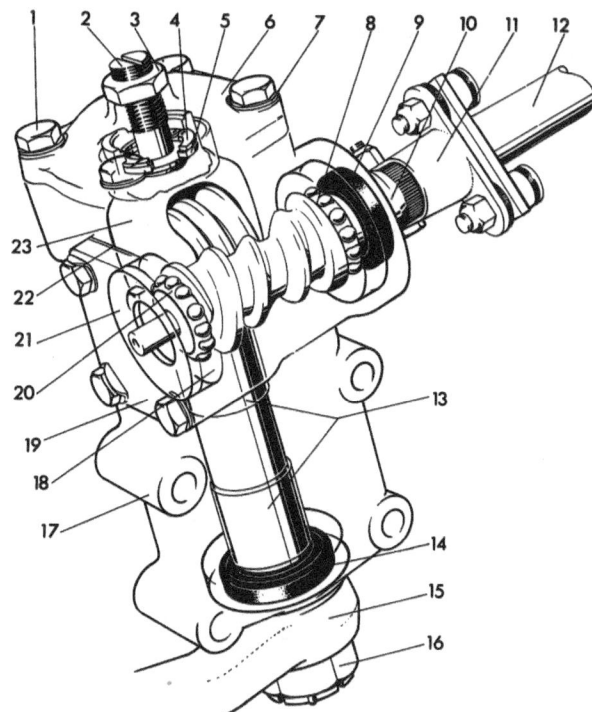

Fig.11.18. Steering box

1 Bolt	13 Bushes, drop arm shaft
2 Adjusting screw, drop arm shaft	14 Oil seal, drop arm shaft
3 Locknut	15 Drop arm
4 Circlips	16 Nut
5 Adjusting washer	17 Steering box
6 Cover	18 Lower bearing race, steering cam
7 Tab washer	19 Worm shaft cover
8 Upper ball bearing, steering cam	20 Lower ball bearing, steering
9 Oil seal, steering cam	worm shaft
10 Steering worm shaft	21 Spacer
11 Flange	22 Spacer
12 Lower steering column section	23 Drop arm shaft

18 Steering rods and ball joints - checking and replacement

1   If bent, the steering rods and tie rod should not be straightened out but should be replaced. The steering rod ball joints are integral with the steering rods so that when these are worn the whole steering rod must be replaced.

2   The steering rods are marked L and R and the marked end should be fitted to the steering knuckle. In left-hand drive cars the relay arm is fitted on the right-hand side and the steering box on the left. In this case, the L and R marks on replacement tie rods may be wrong but they will still show which end should be fitted to the knuckle.

3   The ball joints of the tie rod can be replaced individually. Press them out of their locations in the relay arm and drop arm, remove the tie rod, marking the end that went ot the relay arm. Unscrew the locknuts and the ball joints, remembering that one of them has a left-hand thread. Screw in the new ball joints the same distance as the old ones; this will make less work when - as you must - you re-set the toe-in after replacing the tie rod.

4   The steering column is in two sections, coupled by a safety device which allows them to separate if the front end of the car is pushed in. The arrangement of the upper section is shown in Fig.11.19. It runs in two ball bearings in a jacket which is attached to the body through rubber bushes. The steering wheel lock is shown in Fig. 11.20 which clearly illustrates the way it

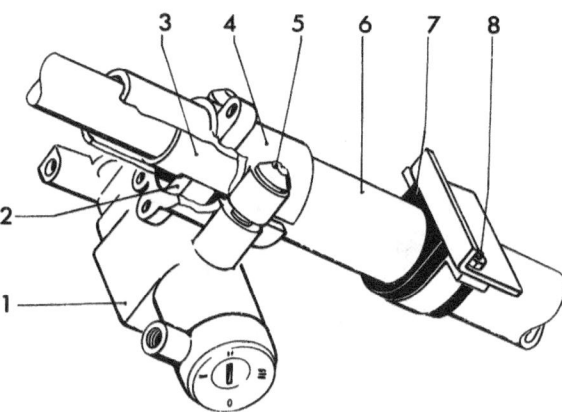

Fig.11.20. Steering wheel lock

1 Steering wheel lock	5 Shear-off bolt
2 Lock pin	6 Steering column jacket
3 Lock sleeve	7 Attachment
4 Cap	8 Shear-off bolt

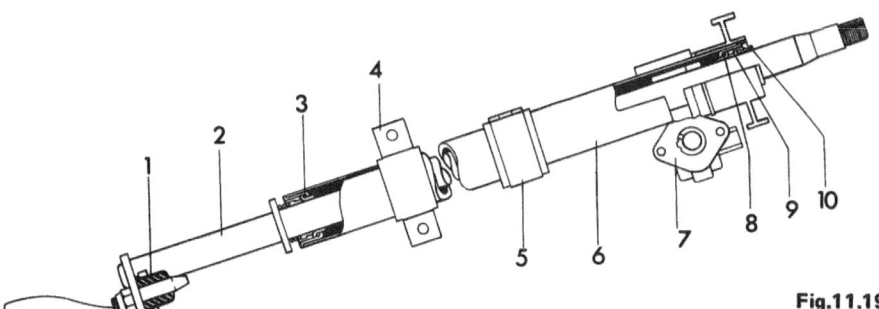

Fig.11.19. Steering column assembly

1 Safety mechanism	6 Steering column jacket
2 Upper steering column section	7 Steering wheel lock
3 Lower bearing	8 Upper bearing
4 Lower attachment	9 Seat
5 Upper attachment	10 Spring

19.1a Remove the upper direction indicator switch housing (held by one screw in the middle)

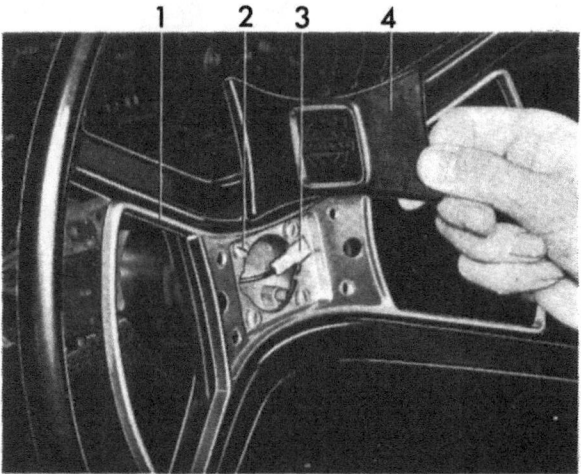

Fig.11.21a. Pull out the impact protector (4) (larger than this in some models) undo screws (2) and remove horn ring (1) with associated bits and pieces. This reveals steering wheel fixing nut which you undo and then.....

Fig.11.21b..... pull off the steering wheel

works. When the ignition key is removed the lock pin is sprung against the steering column and engages in a slot when the steering is set straight ahead. The lock and the upper steering jacket attachment are fitted with shear-off bolts to make tampering difficult. They have been known to cause annoyance to the honest repairer trying to loosen them with a hammer and punch or cold chisel when this slips and hits the paintwork.

19 Steering wheel - removing and installing

1　The removal procedure is clearly shown in the photo and Fig.11.21 and explained in their captions. The remaining paragraphs deal with installation.
2　If you are fitting a replacement steering wheel, remember to attach the indicator switch flange from the old steering wheel before you start.
3　Make sure that the wheels are pointing straight forwards.
4　Place the steering wheel in position and tighten the wheel nut to a torque of 20 - 30 lb ft (3 - 4 kg m).
5　Refit the horn ring and springs. Check that the horn works, and if necessary adjust as described in Chapter 10.

20 Steering column bearings - relacement

1　If the lower bearing is damaged or defective, the whole steering column shaft assembly must be replaced. The upper bearing can be replaced separately as follows:-
2　Remove the steering wheel as just described. Remove the lower part of the directional indicator switch housing.
3　Remove the directional indicator switch and then the switch anchorage from the steering wheel column.
4　Pull out the spring and seat (Fig.11.22).
5　Remove the old bearing and thoroughly clean the shaft and housing.
6　Fit the bearing after having greased it with universal grease (Castrol LM Grease).
7　Reassembly is the reverse of dismantling.

21 Replacing steering column assembly

1　Disconnect the positive battery lead. Only this way can you be certain you will get no damage from shorts. Remove the

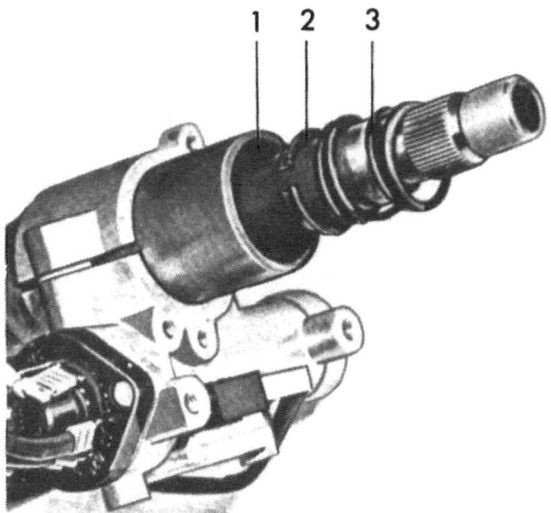

Fig.11.22. Steering column upper bearing

The spring (3) pushes the cone or seat (2) against balls in the bearing (1)

screws between the lower steering column section and the rubber coupling in the safety device.

2 Remove the steering wheel as described in Section 19.

3 Take off the lower part of the directional indicator switch housing, remove the directional indicator switch and its attachment, the ignition/starter switch and, where fitted, the anti-theft warning buzzer switch. Let the switches remain hanging on their wires.(Fig.11.23).

4 Remove the panel under the dashboard which covers a bracket holding the assembly to the main framework. Remove this bracket.

5 Remove the shear-off screws in the upper steering column attachment. The best way to tackle these is with a screw extractor - a device like a taper tap with a left-hand thread. Drill a hole down the middle of the bolt and screw the extractor in anti-clockwise. When it jams in, the screw will start to undo. Be sure you use the right size extractor for the bolt (3/16 inches or 8 mm) and the right size drill for the extractor - otherwise you will be in trouble. If you have not got one a Mole or Vise-grip wrench may well do the trick. The hammer and cold chisel mentioned earlier on shouldn't really be necessary.

6 Having triumphed over the tamper-proof bolts, you can now remove the steering column complete with jacket and bearing.

7 If you are going to use the old steering lock with the replacement steering column assembly, you have two more shear off screws to remove. These are the same diameter as the previous ones.

8 Fit the new parts in reverse order to removal. Adjust the location of the steering jacket so that the distance between the dashboard and directional indicator housing is correct.

9 Be quite sure that everything is in perfect order before you shear-off those four bolts!

22 Replacing the steering wheel lock

1 Follow the procedure in paragraphs 1-3 of the previous Section, except that you don't remove the screws in the safety device.

2 Before removing the steering wheel lock, mark its position on the steering column assembly. You can then put the new one in exactly the same position as the old one and save a lot of fiddling about.

3 Reassemble in reverse order. Finally, when you are prefectly sure that everything is working, 'shear-off' those shear-off bolts.

23 Steering box - removal and dismantling

1 To remove the steering box, first detach the track rod and steering rod ball joints from the drop arm as described in Section 18. Remove the locknut for the drop arm, and pull this off its shaft. Fig.11.24 shows the special Volvo puller in use, but the owner's tool box or his ingenuity will provide an adequate substitute.

2 Mark the position of the steering column flange on the knurled end of the steering worm shaft. Remove the nuts fixing the flange to the flexible joint and unclamp the flange (Fig.11.25). Push the flange as far down the shaft as it will go.

3 The steering box can now easily be removed from the chassis.

4 Start the dismantling of the steering box by removing the flange from the worm shaft. Naturally you know the position in which it must be put back, because you marked it before originally undoing the clamp.

5 Put the steering gear in the middle position as indicated by the mark on the worm shaft shown in Fig.11.26.

6 Remove the four bolts holding the upper cover, pull up the cover a little way (the drop arm shaft will come with it) and drain off the oil from the box. Then withdraw the drop arm shaft and cover.

7 Remove the locknut from the adjusting screw and screw this through the cover. The adjusting screw is retained in the drop arm shaft by a circlip and washer which you can dismantle if

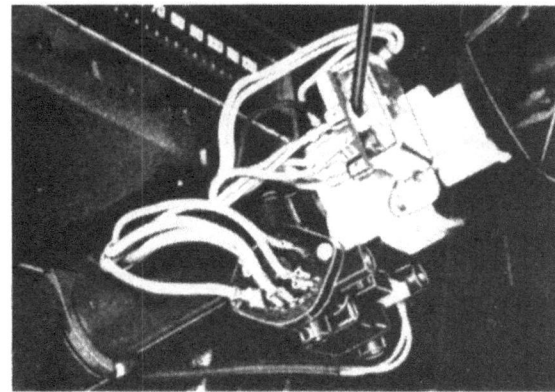

Fig.11.23a. The ignition/starter switch and just above it the direction indicator switch. These are screwed on, whereas.....

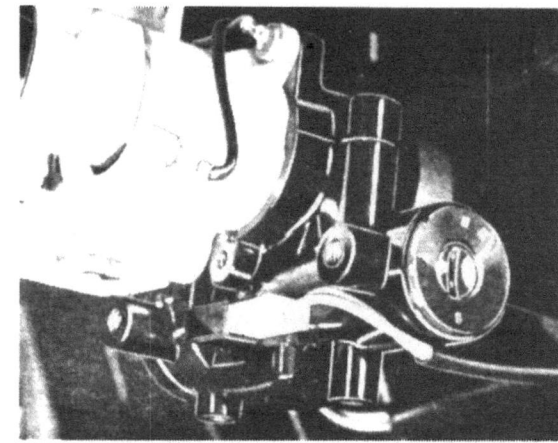

Fig.11.23b. The switch for the anti-theft warning buzzer simply pulls out

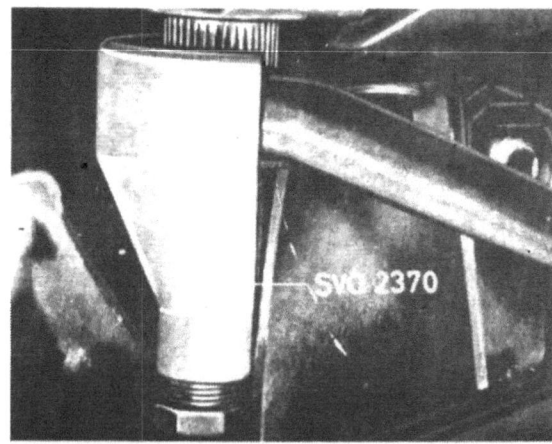

Fig.11.24. Pulling off the drop arm

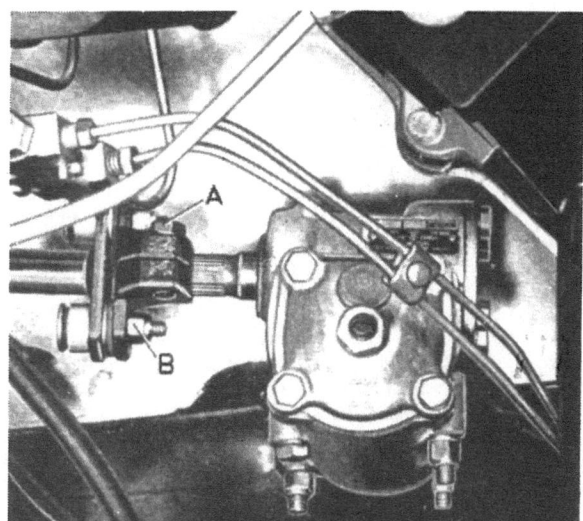

Fig.11.25. Nut 'B' and its opposite number attaching steering flange to the universal joint. Nut 'A' clamps the flange to the steering worm shaft

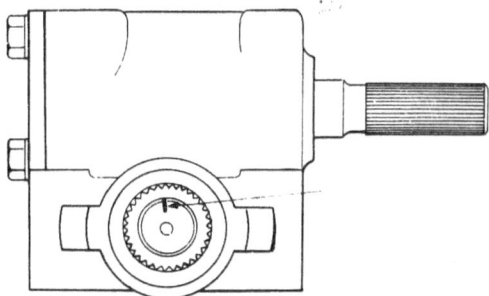

Fig.11.26. Steering worm shaft in centre position

Fig.11.27. The drop arm shaft and roller form an integral unit

1 Circlip   3 Adjusting screw
2 Adjusting washer   4 Drop arm shaft

SVO 2720

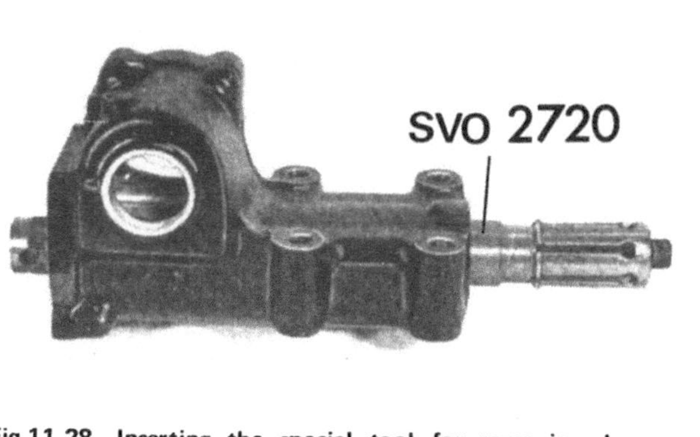

Fig.11.28. Inserting the special tool for removing drop arm bushes. The bush being tackled is in the position shown in Fig.11.29.

necessary. (See Fig.11.27).

8 Remove the cover over the lower end of the worm shaft, taking care not to damage the shims as these control the play in the ball races holding the worm shaft.

9 You can take out the worm shaft and its ball races.

10 The removal of two sealing rings (take care not to damage the steering box casing with your screwdriver) completes the dismantling operation.

24 Steering box - inspection

1 Wash all the parts in white spirit except the gasket and sealing rings which will be replaced anyway.

2 Check the drop arm shaft for signs of heavy wear, scratches or scorings on the contact surfaces of its roller. The roller should not be loose in the shaft. If you see these or other signs of wear or damage, replace the shaft.

3 The same applies to the steering worm and its shaft.

4 Examine the outer rings of the worm shaft bearings (you will have to drift out the outer ring of the upper bearing from the casing) and the ball bearings themselves. If there is any sign of scoring, blueing or wear they should be replaced.

5 If the drop arm shaft is loose in its bushes or if the bushes are damaged, they should be replaced.

6 To remove the bushes, Volvo make a special tool with an expander ring whose leading edges pass through the bush and then click into position on the other side of it, enabling the bush to be withdrawn (see Fig.11.28 and 11.29). Failing this you can drift or press them out both at once from one end.

7 The replacement bushes must be pressed in and reamed in situ. Fig.11.30 shows the Volvo guide and reamer made for the job. If you can't get hold of this, you are faced with the problem of checking the shaft diameter and producing a suitable reamer; if you feel this is beyond you there is no alternative but to seek expert help for this operation, which is an extremely important one.

8 There is also a bush for the drop arm shaft in the top cover of the steering box. This bush cannot be removed, so if it needs replacing you have to buy a new cover complete.

9 Be sure you give the housing a thorough clean after reaming.

25 Steering box - assembly

1 Initial stages of the assembly are simple. Be careful how you fit the rubber sealing rings, and be sure that the outer race of the upper bearing is pressed back into position hard against the

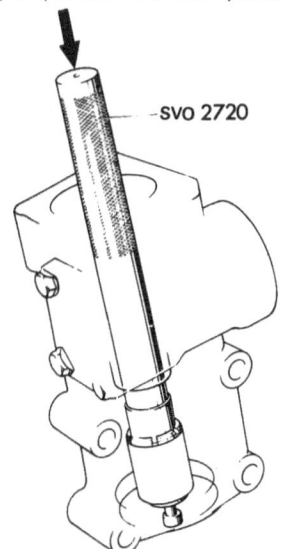

—SVO 2720

Fig.11.29. Pressing out one of the bushes for the drop arm shaft

Fig.11.30. The special Volvo reamer for the drop arm shaft bushes fits into a guide which bolts into the steering lock housing

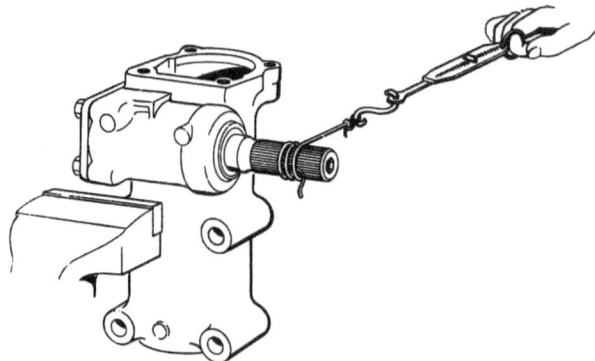

Fig.11.31. Measuring torque on the steering worm shaft

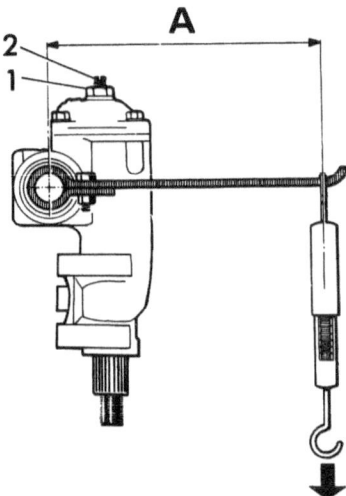

Fig.11.32. Measuring torque on the steering arm shaft with drop arm shaft fitted

1 Locknut
2 Adjusting screw A = 8¼" (210 mm)

shoulder in the housing.

2   Before fitting the drop arm shaft, assemble the steering worm shaft and fit its cover, using the same shims as previously. Tighten the cover while checking that the shaft rotates easily without any play.

3   If the bearings are properly located, the worm shaft should require a torque of 1 - 2 lb in (1 - 2.5 kg cm) to rotate it. You can measure the torque with a spring balance and cord as shown in Fig. 11.31. The balance should read 2.2 - 5.5 lbs (1 - 2.5 kg cm).If this is not the case, adjust by inserting or removing shims. Naturally, you will not have any of the correct shims available, so when you have established the correct spacing you will have to buy or make the shims you want. Don't forget that this cover must be oil tight.

4   Fit the adjusting screw, washer and circlip on the drop arm shaft. The adjusting screw play should be as little as possible and should not exceed 0.002 ins (0.05 mm). The play is reduced by exchanging the washer for a thicker one. Be sure that the adjusting screw can rotate easily after fitting.

5   Oil and refit the drop arm shaft, making sure that the adjusting screw is brought so far through the cover that there is no danger of binding when the cover is screwed down. Don't forget the gasket.

6   Oil the sealing ring and fit it.

7   Centralise the steering gear (Fig.11.26) and screw in the adjusting screw (photo) until a noticeable resistance is felt when the worm shaft is rotated to and fro over the centre position. The correct torque on the worm shaft can be measured with a simple lever and spring balance (Fig.11.32). The balance should read 0.9 - 1.5 lbs (0.4 - 0.7 kg). When it pulls the shaft over the centre position. If you use the cord method described in Section 3 the balance readings should be 18 - 31 lb (8 - 14 kg).

8   Fit the flange on the worm shaft using the position mark if the shaft has not been replaced. Finally, fill with ½ pint (0.25 litre) hypoid oil SAE 80 (Castrol Hypoy Light).

26 Steering box - installing

1   This is quite straightforward. Fit the steering box on to the chassis, and replace the drop arm so that the line-up mark and the drop arm shaft coincides with that on the drop arm. Tighten the nut to 125-145 lb ft (17-20 Kgm).

2   Reassemble the steering flange and flexible joint on the steering shaft, adjusting it if necessary so that the steering wheel is central when the wheels point straight ahead. Check that the distance between the steering box and lower flange is 1 inch ± 3/16 inch (27 ± 5 mm).

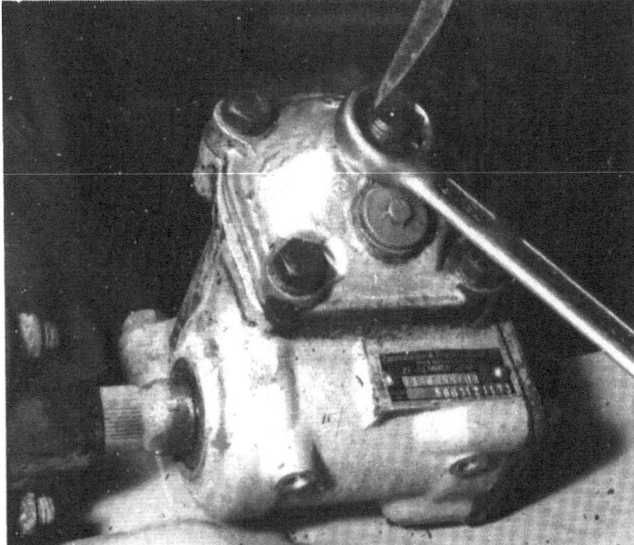

25.7 The steering box as it appears in a right hand drive car. The adjusting screw is being turned while its locknut is held with a spanner

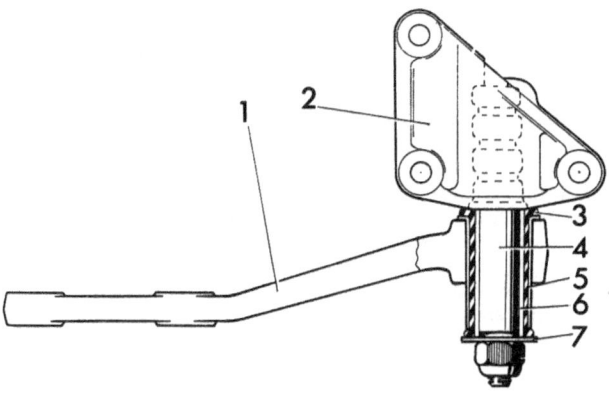

Fig.11.33. Relay arm assembly

1 Relay arm	5 Outer sleeve
2 Bracket	6 Inner sleeve
3 Rubber bush	7 Washer
4 Bearing pin	

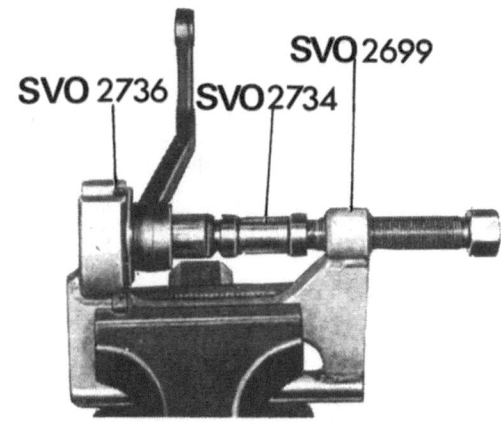

Fig.11.34a. The old bush (which protrudes from the relay arm as shown in Fig.11.33) is pressed through the arm. SVC 2734 is only a distance piece

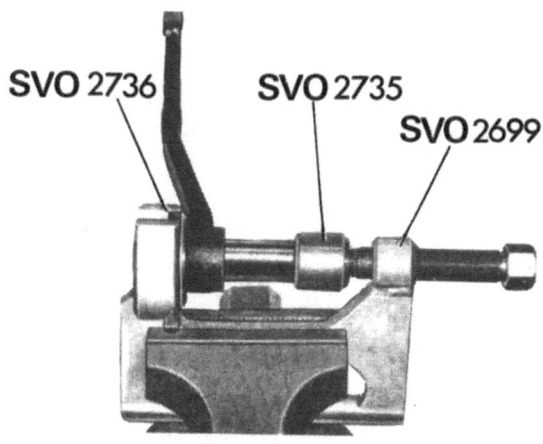

Fig.11.34b. The arm is turned round and the new bush is pushed in

27 Relay arm - checking and replacement

1 The relay arm assembly is shown in Fig.11.33. The inner and outer sleeves of the relay arm bush should not rotate relative to the relay arm shaft or the relay arm itself respectively. If you are satisfied that this is so, and the rubber bush seems intact as shown by an even resistance to rotation, all is well. If not, press out the ball joints from the arm and remove it from the vehicle by undoing and removing its nut and washer and pulling it down. Naturally, you have disconnected the ball joints as previously described before doing this.

2 If the arm and the bracket on the vehicle show no signs of wear, it is possible to replace the bush. It should be pressed on to the arm (Fig.11.34) and the arm can then be reassembled to the bracket.

3 Otherwise the relay arm and its bracket can be replaced as a complete unit. It is attached to the chassis by three bolts.

28 Wheel alignment

1 Life was a lot easier in the good old days when kingpins were kingpins. The angular relationships between the front wheels and the chassis remained the same over wide variations of load; this meant that you could allow a wider margin of error when setting them up in the first place. With today's independent suspension, the angles are varying all the time. This leaves you very little margin of error in setting them up and this in turn makes it essential that measurements should be accurate.

2 We hope our more expert readers will bear with us if we give a brief description of the various angles.

3 **Castor.** This is illustrated in Fig. 11.35. It is the angle between a vertical line and the line through the centre of the ball joints. If the angle is as shown (which is the case with almost all cars, including Volvos) it is known as positive castor. If you think of the castors on furniture you will see how it causes the wheels to run straight forwards if the steering wheel is free to turn.

4 **Camber** is the inclination of the wheel itself outwards or inwards. If outwards, as shown in Fig. 11.36 it is positive. Faulty camber causes uneven tyre wear.

5 **Kingpin inclination** is the angle between the centre line through the ball joints (which is where the kingpin would be in a solid suspension) and the vertical (see Fig. 11.36). Correct

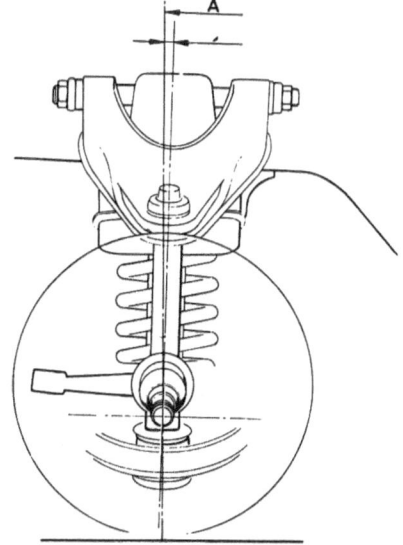

Fig.11.35. Castor angle

Line 'A' is vertical, car is facing right

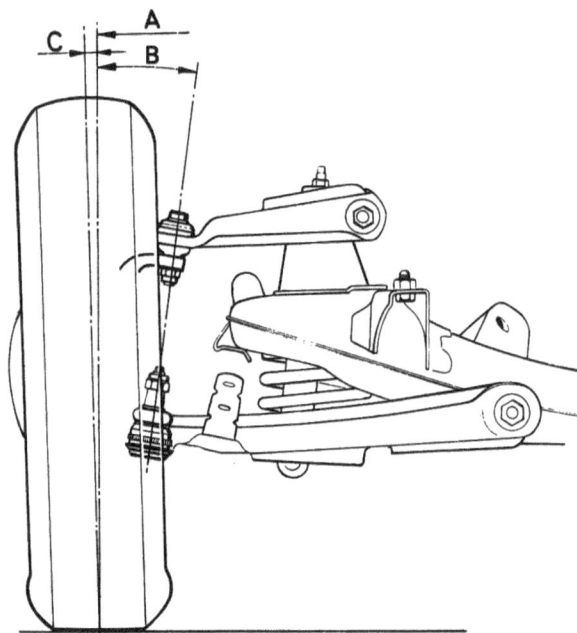

Fig.11.36. Camber and king pin inclination

'A' is vertical, 'B' is king pin inclination, 'C' is camber

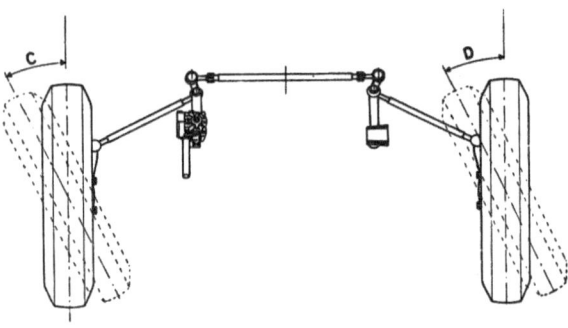

Fig.11.37. Toe-out is the difference between 'C' and 'D'

Fig.11.38. A simple but effective wheel alignment gauge

kingpin inclination is important for two reasons; the centre line of the ball joint passes through the contact area between the tyre and the road which makes the wheel easier to turn, and it also assists the tendency of the wheel to run straight forwards since the car lifts very slightly when the wheels are turned.

6 **Toe-out.** When driving round a bend, the wheels are rolling round different radii. Because of this, they ought not to be parallel and toe-out is the measurement of the extent to which this is true. Correct toe-out minmises tyre wear. Note that when toe-in (see next paragraph) is outwards instead of inwards this is sometimes called toe-out, but that is something quite different. Toe-out is measured by the differences between the angles C and D in Fig. 11.37.

7 **Toe-in** hardly needs defining. It is the difference between the rearmost point of the wheels and their foremost point, measured at the rims with the wheels pointing straight ahead. Correct toe-in is an important factor in reducing tyre wear.

---

29 Wheel alignment - checking and adjustment

1 In this Section we have no alternative but to assume that you have access to the specialised measuring equipment needed for this work. Such equipment is bound to be accompanied by instruction on its use. The one exception is toe-in measurement, which can be done with simple - even homemade - apparatus, although more sophisticated approaches save a lot of time. The toe-in alignment gauge will be familiar to most of our readers, but to make sure that they know what we are talking about, we show a picture of one (Fig.11.38). If you want to make something of the sort yourself, why not - but remember that your measurements should be accurate to one or two parts in a thousand, so your device must be quite rigid and smoothly adjustable.

2 Before checking and adjusting the wheel angles, check the following points and remedy any faults:-
a) Tyre pressure and wear.
b) Play in front wheel bearings.
c) Play in ball joints or wishbone attachments.
d) Broken springs.
e) Abnormal loading.
f) Wheel out of true by more than 0.1 inches (2.5 mm).
g) Faulty shock absorbers.
h) Faulty steering box adjustment.
i) Play in relay arm or steering rods.

3 **Castor** and **camber** are adjusted by altering the shims on the upper wishbones (see Figure 11.10). Shims are stocked in thicknesses ranging from 0.006 inches to 0.24 inches (0.15 mm - 6.0 mm). The **castor** is altered to the same extent by either
a) removing a shim at one of the bolts,
b) adding a shim to the other bolt,
c) moving over half of the required shim thickness from one bolt to the other. Alternative c) does not affect the camber.

4 **Camber** is adjusted by adding or subtracting the same shim thickness at each bolt. This will not affect the castor. Camber becomes more positive when shims are removed and vice versa.

5 For a guide to the shim thickness required to produce a given alteration in castor or camber, see Fig.11.39.

6 The **castor** for each wheel should lie between 0° and $+1^\circ$ and the difference between both sides should not exceed $\frac{1}{2}^\circ$. The **camber** for each wheel should be between 0° and $+\frac{1}{2}^\circ$. This will show you what you are up against if you try to do these adjustments yourself, though we are not saying it is impossible. The difficult part is the measurement of the angles for which you need a level floor and instruments which, though essentially simple, are accurate.

7 **Kingpin inclination** should be 7.5° at a camber of 0°, or a little less if the camber is 0.5°. It is difficult to measure exactly, because it varies so much with loading, and in any case there is no adjustment. If the difference between both sides is less than 1°, it is safe to say that all is well. If it is much more, look to your steering linkages - or may be one of the steering knuckles is distorted.

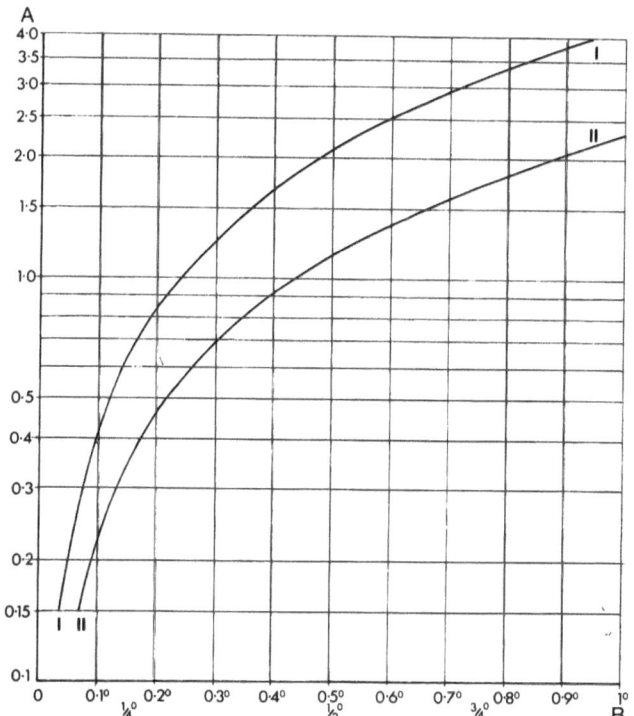

Fig.11.39. Diagram for alteration of castor and camber

'I' = camber, 'II' = castor, 'A' = shim thickness (mm), 'B' = alteration of angle

8 **Toe-out** has to be checked on turn-tables. Turn the wheels to the left until the right wheel has turned 20° inwards. The scale on the left turn-table should then read 22.5° ± 1°. Repeat the procedure in the opposite direction. Both measurements must lie within the stated tolerances. There is no adjustment, but if the toe-out is incorrect, check steering arms and steering rods.

30 Toe-in

1 No doubt you have noted the awful warnings given above, but there is worse to come. Volvo instructions up to 1971 recommend 0-0.16" (0.4 mm) while from 1972 onwards they say 0.08-0.20" (2.5 mm). There seems to be no design change to account for this, but if you want to be on the safe side, you will presumably get it between 0.08" and 0.16" (2-4 mm).
2 To meet this sort of tolerance with a simple alignment gauge only one method will do.
3 Point the wheels straight ahead.
4 Measure the distance between the front points of the wheels and mark the points between which you measured.
5 Now move the car forward until the marked points are at the back and measure the distance there. Only thus will you be able to avoid any effect of the wheels being out of true.
6 Adjust by slackening the locknuts on the tie rod and turning it. If you turn it in the normal direction of rotation of the wheels you will increase the toe-in and vice versa.
7 Tighten the locknuts after adjustment to a torque of 55-65 lb ft (7.5 - 9.5 kgm).
8 Cross your fingers and check the toe-in again after tightening.

31 Adjusting steering limits

1 Turning the wheels in one direction is limited by a stop screw acting on the drop arm, and in the other direction by a stop screw acting on the relay arm. The lock angle should be 43-45°. If it is not, adjust the screws as necessary.
2 Check that brake hoses are not under strain at full wheel lock.

Fault diagnosis

Symptom	Reason/s	Remedy
STEERING FEELS VAGUE, CAR WANDERS AND FLOATS AT SPEED		
General wear or damage	Tyre pressures uneven	Check pressures and adjust as necessary.
	Shock absorbers worn	Test, and replace if worn.
	Steering gear ball joints badly worn	Fit new ball joints
	Suspension geometry incorrect	Check and rectify.
	Steering mechanism free play excessive	Adjust or overhaul steering mechanism.
	Front suspension lacking grease	Check condition and grease or replace worn parts and re-grease.
STIFF AND HEAVY STEERING		
Lack of maintenance or accident damage	Tyre pressures too low	Check pressures and inflate tyres.
	No grease in steering ball joints	Replace.
	Front wheel toe-in incorrect	Check and reset toe-in.
	Suspension geometry incorrect	Check and rectify.
	Steering gear incorrectly adjusted too tightly	Check and re-adjust steering gear.
WHEEL WOBBLE AND VIBRATION		
General wear or damage	Wheel nuts loose	Check and tighten as necessary.
	Front wheels and tyres out of balance	Balance wheels and tyres and add weights as necessary.
	Steering ball joints badly worn	Replace steering gear ball joints.
	Hub bearings badly worn	Remove and fit new hub bearings.
	Steering gear free play excessive	Adjust and overhaul steering gear.

Chapter 12 Bodywork

Contents

Specifications

	142	**144**	**145**
Length	4640 mm (182.7 in.)	4640 mm (182.7 in.)	4640 mm (182.7 in.)
Width	1735 mm (68.3 in.)	1735 mm (68.3 in.)	1735 mm (68.3 in.)
Height	1440 mm (56.7 in.)	1440 mm (56.7 in.)	1450 mm (57.0 in.)
Wheelbase	2620 mm (103.1 in.)	2620 mm (103.1 in.)	2620 mm (103.1 in.)
Ground clearance, empty ...	210 mm (8.3 in.)	210 mm (8.3 in.)	210 mm (8.3 in.)
with 2 persons	180 mm (7.0 in.)	180 mm (7.0 in.)	180 mm (7.0 in.)
Track, front	1350 mm (53.1 in.)	1350 mm (53.1 in.)	1350 mm (53.1 in.)
rear	1350 mm (53.1 in.)	1350 mm (53.1 in.)	1350 mm (53.1 in.)
Turning circle	9250 mm (30 ft. 4 in.)	9250 mm (30 ft. 4 in.)	9250 mm (30 ft. 4 in.)
Curb weight	2618 lb. (1190 kg)	2596 lb. (1180 kg)	2706 lb. (1230 kg)

1 General description

The Volvo 140 series is of integral construction. There is no separate chassis frame, the strength being provided by the various angles and box sections built into the floor section and the sturdy body pillars. Sturdiness is a word which at once springs to mind when you look at the Volvo 140; one is not surprised to learn that the same company produces heavy lorries. Drawings of the floor section and two typical bodies are shown in Fig. 12.1. Though the floor section is shown differently, it is not of course in any way detachable from the rest of the body. The floor section is the same for all models, except that on the 145 it is reinforced with an extra frame at the extreme rear.

Two front side members project from the front floor section. They are supported in the front by a short cross member and carry the front axle assembly and upper support bars.

2 Maintenance - bodywork

1 The condition of the bodywork is of considerable importance as it is on this, in the main, that the second-hand value of the car depends. Maintenance is easy but needs to be regular and careful. Neglect, particularly after minor damage, can lead quickly to further deterioration and costly repair bills. It is important also to keep watch on those parts of the car not immediately visible, for instance the underside, and inside all the wheel arches.
2 The basic maintenance routine for the bodywork is washing -

preferably with a lot of water, from a hose. This will remove all the solids which may have stuck to the car. It is important to flush these off in such a way as to prevent grit from scratching the finish. The wheel arches and underbody need washing in the same way to remove any accumulated mud which will retain moisture and tend to encourage rust. Paradoxically enough, the best time to clean the underbody and wheel arches is in wet weather when the mud is soft.
3 Once a year, or every 12,000 miles, it is advisable to visit a garage equipped to steam clean the body. This facility is available at many commercial vehicle garages. All traces of dirt and oil will be removed and the underside can then be inspected carefully for rust, damaged pipes, frayed electrical wiring and so forth. The car should be greased on completion of this job. The engine compartment should be cleaned in the same way.
4 If steam cleaning is not available, brush 'Gunk' or a similar cleaner over the whole of the engine and engine compartment with a stiff brush, working it well in where there is an accumulation of oil and dirt. Do not cover the ignition system, and protect it with oily rags when the 'Gunk' is washed off. As it is washed away, it will take with it all traces of oil and dirt, leaving the engine looking clean and bright.
5 The wheel arches should be given particular attention, as undersealing can easily come away here, and stones and dirt thrown up from the road wheels can soon cause the paint to chip and flake and so allow rust to set in. If rust is found, clean down to the bare metal with wet and dry paper, paint on an anti-corrosive coating such as 'Kurust' or red lead and renew the undercoating and top coat.

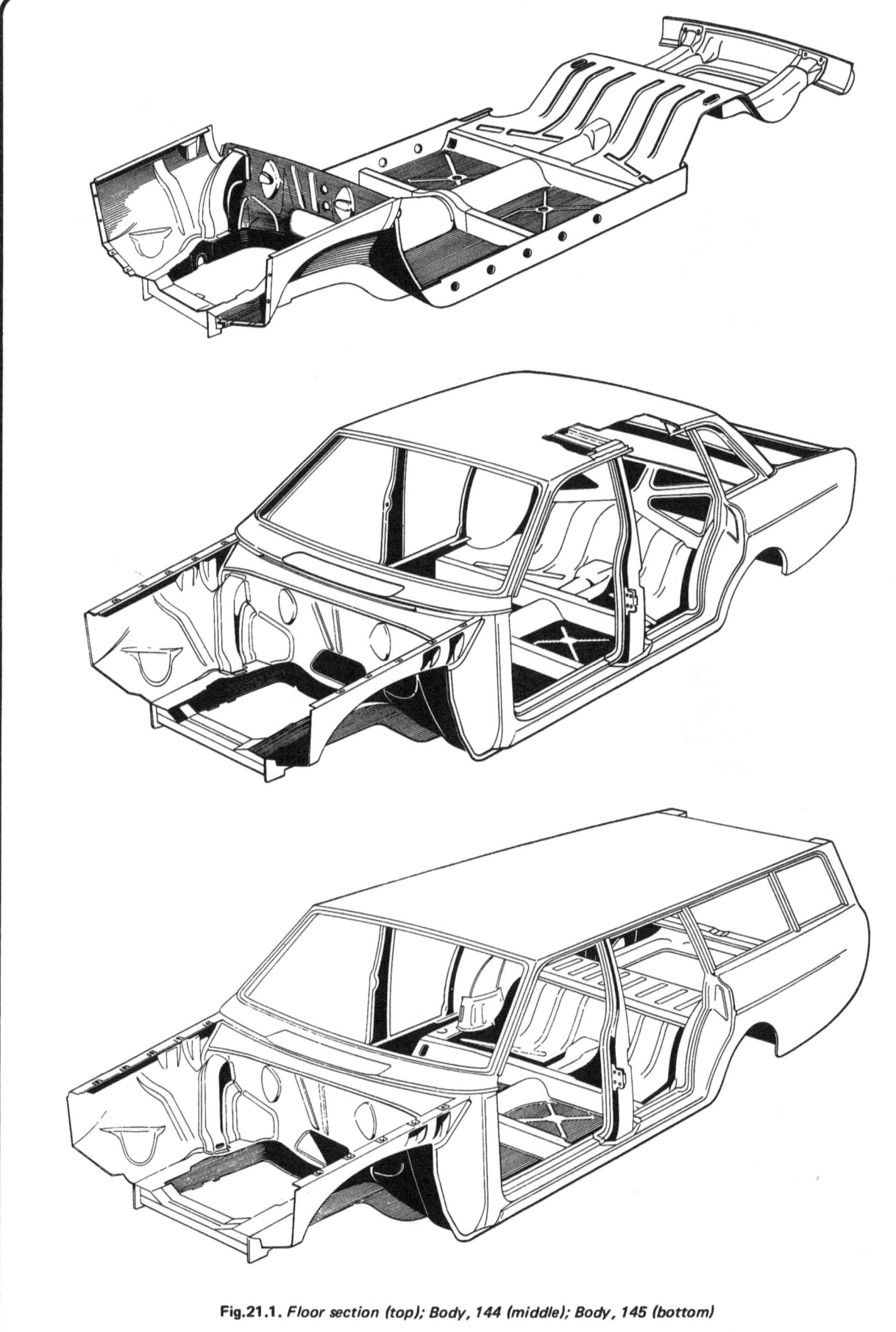

Fig.21.1. *Floor section (top); Body, 144 (middle); Body, 145 (bottom)*

6 The body should be washed once a week or more often if necessary. After washing paintwork, wipe it with a chamois leather to give an unspotted clear finish. If a car is frequently washed, it only needs a very occasional waxing as a protection against chemical pollutants in the air. Wax the chromium plated parts as well as the paintwork. To keep windscreens and windows clear of film, wash them with water to which a little ammonia has been added.

Keep wax polish away from glass - the smallest trace will cause smeariness in wet weather.

7 Spots of tar and grease thrown up from the road can be removed by a rag dampened in petrol. Tar should not be allowed to linger on the paintwork, nor should bird droppings, which sometimes discolour paint.

3 Maintenance - upholstery and floor coverings

1 Mats and carpets should be brushed or vacuum cleaned regularly to keep them free of grit. If they are badly stained remove them for sponging and make sure they are quite dry before replacement. Seats and interior trim panels can be kept clean by a wipe over with a damp cloth. If they do become stained, use a little liquid detergent and a soft nail brush to scour the grime out of the grain of the material.

2 Do not forget to keep the head lining clean in the same way as the upholstery.

3 When using liquid cleaners inside the car do not over-wet the surfaces being cleaned. Excessive damp could get into the seams and padded interior causing stains, offensive odours or even rot. If the inside of the car gets wet accidentally it is worthwhile taking some trouble to dry it out properly, particularly where carpets are involved.

4 Body repairs - minor

1 Major damage must be repaired by specialist body repair shop but there is no reason why you cannot successfully beat out, repair and respray minor damage yourself. The essential items which the owner should gather together to ensure a really professional job are:-
a) A plastic filler such as Holts Cataloy
b) Paint whose colour matches that of the bodywork exactly, either in a can for application by a spray gun or in an aerosol can
c) Fine cutting paste
d) Medium and fine grade wet and dry paper

2 When knocking out small dents, never use a metal hammer as this tends to scratch and distort the metal. Use a hide mallet or something similar, and press on the other side of the dented surface a metal dolly or smooth wooden block roughly contoured to the normal shape of the damaged area.

3 After the worst of the damage has been knocked out, rub down the damage and the surrounding area with medium wet and dry paper and thoroughly clean away all traces of dirt.

4 The plastic filler comprises paste and hardener which must be thoroughly mixed together. Mix only a small portion at a time as the paste sets hard in five to fifteen minutes depending on the amount of hardener used.

5 Smooth on the filler with a knife or spatula to the shape of the damaged portion and allow to dry thoroughly - a process which takes about six hours. If any great thickness of filler is required, it is better to build it up layer by layer, applying each new layer after the old one has partially set - which takes about a quarter of an hour.

6 Finally, smooth down the filler with fine wet and dry paper wrapped round a block of wood and continue until the whole area is perfectly smooth and it is impossible to feel where the filler joins the rest of the paintwork.

7 Spray on from an aerosol can or a spray gun an anti-rust undercoat, smooth down with wet and dry paper and then spray on one or two coats of undercoat - sand papering down each

time - and finally the top coat.

This is the only operation in this section which really needs skill. The others demand care and patience, but are not really difficult. If you have never done any spraying at all, half an hour of experiment with spray gun or aerosol will put you into the way of it. An old five gallon drum makes a good subject to practise on.

Be sure to mask the surrounding area much further in all directions than you think can possibly be necessary.

8 When the paint is thoroughly dry, polish the whole area with fine cutting paste and smooth the re-sprayed areas into the remainder to remove the small particles of spray paint which will have settled round the area.

9 This will leave the area looking perfect and with not a trace of the previous dent.

5 Body repairs - major

1 Because the body is built on the monocoque principle, major damage must be repaired by specialists with the necessary welding and hydraulic straightening equipment.

2 If the damage is severe it is vital that on completion of the repair the chassis is in correct alignment. Less severe damage may also have twisted or distorted the chassis although this may not be visible immediately. It is therefore always best on completion of repair to check for twist and squareness to make sure that all is well.

3 To check for twist, the basic apparatus needed is a clean, level floor. The car should be raised on jacks or stands at each of its four jacking points, arranging matters so that sills are parallel with the ground. Take measurements at the suspension mounting points, and if comparable readings are not obtained on both sides it is an indication that the body is twisted.

4 After checking for twist, check for squareness by taking a series of measurements between the body and the floor. Drop a plumb line and bob weight from various mounting points on the underside of the body and mark these points on the floor with chalk. Draw a straight line between each point and measure and mark the middle of each line. A line drawn on the floor starting at the front and finishing at the rear should be quite straight and pass close through the centre of the other lines. Diagonal measurements can also be made as a check for squareness.

6 Door rattles - tracing and rectification

The most common cause of door rattles is a misaligned, loose or worn latch plate but other causes may be:
a) loose door handles, window winder handles or door hinges;
b) loose, worn or misaligned door lock components;
c) loose or worn door locking linkages;
d) any combination of the above three.

Worn parts should be replaced as described in later parts of this Chapter.

7 Bonnet

1 The bonnet is attached by two bolts to each hinge and removal is a simple matter (photos). The hinges themselves are attached to the body with three bolts (accessible under the mudguards). All the holes in the hinges are elongated in order to permit adjustment of the position of the bonnet.

2 The bonnet sits on four rubber stops at its corners, which can be screwed in and out.

3 The bonnet lock is illustrated in Fig. 12.2.

8 Mudguards

1 The front mudguards are bolted to the body and can easily be changed. It is simplest to remove the bolts in the following

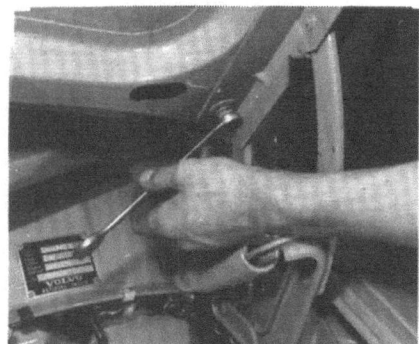

7.1a Undo the bonnet hinge bolts ...

7.1b ... and with the help of an assistant remove the bonnet

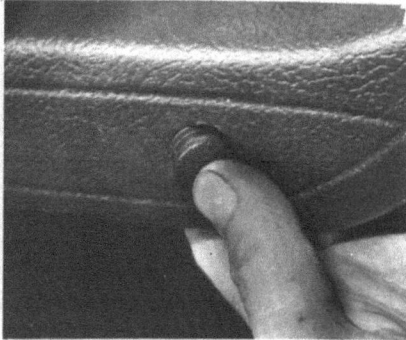

10.1a Remove these plugs from the arm-rest ...

10.1b ... revealing the fixing screws which you remove and then ...

10.1c unscrew the ring on the armrest till you can release the catch

10.2 Winding handle, washer and spring clip

order:
   the bolt between the mudguard and stay at the lower side member;
   the four bolts between the rear edge of the mudguard and body (accessible when the front door is opened);
   the bolts between the mudguard and front plate;
   and finally the bolts in the upper part of the side member.
   Fitting is done in the reverse order.

2   The rear mudguard is integral with the body and replacing this is a welding job.

9   Front section

1   The whole of the front section, carrying the headlamps, the radiator grille and the radiator can be removed complete. It is attached to the front mudguards, wheel arch plates and the lower cross member.

2   To remove it, disconnect and take out the battery and unscrew the bolts between the battery shelf and front section.

3   Remove the radiator grille and the headlights (see Chapter 3).

4   Remove the bolts attaching the front section to the mudguards, cross member and wheel arch plates. The front section can now be removed.

10   Doors - removing upholstery

1   Remove the arm rest in the front door by taking out the two plastic plugs and removing the screws (photos). Then turn the plastic ring at the front end of the arm rest anti-clockwise several turns, leaving the arm rest free to be unhooked from the door (photo).
   The arm rest in the rear door is removed by taking out plastic plugs and undoing the fixing screws.

2   Remove the window winding handle by pressing the spacer towards the door and then along the handle as shown in Fig. 12.3. Be sure when refitting that the spring clip is replaced with the open ends facing the handle. (photo)

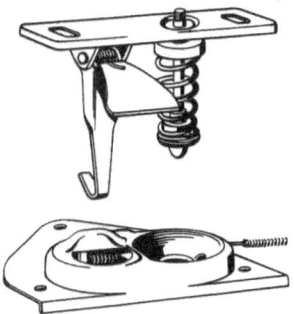

Fig.12.2. Bonnet lock

Fig.12.3. Push handle towards door and you can then push the loop in the spring clip on to the shaft and so release it

This photographic sequence shows the steps taken to repair the dent and paintwork damage shown above. In general, the procedure for repairing a hole will be similar; where there are substantial differences, the procedure is clearly described and shown in a separate photograph.

First remove any trim around the dent, then hammer out the dent where access is possible. This will minimise filling. Here, after the large dent has been hammered out, the damaged area is being made slightly concave.

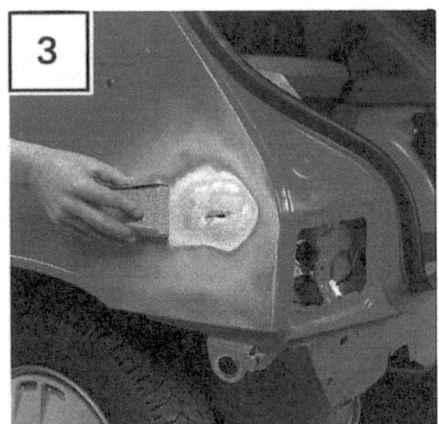

Next, remove all paint from the damaged area by rubbing with course abrasive paper or using a power drill fitted with a wire brush or abrasive pad. 'Feather' the edge of the boundary with good paintwork using a finer grade of abrasive paper.

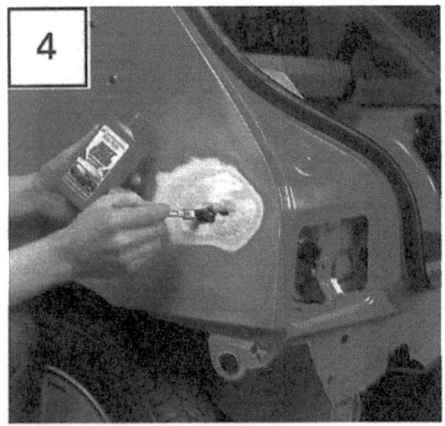

Where there are holes or other damage, the sheet metal should be cut away before proceeding further. The damaged area and any signs of rust should be treated with Turtle Wax Hi-Tech Rust Eater, which will also inhibit further rust formation.

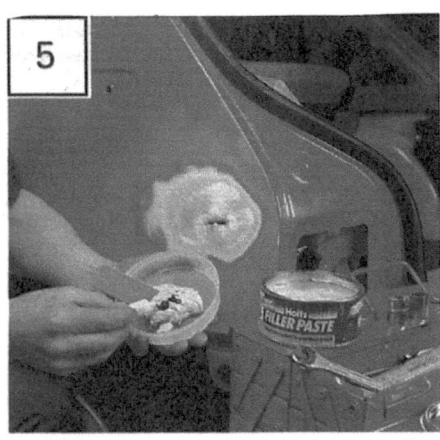

For a large dent or hole mix Holts Body Plus Resin and Hardener according to the manufacturer's instructions and apply around the edge of the repair. Press Glass Fibre Matting over the repair area and leave for 20-30 minutes to harden. Then ...

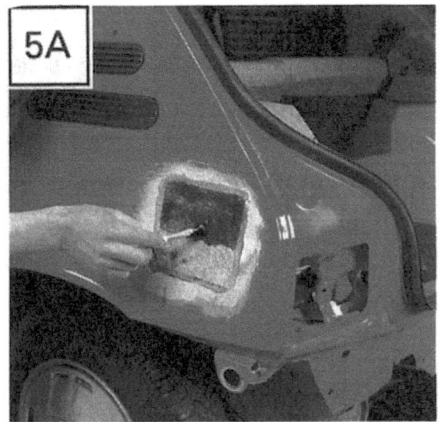

... brush more Holts Body Plus Resin and Hardener onto the matting and leave to harden. Repeat the sequence with two or three layers of matting, checking that the final layer is lower than the surrounding area. Apply Holts Body Plus Filler Paste as shown in Step 5B.

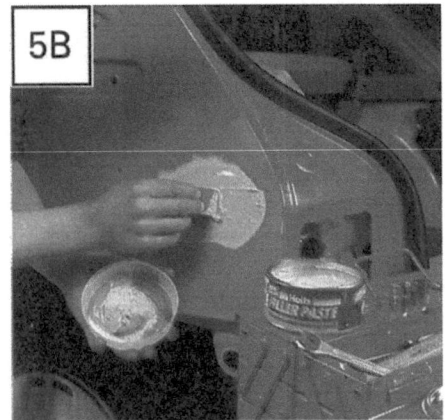

For a medium dent, mix Holts Body Plus Filler Paste and Hardener according to the manufacturer's instructions and apply it with a flexible applicator. Apply thin layers of filler at 20-minute intervals, until the filler surface is slightly proud of the surrounding bodywork.

For small dents and scratches use Holts No Mix Filler Paste straight from the tube. Apply it according to the instructions in thin layers, using the spatula provided. It will harden in minutes if applied outdoors and may then be used as its own knifing putting.

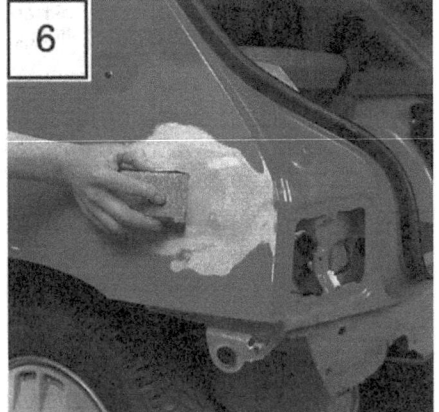

Use a plane or file for initial shaping. Then, using progressively finer grades of wet-and-dry paper, wrapped around a sanding block, and copious amounts of clean water, rub down the filler until glass smooth. 'Feather' the edges of adjoining paintwork.

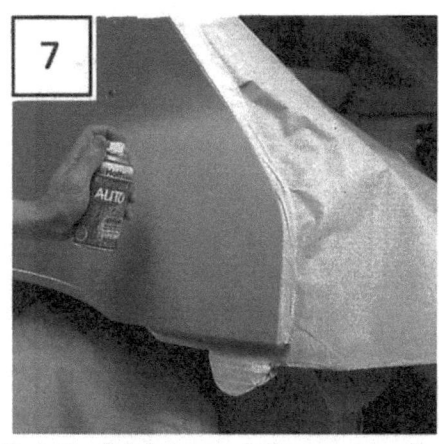

Protect adjoining areas before spraying the whole repair area and at least one inch of the surrounding sound paintwork with Holts Dupli-Color primer.

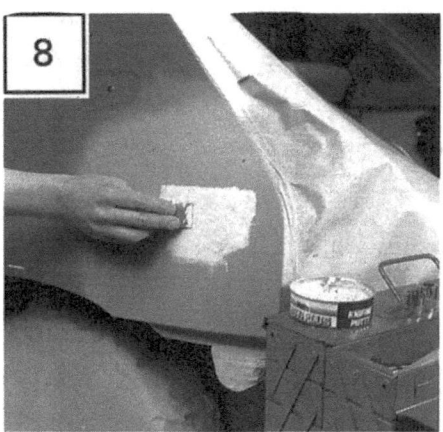

Fill any imperfections in the filler surface with a small amount of Holts Body Plus Knifing Putty. Using plenty of clean water, rub down the surface with a fine grade wet-and-dry paper - 400 grade is recommended - until it is really smooth.

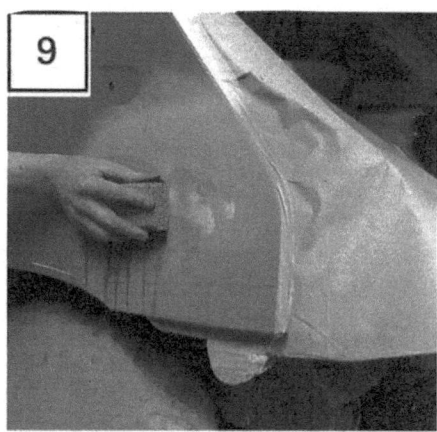

Carefully fill any remaining imperfections with knifing putty before applying the last coat of primer. Then rub down the surface with Holts Body Rubbing Compound to ensure a really smooth surface.

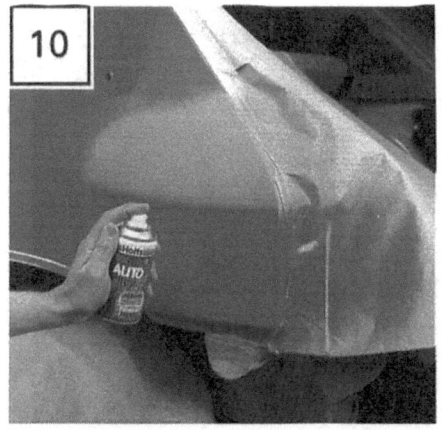

Protect surrounding areas from overspray before applying the topcoat in several thin layers. Agitate Holts Dupli-Color aerosol thoroughly. Start at the repair centre, spraying outwards with a side-to-side motion.

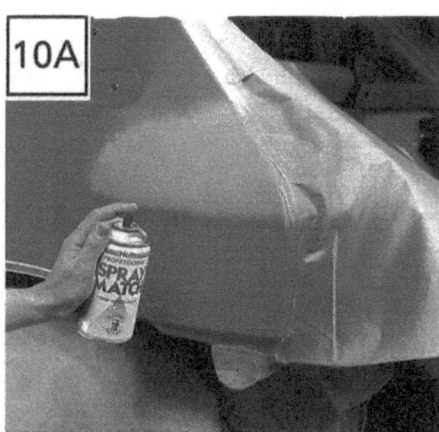

If the exact colour is not available off the shelf, local Holts Professional Spraymatch Centres will custom fill an aerosol to match perfectly.

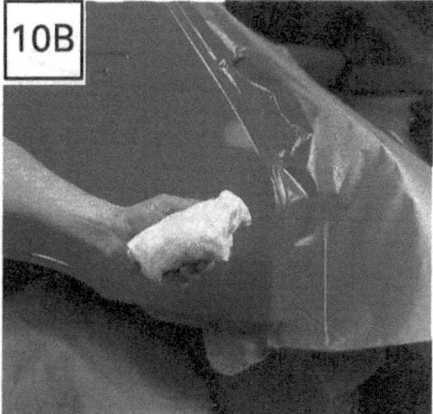

To identify whether a lacquer finish is required, rub a painted unrepaired part of the body with wax and a clean cloth.

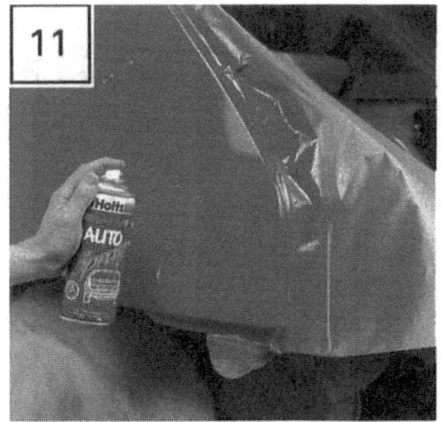

If *no* traces of paint appear on the cloth, spray Holts Dupli-Color clear lacquer over the repaired area to achieve the correct gloss level.

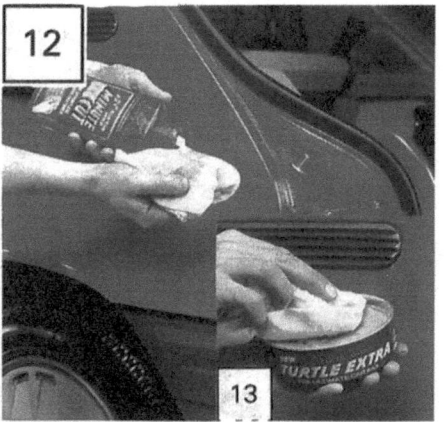

The paint will take about two weeks to harden fully. After this time it can be 'cut' with a mild cutting compound such as Turtle Wax Minute Cut prior to polishing with a final coating of Turtle Wax Extra.

When carrying out bodywork repairs, remember that the quality of the finished job is proportional to the time and effort expended.

3   Unscrew the locking knobs, remove any obvious fixing screws (typically two, near the top edge), carefully prise out the surround for the latch lever and you can then remove the upholstery panel by inserting a screwdriver at the edge and levering it away. (photos)

11 Door stop - removal and fitting

The door stop is visible in the photo just below the upper hinge and is shown in detail in Fig. 12.4. It is fastened to the door by two bolts and to the pillar by a single bolt. When these are removed the complete assembly comes away. When replacing it, don't forget the rubber seal.

12 Front door lock - removal and fitting

1   The door lock mechanism is shown in Fig. 12.5. A look at this Figure in conjunction with the lock itself in position on the door will be enough to show you what positional adjustments are available and how you carry them out.
2   To remove the lock, first remove the lock cylinder by unscrewing its retaining screw (16) (Fig. 12.5).
3   Remove the pull rods and push rod (4, 9, 14 and 1 in Fig.

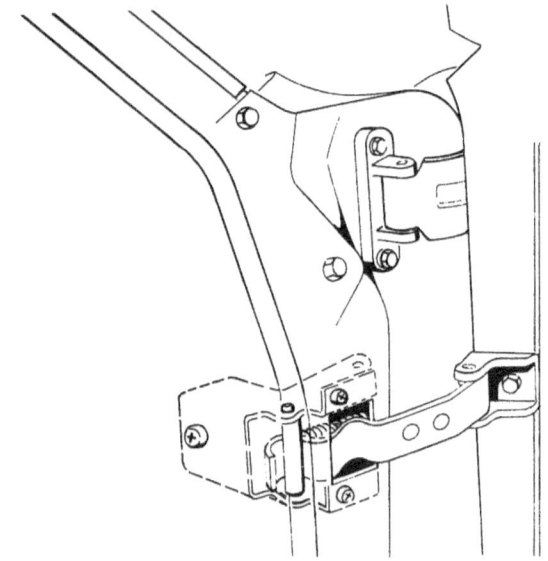

Fig.12.4. Door stop

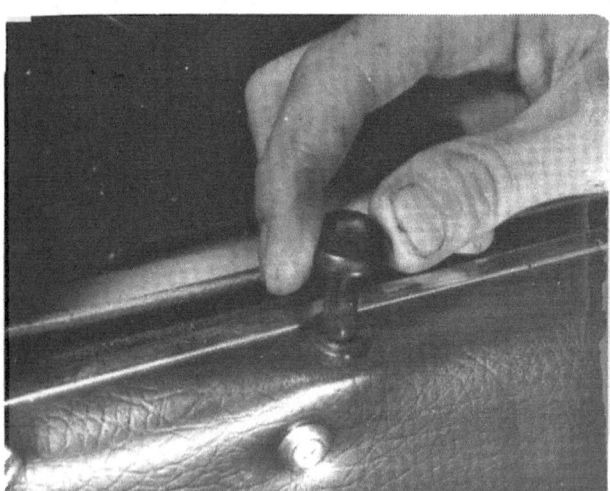

10.3a Unscrew the locking knob. Note fixing screw just below it.

10.3b Gently prise out the surround for the latch lever

10.3c The upholstery panel is now held to the door by clips and can be lifted off

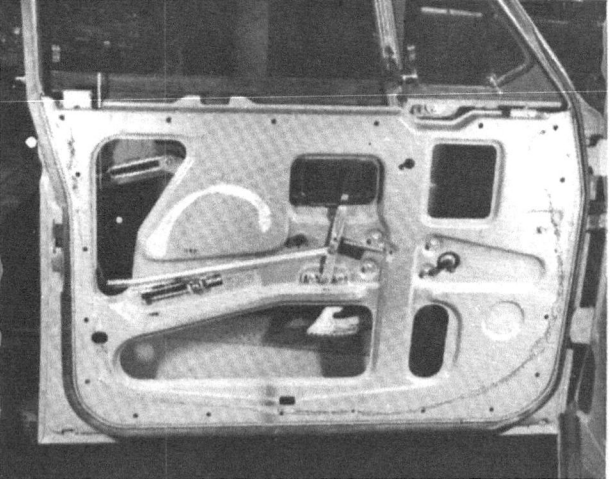

11.1 Door with upholstery panel removed. Note door stop and its rubber seal just below top hinge, and the window raising and lowering mechansim on left (the quadrant is on the right)

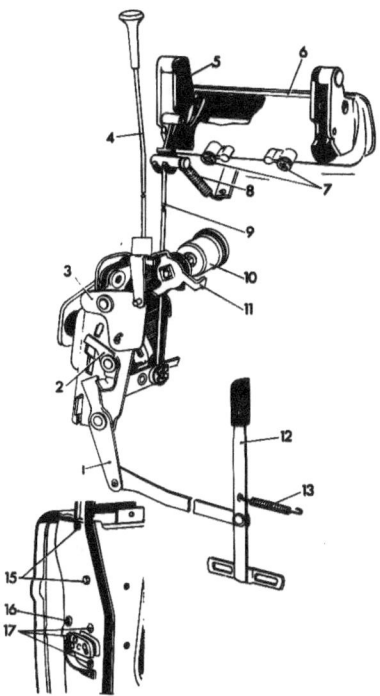

Fig.12.5. Front door lock assembly

1	Lever	10	Lock cylinder
2	Lever	11	Lock device
3	Lever	12	Inner door opener
4	Pull rod for lock button	13	Return spring for inner door opener
5	Outer handle		
6	Cover for outer handle	14	Pull rod for latch
7	Screws for outer handle cover	15	Door frame attachment screws
8	Return spring for outer handle	16	Cylinder attachment screw
9	Pull rod for outer handle	17	Lock attaching bolts

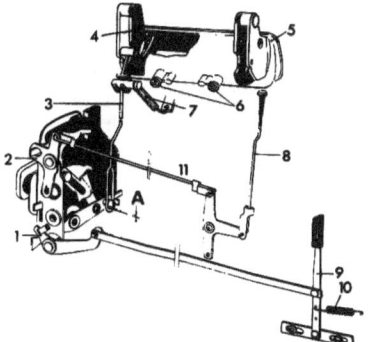

Fig.12.6. Rear door lock assembly

1	Lever	7	Return spring for outer handle
2	Lever		
3	Pull rod for outer handle	8	Pull rod for lock button
4	Outer handle	9	Inner door opener
5	Cover for outer handle	10	Return spring for inner door opener
6	Screws for outer handle cover	11	Pull rod for latch

4   Unscrew the two door frame bolts 15 (Fig. 12.5).
5   Unscrew the three screws attaching the door lock (17) (Fig. 12.5).
6   Ease the lock past the door frame, carefully levering this out of the way. The lock is now free of the door.
7   Refitting is simply the reverse of the removal.

13 Rear door lock - removal and fitting

1   The rear lock mechanism is shown in Fig. 12.6. As with the front lock, a study of this Figure and the lock itself in position on the door will show what adjustments are available and how they can be carried out.
2   To remove the lock, first remove the pull rods and push rod 3, 8 and 11 in Fig. 12.6.
3   Wind down the window so that its lower edge comes level with the upper edge of the door lock.
4   Lift out the weather strip from the door frame, unscrew the door frame attaching screws and lift it off. Two of these will be found on the front edge of the door just as they are for the front door (Fig.12.5) and two more at the rear edge.
5   Unscrew the attaching screws for the door lock (placed similarly to those for the front door, (Fig.12.5), and remove the lock from the door.
6   Refitting is the reverse of the removal process.

14 Other locks - latch plates

1   Figs. 12.7, 12.8 and 12.9 give sufficient detail of these to enable the owner to carry out whatever adjustment or replacement is necessary.
2   An interesting example of Volvo thoroughness is their specification for the tilt of the latch plate, which is actually the same plate whether fitted to front or rear doors.

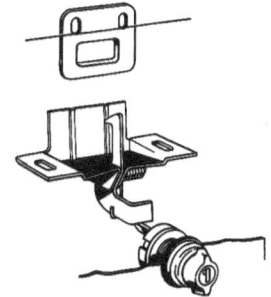

Fig.12.7. Luggage compartment lock assembly

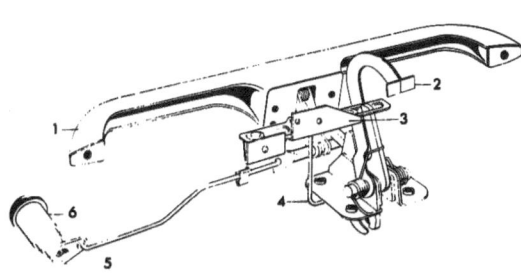

Fig.12.8. Tailgate lock assembly

1	Outer handle	4	Control for latching device
2	Inside opener		
3	Latching device for inner opener	5	Eccentric
		6	Lock cylinder

15 Door frames - removal

The removal of the rear door frame is quite straightforward and has already been considered in Section 13 paragraph 3-7. The front door frame, as well as being attached by two screws at the front edge of the door and two screws at the rear, is fixed to a bracket which will be found inside the door framework close to the window winding quadrant. To get at this of course, you have to remove the upholstery panel.

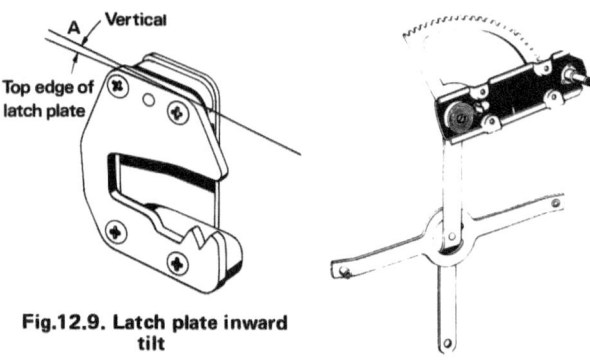

Fig.12.9. Latch plate inward tilt

A = 1.5° (front door)
A = 2.5° (rear door)

Fig.12.10. Window winding mechanism

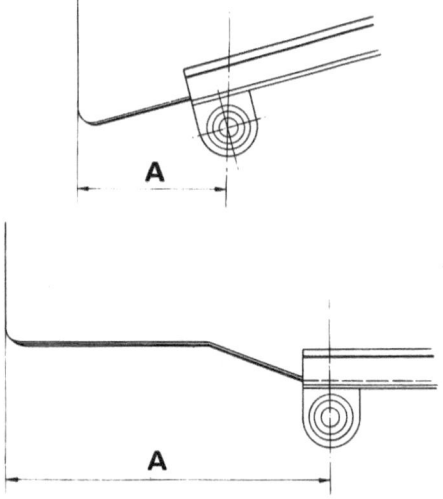

Fig.12.11. Dimensions for setting window glass in lifting rail

(top) side door 142 and front side door 144 and 145
A = 3" ± 0.08" (78.5 ± 2 mm)
(bottom) rear side door 144 and 145
A = 6.7" ± 0.08" (169 ± 2 mm)

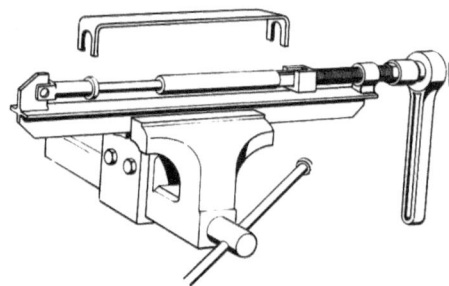

Fig.12.12. Compressing the gas spring for luggage compartment or tailgate

16 Side windows and front quarter windows

1 Examination of the window winding mechanism will soon reveal how it functions, how it is attached to the window and how, if necessary, it can be removed. If, through neglect, it has become so worn that oiling will not restore smooth working, there is no alternative to replacing the affected parts. The basic mechanism is shown in Fig.12.10.

2 The windows can be removed by removing the door frames, detaching the lifting arms from the support rail (there is an excellent view of the end of a lifting arm engaged in a support rail in photograph 11.1) and then lifting the window straight out. Be very careful not to let the window fall into the door, because if you do the edge of the support rail will certainly damage the outer door panel.

3 When fitting a new window glass into the support rail, be sure you follow the dimensions given in Fig.12.8. If you don't the winding mechanism will not work properly.

4 The front quarter windows can be removed after removing the door frame (see Section 15). Remove the grooved strip from the front slide rail, then remove the plate under the window after removing its securing screws. The quarter window can then be removed after the rubber surround has been taken off.

5 Refitting is the reverse of the removal procedure.

17 Doors and tailgate - removal, refitting and adjustment

1 To remove the doors, take out the upholstery panels (Section 10) you have to do this to get at the nuts on the hinge bolts - remove the door stops (Section 11), disconnect the heated rear window and unscrew the bolts between (if fitted) the hinges and the door. Elongated holes in the hinges where they fit to the door and oversized holes in the pillar where the hinges are attached provide for adjustment of the door position.

18 Tailgate - removal and refitting

1 To remove the tailgate, you will have to take off the upholstery panel on the inside. Then remove the left-hand number plate lamp and its cable, disconnect the other out-going cables from the tailgate, remove the gas spring, undo the bolts connecting the hinges to the tailgate and lift it off. The tailgate hinges can be removed from the body by easing the hinge out of its groove at the rear, pushing the electric cables out of the way and thus enabling yourself to get at the nuts holding the hinge bolts. Replacement is straightforward the only problem being to compress the gas spring. To keep it compressed a simple bracket, like that shown in Fig.12.12, is very little trouble to make ; tying it up with wire would be even less trouble.

19 Luggage compartment lid

1 The luggage compartment lid is mounted on two hinges, both of which are attached by two bolts to the inner plate of the lid and by three bolts to the pillar under the rear window.

20 Rear window, rear quarter windows

1 The rear window is held in a rubber moulding in the conventional manner. To remove it, prise out the metal trim (Fig.12.13) and then give it a firm push with the palms of both hands and refitting is by the usual cord method illustrated in Figs.12.14, 12.15 and 12.16.

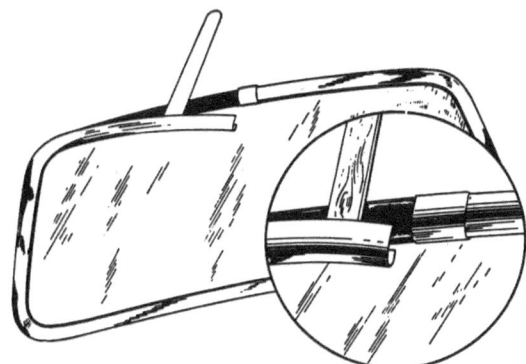

Fig.12.13. Prising out rear window metal trim

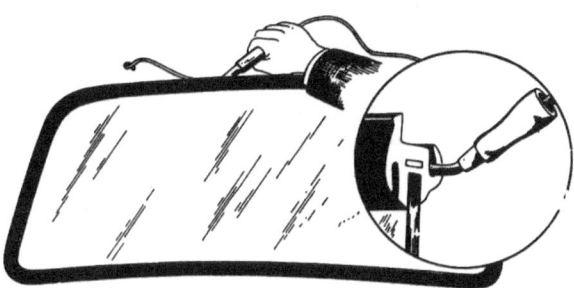

Fig.12.14. Fitting cord into sealing strip after this has been put round the glass. If you haven't got the useful gadget illustrated you can feed the cord in with a screwdriver

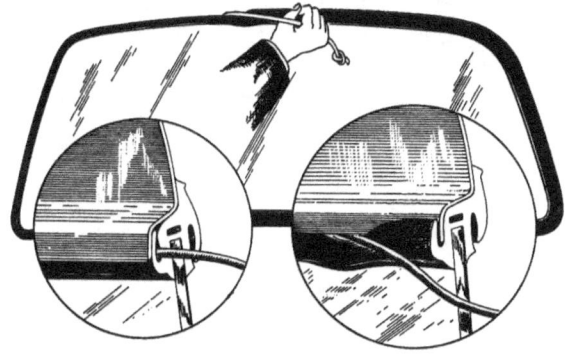

Fig.12.15. Pulling the edge of the rubber strip over the frame with cord

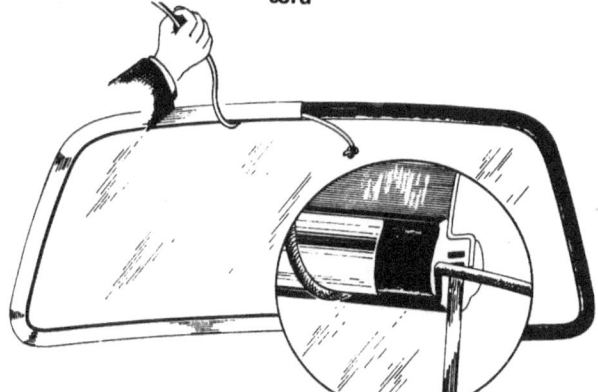

Fig.12.16. Fitting the metal trim

2   When fitting a new window, be sure that everything is entirely free from grease so that when sealing compound is applied later it will have the maximum effect.

3   Place the rear window in position with the rubber strip fitted round it and cord (preferably of terylene) fitted in the groove of the rubber strip in contact with the body as shown in Fig.12.15. Be sure that the window is centred and making good contact all round, persuading it, if necessary, by giving it a few blows with the palm of your **gloved** hand. Then carefully pull out the cord from inside, causing the strip to creep over the sheet metal edge. If it does not come out easily, check that the window is properly centred. There is no need to use much force - in fact if you pull too hard you may damage the strip.

4   Check that the rubber strip seals well all round. If necessary you can adjust the position of the window by striking it with the palm of your hand.

5   Seal the joints between the rubber strip and the body with sealing compound using a gun with a flat nylon nozzle. Make sure the sealing compound fills the joint well.

6   The trim mouldings are fitted in the same way as shown in Fig.12.16.

7   The rear quarter windows are fitted in exactly the same manner as the rear window.

21 Windscreen - removal

1   The windscreen is fitted in quite a different way from the rear window and then removing it you keep your feet firmly on the ground. To remove the windscreen (or the remainder of one) first cover the outside of the car with a blanket or something similar to prevent scratching.

2   Remove the external moulded trim. This clips into slits round the edges of the windscreen and can be prised out. Locate the actual clip points and prise there.

3   Take off the wiper arms.

4   Remove the internal moulded trim and the rear view mirror.

5   The windscreen is held in by an adhesive sealing strip which is best removed by using a soldering iron with a suitably shaped bit as shown in Fig. 12.17. When the windscreen is removed, clean off all traces of sealing, remove any defective clips, inject sealing agent into the holes where new clips are to be fitted and fit them. Note the two spacers on the lower edge between the second and third clip from each side. The best cleaning agent is ethyl or methyl acetate.

22 Windscreen - fitting

1   You will have seen when taking the old glass out that it relies entirely upon contact with a sealing strip to hold it into place. The crucial part in fitting the windscreen comes when you have

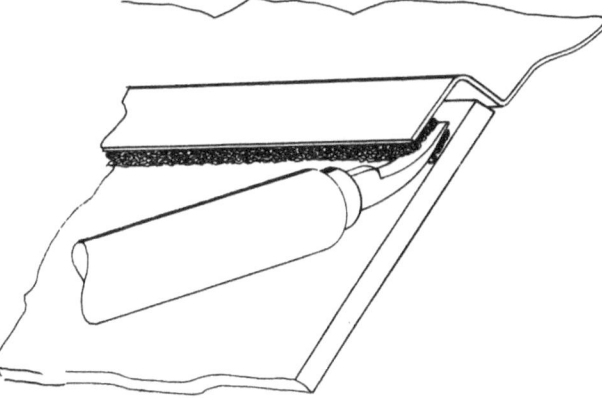

Fig.12.17. Removing the windscreen

to offer it to the sealing. Once it is stuck down, there is very little you can do about adjusting it. We suggest that if you haven't previously done this sort of thing you have a rehearsal before you actually apply the sealing. You will certainly need an assistant - may be you will get on better with more than one. You will probably find that the best approach is to arrange small spacing blocks at the bottom edge of the windscreen opening on to which you can place the windscreen with its bottom edge virtually touching the sealing and then swing it forward so that it makes contact with the sealing almost simultaneously all round. To avoid getting grease on the edges of the windscreen, use clean rubber gloves for lifting it. If you can borrow a glass lifter do so, but making one which is guaranteed not to let you down would probably waste more time than would be saved when using it.

2   For the actual fitting, use Volvo Sealing Agent No 686275 in conjunction with special butyl coated tape. The sealant is applied to the windscreen and to the body, and the tape is sandwiched between the two coatings.

3   Apply the sealant to the body and to the windscreen. The coated strip should be between ¾" and 7/8" wide (18-21 mm) and two coats should be applied in each case.

4   Fit the spacers (ie the ones that are actually fitted to the car - not any temporary ones you may be going to use for placing the windscreen) on the lower edge of the windscreen opening between the second and third clip from each side.

5   Allow the sealant to set for at least ten minutes but not more than an hour. Then roll the tape round the whole of the opening without removing its protective paper (this faces the front of

course). Make a joint at one of the sides, cutting it at an angle and butting the edges. Use a very sharp knife or razor blade, preferably heated. **Do not** stretch the tape.

6   When you are ready to place the windscreen in position, remove the protective paper from the tape without touching the adhesive surface or disturbing the joint. Then place the windscreen in position and push on it for at least a minute.

7   Re-fit the outer and inner mouldings, rear view mirror and windscreen wiper arms and the job is done.

23 Sun roof

1   Enough details are given in Fig.12.18. to enable anyone looking at it, in conjunction with an actual sun roof, to see how the whole thing works. It can be removed as follows.

2   Open the sun roof and release the clips securing the roof upholstery at the front end. Move the upholstery back to leave an opening.

3   Crank the sun roof forwards and slacken the screws at its four attachments (9. and 11., Fig.12.18). Bend the blade springs (10) to one side and remove the reinforcing plates (13) at the rear attachments. The sun roof can now be lifted off.

24 Sun roof - replacing cables

1   Remove the sun roof as described in Section 23.

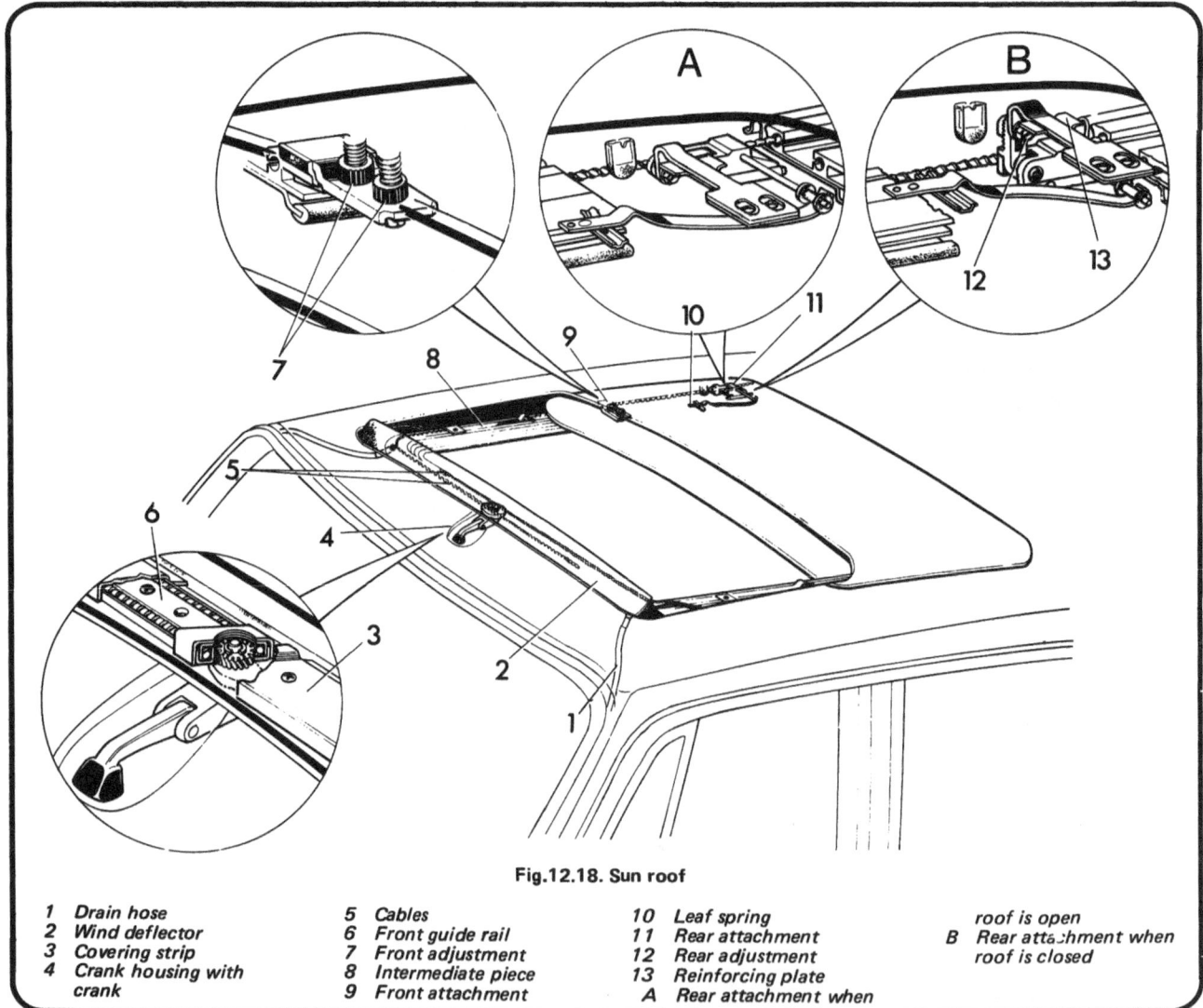

Fig.12.18. Sun roof

1	Drain hose	5	Cables	10	Leaf spring		roof is open
2	Wind deflector	6	Front guide rail	11	Rear attachment	B	Rear attachment when
3	Covering strip	7	Front adjustment	12	Rear adjustment		roof is closed
4	Crank housing with crank	8	Intermediate piece	13	Reinforcing plate		
		9	Front attachment	A	Rear attachment when		

2   Remove the wind deflector (2 Fig. 12.18).

3   Remove the intermediate pieces (8) covering strip (3) and holders above the drive. Release the front guide rails (6) and pull out the cables (5).

4   Fit replacement cables so that the attachments for the sun roof come opposite each other at the rear end of the roof opening. Screw the front guide rails on securely.

5   Refit the intermediate pieces, holders, covering plate and the wind deflector.

6   Screw on the roof securely and put back the leaf springs.

7   Crank the sun roof forwards until it is completely closed and check that it is level with the main roof. If necessary adjust at the front and rear attachments (7 and 12, Fig.12.18). Check that the lifts on the rear attachments are pushed up when the roof is closed. (B, Fig.12.18).

8   When the roof is closed the crank should point straight forwards in the vehicle. If it does not, unscrew the crank and

gear housing, turn the crank to the stop position and replace.

25 Front bumper shock absorbers

1   On recent models the front bumpers are attached to the frame by shock absorbers which enable them to withstand a frontal collision impact of 5 m.p.h. (8 km.p.h.). Figs. 12.19 and 12.20 make it obvious how these are removed and fitted.

2   The shock absorbers are filled with a gel which turns to a liquid when compressed. This means that a defective unit is not going to draw attention to itself by leaking fluid, but since the shock absorber is not going to be working very hard for its living it is not very likely to become defective anyway. No servicing or maintenance is called for - an occasional push on the front bumper will check that the system is working properly.

Fig.12.20. Front bumper shock absorber

Fig.12.21. Front bumper attached to frame
via shock absorber

Chapter 13 Supplement: CI fuel system models

Contents

---

1 Introduction

1 In 1974 Volvo introduced a Continuous Injection (CI) type of fuel system in place of the earlier electronically controlled fuel injection system fitted to some models.

2 The purpose of this Supplement is to include in this manual all information in respect of the fuel system for cars equipped with Continuous Injection fuel systems.

3 The ignition system distributor is basically the same as fitted to carburettor engines and the different specification is listed in Section 2.

---

2 Specifications

The specifications listed here apply to those cars equipped with Continuous Injection (CI) fuel systems. The original specifications given at the beginning of each Chapter in this manual apply unless alternative figures are quoted here.

Continuous Injection fuel system

Fuel filter

Type	Paper
Change interval	50,000 miles (80,000 km)

Fuel pump

Type	Electric, roller type
Capacity	22 Imp gall = 26.5 US gall/hr at 71 psi (100 l/hr at 5 kg/sq cm)
Current consumption	8.5 amps (max)

Auxiliary air valve

Completely open	at −30°C (−22°F)
Completely closed	at +70°C (+158°F) (or after 5 minutes driving with an ambient temperature of +20°C (68°F)
Line pressure	64 - 74 psi (4.5 - 5.2 kg/sq cm)
Rest pressure	24 - 34 psi (1.7 - 2.4 kg/sq cm)
Control pressure	50 - 55 psi (3.5 - 3.9 kg/sq cm)

Air filter

Type	Paper
Change interval	25,000 miles (40,000 km)

CO valve

Warm engine, idling speed:

Except USA	0.5 - 3.5%
USA	1.5%

Ignition system

Spark plugs

B20E engine	Bosch W225 T 35 or equivalent
B20F engine	Bosch W200 T 35 or equivalent

Ignition timing (stroboscopic)

B20E engine	10 BTDC at 600 - 800 rpm (vacuum unit disconnected)
B20F engine	10 BTDC at 600 - 800 rpm

Distributor (B20E engine)

Type	Bosch JFUF
Direction of rotation	Counter-clockwise
Breaker point gap	0.014 in (0.35 mm)
Dwell angle	59 - 65°
Centrifugal unit, advance:	
Total	11$^O \pm$ 1^O
Begins	375 - 550 rpm
3°	625 - 790 rpm
7°	960 - 1125 rpm
Ends	1375 rpm
Vacuum unit (negative control), retard:	
Total	$\pm$ degree
Begins	2.36 - 3.96 in (60 - 100 mm) Hg
3°	3.56 - 5.02 in (90 - 127 mm) Hg
Ends	5.15 - 5.54 in (130 - 140 mm) Hg

Distributor (B20F engine)

Type	Bosch JF
Direction of rotation	Counter-clockwise
Breaker point gap	0.014 in (0.35 mm)
Dwell angle	59 - 65°
Centrifugal governor, advance:	
Total	12$^O \pm$ 1^O
Begins	400 - 525 rpm
3°	610 - 780 rpm
7°	950 - 1125 rpm
10°	1400 to 1970 rpm
Ends	2250 rpm

3 Routine maintenance

1 Clean the fuel tank filter every 15,000 miles (25,000 km).
2 Change the line fuel filter at 50,000 miles (80,000 km).

4 Engine removal

1 Carry out operations 1 to 6 of Section 5, Chapter 1.
2 Disconnect the following fuel hoses:

    a) *Rubber hose to the control pressure regulator.*
    b) *Plastic hose from the control pressure regulator at the fuel distributor.*
    c) *Hose at the cold start injector.*
    d) *Hose at the fuel filter.*
    e) *Fuel return hose at the fuel distributor.*

3 Remove the pipe connecting the air cleaner and intake manifold.
4 Disconnect the leads from the cold start injector, control pressure regulator, auxiliary air valve, coolant temperature sensor and thermal time switch.
5 Disconnect the earth lead for the control pressure regulator.
6 Disconnect the fuel lines from the injectors.

7 Disconnect the throttle cable.
8 Disconnect the leads from the oil pressure sender, the alternator and the starter motor.
9 Disconnect the heater hoses at the bulkhead.
10 Disconnect the brake vacuum booster hose at the intake manifold and the crankcase ventilation hose at the air cleaner.
11 Disconnect the leads at the spark plugs and the distributor. Remove the distributor cap.
12 Proceed as described in Chapter 1, Section 7.

5 Continuous Injection (CI) fuel system - control principle

1 The 1974 Volvo models equipped with a fuel injection system have a CI (Continuous Injection) system, unlike the electronically controlled system fitted to earlier models.
2 The injection valves of the system are always open, that is, are always injecting fuel when the engine is running. The amount of fuel is not controlled by variation of the injecting time, as in the earlier system, but by varying the amount of fuel flowing through the injectors.
3 The CI system principle is to measure continuously the airflow into the engine and let this airflow control the amount of fuel fed to the engine. The measuring of the induced air and the control of the fuel flow is provided by an air-fuel control unit which is the heart of the CI system. The air-fuel control unit

Fig. 13.1. CI Fuel injection system

1	Air cleaner	8	Fuel filter
2	Fuel distributor	9	Injector
3	Air flow sensor	10	Idle adjustment screw
4	Cold start injector	11	Auxiliary air valve
5	Intake manifold	12	Pump relay
6	Control pressure regulator	13	Relay (stops the pump if
7	Thermal time switch		the engine stops)

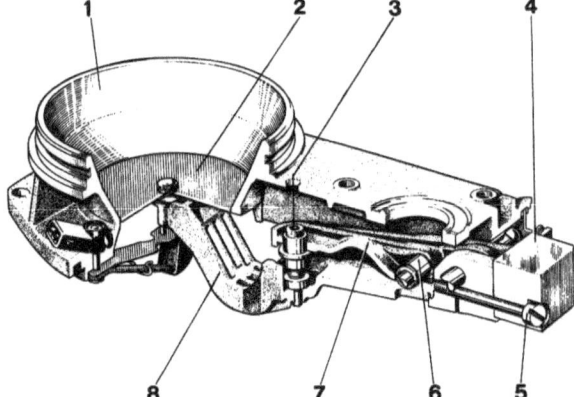

Fig. 13.2. The air flow sensor

1	Air venturi	5	Lock screw
2	Air flow sensor plate	6	Pivot
3	CO adjustment screw	7	Adjustment arm
4	Balance weight	8	Lever

consists of an airflow sensor and a fuel distributor.

4   The airflow sensor consists of a plate in a venturi. The air flows upwards through the venturi and lifts the plate to let air pass through. A large airflow lifts the plate to a high position, a small airflow to a low position.

5   The movement of the airflow sensor plate is transferred by a lever to a control plunger in the fuel distributor. The lever is provided with a balance weight which equalizes the weight of the plate and the lever.

6   The control plunger is located in a cylinder which is provided with four metering slots, one for each engine cylinder. When lifted, the edge of the control plunger head uncovers the metering slots. A high airflow sensor plate position corresponds to a large uncovered metering slot area: a low position to a small area.

7   The difference between the fuel pressure ahead of the slot and after the slot must be constant in order to ensure that the quantity of fuel passing through the metering slots is proportional to the uncovered metering area. This is ensured by four pressure regulating valves, one for each metering slot, which maintain a constant pressure drop of 1.4 psi (0.1 kg/sq cm) over the slot.

---

6   CI fuel system - general description

Air system

1   Besides the airflow control unit, the CI fuel system consists of several other components. A diagram of the system is illustrated in Fig. 13.1.

2   The air cleaner has a replaceable paper type cartridge which should be replaced every 25,000 miles (40,000 km).

3   The air flow sensor controls the flow of air to provide a correct fuel-air mixture at all loads. The throttle is located in the intake manifold and is controlled by the throttle pedal. An idle adjustment screw is located in a channel bypassing the throttle. It increases or decreases the area of the bypass channel and thus controls the idling speed.

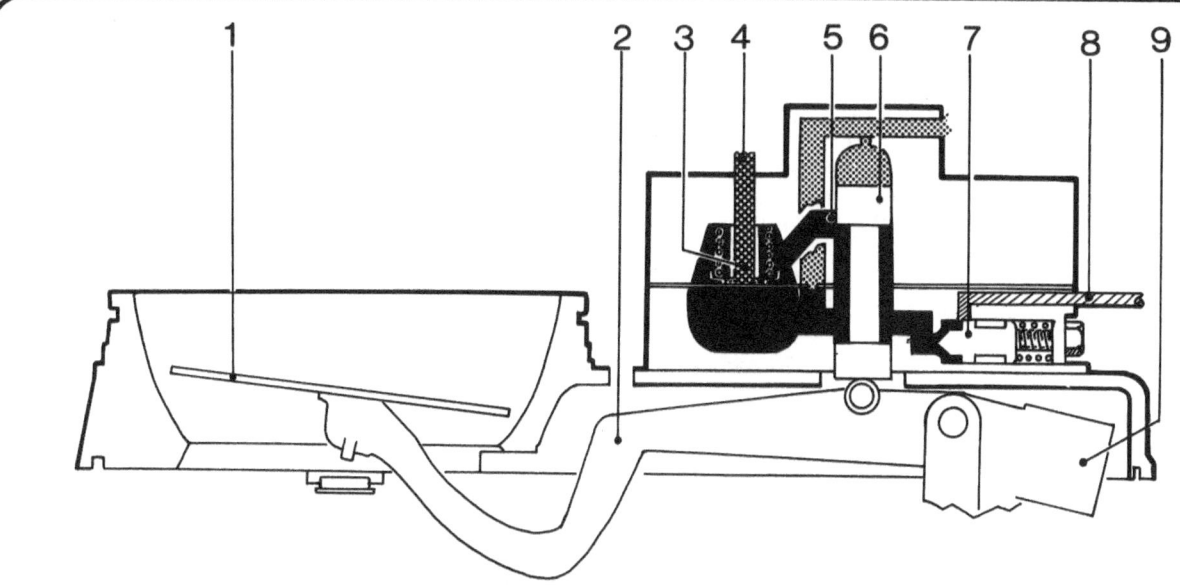

Fig. 13.3. Air-fuel control unit

1 Air flow sensor plate	4 To injector	6 Control plunger	8 To tank
2 Lever	5 Control plunger head	7 Line pressure regulator	9 Balance weight
3 Pressure regulating valve			

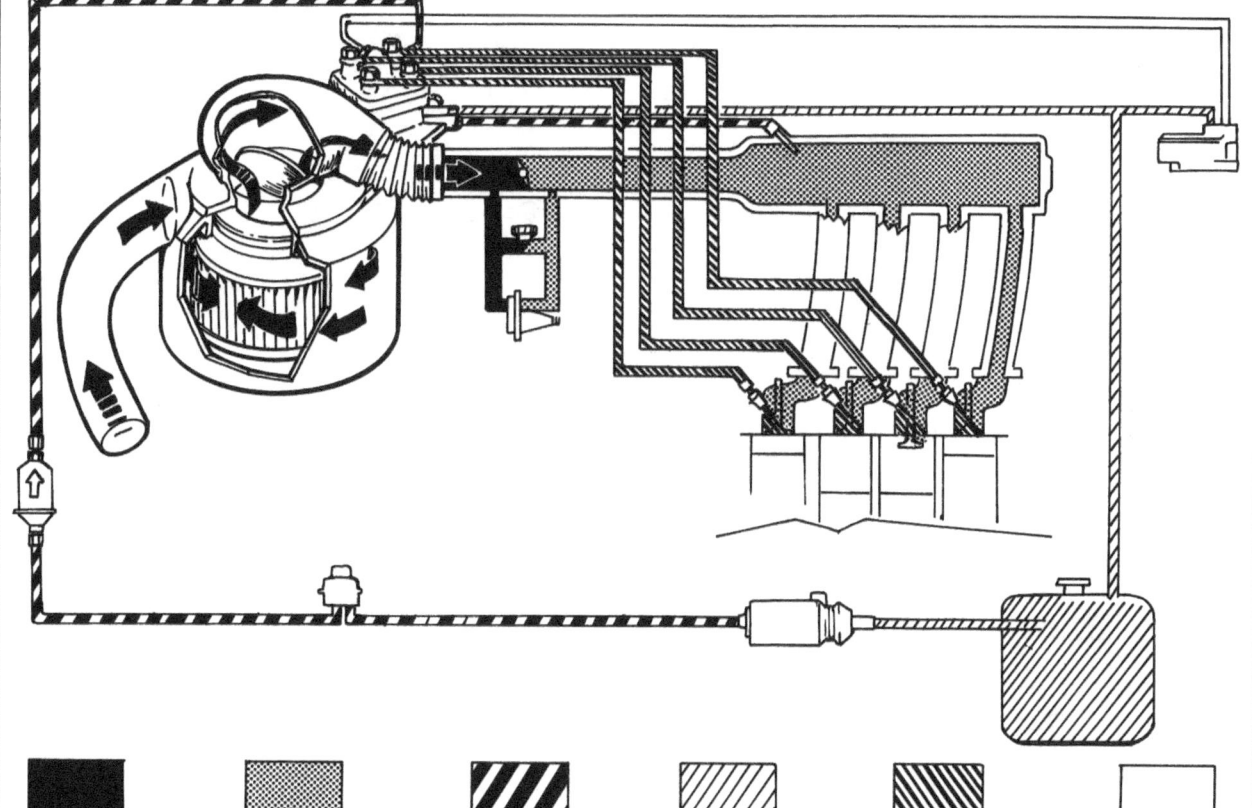

Air Atmospheric pressure	Air Under-pressure	Fuel Line pressure 4.5 kp/cm^2	Fuel Pressure-less	Fuel Injection pressure, approx. 3.3 kp/cm^2	Fuel Control pressure, approx. 3.2 kp/cm^2 (hot engine)

Fig. 13.4. Diagram of CI fuel system

1 Fuel tank	5 Air cleaner	9 Idle adjustment screw	12 Intake manifold
2 Fuel pump	6 Air flow sensor	10 Auxiliary air valve	13 Control pressure regulator
3 Pressure accumulator	7 Fuel distributor	11 Cold start injector	14 Injector
4 Fuel filter	8 Throttle		

4   The auxiliary air valve is located on the intake manifold and like the idling adjustment screw, bypasses the throttle. A bi-metallic spring presses on the valve when the engine is cold and thereby the bypass air channel is kept open. Current flows through the coil when the starter motor is operated and when the engine is running. The coil heats the bi-metallic spring which decreases the pressure on the valve which is gradually closed by the spring.

Fuel system

5   The fuel system consists of the fuel pump, fuel accumulator, fuel filter, fuel distributor and injectors as well as the control pressure regulator and line pressure regulator. The components are described in the order the fuel travels through the system.

6   The fuel pump is a roller-type pump combined with an electric motor and is located in front of the fuel tank. If the fuel pressure should become excessive (pinched fuel line, etc.) a built-in relief valve allows the fuel to circulate inside the pump. In the rest position, pressure is maintained in the system by a check valve in the fuel pump outlet.

7   The fuel accumulator is located close to the fuel pump and helps accumulate and maintain pressure in the fuel system when the fuel pump check valve has closed.

8   The fuel filter is installed in the system between the fuel accumulator and the fuel distributor. The direction of flow is marked by arrows on the housing.

9   The fuel distributor controls the amount of fuel to the injectors in relation to the airflow. It consists of a line pressure regulator which controls the pressure to the fuel distributor; a control plunger, which controls and distributes the fuel to the injectors; and four pressure regulator valves which maintain a constant pressure difference between inlet and outlet of the control plunger.

10 The line pressure regulator controls the fuel pressure to the fuel distributor. It closes the tank recirculation line if the fuel pressure is below 64 psi (4.5 kg/sq cm).

11 The fuel control unit plunger opens the metering slots according to the airflow sensor plate position, when the plate position is high more fuel is directed through the pressure regulating valves.

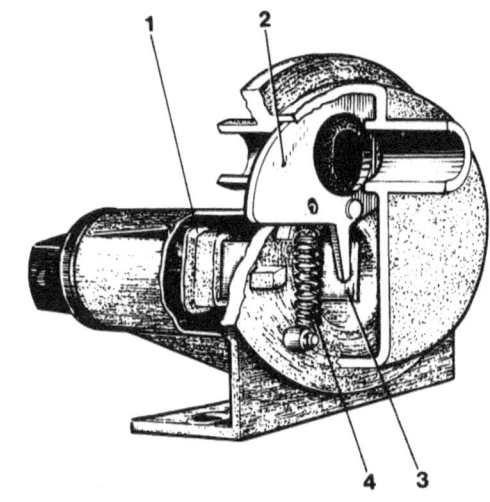

Fig. 13.5. Auxiliary air valve -

1 Coil	*3 Bi-metallic spring*
2 Air valve	*4 Return spring*

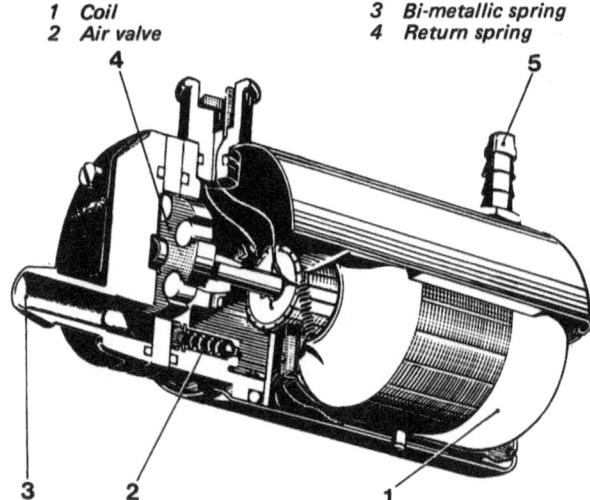

Fig. 13.6. Fuel pump

1 Rotor	*4 Pump rotor*
2 Relief valve	*5 Outlet*
3 Intake	

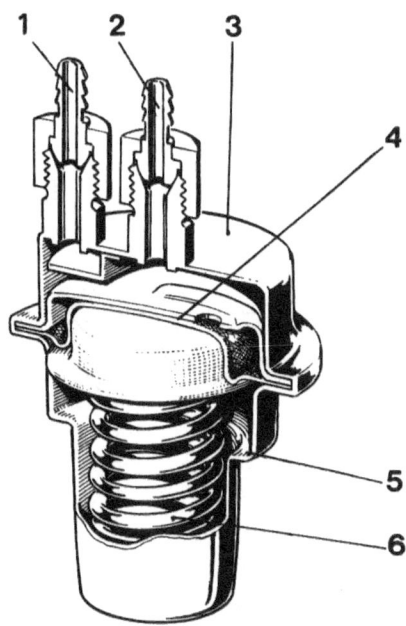

Fig. 13.7. Fuel accumulator

1 Inlet	*4 Diaphragm*
2 Outlet	*5 Stop*
3 Housing	*6 Spring*

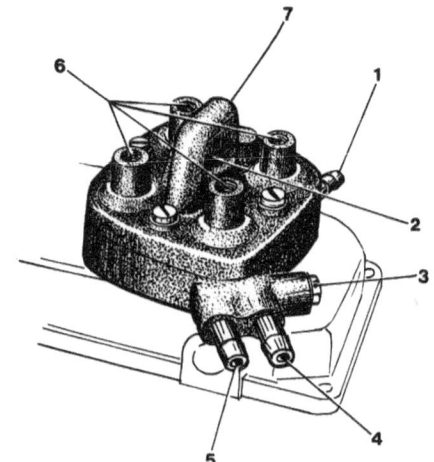

Fig. 13.8. Fuel distributor

1 Fuel supply	*5 To cold start injector*
2 Fuel control unit	*6 To the injectors*
3 Line pressure regulator	*7 To the control pressure*
* Tank return*	* regulator*

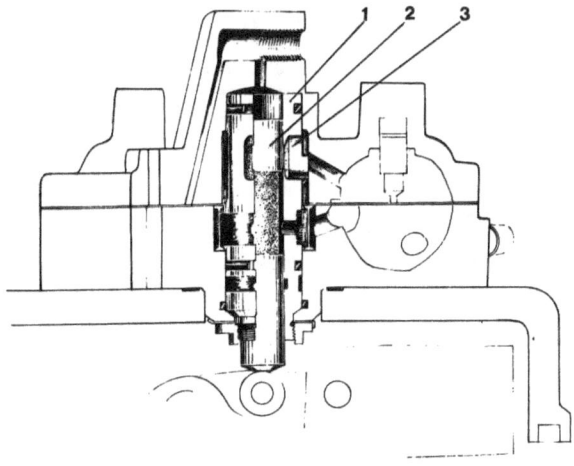

Fig. 13.9. Fuel control unit

1 Cylinder   3 Metering slots
2 Control plunger

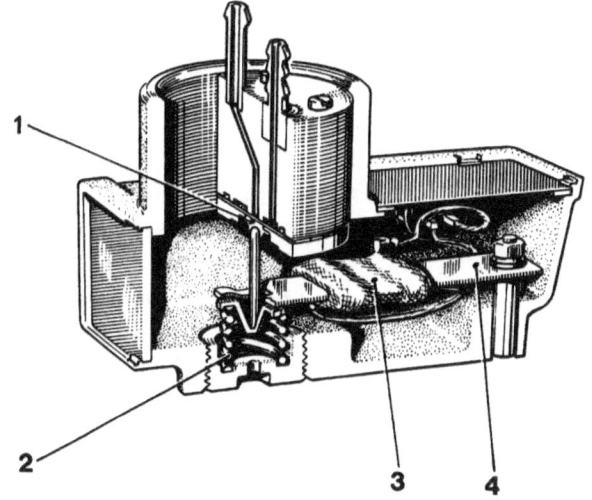

Fig. 13.10. Control pressure regulator -

1 Diaphragm valve   3 Coil
2 Spring   4 Bi-metallic spring

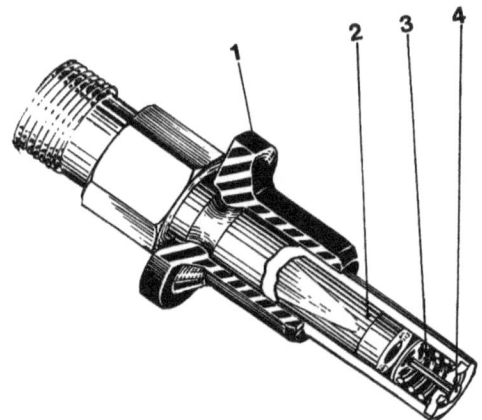

Fig. 13.11. Fuel injector

1 Rubber seal   3 Valve spring
2 Insert   4 Valve

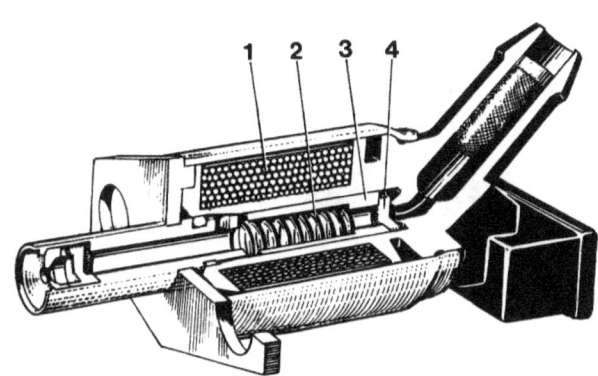

Fig. 13.12. Cold start injector

1 Coil   3 Actuator
2 Return spring   4 Seal

12 Some of the fuel from the fuel distributor inlet is diverted to the control plunger top side. From there it travels first to a control pressure regulator and then to the tank. The control pressure is controlled by the control pressure regulator and is normally 52.5 psi (3.7 kg/sq cm). The control pressure fuel acts on top of the control plunger and dampens the movement of the airflow sensor plate during fast acceleration.

13 The control pressure regulator controls, during warm-up period, the control pressure in relation to the engine temperature so that the fuel mixture is enriched.

14 The pressure regulating valves provide a constant pressure drop across the metering slots, independent of the amount of fuel passing through the slots. This is necessary in order to achieve an injection proportional to the positions of the control plunger and the airflow sensor plate.

15 The injectors have a spring-controlled valve which opens at a fuel pressure of 47 psi (3.3 kg/sq cm). The fuel pressure opens the valve and that makes the injection continuous, while the fuel flow varies according to the air inducted.

16 The cold start injector supplies extra fuel for cold starting. The injection time is controlled by the thermal time switch and provides extra fuel for 12 seconds at −20°C (5°F). The cold start injector is igniting fuel only when the starter motor is operating. It stops injecting fuel if the engine starts, and the

starter motor stops operating, before the time permitted by the thermal time switch is up.

17 The thermal time switch determines the cold start injector operating time. It is a sealed unit, having contacts controlled by a bi-metallic spring. The bi-metallic spring has two coils, one activated from the cold start injector and the other from the starter. The contacts are closed at below +35°C (95°F). When the starter operates current flows from the starter to the cold start injector and, via a coil and the contacts, to earth. At the same time current flows from the starter, via the second coil and the contacts, to earth. The cold start injector operates as long as the contacts are closed and the starter is operating. The current flowing from the starter motor to the coil heats the bi-metallic spring, the contacts open and the cold start injector stops operating. The heating time varies with the engine temperature: the warmer the engine the shorter the heating time for the bi-metallic spring and consequently also the injection time.

Electrical system

18 Fig. 13.15 shows the layout of the electrical system and wiring circuits.

19 When the ignition is switched on, current flows from the ignition coil terminal '15' to the main relay terminal '86', through the relay coil to terminal '85' and finally to the air-fuel

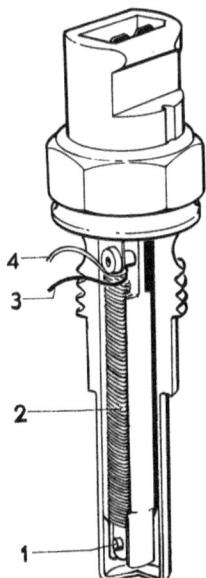

Fig. 13.13. Thermal time switch

1   *Contacts*
2   *Bi-metallic spring*

3   *Lead from starter*
4   *Lead from cold start injector*

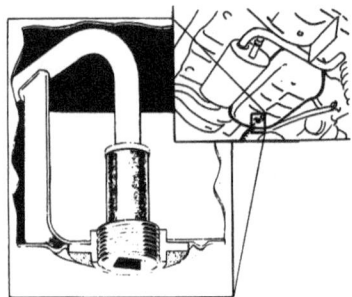

Fig. 13.14. Cleaning the tank fuel filter

control unit and earth. The main relay is thus activated.
20 When the ignition key is turned to the starting position, current flows from the starter terminal '50' to the main relay terminal '87', through the closed contacts to terminal '30' and to the pump relay terminal '86'. From there through the relay coil to terminal '85' and earth. The pump relay is thus activated.
21 Current flows from fuse '7' to the pump relay terminal '30', through the closed contacts to terminal '87', to the fuel pump and earth. The fuel pump is thus activated and pumps fuel. The control pressure regulator and the auxiliary air valve are activated at the same time as the fuel pump.
22 When the starter motor is operating or after the engine has started, the contacts at the air-fuel control unit open, the earth circuit is opened, and the main relay is deactivated. Current now flows from terminal '86' to terminal '87a', through the contacts to terminal '30'. The fuel pump relay is still activated and the pump is operating. There is no current flow to the main relay terminal '87' when the engine is running and the starter motor not operating.
23 If the engine stops (with the ignition still switched on) the contacts at the air-fuel control unit close. Main relay terminal '85' is earthed, the relay is activated, and terminal '30' is connected to terminal '87'. As there is no current flow to terminal '87', the pump relay is deactivated and the fuel pump stops working.
24 The cold start injector is activated only when the starter motor is operating and the engine temperature at the same time is so low that the thermal time switch cuts in.

---

7   Fuel tank filter - cleaning

---

1   The filter should be cleaned at intervals of 15,000 miles (25,000 km).
2   Remove the plug from the bottom of the tank Fig. 13.14 and clean it.
3   When refitting, ensure that the suction pipe is centred in the flange hole, otherwise the filter can get damaged and, at worst this could shut off the fuel supply.

---

8   Air-fuel control unit - removal and refitting

---

1   Clean round all the fuel connections before disconnecting them.

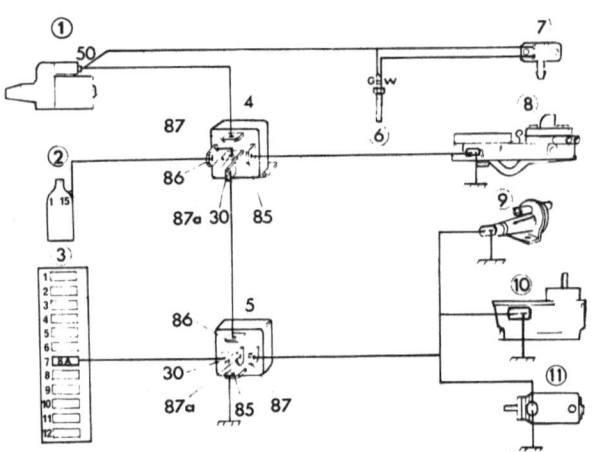

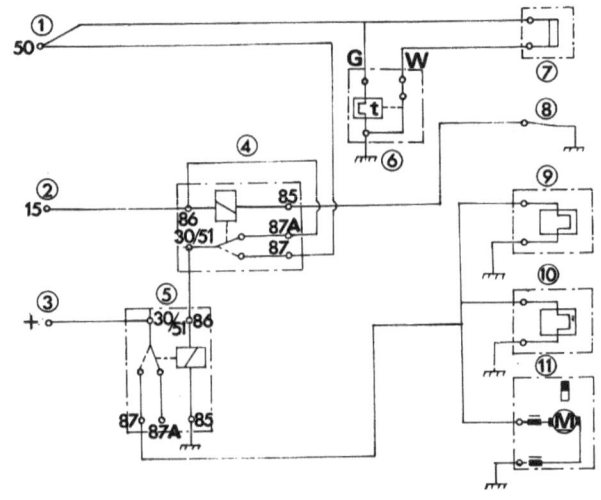

Fig. 13.15. Electrical system

1   *Starter motor*
2   *Ignition coil*
3   *Fuse box (Fuse No. 7)*

4   *Main relay*
5   *Fuel pump relay*
6   *Thermal time switch*

7   *Cold start injector*
8   *Air-fuel control unit*
9   *Auxiliary air valve*

10   *Control pressure regulator*
11   *Fuel pump*

Fig. 13.16. Removing the air-fuel control unit

Fig. 13.17. Removing the fuel distributor

2 Remove the rubber bellows and the strap for the injector pipes.

3 Remove the injector pipes and the control pressure pipe from the distributor.

4 Disconnect the cold start injector and recirculation pipe lines. Pull out the electrical plug connection.

5 Disconnect the fuel line at the filter.

6 Remove the air-fuel control unit retaining screws and lift it out. Collect the gasket.

7 Refitting is the reverse of the removal sequence. Always fit a new gasket.

9 Air-fuel control unit - dismantling and inspection

1 Clamp the unit lightly in a vice, but do not use force likely to damage it.

2 Remove the three securing screws and carefully lift off the fuel distributor taking care that the control plunger does not fall out and get damaged.

Note: The fuel distributor must not be dismantled.

3 Remove the two retaining screws and lift off the bridge piece.

4 Remove the balance weight.

5 Remove the lever with the adjustment arm by removing the circlip, washer, rubber seal, springs and balls as well as the shaft.

6 Wash the control plunger in petrol and blow it off with compressed air. Check the plunger for damage. If the plunger is worn or damaged, the fuel distributor must be renewed. Any attempts to clean the slots will do more harm than good. Renew any worn or damaged parts.

Fig. 13.18. Undoing the bridge piece retaining screws

10 Air-fuel control unit - reassembly

1 Place the lever and adjustment arm in position. The adjustment arm should be positioned so that the roller for the control plunger is towards the fuel distributor. Fit the shaft, balls, springs, rubber seal, washers and circlip.

2 Fit the balance weight and centre the lever. Tighten the balance weight screw.

3 Fit the sensor plate stop so that the spring and contact are on the right side, Fig. 13.22.

4 Centre the airflow sensor plate. The sensor plate must not touch the retainer at any point. If adjustment is needed, loosen the plate screw and reposition the plate.

5 Check that with the airflow sensor plate at rest, it is level or no more than 0.040 in (1 mm) below the venturi edge. Adjust, if

Fig. 13.19. Remove the balance weight

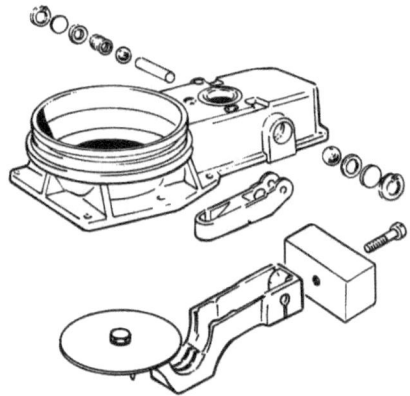

Fig. 13.20. Assembling the air-fuel control unit

Fig. 13.21. Centre the lever

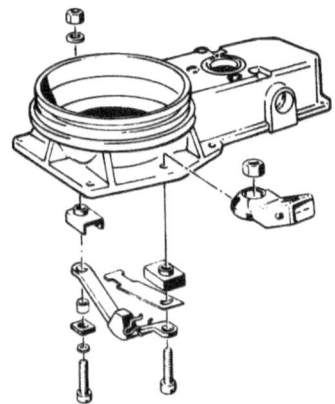

Fig. 13.22. Fitting the sensor plate stop

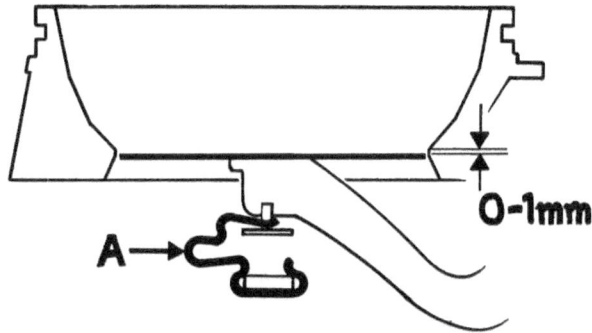

Fig. 13.23. Checking the sensor plate rest position

necessary, at 'A' in Fig. 13.23 with needle-nosed pliers.

6   Check the sensor plate for freedom of movement from low to high positions.

7   Fit the fuel distributor, taking care to avoid damaging the control plunger and O-ring. Always fit a new gasket. Tighten the retaining screws to 2.3-2.7 lb f ft (0.31-0.37 kg f m).

---

11 Line pressure regulator - inspection

1   Refer to Fig. 13.25. Remove the plug taking care not to lose the shims in the plug.

2   Pull out the plunger and the spring. Remove the O-ring from the plunger.

3   Clean the parts and examine them for damage. Renew defective parts, except the plunger which cannot be renewed separately as it is matched with the fuel distributor. If it is defective renew the distributor.

4   Fit a new O-ring on the plunger and refit the assembly using the same shims as were removed.

---

12 Line and rest pressure - testing

Line pressure

1   Connect a pressure gauge, with a three-way control lever as shown in Fig. 13.26, between the fuel distributor and the control pressure regulator.

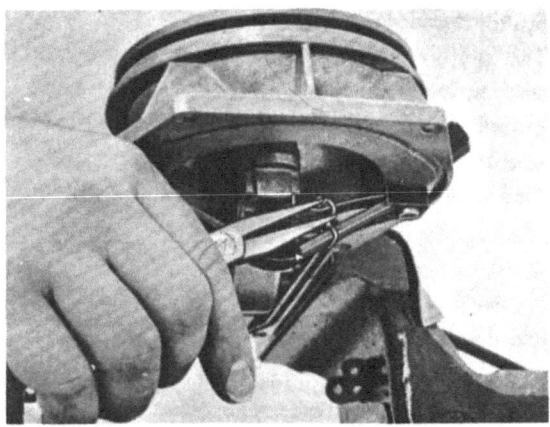

Fig. 13.24. Adjusting the sensor plate position

2 Switch on the ignition and disconnect the lead at the airflow sensor, to start the fuel pump.
3 Check the line pressure on the gauge. It should be 64-74 psi (4.5-5.2 kg/sq cm).
4 If the line pressure is low the reasons could be as follows:

a) Fuel line leakage. Check and rectify.
b) Line pressure regulator incorrectly adjusted. Adjust as described in Section 13.
c) If there is no line pressure with the pump operating, check for blockage of the fuel lines, filters or fuel distributor.
d) Fuel pump defective.

5 Excessively high pressure can be caused by:

a) Blocked recirculation line.
b) Line pressure regulator incorrectly adjusted, refer to Section 13.

Rest pressure

6 Reconnect the electrical lead to the airflow sensor.
7 After a few seconds check the rest pressure reading on the gauge. It should be 24 psi (1.7 kg/sq cm) minimum and 34 psi (2.4 kg/sq cm) maximum (injector opening pressure). Check that there is no noticeable drop in pressure within one minute. If the pressure is incorrect refer to Section 13, and adjust the line pressure regulator.
8 If the rest pressure drops too quickly, check as follows:

a) Turn the lever on the gauge towards the control pressure regulator. If the pressure still drops too quickly the control pressure regulator or its fuel lines are leaking and should be replaced.
b) Block the fuel recirculation line after the fuel distributor. If the pressure stops dropping, the line pressure regulator or its O-ring is faulty. Refer to line pressure regulator inspection, Section 11.
c) Turn the gauge lever at right-angles to the connection from the fuel distributor. Remove the airflow sensor lead for a few seconds to bring up the line pressure, then reconnect the lead. Pinch the fuel feed hose from the tank to the pump. If the fuel pressure stops falling the fuel pump check valve is faulty.
d) Check the fuel lines for leaks.

13 Line pressure regulator - adjustment

1 To adjust the line and rest pressure remove or add shims, as necessary, in the line pressure regulator.

2 There are two thicknesses of shims:

0.0039 in (0.1 mm) = 0.8 psi (0.06 kg/sq cm) pressure difference.
0.0196 in (0.5 mm) = 4.3 psi (0.3 kg/sq cm) pressure difference.

Use mainly the thick shims for adjustment. The thin shims are used when the line pressure is 69 psi (4.9 kg/sq cm) or more and the rest pressure at the same time is more than 24 psi (1.7 kg/sq cm).
Note: Both the line pressure and rest pressure are affected at the same time.

14 Control pressure - testing

The engine must be cold (at ambient temperature) when the control pressure is being checked.
1 Connect the pressure gauge between the fuel distributor and the control pressure regulator with the gauge lever at right-angles to the connection to the fuel distributor.
2 Switch on the ignition and start the fuel pump by disconnecting the lead at the airflow sensor.
3 Check the control pressure against the chart, Fig. 13.27. As you can see from the chart the control pressure at 20°C (68°F) should be 20.6-24.8 psi (1.45-1.75 kg/sq cm).
4 If the control pressure is too low, try a new control pressure regulator. If the pressure is too high, the recirculation line may be blocked. If the line is open, try a new control pressure regulator.
5 Reconnect the lead at the airflow sensor and switch off the ignition.

15 Injector - removal and refitting

1 Clean round the fuel injector and fuel pipe. Disconnect the fuel pipe.
2 Remove the injector retainer and the injector.
3 When refitting the injector fit a new rubber seal.
4 Reconnect the fuel pipe. Start the engine and check for leaks.

16 Injectors - testing

1 Check the injectors at rest pressure.
2 Remove the injector with the fuel line connected.
3 Lift the airflow sensor plate so that the metering slots in the fuel distributor open.

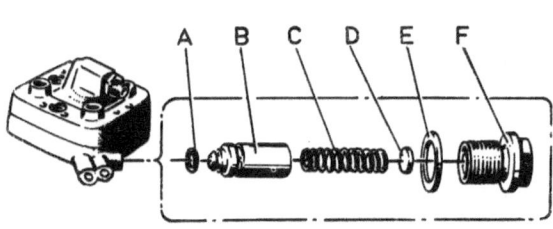
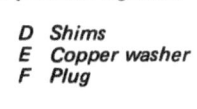

Fig. 13.25. Exploded view of line pressure regulator

A 'O' ring   D Shims
B Plunger   E Copper washer
C Spring   F Plug

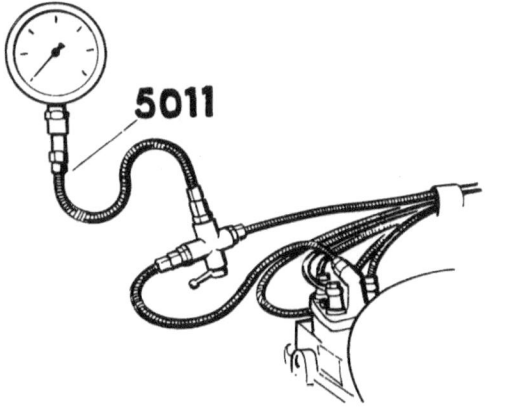

Fig. 13.26. Test gauge and three-way control valve

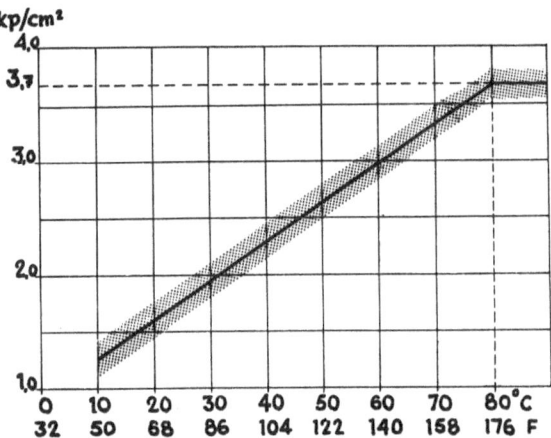

Fig. 13.27. Control pressure at various temperatures

Fig. 13.28. Disconnecting the fuel line from the control pressure regulator with a soldering iron

Fig 13.29. Throttle adjustment

4   Injectors must not leak more than one drop in 15 seconds. Renew injectors leaking at more than this rate.
Note: If all the injectors leak the reason may be an excessive rest pressure, see Section 12.

17 Cold start injector - removal and refitting

1   Disconnect the electrical plug. Clean round the fuel pipe connection and disconnect the pipe.
2   Remove the two retaining screws and the cold start injector and seal.
3   Refit the injector, use a new seal, and fit the retaining screws.
4   Reconnect the fuel pipe and electrical plug.

18 Cold start injector - testing

1   With the engine cold remove the cold start injector, leaving the fuel and electrical supply connected.
2   Hold the injector over a container (a glass jar is ideal), switch on the ignition and operate the starter motor.
3   The cold start injector should spray for 12 seconds at an engine temperature of −20ºC (−4ºF). Higher temperatures decrease the injection time and it ceases completely above +35ºC (95ºF).
4   If no fuel appears, remove the plug and check that when the starter motor is operated, 12 volts is measured across the socket pins. If this happens it indicates that the injector is faulty and will have to be renewed. If there is no voltage the wiring or thermal time switch is faulty.

19 Auxiliary air valve - removal and refitting

1   Disconnect the plug and hoses.
2   Remove the retaining screws and the auxiliary air valve.
3   When refitting the valve do not forget to connect the earth wire to one of the retaining screws.
4   Reconnect the hoses and plug.

20 Auxiliary air valve - testing

1   Remove the hoses and electrical connection.
2   Check that the valve is open, it should be half open at +20ºC (68ºF). It is completely closed when the engine is hot. Use a mirror and light when carrying out the check.
3   Reconnect the electrical plug. The valve should close completely within 5 minutes.
4   If the valve has not closed, tap lightly on the valve, if it closes it is OK (engine vibrations normally contribute to closing).
5   If it stays open check for voltage at the plug, if the voltage is OK, renew the air auxiliary valve.

21 Control pressure regulator - removal and refitting

1   Clean round the fuel line connections and remove the fuel line strap.
2   Disconnect the control pressure regulator hose at the fuel distributor and the electrical connection at the regulator.
3   Remove the control pressure regulator outlet line.
4   Remove the control pressure regulator and clamp it in a vice. Using a soldering iron, remove the line from the nipple. Do not cut the line.
5   Trim the fuel line and fit it to the new regulator.
6   Refit the regulator. Connect the earth lead to one of the retaining screws. Reconnect the hoses and electrical lead.
7   Check the control pressure: refer to Section 14.

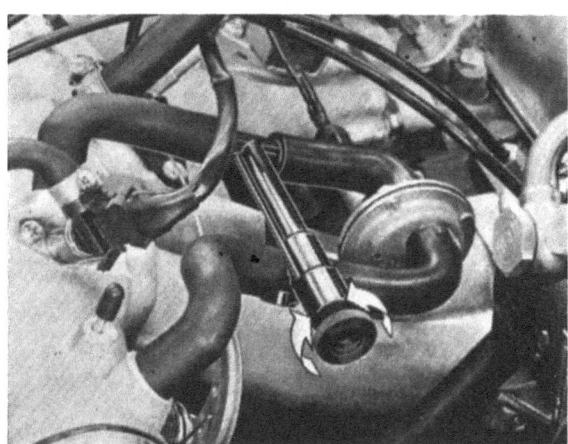

Fig. 13.30. Idling speed adjusting screw

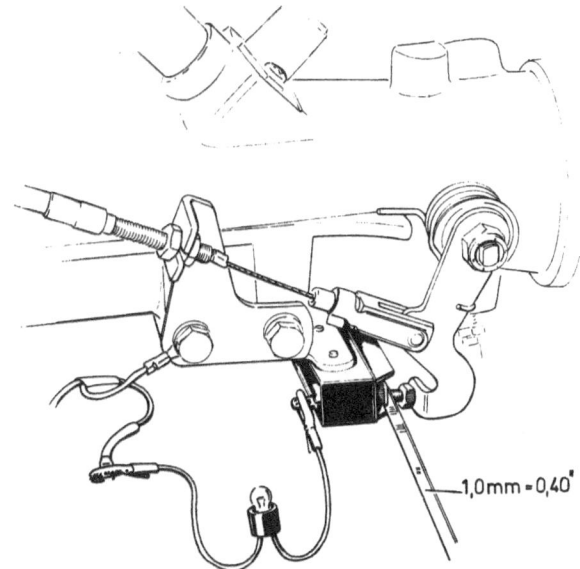

Fig. 13.31 Micro-switch adjustment

22 Fuel filter - removal and refitting

1   Clean round the hose connections.
2   Disconnect the hoses and remove the attaching screws and the filter.
3   Remove the unions and washers from the filter and fit them on the replacement filter.
4   Fit the filter and connect the pipe lines. An arrow on the filter casing shows the direction of flow, make sure it is the right way round.
5   Switch on the ignition. Disconnect the electrical plug at the airflow sensor and check that the fuel filter connections are not leaking.
6   Reconnect the plug at the airflow sensor and switch off the ignition.

23 Thermal time switch - testing

1   Run the engine until the temperature is above +35ºC (+95ºF).
2   Remove the cold start injector and hold it over a glass jar. Operate the starter motor.
3   The cold start injector should not spray, as the engine is hot. If it does spray, the thermal time switch is faulty and should be renewed.
4   Refit the cold start injector.

24 Thermal time switch - removal and refitting

1   Disconnect the electrical lead.
2   Partly drain the coolant system, or have a small plug ready to blank the orifice, then unscrew the switch from the block.
3   Refit the timer and reconnect the electrical lead.
4   Top-up the coolant system.

25 Fuel pump and accumulator - removal and refitting

1   Clean round all the hose connections so that dirt will not get into the pump.
2   Disconnect the battery earth terminal.

3   Pinch the fuel inlet hose with a clamp.
4   Disconnect the fuel inlet and outlet hoses.
5   Remove the retaining nuts, the fuel pump and accumulator, and the guard plate.
6   Disconnect the electrical plug and the fuel accumulator hoses.
7   Separate the bracket, rubber mountings, accumulator and fuel pump.
8   Refitting is the reverse of the removal procedure. Always fit a new fuel hose between the fuel accumulator and the fuel pump at every removal.

26 Fuel pump check valve - renewal

1   Remove the fuel pump, as described in Section 25.
2   Clamp the pump in a vice by its bracket. Never hold the pump other than by the bracket.
3   Screw out the check valve and make sure that no dirt enters the pump.
4   Refit the check valve, using a new gasket. Tighten the valve to a torque of 12-16 lb f ft (1.6-2.7 kg f m). Do not overtighten as you will damage the threads in the fuel pump housing.
5   Refit the fuel pump: refer to Section 25.

27 Throttle plate - adjustment

1   Loosen the locknut and turn the stop screw out until it is clear of the throttle lever stop.
2   Turn the screw in, until it touches the stop, then a further ½ turn. Tighten the locknut.
3   Check that the throttle shaft lever touches the full throttle stop when the throttle pedal is fully depressed. Check that the throttle plate is free and does not stick in the closed position.

28 Idling speed - adjustment

1   Run the engine until it is at normal operating temperature.
2   Adjust the idling speed to 900 rpm, manual transmission, or 800 rpm automatic transmission, with the throttle closed by turning the idling adjustment screw (see Fig. 13.30).
3   If the idling speed cannot be lowered to the specified speed,

the throttle valve plate must be slightly open. Check its setting as described in Section 27.

29 Air filter element - renewal

1   Release the clamps securing the rubber bellows and remove the bellows.
2   Disconnect the electrical plug at the fuel distributor.
3   Undo the clips and remove the air cleaner upper part including the fuel distributor and move it to the side.
4   Remove the air cleaner element and fit a new replacement.
5   Refit the upper part of the cleaner and the rubber bellows. Reconnect the electrical plug at the fuel distributor.

30 EGR (Exhaust Gas Recirculation) system - general

1   In order to reduce engine and exhaust pollution to a minimum, cars destined for territories where stringent control regulations are in force have an EGR emission control system fitted.
2   The EGR system is a method of recycling the engine exhaust gases by returning them to the combustion chambers where they reduce the combustion temperature and restrict the volume of noxious gases produced.
3   The arrangement includes a vacuum-operated valve, an air shutter and connecting pipes.

31 EGR valve - servicing

1   Every 15,000 miles (25,000 km) the EGR valve should be cleaned and checked.

2   To clean the valve, disconnect the connecting pipes, unscrew the valve and remove it. Using a wire brush clean away all the deposits, also clean the intake manifold nipple.
3   The EGR valve should be renewed at intervals of 30,000 miles (48,000 km).
4   To check the operation of the EGR system after refitting the valve, remove the EGR valve vacuum hose at the intake manifold and create a vacuum by sucking the end of the hose. The engine should run unevenly or stall. If this does not happen check that the return pipe and the EGR line are not blocked. If the lines are clear and the engine still runs smoothly renew the valve complete.

32 Throttle with micro-switch - adjustment

1   Adjust the throttle plate as described in Section 27.
2   Disconnect the lead at the micro-switch, see Fig. 13.31, and connect a test lamp in series between the disconnected lead and the micro-switch terminal.
3   Switch on the ignition. Insert a 0.040 in (1 mm) feeler gauge between the throttle adjustment screw and its stop.
4   Loosen the locknut for the micro-switch adjustment screw and screw out the adjustment screw until the micro-switch is free. Then screw in again until the test light just comes on. Lock the adjustment screw.
5   To check the adjustment insert a 0.035 in (0.9 mm) feeler gauge between the throttle adjustment screw and its stop. Open and close the throttle by hand (do not allow the throttle to slap back to the closed position). The test lamp should light up.
6   Replace the feeler gauge with one of 0.050 in (1.3 mm) and again open and close the throttle. The test lamp should not light.
7   Switch off the ignition, remove the test lamp and reconnect the lead to the micro-switch.

33 Fault diagnosis - CI fuel system

The following table details a few of the symptoms of fuel system trouble and possible causes. Always bear in mind that it is difficult to distinguish between ignition faults and fuel system faults in many cases. As ignition faults are easy to check make sure the ignition system is in order before starting on the fuel system.

Symptom	Reason/s
Smell of petrol when engine is stopped	Leaking fuel pipes or unions. Leaking fuel tank.
Smell of petrol when engine is idling	Leaking fuel lines or unions in fuel distribution system.
Difficult starting with cold engine	Leak in the intake system. Airflow sensor plate maladjusted. Fuel distributor or airflow sensor sticking or binding. Line pressure too low. Control pressure too high. Auxiliary air valve not opening. Cold start injector faulty. Thermal time switch faulty. Blocked fuel lines or filter.
Difficult starting with warm engine	Leak in the intake system. Airflow sensor plate maladjusted. Fuel distributor or airflow sensor sticking or binding. Line pressure too low. Cold start injector leaking. Air-fuel unit leaking. Control pressure incorrect. Rest pressure incorrect. Injectors leaking.

Symptom	Reason/s
Uneven running	Control pressure incorrect.
	Cold start injector leaking.
	Air-fuel control unit leaking.
	Auxiliary air valve nut closing.
	Injectors leaking.
	Defective injector O-ring seal.
	Air leak in intake system.
Poor performance, lack of power	Cold start injector leaking.
	Control pressure too high.
	Fuel starvation - blocked fuel lines, filters, injectors or fuel distributor.
	Intake system leaking.
Excessive fuel consumption not accounted for by external leaks	Control pressure too low.
	Cold start injector leaking.
	Faulty injectors.

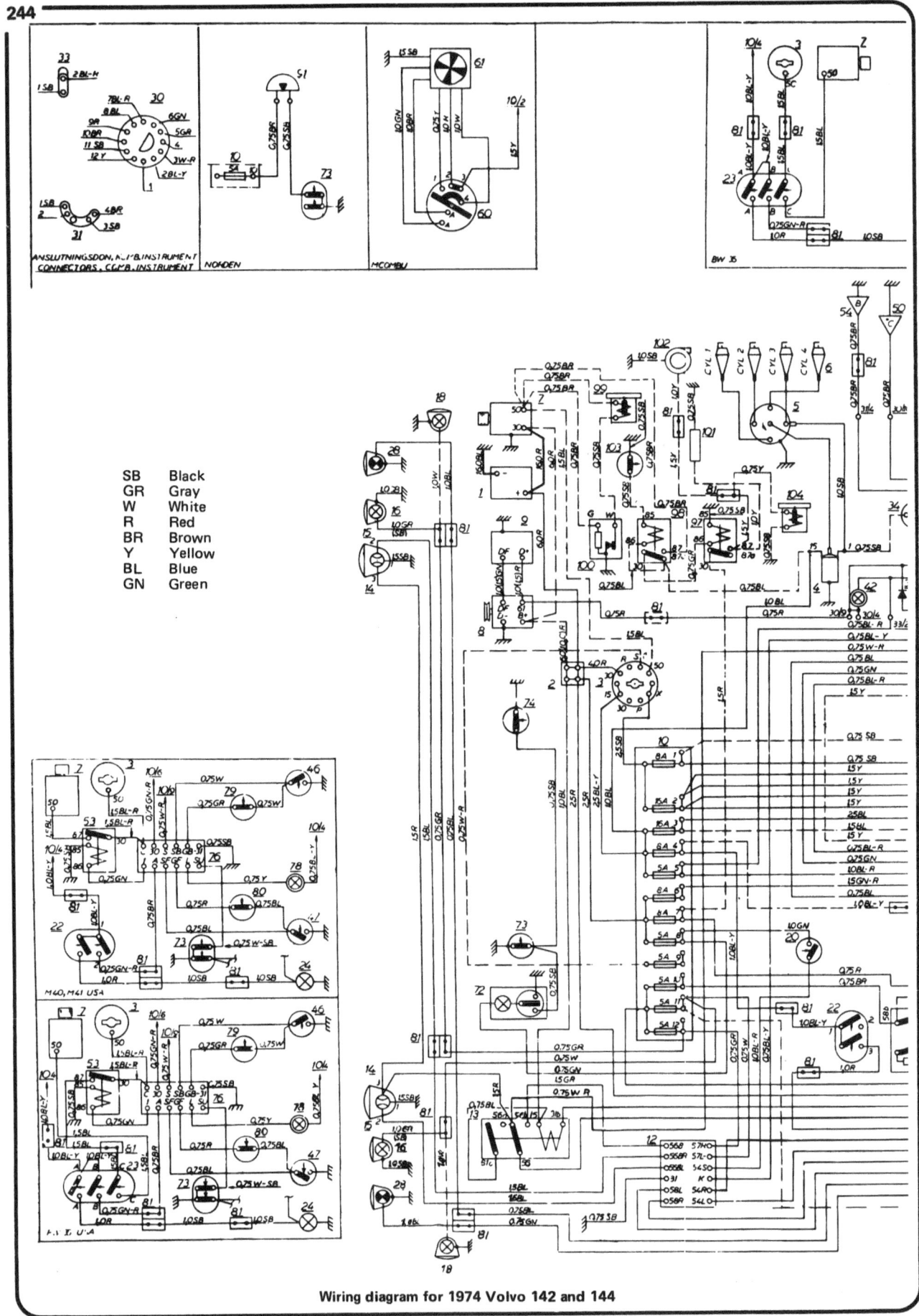

SB Black
GR Gray
W White
R Red
BR Brown
Y Yellow
BL Blue
GN Green

Wiring diagram for 1974 Volvo 142 and 144

Wiring diagram for 1974 Volvo 142 and 144

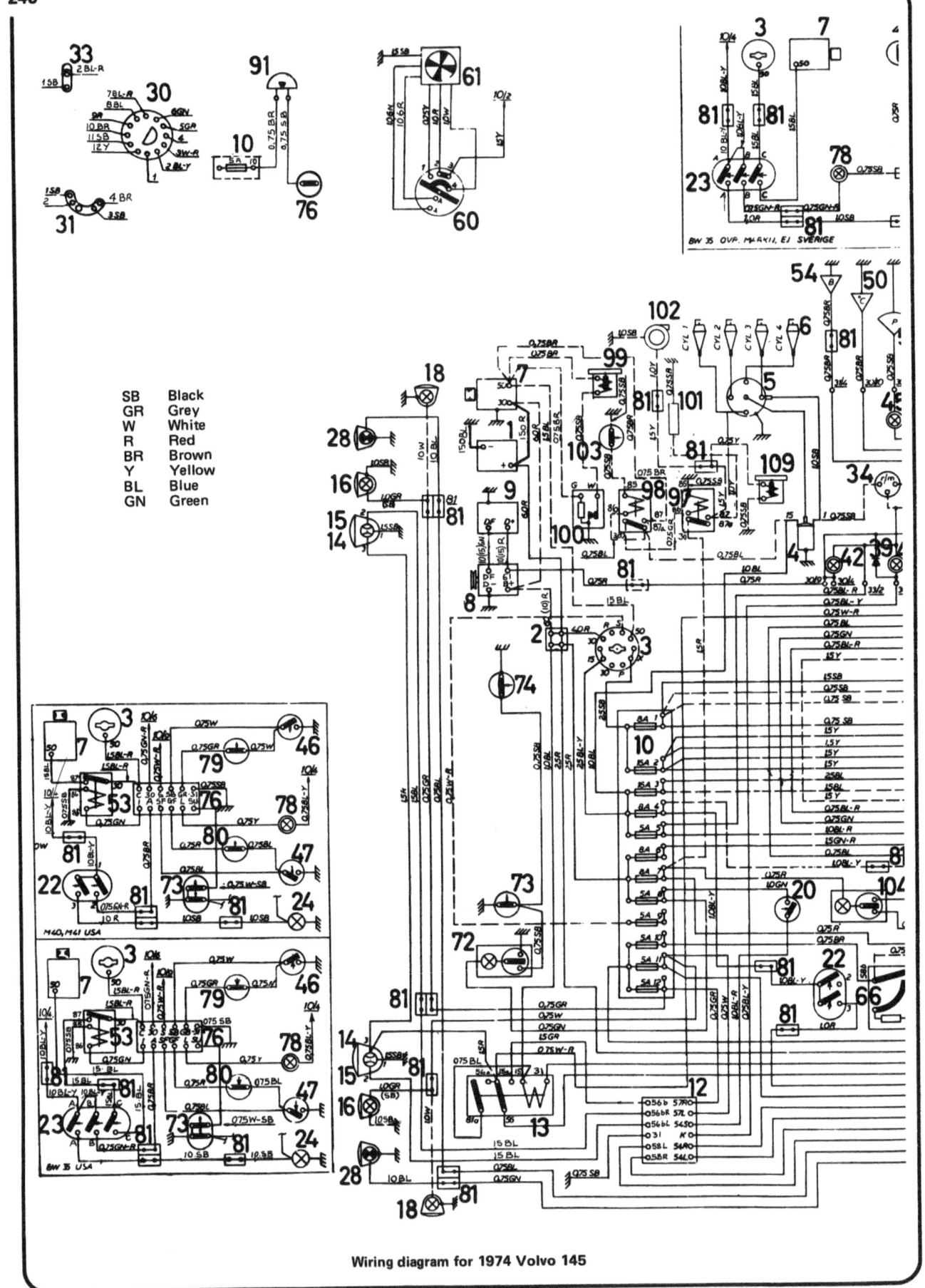

SB   Black
GR   Grey
W   White
R   Red
BR   Brown
Y   Yellow
BL   Blue
GN   Green

Wiring diagram for 1974 Volvo 145

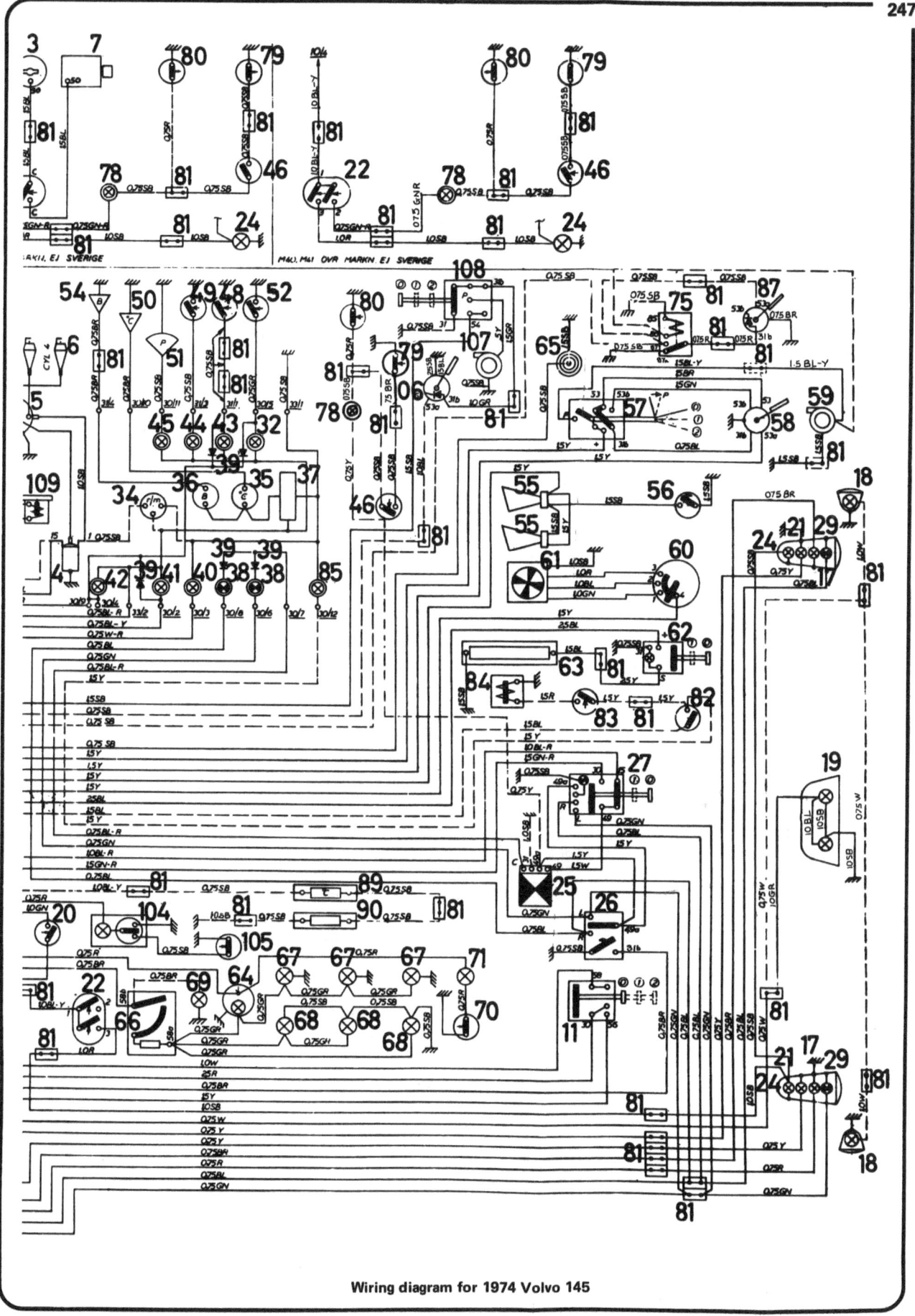

Wiring diagram for 1974 Volvo 145

248

Key to wiring diagram on pages 242 and 243 (Volvo 142 and 144)

1 Battery
2 Connection box
3 Ignition switch
4 Ignition coil
5 Distributor, firing order 1 - 3 - 4 - 2
6 Spark plugs
7 Starter motor
8 Alternator
9 Voltage regulator
10 Fuse box
11 Light switch
12 Bulb Integrity Sensor
13 Switch relay, upper and lower beams
14 Upper beams
15 Lower beams
16 Position light
17 Tail light
18 Side marker light
19 License plate light
20 Stop light switch
21 Stop light
22 Contact on transmission, M40 - M41
23 Contact on transmission BW 35
24 Back-up light
25 Flasher
26 Turn signal switch
27 Hazard warning light switch
28 Front turn signal
29 Rear turn signal
30 Connection at instrument
31 Connection at instrument
32 Brake warning light
33 Connection at instrument
34 Tachometer
35 Temperature gauge

36 Fuel gauge
37 Voltage stabilizer
38 Turn signal control light
39 Diode
40 Upper beam control light
41 Bulb Integrity Sensor warning light
42 Charging warning light
43 Parking brake control light
44 Choke control light
45 Oil pressure warning light
46 Contact, passenger's seat
47 Contact, driver's seat
48 Contact, parking brake
49 Contact, choke
50 Temperature sensor
51 Oil pressure sender
52 Contact, brake warning
53 Starter cut-out relay
54 Fuel gauge sender
55 Horn
56 Horn ring
57 Switch, wiper/washer
58 Wiper
59 Washer
60 Blower switch
61 Blower
62 Switch, electrically heated rear window
63 Electrically heated rear window
64 Clock
65 Cigarette light
66 Instrument light rheostat
67 Instrument light
68 Control panel light
69 Gear shift panel light

70 Contact, glove locker
71 Light, glove locker
72 Interior light
73 Door contact, driver's side
74 Door contact, passenger's side
75 Relay, headlight wiper
76 Interlock Control Unit
77 Buzzer, seat belt
78 Warning light, seat belt
79 Seat belt contact, passenger's side
80 Seat belt contact, driver's side
81 Connection
82 Switch, overdrive M 41
83 Switch for overdrive, on transmission M 41
84 Solenoid for overdrive, on transmission M 41
85 Overdrive control light
87 Headlight wiper
89 Heater pad with rheostat, driver's seat
90 Heater pad, driver's seat
91 Light reminder buzzer
97 Relay, fuel pump
98 Main relay, fuel injection
99 Cold start injector
100 Thermal time switch
101 Control pressure regulator
102 Fuel pump
103 Air flow sensor
104 Auxiliary air valve

Key to wiring diagram on pages 244 and 245 (Volvo 145)

1 Battery
2 Connection box
3 Ignition switch
4 Ignition coil
5 Distributor, firing order 1 - 3 - 4 - 2
6 Spark plugs
7 Starter motor
8 Alternator
9 Voltage regulator
10 Fuse box
11 Light switch
12 Bulb Integrity Sensor
13 Switch relay, upper and lower beams
14 Upper beams
15 Lower beams
16 Position light
17 Tail light
18 Side marker light
19 License plate light
20 Stop light switch
21 Stop light
22 Contact on transmission M40 - M 41
23 Contact on transmission BW 35
24 Back-up light
25 Flasher
26 Turn signal switch
27 Hazard warning light switch
28 Front turn signal
29 Rear turn signal
30 Connection at instrument
31 Connection at instrument
32 Brake warning light
33 Connection at instrument
34 Tachometer
35 Temperature gauge
36 Fuel gauge
37 Voltage stabilizer

38 Turn signal control light
39 Diode
40 Upper beam control light
41 Bulb Integrity Sensor warning light
42 Charging warning light
43 Parking brake control light
44 Choke control light
45 Oil pressure warning light
46 Contact, passenger's seat
47 Contact, driver's seat
48 Contact, parking brake
49 Contact, choke
50 Temperature sensor
51 Oil pressure sender
52 Contact, brake warning
53 Starter cut-out relay
54 Fuel gauge sender
55 Horn
56 Horn ring
57 Switch, wiper/washer
58 Wiper
59 Washer
60 Blower switch
61 Blower
62 Switch, electrically heated rear window
63 Electrically heated rear window
64 Clock
65 Cigarette light
66 Instrument light rheostat
67 Instrument light
68 Control panel light
69 Gear shift panel light
70 Contact, glove locker
71 Light, glove locker
72 Interior light
73 Door contact, driver's side

74 Door contact, passenger's side
75 Relay, headlight wiper
76 Interlock Control Unit
77 Buzzer, seat belt
78 Warning light, seat belt
79 Seat belt contact, passenger's side
80 Seat belt contact, driver's side
81 Connection
82 Switch, overdrive M41
83 Switch for overdrive, on transmission M 41
84 Solenoid for overdrive, on transmission M 41
85 Overdrive control light
87 Headlight wiper
89 Heater pad with rheostat driver's seat
90 Heater pad, driver's seat
91 Light reminder buzzer
97 Relay, fuel pump
98 Main relay, fuel injection
99 Cold start injector
100 Thermal time switch
101 Control pressure regulator
102 Fuel pump
103 Air flow sensor
104 Rear interior lamp
105 Rear door contact
106 Rear window wiper
107 Rear window washer
108 Rear window wipe/wash switch
109 Auxiliary air valve

Safety first!

Professional motor mechanics are trained in safe working procedures. However enthusiastic you may be about getting on with the job in hand, do take the time to ensure that your safety is not put at risk. A moment's lack of attention can result in an accident, as can failure to observe certain elementary precautions.

There will always be new ways of having accidents, and the following points do not pretend to be a comprehensive list of all dangers; they are intended rather to make you aware of the risks and to encourage a safety-conscious approach to all work you carry out on your vehicle.

Essential DOs and DON'Ts

DON'T rely on a single jack when working underneath the vehicle. Always use reliable additional means of support, such as axle stands, securely placed under a part of the vehicle that you know will not give way.

DON'T attempt to loosen or tighten high-torque nuts (e.g. wheel hub nuts) while the vehicle is on a jack; it may be pulled off.

DON'T start the engine without first ascertaining that the transmission is in neutral (or 'Park' where applicable) and the parking brake applied.

DON'T suddenly remove the filler cap from a hot cooling system – cover it with a cloth and release the pressure gradually first, or you may get scalded by escaping coolant.

DON'T attempt to drain oil until you are sure it has cooled sufficiently to avoid scalding you.

DON'T grasp any part of the engine, exhaust or catalytic converter without first ascertaining that it is sufficiently cool to avoid burning you.

DON'T allow brake fluid or antifreeze to contact vehicle paintwork.

DON'T syphon toxic liquids such as fuel, brake fluid or antifreeze by mouth, or allow them to remain on your skin.

DON'T inhale dust – it may be injurious to health (see *Asbestos* below).

DON'T allow any spilt oil or grease to remain on the floor – wipe it up straight away, before someone slips on it.

DON'T use ill-fitting spanners or other tools which may slip and cause injury.

DON'T attempt to lift a heavy component which may be beyond your capability – get assistance.

DON'T rush to finish a job, or take unverified short cuts.

DON'T allow children or animals in or around an unattended vehicle.

DO wear eye protection when using power tools such as drill, sander, bench grinder etc, and when working under the vehicle.

DO use a barrier cream on your hands prior to undertaking dirty jobs – it will protect your skin from infection as well as making the dirt easier to remove afterwards; but make sure your hands aren't left slippery. Note that long-term contact with used engine oil can be a health hazard.

DO keep loose clothing (cuffs, tie etc) and long hair well out of the way of moving mechanical parts.

DO remove rings, wristwatch etc, before working on the vehicle – especially the electrical system.

DO ensure that any lifting tackle used has a safe working load rating adequate for the job.

DO keep your work area tidy – it is only too easy to fall over articles left lying around.

DO get someone to check periodically that all is well, when working alone on the vehicle.

DO carry out work in a logical sequence and check that everything is correctly assembled and tightened afterwards.

DO remember that your vehicle's safety affects that of yourself and others. If in doubt on any point, get specialist advice.

IF, in spite of following these precautions, you are unfortunate enough to injure yourself, seek medical attention as soon as possible.

Asbestos

Certain friction, insulating, sealing, and other products – such as brake linings, brake bands, clutch linings, torque converters, gaskets, etc – contain asbestos. *Extreme care must be taken to avoid inhalation of dust from such products since it is hazardous to health.* If in doubt, assume that they *do* contain asbestos.

Fire

Remember at all times that petrol (gasoline) is highly flammable. Never smoke, or have any kind of naked flame around, when working on the vehicle. But the risk does not end there – a spark caused by an electrical short-circuit, by two metal surfaces contacting each other, by careless use of tools, or even by static electricity built up in your body under certain conditions, can ignite petrol vapour, which in a confined space is highly explosive.

Always disconnect the battery earth (ground) terminal before working on any part of the fuel or electrical system, and never risk spilling fuel on to a hot engine or exhaust.

It is recommended that a fire extinguisher of a type suitable for fuel and electrical fires is kept handy in the garage or workplace at all times. Never try to extinguish a fuel or electrical fire with water.

Note: *Any reference to a 'torch' appearing in this manual should always be taken to mean a hand-held battery-operated electric lamp or flashlight. It does NOT mean a welding/gas torch or blowlamp.*

Fumes

Certain fumes are highly toxic and can quickly cause unconsciousness and even death if inhaled to any extent. Petrol (gasoline) vapour comes into this category, as do the vapours from certain solvents such as trichloroethylene. Any draining or pouring of such volatile fluids should be done in a well ventilated area.

When using cleaning fluids and solvents, read the instructions carefully. Never use materials from unmarked containers – they may give off poisonous vapours.

Never run the engine of a motor vehicle in an enclosed space such as a garage. Exhaust fumes contain carbon monoxide which is extremely poisonous; if you need to run the engine, always do so in the open air or at least have the rear of the vehicle outside the workplace.

If you are fortunate enough to have the use of an inspection pit, never drain or pour petrol, and never run the engine, while the vehicle is standing over it; the fumes, being heavier than air, will concentrate in the pit with possibly lethal results.

The battery

Never cause a spark, or allow a naked light, near the vehicle's battery. It will normally be giving off a certain amount of hydrogen gas, which is highly explosive.

Always disconnect the battery earth (ground) terminal before working on the fuel or electrical systems.

If possible, loosen the filler plugs or cover when charging the battery from an external source. Do not charge at an excessive rate or the battery may burst.

Take care when topping up and when carrying the battery. The acid electrolyte, even when diluted, is very corrosive and should not be allowed to contact the eyes or skin.

If you ever need to prepare electrolyte yourself, always add the acid slowly to the water, and never the other way round. Protect against splashes by wearing rubber gloves and goggles.

When jump starting a car using a booster battery, for negative earth (ground) vehicles, connect the jump leads in the following sequence: First connect one jump lead between the positive (+) terminals of the two batteries. Then connect the other jump lead first to the negative (–) terminal of the booster battery, and then to a good earthing (ground) point on the vehicle to be started, at least 18 in (45 cm) from the battery if possible. Ensure that hands and jump leads are clear of any moving parts, and that the two vehicles do not touch. Disconnect the leads in the reverse order.

Mains electricity and electrical equipment

When using an electric power tool, inspection light etc, always ensure that the appliance is correctly connected to its plug and that, where necessary, it is properly earthed (grounded). Do not use such appliances in damp conditions and, again, beware of creating a spark or applying excessive heat in the vicinity of fuel or fuel vapour. Also ensure that the appliances meet the relevant national safety standards.

Ignition HT voltage

A severe electric shock can result from touching certain parts of the ignition system, such as the HT leads, when the engine is running or being cranked, particularly if components are damp or the insulation is defective. Where an electronic ignition system is fitted, the HT voltage is much higher and could prove fatal.

Conversion factors

Length (distance)

Inches (in)	X	25.4	=	Millimetres (mm)	X	0.0394	= Inches (in)
Feet (ft)	X	0.305	=	Metres (m)	X	3.281	= Feet (ft)
Miles	X	1.609	=	Kilometres (km)	X	0.621	= Miles

Volume (capacity)

Cubic inches (cu in; in³)	X	16.387	=	Cubic centimetres (cc; cm³)	X	0.061	= Cubic inches (cu in; in³)
Imperial pints (Imp pt)	X	0.568	=	Litres (l)	X	1.76	= Imperial pints (Imp pt)
Imperial quarts (Imp qt)	X	1.137	=	Litres (l)	X	0.88	= Imperial quarts (Imp qt)
Imperial quarts (Imp qt)	X	1.201	=	US quarts (US qt)	X	0.833	= Imperial quarts (Imp qt)
US quarts (US qt)	X	0.946	=	Litres (l)	X	1.057	= US quarts (US qt)
Imperial gallons (Imp gal)	X	4.546	=	Litres (l)	X	0.22	= Imperial gallons (Imp gal)
Imperial gallons (Imp gal)	X	1.201	=	US gallons (US gal)	X	0.833	= Imperial gallons (Imp gal)
US gallons (US gal)	X	3.785	=	Litres (l)	X	0.264	= US gallons (US gal)

Mass (weight)

Ounces (oz)	X	28.35	=	Grams (g)	X	0.035	= Ounces (oz)
Pounds (lb)	X	0.454	=	Kilograms (kg)	X	2.205	= Pounds (lb)

Force

Ounces-force (ozf; oz)	X	0.278	=	Newtons (N)	X	3.6	= Ounces-force (ozf; oz)
Pounds-force (lbf; lb)	X	4.448	=	Newtons (N)	X	0.225	= Pounds-force (lbf; lb)
Newtons (N)	X	0.1	=	Kilograms-force (kgf; kg)	X	9.81	= Newtons (N)

Pressure

Pounds-force per square inch (psi; lbf/in²; lb/in²)	X	0.070	=	Kilograms-force per square centimetre (kgf/cm²; kg/cm²)	X	14.223	= Pounds-force per square inch (psi; lbf/in²; lb/in²)
Pounds-force per square inch (psi; lbf/in²; lb/in²)	X	0.068	=	Atmospheres (atm)	X	14.696	= Pounds-force per square inch (psi; lbf/in²; lb/in²)
Pounds-force per square inch (psi; lbf/in²; lb/in²)	X	0.069	=	Bars	X	14.5	= Pounds-force per square inch (psi; lbf/in²; lb/in²)
Pounds-force per square inch (psi; lbf/in²; lb/in²)	X	6.895	=	Kilopascals (kPa)	X	0.145	= Pounds-force per square inch (psi; lbf/in²; lb/in²)
Kilopascals (kPa)	X	0.01	=	Kilograms-force per square centimetre (kgf/cm²; kg/cm²)	X	98.1	= Kilopascals (kPa)
Millibar (mbar)	X	100	=	Pascals (Pa)	X	0.01	= Millibar (mbar)
Millibar (mbar)	X	0.0145	=	Pounds-force per square inch (psi; lbf/in²; lb/in²)	X	68.947	= Millibar (mbar)
Millibar (mbar)	X	0.75	=	Millimetres of mercury (mmHg)	X	1.333	= Millibar (mbar)
Millibar (mbar)	X	0.401	=	Inches of water (inH₂O)	X	2.491	= Millibar (mbar)
Millimetres of mercury (mmHg)	X	0.535	=	Inches of water (inH₂O)	X	1.868	= Millimetres of mercury (mmHg)
Inches of water (inH₂O)	X	0.036	=	Pounds-force per square inch (psi; lbf/in²; lb/in²)	X	27.68	= Inches of water (inH₂O)

Torque (moment of force)

Pounds-force inches (lbf in; lb in)	X	1.152	=	Kilograms-force centimetre (kgf cm; kg cm)	X	0.868	= Pounds-force inches (lbf in; lb in)
Pounds-force inches (lbf in; lb in)	X	0.113	=	Newton metres (Nm)	X	8.85	= Pounds-force inches (lbf in; lb in)
Pounds-force inches (lbf in; lb in)	X	0.083	=	Pounds-force feet (lbf ft; lb ft)	X	12	= Pounds-force inches (lbf in; lb in)
Pounds-force feet (lbf ft; lb ft)	X	0.138	=	Kilograms-force metres (kgf m; kg m)	X	7.233	= Pounds-force feet (lbf ft; lb ft)
Pounds-force feet (lbf ft; lb ft)	X	1.356	=	Newton metres (Nm)	X	0.738	= Pounds-force feet (lbf ft; lb ft)
Newton metres (Nm)	X	0.102	=	Kilograms-force metres (kgf m; kg m)	X	9.804	= Newton metres (Nm)

Power

Horsepower (hp)	X	745.7	=	Watts (W)	X	0.0013	= Horsepower (hp)

Velocity (speed)

Miles per hour (miles/hr; mph)	X	1.609	=	Kilometres per hour (km/hr; kph)	X	0.621	= Miles per hour (miles/hr; mph)

Fuel consumption*

Miles per gallon, Imperial (mpg)	X	0.354	=	Kilometres per litre (km/l)	X	2.825	= Miles per gallon, Imperial (mpg)
Miles per gallon, US (mpg)	X	0.425	=	Kilometres per litre (km/l)	X	2.352	= Miles per gallon, US (mpg)

Temperature

Degrees Fahrenheit = (°C x 1.8) + 32   Degrees Celsius (Degrees Centigrade; °C) = (°F - 32) x 0.56

*It is common practice to convert from miles per gallon (mpg) to litres/100 kilometres (l/100km), where mpg (Imperial) x l/100 km = 282 and mpg (US) x l/100 km = 235

Index

FSC
www.fsc.org
MIX
Papier | Fördert
gute Waldnutzung
FSC® C083411

Zeitfracht Medien GmbH
Ferdinand-Jühlke-Straße 7
99095 Erfurt, Deutschland
produktsicherheit@kolibri360.de